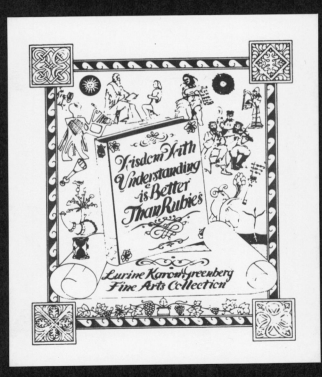

Blowin' Hot and Cool

Blowin'
Hot and Cool

Jazz and Its Critics

JOHN GENNARI

The University of Chicago Press
Chicago and London

John Gennari is assistant professor of English and director of the ALANA U.S. Ethnic
Studies Program at the University of Vermont.

The University of Chicago Press, Chicago 60637
The University of Chicago Press, Ltd., London
©2006 by The University of Chicago
All rights reserved. Published 2006
Printed in the United States of America

15 14 13 12 11 10 09 08 07 06   1 2 3 4 5

ISBN : 0-226-28922-2 (cloth)

Library of Congress Cataloging-in-Publication Data

Gennari, John.
    Blowin' hot and cool : jazz and its critics / John Gennari.
      p. cm.
    Includes bibliographical references (p.) and index.
    ISBN 0-226-28922-2 (cloth : alk. paper)
    1. Jazz—History and criticism. 2. Music—Social aspects—United States. I. Title.
  ML3506.G46 2006
  306.4'8425—dc22

                         2005030539

For my parents,
Remo Gennari and Clara Dal Cortivo Gennari

CONTENTS

ACKNOWLEDGMENTS

This book wouldn't have been possible without the support of a number of individuals and institutions it is now my pleasure—finally!—to thank. None of those I name here are responsible for any of this book's errors, defects, misjudgments, or infelicities. Surely I've forgotten to name others who deserve warm recognition for helping me out somewhere on this long journey.

The work for this book began in the late 1980s, when I was a graduate student in the American Civilization Department at the University of Pennsylvania. One of the glories of that now defunct department was its popular History of Jazz course, taught for many years by Neil Leonard, a pioneer of jazz studies and a perceptive student of American arts and culture. If not for Neil's example, I wouldn't have known that American Studies was a good home for someone who wanted to tackle jazz from a cultural angle. It was as an assistant and sabbatical teaching replacement in Neil's course that I first began to read deeply in jazz history and criticism and to think about the people and issues I've addressed in this book. Neil told me that a book on jazz criticism was an important project, and that I should write it in my own voice. Other Penn faculty members taught me important things about how to study American culture, especially Jan Radway (now at Duke), Drew Faust (now at Harvard), Bruce Kuklick, Murray Murphey, and Al Filreis.

In 1990, Neil put me in touch with Gary Carner, who was looking for someone to contribute an article on the history of jazz criticism to a special issue of *Black American Literature Forum*. Catalyzed by Gary's rich suggestions, I wrote and wrote and ended up with a sprawling, seventy-five-page article that became the blueprint for all the jazz work I've done since. Around the same time, Harvard Law School professor Randall Kennedy invited me to write about jazz in *Reconstruction*, his much missed journal of African American affairs. It frankly astonished me that two such capable people as Gary and Randy thought I had something interesting to say about jazz. Maybe I was on to something.

The *BALF* and *Reconstruction* publications came at a critical time, leading to fellowships that underwrote my research and expanded my circle of contacts in jazz studies, American Studies, and African American Studies. As a Smithsonian Institution Predoctoral Fellow, I soaked up the wisdom and generosity of Charlie McGovern, who urged me to think about jazz as part of a larger, American-cultural narrative, and offered especially acute insights about Martin Williams. I gathered helpful advice from John Hasse, whose passion for Duke Ellington rubbed off on me. I watched Walter Van de Leur scour the Smithsonian's Ellington archive for evidence of Billy Strayhorn's compositional hand. I teamed up with Bob Haddow to interview Willis Conover in his USIA office. I floated a number of Guinness Stout–soaked ideas at the Tuesday pub outings presided over by Pete Daniel.

A grant from the National Endowment for the Humanities enabled me to spend a year as a visiting fellow at the W. E. B. Du Bois Institute at Harvard University, where this book really took shape. I owe a special debt of gratitude to the late Richard Newman, fellows' officer and unofficial "mayor" of the Du Bois Institute, whose love of black culture was something to behold. Thanks as well to Lisa Gates, for her administrative support and immense good cheer; and to Du Bois director Skip Gates, Cornel West, Evelyn Higginbotham, and Randy Matory, who engaged and supported my work during that fellowship year. It was a special joy to reunite with Randy, who had witnessed my growing passion for jazz when we roomed together in college. The Du Bois Institute was where I met Guy Ramsey, Daphne Brooks, Farah Jasmine Griffin, Elizabeth McHenry, and Brent Edwards, fresh voices in African American Studies whose work has challenged and inspired me. It was where I had my first research assistant, Gabriel Mendes, who reorganized my files and helped me locate some important press clippings on the Newport Jazz Festival. And it was where I came to know Pat Sullivan and Mary Hamer, treasured friends whose spirit breathes over these pages.

A fellowship at the Carter G. Woodson Institute at the University of Virginia enabled me to research and write the Charlie Parker chapter and begin to rethink one or two others. Reginald Butler, Scot French, and Gail Shirley-Warren provided terrific institutional support, while Kyra Gaunt, Grace Hale, Natasha Gray, Vania Penha-Lopes, Greta deJong, Phil Troutman, Andy Lewis, Eve Agee, and Lisa Swales made Charlottesville swing. I must give special thanks to Scott DeVeaux, John Mason, and Eric Lott for reading and commenting on my work; Reg Butler for giving me the chance to teach my first jazz cultural studies seminar, and the UVA African-American Studies students who made that experience so enriching.

I've taught at a few different institutions while working on this book, and I would like to thank several former and present colleagues and students for providing material, intellectual, and emotional support for the project. Steve Morillo, of Wabash College, and Toni Rosato, of the University of Colorado, were there for me when I most needed their rare kind of affection and wisdom. Erika Doss and Rickie Solinger offered the example of their fierce intellectual discipline, and also of their warm generosity. Perhaps most importantly, each of the above fed me often and well. William Wei, director of the Sewall Residential Program at the University of Colorado, found me funds for some research travel and to pay Erin Hicks, a student research assistant who did exemplary work finding and copying *Down Beat* columns from the 1950s and '60s. Sewall administrator Linda Kerr-Saville helped me in any number of ways, including packing and shipping my belongings as I moved from place to place. At Penn State–Harrisburg I benefited from the mentoring of Simon Bronner and Bill Maher, and from the friendship of Simon and Bill as well as of Louise Hoffman, Matthew Wilson, Michael Barton, Irwin and Susan Richman, Sam Winch, and especially my neighbor and fellow long-suffering Red Sox fan Jessica Dorman.

At the University of Vermont, a junior research leave and professional-development monies have been critical to the completion of this book. My colleagues in the UVM English Department and the ALANA U.S. Ethnic Studies Program have given me a home and have inspired me with their commitment to ideas, creative expression, and social justice. The students in my "Jazz, Literature, and the Cultural Imagination" seminar have often reminded me, with their keen interest and passion, what a rare privilege it is to teach this material. Katherine Layton and Stella Moyser have dealt heroically with the intricacies of my research funding. Stella, my superb administrative assistant, has kept me humored with stories about her "naughty and agile" cats.

The research for this book began in earnest at the Institute of Jazz Studies at Rutgers–Newark, where Dan Morgernstern and his staff encouraged my probing of their invaluable archive and pointed me in the direction of materials I otherwise wouldn't have found. I also owe thanks to archive and library staffs at the following institutions: Van Pelt Library at the University of Pennsylvania; Widener Library at Harvard University; Bobst Library at New York University; Low Memorial Library at Columbia University; the University of Colorado Music Library; the University of Virginia Music Library; Bailey-Howe Library at the University of Vermont; the Center for

Black Music Research Library at Columbia College (Chicago); the Smith-sonian Institution's National Museum of American History; and the Harry Ransom Humanities Research Center at the University of Texas (with spe-cial thanks to Dell Hollingsworth and Richard Workman). When they were still graduate students at UT–Austin, Siva Vaidyanathan and Joel Dinerstein told me about the Ross Russell archive at the Harry Ransom Center, then generously guided my use of it. Later, Siva put me up in his NYU apart-ment several times when I had business for this book in New York. And he helped me—a hopeless neo-Luddite—buy my first computer, the one on which most of this book has been written.

A number of individuals from the jazz world who granted me interviews or talked to me informally gave me insights and a scope of understanding I couldn't have gained from just the written sources. These include the late Barry Ulanov, Nat Hentoff, George Wein, George Avakian, Whitney Balliett, Dan Morgenstern, the late Martin Williams, Robert Farris Thompson, Albert Murray, George Russell, Jimmy Giuffre, the late Percy Heath, Jon Hendricks, Oliver Lake, Bob Blumenthal, Gary Giddins, Peter Watrous, Henry Martin, and Sharony Andrews Green. I'm deeply indebted to Bryant Dupre for shar-ing with me the interviews he taped with Martin Williams, Stanley and Helen Dance, George Simon, and Walter Schaap.

I'm especially fortunate that Robert O'Meally invited me to join the Jazz Study Group at Columbia University's Center for Jazz Studies, an extraor-dinary group of scholars, musicians, visual artists, and dancers who gather twice a year to explore jazz's multiple and fascinating cultural meanings. Bob's surpassing grace and diplomacy create an ideal environment to think about jazz, and every meeting brings an epiphany that finds its way into our work. When I first entered this field, Krin Gabbard was boldly pushing it into fascinating new areas of cultural inquiry. I knew him then as the editor of two pioneering volumes on the new jazz studies and as author of a seminal work on jazz and the American cinema; I know him now as a trusted close reader of all my work and as a good friend. Through Krin I met Bernard Gendron, who incisively vetted an early draft of my chapter on the 1960s.

Ron Radano, William Kenney, Lewis Erenberg, Herman Beavers, and Robin D. G. Kelley took an interest in my work when I was finishing up my dissertation, and they've remained stalwart supporters ever since. The late Mark Tucker offered warm encouragement and invited me to participate in a pair of splendid symposia on Duke Ellington and Thelonious Monk he organized at the University of North Carolina. I met Sherrie Tucker some-where on the conference circuit just when her groundbreaking work on jazz and gender was beginning to shake up the field. Somehow in the midst of a blistering schedule last year she found time to read and comment on two of my chapters. Ben Cawthra invited me to participate in the planning of the Missouri Historical Society's exhibition on the life and work of Miles Davis, which gave me a chance to learn a great deal from Gerald Early, Quincy Troupe, Eugene Redmond, Ingrid Monson, and Ben himself. Conference get-togethers with Rich Crawford, David Sanjek, Burt Peretti, Gena Caponi Tabery, Eric Porter, Nichole Rustin, Salim Washington, Penny Von Eschen, Meta DuEwa Jones, Tanya Kalmanovitch, and Paul Allen Anderson have significantly enriched my work.

I've been blessed to have as my editor Doug Mitchell, a man of unusually deft rhythm and wit, whose faith in me has been a sustaining comfort, and whose patience has been nothing short of miraculous. Evan Young copyedited the manuscript with perfect touch. Martin White expertly crafted the index. Tim McGovern and Leslie Keros guided me through the production process with uncanny finesse. Three outside reviewers engaged by the University of Chicago Press helped me—really, really helped me—figure out what I was trying to do.

María de Lourdes Dávila was with this book at the beginning, believed in it, and gave a piece of her heart to it. Brett Gary has been my padrone—tout, counselor, and soulmate—since the Philly days. He and his wife Amy Bentley, another Penn friend and Colorado crony, graciously hosted me in their New York apartment many times during the course of my research. Not the least of their gifts was introducing me to Gary Ferrini, a paesan who shares my love of jazz, sports, and sopresatta. Nancy Bernhard, another of my grad school chums, put me up when I rolled into Cambridge for my Du Bois fellowship year, and also brought her formidable editorial skill to bear on a couple of my chapters. George Daley, a pillar in my life since college, regularly fed and watered me through that year. Barry Shank tried to bring out the musician in me, and he has read my work carefully and challenged me to think about music and American culture more deeply. So too have Jim Hall (who read most of the manuscript) and Tom Ferraro, who seem like lifelong friends though we've only known each other since this work brought us together a decade ago. Elizabeth Alexander has given me—well, everything. Old friends Jim Hurley, Stan Schmidt, Shirley Wajda, Gretchen Hackett, Saul Cornell, Nancy Bercaw, and Alex Lichtenstein continue to teach me new things. Dan Horowitz and Laban Carrick Hill came to my rescue at a critical juncture, and Laban offered especially helpful commentary on late drafts of my first few chapters. When I moved to Burlington, Amor Kohli was already here planting jazz-literature seeds; later, Major Jackson came around to fertilize them. Alex Stewart read most of the manuscript and gave it his valued blessing. Dr. Lawrence McCrorey has inspired me with his social conscience and courage, his stories, his undying love of this music, and his sweet and husky tenor sax croon.

I grew up in a family in which love expresses itself most powerfully in silent communion over food. And so it feels awkward to try to use words to express my heartfelt thanks for their love and faith in me, when what I really want to do is break bread and quaff wine. There will be plenty of that, but words are the coin of *this* realm, and every one of them in this book is a tribute to my parents Remo and Clara Gennari, my brother James Gennari and sister Joan Tyer and their families, and my wife Emily Bernard.

Nobody believes more strongly in the power of words than Emily. And yet words cannot possibly repay the debt I owe her—for her love and caring, for her patience and faith, but most of all for the sublime beauty and fierce honesty of her own words, and her amazing devotion and support as I've labored to get mine right.

Portions of this book appeared in preliminary form in previously published essays: part of chapter 2 as "'A Weapon of Integration': Frank Marshall Davis and the Politics of Jazz," *Langston Hughes Review,* Fall 1995/Spring 1996, 15–32; part of chapter 4 as "Miles Davis and the Jazz Critics," in *Miles Davis and American Culture*, ed. Gerald Early (St. Louis: Missouri Historical Society Press, 2001): 66–77; part of chapter 5 as "Hipsters, Bluebloods, Rebels, and Hooligans: The Cultural Politics of the Newport Jazz Festival, 1954–1960," in *Uptown Conversation: The New Jazz Studies*, ed. Robert G. O'Meally, Brent Hayes Edwards, and Farah Jasmine Griffin (New York: Columbia University Press, 2004), 126–49; part of chapter 6 as "Baraka's Bohemian Blues," *African American Review* 37, nos. 2 and 3 (Summer/Fall 2003): 95–101; and part of chapter 7 as "Pulp Addiction: Tracking the Bird Obsession in Ross Russell's *The Sound*," *Brilliant Corners* 2, no. 1 (December 1997): 38–51. I am grateful to the publishers of these earlier essays for their permission to reprint.

(Much More than) a Few Words about Jazz

An Exquisite Corpse

As the story goes, the drummer Art Blakey was driving to a job in Pennsylvania, passing through a small town, when he got stuck behind a funeral procession. Unable to drive past the cemetery until the service was over, he pulled over and got out of his car to listen to the eulogy. After the minister finished speaking on behalf of the deceased, he asked if anyone had anything to add. A heavy silence ensued, until Blakey stepped forward and brightly intoned: "If nobody has anything to say about the departed, I'd like to say a few words about jazz!"[1]

Many are the words that have been spoken, the bodies laid to rest, and the corpses exhumed in the telling of jazz's story. In 1939, the jazz and dance critic Roger Pryor Dodge rued that "as soon as jazz became disturbingly identifiable as something more than 'our popular music,' countless uninformed commentators sprung up with something to say about it."[2] Fifteen years later, Whitney Balliett noted that "although America has always tried to keep jazz in the same national tower with other queer relatives like the Spanish-American War and the American Indian, it has never been able to stop talking about it."[3] In 2001, in Ken Burns's PBS documentary on the cultural history of the music, several of jazz's most garrulous spokespersons held forth for more than nineteen hours, brandishing a vocabulary full of such juicy words as "heroic," "erotic," "majestic," and—the film's mother of all jazz words—"genius." And yet the film couldn't carry the jazz story past the 1960s, which meant virtually excising nearly a third of the music's

1

century-long history and strongly implied that jazz is now entombed in a condition of permanent epilogue. One critic of the film has likened it to a "funeral celebration," while another has characterized the curatorial, neoclassical aesthetic of the film's main talking head—the trumpeter and Lincoln Center jazz program artistic director Wynton Marsalis—as a form of "musical necrophilia."[4]

When I first became interested in jazz as a college student in the late 1970s, word of jazz's death was all around—whether in the sound of printed or spoken words lamenting the passing of a hallowed tradition, or the silence of unspoken words marking the absence of jazz in places (dance halls, hotel ballrooms, neighborhood bars, coffee shops, radio programs) where previously it had been a vital presence. I found this talk both captivating and puzzling—captivating because of the solemn earnestness of the jazz-is-dead discourse, puzzling because the jazz that I was discovering and loving seemed like the essence of life itself. How could jazz be dead if Dizzy Gillespie, Max Roach, Art Blakey, and Sonny Rollins were still alive? How could jazz be dead if every summer brought jazz festivals and outdoor concerts, providing a more rarified experience than the weed- and booze-suffused open-air rock concerts that were defining rituals for adolescents of my generation. More to the point: how could jazz be dead if, as a college student, I could go to a club in the Village, shell out an entire semester's work-study wages on the cover charge and a couple of scotches, sit close enough to drummer Jack De Johnette to hear him breathe, and between sets try to impress my girlfriend with how much I knew about Jack's early-career breakthrough with Miles Davis. If jazz was dead, so was my chosen path into hipness and enlightenment.

In my Italian-American working-class home, music was second only to food as a sacrament of family life. In fact the two were ritually intertwined: family dinners usually involved impromptu dancing, while the canning of garden vegetables, simmering of pasta sauces, and grating of cheese all unfurled to the sound of the Valtaro orchestra, Frank Sinatra, Glen Miller, Dean Martin, Johnny Mathis, Motown, The Beatles, The Rolling Stones, James Brown, Aretha Franklin, Chaka Khan, and Tito Puente. As a fledgling drummer, I played in school stage bands, rock and funk garage bands, and theater pit bands. Jazz—at least the jazz canon as then represented in something like *The Smithsonian Collection of Classic Jazz,* which I knew about only because my high-school English teacher recommended it as a gift for our departing school band director—was not a central part of my musical life. My budding interest in jazz during my college years took me ever further afield from the familiar territory of everyday mainstream American culture: to the far left of the FM radio dial, to used-record stores run by aging hipsters, to the dorm rooms of a few nascent aficionados whose stacked wooden boxes full of carefully organized LPs I deeply envied. What I found in those fugitive spaces surely didn't smell like death; it seemed bracingly alive and exciting.[5]

Indeed, it seemed alive and exciting beyond words, or at least beyond *my* ability to capture it in words. Hence my fascination with the people I was reading during that time who had undertaken to write about jazz—jazz as music, jazz as culture, jazz as history. LP liner notes were the starting point. Twenty-five years later, I still vividly remember finding a copy of Eric Dolphy's *Out to Lunch* in a subterranean used-record shop, then standing there to read and reread A. B. Spellman's description of drummer Tony Williams playing "pulse" rather than "time." A college buddy turned me on to a couple of Nat Hentoff's books; these in turn led me to books by Spellman, Martin Williams, Amiri Baraka (LeRoi Jones), and Whitney Balliett. This material gave me historical background for the younger jazz writers I began to read in *The Village Voice* (Gary Giddins, Stanley Crouch, Francis Davis, Howard Mandel, and others), the *Boston Phoenix* (Bob Blumenthal), and in *Down Beat, Jazz Magazine*, and other organs of the jazz press.[6] Each writer—they were all men—had his own writing style, favorite musicians and causes, and pet peeves. Sometimes they argued directly with each other; always they seemed aware of each other. Discussion among my jazz-minded friends often started with "Did you read what __ said about __?" Somehow this jazz writing seemed more important, more necessary than the writing about rock and pop music. Many rock musicians were well-known celebrities; we saw them on television. We loved their music because it was accessible. Those of us who were musical dabblers played rock and funk because they felt like native languages, and because we knew we could connect with an audience of our peers. If we ventured into jazz, it was as a second language, and it came with no guarantee of an audience. These jazz writers crucially helped us to understand jazz and, equally important, to imagine ourselves part of a community of people for whom the music mattered more than almost anything else.

These writers are the inheritors of a calling that since the 1930s (I propose in this book) has been crucial to the history of jazz, to the lives and careers of jazz musicians, and to the shaping of ideas about jazz's significance in American culture. As proselytizers, intermediaries, gatekeepers, translators, rhetoricians, conceptualizers, producers, and analysts of jazz, jazz critics have been undeniably powerful voices—some would say too powerful—in the music's public discourse. When we talk about jazz as American music, world music, black music, mulatto music, popular music, art music, democratic music, freedom music, rhythmic music, melodic music, romantic music, tragic music, dead music, or living music, we're talking in a language and through conceptual categories that have been established by critics. Indeed, the very question of which music is jazz, and which is not, is one on which critics usually get the last word.

Jazz has never been just music—it's been a cornerstone of the modern cultural imagination, an archive of mythological images, and an aesthetic model for new modes of writing, seeing, and moving. Across the spectrum of high, middlebrow, and low culture, from symphonies and modern dance to cartoons and advertising, jazz has been appropriated, remembered, dismembered, loved, and abused. The jazz historian Ted Gioia has noticed that for all of the extraordinary attention paid to Wynton Marsalis in recent years, very rarely does the discussion center on a particular piece of his music; "Marsalis the musician," he writes, "has been eclipsed by Marsalis the institution." And this is part and parcel of a larger process of institutionalization—jazz education, repertory orchestras, documentary films, CD reissue programs, museum exhibits, etc.—that Gioia sees as heavily tilted toward the past, threatening to turn jazz into a "historical artifact." He worries further that the dominant approach to jazz history "has become a form of hagiography," a "litany of the saints." And he suggests that critics, historians, educators, and other members of the "jazz superstructure" often embrace "static models of jazz" because doing so simplifies their job of making sense of the complex world of improvisation.[7]

I share these concerns, and I propose in this book that one of the ways to create a less static model of jazz—and perhaps even to grant more agency and power to jazz musicians—paradoxically is to shift the focus from the musicians to the jazz superstructure. Or, rather, to focus on the complexity of the negotiations and interactions that take place between musicians and the superstructure as jazz is delivered to the audience—to follow the sounds of the music, as it were, from their point of production through channels of distribution out into the public sphere. This is because it seems to me undeniable that the meanings we attach to the music and the musicians—how we make sense out of what we hear and see and feel—are very deeply influenced by the filters that stand between us and the sound that comes out of the musicians' bodies and instruments. This is not just a matter of physical or temporal proximity: even when we occupy the same space as performing musicians, our perceptions of what we are hearing are indelibly, if invisibly, mediated by what we have heard before, including critical discourse. There's something finally mysterious and unintelligible about the relationship between artist and audience, and the critic's job is to provide words for an experience for which there are no words. Critics try to locate words for an experience that is finally elusive. ("Writing about music is like dancing about architecture," goes the phrase variously attributed to Thelonious Monk, Elvis Costello, Clara Schumann, and many others I haven't heard about.) The circle—musician, critic, audience—composes a dynamic that is perpetually in motion, always fulfilling and always unsatisfying. And it's this dynamic tension—of a desire awakened but only partially met—that makes jazz performance meaningful and demands its repetition.

As in an African dance ritual or an African American preacher's sermon to the congregation, jazz performance functions as a dialogue among the musicians, as well as between the musicians and the dancing or listening audience. Jazz musicians learn to listen and communicate with each other, to be deeply attuned to the nuances of time, gesture, attitude, and sound that each player brings to the performance. This spirit of interactive collaboration often makes the instruments of the band sound like so many voices engaged in a conversation—horn sections spraying riffs across the bandstand; a pianist "comping" behind a soloist; a drummer "dropping a bomb" to kick the band forward; horn players and the drummer "trading fours" or eights like sentences building themselves into a paragraph.

Jazz *speaks*, in other words, through means that can make post-performance written accounts seem secondary or even superfluous. Every musician I know habitually enacts a ritual that seems to have been adopted as a craft requirement: to dismiss critics out of hand, to deny their power of knowledge in this realm. And yet many of these musicians can tell me, sometimes almost word for word, what a particular critic has said about them. Much as jazz has remained rooted in African-derived performance traditions that stress in-the-moment oral and gestural communication, it is also a commercial product whose fate hinges on public understanding (or misunderstanding). It is also, especially for African American musicians and audiences, a hugely important form of historical memory, a vessel of deep meaning testifying to the heroic survival and cultural distinction of an oppressed minority group. Jazz critics may think of what they are doing as an exercise in formal analysis, but musicians read jazz criticism as a first draft of *their* history. This has led to complicated, fraught, and fascinating relationships between musicians and writers. The two black musicians who were most ferocious in condemning white critics, Miles Davis and Charles Mingus, were among those who had the most intimate personal relationships with the white critics they considered exceptions to the general rule. Davis's autobiography, whose bid for raw voice-of-the-musician authenticity dictates regular spasms of critic-bashing, is in fact a highly mediated narrative that contains—as part of the editorial intervention of collaborator Quincy Troupe—whole sections of musical analysis and career emplotment lifted directly from the work of one of Davis's biographers.[8]

It *was* Thelonious Monk who said: "If you want to know what's going on in jazz, ask a musician." Many musicians have been fine writers and powerful spokespersons for the music. Black musicians especially have found it important to speak for and about jazz, and their own contributions to it, in ways that challenge or correct what they see as distortions, evasions, and calumnies generated by the white-dominated critical establishment. Nat Hentoff, one of the white writers who has been most sensitive to this dynamic, wrote in the early 1960s: "the Negro player frequently does not believe that the critics—nearly all of whom are white—have paid the emotional 'dues' he has been assessed from the time he was born. Therefore, he reasons, not always with justice, how can the critics possibly understand his message, which is so much more than the notes he plays?"[9] Many black musicians—including W. C. Handy, Louis Armstrong, Duke Ellington, Herbie Nichols, Billy Taylor, Jon Hendricks, Charles Mingus, Abbey Lincoln, Archie Shepp, Art Taylor, David Baker, Anthony Braxton, Leo Smith, Marion Brown, George Lewis, Wynton Marsalis, Salim Washington, and Guthrie Ramsey Jr.—have written about jazz in the idioms of memoir, journalism, interview, criticism, and scholarship.[10] There's nothing essentially "black" that unites these black musician/writers; there's also no mistaking that these voices are collectively distinct from those of the white critics. In particular, black musician/critics have tended to emphasize the social messages embodied in the music ("so much more than the notes") and usually have been more concerned with jazz's function as a form of communal bonding, ritual, and social interaction—jazz not just as a collection of sounds, but as a way of living in the world. In this approach to jazz, criticism is a form of participatory discourse embedded within the social process of music-making, not a form of judgment or analysis delivered from on high.

Art Blakey carried the language of jazz forward as a master drummer, bandleader, teacher, and orator. For nearly half a century, his group, the Jazz Messengers, functioned as a kind of workshop guild where younger musicians (including Wynton Marsalis) served an apprenticeship in rhythm, harmony, professional deportment, and jazz evangelism. Blakey was like a preacher who first tended to the souls of his flock, then delivered the good word to anyone who would listen. His concern was not primarily for my hipness and enlightenment, but for the survival of a cultural form that carried the history of his people.

Romance and Race

Jazz critics, alas, can be ignored, reviled, resented, misunderstood, or appreciated. What they cannot be—if one is to reckon fully with the cultural history of jazz—is avoided. The British writer Geoff Dyer, in *But Beautiful: A*

Book about Jazz (1996), a set of "poetically charged vignettes" about jazz musicians and their pathologies, calls his approach "imaginative criticism" to distinguish it from the "enacted criticism" practiced by musicians themselves as they continually absorb, interpret, revise, amplify, and reject the existing jazz canon. The tradition of jazz criticism per se, as it has come to be known, Dyer does not explicitly engage—with the result that he fails to acknowledge that his imaginative criticism is crucially dependent on anecdotes, notions, images, and arguments that have come from the trench work of jazz critics.[11]

Dyer is an adherent of the Romantic tragic view of jazz, one that likens Charlie Parker, John Coltrane, and Eric Dolphy to Shelley, Keats, and Schubert, seeing in all both a talent "consuming itself even as it flourishes" and the grounds for an argument that "premature death is a condition of creativity." He sees the jazz life as one defined by "drink, drugs, discrimination, grueling travel, [and] exhausting hours" but muses that "the damage wrought on jazz musicians is such that you wonder if there is not something else, something in the form itself which exacts a terrible toll from those who create it."[12] The critics I study in this book by and large have taken a different view of the music and the musicians. While obituary writing has always been a staple of their trade, and while their impassioned eulogizing of favorite musicians might sound like so many nails being driven into jazz's coffin, even this part of the job usually radiates the exalted hopes they've attached to the music's potential as a force of joy, redemption, and transcendence. Peruse the work of any of major jazz critic, and it won't be long before you find an essay arguing that Armstrong, Ellington, Earl Hines, Billie Holiday, Dizzy Gillespie, Benny Carter, Red Rodney, and Doc Cheatham improved with age, that it's their late-career performances—usually trashed by greenhorn critics itching for the shock of the new—that truly reveal the fullness of these musicians' artistry. For every sensational example of a famous musician's tragic decline, these critics offer multiple counterexamples of "outcats" gamely staying afloat in obscurity or exile, then suddenly breaking out in a burst of fugitive glory.

The sensibility at work here might be described as passionate rather than tragic, romantic rather than Romantic. This has something to do with the exigencies of the trade. The people we call jazz critics have never enjoyed the occupational security that goes with the tenured academic positions available to elite literary critics, or with the handsome paychecks available to savvy rock critics who know their way around the media conglomerates that undergird rock's multibillion-dollar industry. Like the vast majority of jazz musicians, they've had to scramble and scuffle to stay afloat in their chosen discipline. As noted by Dan Morgenstern, the jazz critic and editor who now directs the Institute of Jazz Studies at Rutgers/Newark, jazz critics have worked as "editors and a&r [record company artist-and-repertory] men, broadcasters and emcees, publicity flacks and personal managers, concert producers and TV script advisors, songwriters and lecturers."[13]

No writer has ever made a living writing exclusively about jazz, and most of the jazz writing that brings any decent remuneration is not the rhetorical analysis and aesthetic judgment that has defined "criticism" in the Western intellectual tradition since Aristotle, but rather the reportorial human-interest stories and celebrity profile magazine pieces that add splash and color to modern journalism. Morgenstern's jazz critic job description doesn't include the non–jazz world employment—encyclopedia editing, adjunct teaching, and the like—that even some of the most famous U.S. jazz critics have needed to pay their bills.

In a field of black creative leadership, most jazz critics are white, and they've often brought to their work a heightened sense of social purpose in a culture in which crossing the color line historically has been fraught with complications. (Jazz, said Martin Williams, represents "our unsolved problems, all our lack of self-knowledge, all sorts of things . . . we refuse to admit or refuse to face up to.")[14] Precisely because of the relatively smaller number of black voices (and other voices of color) in this discourse, black critics have carried even more of a burden—the burden of "representing the race" in a way that answers to the complex and often contradictory demands of their communities. Across lines of color, there's a romanticism that imbues every jazz critic's engagement with the music, usually starting with an intense, life-changing shock of discovery that comes during adolescence, packing all the power of a religious epiphany. For white critics, the challenge is to talk about their enchantment with black hipness, rhythmic finesse, sensuality, and emotional expressiveness—sometimes expressed through their attraction to white musicians who've absorbed black style—without coming off as lame caricatures of the White Negro or Wigger. For black critics, the challenge is to marshal and distill their privileged access to black culture without buying into notions of racial mystique born of white envy or blacker-than-thou purity. Understanding and honestly discussing the emotional complexities of this challenge is quite difficult.

Against endemic suspicion of their motives and qualifications—"the jazz critic is at best tolerated and at worst despised by the great majority of jazz musicians," Morgenstern has said[15]—the critics I've studied (race aside) have achieved insider status on the jazz scene, an exceptional status that hasn't guaranteed their veracity or trustworthiness nor insulated them from musicians' abuse and censure. Still, as intimates and confidants of the musicians, they've known a great deal about the hardships and dissipations that have been a part of the jazz life. But they've also known something about the prosaic day-to-day struggles and the simple pleasures of musicians' lives. They've known that musicians have bills, hobbies, political views, and favorite foods, movies, and sports teams. They've known about this musician's unruly affairs of the heart and that one's engrossing idiosyncrasies of mind.

These matters of heart and mind can't be reduced to narrow notions of race, but neither can they transcend race in a society that has built itself on a racial fault line. Until the advent of the Lincoln Center jazz program under Wynton Marsalis, no major U.S. cultural institution having anything to do with jazz has had black leadership. U.S. jazz magazines—*Down Beat, Metronome, Record Changer, The Jazz Review, Jazz* (later *Jazz & Pop*), *Jazz Magazine, Jazz Times,* and *Jazziz,* among others—historically have been dominated by white ownership and editorial control. White voices likewise have dominated jazz's representation in the mainstream print and broadcast media. Record companies and booking agencies have always been white-controlled. In the face of this, it's hardly surprising that some black jazz musicians would liken the jazz world to a plantation economy or would group white critics along with record executives, agents, and club owners as members of the master class.

At the same time, precisely because of this white hegemony in the jazz business and in U.S. culture more generally, it's been crucial for black musicians to gain white critics as allies, and for these critics to use their white privilege on behalf of the musicians. The black writer Amiri Baraka remembers the night in 1960 "when I was a little boy of 25 trying to be a jazz critic I had gone without benefit of a sponsor to the Village Vanguard where [Miles] Davis was playing." Baraka—then LeRoi Jones—wandered into the dressing room, hoping to get an interview with the man he had idolized in his youth in Newark as a fledgling trumpeter and bebop fan. He was left high and dry. "He waved off my request, mumbling something, I guess about how he didn't want to be bothered." The disappointed but daring Baraka shot back at Davis: "I'd bet you'd do it if I was Nat Hentoff!"[16] Even when they've most wanted to assert their autonomy and develop more authentic forms of black art (during the Harlem Renaissance of the 1920s and the Black Arts Movement of the 1960s, for example), African American artists have never fully exempted themselves from white patronage, critical support, or creative influence. It is the lot of the black artist in America to come to terms with what Langston Hughes called the "white shadows."[17] This includes cultivating what Emily Bernard calls "the white exception"—which for black jazz musicians has usually meant a white critic who has demonstrated a knowledge of black culture, a social ease with black people, and a proven ability to change minds and shape tastes in the broader culture.[18] For the black musician, the terms of this relationship cannot help but be marked by a certain ambivalence, even if it is also an intimate and rewarding personal friendship.

Just as I want to complicate idealized notions of interracial harmony, I want also to challenge and revise the hoary image of the white jazz critic as a parasite or vampire sucking blood and loot off of black musicians. For one thing, this image has the effect of casting black musicians as abject victims and denying their ability to shape and control their own careers. It also denies the artistic and intellectual freedom of black musicians who may, for their own reasons, find the cultural differences between themselves and white critics a matter of productive curiosity. Because black culture itself is multiracial, polyethnic, and class-stratified, most black musicians have no difficulty recognizing the cultural differences *between* white critics. Just as the *frisson* of difference so often sparks the music itself—think not only about the cross-racial collaboration between Miles Davis and Gil Evans, but of the different "black" identities in the Ellington orchestra or The Modern Jazz Quartet—so too does the play of ethnicity enliven musician/critic social intercourse. Leonard Feather knew that his identity as an Englishman and as a Jew affected his relationships with black musicians in different ways— the first identity invoking their cosmopolitanism, the second their sense of a shared minority experience. Musicians have known that Nat Hentoff, Ira Gitler, and Gary Giddins are not just white but Jewish; that John Hammond, Marshall Stearns, and Whitney Balliett were northeastern WASPs, while Martin Williams was a southern one; that George Frazier was a Boston Irish "southie" posing as a Harvard don; that Ralph Gleason was a New York Irishman posing as a San Francisco love child. It may or may not be true, as Ishmael Reed put it, that "most jazz criticism is a form of white-collar crime."[19] But if it is true, it's only the beginning of the story, not the conclusion.

Where does this leave the black jazz critic? Very often throughout the history of jazz, invisible, or, like LeRoi Jones in 1960, struggling for a piece of the action. In 1957, the African American pianist Billy Taylor published an essay titled "Negroes Don't Know Anything about Jazz." Taylor lamented that the jazz audience was overwhelmingly white and argued that more blacks would appreciate the music if only more black writers would write about it. "Will Negro writers be content to let writers like Nat Hentoff, Bill Coss, Marshall Stearns, Whitney Balliett, Orrin Keepnews and other interested and talented white writers tell the whole story of jazz?" Taylor asked, adding, "Don't they have anything to say as Negroes?"[20] Taylor had to know that within black America there were forms of "criticism" organic to neighborhood and family social life—the word on the street and around the dinner table about who was really blowing. There's never been a more efficient form of community criticism than amateur night at the Apollo Theater, where performers who can't cut the mustard are unceremoniously booed off the stage while those who do are ecstatically embraced. It's always been shocking to the person who thinks of film criticism only as magazine and newspaper movie reviews to discover in a black neighborhood movie theater a quite different mode of critical engagement—an audience in constant dialogue with the movie as it is being screened. So too do black mass audiences tend to relate to music—in real time, orally and physically, asking it to speak directly to them and to move their bodies. But Taylor, who was just then hatching what has become a career-long commitment to jazz repertory and formal jazz education, was interested in the more "serious" mode of appreciation that formal jazz criticism represented.

If we are to understand the history and political economy of jazz, we must probe and untangle knotty intersections of black, brown, beige, and white; complex dynamics of race, gender, class, nationality, and power; interlocking cultures of sound, image, and word. This is what I propose to do in this book, through the figure of the jazz critic.

Canonizing Jazz

I begin in chapter 1 with a focus on John Hammond and Leonard Feather, arguably the two most consequential behind-the-scenes players in the music's history. This chapter details how Hammond and Feather established the field of U.S. jazz criticism as a multi-pronged mission involving artist management, record production, concert promotion, mass media advocacy, and liberal political activism. I examine how these two white critics—Hammond the Vanderbilt scion, Feather the emigré British Jew—countered both the bohemian and the primitivist conceptions of black culture that had flourished in the 1920s, and I examine the complex politics of race, class, and nation that sometimes united and sometimes divided the two men.

In chapter 2 I construct a more sweeping portrait of the 1930s and 1940s jazz world, mapping the development of a swing-era fan discourse in *Down Beat* and *Metronome* against the advent of an anti-commercial critical discourse that begins (in the work of Milt Gabler, Marshall Stearns, Barry Ulanov, George Simon, Ralph de Toledano, Eugene Williams, and others) to develop a formal aesthetic paradigm of jazz. I explore the dynamics of race, class, and gender that inflect the experiences of young white male fans Nat Hentoff, Martin Williams, Ralph Gleason, and an army of "hot collectors" who crossed the color line into black neighborhoods in search of blues and jazz records and performances. I further consider how swing-era African

American fans and writers (especially the poet and newspaperman Frank Marshall Davis) thought about the meaning of jazz and the role of jazz criticism in different ways than whites did. Chapter 3 examines the emergence of jazz history in the late 1930s, focusing on the signal importance of the 1939 book *Jazzmen*, and then tracing the ensuing historiographic debates that intersect with the traditionalist/modernist sectarian wars of the 1940s and 1950s in the work of Rudi Blesh, Sidney Finkelstein, Barry Ulanov, Marshall Stearns, and Ralph Ellison.

In chapter 4 I focus on the critics who came of age in the 1950s, especially Nat Hentoff, Whitney Balliett, Martin Williams, Gunther Schuller, and Ralph Gleason. I connect their call for a more "serious," intellectualized jazz criticism to cold war–era cultural politics, and I consider how this stance shaped aesthetic preferences and complicated the critics' attachments to the music and the musicians. Chapter 5 links this new trend in postwar jazz criticism with broader cultural developments that helped to strengthen the association between "the jazz mainstream" and "mainstream America." I focus on the advent of the Newport Jazz Festival and the Lenox School of Jazz as sites where critics and other gatekeepers evangelized the music as fine art and as a force of racial harmony and bourgeois normalcy.

In chapters 4 and 5 I'm trying to capture a moment in jazz history when aesthetic and sociopolitical borders were constantly under revision. As the bebop revolution of the early 1940s spawned a panoply of stylistic directions for modern jazz (hard bop, Afro-Cuban, cool, soul, Third Stream, free), jazz criticism cultivated new rhetorics to describe the artistic/intellectual ambitions of the new music while also challenging the analytic frames of European musical tradition. Just as this "mainstreaming" of jazz was unfolding in the 1950s, pitched political battles for civil rights in the United States and African independence endowed blacks with ideas about creative freedom and cultural autonomy that clashed with the cold war integrationist agenda that had come to dominate jazz criticism. In chapter 6, I analyze the white critics' ambivalent response to jazz's black freedom movement, as well as black critics' (especially Amiri Baraka's) difficult challenge in answering the political demands of the 1960s. This chapter shows how jazz criticism began the 1960s embroiled in partisan debates over the relationship between free jazz, black freedom, and the cold war, and ended the decade trying to make sense of jazz's fate in the wake of the British Invasion, the ascendancy of rock, Black Power, and the counterculture.

The last two chapters take distinct angles on the dynamics and difficulties of jazz's canonization. In chapter 7 I consider the critical discourse on a single musician, Charlie Parker, exploring how some of his key interpreters have struggled over the terms of his memorialization. My central focus is on Ross

Russell, the record producer and critic who nursed an obsessive desire to deliver the most definitive critical, imaginative, and historical statements on Parker, one of the most intriguing and elusive of jazz's major figures. Russell's vexed personal relationship with Parker and his intimacies with other white male critics allow me to sharply pinpoint questions about race, masculinity, and asymmetries of power in the critic/musician relationship. Chapter 8 closes the book with a discussion of the jazz culture wars of the 1980s and 1990s. I examine Gary Giddins, Stanley Crouch, Albert Murray, and other critics who have elaborated and extended the postwar frameworks developed by Ralph Ellison, Marshall Stearns, Martin Williams, and others, and I consider various strains of disenchantment with this new dominant jazz criticism.

My focus on jazz critics contributes to an exciting and burgeoning scholarly field, a new interdisciplinary "jazz studies" that, like the most valuable jazz criticism itself, aims to take the discussion of the music beyond the cabalistic ephemera of record collectors, the hagiographic writhings of aficionados, the sober formalism of traditional musicology, and the impressionistic treatments of popular journalism. In what has emerged as a clarion call for jazz scholars across the disciplines, the music historian Scott DeVeaux wrote in 1991 that "the time has come for an approach that is less invested in the ideology of jazz as an aesthetic object and more responsive to issues of historical particularity. Only in this way can the study of jazz break free from its self-imposed isolation, and participate with other disciplines in the exploration of meaning in American culture."[21] Contemporary jazz scholarship—whether affiliated with ethnomusicology, English, American studies, cultural studies, or history—investigates the ways jazz has been imagined, defined, managed, and shaped within particular cultural contexts. It considers how jazz as an experience of sounds, movements, and states of feeling has always been mediated and complicated by peculiarly American cultural patterns, especially those of race and sexuality.[22]

Critics have been among the most important jazz mediators, crucially shaping the terms and conditions on which the music and the musicians reach the public. Some of the most influential statements in jazz criticism have been rendered in the form of liner notes, the product packaging prose form audiences encounter even before they cue up a record or a CD. In Burlington, Vermont, the small New England city where I live, in recent years the jazz festival that runs every June has featured Bob Blumenthal as its critic-in-residence; he moderates "meet the artist" and lecture/demonstration events and leads a session in which audiences listen to a classic recording, then conduct an analytical discussion of it—recalling the United Hot Clubs listening sessions pioneered in the late 1930s by Marshall Stearns, John Hammond, and George Frazier.

Jazz history teems with these kinds of scenes: Stearns's jazz history classes at NYU and the Lenox School of Jazz (where his students included Ornette Coleman and Don Cherry); Barry Ulanov and Rudi Blesh leading bebop and traditional New Orleans musicians in a radio battle-of-the-bands; Leonard Feather conducting his "blindfold test" to get musicians to assess and discuss each other; Ralph Gleason, as TV host of "Jazz Casual," lingering insouciantly on the edges of the picture frame, Zelig-like, as John Coltrane and Elvin Jones scream and thrash and raise the skies in a performance of "Afro-Blue"; Gary Giddins fronting the American Jazz Orchestra with spoken obbligatos on Ellingtonia; a Stanley Crouch sermon on "the majesty of the blues" appearing on a Wynton Marsalis recording.

There are excellent rock, pop, and hip-hop critics, but it's hard to imagine one of them serving as critic-in-residence at a festival. For that matter, I can't remember ever hearing the term "gospel critic," though I'm quite sure that black folks who leave church on Sunday know whether the music was better this week than last. Of all the great American vernacular musics, only jazz has cultivated intellectual discourse as a core element of its superstructure—which is not to say that the other musics are not of intellectual interest, or that they are of any less artistic worth, as many jazz enthusiasts believe. Indeed, that jazz alone is trumpeted as "a uniquely American art form"—when the same thing could be said about rock, gospel, country, and bluegrass—underscores more than anything else how successful jazz critics have been in bootlegging the discourse of high art to argue for the music's aesthetic superiority. It may be true that jazz really is aesthetically superior, but it also may be true that jazz's early association with artistic modernism and urban sophistication—compared to, say, country blues—gave it enough capital among European and white American intellectual elites to last it through the twentieth century. As blues, rock, country, and other American vernacular musics take their own paths to canonization, it will be interesting to see how concepts of art, culture, race, and criticism are reconfigured.[23]

Much as I think the story I tell in this book is an important one for understanding the history of jazz, during my research and writing, and through my exchanges with fellow jazz studies scholars, I've also sensed the limitations and heard the silences of this project. For one thing, though this book is an ambitious study of U.S. jazz criticism, there are many notable American jazz critics unrepresented or underrepresented in these pages.[24] I know about such critics because they've been published in U.S. jazz magazines and the national press. An untold number of others—writing for regional newspapers, college newspapers, jazz appreciation society newsletters, and the like—have flown beneath the radar of my research design, though they richly deserve further study.

My central theme—jazz's canonization as an art—has tilted my focus not just toward elite sources, but toward elite sources in a small number of major urban centers, especially New York. I think this is a necessary bias, given New York's importance since the 1930s as a cultural capital and a proving ground for musicians and writers alike. But having studied, taught, and written about jazz while living in metropolitan New York/New Jersey as well as other locations (Massachusetts, Pennsylvania, Indiana, Colorado, Virginia, and Vermont), I know very well that there are vibrant local jazz cultures outside of Manhattan. I've come to know distinctive jazz cultures in Brooklyn, Boston, and even Burlington, Vermont, which produces an avant-garde magazine (*Signal to Noise*) and has become a destination location for such musicians as William Parker, Matthew Shipp, and Oliver Lake. In Harrisburg, Pennsylvania, I encountered a local jazz society that sponsors concerts, jam sessions, and jazz education in the public schools, and a local historical society that has mastered the "Duke Ellington-once-performed-here" rhetoric of jazz historiography. Multiply these scenes and activities to cover the expanse of the country, throw in Internet jazz discourse, formal and informal record collector networks, and jazz radio programming, and the story of jazz's canonization grows exponentially.

But even that's only the beginning of a much larger story. Like Ken Burns's jazz documentary and the vast majority of jazz history texts, this book is not only New York-centric but U.S.-centric in focus. I mention non-American critics (Hugues Panassié, Charles Delauney, André Hodeir, Eric Hobsbawn, Philip Larkin, and Max Harrison) only as they appear in the U.S. jazz discourse. This is a serious limitation. Putting aside the vexed question—one that has been raised in a particularly tendentious fashion by James Lincoln Collier[25]—of whether or not jazz has been properly appreciated in the United States, there's no question that its exalted image has much to do with the reception it has received the world over. Since World War II, every European and Asian capital has had a jazz scene, some attracting U.S. expatriate jazz musicians of major consequence (Kenny Clarke, Dexter Gordon, Johnny Griffin, George Russell, Don Cherry, and Jon Hendricks, to name just a few). John Hammond started his career in the 1930s writing for British music magazines and making records for the UK market. The French company BYG recorded some of the singular music of the late 1960s avant garde, and much of what was considered U.S. jazz's cutting edge in the 1970s and 1980s was recorded on the Italian Black Saint and German ECM labels. Today's serious jazz consumer, even if located in New York or Vermont, buys CDs that are produced in Italy, Japan, Germany, France, Denmark, and the Netherlands. Given the transnational scope of the jazz superstructure, it stands to reason that some of the most searching jazz criticism has been written by citizens of countries others than the United States.[26]

Though I believe that a focus on the United States, and on the exchange and interaction between blacks and whites, is especially important to the history of jazz, I think that the very idea of jazz's Americanness should be critically analyzed rather than simply taken for granted. John Szwed argues that jazz began as a world music, noting that early New Orleans jazz polyphony and rhythms had more in common with the music of Martinique, Brazil, and Argentina than anything that was heard in the rest of North America at the beginning of the twentieth century.[27] By enlarging our concept of "American" to include all of the Americas, and not just the United States, we give ourselves a sturdier framework for understanding jazz as a New World mulatto music that carries forward the already Africanized, multicultural soundscape of the Spanish and Portuguese colonial powers. Here's the deeper historical foundation for what we now call "Latin Jazz" (which, incidentally, gets more play in books like *Jazz for Dummies* and *The Complete Idiot's Guide to Jazz* than in the standard college jazz history textbooks).[28] Only by fully reckoning with the Latino presence in jazz and other black American musics can we avoid simply replacing a limited narrative of white American exceptionalism with a limited narrative of black American exceptionalism.[29] And the rich nuances and complexities of "race" in Latino culture—not to mention creolized New Orleans—ought to compel a further assault on the simple white-black dyad that dominates U.S. race discourse. Very often the "white" musicians discussed in jazz histories were Italians and Jews whose whiteness was of a very different color than that of Irish, Anglo, and German Americans.[30]

By far the loudest silences in this book are female and feminine voices. While female jazz critics have been even fewer in number than female jazz musicians, the issue is not simply a matter of sexual identity, but also of gender dynamics. From the violent gangster milieu of jazz's early sporting life environs; to the urbane, stylized machismo of the jazz-inflected New Frontier; to Wynton Marsalis and Stanley Crouch's tendentious feminization of the 1960s counterculture, jazz culture has been dominated by masculinist voices and sensibilities. I've noted in this book several important instances in which male critics have buttressed their masculinist authority by distancing themselves from sentimental attachments to the popular music of their youth. This feeds a larger pattern in which jazz's reputed high art autonomy and profundity are complemented by a concept of criticism that stresses taut discipline, rationality, and judiciousness—qualities assumed to be part of a masculine intellectual seriousness set off from the infantilized and feminized emotional realm of mass popular culture. On a more practical level, women have been resented as intruders on the homosocial boisterousness and easy profanity of jazzmen in the dressing room and on the road. Women in the jazz world very often are pigeonholed either as maternal figures or as sexual objects. The artist and writer Sharony Andrews Green has spoken to me with great pride about helping young New York male jazz musicians with domestic chores they can't handle because of their busy traveling schedules. But she has also told me that, as a serious professional writer, she can't help but resent it when she senses that a musician looks at her first as a woman.[31]

Women who deserve further study include the Canadian-born Helen Oakley Dance, a major figure on the jazz scene of the 1930s and 1940s as a writer, producer, and publicist; and Valerie Wilmer, the British writer and photographer, whose book *As Serious as Your Life: The Story of the New Jazz* (1977) provides both an indispensable view of the post-1960s avant garde and a bracing look at race and gender relations in jazz. It's important to recognize the work produced by these women as quality work, not just as women's work. But it's also important to recognize how such work might be different because it has been produced by women working in a realm dominated by men and by patriarchal ideologies. What's striking about both Wilmer's book and Sharony Andrews Green's biography, *Grant Green: Rediscovering the Forgotten Genius of Jazz Guitar* (1999), is the attention they pay to the vital roles played by girlfriends, wives, and other family members in sustaining a male musician's career. Often the costs are very high and the rewards uneven. But Wilmer and Green are not trying to demonize the men or sentimentalize the women and children—they're trying to give us a clear and truthful account of jazz lives in all of their wonderful and terrible messiness. In doing so, they achieve something that has eluded even the most perceptive male jazz writers, and they raise the bar for all jazz writers.[32]

Jazz is a very big story indeed, bigger than even the critics have let on. But theirs is a very important story too. Here's my version of it, in much more than a few words.

CHAPTER 1

"Not Only a New Art Form but a New Reason for Living"

Needed: White Guys without Dates

In July 1935, a twenty-one-year-old Englishman named Leonard Feather set sail for New York for the first of two visits that year intended to spark his fledgling career as a jazz writer. Feather had cut his writing teeth apprenticing for German and French movie trade magazines, but for the previous eighteen months he had turned his focus to jazz, publishing articles in Britain's *Melody Maker*, *Gramophone*, *Tune Times*, and *Swing Music*. Also a budding pianist and songwriter, Feather's knowledge of jazz had come mainly through records. For European jazz cognoscenti of the 1930s, a pilgrimage to New York, the jazz recording capital, was *de rigueur*. As Feather relates in his 1987 autobiography, his first 1935 trip held especially great promise because of the person who was waiting for his ship to dock in New York harbor, ready to shepherd him around to the city's jazz spots: John Hammond.[1]

Hammond, then twenty-five, was well known in British jazz circles as a record producer, talent scout, journalist, and social critic. He had been commissioned by Columbia to produce a series of sessions from 1933 to 1935 for British release, and he had started his career as a jazz writer in the early 1930s in *Melody Maker*, *Gramophone*, and another British publication called *Rhythm*. It would still be a few years before Hammond established his dominion over the U.S. jazz scene, but the foundation had been firmly laid in 1933. In a feverish seventy-two-hour stretch in November of that year, Hammond supervised the last recordings of Bessie Smith and then the first recordings of Billie Holiday. These sessions employed a racially mixed group of sidemen, including the Jewish clarinetist Benny Goodman—an early example of the integrationist agenda that would become Hammond's hallmark.

Before his first 1935 transatlantic journey, Feather, who came from a wealthy Jewish family in London, had met only one black person in his life—Louis Armstrong, whom he had contrived to meet at a bar near London's Palladium the night of Armstrong's first British concert in 1932. Feather encountered Armstrong—he says in the autobiography—as "a mature and greatly respected artist," unconcerned about his racial identity and unaware of the history of American race relations. But mainly through reading Hammond's dispatches in the British music press over the next few years, Feather learned about the existence of Jim Crow segregation and racial oppression. This knowledge did not dampen his enthusiasm for crossing the racial border in search of cultural riches.

This meant Harlem. Within hours of his arrival, Feather found himself at the Apollo Theater, the leading shrine of black vaudeville entertainment. In spite of the building's "exotic, funky appeal," Feather found the evening's bill to be a let-down. While comedian Pigmeat Markham was "raw and raucously funny," that week's house orchestra, Erskine Hawkins and his Bama State Collegians, struck Feather as "not the equal of the black bands whose records I had been collecting." Even more disappointing was Bessie Smith, whose performance Feather deemed "pathetically unrepresentative of her early grandeur." Feather wondered what this meant to the reputation of a performer whom Hammond regarded as the greatest artist that his country had produced. Would she be remembered as the great blues empress of the 1920s, or as the woman he had seen on this night, who had drunk too much and had "proclaimed racy lyrics in a strange, throbbing voice"? Would she be remembered at all? What good was it that he and Hammond knew of her former glory when "to almost all whites she was unknown," while "to most blacks she was an insignificant, half-forgotten vaudeville performer"?[2]

Leonard Feather's remembrance of his arrival in the United States, with its racial self-reflexivity and its dual foregrounding of John Hammond and Harlem, spotlights several themes rich in meaning and implication for the canonization of jazz. First is the image of Europe as a standard-bearer of high art, ostensibly transcendent civilizational values, and superior skills of cutting-edge artistic awareness. Well into the twentieth century, this image endured as a rebuke to American philistinism, whether the latter was attributed to the lingering effects of Puritanism or to the poison of a business-dominated popular culture. During the first decades of the century, as Progressive middle-class reformers held jazz responsible for rising rates of drug addiction and illegitimate birth and as Protestant ministers (black and white) ranted apocalyptically about jazz's association with devil worship, word filtered back from Europe of Brahms and Stravinsky's excitement over ragtime and of the Swiss conductor Ernst-Alexandre Ansermet's pronouncement that clarinet virtuoso Sidney Bechet was an "artist of genius" who was marking "the highway the whole world will swing along tomorrow."[3]

When the American press reported that Prince George owned one of the world's largest collections of Ellington records, and that—as if to preempt accusations of noblesse oblige dilettantism—he was "often found bending over a revolving disc so that he can hear more clearly . . . the intricate sinuosity of a tenor saxophone as it curls in and out of the ensemble," the implication was that jazz consumption in Britain was at once a more serious and a more credentialed affair than it was at home.[4] In France, jazz had enjoyed a vogue among the intellectual avant garde since the 1920s. The notion that black rhythmic artistry pullulates exclusively from the lower half of the human anatomy—a holdover from the Josephine Baker rage of the 1920s, when, as Phyllis Rose puts it, "the erotic gaze of a nation moved downward" to contemplate the dancer's exquisite rear end[5]—appeared to be contradicted by the kinesthetics of Parisian audiences at Ellington and Armstrong concerts in the 1930s: holding chins in hand in statuesque poses reminiscent of "Il Penseroso," French listeners maintained a hushed immobility from the beginning of the show to the end, the better to apprehend the music's *cerebral* qualities. One listener doubtless so postured during a 1939 Ellington concert, critic Jacques-Henri Lévesque, professed to hear in the band's ensemble flourishes and rhythmic pulse the "very secret of the cosmos." Surrealist poet Blaise Cendrars, illustrating the French intellectual's proclivity for manifesto, said of the same concert, "Such music is not only a new art form but a new reason for living."[6]

"It cannot be too often repeated, to our shame, that Europeans realized the importance and value of jazz many years before the Americans who originated it," wrote Ralph de Toledano in 1947.[7] If this widespread sentiment explains why John Hammond found a sympathetic audience in Britain, and why Leonard Feather was able to hatch and nurture his jazz interest there, it also raises the ante on the significance of their pilgrimage to Harlem. For in depositing themselves at the very symbolic center of black culture, these two young white men set spinning a whirling kaleidoscope of race, class, nation, and culture. Here were white cultural colonialists bent on a mission of discovery and resource extraction, their artistic booty to enter circulation among audiences who wouldn't think of making their own foray into these darker regions. And yet embedded in this dynamic of U.S. racial colonialism

were the seeds of an emergent U.S. cultural nationalism, a postcolonial nationalism of sorts, resting on an inter-class as well as cross-racial foundation.
Here the story is of two white men—one the scion of one of America's sto-
ried old-money families, the other a London bourgeois who would soon
emigrate and trade the genteel luxury of his upbringing for the pell-mell
lifestyle of the U.S. entertainment industry—who set out to convince the
world that a music born of slavery and segregation was the true American
art, the singular twentieth-century art, and as such a symbol of America's
emergence as a self-sustaining cultural entity. But self-sustaining does not
yet mean self-understanding: hence the hand-wringing over the infantile
state of U.S. jazz criticism.

It was a curious collision of cultural forces: the art that vindicates American civilization is the one that points up the tragedies of American history
and the hypocrisies of American culture; the voices loudest in public praise
of the art belong to men hailing from social stations far removed from that of
the artists. Fueling Hammond and Feather's sense of purpose, invigorating
their conviction about the justness—no, the necessity—of their mission,
was a looming specter of loss and a faith in the possibility of remembrance
and recognition. Who will remember Bessie Smith? Who will recognize
Bessie Smith's successors and convince an indifferent America of their vital
importance? Just what sort of attention do these artists deserve?

Questions of this sort licked at Feather as Hammond guided him deeper
into the Harlem night. Next it was fifteen blocks north to the Savoy Ballroom,
the "Home of Happy Feet," where swing, the stomping, dance-oriented
music that originated in Harlem, captivated the bodies of hundreds of the
young and the young at heart. Here things really came alive:

> The impact of the moment I walked into the Savoy was immediate and too
> startling ever to be forgotten. The sensation was one of removal from any world
> I had known. During the first five minutes I felt I had absorbed more music than
> I had heard in all my years of listening to jazz impersonalized by the obstacle
> of the phonograph.

As the Teddy Hill Orchestra swung hard, Feather marveled at the cohesion
of the rhythm section and the power of the soloists, especially Chu Berry
on tenor sax, Roy Eldridge on trumpet, and Dickie Wells on trombone.
Oddly, to Feather, the dancing "jitterbugs," caught up in a stomping groove
that literally shook the parquet floor, seemed little interested in the finer
points of the music. "The music that made such a feverish emotional impact
on my sensibilities," he observed, "appealed to this audience mainly on
utilitarian grounds." Not until "John and I, joined soon by a few others who

perhaps were encouraged by our initiative," did anyone sidle up close to the bandstand, the better to scrutinize and appreciate the musicians at work.

Two young white men without dates, in a room full of good-timing cheer and ecstatic bodily release, position themselves between the musicians and the audience—here, in microcosm, was the *Ur*-stance of the jazz critic: poised on the seam between artistic creation and popular consumption, close to but also crucially distinct from the dancing mass body, caught up in an imagined sense of privileged intellectual and emotional communion with the music. Overlaying this subtle geography of inside/outside was both a self-consciousness about racial and class difference and a correspondingly self-justifying sense of exceptionalism, a conceit that the critic's exalted purpose exempted him from the conventional patterns of cross-racial exchange. So, while surprised by the Savoy patrons' seeming indifference to the music *qua* music, Feather was pleased by the crowd's interracial composition and egalitarian dynamic. He made a point during this sojourn of *not* visiting the Cotton Club, offended by its policy of admitting blacks only as performers and uncomfortable with the thought of being confused with the rich whites whose "slumming" filled the coffers of the club's mobster proprietors. Feather knew that Hammond came from great wealth, that his mother was a Vanderbilt and his father an heir to a Southern fortune and one of the high-powered corporate lawyers of the day. He was sure, however—or at least needed to believe—that Hammond went to Harlem not to service his own decadent pleasures, but to work earnestly and valiantly toward racial equality and recognition of black artistic excellence.

In Feather's eyes, Hammond was "more at ease in Harlem than almost any other white American could feel." Fancying a similar reputation for himself, Feather was pleased to discover that, paradoxically, his outsider status might help him become a privileged insider:

> The Savoy engendered in me oddly mixed emotions of alienation (due to my British reserve rather than my whiteness) and of belonging, for it was at the ballroom, and at other retreats north of Central Park, that I would quickly learn to feel more at one with my surroundings than anywhere else either at home or abroad. There was an immediate sense of being welcome in a community where, as Hammond and others had warned, people from downtown might expect to find themselves regarded with acute suspicion. Not being an American, as I soon found out, fortified my credentials.[8]

Through Hammond, Feather met and befriended a number of "accessible and hospitable" musicians, including trumpeter Red Allen and pianist Teddy Wilson, and made strategic contacts with other music and entertainment industry personnel. Clarence Williams, the early blues and jazz songwriter and pianist then operating as a music publisher, bought two of Feather's songs, boosting his confidence to continue writing blues and jazz material. Romeo Dougherty, the entertainment editor of the *New York Amsterdam News*, made Feather the paper's first white contributor, giving him a column as a London correspondent reporting on that city's West Indian club scene. *Metronome* editor George Simon also retained Feather as a London correspondent reporting on British jazz recording and concert developments, including his own role in helping Benny Carter assemble the first interracial and international jazz orchestra.[9]

Leonard Feather had found his calling. He would not be the dutiful Jewish son, joining his father's business in clothing and real estate. In late 1939, he would move permanently to the United States, where, until his death in 1994, he was a ubiquitous presence on the jazz scene as a journalist, record and concert producer, publicist, radio programmer, encyclopedist, composer, lyricist, and educator. "Over the amazingly long, prolific, and frequently controversial run of his career," Gary Giddins eulogized, Feather "decisively supplanted Hammond as jazz's most important critic and chronicler."[10] Feather's career would include several acrimonious public feuds with Hammond, the earliest coming over Duke Ellington's creative direction when the composer and bandleader began to explore scored-through concert forms. While Feather became a herald of "progress" and "freedom" in jazz and supported most of its stylistic innovations until souring on certain strains of the post-1960 avant garde, Hammond—who carried his scouting, promotional, and production talents into the genres of gospel, blues, rhythm-and-blues, and rock into the 1980s—scorned bebop and other post–World War II modern jazz styles, sounds he regarded as "cerebral gymnastics" that emphasized "technique at the expense of musical emotion."[11] But no critic has ever wielded as much influence over the development and direction of jazz as Hammond did during the Swing Era. Feather, in 1964, attempted to summarize this influence:

> Hammond's importance [was] inestimable. It is worthwhile speculating what the course of jazz might have been without him. Benny Goodman, for whom jazz in 1934 was not a consuming passion, might have lived out his life as a house musician at NBC or CBS. The swing era, at least by that name or that figurehead, would never have arrived. Meade Lux Lewis would probably have spent the rest of his days as a cabdriver or janitor, and we critics who have written about it with such self-righteous knowledge might never have heard that boogie-woogie existed. Count Basie might have stayed in Midwestern obscurity. Teddy Wilson certainly would not have joined Goodman, and it might have been years before

the color line was broken. As for Billie Holiday, it is chilling to contemplate what her fate could have been had Hammond not sponsored her . . . . The argument that talent will out—that if Hammond had not launched these artists, someone else would have—is glib and totally unconvincing.[12]

Hammond, as Dan Morgenstern has said, needed to be needed.[13] Duke Ellington clearly didn't need him, nor did the beboppers and other modern jazz musicians whose ideas about jazz's post–World War II future left Hammond behind. Did Billie Holiday need him in the desperate way that Feather suggests? Did Bessie Smith need him as badly as Hammond always thought she did? Did Hammond need *them* just as badly? These are thorny, probably unanswerable questions. But in 1935, when Leonard Feather needed a Virgil to guide him through swinging Harlem, John Hammond was his man.

WASPs, Jews, and Jitterbugs

At the time they established positions of influence in the jazz world, Leonard Feather and John Hammond were very young men. Hammond, in particular, with his trademark crewcut and inveterate eagerness, always seemed younger than he actually was. As David Stowe has noted, when Hammond hit the public spotlight as the impresario and master of ceremonies of the 1938 "From Spirituals to Swing" concert at Carnegie Hall, profiles in the *New Yorker, Harper's, Collier's,* and elsewhere portrayed him as having the mannerisms of a callow schoolboy.[14] Both had been precocious adolescents, chafing against their class and ethno-religious pedigrees. Feather writes in his memoir of his resistance to "the forced attitudes, beliefs, and superstitious practices" of his childhood Hebrew instruction and of an early epiphany in his family's synagogue, where "the sight of women all seated in the balcony, like some lesser breed not fit to associate with men, taught me a lesson, not only about sexism but about segregation in whatever form it might appear." He soon became a "devout lifelong agnostic" and tested his parent's indulgence by bringing "goyisher" friends home from school. His early romances were with non-Jewish women, including a dalliance with the African American dancer Vivian Dandridge—Dorothy's older sister—during the summer of 1939, when the Dandridge Sisters had an engagement at London's Palladium.[15]

Feather's interest in American popular culture, which began in adolescence when an uncle visiting the United States sent him comic books, was itself a mild transgression against his parents. They boasted of their son's facility on the piano, prizing his mastery of Grieg and Chopin as the proper parlor culture of a well-bred European bourgeois. But Feather had different ideas. When he was fourteen, a school chum had taken him to a Kensington record shop to hear a new 78 just over from the States. Listening to the record—Louis Armstrong's "West End Blues"—sealed Feather's romance with jazz and America. "Nothing mattered except the sheer, pure beauty," he later wrote. "I was hooked . . . . [The record] provided a sense of direction, a lifestyle, an obsessive concern with every aspect of jazz. All that mattered from that moment was the next record release or the latest transatlantic news item."[16]

John Hammond Jr. inherited from his patrician mother a sense of noblesse oblige, a reformist zeal, and a strict moral code that frowned on the use of alcohol and tobacco. But he transmuted her Christian Science fervor into political and cultural activities that challenged his parents' WASP loyalties. As an adolescent, he sneaked out of the family's palatial mansion on East 91st Street on Manhattan's Upper East Side to head for the forbidden pleasures of Harlem's burlesque houses and to shop for African American blues and jazz "race" records. Early on Hammond developed a ferocious distaste for the polite, peppy dance music of white "sweet" bands that played upscale hotel ballrooms, debutante balls, and other cocktail-swilling functions of the leisure class. He found this music insipid, sentimental, and perfectly representative of the hollow artificiality of the socially privileged. What inspired his fanatical devotion was the emotional honesty and gritty realism of the blues, the rhythmic vitality and intense improvisational freedom of hot jazz. He continued building his formidable record collection and his blues and hot jazz purism while prepping at Hotchkiss and during an abbreviated college career at Yale. On the pretext of returning to the city for violin lessons, he scoured Harlem and other black neighborhoods for the latest "race" record releases.

In 1931, at the age of twenty-one, with a $10,000-a-year trust fund to ease him through the Depression, Hammond dropped out of Yale, moved to Greenwich Village, and began his work in the music industry. While working for the powerful music publisher and talent manager Irving Mills, Hammond honed his skills as a record producer and wrote about his favored jazz musicians in the British music press, the *Brooklyn Eagle*, and elsewhere. In defiance of his parents' segregationist and pro-Hoover convictions, he also worked as a disc jockey at New York radio station WEVD (the call letters standing for socialist Eugene V. Debs) and became a contributing writer for the Left-radical *Nation,* where he covered the case of the Scottsboro Nine, and the *New Masses*, the quasi-official cultural journal of the Communist Party of America (CPUSA), where he hyped his own musical activities and exposed racist practices in other sectors of the recording industry. Practicing the politics he wrote about, Hammond raised money for the defense of the Scottsboro Nine, organized for the Congress of Industrial Organizations (CIO), and served as a board member of the National Association for the Advancement of Colored People (NAACP).[17]

For Leonard Feather, jazz and American popular entertainment diverged from his parents' upper-middle-class European Jewish culture. For Hammond, in contrast, jazz and American popular entertainment represented an embrace of working-class American Jewish culture, in alliance with African American folk culture, against his WASP roots. As Lewis Erenberg notes, while Hammond developed a strong admiration for Jews through his love of popular theater and burlesque, his mother, in a rearguard effort of neo-Victorian Progressive reform, spearheaded a theater censorship society aimed at precisely the kind of déclassé shows her son relished. He developed relationships with many Jews prominent in show business and Leftist politics. "I admired them as I admired the black artists on my favorite records. I wanted to be Jewish," Hammond wrote in his autobiography. To his parents' displeasure, Hammond began to search for Jewish tributaries in the family's bloodlines and removed his name from the anti-Semitic Social Register. Given this strong desire to puncture his family's WASP pretenses, it was a deliciously satisfying day for Hammond when, in 1942, his sister Alice married Benny Goodman, whose family was not just Jewish, but working-class immigrant Jewish.[18]

That Feather and Hammond would use music to mark cultural distance from their parents is not itself exceptional: throughout the twentieth century, the consumption of American popular music has been perhaps the most important element in defining and shaping youth culture. What's notable is that two ambitious, well-heeled young men would think of jazz not just as something pleasurable, but as something on which to build a career, something to which they could devote their lives. This music was not *just* fun, they insisted: it was serious, it had deep cultural and historical significance that had to be understood and honored, and it was an important force for positive social change. Hence Feather's ambivalent perceptions that first night at the Savoy with Hammond: it's great that these black and white folks are sharing the dance floor, but why aren't they more interested in the music for its own sake? Don't they understand that these musicians are artists?

To bolster their authority, swing-era jazz critics were at pains to distinguish themselves from mere "fans"—defined as those who had enthusiasm but not expertise—and others given to gravitas-deficient modes of musical consumption. In the late 1930s, as swing music and dancing moved to the center of American youth culture, no figure more threatened the conceit of the jazz critic as a mature arbiter of high-tone artistic activity than the "jitterbug," the dancer whose body splenetically registered swing music as so many jolts of electric current. Hammond evinced an especially strong animus toward the figure, perhaps because his own kinesthetic reactions to the music were not very different. "Hammond in action is the embodiment of the popular conception of the jitterbug," said the *New Yorker*. "When the music jumps, he begins to move his head, his feet, and sometimes his whole body. His eyebrows go up, his mouth opens wide and reveals a set of even, gleaming teeth, and a long-drawn-out 'Yeah' slides out of his throat." As David Stowe notes, Hammond "angrily disclaimed the jitterbug label," telling a reporter, "A jitterbug is an exhibitionist, I'm not. I just like the music, that's all."[19]

Hammond's work habits were well captured in a profile in *Harper's* by Irving Kolodin, who described the young critic on a routine visit to a jazz club:

> If the music appeals to him he will listen intently, responding with a transfixed grin and a metronomic movement of the right foot, from a position as close to the bandstand as any nonunion member can achieve. If he is displeased with the playing, or what is even worse, bored, he will while away the time until things improve in perusal of the *New Masses*, the *New Statesmen*, or *Variety*; for his standard equipment includes a firm bundle of all the interesting publications that have appeared on the newsstands in the preceding twenty-four hours. It is an unpardonable breach, however, for any companion of Hammond's to so much as glance at the weather prediction in his newspaper while a soloist whom John considers "right" is performing.[20]

"For the Race"

Such diligence distinguished Hammond not only from the jitterbugs, but also from slummers, middle-class and upper-class whites who prowled African American neighborhoods for exotic entertainment, sexual adventure, and vice. During the "Negro vogue" of the 1920s, Harlem became the focus of white leisure and fantasy, a kind of imagined jungle of forbidden pleasures. There were at least two Harlems in the 1920s: black Harlem, where working-class and middle-class African Americans lived, worked, prayed, and entertained themselves; and—as Kevin Mumford has termed it—an "all-white leisure zone" of establishments where the only African Americans were the entertainers and the service personnel. At the Cotton Club, the flagship of slumming, a burly black bouncer stood at the door to bar other blacks from entering, while inside, white patrons reveled in the spectacle of scantily clad "tall, tan, terrific gals" dancing with erotic suggestiveness to the "jungle" sounds furnished by the orchestras of Duke Ellington, Cab Calloway, and others. The decor, combining references to the Old South plantation and the primitive "heart of darkness," contributed to the aura of colonial fantasy. The experience for whites, Mumford suggests, was "the cultural equivalent of taking a Cunard cruise to Africa, an exciting excursion into another social world."[21] This phenomenon of urban slumming was in many ways a subset of the larger vogue of "primitivism" in post–World War I Western culture, a turn to the racial Other—always imagined as a hypersexual being—as an escape from the sexual repression and the soul-deadening impact of industrialization and bureaucratization.[22]

The high point of slumming and the "Negro vogue" coincided with the Harlem Renaissance—or, as it was known at the time, the Negro Renaissance—the flowering of black literature, culture, and intellectual self-examination associated with such figures as W. E. B. Du Bois, Alain Locke, James Weldon Johnson, Zora Neale Hurston, Jesse Fauset, Nella Larsen, Charles Johnson, Langston Hughes, Claude McKay, and Countee Cullen. As a cultural movement, the Harlem Renaissance was richly layered, multifarious, and full of fascinating internal debate and division. The central questions were these: What is authentic African American art? Which expressive practices and artistic forms will contribute most to the cultural progress of the race? How should "the Negro" be represented to the larger world?

To oversimplify a set of complex debates and shifting alliances, the movement essentially clustered around two cultural ideologies. The first was associated with the older figures Du Bois and Locke and represented in the pages of *Opportunity*, *The Messenger*, and *The Crisis,* the Du Bois-edited official magazine of the NAACP. This position advocated a vanguard of what Du Bois called "the talented tenth," a group of exceptionally gifted black leaders and artists who would dissolve white stereotypes about black cultural inferiority by upholding a Victorian-derived "politics of respectability" and by creating a distinctive racial art that cultivated vernacular themes and idioms within the framework of elite European forms. Black art should draw on the cultural inheritance of the race but should aspire to Euro-American high-culture aesthetic norms of discipline, restraint, austerity, and resolution. Du Bois, for instance, saw the slave spirituals as the soul of the black people, the basis of a folk-centered nationalist art that would lead to the cosmopolitan "kingdom of culture." As a buttoned-up Victorian bourgeois, on the other hand, he condemned the "pythian madness" of black evangelical religion and resisted the ecstatic rhythms and sensuality of jazz and blues. This was a racial uplift ideology that loathed slumming, primitivism, and any other form of white fantasy or white consumption that associated black culture primarily with sex and vice.[23]

The second Harlem Renaissance cultural ideology announced itself forcefully in Langston Hughes's 1926 essay "The Negro Artist and the Racial Mountain," and that same year, in the journal *Fire!!*, an artistic manifesto produced by a younger school of writers and artists, including Hughes, Hurston, Wallace Thurman, Aaron Douglas, Bruce Nugent, John P. Davis, and Gwendolyn Bennett. Hughes's "Racial Mountain" essay was published in the *Nation* as a response to George Schuyler's satirical essay "The Negro Art Hokum," which rejected the idea of a separate black aesthetic. But Hughes's essay took aim at a deeper vein of black cultural conservatism, Eurocentric aesthetics, and hidebound puritanical morality. He implicitly mocked Du Bois's "talented tenth" concept, arguing that the "better-class Negro" is typically someone trying to be just "like white folks." He located racial authenticity in the "heritage of rhythm and warmth" and the "incongruous humor" of the blues, and he describes his own poetry as an effort "to grasp and hold some of the meanings and rhythms of jazz." "Let the blare of Negro jazz bands and the bellowing voice of Bessie Smith singing Blues penetrate the closed ears of the colored near-intellectuals until they listen and perhaps understand," the essay defiantly proclaimed. "We younger Negro artists who create now intend to express our dark-skinned selves without fear or shame."[24] *Fire!!* was an even more defiant nose-thumbing at the Harlem intellectual establishment: a collection of poetry, short stories, polemical essays, and art work saturated with the taboo theme of black sexuality, including homosexuality and interracial sex. Together, the two documents heralded a new cultural sensibility in which black rhythm, humor, emotional spontaneity, eroticism, and sexual desire would figure prominently.[25]

At the center of the rupture in Harlem Renaissance ideology was one of its white patrons and chroniclers, Carl Van Vechten, and his controversial 1926 novel *Nigger Heaven*. Van Vechten is important to an understanding of John Hammond, Leonard Feather, and other white jazz critics not just because he was himself a music critic—his articles in *Vanity Fair* on the spirituals and the blues were seminal appreciations of those forms as authentic American art[26]—but because his style of intercession, mediation, and patronage was significantly different from that of the jazz critics, even as all were engaged in the process of shaping black art. Van Vechten, a transplanted Midwesterner who lived at a tony address in midtown Manhattan, was the leading white mainstream symbol of Harlem slumming and the "Negro vogue." A novelist and photographer as well as a music and theater critic, Van Vechten was equally known for leading white sophisticates on guided tours of Harlem cabarets. So strongly was he associated with white exploration of uptown nightlife that one history of New York, written in the early 1950s, credited Van Vechten with "discovering Harlem." A popular song about slumming, "Go Harlem," jauntily encouraged white New Yorkers to "go inspectin' like Van Vechten."[27] As Emily Bernard argues, however, Van Vechten's interest in black culture was much deeper than that of the slummers he brought uptown.[28] He was famous for throwing parties that brought young black artists and writers downtown and gave them exposure to influential, moneyed whites. As a literary midwife to the Harlem Renaissance, Van Vechten was responsible for his friends Alfred and Blanche Knopf publishing the first works of Langston Hughes and Nella Larsen and reissuing James Weldon Johnson's *The Autobiography of An Ex-Colored Man* (1927). In 1939, Van Vechten established the James Weldon Johnson Collection of Negro Arts and Letters at Yale University, which became what it remains to this day: the premier archive for the study of African American literature and culture. More than a decade earlier, Johnson—who died in a car accident in 1938—wrote to Van Vechten: "Has anyone ever written it down—in black and white—that you have been one of the most vital forces in bringing about the artistic emergence of the Negro in America?" Nella Larsen proclaimed Van Vechten "the best thing that ever happened to the Negro race."[29]

Notwithstanding these accomplishments and encomiums, Van Vechten's name became, as Bernard puts it, "synonymous with white exploitation of black culture," a reputation that "still holds today—that is, when he is remembered in connection with the Harlem Renaissance at all."[30] This demonization of Van Vechten began with the controversy that surrounded his book *Nigger Heaven* and continues down to our own time in scholarship and fiction that portray Van Vechten as a parasitic, corrupting figure who exploited Harlem for material gain and sexual pleasure.[31] The very title of the novel was (and is) taken by some to be offensive and to render mute any further discussion of its contents.[32] Perhaps equally salient was the fact that Van Vechten was known to be homosexual, as were many of the men associated with the Harlem Renaissance, though few were openly so in a climate in which the "politics of respectability" mandated that Race Men conform to bourgeois norms of sexuality.

In this respect, as Kevin Mumford argues, Van Vechten was less the symbol of white mainstream slumming, which offered nothing of value to black culture, than he was a representative of the bohemian avant garde, which helped enable certain transgressive black artists and writers to challenge bourgeois authority and convention. Mumford suggests that Van Vechten's bohemianism oscillated between the overtly sexualized gaze of the voyeur and the discriminating connoisseurial gaze of the aesthete. In Van Vechten's 1930 novel *Parties: Scenes from Contemporary New York Life*, for example, his white bohemian characters look at blacks dancing the Lindy Hop with an appreciation of the artistic quality of the performance, but then they also spout lines about the blacks' "lithe African beauty" that suggest an underlying primitivist fantasy. "In the end, " Mumford writes, "Van Vechten vacillates between portraying the bohemian as being above the typical slummer, someone who appreciated Harlem on an artistic level, but also someone who succumbed to the impulse to sexualize and sensationalize black Harlemites."[33]

Against this backdrop, what is significant about John Hammond and Leonard Feather is the extent to which their experience in Harlem and their approach to black culture diverged from the slumming and bohemian models. One of the main reasons for this is that these jazz critics never engaged in the fantasy of "passing" for black and were never represented as such by those who helped frame their images in the public mind. Van Vechten relished the *Vanity Fair* jest that he was getting a "tan" from spending so much time in Harlem; he cherished the Miguel Covarrubias caricature of him in blackface, titled "A Prediction"; he coyly referred to himself as "cullud" in his correspondence with Langston Hughes.[34] Van Vechten's effectiveness in brokering black culture to a wider audience hinged on the power of his white privilege. It was his use of this white privilege "for the race," after all, that was the reason for his being feted as an "honorary Negro." Yet he played with the notion of inhabiting or embodying a symbolic blackness himself. In contrast, John Hammond's crossover fantasy, as we've seen, was to be a Jew—the kind of Jew who helps blacks, not who transmutes himself into one. Feather, from that first night at the Savoy, understood that the key to his insider status was his foreignness. His cachet in the black community came from his whiteness—a whiteness that was different from the American whiteness that blacks couldn't help but distrust.

As adolescents, Hammond and Feather used jazz to distinguish themselves from their parents. But as young adults, it was their inherited bourgeois whiteness that gave them the leverage to proselytize and canonize jazz and to agitate for black civil rights, campaigns that hinged on the clout they could wield in mainstream and elite quarters. What made Hammond and Feather useful to the black community, in other words, was that they were *not* "white Negro" bohemians. In this regard, it is telling that Hammond and Feather defined themselves against not just Van Vechten's model of the avant-garde primitivist aesthete, but also Milton "Mezz" Mezzrow's model of the race-crossing hipster. Mezzrow's 1946 autobiography *Really the Blues* is the canonical text of white rebellion through a transformative affiliation with romanticized blackness. After a rowdy, delinquent adolescence that landed him in reform school and jail, Mezzrow (né Milton Mesirow) completed the mutiny against the middlebrow regime of his drugstore-owning,

Russian-Jewish immigrant parents by embracing blues, jazz, and black culture as the ecstatic embodiment of freedom, spontaneity, and authenticity. During a swing-era career as a jazz clarinetist and soprano saxophonist characterized by a desperately self-conscious effort to mimic traditional New Orleans–style black musicians, Mezzrow became best known as a peddler of marijuana, counting Louis Armstrong as one of the regular customers for his "mezzrolls." Mezzrow settled in Harlem with a black wife and became, by his own account, a "voluntary Negro." So intense was Mezzrow's identification with blackness that he deluded himself into believing his skin actually turned darker the longer he lived in Harlem. In his autobiography, Mezzrow strained to demonstrate his insider status by translating black jive language for his presumably square and clueless white readers.[35]

It's hard to imagine Hammond and Feather dabbling in black slang. Feather, in fact, took some measure of amused satisfaction when black jazz musician friends like Charlie Parker mimicked *his* Anglo accent and mannerisms. In their autobiographies, both Hammond and Feather position themselves in relation to Mezzrow in ways that suggest allegiance to the bourgeois rectitude of their own parents. Hammond does this in a passage in which he identifies Mezzrow as Armstrong's pot dealer and reflects on how he failed to endear himself to Armstrong when he tried to convince him that he didn't need the "mezzrolls" to play or feel well. "I was, after all, my mother's son," Hammond writes, "not quite free of her proselytizing impulse or the certainty of knowing what was good for other people."[36] Feather, for his part, develops a friendship with Mezzrow based, he says, on "our intense opposition to racism and our shared love of the blues." He admits that Mezzrow (not just Hammond) was instrumental in his gaining insider access to the Harlem jazz world: "Making the uptown rounds with Mezz . . . was a special pleasure," he writes, "since Mezz was well liked in the circles where his product was traded, which made us both feel welcome." While copping to having once delivered a "mezzroll" to a mutual musician friend in London, Feather carefully notes that Mezzrow never offered marijuana to him, and that his only experience with the substance amounted to a few puffs on one joint given him by Charlie Barnet and another passed to him at a social event at Louis Armstrong's house. The friendship with Mezzrow, Feather concludes, "was beyond any rational explanation" given their different upbringings: Mezzrow was "the product of a rough Chicago neighborhood," whereas "I had grown up protected by a staid middle-class family in London."[37]

This was no greater social distance, of course, than that which separated Feather from any number of musicians. What more decisively distinguished Feather and Mezzrow was the way they conceptualized their relationship to blacks. Mezzrow imagined that relationship as a shared desire for the warm intimacy and easy pleasures of the subcultural margin. His was a romantic racialist perspective that fancied African Americans as happier and spiritually purer for living outside the uptight middle-class mainstream. Feather, by contrast, assumed that African Americans were like other Americans in their bourgeois individualism and desire for upward class mobility; his role was to help them break down the barriers of segregation that prevented most of them from leading middle-class lives. For Feather, social and political alliances between blacks and Jews existed for the purpose of overcoming not just segregation but, ultimately, the very concepts of race and racial difference.

Swinging Left with the "Great White Father"

Coloring and shaping these various cross-racial stances and alliances were the progressive politics of the Depression and World War II eras. John Hammond and Leonard Feather were anticommunist liberals whose civil rights activism grew out of a tradition of Leftist politics in the jazz world that started in the early 1930s and intensified with the Popular Front initiative of the Communist Party after 1935. Throughout the 1930s and early 1940s, Harlem CP-sponsored dances, Scottsboro benefits, Lincoln Brigade and Russian war relief events, union rallies, and other Left-oriented functions featured prominent jazz artists such as Benny Carter, Duke Ellington, Count Basie, Benny Goodman, Chick Webb, Cab Calloway, and Bessie Smith. At the center of this activity was John Hammond. Hammond was never a card-carrying party member; as Feather later put it, he "regarded the Communists as opportunists who blew hot and cold on the race issue."[38] As an ardent integrationist, Hammond was especially at odds with the party's Black Belt Thesis, which called for the establishment of a separate black state in the American South. He was also, along with Charles Edward Smith and other jazz proponents on the radical Left, in opposition to the Communist Party hierarchy's doctrinaire view of jazz as a debased commercial mass culture and secular opiate of the masses. Smith, writing in the *Daily Worker*, argued that spirituals, the blues, and hot jazz were the authentic folk musical forms of the black working class and that the Marxist critique was more properly aimed at popular sweet music.[39] Hammond was part of a group of young blacks and Jews associated with the Harlem branch of the CPUSA who, in tandem with radical student movements on college campuses across New York City, diverged from the party line in embracing jazz as an authentic, unadulterated popular art.[40] While some on the

Communist Left—including many at the *New Masses*—continued to regard jazz as irredeemably bourgeois, the Popular Front opened up a space for jazz as a politically expedient tool of interracial coalition-building. Hammond adroitly used this opportunity to publicize his interlocking campaigns on behalf of black jazz musicians, integration, and social justice. "The people at the *New Masses* just hated jazz," Hammond said, "but, since it was the days of the United Front . . . they thought [it] would be good for their cultural image to have somebody write about jazz, particularly black jazz."[41]

By aligning himself with the Leftist politics that flourished in Harlem in the 1930s as the Depression exacted a heavy toll on the lives of ordinary blacks, Hammond practiced a different kind of mediation of black culture than did the fiercely apolitical Van Vechten. Under Hammond's influence, jazz gravitated from the primitivist aesthetic discourse of the Harlem Renaissance to the folkloric and popular culture discourses of the 1930s; the jazz musician, in this new paradigm, was less an unrepressed exotic than a voice of the people. While the 1930s vogue of the "folk" had diverse political shadings—including the conservative projects of white southern folk song collector John Lomax and black southern folklorist Zora Neale Hurston— its strongest articulation came from a Leftist thrust that related notions of vernacular cultural authenticity to the social struggles of the downtrodden.

As James Smethurst suggests, the folkloric "collecting" done in the late 1920s and 1930s by Hammond, Alan Lomax, B. A. Botkin, Melville Herskovits, and Lawrence Gellert was crucial to the "construction of an 'authentic' oppositional folk voice" that provided black and white artists and intellectuals with a palpable sense of political resonance in the cultural expressions of the black masses.[42] Gellert's *Negro Songs of Protest*—published in 1936 by the CPUSA-influenced American Music League—spotlighted protest themes in the work songs and other folk music of black southern farmers and laborers. But the explicit articulation of resentment against racial and economic injustice on the part of the most oppressed classes was just one dimension of 1930s Leftist discourse. While Langston Hughes's social poetry of the 1930s included a heightened thematic focus on black poverty, racism, and political struggle, it also valorized cutting-edge urban black vernacular language, rhythm, and style that was flourishing among the masses of blacks who had recently migrated from the South to northern and Midwestern cities. Whereas Zora Neale Hurston and Sterling Brown continued to look to the rural, hardscrabble South as an irreplaceable mother lode of the authentic folk vernacular, both Hughes and the Chicago poet Frank Marshall Davis looked to jazz, vaudeville, radio, movies, advertising, and popular journalism as the building blocks of an emerging modern urban black folk culture.[43]

In his work as a record producer, Hammond helped validate the cultural authenticity of musical art that was being created in one of the major commercial communications industries and circulated to a mass public using the most sophisticated techniques of modern capitalism. This was an especially tricky but crucial matter for Leftist ideology, as swing music became a hugely popular phenomenon that helped significantly to bring about the national consolidation of a horizontally integrated mass culture industry linking the record companies with radio and Hollywood.[44] To doctrinaire 1930s Marxists, the sudden appearance of swing music and its jitterbugging audience looked suspiciously similar to the fad for chewing gum: both were read as cases of an all-powerful and venal culture industry imposing a false happiness on a mass of easily duped, passive consumers. Hammond was himself a sharp critic of the capitalist organization of both production and consumption in the culture industry. Part of his pro-union activism targeted oppressive labor conditions in the record companies' manufacturing facilities. And, with his intense hatred of sweet music, Hammond was among the first to popularize the word "commercial" as an epithet. Under the protective cover of his amply publicized commitment to social justice and artistic integrity, Hammond ventured to use the corporate beast against itself.

Working first as a freelance affiliate and then as an associate recording director of Columbia Records, Hammond mastered the technologies of big business production and publicity, later applying these tools in smaller entrepreneurial ventures such as Vanguard Records. What ensured Hammond's credibility on the Left was not just his ability to deliver righteous criticism of the music industry with the authority of an experienced insider, but also the way that his work habits flouted the image of a corporate executive hatching his schemes from the sanitized remove of a Manhattan skyscraper office. The preferred image of Hammond was of a man out in the field, among the people, his ear tuned to the indigenous folk sounds welling up from below. When one of his records made it to the juke box, the sense was that it carried the organic spirit of the juke joint, the honky tonk, the speakeasy, the rent party, and other community spaces Hammond regularly visited in his search for authentic, grass-roots music. That's the image that best served the Popular Front campaign to recognize black folk culture as one of the bedrock pillars of a democratic American national culture.[45]

Fellow critics invested in the sanctity of Hammond's purist mission by characterizing his work in corporate precincts as a kind of strategic guerilla offensive. In 1940, when a group of self-proclaimed "California hot music addicts" circulated a petition protesting Hammond's Columbia affiliation on the grounds that it compromised his professed anticommercialism—at Columbia Hammond was obliged to record "sweet" bands as well as the "hot" bands he much preferred—*Down Beat* critic Dave Dexter Jr. jumped to Hammond's defense, arguing that Hammond's position had in no way diminished his "hell-bent-for-leather" style, and indeed had given him a choice opportunity for voicing his jazz purism:

> [Hammond] goes about it [recording sweet bands] in a business-like matter of fact way. No raves about the music. No false compliments. He cuts the sides, nods an okay from the control room, and calls it a day. If one of the schmaltz maestros should ask him "how do you like that waterfall effect I get with my saxes?" John would look the guy straight in the eye and say "it stinks." But most of them, knowing Hammond, don't ask questions like that.[46]

Hammond's trickiest and most consequential project—an act of black folk reclamation that infused one of his most blatantly commercial endeavors—was his influence on the career of Benny Goodman. Hammond began shaping Goodman's career in 1933, when he advised the clarinetist to abandon the security of playing sweet music. This was a life that suited Goodman just fine, coming as he did from a poor immigrant family and trying to launch a career in the middle of the Depression. Goodman took the advice and, under Hammond's supervision, cut some records for the English market using hot-oriented white musicians, including trombonist Jack Teagarden and drummer Gene Krupa. Sold on hot jazz, Goodman turned down a seat in Paul Whiteman's thriving band and put together his own twelve-piece outfit. The musicians were all white, but Hammond convinced Goodman to base his repertoire on the work of black arrangers Fletcher Henderson, Edgar Sampson, and Jimmy Mundy. Henderson's band of the late 1920s and early 1930s, a favorite of Hammond's and one of his early recording projects, was particularly important. Even before Ellington, Henderson had figured out how to make a big band swing with the rhythmic power and finesse of a smaller group. He also knew how to provide rich ensemble backing for the solos played by the extraordinary improvisers who passed through his organization, including trumpeters Louis Armstrong and Roy Eldridge and saxophonists Chu Berry, Coleman Hawkins, and Lester Young. This became the model for Goodman, even though he knew his band wasn't yet at the level of Henderson's best.[47]

Hammond's recordings of the Henderson orchestra—particularly the 1932 waxing of "King Porter Stomp"—were historically significant, but what really consolidated his reputation as a scout and producer of black talent were his 1933 recording sessions with Bessie Smith and Billie Holiday, released on the Okeh "race" subsidiary label of Columbia's American division.[48] The Smith records, which offer the only opportunity to hear the singer in a swing context, revived the career of the 1920s blues empress. Hammond always thought he did more than just that—that he had rescued Smith from a demeaning, penurious existence singing pornographic songs for tips in a North Philadelphia gin mill. Smith biographer Chris Albertson has challenged that account, quoting Smith's sister-in-law that the establishment in question was "just a nice little club that nobody had to be ashamed to work in," and suggesting Smith had figured out how to "play" Hammond by feigning abject poverty and capitalizing on his need to see himself as her savior.[49] This dynamic also colored Hammond's strained effort to publicize Smith's tragic death as a case of racial martyrdom. Smith died at age forty-three after an automobile accident on a country road in Mississippi, outside of Memphis. In the research for his biography, Albertson turned up a death certificate and other supporting evidence to demonstrate that Smith died after being transported to a black hospital in Clarksdale, Mississippi. Hammond's story in *Down Beat*—headlined "Did Bessie Smith Bleed to Death While Waiting for Medical Aid?"—alleged that Smith had bled to death in the waiting room of a white Memphis hospital after being refused treatment because of her color. The story became a *cause célèbre* among civil rights advocates of the day who seized on it as startling evidence of Southern bigotry. In 1960, playwright Edward Albee's play *The Death of Bessie Smith* dramatized the story that Hammond told in 1937.[50]

Hammond's *Down Beat* article was notable not just for its myth-making significance, but for what it reveals of its author's overlapping roles as jazz missionary, social activist, and salesman. The article began

> Bessie Smith was killed during the last week in September, and perhaps the greatest and least appreciated artist in American jazz is gone. My own admiration for her has been expressed too often to warrant repeating here again, but I feel like kicking myself for not having done more to make her art known to thousands who might really have appreciated her had they only had the opportunity.

Hammond then floated the unsubstantiated rumor that Smith had died in the white Memphis hospital. "If the story is true," Hammond wrote,

> it is but another example of disgraceful conditions in a certain section of our country already responsible for the killing and maiming of legitimate union organizers. Of the particular city of Memphis I am prepared to believe almost anything, since its mayor and chief of police publicly urged the use of violence against organizers of the CIO a few weeks ago.

This reference to his own brush with Southern inhospitality—it came when Hammond was engaged in union organizing activity with a group that included Malcolm Cowley, John Dos Passos, Edmund Wilson, and Waldo Frank—was followed by this piece of salesmanship:

> Be that as it may, the UHCA [United Hot Clubs of America, the collector's organization of which Hammond was an officer] is busy sponsoring a special Bessie Smith memorial album . . . . [T]he album will be released by Brunswick-Columbia [i.e., by Hammond] around the middle of November with pictures of performers and details about each of the discs. Take it from one who cherished all the records that this will be the best buy of the year in music.[51]

Hucksterism of this sort reveals just how commercially savvy—or craven—Hammond could be in the service of his mission on behalf of "neglected" art.

Equally crucial to that mission were the Billie Holiday recordings that Hammond produced just days after the final Bessie Smith recording date in November 1933. These recordings launched the career of the precocious eighteen-year-old whom Hammond, on a tip from Red Norvo and Mildred Bailey, had found in a Harlem after-hours club singing in a style that combined Smith's former bodacious sensuality with a horn-like vocal quality suggestive of Louis Armstrong's trumpeting. Hammond cut hundreds of records with Holiday on Columbia and its affiliate labels throughout the 1930s. Hammond, Holiday, and pianist Teddy Wilson selected sidemen for the sessions from the Goodman, Basie, Ellington, and Teddy Hill bands, depending on who was in town.

In these recordings, Hammond turned the recording studio into a space where the musicians reproduced the ambience of the jam session. Most of the records were produced with no rehearsals or second takes. Trumpeter Buck Clayton and drummer Jo Jones, sidemen on some of the key dates, said that they arrived at the studio unburdened by any knowledge of what was to happen, took a few sketchy cues from Wilson on the order of solos and how to begin and end the songs, and then, in musician's parlance, "hit" the songs. The paradox here is that recordings that soon became "classics," and that years later figured deeply in the sense of a jazz tradition, appear to have been the product of a casual get-together. Albert Murray and Robert O'Meally have deftly unraveled the paradox by making the point that Holiday was—in Murray's words—"working with people whose styles and whose approaches and whose feelings and whose values she knew." For musicians who slept with their instruments at their bedside, who participated in jam sessions in the kitchens and living rooms of each other's homes, the recording studio was an extension of social space in which music-making was an activity just as ordinary—and just as serious—as eating or making love.[52]

Hammond preferred this kind of intimate, familiar, unmannered feeling to the slicker, machine-like spectacle of the big bands. Throughout the 1930s, as Benny Goodman's big band grew more and more popular, Hammond used Goodman's success to showcase small-group, chamber jazz units that featured some of the black musicians he wanted to promote. The first of these small groups was a trio, with Teddy Wilson on piano, that Hammond had first recorded in 1934. The trio, with the white drummer Gene Krupa, had its first public appearance at the Congress Hotel in Chicago in 1936, in a concert produced by Helen Oakley and "Squirrel" Aschcroft of the Chicago Hot Club. Soon the trio added vibraphonist Lionel Hampton, whom Hammond had discovered in a club in Los Angeles, and became a quartet. Later, when Goodman rejected Hammond's suggestion to add a guitarist from Oklahoma named Charlie Christian, Hammond, undeterred, snuck Christian on stage between sets, having conspired with the other members of the group to give the young electric guitar phenom the first solo. Christian impressed Goodman, and thus was born the Benny Goodman Quintet. As Lewis Erenberg notes, these smaller units "proved necessary to circumvent the rules of segregated venues that might accept some black 'guest' players but were uncomfortable with a large integrated band that symbolized permanent equality between the races."[53] Goodman didn't integrate his big band until 1939, when he added Christian on guitar and Fletcher Henderson on piano.

For Hammond, it wasn't Goodman's big band, nor Duke Ellington's, that best captured the swing ideal that he located in the small-group jam session format. That honor fell to Count Basie's band, which Hammond first heard from the Reno Club in Kansas City on his twelve-tube Motorola car radio while sitting outside the Congress Hotel in Chicago one night in 1936. Hammond "couldn't believe" what he heard: Basie's deft, economical piano; a fleet and propulsive rhythm section led by drummer Jo Jones; horn sections that talked back and forth in vigorous call-and-response patterns; and bracing soloists, especially Lester Young on tenor—the absolute essence of swing.[54] Within weeks Hammond drove his Terraplane out to Kansas City to see for himself. Hammond began hyping the band in Down Beat, praising its "rough edges" as a mark of its unmannered authenticity and positing the Reno Club as "the ideal stage" for Basie's "unselfconscious and direct music."[55] Hammond's missionary instincts told him that it was his job to deliver this band to the world beyond Kansas City, but his Down Beat dispatches hinted at his worry that uprooting the band from the fertile southwestern soil would threaten its natural "unselfconscious," headlong style. "Basie's band is at its best when it is playing a single good tune for about twenty minutes, with the rhythm section exerting a drive unlike that of any other, and a couple of good soloists playing against brass figures which could only originate in Kansas City," Hammond wrote, adding "Once it becomes mannered and pretentious the group will have lost its only reason for existence."[56] But Hammond soon swallowed his worries and prevailed on his friend Willard Alexander of Music Corporation of America—the agency that also handled Goodman—to find premier bookings.

Hammond's relationship to Basie traced a fine line between healthy advocacy and paternalistic meddling. Basie couldn't have minded Hammond's efforts to publicize and protest the exploitative nature of the record contract he had signed with Decca Records. The contract paid Basie a straight $750 a year for twenty-four sides, with no royalties. To Basie, who had been making $15 a week at the Reno Club, this seemed like a lot of money. Hammond knew that the contract fell below the American Federation of Musicians' minimum scale for recordings, and he understood that the real money was in the royalties that accrued from Basie hits like "One O'Clock Jump" and "Jumpin' at the Woodside." When Hammond couldn't get *Down Beat* to publish an exposé on the matter, he turned to the *New Masses*, where, under the pseudonym Henry Johnson, he accused the recording industry of running a Jim Crow system that treated black performers like sharecroppers.[57]

What's curious about Hammond's display of righteous concern for the terms of Count Basie's Decca contract—and one of the things that makes it difficult to reach any clear conclusion about Hammond's role in the matter of artist compensation—is the evidence of similarly exploitative arrangements with artists who worked under Hammond's sponsorship at Columbia Records. According to Chris Albertson, for instance, Bessie Smith was never paid artist royalties by Columbia, and in some cases was not paid even a basic one-time recording fee for selections the company later used in posthumous reissues. In the early 1980s, the Smith estate filed a lawsuit against Columbia Records' parent corporation, CBS, alleging that Jack Kapp, a Columbia Records official during the period when Bessie Smith was recording, used a dummy publishing company to copyright Smith's tunes and then collected the royalties himself. Hammond has never been accused of this kind of raw swindle, but the Bessie Smith case—how could Hammond not have known the details of Smith's Columbia contract?—raises the question of whether Hammond's initiative on Count Basie's behalf against Decca was less a case of principle than of strategic lobbying against a record industry competitor.[58]

The flip side of Hammond's solicitude for Basie was his reputation for heavy-handed intervention in the band's operation, especially when it came to personnel decisions. In 1937, Hammond convinced Basie that adding Billie Holiday as a second singer to complement the blues shouter Jimmy Rushing would enhance the band's popularity. In her short stint with the band, Holiday established herself as a consummate jazz singer, possessed of a uniquely astringent voice, an unerring sense of time, and a fearless ability to trade swinging riffs with Basie's superb hornmen, tenors Young and Herschel Evans and trumpeters Buck Clayton and Harry "Sweets" Edison. Holiday left the band in 1938, however, and soon took a job with white bandleader Artie Shaw. There was more money for Holiday in Shaw's otherwise all-white outfit, which rivaled Goodman's band for popularity. But there was also a great deal of hassle and heartache in facing white audiences that were offended by race mixing on stage; in having to share the spotlight with white singer Helen Forrest; and in the daily abuses of segregation. "I got to the point," Holiday said in her ghosted memoir *Lady Sings the Blues*, "where I hardly ever ate, slept, or went to the bathroom without having a major NAACP-type production."[59] Touring with the Basie band had brought its own brushes with bigotry, to be sure. For a performance at Detroit's Fox Theater, she had to darken her skin with greasepaint—in the style of blackface minstrelsy—to placate management's concern that the audience would mistake her for white and take offense at her singing with a black band.[60]

Despite the pain of such incidents and the arduousness of one-nighting the country in a beaten-up bus, Holiday loved performing with the band and cherished her close relationships with some of the men, especially guitarist Freddie Green, with whom she had a romance, and Young and Clayton, whom she regarded as surrogate brothers. So why did she leave? Basie drummer Jo Jones insisted that Hammond fired Holiday because she didn't want to sing the blues, as he wanted her to. Jones contended that while Holiday didn't eschew the blues style, she didn't want to steal the spotlight from Jimmy Rushing, and so limited herself to "rhythm" numbers. Whether true or not that Holiday was fired from the band for this reason— and there are competing versions of what happened—Jones and Holiday herself held to the story that Hammond was responsible for her leaving the band. "[N]obody's got guts enough to tell the people because he's the great white father," Jones complained.[61]

Hailing from the opposite end of the class spectrum than many of the musicians in his orbit, and prone to an imperious style, Hammond generated plenty of criticism that labeled him a paternalist and a tyrant. Some saw a holier-than-thou edge to his political zeal and his solicitude for black musicians. Hammond helped Benny Goodman and other white musicians who had a strong swing and blues orientation, like Red Norvo and Mildred Bailey. But it was black musicians, particularly those he could take credit for discovering or rediscovering and those whose poverty and neglect he could publicize with muckraking fervor, that most fueled Hammond's sense of self-righteousness. Otis Ferguson, who wrote on jazz and the popular arts in the *New Republic*, came from a working-class background and shared much of Hammond's politics, but he thought Hammond—whom he depicted as a pampered rich boy—sacrificed his critical integrity to his ideological convictions:

> He is all for the working class. Fine. He's dedicated to the cause of the Negro. Fine. But he's too apt to shut his ear to the music of someone who didn't pay off on a date or said nuts to the lettuce pickers and call it criticism. And when he goes around saying "white musician" the way you'd use the term "greaseball," he not only confuses his readers and upsets his own standards but starts the Jim Crow car all over again, in reverse.[62]

The *Nation's* classical music critic, B. H. Haggin, who had worked with Hammond at both WEVD and the *Brooklyn Eagle* in the early 1930s, thought Hammond's political concerns had destroyed his talent as a critic. "Hammond," he wrote, "began with his mind, his sharp ears, his fine musical sensitiveness fixed on the music," but over time had allowed himself to be concerned with "innumerable extraneous and irrelevant considerations, such as whether a company's plant was unionized or a player was a Negro."[63]

Hammond, Duke Ellington, and the "Lost Cause"

One of the strongest attacks on Hammond came from Duke Ellington, writing·in *Down Beat* in 1939. Ellington acknowledged that Hammond had earned the gratitude of some musicians but charged that his judgment had become "slightly warped" and his "prejudices a little bit unwieldy" because of his work as "an ardent propagandist and champion of the 'lost cause,'" identifying himself with "the interests of the minorities, the Negro peoples, to a lesser degree, the Jew, and to the underdog, in the form of the Communist party."[64] Ellington soon retracted the red-baiting charge: "It was my intention to merely infer that the political affiliations of Mr. Hammond bordered on the 'left wing.' "[65]

Hammond was then riding high on his image as "Number One Swing Man," so· dubbed by Irving Kolodin in *Harper's* not just for his well-publicized patronage of Billie Holiday, Benny Goodman, Count Basie, and others, but for his staging at Carnegie Hall of two concerts that proposed a narrative of the history of jazz rooted in the African American experience.[66] In the first "From Spirituals to Swing" concert, held at Carnegie Hall in December 1938 under the sponsorship of the *New Masses*, Hammond's program began with recorded West African music, followed in the first half by live gospel, boogie-woogie, blues, and New Orleans jazz. The second half was given over entirely to the Count Basie band. The effect was to demonstrate that swing hadn't burst spontaneously out of Benny Goodman's clarinet, but grew instead out of a long tradition of black music going back to the slave spirituals. The second "From Spirituals to Swing," held in 1939 under the sponsorship of the Popular Front–connected Theater Arts Committee, included Goodman and ended with a racially mixed jam session, but the concert was otherwise dominated by African American personnel, including Sterling Brown as master of ceremonies.

The first concert evening started inauspiciously when a palpably nervous Hammond faltered in his spoken introduction, Carl Van Vechten yelled "louder" from his front-row seat, and the sound technician inadvertently blasted a record of "wild African chanting" at a volume that completely drowned Hammond out.[67] But as attested in uniformly positive reviews of the sold-out, three-and-a-half-hour concert, Hammond's shortcomings as a public speaker didn't overshadow his accomplishments as an impresario.[68] His concert program included the boogie-woogie pianists Albert Ammons, Meade Lux Lewis, and Pete Johnson; gospel singer Sister Rosetta Tharpe; the Mitchell's Christian Singers gospel vocal quartet; New Orleans jazz soprano saxophonist Sidney Bechet; stride pianist James P. Johnson; blues singers Big Joe Turner and Big Bill Broonzy; and blues harmonica player Sonny Terry. An all-star jam session anchored by the Basie rhythm section brought many of these stylistically distinct musicians together in an effort to demonstrate an underlying shared affinity of black musical feeling.

As Paul Allen Anderson argues in the masterful discussion of "From Spirituals to Swing" in his book *Deep River: Music and Memory in Harlem Renaissance Thought*, the concerts served as a corrective to the whitewashed historical narrative for jazz represented in Paul Whiteman's "Experiment in Modern Music" concert at New York's Aeolian Hall in 1924. That concert began with a caricatured performance of "Livery Stable Blues" (the song made famous in a 1917 recording by the white Original Dixieland Jazz Band) and ended with the premier of popular Jewish songwriter George Gershwin's first concert work, "Rhapsody in Blue."[69] Whiteman, the jovial, rotund bandmaster from Denver, had garnered acclaim as the "King of Jazz" with his presentation of a new American symphonic music that brought an air of polite bourgeois refinement to the rhythms and spirit of native folk music and the melodic ideas of Tin Pan Alley. Whiteman's symphonic jazz, a hybrid of American popular music and European compositional and performance techniques leavened by the "sweet" sound of violins, carefully concealed its indebtedness to African American folk sources behind a façade of middle-class white respectability, sidestepping the moral panic that dominated jazz's reception in the 1920s.

Gerald Early provocatively suggests that both Whiteman and Benny Goodman are best understood not simply as white expropriators of black creativity, but as mediating figures who helped dissolve white middle-class prejudices against jazz, enabling it to accrue cultural capital that eventually paid interest to black jazz musicians as well. Whiteman's contribution, Early argues, was to establish jazz as a legitimate American music in the face of Eurocentric elite and neo-Victorian middle-class denunciations of the music as crude, uncivilized, and immoral.[70] By showing that something called jazz could work as respectable bourgeois entertainment, Early argues, Whiteman helped to ensure that the music could be packaged as something other than blackface minstrelsy. But the cost of this mediation was in having a white man (Whiteman) become the face of jazz. Early writes:

> What Whiteman's 1924 concert was trying to establish was the idea that from its beginnings to its most fully realized form as symphonic concert music, jazz was and is undeniably *American* music; and inasmuch as Whiteman wanted to convince himself and his audience that it was an American music, he was bound to convince both himself and others that it was, officially, a white music. Otherwise, history taught him that the only way he could perform black music would be in blackface or as a kind of minstrel. Whiteman, whatever his faults, did not want jazz to become another minstrel music and it is, in part, through his popularizing efforts that the music did not become that.[71]

Whiteman's own prejudices against black folk culture were those of the middle class—both white and black—of his time. His formula for elevating vernacular folk sources through the use of scored compositions and orchestral instrumentation was similar to the "folk-to-formal" racial uplift approach favored by Alain Locke, a graduate of Harvard and Oxford, professor of philosophy at Howard University, and editor of the landmark 1925 collection *The New Negro*.[72] In his 1936 monograph *The Negro and His Music*, Locke expressed concern that it was white composers like Anton Dvořak, George Gershwin, and Paul Whiteman who were capitalizing both artistically and commercially on the use of black folk idioms in scored works for concert presentation.[73] Even as Locke brooded about the appropriation of black folk sources by Whiteman and other white bandleaders and composers, he also saw Whiteman's success as a healthy challenge to African American composers. Duke Ellington, who expressed admiration for Whiteman, was one who rose to that challenge, developing an African American symphonic jazz that fulfilled the New Negro vision.

Hammond wasn't alone in viewing symphonic jazz as both a threat to hot jazz purism and as a misguided bid for cultural refinement. Roger Pryor Dodge, a dancer and an astutely intelligent dance and music critic, railed against "Whiteman-Gershwin faddism," which he saw as a "white-collar meddling" that stripped popular music of its dance-oriented vitality and substituted the pretentious, ornate drapery of watered-down classical music. The problem with symphonic jazz for Dodge—especially the rhapsody form favored by Gershwin—was its emulation of nineteenth-century Romantic music, in which tonal sensuousness and plush arrangements predominated over rhythmic and melodic power and terseness. Unfurling his aesthetic theory in a highly gendered and racialized vocabulary, Dodge described his preferred hot jazz as a "virile non-emasculated" music "produced by the primitive innate musical instinct of the Negro and of those lower members of the white race who have not yet lost their feeling for the primitive." "Primitive" was the highest tribute Dodge could pay; it's the same word he used to describe Bach, who stood in this critic's system as a paragon of contrapuntal, improvisatory virtuosity, centered on popular dance rhythms and "bare" melodies "driving with a continuous flow of musical thought to a natural and inevitable conclusion." Such virility had been achieved by Bessie and Clara Smith, King Oliver's Jazz Band, Louis Armstrong and His Hot Five, Red Nichols and His Five Pennies, and Jimmy O'Bryant's Famous Original Washboard Band, among others. It was *especially* evident in the Duke Ellington performances that featured James "Bubber" Miley's growling, blues-drenched hot trumpet solos on "Black and Tan Fantasy" and "East St. Louis Toodle-Oo." But this virility and vitality were giving way to an "invading sweetness" in Ellington's arrangements as the composer—sharing with "the later Goodman clarinet, the Wilson piano, [and] much of the Dorsey and Teagarden trombone work" in what this sternest of critics deemed a period of jazz decadence in the late 1930s—drowned hot jazz in "an unfortunate demonstration of a superimposed, cheap, classical experience."[74]

Ever mindful of his own distinctions between the real and the ersatz, Hammond intended to put a black face on jazz that wasn't the degraded blackface of minstrelsy, and also wasn't the sophisticated black face of Duke Ellington. In staging the Count Basie band as the paragon of hot jazz, Hammond's paradoxical goal was to exploit the bourgeois cultural capital of the elite Carnegie Hall setting while also burnishing the band's image as an unmannered, freewheeling outfit that embodied the values of the rough-and-tumble southwest. It was helpful to Hammond that this would not be the first time hot jazz was performed at Carnegie Hall. In January 1938, Benny Goodman headlined a highly successful evening of jazz at the New York concert hall featuring both his big band and his racially integrated small groups, capped off by a jam session that included members of both the Basie and Ellington bands. The concert offered its own revision of the Whiteman event fourteen years earlier. A section that offered a historical overview of the evolution of jazz included pieces by the black composers Will Marion Cook and Ford Dabney. Symphonic jazz was conspicuously absent from a program that instead culminated in a rousing jam session version of "Honeysuckle Rose," with exciting solos by Lester Young, Buck Clayton, Goodman, and Harry James. Early argues that it was a historic event for two reasons: first, it presented jazz as a racially syncretized art "with whites as popularizers and blacks as cocreators, coperformers, and atavistic spiritual source"; second, it showed that dance music, and not just symphonic music, could be transformed into an art music. Goodman "made people listen to dance music and thus, even more than the beboppers who came later, he effected the transformation of hot jazz music into an art music and reoriented the public to accepting jazz as high art without the trappings of classical European art music."[75]

Less than a year later, Hammond's first "From Spirituals to Swing" concert underscored the black folk provenance of this newly legitimized art music. With the sponsorship of the *New Masses*—where he turned after failing to secure backing from the NAACP and the International Ladies Garment Workers—Hammond programmed a concert that represented black jazz as an authentic urban art, organically connected to localized, regional black folk cultures untainted by commercialism. In the parlance of 1930s Left populist rhetoric, Hammond's black face of jazz was the face of "the people." More than signifying the Left's embrace of jazz, however, "From Spirituals to Swing" served as a monument to Hammond's own efforts as a talent scout and missionary on behalf of downtrodden, neglected, and oppressed black musicians. Hammond had been assured by Eric Bernay of the *New Masses* that the magazine "would not make political capital of our association" and that the concert would be "advertised and presented simply as the musical event it became."[76] But the publicity and packaging of the concert—as well as reviews of it—consistently foregrounded Hammond's role in the musicians' lives, his politics, and his ideas about black musical authenticity. "Most of the people you will hear are absurdly poor," Hammond and James Dugan asserted in the program notes for the first concert , and "the greatest of these artists die of privation and neglect." The notes detailed how black musicians, including some of that evening's performers, suffered under the yoke of "Jim Crow unions and unscrupulous nightclub proprietors."[77]

The evening was dedicated to Bessie Smith, reminding the most knowledgeable members of the audience of Hammond's own role in reviving her career and in publicizing the shady circumstances of her death. In the weeks leading up to the concert, the *New Masses* published advertisements, editorials, and articles that burnished Hammond's image as an intrepid discoverer of black talent while at the same time exalting the musicians as standard-bearers of a folk purity and sincerity not to be found in the glibly commercial productions of Broadway and Tin Pan Alley. One editorial told the story of boogie-woogie pianist Meade Lux Lewis. The boogie-woogie style, the editorial explained, "came out of the poverty of the American Negro who could not afford an orchestra on his festive occasions," and so "one player of a battered piano had to furnish the drive of a jazz orchestra." Lewis had made a record in the early 1920s that was deemed a classic by American and European jazz aficionados, but then had disappeared from the music world. In 1937, Hammond, after a five-year search, found Lewis working in a car wash on Chicago's South Side. He brought him to New York and recorded him for English Parlophone, "because no American phonograph company would take a chance on such records selling."[78]

In a post-concert piece in the *New Yorker* focusing on the boogie-woogie pianists Lewis, Albert Ammons, and Pete Johnson, Hammond exalted their natural talent and unselfconsciousness: " 'They're terrific,' he said. They can't read music, which Hammond thinks is a good thing, on the theory that if they ever studied technique and harmony, they might lose their natural feeling for their art. 'You can't intellectualize boogie-woogie,' Mr. Hammond said."[79] Hammond's insistence on the unselfconscious innocence, sincerity, and purity of authentic black music was at the heart of his connoisseurial mission. It seemed not to worry him unduly that this authenticity might be compromised by the very act of bringing black folk performers to New York to make records and perform for predominantly white audiences at elite institutions like Carnegie Hall. "The Music Nobody Knows"—the title of Hammond and James Dugan's lead article in the "From Spirituals to Swing" concert program—was a self-congratulatory irony, for with the benefit of Hammond's social connections and music industry muscle it was inevitable that this music would become known in cosmopolitan circles. The music was already known, of course, in the local communities where these musicians performed before coming to New York. Hammond seemed untroubled by the tension at the heart of an integrationist mission that sought to deliver black musicians into mainstream and elite white institutions, but then valorized and supported those musicians only to the extent that they demonstrated their distance from both white and black middle-class culture.

Duke Ellington was not a good candidate for this patronage model. Ellington came from a black middle-class Washington, D.C. community with contacts to the city's white elites and with its own well-entrenched canons of refinement and institutions of learning and culture. During the first decades of the twentieth century Washington, D.C. was, in the words of historian Constance McLaughlin Green, "the undisputed center of Negro civilization." Howard University stood at the apex of a sturdy infrastructure of black churches, schools, civic organizations, and theaters that gave institutional weight to the pride and privilege of the community. Music education and performance were the *sine qua non* of cultural distinction, with church choirs, choral ensembles, operatic societies, and musical theater groups offering spirituals and jubilees along with Tchaikovsky and Dvorak.[80] While Ellington's 1932 recording "It Don't Mean a Thing If It Ain't Got That Swing" heralded the swing craze that defined American popular culture for the next decade, it was a successful 1933 European tour, marked by critical appreciation of his skills as a composer, that helped kindle the artistic ambitions he carried from his childhood.

Ellington knew that jazz was a viable popular music; his ambition was to turn it also into an African American concert music, featuring longer compositions with narrative themes related to the historical experience of African Americans. Ellington's interest in the history of his people had been sparked by his teachers at all-black Armstrong High School; there, as he recalled in his memoir, "Negro history was crammed into the curriculum, so that we would know our people all the way back."[81] His coming-of-age occurred at a time when black intellectuals worked strenuously to unearth the African American history that had been obscured by the pro-slavery ideologies that dominated American historiography well into the twentieth century. The Washington, D.C. black community that produced Duke Ellington also was home to Carter G. Woodson, a Harvard Ph.D. who in 1915 founded the Association for the Study of Negro Life and History and started *The Journal of Negro History*. Also located in Washington was the aforementioned Alain Locke, editor of *The New Negro* (1925), a major anthology of African American literature and culture that became a kind of blueprint for the racial uplift thrust of the Harlem Renaissance.

The Harlem Renaissance and 1920s black culture in general percolated with a sense that, as bibliophile Arthur Schomburg put it in *The New Negro*, "The American Negro must remake his past in order to make his future."[82] Jamaican immigrant Marcus Garvey tried to mobilize the black masses for a self-financed return to Africa on a mission to rescue black civilization from the ravages of European imperialism. Locke and Du Bois rejected Garvey's separatist economic agenda but shared his anticolonial political message while developing their own pan-Africanist cultural views. *Opportunity, The Crisis,* and other venues of black intellectual discourse featured articles and graphics celebrating the grandeur, beauty, and civilizational primacy of African art. At the same time came a proliferation of books whose purpose was to authenticate black contributions to American culture, most importantly James Weldon Johnson's *The Book of American Negro Poetry* (1922) and (with his brother J. Rosamond Johnson) *The First Book of Negro Spirituals* (1925) and *The Second Book of Negro Spirituals* (1926).[83]

Ellington was not an intellectual, but as an ambitious, self-conscious artist imbued with race pride, his work in the 1930s and early 1940s—especially his score for the nine-minute short film *Symphony in Black* (1935) and his fifty-minute extended suite *Black, Brown, and Beige* (1943)—resonated strongly with the New Negro program of racial uplift, historical consciousness, and artistic progress. John Hammond may have cut a less controversial figure in Harlem than Carl Van Vechten did, but he paid little respect to its cultural elites, focusing more on its cabarets than on its churches, magazines, and salons. Alain Locke played to fellow Washingtonian Ellington's competitiveness when he invited the orchestra to perform the entire second half of a concert of African American music scheduled for January 1940. Locke appealed to Ellington's race pride: the concert would give Ellington "a chance at last to give a real Negro version without having to have any white producer intruding his ideas or particular whimsies." The concert—also to have been sponsored by the *New Masses,* Locke's politics at the time being further left than Hammond's—never came off. Nevertheless, as Anderson suggests, "the prospect of circumventing Hammond must have delighted Ellington."[84]

Squawking between creators and critics may be the background noise of the modern arts, perhaps especially so in jazz, but this particular battle deserves special scrutiny for what it reveals of two of the most powerful voices in the swing-era discourse on jazz aesthetics and racial politics. Each combatant is plenty fascinating in his own right, of course, but Ellington and Hammond are even more interesting in their relationship to each other, and in the ways that their overlapping and competing ambitions channeled larger currents of race, class, and culture. Both were audacious in their assault on social boundaries—Hammond, the WASP class traitor who defied his parents' segregationist convictions; Ellington, the bourgeois race man whose black-tie symphonic concertizing typified the racial uplift strategy favored by Locke, Du Bois, and the New Negro wing of the Harlem Renaissance, but who was also an urbane hipster, proud of what he called his "pool-hall education," a quality that connected him to the emergence of a new urban folk sensibility championed by Langston Hughes and other younger members of the movement. Both were canny, even slippery operators: Hammond, who saw the fight for racial equality and labor rights as indistinguishable from the fight for recognition of the superiority of the Count Basie rhythm section; Ellington, whose constant morphings challenged and confounded static definitions of jazz and black artistry—now the "primitive" purveyor of "jungle" sounds, now the artist-intellectual writing both musical scores and critiques of jazz critics, now the media-savvy commercial entertainer. Such was the performative brilliance of the man who was fond of calling himself—in an upper-class British accent—a "primitive pedestrian minstrel."

Ellington's attack on Hammond in *Down Beat* in 1939 followed Hammond's blistering 1935 assault on the extended work *Reminiscing in Tempo*. In an article titled "The Tragedy of Duke Ellington," Hammond said the thirteen-minute piece was "formless and shallow" and signaled Ellington's capitulation to European influences like Debussy and Delius. Calling the piece "un-Negroid," Hammond brazenly argued that the "trouble with Duke's music is that fact that he has purposely kept himself from any contact with the troubles of his people or mankind in general." Ellington's music "has become vapid and without the slightest resemblance of guts," Hammond argued, because Ellington "keeps himself from thinking about such problems as those of the southern share croppers, the Scottsboro boys, [and] intolerable working and relief conditions." Hammond concluded: " It would probably take a Granville Hicks [the literary editor of the *New Masses*] or a Langston Hughes to describe the way he shuts his eyes to the abuses being heaped upon his race."[85]

A monument to Hammond's self-importance as an arbiter of both political virtue and racial authenticity, the review defined "black music" in narrow ideological and formal terms that Ellington and many other African American musicians have challenged in a number of ways. By implying that the vitality of jazz was necessarily connected to both a specific political program and an exacting definition of "negroid" aesthetics, Hammond's review posited a standard of purity that not even Hammond's favored musicians could attain. Count Basie's band, with its freewheeling riff style and eschewal of written charts, best matched Hammond's prescription for authentic black jazz. But not even Hammond ascribed the superiority of Basie's rhythm section to its players' concerns about the problems of southern sharecroppers. Ellington had his own ideas about what he called "Negro music," and they were not limited to the three-minute swing dance tunes Hammond would have preferred that he play. Though unwilling to submit to Hammond's litmus test, Ellington harbored his own ideas about racial authenticity. He asserted that his aim "has always been the development of an authentic Negro music, of which swing is only one element." Whether performing for social dancers or concert listeners, reveling in syncopated rhythms or writing complex harmonies, Ellington maintained that his musical aesthetic was "definitely and purely racial."[86] Whether as a jazz composer and band-leader or as a public celebrity, Ellington felt he certainly didn't need John Hammond to instruct him on how to represent his race.

The *summa* of Ellington's explicitly race-conscious writing was the solemn and sweeping portrait of African American experience in his extended suite *Black, Brown, and Beige*, which premiered at Carnegie Hall in January 1943.[87] Subtitled "a tone parallel to the history of the Negro in America," the suite was a series of musical moods invoking the experiences of enslavement, whippings, escapes, emancipation, Jim Crow segregation, mass migration, urbanization, religious conviction, and patriotic loyalty. The performance was one of a number of World War II–era cultural productions that con-structed an image of African Americans as hardworking, pious, diligent, courageous people who represented the best values of American culture.[88] While pointing to the history of racial oppression and the exclusion of blacks from U.S. citizenship, the suite framed the African American story as a heroic struggle for freedom that crucially supported the nation's own battle for independence and more recent emergence as a bulwark against interna-tional tyranny. Ellington's narrative gave special attention to black military participation in previous U.S. wars, and the "Beige" movement culminated in a patriotic apotheosis, with Jimmy Britton singing the line: "We're black, brown, and beige but we're red, white, and blue."[89]

While such topical flourishes in *Black, Brown, and Beige* played to wartime ideological considerations—including the "Double V" campaign to couple the global battle against fascism with the domestic battle against anti-black racism—Ellington's basic thinking about the piece predated the war and reflected his longstanding interest in racial memory as an artistic resource. The Carnegie concert program notes by Irving Kolodin noted that *Black, Brown, and Beige* grew out of an unproduced opera Ellington had started in the early 1930s under the working title "boola"—a term, the notes said, that "Negroes use to symbolize the perpetual spirit of the race through time."[90] Ellington's invocation of a transhistorical racial spirit, as well as his use of racially inscribed folk materials such as work songs and spirituals in his for-mal compositions, made him the kind of figure Alain Locke envisioned when he called for jazz to develop into a scored-through concert music that trans-formed African American vernacular traditions into cosmopolitan art. With *Symphony in Black*; *Black, Brown, and Beige*; and other extended compositions such as *New World a-Coming* (1943), *Harlem* (1951), and *My People* (1963), and with his sacred concerts, Ellington devoted a substantial portion of his career to work that embodied the New Negro vision of symphonic jazz.

This was the Ellington that John Hammond regarded as a traitor to the purist values of hot jazz. Continuing the assault he had launched with his pan of *Reminiscing in Tempo*, Hammond ripped into *Black, Brown, and Beige* in a review article bearing the portentous title "Is the Duke Deserting Jazz?" Hammond deemed it "unfortunate that Duke saw fit to tamper with the blues form in order to produce music of greater 'significance'" than his swing tunes of the early 1930s. Ellington's interest in complex harmonies, Hammond argued, "alienated a good part of his dancing public." He concluded: "I hope that some day [Ellington] will be able to find himself once again and continue his contributions to the folk—or people's—music of our time."[91] Hammond's review appeared in *Jazz* magazine, whose young editor, Bob Thiele, agreed with Hammond's view that the concert suite was a pretentious effort to reach beyond the inherent resources of the jazz idiom. Thiele found Ellington's arrangements marred by "exaggerated coloring" and an "over rich layer cake of ideas and tones" that were "in direct opposition to the fundamentals of jazz."[92]

When Victor issued a recording of *Black, Brown, and Beige*, Roger Pryor Dodge condemned it as an unfortunate example of "arranged jazz" that rendered interpretations of moods and styles rather than unselfconscious musical expression unto itself. Instead of blues, for example, Ellington offered a movement called "The Blues," leading Dodge to "wonder what use was served the whole era of Bessie Smith as a contribution to the blues in jazz." Conspicuously absent throughout the composition was precisely the element that for Dodge constituted the *real* in composed music: passages that faithfully captured the creative origins of the music in the dance context, and that "stood on the same ground" as the improvisations performed in those originary moments. "This the Duke's composition cannot do," Dodge averred, "because he has not developed the jazz idiom but has *borrowed* from both the 'arrangement' and the last echo of Debussy." He concluded with characteristic acerbity: "This Duke composition should be listened to as a piece which exemplifies the path that jazz should not take."[93]

"The Myth of Race"

The debate over *Black, Brown, and Beige* occasioned a schism between John Hammond and his friend Leonard Feather, who was then working as Ellington's press agent. Feather wrote a blistering rejoinder to Hammond's review in which he praised Ellington's composition as a "deep and stirring" piece with "many complexities of form and fascinating developments in melodic continuity." Responding to Hammond's complaint that the piece didn't lend itself to dancing, Feather quipped: "Who the hell wants to dance in Carnegie Hall? And what does Hammond know about music for dancing, since he doesn't even dance?"

Feather championed Ellington's interest in extended concert forms using the same argument he would use a few years later in his endorsement of bebop, a critical stance that would also put him at odds with Hammond and other staunch adherents of older styles: the aesthetic mission of jazz was to keep moving forward in its exploration of new stylistic possibilities. For Feather, Ellington's music was—in the early 1940s at least—the leading edge of jazz's evolutionary thrust: "It is the only jazz that has combined the fundamental qualities of this musical idiom with the progress and advancement that are necessary to save it from stagnation." Aside from aesthetic considerations, Feather's review was a shrill polemic aimed at Hammond's imperial power in the jazz world. Feather charged that "Hammond's prejudices against certain musicians and bands are mostly motivated by his inability to run their bands or careers for them." To back up the charge—which referred implicitly to Hammond's strong influence over the Goodman and Basie bands—Feather recounted an episode in the Columbia recording studios a few years earlier in which Ellington had rejected Hammond's advice about hemming in a recalcitrant soloist. "John never quite got over that," Feather alleged.[94]

The running of his band was not the only matter on which Ellington asserted his autonomy by resisting or working around Hammond's influence. Ellington had his own ideas about how best to advance the cause of African Americans and other oppressed and aggrieved peoples, and, like Hammond, he worked out his own relationship with the Popular Front. Notwithstanding his ritual disavowals of the organized Left—"the only Communism I know is that of Jesus Christ," he was fond of saying—Ellington was a frequent enough participant in Popular Front–sponsored events of the late 1930s to earn him (along with Hammond) surveillance by the FBI.[95] While not *of* the Left, Ellington circulated *through* the Left, and this casual fellow traveling helped inspire what he called his "social-significance thrusts" of the early 1940s. These included not only the Carnegie performance of *Black, Brown, and Beige* (the proceeds of which went to Russian war relief), but also his 1941 musical revue *Jump for Joy*, a show Ellington hoped "would take Uncle Tom out of the theater, eliminate the stereotyped image that had been exploited in Hollywood and Broadway, and say things that would make the audience think."[96]

Hammond's wrangling with Duke Ellington revealed his unwillingness to embrace multiple streams of black culture, especially the tradition of cultural and intellectual self-sufficiency that middle-class blacks had built in Washington, D.C. and the New Negro ideology of cultural evolutionism that shaped the Harlem Renaissance. Hammond's strict demands for id-iomatic purity—his unyielding formula for authentic musical blackness—often meant that he trusted himself more than he did black musicians to know how black music could be used to advance black social causes. When Billie Holiday started performing the anti-lynching ballad "Strange Fruit," Hammond thought it was "artistically the worst thing that ever happened to her," even as he admitted that its "shock value" both helped her career and raised consciousness about the horrors of American racism. Echoing his criticism of Ellington's concert suites, he regarded the song as a mannered reach for "significance."[97]

As the title *Black, Brown, and Beige* suggests, Ellington thought in ex-pansive terms about the wide range of identities and experiences—the full spectrum of color, as it were—that made up African American culture and history. But he did not think it was his responsibility, as Hammond believed, to break the Jim Crow color line by hiring white musicians into his band, especially at a time when that same color line prevented black bands from performing in the most lucrative hotel jobs and commercially sponsored radio programs. Ellington was no foe of integration as a general social goal, but as long as the society and the music world continued to be segregated he saw the integration of bands as working mostly in favor of white bands and musicians. Hammond felt differently and urged Ellington to integrate his band. Later recalling his quarrels with Ellington on this issue, Hammond said that "jazz always has had a duty to promote racial understanding and interracial cooperation."[98] It's not hard to understand why Ellington would have been puzzled by Hammond's exhortations on this issue. The same priv-ileged white man who criticized him for making music that wasn't "black" enough also wanted him to add white musicians to his band. The same white man who was so eager to discover and preserve black folk authenticity—to mark its otherness and difference from white culture—also wanted to be known as the one who brought blacks and whites together in the jazz world.

Leonard Feather took up where Hammond left off in promoting jazz interracialism, and it was he who became, from the 1940s on, perhaps the most famously righteous and effective critic of Jim Crow segregation and white supremacy in the jazz and entertainment industries. After he relocated to Los Angeles in the late 1950s, Feather, in league with his close friend Benny Carter as officers of the local chapter of the NAACP, relentlessly battled institutionalized racism in the musicians' union and the Hollywood movie studios. Like Hammond, Feather would serve as an important ally of black musicians; unlike Hammond, Feather would endeavor to do so in a way that stressed what he shared with these musicians, both as an artist and as an ethnic minority, rather than what marked their social difference—even, as I suggested earlier, when in a white supremacist and class-stratified culture Feather's British bourgeois whiteness was a difference that could make *all* the difference. Colorblindness was the ideology that grounded Feather's Jewish liberalism. Being himself a white musician working in the jazz and blues idioms, Feather challenged the idea that race was a determining factor in jazz performance. He would become a fierce propagandist for his conviction that there was no color line in the music, most famously in one of his "blindfold test" columns. The column—which Feather originated in *Metronome* in the 1940s and then took with him to *Down Beat*, which copyrighted the concept and continues to publish the column to this day—asked noted musicians to "blindly" listen to records, then identify and assess them. In 1951, black trumpeter Roy Eldridge, who had become embittered by his experiences playing in white bands and, according to Feather, was "imbued with some of the cultural confusion still manifest in critical circles in France," told Feather he was sure he could distinguish white musicians from black ones. "At the end of the test," Feather later recounted, "he admitted that he had been wrong; he had failed even to achieve the 50% ratio of correct guesses to which the law of averages entitled him."[99]

As jazz criticism's liberal conscience, Feather peppered nearly all of his writing—even his ostensibly value-free, fact-driven jazz encyclopedias—with the grim details of racism ("no study of jazz can be complete without a consideration of the socio-historical factors that determined the associations and the frustrations of the man who created it") but also with a self-satisfied reckoning—often a literal counting—of the number of interracial associations producing high-quality jazz.[100] One wonders whether interracialism as an end in itself became an *idée fixe* that undermined the objectivity Feather was so keen to claim for himself. "It would seem to be an inescapable fact that some of the most valuable jazz of recent years has been produced by interracial teams," Feather wrote in the early 1960s, citing the productive collaborations of Miles Davis and Gil Evans, John Lewis and Gunther Schuller, Dizzy Gillespie and Lalo Schriffin, and Sonny Rollins and Jim Hall. Artistically fruitful as these collaborations were, Feather's assessment could hardly be read as objective, coming as it did at a time when he was inveighing against a black nationalist movement in which he claimed to hear ominous "fascistic overtones." This may help to account for why he had seemed deaf to the intrinsic quality of the soul jazz movement of the 1950s, with its race-conscious musical vocabulary and public image, and why throughout the 1960s his opinions of musicians often seemed deeply entangled with his perception of their racial politics.[101]

Feather was far from alone among jazz's white liberal integrationists in chafing under the heat of 1960s black nationalism. What gave Feather's experience resonance and a certain pathos was his perspective as a Jew who had emigrated to the United States and into the jazz life during the ascendancy of European fascism in the late 1930s and early 1940s. "Most of us no longer speak of 'white jazz' and 'Negro jazz,'" Feather wrote in a 1965 lament. "The myth of race, a curious distortion of Hitler's theories, almost disappeared in jazz until the stirring of a chauvinistic theory that Negroes are the only real 'blues people' caused an alarming new rift."[102] This allusion to *Blues People* (1963), by LeRoi Jones (Amiri Baraka), imagined a jazz world in the 1940s and 1950s practically free of racial conflict—a hopeful vision of the *dream* that Feather, Barry Ulanov, Marshall Stearns, Nat Hentoff, Ralph Gleason, and other jazz critics cultivated in league with Dizzy Gillespie, John Lewis, Dave Brubeck, and other musicians who shared in jazz's postwar consensus liberal ideology; not, as Feather would be the first to admit, an accurate assessment of the day-to-day, on-the-ground experience of musicians who worked in a manifestly racist industry and lived in a United States still riven by Jim Crow segregation. But Feather was here concerned with the mythology of racial difference, a matter he had been speaking about since positioning himself against French jazz criticism during the World War II years, when he found notions of racial superiority—even notions that valorized his black musician friends—dangerously akin to Nazi ideology. When Feather, in this same 1965 essay, sounded an alarm "that black nationalist leaders and the American Nazi Party had a relationship of mutual respect" and "that both had expressed similarly antagonistic views on the Jews," he was expressing a deeply personal sense of horror at the twentieth century's most chillingly consequential racial ideology.

Feather was by this time the strongest critic of the notion that black musicians were innately superior to white musicians *because of* their natural racial endowment. This racially essentialist notion of black jazz, which had been implicit in much 1920s transatlantic primitivist discourse, became codified in French jazz critic Hugues Panassié's 1942 book, *The Real Jazz*. Panassié's 1934 book *Le Jazz Hot* (published in the United States in 1936 as *Hot Jazz*) had been a groundbreaking effort to explain what made jazz an important and distinctive music. Panassié's focus in the earlier book was not racially exclusivist: while he held up Louis Armstrong as the prime example of the vitality and emotional power of the hot soloist, he also praised such white jazz musicians as Benny Goodman, Jack Teagarden, and Gene Krupa. In 1938, Panassié came to New York to produce a series of records for RCA with Mezz Mezzrow as his associate. Under Mezzrow's influence, Panassié significantly revised his view of jazz authenticity. In *The Real Jazz*, he ranked Goodman as a "detestable" clarinet player whose sterile intonation was inferior to that of black players Jimmie Noone and Omer Simeon—and white player Mezz Mezzrow, who became Panassié's lone example of a white musician who played jazz authentically.[103] Feather's rebuke of Panassié was much graver than his fraternal sparring with John Hammond over the Duke Ellington matter or with Mezz Mezzrow over White Negro posturing: in *Metronome*, he and co-editor Barry Ulanov published an unsubstantiated rumor (later retracted) that Panassié—an arch-conservative who wrote for *Action Française* in addition to his own magazine, *Le Jazz Hot*—collaborated with the Vichy regime during the Nazi occupation of France.[104]

Such were the heavy personal stakes (as we'll see further in coming chapters) in jazz sectarian polemics that took on the urgency and intensity of the larger ideological battles of a world at war. While Feather throughout his long career remained committed to the progressive civil rights agenda and to the diligent sense of purpose he observed in John Hammond in 1935, by the early 1940s Feather clearly had broken from his mentor in several crucial respects. Not for Feather was Hammond's obsession with folk authenticity, his romantic notions of the pure and the untutored waiting to be "discovered" and patronized. As a musician among musicians—or, as in the Ellington case, as a publicist working on behalf of a famously self-secure musician—Feather sensed the condescension inherent in such a conceit. More subtly, as a Jew during the Hitler years, he had to have been concerned about the untoward possibilities inherent in any folk-centered nationalist project, notwithstanding the strategic anti-fascism of the Popular Front Americanism in which Hammond figured so prominently. Still, for all of these divergences, as a jazz critic and missionary Feather retained at least a piece of Hammond's primary conceit: the idea that he was needed in the jazz world, and that he could do some good.

Tellingly, when the *Negro Digest*, in 1945, asked Feather to contribute a column to their series "If I Were a Negro," his strategy was to cast himself in the role of a young black professional—a lawyer who had "the educational equipment to fight Jim Crow," say, or a doctor who maintained an all-white client list. This well-educated, financially successful black man would live in one of the snobbish "high-class" districts in a house that he was able to buy only after mounting a noisy challenge to the discriminatory real estate practices that had kept other blacks out of that neighborhood. In this battle and others, the black man would make a special effort "to cultivate Jewish people and point out the many similarities between their problems and mine." Then he would cultivate as many white friends as possible as a way of proving that "people are people, and skin is only skin deep."[105] In this advocacy of a "colorblind" black-Jewish alliance in the struggle for a patently bourgeois vision of freedom and equality, Feather was proposing something akin to what he took to be his own usefulness in the jazz world, something that gave social purpose and meaning to his life, something parallel to his own substantial achievement.

In this, the passionate embrace of jazz as not only an art form but a new reason for living, Leonard Feather and John Hammond had plenty of company.

CHAPTER 2

"As If It Were Artistic and Not Just a Teenage Enthusiasm"
Hot Collecting across the Color Line

Jazz, for the true fan, is not merely to be listened to, but to be analyzed, studied, and discussed. The quintessential location of the fan is not the dance hall, the night club, or even the jazz concert or club, but the private room in which a group of young men play one another records, repeating crucial passages until they are worn out, and then endlessly discussing their comparative merits. For every jazz fan is a collector of records, within his financial means.

—Eric Hobsbawm, *The Jazz Scene*

"A Conspiracy of Appreciation"

The great British Marxist historian Eric Hobsbawm was no stranger to those private rooms where purposeful young men dissected the Hot Fives and Sevens, swelled to Bix and Tram, pondered Ellington, and cursed the commercial corruption of true art in stray discs that weren't worth the wax on which they were cut. Decades before taking the *nom de plume* Francis Newton to write about jazz in *The New Statesman*, Hobsbawm found his passion for the music at age sixteen in nocturnal male bonding rituals carried out with a cousin of the same age in the attic of his family's house in a Victorian white-collar suburb of London. The Jewish family had just recently returned to England after a crack at the movie business in Berlin that happened to coincide with the flowering of German fascism. This cousin conformed almost exactly to the ideal type of 1930s British jazz fan that Hobsbawn later profiled in his 1959 book *The Jazz Scene*: "the intelligent, self-educated young man from the lower middle-classes, preferably a little bohemian." The two teenagers worked on each other's belief systems: while Hobsbawm tried to convert the cousin "to the communism to which I had been converted while living through the rise of Hitler," the cousin converted him to jazz. He did this with a hand-cranked gramophone and a cache of about twenty 78-rpm heavy black discs, including the British releases of Fletcher Henderson's "Sugar Foot Stomp" and Don Redman's "Chant of the Weeds." "In between records and intensive discussions about how great they were, we restored our strength with potato crisps and spoonfuls of heavily sugared canned milk, the kind that was firmly labeled 'unfit for babies.' We preferred to have these sessions at night. When the days were too long, we drew the curtains."[1]

When we draw back the curtains on private homosocial encounters of this kind, we reveal something important about popular music's crucial role in the construction of gender. "For many men, and surely for a few women, mastering the discourse of record collecting has always been a way of establishing a masculine identity," writes Krin Gabbard, adding that "it's no wonder a major fixation on record-collecting almost inevitably attracts a young man's fantasy when he turns fourteen or fifteen." That's the age at which many young men and a smaller number of equally determined young women "work at acquiring a commanding knowledge that can be carefully deployed in the right surroundings," such displays of "authoritative information" constituting "a well established sign of masculine power in contemporary . . . culture."[2] If Hobsbawm was a year or two late in his jazz conversion experience, he quickly made up for lost time by joining his cousin in a pilgrimage to a South London ballroom where Duke Ellington was performing a midnight-to-dawn "breakfast dance." ("Of course," Hobsbawm quaintly says in his 1992 remembrance of the occasion, "we knew the great man's record 'Breakfast Dance' forwards and backwards.")[3] Nursing the one glass of beer he could afford, Hobsbawm became absorbed in the "spirit of dedication" he would later describe, in The Jazz Scene, as an essential affective posture of the jazz fan: "Jazz fans do not listen to their music to dance, and often avoid dancing, unless pressed into it by their girlfriends, whose approach to the music is normally more utilitarian. They stand or sit by the bandstand, soaking in the music, nodding and smiling at one another in a conspiracy of appreciation."[4]

This was 1933. For the next twenty years, as a dispute between musicians' unions kept American musicians out of Britain, Hobsbawm and other British jazz fans subsisted on records ("this stored and unreal form"), forming an aficionado network that exercised decisive influence over the development of jazz in Britain. "We were convinced that only Americans, preferably black, were worth listening to," Hobsbawn recalled.

To this point Hobsbawm's story is a familiar one of the white male ado-lescent securing his masculinity—note the shift from the sugary condensed milk to beer—through his identification with black performers. But then his story breaks pattern. Instead of digging deeper and deeper into disco-graphical minutiae, straining his financial and spatial resources with a steady accumulation of record platters, and brandishing his bona fides in conspic-uous displays of jazz arcana, Hobsbawm through the war years and well into the 1950s contented himself with being a "fringe observer of the jazz scene."

> I was no expert. I was neither a collector nor the sort of guy whose name collectors knew, and I neither wanted to write about jazz nor did anyone ask me to. Not even in any of those tiny, short-lived, fact-filled, and denunciatory jazz magazines in which the experts poured out their information and squared up to each other on such issues as black vs. white or the acceptability of swing bands, like entrants for a local bantamweight contest.[5]

In forgoing serious jazz connoisseurship as the driving obsession of his post-pubescence, Hobsbawm may have saved himself from a cache of pub-lished opinions he would later regret when he assumed the mantle of ma-ture jazz analyst, this after having established his reputation as a leading academic historian. If we credit common stereotypes along with sensitive portrayals of record collectors in Anglo-American cinema and literature, we might suspect that Hobsbawm also spared himself a certain amount of em-barrassment in matters of male bonding, romantic intimacy, coupling, and sexual performance.[6]

Consider the character Josh Edwards in the classic juvenile delinquency film *Blackboard Jungle* (1955). Edwards (Richard Kiley) is a hapless, be-spectacled math teacher, resigned to the futility of his traditional pedagogic methods, who tries to assuage his students by playing some discs from his copious jazz record collection. In a painful display of the disconnect between moldy fig jazz connoisseurship and postwar youth culture, the black-leather-jacket-clad students respond to the teacher's close reading of Bix Beiderbecke's "Jazz Me Blues" ("Pay attention to that cornet. Beiderbecke came before James and Ellman") by smashing both his records and his eye-glasses to smithereens. What's clear from the scene is not just Edwards's ob-session with white musicians—earlier we see him listening to Stan Kenton with a rabid intensity that suggests "Stan the Man" has discovered the for-mula for the music of the spheres—but how wanting is his masculine au-thority in the face of street-smart urban toughs running roughshod over the school. If we are to assume that Edwards's record collecting had begun in his own adolescence as an expression of his emerging masculinity, we are now faced with the acute crisis of masculinity to which his precious collecting hobby consigns him. It goes without saying that Josh Edwards has no girlfriend, nor, from the look of things, any conceivable prospect of finding one.[7]

More recently, in *Ghost World* (2000), we witness an early blues and jazz record collector named Seymour, played to nebbishy perfection by Steve Buscemi, bollix up two hetero-relationship possibilities and end up, by the movie's end, prostrate in a female psychiatrist's office, presumably struggling to untangle the intricacies of his over-identification with his mother. Seymour's social life consists of collectors' soirées where middle-to-old-aged, badly dressed men stand around trading tidbits of precious information about vintage recordings. A desperate foray into the personal ads inadvertently connects Seymour with a young woman named Enid (Thora Birch), an ennui-ridden malcontent looking for offbeat experiences to counteract the vapidity of the southern Californian suburban teenage wasteland. Enid, it turns out, is soulful and *simpatico*: this is signaled to us in the epiphany she undergoes while listening to an old Skip James recording of "Devil Got My Woman" that she's bought from Seymour at a garage sale. After sleeping with Seymour, she questions the appropriateness of a sustained relationship with a man twice her age and begins to try to set him up with other women. At a bar, she delivers a hot-to-trot redhead to Seymour's table, but all he can do is harangue her with a lecture on the difference between ragtime and the blues.

There's a disturbing racial subtext to Seymour's collecting fetish that surfaces when he shows Enid some of the visual material in his possession. Seymour has assembled a history of advertisements and figurines from Cook's Chicken, the chain restaurant company where he works as a middle manager at the corporate office. Back when the company was called Coon's Chicken, the company's signature image was a huge, grinning minstrel black face. Enid is intrigued by the blackface image and brings a poster bearing it to her art class. The art teacher is equally fascinated by the image and insists on mounting it in an exhibition of student art. Some people object to the display of the image and it is removed, but not before a photographer from the local newspaper snaps a shot of it. When the picture appears in the newspaper, Seymour is fired from his job.[8]

Gabbard suggests that "Seymour is implicated in this racist past not just because he works for Cook's Chicken but because his polymorphous fascination with blackness has led him to preserve the old documents."[9] He argues more generally for a larger pattern in twentieth-century culture in which white fans of black music, in an effort to inoculate themselves against charges of "snobbery, slumming, colonizing, voyeurism, and even a form of racism," attempt to shift the rhetoric of collecting in the direction of art and aesthetics, insisting that "jazz and blues are simply great art musics and that [the white collector] is sufficiently free of racial and cultural prejudice to be capable of recognizing the achievements of distinguished black artists." For Gabbard, this aestheticized rhetoric of high-art connoisseurship hinges on "massive acts of repression" to conceal the collector's erotic interest in the physical prowess and hip attitude of the live black artist. As long as the white male jazz fan stands by his claims of a purely artistic appreciation, he "need not concern himself with the homoerotic and voyeuristic element of his fascination with black men as they enact their masculinity with saxophones, trumpets, guitars, and other phallic instruments."[10]

The presence and power of erotic voyeurism in jazz consumption and spectatorship is, I think, undeniable; so much so that we would also want to recognize its importance in exchanges other than between the white male fan and the black male musician—for instance, in black heterosexual male fascination with white female singers, or in black female and black male homosexual interest in white instrumentalists. Like Gabbard, my focus here is mainly on white male homosociality, in this case in a history that reaches back to the 1930s and early 1940s, a history in which young white men of the same generation as Eric Hobsbawm, John Hammond, and Leonard Feather participated avidly—often fanatically—in the phenomenon of jazz record collecting and its allied discourses. Fanatical is just the word for a fan discourse that helped make the swing movement the rowdy cultural explosion that it was in this country. Much like the passionate, sometimes maniacal fans of spectator sports, swing fans—in magazines like *Down Beat* and *Metronome*—pursued their hobby with raw adolescent fervor, fierce partisanship, and blunt talk of winners and losers. At the same time, not at all coincidentally, there emerged an aestheticized discourse of jazz as an art music, a discourse—carried out in collectors' "hot clubs" and in the Modernism-inspired "little magazines" attached to them—that became central to the establishment of a jazz canon centered on recordings other than the most commercially successful, largely white acts of the swing era. This anticommercial, connoisseurial discourse has been central to jazz—has, in fact, defined the very idea of jazz—down to our own time.

Still, I am not quite as ready as Gabbard to explain jazz's art discourse as largely the product of the repression of interracial homoerotic desire, or—to name the stereotype that Gabbard himself disproves in living a life that happily accommodates both his copious vinyl collection and his wife— of the cloddish inability of the white male jazz record collector to sustain healthy heterosexual relationships. This is not because the men I will discuss were not notably deficient (so far as I have been able to determine) in their normative heterosexual self-presentations; the whole point of the concept of repression, after all, is to address not what we see, but what we don't see, on the supposition that it is precisely what we don't see that might tell us the most about what we need to know. But what I *do* see in the late 1930s and early 1940s swing and jazz collector's culture is a dizzying swirl of desires and passions in which erotic voyeurism and the white fascination with blackness took shape through a variety of cultural exchanges inflected with complex social and historical factors.

Foremost in visibility, to be sure, was the emergence of a collector's culture in which young, mostly white men, much like Eric Hobsbawm and his cousin, engaged in fraternal associations around and through rituals of intense listening and verbal expression. Much of this boisterous discourse was fueled by the runaway testosterone of adolescent males arrayed in a kind of Darwinian competition, the young rivals locked into contests of phallic one-upmanship. The governing dynamic was one in which young white men fronted for each other in displays of superior knowledge and righteous indignation at hopelessly uninformed tastes running wild in the general population. The men who emerged as most committed to a formal and aestheticized paradigm of jazz history—those who adopted what I call the critic's pose—consciously distinguished themselves from the popular mass culture of swing, with its emphasis on jitterbugging, autograph-hounding, and celebrity worship. All of this the proto-critics regarded as hysterical and infantile. Paradoxically, even the phallic one-upmanship of swing fan verbal volleying was read in a pejorative sense as an abjectly feminized pursuit, in contrast to the ostensibly sober, intellectually hard-edged, masculine authority they assigned to their own hot collecting and canon-building efforts.

The term "intellectual" is important here, for it speaks to both the objective location and the subjective desires and pretenses of the men who emerged alongside Hammond and Feather as important figures in U.S. jazz criticism. Whereas Hammond and Feather fashioned their critic's poses from deep inside the commercial entertainment industry, men like Marshall Stearns, Ralph Gleason, Barry Ulanov, Ralph de Toledano, Eugene Williams, and, a bit later, Nat Hentoff and Martin Williams honed their jazz appreciation skills while enrolled in Ivy League and other elite colleges. The righteous passion these men brought to jazz was to no small degree energized by their sense that this music belonged in the cultural pantheon that a sound liberal arts education—whether institutional or personal—ought to represent. In this, these men were modernist organic intellectuals, not unlike the earlier champions of Picasso, Joyce, and Stein, working outside or on the edges of the education system and the cultural establishment to support and enshrine an artistic vanguard. But in most cases, like Hammond and Feather their initial attraction to the music ran to an even deeper, more personal sense of outsider-ness or edginess, owing to a palpable sense of distinction from the social world and the culture of their parents. And this had largely to do with race.

In the late 1930s and early 1940s, swing, hot collecting, the birth of jazz magazines and fan culture, and the development of jazz criticism were all overshadowed by the politics of race, and the politics of race were overshadowed by the rise of fascism and the onset of world war. While the mass-circulated *Down Beat* and *Metronome* were aimed at an American youth market not primarily concerned with the ideological intricacies of fascism and communism, and while smaller, more specialized publications such as *Jazz Information* reveled in discographical debates of such intensity that one can hardly imagine readers having had much energy left over to worry about epochal world events, the most thoughtful of these readers were young people caught up in what Warren Susman called the era's "culture of commitment." This was a historical moment when belief systems and loyalties were constantly being put to the test. In such a climate, popular culture can take on much the same level of seriousness and import as political culture. This was certainly true for John Hammond and Leonard Feather in their linkage of jazz with civil rights advocacy, a Left-leaning campaign carried on by some of the figures I introduce in this chapter, such as Nat Hentoff and Ralph Gleason. But it was also true, if in different ways, of Ralph de Toledano, who became an arch-conservative with access to the highest circles of government, or of Martin Williams, who became a cultural conservative with a sinecure at the Smithsonian. It was *especially* true for black American jazz fans and critics who tried to leverage white interest in jazz into economic and cultural capital that was crucial to their campaign for social and political equality. For all of these actors, jazz, and the legitimation of jazz as an art, mattered profoundly in ways that included but also reached beyond the erotic and the psychosexual.

And it all started with the records.

"The Back of My Hand to Yiz"

Growing up in the 1930s, Nat Hentoff was a swing fan, which meant that when his teachers at Boston Latin High School turned to face the blackboard, he stole a look at the copy of *Down Beat* hidden under his schoolbooks. At the risk of missing a crucial algebra problem or civics homily, Hentoff lost himself in blaring tabloid headlines, heartthrob-of-the-month girlie pictures, and a cultish lexicon in which "hep cats" spoke of being "sent" by the "platters" recently "waxed" by their favorite "hot," "sweet," or "corn" bands. Hentoff had discovered swing one day at age ten when his walk through Kenmore Square was interrupted by a "fierce wailing of brass and reeds, a surging, pulsing cry of yearning," which he traced to a record of Artie Shaw's "Nightmare" playing on a phonograph in Krey's department store. Hentoff's impulse upon hearing the record was to cry out himself. But he held back, as he later explained, because "it was not something a Boston boy, especially a Boston Jewish boy wandering outside of the ghetto, could ever satisfactorily explain to one of *them*." From that point on the small change he earned assisting his neighborhood Yiddish-speaking fruit peddler went toward purchases of the Shaw, Duke Ellington, Louis Armstrong, and Billie Holiday records he heard while hanging out at Krey's, and while listening to the local jazz radio show hosted by Krey's clerk, Bill Ingalls. The fact that Hentoff's Depression-era household didn't have a phonograph on which to play these records proved to be no deterrent: from reading the lively discussions of them by critics and fans in *Down Beat*, he knew that he had to have them.[11]

Along with the tens of thousands of other swing fans reading *Down Beat* and *Metronome* in the late 1930s, Hentoff closely followed updates of each magazine's reader's poll to see what proportion of the swing audience had voted correctly, as he had, in their choices of the best bands and musicians. He savored the arguments about the relative merits of the Benny Goodman and Duke Ellington bands, whether Casa Loma was a swing or a sweet band, whether Davey Tough or Chick Webb was the better drummer. He was intrigued by *Down Beat*'s ongoing John Hammond chronicle, a saga of one man's heroic fight for an America that was fair to its workers and minorities and that recognized the superiority of the Count Basie rhythm section. While Hentoff found both Hammond's musical taste and his politics unimpeachable, he thought he detected a whiff of aristocratic arrogance in the manner in which the Vanderbilt scion Hammond was going about trying to lord it over the swing business. In Hentoff's mind the true jazz aristocrat was Duke Ellington, and when the Duke denounced Hammond as a "causified critic" and "ardent propagandist," Hentoff assumed that Ellington was opposed not to the cause of racial equality, but to people who tried to tell him what to do. He read with interest Marshall Stearns's fifteen-part series, "The History of 'Swing-Music,'" which traced jazz's historical roots back to the African American slave experience. Feeling, however, that "the writing about jazz should be as exciting as the music itself," Hentoff found Stearns, a budding scholar of medieval English literature, an unfortunately pedestrian writer.[12]

Much more to Hentoff's liking was *Down Beat*'s Boston correspondent, George Frazier. Though his politics were unclear and his musical tastes unpredictable, Frazier's writing style could affect a young jazz fan's hormones in much the same way as the heartthrob-of-the-month girlie pictures. The purpose of jazz criticism, in Frazier's view, was to "send you."[13] And Frazier, through *Down Beat*, *Mademoiselle*, and newspapers that syndicated his *Boston Herald* column "Sweet and Lowdown," was sending more swing fans than any other critic, save perhaps the ubiquitous Hammond. In singularly cavalier language, Frazier told his readers what he liked and what he disliked. He didn't like Martha Tilton when he heard her sing with Benny Goodman in 1938, and so the headline on his next *Down Beat* column read "Martha Tilton Stinks."[14] He didn't like the idea of Boston becoming a jazz backwater, and so he wrote in another *Down Beat* column:

> Boston remains as dull and stupid as ever . . . . The night club owners invariably pick up the stinkiest talent and the patrons fail to realize it . . . any Boston band that plays in tune is a rarity.[15]

He liked singer Lee Wiley, and so he described her as

> 'one bitch of a singer' . . . [a singer who] has a voice and a style that have long since made me extremely eager to go to bed with her—but in a nice, noble way, you understand.[16]

Taking jazz criticism's masculinist impulses beyond Hammond's earnest political yearnings and Stearns's scholarly cool, Frazier's hard-boiled pulp prose portrayed the jazz world in explicitly gendered and vulgarly eroticized terms. Frazier liked musicians who admired his clothes and who aspired themselves to a certain sartorial elegance. And so his panegyric to Lee Wiley noted the "marvelous skirts from I. Magnin's, the little white straw hat and the navy blue dress with white piping that she wore to the Stork for brunch last Easter Sunday,"[17] while the upshot of his lukewarm assessment of Frank Sinatra was a mild censure of the singer's youthful ignorance of the finer points of men's neckwear:

> Frank Sinatra looks like nothing so much as he looks like a Frank Sinatra fan. He favors big knots when he wears four-in-hand ties, and the collars on his shirts are either very short (like Cary Grant's) or very long (like George Raft's.)[18]

What Frazier liked most of all, however, was to incite controversies that made himself the center of attention. There was no surer means for a swing critic to do this than to register disapproval of the so-called "King of Swing," Benny Goodman. After championing Goodman in the early- to mid-1930s, first for being faithful to his Chicago roots and then for having the artistic taste and social tolerance to hire black musicians, Frazier later in the decade voiced a sense of betrayal over what he considered Goodman's commercial sell-out. When Goodman's supporters flooded *Down Beat* with letters questioning Frazier's critical integrity, he shot back in kind:

> I'd like a word with those of you who accuse me of unfairness to Benny Good-man. As you may have gathered by now, I've never been one to go around organizing fan clubs for [Benny] and his picture is one picture that I positively do not keep under my pillow, but I don't think that constitutes unfairness. It's simply that I'm a big boy now and no longer allow myself to be overawed by the big bigness of his name. Benny this and Benny that and the back of me hand to yiz, as I once warned my audience of smart young women.[19]

It was writing like this that hit the adolescent Nat Hentoff right where he lived. Frazier, Hentoff thought, wrote "like Errol Flynn playing Captain Blood."[20] Aside from the brassy, take-no-prisoners style that tapped into the same visceral energies unleashed by the music, what Hentoff found so alluring about Frazier was the fact that this Harvard man, this man who looked "as if he might be the direct descendant of William Bradford,"[21] was so fully invested in the same culture Hentoff himself was. Hentoff later was astonished to discover that Frazier was not, as he supposed, Boston Brahmin, but rather Boston Irish, the son of a Southie fire department inspector. But questions of pedigree were less important than shared passions: what mattered was that Frazier was being "sent" by the same music that was "sending" Hentoff himself. Frazier had an arrogance that often shaded into condescension, yet he remained obsessed with what a teenager thought about him and his opinions—as Hentoff discovered when Frazier dutifully answered each of the teenager's letters with missives powered by the same levels of indignation and vitriol that he poured into his published articles. George Frazier writing about jazz was really George Frazier writing about the experience of being a jazz fan, and of wanting to be perceived as that most privileged of jazz fans, the jazz critic.

"Not Just a Teenage Enthusiasm"

It happened sometime during the 1949–50 academic year, the year Martin Williams spent earning a master's degree in English at the University of

Pennsylvania, a year in which he was "trying to resist jazz." After a great deal of soul-searching, he had decided on a career as an English professor. He had tried law school—at the University of Virginia, his alma mater—but had found it insufferable, his only reason for enrolling, he soon realized, being to placate his parents. His gentrified Richmond upbringing, the education at the St. Christopher Episcopal Preparatory School, had instilled in him "a sense of standards" that he deeply valued. But his parents' "delusions of aristocracy"—his mother's old-line Virginian gentry bloodlines counting for more than the professional status of his father, a Richmond dentist—were proving to be a chafing encumbrance. He had no problem with being perceived as a leader, nor even with thinking himself superior, but he resented being a "tool of [his] parents' ambitions."[22]

One of the lessons Williams had learned from his parents typified for him the meretriciousness of their social aspirations. It had to do with the decorum he was expected to maintain in his relations with black people. As a matter of honor, of the dignity of his social station, he was never—*never*—to be heard publicly using the "N word." That word was a vulgar, lower-class word, a redneck word. Uttered publicly, that word could instantly sweep open the curtain and reveal all of the backstage props the family had so carefully constructed for its performance on the Virginian social stage.

Martin Williams—Martin Tudor Hansfield Williams—knew about the curtain, because he had been backstage. One day when he was sixteen or seventeen he had asked his mother to come back to his bedroom. He wanted her to hear some of the music that was firing his imagination so. Since his parents rarely listened to music and didn't even have a phonograph player, he had bought a phonograph of his own which he kept in his bedroom, where he spent countless hours listening to the jazz records he had begun collecting. He played for his mother one of his favorite Louis Armstrong records. She sat dutifully, showing little outward emotion other than what seemed a touch of impatience that the record was taking so long. When the song finished, young Martin lifted the needle off of the platter. With a deep sigh, he said to his mother, "Isn't that just beautiful?" She looked him straight in the eye and responded crisply: "Martin, I think you've got nigger blood."[23]

Williams told this story about his mother's breach of linguistic decorum many years later by way of explaining how his career as a jazz critic troubled and disappointed his parents, who could never—even after their son became the head of jazz programming at the Smithsonian—overcome their disdain for their son's love of black culture. As a naval officer serving in the Pacific theater during World War II, Williams did his parents proud, but he also stoked and enlarged his jazz interest. The deep nationalist pride he took from the war owed something to the time he spent on shore in Los Angeles jazz clubs fine-tuning his appreciation of Kid Ory's traditional New Orleans style and struggling to come to terms with the avant-garde experimentalism of the Charlie Parker–Dizzy Gillespie band. Not resisting jazz during the war meant that a handsome percentage of his navy stipend had gone toward vintage and used copies of 1920s race records that he found in Ross Russell's Dial Record Shop in southwest Los Angeles, a hobby that allied him with the Ivy League students and second-generation white ethnics who had canvassed black neighborhoods and Salvation Army stores throughout the 1930s in search of authentic jazz and blues records.

And so in Philadelphia, his resistance to jazz being not as stout as it might have been, Williams now and then had climbed down from the ivy tower and ventured forth to the black neighborhood bars that hosted the city's jazz scene. The cultural barriers he traversed in these instances were not unfamiliar. Growing up in Richmond, he had attended dances in the basement of a black Baptist church, standing in the area cordoned off for white patrons right next to the bandstand, peering over the musicians' shoulders. One time, when he was so positioned during a performance by the Count Basie band, he watched Lester Young reading from a piece of sheet music that was identified at the top with the big letter "X." After the band finished the tune, one that Williams hadn't heard before, he asked Young for its name. In the airy, slow drawl for which he was legendary, Young said to the teenage Williams, "I guess we're calling that one 'X' . . . 'Ms. X.'"[24]

In Philadelphia there was the Aqua Lounge, nearby in West Philly the Blue Note around 15th and Ridge, Pep's, the Showboat, Joe Pitt's Musical Bar, the Zanzibar. Commercial establishments rather than temples of art, some of these clubs had been moving away from a straight jazz policy, booking more of the rhythm-and-blues acts that now seemed more popular with their young, predominantly black clientele than the bebop bands that had been their bread and butter through the 1940s. Some of them had positioned their bandstands right behind the bar, leaving just enough space on the bar itself to allow honking, squealing, squawking saxophonists to careen and gyrate up and down it without stepping into customers' drinks or on their hands.[25]

One saxophonist who was becoming known in Philly around this time for "walking the bar"—better known than he was for the music theory and composition studies he was taking at the Granoff School of Music—was a young man named John Coltrane. Martin Williams never saw Coltrane in the short time he was in Philadelphia, nor did he see any of the more committed R&B "honkers." If he had, he might have appreciated their skills as entertainers, and might even have enjoyed them. But he would have been wondering whether behind the mask of the entertainer there was something more, something of more permanent value. This was the way he had approached swing, the popular music of his youth. "We were interested in different aspects of the music," Williams said of the times he escorted young women to dances. "If when we went to see someone like Tommy Dorsey, what they [his dates] wanted were the romantic ballads; what I wanted were the jazz instrumentals." Similarly, in his radio and record listening at that time, Williams began to discern "jazz" elements contained within "swing" performances. He counted as his first recognition of jazz per se his appreciation of the piano work of Teddy Wilson on one of Benny Goodman's small-group recordings. And in his first piece of writing about jazz, an article for his prep school paper in 1941, he talked about his discovery—from listening to a reissue record of the Fletcher Henderson band in the late 1920s—of the stylistic debt Benny Goodman owed to this seminal black bandleader and arranger.

From a very early age, in other words, Williams was concerned with how jazz had evolved as an artistic tradition:

> I was not only interested in current hits. The idea that there were roots here, the idea that there were great figures from the past, there were great ensembles and great styles, before the time of the currently popular stuff, always appealed to me. I began to collect Armstrong and Beiderbecke records when I was still in my teens. I was curious about all that. And also the idea that if this was really artistic, as people were saying, I wanted to know how and why. I wanted to be able to discuss it as if it were artistic and not just a teenage enthusiasm.

This primary emphasis on the tradition of jazz had stayed with Williams. But it had to do with more than his precocious sense of aesthetics. When Williams first heard bebop pioneers Charlie Parker and Dizzy Gillespie at Billy Berg's in Los Angeles, he was taken aback. "It had to do with what that music was saying," Williams said years later:

> I'm a southern kid. I've still got all that latent stuff in me [about race] that I haven't dealt with. I'm living in this paradox. That [bebop] sounded arrogant, uppity.... [When I] saw Bird's combo, what struck me even more than the music was the *attitude* coming off the bandstand—self-confident, aggressive. It was something I'd never seen from black musicians before.[26]

Since then he had come to a better understanding and appreciation of bebop, but he remained strongly beholden to the 1930s swing and the pre-1930s traditional jazz he had been listening to since he was a teenager. It was performances of these residual styles that Williams favored in his escapes from the groves of academe.

And so it was that one night when one of jazz's biblical characters, the veteran New Orleans reedman Sidney Bechet, came to Philadelphia, Martin Williams was there to see him, and it was then that it happened:

> Sidney Bechet was on the bandstand one night . . . . I saw him up there, playing so passionately. Probably a slow blues, but it wouldn't have to be. I realized in a flash that the man, and the instrument, and the sound coming out of it, and the passion, and the music were all one thing . . . one aesthetic whole . . . . I was just staggered . . . . It was an epiphany for me . . . . I think it was then that I was first in touch with the essential miracle of the music.[27]

The significance of Martin Williams's Bechet-induced epiphany was not about sectarian loyalties; it was not about Williams backsliding into a moldy fig absolutism that would require him to reject as inauthentic any jazz not played by somebody born in New Orleans before the turn of the century. The significance of Williams's experience of being "just staggered" by Bechet, rather, was that it signaled the beginning of the end of his resistance to jazz, and set him upon the course of turning his interest in the music into something more than a hobby—indeed, into the defining feature of his life.

"As If It Were Artistic"

Just what had happened to Martin Williams this mid-century night in a Philadelphia jazz club? In some ways, what happened sounds a lot like what Fredric Jameson has described as the archetypical audience experience of artistic modernism:

> At its most vital, the experience of modernism, was not one of a single historical movement or process, but of a "shock of discovery," a commitment and an adherence to its individual forms through a series of religious conversions.[28]

Ever since audiences other than its primary one of first-generation urban African Americans had begun to embrace jazz, they had done so with the zealotry usually attributed to religious conversion experiences—with a sense of the music as the touchstone of a new belief system, a new way of life far more spontaneous and life-affirming than that of their parents, a new culture more emotionally authentic than the one propagated in the churches, universities, and corporations. These were multisensory experiences—sonic, visual, physiological—that stirred the imagination and vibrated in the chambers of the body. When Martin Williams's mother quipped that he might have been touched by the tar brush, little did she know that she was tapping one of his deepest desires, a desire that begins to articulate itself—but also remains partially repressed under the protective shield of "Art"—when he describes the "aesthetic whole" he perceived in the body and the sound of Sidney Bechet. When Nat Hentoff was called by the "surging, pulsing cry of yearning" he heard in Artie Shaw's clarinet, he was responding to an inchoate swirl of emotions, a hunger for states of feeling not sanctioned in the social institutions that were disciplining his adolescent desires.

Before coming to New York to study at Columbia University, Ralph Gleason was not unlike millions of other Depression-era teenagers for whom the radio served as a magical force, bringing fresh new sounds into their private spaces, tickling their ears and moving their bodies, endowing their lives with cadence and melody, stoking their yearning to get deeper into the music and closer to the people who made it:

> A remote broadcast from some long-forgotten ballroom somewhere in the Middle West, a wild, throbbing sound in the night by people I never heard of, absolutely killing me with its subtlety and its insinuating rhythms.... And when I got to the Big Apple and found you could go to see a band . . . in person at the Apollo or the Savoy Ballroom or the Renaissance or the Strand or the Paramount theaters, I simply couldn't believe it. It was too good to be true.[29]

For the jazz canon to take shape, and for jazz criticism to develop into a field of sanctioned cultural discourse, it was necessary for the incipient desires of young men like Williams, Hentoff, and Gleason to become aestheticized and formalized. For the discussion of jazz to take place—as Williams put it—"as if it were artistic and not just a teenage enthusiasm," the very passions that were unleashed by the music needed to be mastered and tutored. If the "shock of discovery" was the experience that hardwired jazz with its modernist charge, it was only through the engineering of more routinized circuits of consumer energy that the music would secure its hold on the American cultural imagination. Hence the elemental importance of record collecting and the networks of fan discourse connected with the connoisseurial impulse.

In 1935 George Frazier, John Hammond, and Marshall Stearns joined Milt Gabler, a New York–based record retailer, in founding the United Hot Clubs of America, an organization patterned after the French jazz aficionado group started by Hugues Panassié earlier in the decade. Founded "on a desire to facilitate the universal progress of swing music" and "backed by the conviction that [jazz] is a worthy cultural object of study," the Hot Clubs aimed to serve a select, intensely committed audience for hot jazz. Hot Club meetings established a kind of informal jazz pedagogy.[30] George Frazier, leader of the Boston Hot Club, was described as resembling "Aristotle in his lyceum," tutoring Boston-area college students in the fundamentals of hot jazz.[31] The Hot Club listening sessions at Marshall Stearns's New Haven grad school apartment were considered by participants—such as George Avakian, then a Yale undergraduate, later a major jazz record producer, who several years later joined Stearns and Hammond in teaching a jazz history course in New York University's adult education division—to be among the finest educational experiences available in that town, not excluding the edifying possibilities afforded by the regular Yale curriculum.[32] Stearns remembered those meetings as affairs in which participants feverishly conveyed their enthusiasms:

> Bob Sun [for instance] was madly in love with Willie the Lion Smith. He'd put a record of Willie's on whenever he got the chance and then he wouldn't take it off. He'd just play it over and over and over and buttonhole everyone and say, "Listen. Listen to this." And then perhaps you'd find one bar in the whole record that he thought was particularly out of the world (out of the world was the word that you used) and he'd just sit you down and listen to it and you couldn't fight it.[33]

Such rigorous attention to musical "texts" appeared to justify the Hot Club charter's claim that jazz was a "worthy cultural object of study." But the question arose as to just which should be the objects under study. The texts for the Boston, New Haven, and New York Hot Clubs curriculum were, literally, the private record collections of George Frazier, Marshall Stearns, John Hammond, and the jazz aficionados who attended club sessions. To facilitate the "universal progress" of the music, it was necessary to disseminate these texts beyond the inordinately narrow geographic and social parameters of the jazz collector's establishment. To this end, a crucial Hot Club project—not only for its time but for its lasting impact on the jazz canon—was the organization's sponsorship of jazz record reissues.

When a record produced by one of the major record companies failed to sell more than a thousand copies a year, it was customary for the company to cease pressing new copies. Since nearly all of the jazz records cut in the 1920s and early 1930s were unable to meet this sales threshold after a year or two on the market, much of the music that subsequently became canonized as the classic jazz of the period (primarily the recorded work of New Orleans and Chicago bands) was out of print by the late 1930s, the master recordings of those records left languishing in the vaults of the record companies. Milt Gabler persuaded the record companies to release a few sets of reissues by guaranteeing to sell at least a thousand copies of each record through his Commodore Record Shop. Stearns and the other critics prompted yet more reissues by successfully marketing records through the Hot Clubs. This success in turn inspired the large record companies (Columbia, Victor, and Decca) to market reissues themselves, without using the Hot Clubs as an official distribution network. Even this strategy carried a tacit Hot Club imprimatur, however, as it was John Hammond, George Avakian, and Milt Gabler who produced the records for the major labels. By the end of the decade, Gabler was pressing reissues himself under the Commodore record label. By 1941, reissues of King Oliver, Louis Armstrong, Bessie Smith, Bix Beiderbecke, Fletcher Henderson, the New Orleans Rhythm Kings, various representatives of the Chicago school, and others were widely available in the American market.[34] This effort, the United Hot Clubs' most significant achievement, was at once an act of cultural archaeology, an unearthing of the *Ur*-texts of the jazz tradition, and an act of cultural diffusion, a dispersal of copies of these texts to a wider audience.

An important dimension of the jazz conversion experience, then, was the talismanic power that was thought to inhere in the records *themselves*. The very act of gaining ownership of a valued jazz record became an integral part of the meaning a fan attributed to the music. In the early 1930s, Walter Schaap was part of a group of Columbia University student jazz buffs that included Ralph Gleason, Barry Ulanov, Eugene Williams, and Ralph de Toledano, all of whom went on to make their mark in jazz criticism. In an interview fifty years later, what Schaap remembered most about the Jimmie Lunceford 78-rpm disc with "Stardust" on one side and "Rhythm Is Our Business" on the other—he still referred to the record by its matrix number, Decca 369—was the fact that his copy was a used one he picked up out of a jukebox on Brooklyn's Kings Highway.[35] While dating the woman who later became his wife, Schaap was able to gauge her jazz tastes by the condition of her records. The fact that she was a *prodigious* listener was evident from her habit of "turning the record white," the aficionado term for a record played so often that its grooves were completely worn out; that she was a *discerning* listener was demonstrated by the condition of her copy of Ellington's version of "Stormy Weather," with the stellar Cootie Williams solo in the first chorus worn smooth, the so-so vocal in the second chorus like new. Marshall Stearns similarly remembered such discerning listening from his adolescence in Cambridge, Massachusetts in the late 1920s: "In Cambridge you couldn't find many records by Negro bands. We'd buy a Whiteman record and we'd play ten grooves toward the end where Bix had six bars and we'd wear out that part of the record."[36]

Ira Gitler tells of a childhood experience that reveals the strong emotional significance records held for the young fan. When Gitler was still in grade school in Brooklyn in the late 1930s, he began following his older brother around to used-record shops. Intimidated by his brother's superior expertise and savvy, young Ira kept putting off buying his own records for fear of having his taste and his connoisseurial instincts questioned. It was a memorable day, then, when Gitler finally got up the confidence to make his first used record purchase.

> I heard "Flying Home" by Charlie Barnett and it gassed me. I think it was on Bluebird. The end of the record was what really knocked me out, but it had also done the same thing to the person who had owned the record first because that part was pretty worn. I realized the condition of the record and the enormity of the price (nineteen cents, I believe) but I wanted it pretty badly and also wanted to impress the clerk with my hipness and my ability to make a decision.[37]

Sadly, though Gitler's older brother liked the record, he found its condition unsatisfactory and insisted on returning it that very evening. "I remember the feeling of defeat I had as we walked through the snow on our way to the store," Gitler rued. "My choice, for whatever reason, had been rejected and I was crushed."[38]

For Gitler and certain others, the exacting protocols of collecting jazz records and demonstrating a proper reverence and maturity in using and discussing them led naturally to a desire for more formal expressive outlets. Ralph Gleason explained how he started writing a record column in his college newspaper: first came the obligatory fraternal bonding experience, in Gleason's case with a premed student named Keery Merwin. Sharing breakfast busboy duties in the dorm dining room, the two mitigated the tedium of their cleaning duties with chatter about the previous night's radio shows or outings to the Apollo or Savoy. Then they got down to business:

> We went straight up to his room at ten, cut classes and played records all day long. When we met, he had all the early Luncefords—"Sophisticated Lady" (that was Decca 129!), "Rose Room." . . . We dug them deeply in an era before the verb "to dig" had emerged into the general slang. What I mean is, we hardly listened to anything else.

Then came an impulse to spread the joy of their truancy to fellow students:

> We went out and found other people to play [the Lunceford records] to. A chance conversation in the corridor outside Irwin Edman's philosophy class and the lunch hour was spent up in Keery's room with the turntable spinning away.

Finally, Gleason's headlong plunge into the jazz life, to the grave detriment of his undergraduate studies:

> Two things became immediately apparent. I had to have a phonograph and I had to have the records. I got them both as fast as I could. Later, I conned the editor of *Columbia Spectator* into letting me take over the record column from the departing tenant and I was in business. Now the Lunceford discs came to the door gloriously free, sometimes even before they were available at the bookshop . . . . It ruined me, of course. I never felt the same about the classroom. I spent more time at the Apollo Theater when Lunceford was there than I did at school.[39]

And so what started as a ploy to get free records set Gleason on the course that would become his life's work as a jazz and pop critic, culminating many years later in his role as a high priest to the Berkeley students—some of them dropouts—who started *Rolling Stone* magazine in the late 1960s.

But academic failure wasn't a prerequisite for membership in this club. After taking his bachelor's degree and staying on at Columbia for graduate work in economic history, Walter Schaap took a year abroad at the Sorbonne working under C. E. Labrouse and Marc Bloch researching the economic history of the French Revolution. While charting fluctuations in bread prices in eighteenth-century Champagne, Schaap spent his spare time working as a translator for the seminal French jazz magazine *Le Jazz Hot*. Before leaving for France, Schaap had been urged by Barry Ulanov to make contact with Hugues Panassié and Charles Delauney, the magazine's editors, and Ulanov gave Schaap the address of the Paris chapter of the Hot Clubs of France. Schaap had read Panassié's book *Le Jazz Hot* soon after it was published in the United States and found the book indispensable as a guide to record buying and discography. "It [gave] us a lot of names to follow up. Panassié would list his favorite musicians on each instrument, and you'd do your best to find the records."[40] Envisioning the Paris office of the Hot Clubs of France as a tony cultural site, Schaap set out in search of the address Ulanov had given him expecting to find a building of no less architectural stature than, say, a foreign embassy. He discovered that the Paris office of the Hot Clubs of France (which doubled as the offices of *Le Jazz Hot*) was nothing more than Hugues Panassié's apartment, and that the protocols of jazz appreciation enshrined there were not so very different from those he knew from his college days. After returning to the United States in 1939, Schaap continued to translate for *Le Jazz Hot* while also submitting an occasional piece of his own to that magazine and to the American jazz magazines. When Charles Delauney came to New York several times over the next couple of years to research the second edition of his *Hot Discography*, Schaap and George Avakian escorted him around to record companies, to music publishers, and to the jazz musicians themselves to seek out information about just who played what on which jazz records. The fruit of these efforts was a volume of discography that survived for several decades as the key source for jazz collectors and for researchers undertaking systematic study of particular musicians and styles, or of the trends governing the music's broader evolution.[41]

"That Rare Breed of Men"

One of the most intellectually ambitious of the Columbia jazz enthusiasts, Ralph de Toledano, later became a noted writer and thinker, albeit of a markedly different ideological stripe than others of his campus bohemian set. Whereas Ralph Gleason, in the early 1970s, wore his inclusion on the infamous "enemies list" of liberals and alleged subversives monitored by Richard Nixon's White House as a badge of honor, de Toldano had been a Nixon confidante since writing admiringly of him during the Alger Hiss trial in 1948. Then an editor at *Newsweek*, de Toledano soon became an influential figure in anticommunist conservative circles, befriending not just Nixon but also Whittaker Chambers and William F. Buckley Jr., and becoming one of the founding editors of *National Review*. A skillful and prolific writer, de Toledano has published twenty-four books in a variety of genres, including biographies of Nixon and J. Edgar Hoover—in which he paints Martin Luther King Jr. as a communist dupe and defends Hoover's persecution of the civil rights leader—and a volume of his personal correspondence with Chambers. He was also a contributor to the publications of the John Birch Society and remains, into his late eighties, a syndicated columnist for a bevy of arch-conservative publications.[42]

De Toledano's first postgraduate journalistic venture was the founding, along with Ralph Gleason and Eugene Williams, of *Jazz Information*, a collector's sheet that was edited and assembled in Williams's apartment in Greenwich Village, which had become something of a jazz salon for the Columbia crowd and had acquired special cachet in the summer of 1942 when Williams hosted legendary New Orleans trumpeter Bunk Johnson and produced a set of recordings on a newly hatched label also called Jazz Information. De Toledano's first book was the edited collection *Frontiers of Jazz,* originally published in 1947 and most recently reissued in 1994. In an introduction written for the 1960 edition, de Toledano wrote that "every anthology of jazz criticism must make its curtsey to that rare breed of men who thrive on the dust of Salvation Army depots, hock shops, thrift shops, and the backwaters of the record trade, who live for the pleasure of turning up an unknown master, a well-known soloist on a forgotten label, who feel that of such is the kingdom of heaven if they unearth a cache of Claxtonolas or a King Oliver Gennett."[43]

This "rare breed of men" pursued jazz records and absorbed the music with a romantic fervor that was part and parcel of the heady experience of modernism. "If Joyce was their literary hero, jazz was their music," Mary Cummings recently wrote of the Columbia collegians in an alumni publication:

> Everyone listened to recordings by Bessie Smith, Louis Armstrong, King Oliver, Bix Beiderbecke. They frequented jazz joints and stole time from their studies to steep themselves in the jazzy atmosphere of Gene Williams's hip Village salon. When Williams brought trumpeter Bunk Johnson up from New Orleans, they all went to Stuyvesant Casino to hear him. If nothing special was on, Nick's on Sheridan Square was usually rocking with jazz, or there was a party somewhere with enough booze, weed and women to keep the wild anti-establishment ethos alive.[44]

De Toledano continues to this day to regard the postwar conservative movement as a noble and necessary antidote to a liberal establishment that took root with FDR's New Deal, allegedly shielded communist sympathizers like Alger Hiss during the war years, and fostered the countercultural excesses of the 1960s and then the political correctness and multiculturalism ideologies of the 1980s and 1990s. (Here, in the terrain of rabid cold war anticommunism, lies one of the intellectual seedbeds for a conservative school of jazz appreciation that leads in our own time to Terry Teachout's criticism in *Commentary* and the *New York Times* and the occasional jazz commentary of a George Will or a George Gilder.) He regards as his most formative intellectual experience at Columbia the senior colloquium he took with Jacques Barzun and Lionel Trilling, and he is at work on an autobiography whose title—*Exit, Pursued by a Bear*—comes from Trilling's book on E. M. Forster.[45] One of his classmates was Thomas Merton, later to achieve fame as a Trappist monk whose book *The Seven Storey Mountain* was credited with humanizing the Catholic message and inspiring a rush of converts to the church. Before his own conversion, Merton was part of the "hard-drinking, jazz-loving, movie-crazed, soul-searching, fiercely competitive group" that clustered around the Columbia humor magazine *Jester*.[46] Merton, a fierce antifascist, was regarded as the most confident, authoritative, and verbally cantankerous of the group, while de Toledano was known for a polemical wit (quipping that a Columbia correspondence course in social conversation had "caused more trouble than the New Deal and the Rhythm Method") and a satirical self-consciousness about sophomoric Romanticism ("He tumulted from Keatsian heights to sexual excess with Elizabethan fervor, mixing love and the intellect and the phallus as freely as he mixed his joyous metaphors").[47]

It fell to another of the *Jester* wags, the young Barry Ulanov, to make explicit the jazz dimension of the magazine's smart-set immersion in the masculinist pursuits of tobacco, liquor, and Barnard women. In "The Swing of Man," an essay in the January 1936 volume, Ulanov praises the "sentient shake" of Ellington's "sophisticated dirges"; bemoans the "exquisite glibness" of the Benny Goodman big band's "amazing razzmatazz savoir-faire"; and anoints Ella Fitzgerald "the best cooncrooner I've ever heard."[48] In September 1936, he rues that Jimmie Lunceford's "Jazzocrats are going overboard on the side of mechanization and the vice of 'Big Money'" while announcing that Artie Shaw's band "deserves mass approbation for their smooth dansapation (*sic*) and sinuous fabric of gutbucket."[49] In October 1936 comes a scathing critique of "His Royal Hammond" and his "dictatorship" over swing music.

> [John Hammond] has done his philanthropic bit for the cause: pushing deserving orchestras to the various record and dance hall types, befriending (a very philanthropic word) individual artists . . . and so on. But know him, for ye must fear him. He is the boy who shapes your opinions for you, swing opinions anyhow, by his articles in the musical dopesheets. . . . His opinions along with those of a few other swing dopesters are the distinct gospel of the night club managers, radio broadcasters and the phonograph record companies, who more often than not choose their bands from among his recommendations. . . . This year swing is king, and like all other rackets it must have its czars.[50]

Ulanov's use of the term "cooncrooner" is of a piece with the casual bigotry of the preppie set; if he remembered using the term, it must have embarrassed the man who soon became—very often in league with John Hammond and Leonard Feather—one of the most forceful antiracist white liberals in the jazz world of the 1940s and 1950s. That racial liberalism and a larger relativistic approach to culture had its formation in a Columbia education that torqued differently than de Toledano's and was integral to the academic studies in the history of the arts, literature, and culture that Ulanov pursued at the same time that he edited a series of music publications— *Swing* (1939–41), *The Review of Recorded Music* (1941–43), *Listen* (1940–42), and *Metronome* (1943–55), where he gained fame as a staunch supporter of bebop and modern jazz—and wrote four books on jazz music and culture— *Duke Ellington* (1946), *The Incredible Crosby* (1948), *A History of Jazz in*

America (1952), and *A Handbook of Jazz* (1957). Before his retirement in the late 1980s, Ulanov had been an English professor at Barnard for more than three decades, having earlier taught at Columbia and Princeton. At Barnard he created the Joint Program in the Arts, and throughout a career in which he authored and edited close to fifty books, Ulanov's stock-in-trade was an interdisciplinary approach to the arts, culture, and religion. After leaving Barnard, he taught at the Union Theological Seminary and, with his wife, wrote a series of books on the intersection of religion and psychology. In short, Ulanov—who died in 2000 at age eighty-two—was a major U.S. intellectual of the twentieth century.[51]

Ulanov, whose father was a violinist who served as concertmaster of the NBC Philharmonic under Arturo Toscanini, attended the Brooklyn Ethical Culture School as a youngster, studying the art and material culture of a variety of world civilizations. "From a very early age I thought in terms of civilizations, and I gained a concept of the development of modernity." This included the radio broadcasts he heard in the early 1930s of live jazz from the Savoy Ballroom and other locations. "The music just knocked me out, and what struck me was the directness of experience, the penetration of the psyche," he remembered. "Duke's ability to get inside the music spiritually and physically; the introspection, the constant conversation with themselves carried on by a Coleman Hawkins or Lester Young—these men were superb moderns." Choosing Columbia over Harvard because of its proximity to Harlem and the creative center of jazz, Ulanov did his best to integrate his jazz interest into his formal studies. In a freshman course on aesthetics with Irwin Edmond, he wrote a paper on the "philosophy of jazz" using Panassié's *Hot Jazz* and Roger Pryor Dodge's essays as source material. Edmond wrote back that he was favorably inclined toward Ulanov's argument, "but then Benny Goodman isn't Bach."

In addition to his literature studies with Lionel Trilling and Raymond Weaver ("a Melville scholar who liked jazz"), Ulanov recalled the formative influence of a senior seminar with Dwight Minor on the U.S. Civil War. The seminar challenged the then dominant "lost cause" historiography that viewed the war—in the vein of D. W. Griffith's epic film *Birth of a Nation*— as a tragedy and cast both the noble southern white slave-masters and the uncivilized black slaves as its tragic victims. Ulanov was inspired to learn more about the everyday lives and cultures of nineteenth-century blacks and whites and the racial ideologies that complicated the relationship between these cultures. Enriching this line of inquiry were Ulanov's studies with Franz Boas, the pioneering scholar of cultural anthropology who inveighed against biologically determinist concepts of race and insisted on the intrinsic value of all cultures. "Hitler is in power," Ulanov recalled, "and I'm learning the most powerful arguments against racial reductionism, arguments I later used to try to combat racism in the jazz world. My feeling was that the very concept of race doesn't serve the black world, and promotes bigotry in the white world. When I went on the road with Ellington [in preparation for Ulanov's 1946 book], Duke and I talked about this every night."

For the young Barry Ulanov, jazz, culture, and politics were "all of a piece."[52]

"He Who Knows All"

It did not escape attention that the emerging field of U.S. jazz criticism appeared to be something of an Ivy League cottage industry. In *The New Republic* in February 1940, a fan named Bob White complained that he was tired of "having to accept as gospel the *ex cathedra* pronouncements of the scion of an old New York family [John Hammond], of a sometime Harvardian [George Frazier], of an English instructor at New Haven [Marshall Stearns]."[53] After allowing his plebeian resentment to fester through the spring and early summer of 1940, White in August wrote to *Down Beat* and uncorked this blistering indictment of the newest old-boy network:

> A formula of how to become a great critic might run something like this: spend four years at least in an expensive eastern college. Become acquainted with old Bix and Louis records and talk about these men in hushed whispers. Never listen to a record made after 1936 . . . it just can't be good, it's too new. Get to know a few old musicians and give them some publicity. It doesn't matter if they can only play in two keys and have no technique. Remember, if it's old, it's good. Sneer at all records made by Dorsey, Goodman, Miller, Barnet, Herman, Crosby. Make some musician your god (some old musician—don't forget) and refuse to talk to any other musician in the same breath. Above all, remain completely ignorant of music. Don't know anything about chords, about tone, about keys. That's all *commercial*. In short, become a romantic, a charlatan, a poseur, a pseudo-intellectual, an aesthetic snob, and you are well on your way to success.[54]

There was indeed merit in White's claim of a preppie cabal at the upper reaches of the jazz critical pecking order. The best proof was that White, himself a recent Dartmouth graduate, now began showing up in *Down Beat* as a critic, promptly showing that Cambridge and New Haven weren't the only breeding grounds of snobbery and pseudo-intellectualism. The reality, however, was that *everyone* writing in the jazz press, critics and fans alike, regardless of class and education, came off sounding like a snob, a pseudo-intellectual, or a charlatan—it was the defining feature of the discourse.

George Simon—son of a prosperous businessman, brother of the founder of Simon and Schuster and of an English professor who moonlighted as an opera critic—was a year out of Harvard when he tapped a family connection to set himself up with a dance-band column in *Metronome*, hitherto a rather staid musician's trade paper.[55] Drawing on his experience as a drummer in his college dance band, Simon evaluated the musicianship, style of presentation, and general artistic and entertainment value of the bands playing New York's hotel ballrooms and dance halls. Simon's reviews, culminating in a "Simon Says" grade on a scale of A to D—true to his Harvard education, Simon never ventured below the "gentleman's C"—became famous among musicians and fans for their razor-sharp edge. Either a band could swing or it couldn't, played in tune or didn't, and Simon told you one way or the other.

But if Simon delivered his critical opinions with blithe self-assurance, it was the readers he drew to *Metronome* who raised swing commentary to Olympian heights of self-righteousness. Less than a year after the inception of his dance-band review column, Simon (under the pseudonym Gordon Wright) started two new columns, "DISCussions" and "Impressions in Wax." "DISCussions," employing the same strategy as Simon's dance-band column, featured reviews of the latest phonograph recordings, while "Impressions in Wax" invited readers to "present their viewpoints of phonograph records." Through this column, swing music fans made known "their viewpoints" not only of phonograph records, but of the fictional Gordon Wright's critical blind spots, and especially of the deficiencies of each other's views on swing musicians and records. Typical in its author's assumption of critical omniscience was a respondent calling himself "He Who Knows All," offering his "complete analyzation of the tenor question" as a service to other fans sharing his incredulity over "how you gentleman can rave about a lot of meaningless and out of tune tenor," such as the playing of Bud Freeman, "just about the world's worst tenor man."[56] Breathless outrage and personal affront coursed through these letters. "How can he say," asked Norman Simpson of Little Falls, N.Y., about Keene Penth of Edgewood, R.I., "that Chu Berry, undoubtedly one of the greatest of the day, and Pat Davis, who is o.k. with the other four Casa Loma saxes, but who is absolutely rank as an individual, sound alike in style? Davis has absolutely no tenor tone. He sounds like he cuts a hunk of shingle off someone's roof for a reed. I think he, pardon me, smells."[57] One respondent saw fit to question the credentials of a swing fan who had criticized Harry James and Vido Musso. "It's plain to see that you could never be a swing cat because of your perverted impressions of some of the swingiest bands in the country," wrote this *real* swing cat. "[J]ames and [M]usso are both great musicians and if they fail to send you I don't see how you can be sent."[58]

To its adolescent fans, swing was *their* culture. It was theirs because they had made it theirs, and in the process of doing so had forced America's cultural gatekeepers to recognize their power as autonomous cultural consumers. The event that launched swing into the mass popularity that has subsequently made it synonymous with 1930s popular culture stands as a singular example of a youth audience forcing its will on America's culture industry. On the night of August 21, 1935, at Los Angeles's Palomar Ballroom, middle-class white kids, as Gary Giddins puts it, "said yes in thunder and hard currency" to the Benny Goodman orchestra's renditions of tunes arranged by the African American bandleader Fletcher Henderson. These tunes—"Sugar Foot Stomp," "Down South Camp Meeting." and others—exemplified the hot jazz side of the Goodman band's book, the side Goodman and his younger audience preferred to the sweet waltzes, rhumbas, and novelties his hotel ballroom employers were forcing him to play for the benefit of an older set of patrons. Goodman's orchestra, which had formed in March 1934, had been on a national tour, testing the waters with a swing big band style that had been created by Henderson and other black arrangers in the late 1920s and early 1930s. The tour followed a twenty-six-week engagement on NBC radio's *Let's Dance* program, which featured the "sweet" Kel Murray orchestra and Xavier Cugat's Latin stylings along with Goodman's jazz. At almost every stop of the tour, the band had met with disappointment. In Denver, in what Goodman called "the most humiliating experience of my life," patrons demanded their money back. At the Palomar, Goodman feared the same outcome when the crowd responded indifferently to the band's opening number, a safe and sugary melodic confection. But urged on by trumpeter Bunny Berrigan, Goodman decided to go for broke one last time with the hard swinging Henderson arrangements. The crowd roared and rushed the stage—affirmation at last. This "hot" Goodman material was known to these California fans only because of the extra two hours that Goodman's segments had aired on NBC radio on the West Coast, after the networks' jazz-leery producers had gone to bed. Emboldened by the Palomar triumph, Goodman abandoned sweet music and cast his lot with the black-influenced dance rhythms and improvisational creativity of hot, swinging jazz. Radio programmers, dance hall bookers, record company executives, and magazine editors stood up and took notice: far from being some fly-by-night fad, like the post–World War I marathon dancing craze, this music and this audience together constituted a force in American entertainment that appeared to have real staying power.[59]

It was this very success that made swing a target of censure for a cadre of self-styled elite fans who feared that Goodman's commercial triumphs and savvy, businesslike approach to managing his affairs posed a danger to jazz's hallowed artistic integrity. Stanley Dance, a British emigré who was to emerge as an important critic as well as an all-purpose aide-de-camp to Duke Ellington, first appeared in the American jazz press in a 1940 letter to *Down Beat*, written "with the greatest regret and disgust," protesting the terrible transgression Benny Goodman committed by "enticing Cootie Williams away from the Duke Ellington orchestra."

> I find [Goodman's] action as contemptible as his clarinet playing. Evidently the "King of Swing" has no artistic conscience whatsoever. However, I've no doubt that in comparison with the Duke, Mr. Goodman's band will continue to sound like a bunch of tired business men and usurers seeking recreation in the music. The trouble with jazz today is that there are more business men than musicians engaged in it.[60]

Anti-Goodman sentiment—here colored with a tinge of *au courant* damnation of the businessman—was an especially effective marker of jazz authority when articulated by onetime Goodman supporters who felt betrayed by the bandleader's commercial sallies in the late 1930s. While a student at New York's Horace Mann High School in the early 1930s, George Avakian had published a sympathetic interview with the "King of Swing" in his school newspaper.[61] A couple of years later, while at Yale, the precocious Avakian, now identified as a "noted critic, writer, [and] collector," was cited in *Down Beat's* "Critic's Row" column as thinking that Goodman had been on an artistic slide since 1930.[62] Avakian's first *Down Beat* piece, a heated anti-commercial polemic arguing that "jazz is jazz: it can't be modernized or streamlined,"[63] did not need to mention Goodman by name in order for readers to grasp his implication.

At work here was the fashioning of the critic's pose, a rite of passage into cultural authority founded on an obligatory disavowal of untutored adolescent passions. For the Frankfurt School critic Theodor Adorno, who targeted the swing craze as a prime example of the Culture Industry's sinister and systematic manipulation of mass consciousness, such critical authority in the jazz world was unimaginable. Swing fans, according to Adorno, were hopelessly infantilized and feminized dupes:

> In general they are intoxicated by the fame of mass culture, a fame which the latter knows how to manipulate; they could just as well get together in clubs for worshiping film stars or for collecting autographs. What is important to

them is the sense of belonging as such, identification, without paying particular attention to its content. As girls, they have trained themselves to faint upon hearing the voice of a "crooner." Their applause, cued in by a light-signal is transmitted directly on the popular radio programs they are permitted to attend. They call themselves "jitter-bugs," bugs which carry out reflex movements, performers of their own ecstasy. Merely to be carried away by anything at all, to have something of their own, compensates for their impoverished and barren existence. The gesture of adolescence, which raves for this or that on one day with the ever-present possibility of damning it as idiocy on the next, is now socialized.[64]

Adorno has been roundly condemned for his misunderstanding of jazz, particularly for his tendency to lump jazz together with the mass popular musical styles that jazz critics and aficionados have always been at such pains to hold at arm's length in their arguments for jazz's superior artistic value. But here Adorno gives voice—albeit the clinical, disinterested voice of high theory—to a sentiment shared by the young male swing consumers who adopted the pose of the critic, often a pose of pseudo-intellectual masculinist authority arrayed against the supposedly infantilizing or feminizing tendencies of mass fan culture.

"A Montague-Capulet Situation"

The fate of the magazines *Down Beat* and *Metronome*, which both absorbed and catalyzed the throbbing populist energy unleashed by swing's youth audience, exemplified these cultural tensions wrought by the swing craze. *Down Beat* began in 1934 as a trade sheet for Chicago dance-band musicians, featuring such fare as instrument manufacturer and booking agent advertisements, musician-authored columns on performance technique, and news coverage of the musicians' union. Publisher Carl Cons began by personally peddling the publication outside the offices of the American Federation of Musicians. Five years later, *Down Beat* was a nationally distributed publication with a readership estimated at 80,000 (*Metronome*'s readership at this time was around 50,000).[65] While continuing to refer itself as the "musician's bible"—its advertisements remained targeted at readers who were consumers of musical instruments and music industry services—the magazine had become a forum for critics and fans to engage in lusty debate over each other's musical tastes.

Down Beat's 1930s metamorphosis from a staid musician-oriented trade journal into a combination trade journal/fan magazine—a medium in which the lines between musician and listener, professional and amateur, producer and consumer, and critic and fan were blurred—was paralleled by an abrupt reorientation at *Metronome* in the middle years of the decade. *Metronome* started in the 1880s as a trade journal devoted to traditional European music, offering information about concerts, auditions, the thoughts and lifestyles of both upstart and lionized figures in the music world, the latest in instrumental technology and technique. The very look of the magazine, its advertising largely segregated from news copy arrayed in four long columns of unbroken print, conferred an air of academic substance.

After World War I, as the spread of the phonograph, the advent of radio, and the dance craze began to transform American musical culture, *Metronome*'s highbrow aspirations became increasingly strained. In a May 1935 editorial, *Metronome*'s editors railed against radio amateur hours, complaining that "the radio stars of today are a lot of street cleaners, clerks, garbage removers, barbers, stenogs, stevedores, hog callers, and housewives," and that "the greatest scientific marvel of the age" is "being used to display the great art of some barber in the Bronx who can play on the pig whistle."[66] Despite this resistance to the Whitmanesque possibilities of the mass media, however, *Metronome*'s economic interests increasingly dictated an ever more inclusive definition of "legitimate" music. By the early 1930s editor Doron Antrim's "Radio Reviews" column covered everything from the Chase and Sanborn Opera Guild and Waltz Time to radio "dancing parties" featuring the likes of Paul Whiteman, Guy Lombardo, and Xavier Cugat. Just as these dance bands masked their lowbrow musical influences in black-tie formality, so *Metronome* tried to paint a veneer of classicism over the hustle and bustle of New York's increasingly commercialized musical scene. But in its effort to carve out a middlebrow niche in which it could sustain its intellectual pretenses while also reaching out to the mounting numbers of jitterbugging youth, *Metronome* found itself caught in a cultural contradiction. A reader's letter in January 1937 captures this contradiction well:

> Look at your own cover page. What does it say there? "METRONOME, Modern Music and Its Makers." Very well. But now open it, and look. What do you see? Names, and names, and names, of bands, musicians, publishers, tunes; that Billy Swingit has joined Maxie Veilchenduft's ork, and what is swing is swing is swing, defining swing when there is no such thing (oh, yes there is, says someone else) and that whites started jazz (no, the colored lads did, no the whites, no the Negroes, aw, shucks . . . .) . . . I should like to suggest [that you] write about modern music, but its serious aspect, form and construction of a major work,

and you will do something you'll be proud of in 5 or 10 years from now. It will make all our American youngsters more serious-minded in their music, and they won't admire every freak clarinet passage that any symphony player could play with his eyes shut, if you'd write it down for him.[67]

This reader wanted his magazine espousing traditional cultural values as a bulwark against adolescent trendiness. What he perceived instead was a magazine careening down a slippery slope toward *Photoplay*-style tabloidism. But the real problem for this reader, and for all of *Metronome's* older readers, was the futility of his hope for making "all of our American youngsters more serious-minded in their music," in the way that *he* was defining "serious-minded" and "their music." For one of the signal characteristics of this new generation of *Metronome* readers was their desire to define "their music" for themselves, in their own "serious-minded" fashion. George Simon characterized this desire with an interesting analogy to sports spectatorship:

> The [swing] bands were like big league ball teams, and the kids knew all the players—even without a scorecard. Ask them to name Casa Loma's clarinet player and they'd tell you Clarence Hutchenrider. Ask them what trombonist played jazz for Bunny Berrigan and they'd tell you Sonny Lee. Ask them what trombonist in Benny Goodman's band never played jazz at all and they'd tell you Red Ballard. Ask them who sang and played lead alto for Count Basie and they'd tell you Earle Warren. Ask them who played drums for Tommy Dorsey and—after *they'd ask you* on what records and you'd told them "Song of India" and an "Opus No. 1"—they'd tell you Davey Tough and Buddy Rich.[68]

A good illustration of the way the swing-era jazz magazines tried to finesse the line between populist youth consumerism and elite art connoisseurship—to negotiate the terrain between a fan culture driven by adolescent enthusiasms, on the one hand, and a purist aficionado culture dedicated to the notion of jazz as an art form, on the other—is the way *Down Beat's* editors introduced George Avakian to its readers. "A young guy still in school at Yale," read the profile of Avakian in *Down Beat's* "Who's Who in the Critics Row column, "[Avakian] is just 22, comes from a wealthy family, lives in New York on Wadsworth Avenue, has been collecting records ever since Marshall Stearns gave him the jazz bug . . . . His enthusiasms and spot decisions have made him look foolish more than once. But the years should bring him around to being one of America's very best critics and connoisseurs."[69] *Down Beat's* packaging of Avakian reveals as much about the magazine's perception of its *own* position in the American cultural discourse: along with the youthful petulance, the donnishness, the proneness to misjudgment characteristic of this discourse, there was also—the message goes—the inchoate potential for contributing something of lasting cultural significance. A similar message can be inferred from the way *Metronome* introduced its readers to Hugues Panassié on the occasion of the French critic's visit to the United States in 1938: "We thought of Panassié as a man of around 40 with a receding hair line and the general air of the class room. The erudition and extent of his knowledge as revealed in his writings would leave one with just that impression. What a jolt. M. Panassié is just 26 and looks even younger. Which may be due partly to the fact that he is blonde and is smiling most of the time." But this surprisingly coltish Frenchman was clearly a man of cultural substance:

> One does not talk to Panassié long (he speaks good English), before you realize that he has the fine sensibilities of an artist. It's partly in the way he holds his hands. He looks more like a critic of the old classical school than one of swing. In fact, he likes Bach, Mozart, Schubert, especially Erik Satie among the moderns. He might have become a long-haired critic had he not met Mezz Mesirow [sic] and took some sax lessons from him. Mezz showed him the difference between good and bad jazz. That was the beginning. He started to assemble and study jazz recordings, to write for French publications. He got to be a crusader for jazz. It was getting a bum deal. Its real artists were underappreciated. The public knew little about these artists, the critics knew even less.[70]

Doubtless some *Metronome* readers would have disputed Mezzrow's authority as a judge of good and bad jazz, but the broader implication was clear: notwithstanding swing's johnny-come-lately status and its deep immersion in youth culture, jazz might achieve vaunted artistic legitimacy if only it developed a critical discourse that tapped into the cultural capital signified by classical learning and a cosmopolitan appreciation of all the finer things in life.

But of course even the purist circles of jazz appreciation were operating in a commercial milieu rather than an academic one; much as a Barry Ulanov might have worked toward an integration of jazz into his larger scholarly pursuits, and however much the Ivy Leaguers invested jazz with intellectual pretensions, it would take a good long time for jazz to be considered a part of the Western cultural tradition canonized in the liberal arts curriculum of elite universities. It was, in fact, the widespread ignorance and denigration of jazz among U.S. intellectuals that spurred young scholarly types like Ulanov to seek out European intellectuals who appeared far more interested in the music and alert to its cultural importance. Jazz was "without friends at home," Ulanov thought, and he resented the "condescending and supercilious tipping of the hat" that American intellectuals gave the music. His friendship with the Belgian writer and pioneering jazz critic Robert Goffin started with the two of them discussing the tragedy of "tone-deaf Americans" not paying attention to the "music of the century." Indeed, much of the polemical energy and exalted purpose among the first generation of young U.S. jazz critics owes to their image of themselves as true prophets of American modernism. That their cultural work took place on the edges of the academy, often in some of the least genteel precincts of the American city, added to their sense of renegade virtue.

Of all the Hot Club originators, the one most deeply implicated in the commercial aspects of the trade—the one literally with the most to lose—was Milt Gabler. Ulanov, Marshall Stearns, and George Frazier sported Ivy League credentials that afforded them the luxury of propagandizing jazz's cultural significance; John Hammond's independent wealth underwrote his self-vaunted artistic integrity. Gabler couldn't match this kind of cultural privilege, but his credentials as a jazz purist were indisputable. While working in his father's 42nd Street radio shop in the late 1920s, Gabler listened extensively to his father's stock of records, finding the Louis Armstrong, Red Nichols, and Duke Ellington discs far more interesting than the more popular recordings of Rudy Vallee, Paul Whiteman, and Guy Lombardo. After opening his own retail record store on 52nd Street—the famous Commodore Record Shop—he concentrated on selling what he considered the better music, leaving Lombardo and Whiteman to the big stores. Known as a man of taste and integrity, committed above all to the music, Gabler became a close friend to many musicians and serious fans. "I have been associated with those flat round concentric objects, the men who make them, and the people who play them for the past twenty years," Gabler wrote in 1947. "I know most of them personally and someone once tabbed me the critic's critic. My place was a haven for them . . . . They all came to me and I listened and I learned."[71] In a paradoxical way, Stearns's and Ulanov's erudition, Frazier's flamboyance, and Hammond's earnestness endeared each of these men to musicians. The idiosyncrasies of these men, coupled with the very fact that they hailed from social backgrounds different from those of the musicians, seemed to arouse musicians' curiosity. In the Bronx-reared Gabler, by contrast, many musicians (particularly the white Chicago musicians) found a man not so different from themselves: a down-to-earth, streetwise, soulful character, at his happiest emcee-ing a Sunday jam session at Jimmy Ryan's, talking shop and trading laughs between sets.[72]

Gabler, however, was also a businessman, a small businessman operating in a specialized niche market in which profit margins were notoriously slim. In the years before World War II, Gabler faced stern competition from a hot jazz collector named Stephen Smith, proprietor of the Hot Record Society shop on Seventh Avenue and 53rd Street. The Hot Record Society was founded expressly as a rival of the United Hot Clubs. Aggressively contemptuous of each other's ideas about *real* jazz, the two aficionado groups locked horns in a sectarian battle described fifty years later by one participant, Russell Sanjek, as "a Montague-Capulet situation."[73] Sanjek, then an HRS man and advertising agency copy writer, later the founder of Broadcast Music Incorporated, was hard pressed to recall any clear-cut standards of taste held by each group:

> There was a standard of prejudice, and you had to adhere to it. Jelly Roll Morton was no good. Red Allen is a clown. There is no God but Louis . . . . You walked down the street, and [if you spotted someone from the rival camp] you'd have to cross to the other side if you didn't want a confrontation.[74]

The HRS crowd tended toward a pristine New Orleans purism, finding the Commodore–Hot Club partisans both too Chicago-oriented and excessively tolerant of late 1930s small swing bands. It is a mistake, however, to believe that this sectarian dispute hinged on decisive aesthetic distinctions. What these groups had in common far outweighed their differences.[75] For all the participants in this culture war, hot jazz of any stripe was marginalized and debased by the cultural establishment, distorted and trivialized by the commercial establishment. An HRS/Commodore–Hot Club debate on the comparative virtues of Armstrong and Beiderbecke might have been fueled by informed, deeply held convictions on the aesthetics of hot jazz trumpeting, but the real heat in such a debate came from the strong polemical bent and spirit of sectarian exclusiveness intrinsic to the cult mentality. At a certain level, moreover, the polemics of what Ernest Borneman called "the jazz cult" functioned as a gloss on the economic contingencies of this small jazz market.[76] The fact is that consumers looking for Armstrong and Beiderbecke records—not to mention Jelly Roll Morton, Bessie Smith, Muggsy Spanier, Original Dixieland Jazz Band, and Wolverines records—could find them at *both* Commodore and HRS. In the absence of significant material distinctions between the two shops, it was necessary to create ideological distinctions. A customer who wanted a copy of Bix Beiderbecke"s "Jazz Me Blues" could buy it from either Milt Gabler or Steve Smith, and usually at about the same price. But did he want to buy it from a man linked to an organizational party line that deemed Beiderbecke inferior to Armstrong? Or that endorsed Beiderbecke but wished to isolate him from the rest of the so-called Chicago school? Or that believed the value in "Jazz Me Blues" to rest not with Beiderbecke's performance, but with the collective swing feeling achieved by the sidemen?

Discourse of this nature was to be found in two short-lived jazz "little magazines," each affiliated with one of these retail stores. The aforementioned *Jazz Information*, started by Ralph Gleason, Ralph de Toledano, and Gene Williams, began as a purveyor of discographical and collector's information, leavened by vitriolic responses to *Metronome*'s or *Down Beat*'s latest outrages. A year later, with the help of Milt Gabler, the publication graduated to a more dignified typeset format. In turn Commodore's record releases, though not advertised per se, received in *Jazz Information* the kind of favorable commentary that amounted to de facto promotion. Catalyzed by this Commodore/*Jazz Information* bond, Stephen Smith set about publishing a house organ for his record business, which took the name *HRS Society Rag*. In the same way that the *Down Beat* and *Metronome* readers' polls kept swing fans interested in both those magazines, the reader who started with either *Jazz Information* or *HRS Society Rag* was all but obligated to read the other magazine as well: it would have been difficult to understand much of the critical commentary in any given issue of either magazine without having been immersed in the web of discourse spun between several back issues of both magazines. In this sense, the *Rag* and *Jazz Information* were symbiotic creatures; the friction sparked by their symbiosis engendered a *frisson* of jazz discourse that, in the end, probably bolstered the economic fortunes of both Commodore and HRS.[77]

"By Harlem Standards"

The most enduring legacy of this purist jazz discourse was its attention to musicians—especially black musicians—whose body of work and reputations might otherwise have been overlooked or shunted to the margins in the more commercially focused fan magazines. It is unclear just how much impact John Hammond, Leonard Feather, and other Left-leaning white critics had on the political consciousness of their swing fan readers. What *is* clear is that these critics' preference for black swing musicians had minimal impact on the fans' musical tastes. This is in distinction, as Eric Hobsbawm has noted, to the situation in Europe, where the dominating influence of a handful of critics (Panassié, Goffin, and Delauney in Paris; Edgar Jackson,

Spike Hughes, Stanley Dance, Feather, and Hammond in London) determined which jazz records were available to the public and hence made a critic-centered, black-dominated jazz canon a virtual *fait accompli.*[78] In *Down Beat* and *Metronome* readers' polls the white bandleaders Benny Goodman, Artie Shaw, Bob Crosby, and Casa Loma routinely amassed several times as many votes as black bandleaders like Duke Ellington, Count Basie, Jimmie Lunceford, and Chick Webb.[79] Whereas Louis Armstrong *never* won the best trumpeter category in the first twenty years of the *Down Beat* poll—losing out to Harry James and Ziggy Ellman in the years before the war, to Roy Eldridge and Howard McGhee in the years right after it, and to Maynard Ferguson and Chet Baker in the early 1950s—in European polls he held the top spot in virtually every published poll from the 1930s through the 1950s. In a fifteen-month stretch in 1936 and 1937, of the swing artists *Metronome* inducted into its "Musician's Hall of Fame," fourteen were white and only one black—and that one, Teddy Wilson, primarily because of his affiliation with Benny Goodman.[80]

Before Barry Ulanov took over as editor of *Metronome* in 1943, the magazine largely reflected editor George Simon's preference for white swing bands. Whereas for John Hammond, Marshall Stearns, Paul Edward Miller, and other champions of black swing the intonation of the saxophones and brass in the Chick Webb, Count Basie, and Jimmie Lunceford bands—coarser than that of both sweet bands like Guy Lombardo's and hotter swing units like Bennie Goodman's—was a key to their appeal, for Simon it was evidence that these bands needed better instruments, more rehearsal, and a finer sense of tonality. In a January 1936 *Metronome* column discussing his selections of "the best bands of the year 1935," Simon congratulates Chick Webb's band (the only black band of the seven on Simon's list) for "intonations and phrasing that are truly exceptional when measured by Harlem standards."[81] Otherwise, in the pages of *Metronome* during the 1930s and early 1940s, black musicians were rarely discussed and hardly ever pictured. The exceptions tended to be generated by Hugues Panassié—in fact, they were instances when Panassié's preference for black jazz was itself the focus of attention. Soon after the U.S. publication of Panassié's *Le Jazz Hot* in 1936, the C. G. Conn musical instrument company ran a three-page advertisement picturing those of Panassié's "swing stars" who used Conn saxophones, trumpets, and trombones.[82] For each of the black musicians pictured in the advertisement—Chu Berry, Benny Carter, Ben Webster, Howard Johnson, and Eddie Barfield on sax; Doc Cheatham, Red Allen, Eddie Anderson, and Cootie Williams on trumpet; and Joe Nanton, George Washington, Sandy Williams, Claude Jones, and Henry Wells on trombone—this was the first

time their photographs had appeared in the magazine. For most of them—
Carter, Webster, and Williams being the exceptions—it was also the last.

In 1938, Panassié named an all-star band for *Life* magazine that included
Louis Armstrong, Sidney Bechet, Earl Hines, Pop Foster, and Zuttie Single-
ton, black musicians left out of *Metronome's* All-Star Bands, the *Metronome*
Hall of Fame, and most the magazine's general coverage of swing during
the 1930s. *Metronome* attacked Panassié's choices on the grounds that his
notion of jazz's rootedness in black culture was a novel, highly debatable
theory. "This is the group," the article reads,

> that, according to Mons. Panassié, plays from "within"—expresses soul—plays
> from the heart. Only this group transfers to the listener what he considers the
> true expression of jazz. And, apparently, the true expression of jazz means to
> Panassié the soulful crying of the American Negro as exemplified, more than in
> any other way, by the playing of the blues.[83]

Glossed over in this assessment is the fact that Panassié's band also included the white trombonist Jack Teagarden and the white clarinetist "Mezz"
Mesirow, both of whom seemed to Panassié to have completely absorbed a
black sensibility. *Metronome's* strongest skepticism about Panassié's notion
of "real" jazz came in its discussion of Panassié's choice for drummer:

> The choice of [Zutty] Singleton, who, technically, is far from being a polished
> drummer, occasioned much disfavor [among the *Metronome* editors' circle of
> musician-friends]. But Zutie [sic], like the rest in the band, inculcates a savage
> simplicity (typically negroid) into his playing that fits right into the Panassié
> approved "blues" or "pure jazz" pattern.[84]

Metronome's ambivalence toward Panassié—first extolling him as a model of
civilized bearing and learning, then condemning his aesthetic preferences as
racially biased—is illustrative of a larger contradictory pattern in swing-era
race relations. Hand in hand with the symbolic crossing of racial boundaries entailed by jazz consumption and connoisseurship, pre–World War II
jazz critics and fans often expressed integrationist sympathies remarkably
progressive for the time—yet at the same time many fans and certain critics
appeared to resent the successes of black musicians and bands. As an artistic
practice that challenged the boundaries between performers and audiences,
intellectuals (or patricians) and the "masses," and blacks and whites, swing
embodied a welcome symbol of social integration—a universal language
and cultural practice that cut across lines of race, class, nation, and cultural
hierarchy. In 1939 New York's leading black newspaper, the *Amsterdam*

News, waxed enthusiastic about the Savoy Ballroom—"The Home of Happy Feet"—as an example of democratic multiculturalism:

> Perhaps no other spot in this great country is so symbolic of the American ideal. The Savoy is truly a melting pot—a cross section of American life. There, every night in the week, every race and nationality under the sun, the high and the low, meet and color lines melt away under the influence of America's foremost sepia swing bands.[85]

But this multicultural mecca was gone by 1943, when New York City shut down the Savoy Ballroom out of a specific fear of race mixing, and under a general wartime climate of anxiety about Harlem radicalism.[86] Still, to a greater extent than professional sports, Hollywood, or national politics, the prewar jazz world offered a vision of a racially integrated mass culture, if not a racially integrated society. Duke Ellington was not only a successful bandleader and matinee idol; he was a cultural hero whose charisma and authority appealed to black and white youth alike. When a racially mixed crowd of 4,000 packed the Savoy for a "Battle of the Bands" between orchestras led by "The King of Swing," Benny Goodman, and the "Idol of Harlem," Chick Webb, the significance of the event, according to historian Edward Pessen, then a Brooklyn high school student, was not so much the partisan arguments over the outcome as "the exemplary colorblindness of the musicians themselves, and of the fans of the music, at a time when recording companies, hotel and nightclub owners and theater managers tried their damnedest to retain the color line that was often prevalent throughout American life."[87]

This thrust for racial integration was, as David Stowe, Michael Denning, and Lewis Erenberg persuasively argue, a cornerstone of Depression- and World War II–era Leftist ideology and practice.[88] It was also, however, a *de facto* outcome made inevitable by an inequitable distribution of material and symbolic resources. Swing's ideology of colorblindness was indeed an exemplary ideal of cultural democracy and a laudable goal for American social relations, whether in the military barracks or on the bandstand and dance floor. Given the legacies of slavery and Jim Crow segregation, however, it was an ideal toward which blacks and whites moved from radically different positions. Certainly the symbolic integration of the bandstand and dance hall served both blacks and whites as both a source of pleasure and a positive gesture of democratic ideology. Nevertheless, to suggest that racial integration was the hallmark of the swing era—as though the music came into existence for the express purpose of bringing whites and blacks together—is to embrace a naive view of racial politics. Black musicians in territory bands, scrounging for work in the throes of the Depression, or even relatively successful black musicians working in Chicago and New York, seeing the white swing band dominance of radio and downtown hotels, were happy to embrace the glories of integration if it meant getting better gigs.

Throughout his career Louis Armstrong performed alongside whites, in front of predominantly white audiences, in music and film industries controlled by white capital. His infrequent political enunciations—most famously a biting critique of Arkansas governor Orval Faubus during the 1957 Little Rock school desegregation battle—demonstrated a strong integrationist faith. But it does not follow logically that Armstrong and his music symbolize the triumph of interracial democracy. Granting, axiomatically, that for Armstrong, Ellington, Basie, and Billie Holiday to make any decent money they would have to seek an audience outside the relatively impoverished black community, it does not follow that their successes in the American entertainment industry ought to be chalked up to the glories of either capitalism or interracial cultural democracy. Likewise, the fact that many black swing fans who embraced the music's integrationist ideology does not mean that jazz stood triumphantly apart from and somehow transcended American racism. Rather, given that jazz's political economy reflected the white hegemony of the broader culture, the fact that the music *itself* had proved able to cross the color line held out the hope—and that is the key word—that jazz might pave the way for broader reforms.

The market power of swing's predominantly white youth audience, coupled with white jazz critics' work as canon-builders and culture industry mediators, underscores the complicated relationship between the bourgeois Left, the popular culture industry, and the political struggle for black equality. Did the swing craze and the "hot collecting" phenomenon of the 1930s and early 1940s—the former a broad-based, youth-dominated popular cultural movement of dance rituals and consumerist practices organized through mass-mediated technologies of radio and cinema, the latter a form of elite connoisseurship invested in preserving jazz's artistic properties against a perceived threat of mass culture pollution—represent healthy developments in pluralist, democratic cultural exchange, or did they represent a plundering of African American cultural wealth by dance-crazed white youth and privileged white dilettantes? The problem with such a question is not only that it threatens to obscure the important difference between the dilletantism of many white jazz consumers and the deeper commitment to black music on the part of a Leonard Feather, a Marshall Stearns, or a John Hammond, but also that it fosters the erroneous impression that the musical universe and evolving cultural heritage of northern urban blacks in the 1930s and 1940s was constituted exclusively of purely "black" music. And it ignores one of the most significant meanings the black audience itself attached to swing: the music's power as a claim on American capital, both cultural and economic.

"A Weapon of Integration"

"I remember one time coming into a house on 126th Street behind the Apollo, a private house," Russell Sanjek recalled of one of his treasure hunts for old records. "The woman obviously rented apartments upstairs. She told me that she had records that her husband had, and she never played them. She just didn't like the music; it wasn't God's music; and she decided she'd get rid of them, and I looked like the kind of person who maybe ought to have them."[89]

Sanjek and other white jazz enthusiasts who canvassed black neighborhoods in search of vintage jazz and blues records illustrated jazz's racialized cultural and economic geography. Though most of these "race" records were manufactured by the white-owned companies Columbia, Decca, Okeh, Paramount, and Victor—the black-owned company Black Swan, originator of the term and the concept of race records, went out of business after being unable to compete with these larger and better-financed companies[90]—their marketing involved lavish advertising in the black newspapers (especially the nationally distributed *Chicago Defender*), the commissioning of distributors who operated on a semi-independent basis in black neighborhoods, and the forging of connections with retailers located in those neighborhoods. Cultural historian Lizbeth Cohen has argued that blacks in Chicago during this period used cultural consumption to leverage their way into the dominant social and economic order; paradoxically, the very fact of racial segregation, and the corresponding resistance to it, made blacks more likely than white ethnics—immigrant Jews, Italians, and Poles—to use their music as a currency of interethnic exchange, less invested in using music as a form of ethnic cultural preservation. "Because assimilation into the mainstream was possible for white ethnics," Cohen writes, "they used mass culture to stave it off by keeping their own culture alive. Ethnic records, like stores, theaters, and radio programs, set out to reinforce traditional culture in the face of threatening alternatives. Racial discrimination, on the other hand, kept blacks from the same opportunities, and pressures, to assimilate. Given that very different context, black jazz recordings, or black employment in chain stores, became a vehicle for making a claim on mainstream society that racism had otherwise denied."[91]

In the early 1920s, the black poet and journalist Frank Marshall Davis worked as a distributor for Black Swan, going door to door on the south side of Chicago with demonstration copies of the latest Ethel Waters and Trixie Smith platters, taking orders for later delivery. Later in the decade he also peddled Okeh and Paramount records, including Ma Rainey, Sara Martin, Mamie Smith, and Clara Smith waxings.[92] The pianist and composer Clarence Williams, who opened a record store on the south side of Chicago in 1924, witnessed another set of music acquisition practices: "Colored people would form a line twice around the block when the latest record of Bessie or Ma or Clara or Mamie come in . . . sometimes these records they was bootlegged, sold in the alley for four or five dollars a piece."[93] In the 1930s, when "Squirrel" Ashcroft III and his circle of north side Chicago jazz connoisseurs from the Chicago Rhythm Club went hunting for early jazz and blues treasures, what they were hunting were objects that had been part of this brisk consumer market on the south side less than a decade earlier.

Sanjek's report that he found more Guy Lombardo records than Fletcher Henderson ones in black Harlem households may have been intended more for its anecdotal color than for its suggestion of an integration of musical tastes across the color line, but such a suggestion is consistent with the experience and testimony of African Americans in the prewar years.[94] Even as the critics were embracing Ellington as the progenitor of a distinctly African American musical form, Ellington himself was to be found in the pages of *Down Beat* lavishing praise on Paul Whiteman, Glen Miller, Artie Shaw, Benny Goodman, and, yes, Guy Lombardo.[95] At this stage in his career, Ellington's creative challenge was to make music that appealed to a dancing audience while also carrying a patina of elegance and sophistication, and Ellington admired these other bandleaders for their success in meeting that same challenge.

Timuel Black, a Chicago educator, recalled that the phonograph record collections in his home and in the homes of his teenage friends in the 1920s and 1930s included not only the latest Louis Armstrong and Ethel Waters releases, but also many of the same Victors, Paramounts, and Columbias as would be found in a typical white middle-class household: the light classics, Caruso, Gilbert and Sullivan. "Music was all around us," says Black. "It was considered good taste to have classical music. I mean, Paul Robeson gave us a lot of pride, and it wasn't *only* because he sang the spirituals. Even jazz musicians, guys like Fats Waller, they were trained in the classics. Fats was heartbroken when he couldn't make it as a classical player, on account of the racism. He loved that music."[96] An episode that loomed large in Black's development as a jazz fan illuminates the way musical tastes transcended the color line. Black was "endeared" to Benny Goodman because Goodman "took the chance [to hire blacks]," an action Black considered, in light of the social climate of the time, "a miracle." Black found Goodman's skills as a clarinetist, on the other hand, something less than miraculous. He preferred Ellington's clarinetist, Barney Bigard. But when many of the black musicians that Black knew told him that Goodman was better than Bigard—Black counted among his friends Louis Armstrong, Billie Holiday, Lester Young, Fats Waller, Milt Hinton, George Dixon, Eddie South, Johnny Griffin, and Johnny Hartmann; he doesn't remember precisely which of these musicians expressed their preference for Goodman over Bigard—he found it necessary to reconsider his position.

African American jazz fans like Timuel Black knew Goodman's success would not have been possible if not for Fletcher Henderson's pioneering band arrangements, not to mention the entire legacy of blues-inflected, improvisational, and dance-oriented music that several generations of black musicians had contributed to the cultural environment Goodman inherited. They knew as well that the celebrity-worship of Goodman and other white bandleaders in the swing magazines typified the problem of measuring and honoring black achievement in a white-dominated public culture. But rather than accusing white swing musicians, critics, and fans of stealing a cultural product that belonged only to African Americans, black fans instead hoped to turn swing's massive popularity to their own advantage. True, *Down Beat* and *Metronome* trafficked heavily in disposable publicity stunts that did nothing to increase awareness of black cultural achievement: in addition to George Frazier's more extravagant submissions, there were editorials on the question "Is Benny Goodman's Head Swollen?"[97] and multi-issue debates set off by articles with titles like "Disc Collectors Are Jerks."[98] True, some powerful critics seemed to harbor cultural biases that blocked their understanding of what black musicians were trying to achieve. True, swing magazine fan letters often came off as the frivolous sport of overprivileged preppies with too much free time and too little responsibility— a bunch of "rich men's sons," swing musician Benny Carter complained, "[who] buy batches of phonograph records with the money which their dads had them sent at college to pay laundry bills, [who then] listen to the records, not knowing what to listen for, and proceed to form all sorts of opinions."[99]

But also to be found in the swing magazines was George Frazier's assertion that of the big bands, only Ellington's and Basie's were worth listening to.[100] There were the numerous articles by and about John Hammond in regard to his actions on behalf of black musicians.[101] And there was Marshall Stearns's *Down Beat* series on "The History of 'Swing Music,'" the first history of jazz written by an American that was unequivocal about the pioneering role of black musicians at every stage of the music's evolution.

Strongly influenced by an exchange of letters with a black man named Harrison Smith, Stearns's series provided key details about exchange between black and white musicians.[102] "The best of Goodman's arrangements today," Stearns wrote in one column of the series, "are by colored musicians, notably Fletcher Henderson, and its band has taken its style from colored orchestras."[103] After Stearns traveled to Chicago in the summer of 1936 to research the origins of Chicago white jazz, H. M. and Boyce Brown, members of the aforementioned Chicago Rhythm Club, made light of Stearns's trip in a letter to *Metronome*, saying that "Stearns could have secured all of the material he would need for several books [on the Chicago style] by spending a few hours chinning with Eddie Condon in New York."[104] But the Browns, the Ashcrofts, and other of the Rhythm Clubbers who equated the history of Chicago jazz with Eddie Condon's and Red McKenzie's Chicago Rhythm Kings' gig at Friar's Inn in 1927 had a lot to learn from Marshall Stearns. In his swing history installment on Condon and McKenzie's band (which included Dave Tough, Bud Freeman, Jimmy and Dick McPartland, and Frank Teschmaker), Stearns pinpointed the key source of inspiration for this music:

> The real thrill came when Dave Tough brought the boys over to hear Louis Armstrong playing with Joe Oliver. They found Earl Hines playing at a beat-up joint called the "Elite." At the Paradise they listened attentively to Bessie Smith, who was their favorite.... [Mezz] Mesirow was the yeast in the swing brew. It was he who kept the boys on their toes by taking them to hear every good colored band within a hundred miles.[105]

Some black musicians were gratified by the positive assessments critics like Frazier, Hammond, and Stearns gave them. Others were not. In the *Down Beat* article in which Duke Ellington took his aforementioned swipe at John Hammond, he also asserted that Marshall Stearns's opinions "are often influenced by misinformation or inaccuracy," and that George Frazier "indulges in flagrant overstatement."[106] Benny Carter was no more convinced of the critics' insights into swing than he was of the schoolboy fans':

> [The critics'] claim is that they are pushing a cause that few people understand; that they know what it's all about; they "feel" swing and write what they feel. At a recent get-together a writer, recognized to be one of the very great "authorities on swing," played his favorite record for others to listen to. He sat before the phonograph, listening intently, outwardly completely inspired by the music. Few noticed him beating his foot; even fewer noticed that he was beating it entirely out of rhythm. Yet, time and again, he has stated blatantly that "such and such a rhythm section stinks."[107]

If the subtext of Carter's remarks on swing fans and critics strongly suggests that he meant to refer mainly to white fans and critics, we shouldn't thereby assume that young blacks were not reading the swing magazines. For African American audiences, it is true, the most important critical evaluations of music were embedded in communal social responses: if a swing band's rhythm section really did stink, a review in *Down Beat* or *Metronome* saying as much would be gratuitous—the point would already have been made on the dance floor. Nevertheless, Timuel Black and his African American teenage friends on the south side of Chicago read *Down Beat* and *Metronome* religiously, Black says, because "we had to be informed about the latest literature." Black became friends with musicians like Ray Nance, Fats Waller, Billie Holiday, and Louis Armstrong, a fact he passes off as being a normal part of living in the black community.[108] "All you'd have to do was stand on the corner in the neighborhood in the afternoon, and they'd come driving by and stop and talk to you." Black was amused when he'd see these people talked about in the swing magazines as though they were gods: "Nobody around here talked about these people that way—unless you were talking about Art Tatum. We knew he *was* God." Neither Black nor his friends ever wrote in to the swing magazines, even when they took issue with a statement about a black band or musician they thought showed a white cultural bias. "We might say 'If a Negro was writing this, he would have known better,' and just go on to the next thing," Black explains. "Or else we'd take that statement and play around with, use it to get into our own discussions. It'd be like, 'Man, did you see what that guy said about so and so,' and then we'd be off and running."

One might interpret the way Black and his friends were using the swing magazines as being analogous to the way Billie Holiday and Fats Waller were using Tin Pan Alley songs: as fungible raw material to be worked over, transformed into something more meaningful to their own cultural milieu, one in which oral communication historically has held an authority equal to or greater than that of the written word. A critique of the *Down Beat* and *Metronome* writers by Billy Rowe, whose long career as an entertainment writer for the Associated Negro Press began in the early 1930s, lends support to this notion: "They fit whatever they heard to the words that they knew about or the words they would like to use. They were not inspired by the music, [never] really understood the music itself . . . to me they were word merchants, not jazz critics."[109]

Rowe here demonstrates a keen perception of the problem of trying to represent an oral, kinesthetic, and spiritual medium through the written word. But Rowe, who made his living writing, as he himself puts it "à la Walter Winchell," was also, occupationally speaking, a "word merchant." Only by

employing the most abjectly essentialist and categorical of assumptions—
that oral communication is for blacks and written communication is for
whites—could one argue that Billy Rowe and other black journalists had
no desire to engage in *written* forms of jazz criticism themselves. Why, then,
didn't Rowe sell some of his words to *Down Beat* and *Metronome*, or write
about jazz in the black newspapers the way it was being written about, with
great popular success, in those magazines? "For the basic reason," Rowe says,
"that in those days and even now, black critics could not afford the luxury
of being critics, because we were so happy when one of our fellows got a job
someplace, at some of those posh hotels those days, that we never criticized
them."[110] "You see," said Frank Marshall Davis, the only black writer who
did sell some words to *Down Beat* in the 1930s, "the primary function of the
black press then was to counteract the racist propaganda of the daily press.
Those who did write felt it their duty to either praise or ignore."[111] By "racist
propaganda," Davis meant the white press's perennial image of the jazzman
as a dissolute rake, an image at complete variance with the smartly dressed,
hard-working, pillar-of-the-community depictions of jazz musicians in the
Chicago Defender, the *Pittsburgh Courier*, and the New York *Amsterdam News*.
But Davis was also sensitive to the subtler propaganda of the swing magazines. The problem was not the explicit propaganda of a uniformly negative
representation of black musicians, but the implicit propaganda of a uniform
underrepresentation of black musicians, positive *or* negative.

Here lies the explanation for the crucial difference between the way jazz
was being discussed in *Down Beat* and *Metronome* and the way it was being
discussed in the black press. It is the difference between discussants, in
the case of the swing magazines, who had the luxury of being able to use
the print media to argue about whether jazz was a serious art form or a
source of entertainment; and discussants, in the case of the black press, who
knew that jazz was *both* serious art and serious entertainment, and instead
used the print media to foreground jazz's role in advancing black economic
and political interests. When Benny Goodman hired black musicians Teddy
Wilson, Lionel Hampton, and Charlie Christian, critics and fans writing
in *Down Beat* and *Metronome* focused their attention on the music: how
would the band sound now that it employed these black musicians?[112] It
was necessary to have this discussion—a crucial point—because the vast
majority of the readers of these magazines had, through the readers' polls,
expressed strong preferences for all-white bands. In the black press, the
musical issue was a given: *of course* the Goodman band would now sound
better—how could it not, now that it would have a direct connection to
the musical milieu that had been the indirect source of its success all along?
Black readers could be expected to understand for themselves what a racially

integrated band signified as a musical issue. What needed to be emphasized in the public discourse was the politico-economic issue: black individuals had crossed the color line, and the black community now would be able to reap at least some of the financial rewards and social status denied it by a segregated society.

For all of the genuine progressivism of their position on the race issue, some of the key white jazz critics failed to understand this important distinction between the white-dominated jazz press and the black press. Their perceptions of the way jazz was discussed in the black press make it appear that white critics expected the black press to address *their* concerns rather than the concerns of black readers. Leonard Feather, for instance, criticized the black press for not being more accommodating of his mission to enhance jazz's high-art legitimacy:

> The only writing about jazz I saw in the black press, which virtually ignored jazz as an art form, was some pieces I wrote as a London correspondent (unpaid) for the *New York Amsterdam News* in 1935–6. But I read several black newspapers regularly in the early 1940s because at least they ran news items or press releases telling me who was where, etc.[113]

When John Hammond said that

> I would buy all the black papers, the *Amsterdam News*, the *Interstate Tattler* out of Philadelphia, the *Pittsburgh Courier*, the *Norfolk Journal & Guide* .... I knew I couldn't write for the black press, because ... the black press was only interested when there was advertising.[114]

—he revealed not only a colossal delusion about the objectivity of his own criticism, but a misunderstanding of the role he played for black swing fans. Among white jazz fans, Hammond, Feather, and other white critics sympathetic to black musicians were important both as tastemakers and as lightning rods for white liberal guilt: their role in the white community was as cultural and psychological arbiters. Among black jazz fans, by contrast, for whom an appreciation of black musicians and a belief in racial equality were givens, these critics were important primarily because of the power they had to help black musicians in the marketplace: their role in the black community was as economic and political arbiters. Though they seem not to have realized it, to the extent to which white jazz writers aspired to the title of "critic," with that term's implication of objective intellectual authority standing above the world of commerce, they were seeking to divorce themselves from the very role that was most responsible for such esteem as they enjoyed among black swing fans—the role of patron and proselytizer for underappreciated black musicians.

Indeed, black journalists who wrote about jazz in the black press took as their primary purpose to petition the black community to provide better support for its own musicians. Dan Burley, the best known of the black newspaper writers who dealt with jazz, strongly criticized black bandleaders for failing to patronize black songwriters. "It has been said," Burley wrote, "that the white orchestras will play a song by a Negro much quicker than a Negro band will play one. It seems that when our bandleaders hit the top, they suddenly forget themselves and develop a 'white philosophy' which means that anything Negroid is to be avoided as much as possible."[115] In his radio column "All Ears" in the *Amsterdam News*, Bill Chase carefully monitored the New York airwaves for the inclusion of black performers and frequently implored his readers to apply pressure to radio stations to increase their use of black talent.[116] To be sure, Hammond's and Feather's campaign for enhancing jazz's high-art legitimacy was not without its own tacit economic component. If jazz were to become a regular feature at Carnegie Hall—not, as in the case of the "From Spirituals to Swing" Carnegie concerts, the Hammond-organized benefits for the *New Masses*, but rather a long-term concert series that would become an integral part of Carnegie's own institutional identity—the real benefit might not be so much the higher cultural esteem jazz musicians would now enjoy by virtue of performing in the same space as European concert musicians. The real benefit might be that jazz musicians would now be paid as well as those classical musicians. And this *was* one of the arguments Hammond made when, in his capacity as a board member of the NAACP, he attacked the "typical black bourgeoisie" attitude that prevented that organization from using its organ, *The Crisis*, to do all that it could to promote jazz. It was not just the implication of his own failure as a jazz proselytizer that made Hammond rueful over the fact that Roy Wilkins "didn't like jazz, even though he had been an editor of the *Kansas City Call*,"[117] or that Walter White, despite being a classmate of Fletcher Henderson's, couldn't disabuse his wife of her enthusiasm for Guy Lombardo. It was also that Hammond knew that black jazz musicians would fare much better in the broader American cultural market if they had more support from black political leaders.

Hammond's frustration was shared by Frank Marshall Davis, who deplored "the lack of acceptance of this music by the Afro-American upper crust who, following the example of white leaders, wanted to put down jazz and the blues."[118] Known since his days at Kansas State University as "the poet who looks like a prizefighter and Charlestons like hell,"[119] Davis found in jazz not only the foundation of his identity as a black man, but also a potent weapon for improving the position of blacks in white-dominated society. Living in Chicago in the 1920s for Davis meant going to the Sunset Theater to hear Louis Armstrong "challenge the whole world with his defiant horn" by "distilling the meaning of black in sharps and flats,"[120] or to the Metropolitan, where Fats Waller, as an organ accompanist for silent films, took "the pretty aural confections of Tin Pan Alley and shov[ed] them down the white world's throat, dipped in the sardonic salt and vitriol of black living."[121] In the 1930s he enjoyed the Goodman band but thought they "constantly blew to capacity," and lacked the "subtlety, reserve, and controlled power" of the group Fletcher Henderson brought into the Grand Terrace in Chicago, a "stupendous unit" featuring Roy Eldridge, Chu Berry, and Big Sid Catlett.[122]

Like Dan Burley, Billy Rowe, and other black newspapermen, Davis was a political commentator, theater and sports columnist, editorial writer, and occasional news photographer. In the late 1930s Davis added to his other assignments for the Associated Negro Press a column called "Rating the Records," similar to George Simon's "DISCussions," with its pithy two-line reviews of the latest releases. Davis believed that the amount of attention given white bands in the swing magazines was vastly disproportionate to their artistic merit, an argument he made in his lone *Down Beat* article, titled "No Secret—Best White Bands Copy Negroes."[123] The article affirmed the creative primacy of Armstrong, Ellington, Lunceford, and Basie, while also implicitly critiquing the fan magazine discourse as itself constitutive of the institutionalized racism that plagued American culture writ large, notwithstanding the important breakthroughs in popular consciousness and social practice that jazz seemed to be making. Davis's own column was avowedly integrated. He wrote approvingly of the Goodman, Dorsey Brothers, Artie Shaw, Charlie Barnet, and Woody Herman bands, and he knew that many of his black readers—this was certainly true of Timuel Black—thoroughly enjoyed these white bands, as he did. As disc jockey, in the mid-1940s, of a short-lived radio show on the Marshall Field station WJJD called "Bronzeville Brevities," Davis made a point of playing recordings of white, black, and mixed bands so as to, as he puts it, "propagandize on the democracy of jazz and suggest increased integration in other fields."[124] He also used the show to put the word out about jam sessions sponsored by the Chicago chapter of the United Hot Clubs, of which Davis was the only black member. The radio show's best publicity was a story in the Chicago *Daily News* titled "Swing Fan Gets a Helping Hand to a Concert—Not on the Radio," telling how a white youth suffering from multiple sclerosis had sent a note to Davis asking for his help in getting to one of the Hot Club jam sessions, and how Davis had picked him up—literally—and carried him out of his apartment and then into Moose Hall, the site of the jam session.[125]

In his days as a distributor for Black Swan, Okeh, and Paramount in the 1920s, Davis wasn't thinking about the long-term value of the records he was hawking. Joining the Hot Club in 1937 sparked his interest in these records as historical artifacts, however, and he began to spend much of his free time on the "hot collecting" circuit of secondhand stores and junk shops. But Davis's notion of jazz history reached back much further than pre–World War I Storyville. Davis saw jazz as a modern urban folk music descended from African tribal culture. At the same time Davis was writing for labor and black newspapers and serving as a vice-chairman of the Chicago Civil Liberties Committee and as a member of the board of the Civil Rights Congress, he was also a performer in a Chicago men's choir that performed African war chants, and tribal, hunting, and fertility songs. Davis's convictions about jazz's African roots were deepened by his relationship with renowned Northwestern University anthropologist Melville Herskovits, whose book *The Myth of the Negro Past*, when it appeared in 1941, became for Davis "a Bible, providing facts to refute confused blacks who believed we were merely carbon copies of Whitey."[126] Davis met Herskovits following a lecture the anthropologist gave at the Hall Branch Library on Chicago's south side in which he played private recordings of Trinidadian and Jamaican music. Davis himself had recently begun giving lectures at the library, as well as full classes at the Abraham Lincoln School, on the history of jazz. Herskovits lent Davis recordings and other materials he had collected pertaining to native African music and its survivals in Brazil, the Caribbean, and North America. In return, Davis appeared as a guest lecturer in Herskovits's social studies class at Northwestern, enlightening a group of North Shore well-to-do white students with what Herskovits called "a realistic, hardboiled approach" to race relations.[127]

The classes at the Lincoln School, a community-oriented adult education program affiliated with the socialist labor movement, came about at the suggestion of Art Stern, whom Davis described as "a young Jewish intellectual who realized the significance of the music in our continuing struggle for equality."[128] It was Davis's hope that these classes would attract an equal number of black and white students. He proposed to show how an art form with roots in native African culture and the slave experience had become a defining cultural expression not only for twentieth-century African Americans, but also for other American minority groups, and ultimately even for privileged Europeans. Jazz's African and African American origins were, in Davis's Marxist-influenced formulation, a product of social and political experience rather than of racial essence. Early jazz represented for Davis an urban, multiracial working-class achievement, a powerful populist critique of the dominant Anglo-American bloc. "It is no accident that Jews and

Italians became excellent jazzicians," Davis observed, explaining that many of jazz's "best early white practitioners were members of minorities suffering, like us, from prejudice."[129] But if Davis's class analysis led him to celebrate cultural exchange between Italians, Jews, and blacks in 1920s New Orleans and Chicago, it also inclined him to an unfavorable view of European and African American artistic hybridization in the bebop community in 1940s New York. Contrary to later interpretations of bebop as an assertion of black identity, Davis saw bop as an attempt to make jazz more appealing to elite white tastes—more of a "respectable" concert music. "If Mr. Gillespie knew much about the socio-economic factors which produced jazz," Davis wrote in a three-way exchange in *People's Voice* with the pioneering bop trumpeter and with Leonard Feather, "he would evolve a trumpet style different from the scalar meanderings which identify him today."

Davis, Feather, and Gillespie were all on the same page in seeing jazz as a political tool; the debate was over how jazz could best serve the political agenda. For Davis, the struggle for racial equality was best served by valorizing the expression of the folk. For Gillespie and Feather, racial equality would only be meaningful if black musicians felt free to pursue whatever creative directions they chose. This debate was part of a larger modernist-fundamentalist divide in 1940s jazz discourse (about which much more in chapter 3), with bebop adherents like Feather and Barry Ulanov pitted against the defenders of various forms of pre-1940s jazz. All the parties in this debate, which raged on with great polemical heat in the jazz magazines, considered themselves politically progressive, especially regarding race issues. Bootlegging the Trotskyite rhetoric of the 1940s Leftist cultural wars, each side in this jazz sectarian slugfest denounced the others as "fascists" and "bourgeois reactionaries." As Bernard Gendron has argued, it is important to note that both the fundamentalists (or "moldy figs") and the bebop enthusiasts were part of the Modernist movement in Western art discourse; they simply "accentuated certain tendencies of the 'modernist' impulse at the expense of others."[130] Frank Marshall Davis's folk authenticism was part of an urban modernist vision that sought to endow contemporary social and political struggles with historically informed artistic values.

Davis's presentations on the history of jazz had been well received by predominantly black audiences at the Hall Branch Library and the South Side Community Center, and by all-black audiences at special events held in private homes in south side black neighborhoods. To his great chagrin, however, only two or three blacks enrolled in his Lincoln School classes over the several years that he taught them. Davis could think of several explanations for this low black enrollment. He felt that blacks, owing to their sense of jazz as being a part of the basic stream of their lives, lacked an interest in the music's "anatomy." "As a group," Davis thought, "we were too close to the music. Jazz was an emotional part of our daily lives. We made it happen and were not too interested in why."[131] But equally important were other factors that had to do with the Lincoln School's location. Located on the top floor of a building in the heart of Chicago's downtown Loop, the school was far enough away from the city's black neighborhoods, Davis surmised, to have in some degree deterred potential black enrollees. In addition to the problem of the Lincoln School's literal physical location, there was the more subtle, but ultimately perhaps more determinative, issue of its location on the map that charts the cultural and psychological geography of American black-white relations. There was, Davis felt, "the tendency on our part, born of experience, to feel uncomfortable around whites no matter how liberal their attitude."[132]

With this single sentence, Davis throws full light on the naiveté of the white jazz critics' grandest vision. While swing's "rhythmic integration" might indeed have become a greater force for a genuine and thoroughgoing social integration of blacks and whites than were other social movements born of liberal impulses, it too had its limitations. And one of them was the inability of the white jazz critic to perceive how his message was shaped by his medium; how the content of what he was saying about jazz could be less important than the form in which he was saying it, and even the place where he was saying it. Frank Marshall Davis was an admirer of John Hammond, just as Langston Hughes and Sterling Brown were admirers of Marshall Stearns. Davis was sorry that he wasn't able to accept Hammond's offer to come to New York as his guest for the Carnegie Hall "From Spirituals to Swing" concert in 1938.[133] Years later, Hughes and Brown were happy to oblige Marshall Stearns's request that they participate in seminars Stearns organized for the Newport Jazz Festival, and in a series of summer roundtable discussions in Lenox, Massachusetts that led to the formation of the Lenox School of Jazz. As black intellectuals who understood jazz's significance not only to American history but to African American cultural identity—indeed, to their *own* self-identity—Davis, Hughes, and Brown knew that their audiences at Lenox and Newport needed to hear what they had to say, every bit as much as, a century earlier, Frederick Douglass's audience at Newport needed to hear what *he* had to say.

"The Feeling of Acceptance"

Timuel Black was sitting in a friend's living room listening to a jazz radio program one day in 1939, when all of a sudden a broadcaster broke in with a stunning announcement: Germany had just invaded Poland. Black knew immediately what this meant. His teachers at DuSable, the all-black Chicago high school he attended, had instilled in him a keen awareness of the foreboding international scene. The Polish-Jewish owners of the grocery store where Black worked lent depth and perspective to his widening horizons by telling him the stories they heard from their relatives of the horror engulfing Europe. "It won't be long before we're in that war," Black told his friends, sounding a solemn note that contrasted sharply with the buoyant, swinging rhythms that now came back on the radio.

Born in Mississippi, Black and his family were part of the post–World War I Great Migration, settling in Chicago in the late 1920s. An excellent student, Black graduated from the University of Chicago and went on to a distinguished career as a high school and college history teacher and political organizer. Black met the Chicago radio broadcaster Studs Terkel on a train headed to Washington for the 1963 civil rights march. He told Terkel of his bittersweet memories of the war. Drafted in 1943, Black was not unhappy to be leaving a Chicago that had just recently been consumed by race riots. He saw the military as an opportunity to develop his leadership skills. Despite achieving officer-level scores on the Army classification test and voicing a strong desire to serve in a combat unit, however, Black, like most African American GI's serving in a military every bit as segregated as the broader American society, was consigned to duty in the quartermaster corps servicing combat troops with food, clothing, and equipment. In the very act of contributing to the defeat of fascism and imperialism, Black became more aware than ever of his own status as a colonial subject. He returned from the war with deeply ambivalent feelings, his gratification with the war's outcome and his longing for home tugging his emotions one way while his heightened awareness of the failures of American society vis-à-vis its African American citizens pulled him in another.

One experience stood out in Black's mind as particularly emblematic of the ambivalence he felt as an African American participant in the events that brought the United States to a pinnacle of world power and prestige. After the Allied assault on Normandy, Black's outfit accompanied Patton through the French countryside and on to Paris. Black told Terkel about his experience at the liberation of the French capital:

> We came there on this beautiful day. How can I describe it? Know how I know they'd retained hope and dreams? They'd buried their jazz records of people like Louis Armstrong and Duke Ellington and Coleman Hawkins. (Laughs.) They said, (tries a French accent) "M'sieur, ze music, le jazz." They hugged and embraced us. It was the feeling of acceptance. I seriously considered not

returning to the United States. They respected something from my own culture so openly, jazz music.[134]

Black was witnessing at first hand the seemingly superior commitment to jazz on the part of Europeans that had been advertised in the U.S. jazz press throughout the late 1930s. In November 1939 readers of *Down Beat* were apprised that Hugues Panassié, Charles Delauney, and many French collectors had "worked feverishly a few days after the war began burying their priceless jazz records—mostly American ones—underground, safe from Nazi bombs."[135] In May 1940, *Down Beat* published a dispatch from Delauney, sequestered "'somewhere in France,' where for months in the mud and fog man seems to have lost all relation to civilized life and appears to be slowly sinking into the primeval ooze."[136] All that stood between the heroic Delauney and this "primeval ooze," American jazz fans read, was his memory of first hearing Louis Armstrong, "a voice now . . . distant . . . [but] really . . . within you, a world which *was* human." Heed this voice, Delauney implored American jazz fans, for in it they would "recognize . . . a social and artistic phenomenon of universal significance."

What began as an inspiring, if melodramatic, exhortation suddenly turned into an anti-American diatribe of the sort that seems an obligatory gesture of French cultural criticism. Reminding his American readers that it was "the intellectuals of 'old Europe,' the French artistic *Avant-garde* to be specific," that had first discovered jazz's "originality and promise," Delauney excoriated American culture for undermining jazz's artistic qualities by handing it over to the exploitative machinery of the entertainment business. "[T]here is something else to jazz," Delauney wrote,

> besides the pretext for emancipation which permits you to abandon your Anglo-Saxon reserve, to assume the nervous, almost neuropathic, characteristics of the jitterbug (the physical reaction of those who, although still young, lead too sedentary a life). Similarly, by equating jazz to a form of sport, you have created contests, rankings of soloists in which spectacularity (effect, outward appearance) and technique (artificiality) alone seem to count. You have started a competition for high notes and drum solos. You have fertilized the ground for the army of hangers-on, managers, and publicity agents, who stage the great meets in the stadia (Randall's Island concert, etc.), draw up budgets of thousands of dollars to launch some new orchestra, and bargain in the slave market for musicians who are snatched away from rival orchestras by the promise of easy money.[137]

After the war, American jazz fans sympathetic to Delauney's mass culture critique were rewarded with an extraordinary final act to the French critic's wartime performance. It emerged in the American press right after the war that diehard French jazz collectors, following Delauney's lead, had contributing to the French resistance by devising an underground network employing American "jive" talk as code for its clandestine communications. Even more remarkable was the role played by a few officers in the German occupying army who chose, in defiance of official Nazi policy, not to fully conceal their enthusiasm for swing music. During the occupation a lieutenant named Dietrich Schultz-Kohn—who in 1936 had undertaken to translate Panassié's *Le Jazz Hot* into German—spent all his spare time helping Delauney work on the 1943 edition of *Hot Discography*. Later, on hand for the surrender of German troops at St. Nazaire and Lorient, he upset the negotiations by inquiring of all the Allied personnel assembled whether they collected Benny Goodman recordings.

In October 1943 the Gestapo raided the federal headquarters of the Hot Club of France in the Rue Chaptal in Paris—the organization had by then graduated from Panassié's apartment to a three-story building—in an effort to root out American and British agents posing as record collectors. Everyone found on the premises was herded off to the Fresnes Prison; two unlucky French jazz connoisseurs, a secretary of the Paris Hot Club and the president of the Marseilles chapter, were sent off to the gas chambers. Delauney was held for four weeks and then released for lack of evidence, presumably spared a worse fate because of solicitations on his behalf by Lieutenant Schultz-Kohn. After getting out of jail, he finished editing the fifth edition of *Hot Discography*, then printed 2,500 copies on black-market paper furnished him by a group of Belgian jazz collectors.[138]

The meaning of such drama was not lost on Timuel Black. On the Washington Mall in 1963, it was the old spiritual "We Shall Overcome" harnessing bodies and voices and spirits into a mass spectacle of hope; on the Champs-Elysées in 1945 hope was Louis Armstrong's "Struttin' Some Barbecue," Duke Ellington's "Black and Tan Fantasy," and Coleman Hawkins's "Body and Soul." Here were people half a world away commemorating *their* recuperated nationhood, marking *their* sense of freedom, through the medium of African American music. For Timuel Black, in whose subsequent endeavors as a teacher and activist spirituals, work songs, blues, and jazz figured as both narratives of past social experience and inspiration for current social struggles, the music was not a symbol of nationhood and freedom; the music *was* nationhood and freedom. And yet, far from begrudging the French their powerful identification with this music, Black found in their jazz-mediated jubilation an affirmation of his own identity.

Why did Timuel Black think similar affirmation was not available in his own country? As we've seen, in his hometown of Chicago in the 1920s, the release of a new Bessie Smith or Ma Rainey disc would find black people lining the blocks outside of south side record stores. The pages of the *Chicago Defender*, the newspaper of record throughout black America, teemed with mail-order ads for "race records" released by Black Swan, Paramount, Columbia, Okeh, and Victor. In the twenty years before Black left Chicago for Europe in 1943 jazz had firmly established itself as one of the most influential forces in American culture. Defying credentialed authorities from both white and black middle classes who denied the music's aesthetic value and stigmatized its social milieu, jazz inspired a sweeping restylization of sound, movement, dress, and language that revolutionized mainstream American popular culture. Throughout World War II the Armed Forces radio network broadcast records by the Benny Goodman, Count Basie, Jimmie Lunceford, Glen Miller, Duke Ellington, Artie Shaw, and Woody Herman bands. Shiploads of GIs docked in New York Harbor lit out for the Paramount Theater, for the clubs on West 52nd Street, or—until its closing—for the Savoy Ballroom in Harlem to capture these bands in live performance. Overseas, the Special Services Division of the Army and the Bureau of Naval Personnel for the Navy distributed an Armed Services Edition of the book *Jazzmen*, an influential collection of essays detailing the history of jazz and its movement from New Orleans to Chicago and New York.[139]

The more serious jazz consumers among these servicemen—perhaps inspired by the *Jazzmen* essay on hot collecting by Hot Record Society proprietor Stephen Smith—took advantage of their sojourns in various American cities to extend their searches for jazz treasures beyond their home territories—witness naval officer Martin Williams's onshore loitering in Ross Russell's Dial Record Shop. Had Los Angeles, Chicago, or New York been subject to the Luftwaffe bombings that devastated London or the Nazi occupation that menaced Paris, it would not have been surprising to find an Ellington or Armstrong record in the heirlooms squirreled away for safekeeping in the backyards of both genteel and *arriviste* households. But in the absence of such a dramatic illustration of jazz's subterranean burrowing into the national cultural patrimony, and in the presence of an official, above-ground culture largely bereft of positive African American content, Timuel Black turned to Europe for, as he termed it, "a feeling of acceptance." In this gesture he followed the cue of jazz musicians Sidney Bechet, Coleman Hawkins, and Benny Carter (each of whom chose to locate in Europe in the 1920s and 1930s) and anticipated the overwhelming feeling of disillusionment that black jazz musicians who served in the war felt upon returning home.

The symbolic fellowship uniting African American freedom fighter Timuel Black with the jazz lovers of post-Vichy France, a fellowship forged in a mutual spirit of engaged resistance, was as yet unrealized in an America where the complexities of black-white relations continued to mitigate against such unequivocally celebratory outcomes. In this country, swing had opened up important symbolic spaces of interracial communication; the U.S. Hot Clubs had begun the crucial work of shaping the jazz canon; the record trade had given young men and women a lively and syncopated soundtrack for their adolescence; and the jazz magazines had given a few young men a chance to hone their intellectual skills and consolidate a sense of masculine authority. But full interracial understanding and sympathy remained—as ever in U.S. culture—a goal that was noble and necessary, but also frustratingly elusive.

CHAPTER 3

Hearing the "Noisy Lostness"

Telling the Story of Jazz

With jazz, we are not yet in the age of history, but linger in that of folklore.

—Ralph Ellison, 1959

In his 1959 essay "The Golden Age, Time Past," the great African American novelist, essayist, and jazz interpreter Ralph Ellison memorialized the Harlem club Minton's, where Charlie Parker, Dizzy Gillespie, Charlie Christian, Thelonious Monk, Max Roach, and others midwifed the birth of bebop in the early 1940s. Ellison stressed how important it was for these young artists to have a place where they could court challenge, test out their new ideas and techniques, hone their craft, and educate themselves in a musical tradition they were both absorbing and revolutionizing. Minton's, Ellison wrote, "was a continuing symposium of jazz," its jam sessions "the jazzman's true academy." Ellison was writing at a flush moment when a burgeoning LP trade, college concert bookings, jazz festivals and schools, new jazz magazines and books, and State Department–sponsored jazz tours gave the music a strutting, triumphal presence in the expanded postwar cultural marketplace and in the national imagination. Even so, Ellison's essay had a certain mournful, elegiac subtext, not least in its suggestion that an "aura of death" permeated jazz culture in the wake of the premature passing of young men like Parker, Christian, and Fats Navarro not long after their Minton's exploits. These men were "dedicated to chaos" in a music that was defined by quicksilver improvisation and rapid-fire stylistic change, and they lived in a culture where "too much happens too rapidly, and before we can evaluate it, or exhaust its meaning or pleasure, there is something new to concern us." Ellison wondered whether these artists' achievements had registered in the national memory, especially given the American tendency to "give but a limited attention to history."

As a swing man who loved Armstrong, Ellington, and Basie above all else, Ellison had been ambivalent about the jazz future Minton's had augured, and he was outright alienated by the late 1950s avant garde taking shape at the Five Spot, Slugs, and other downtown New York clubs. These places seemed far removed from the roots of jazz, as Ellison knew and experienced them growing up in Oklahoma City. Minton's, on the other hand, had sounded and smelled and felt like home, a place for southern-born black musicians, migrants to the big city, to dig deeper into the resources of their own culture. Accordingly, Ellison summoned all of his celebrated literary powers to extract from Minton's a sense of jazz's "noisy lostness," and with it some sense of a tangible and perhaps even usable past.

The notion of a jazz tradition or usable past calls to mind Eric Hobsbawm and Terence Ranger's argument that the viability of the modern nation hinges on the invention and diffusion of foundational cultural symbols that lend substance and legitimation to politically motivated feelings of peoplehood.[1] For Ellison, jazz's very resistance to conventional procedures of historical investigation was itself emblematic of the music's Americanness. If jazz's protean, processual, spontaneous, fleeting, and elusive practices and meanings confound the notater, the critic, and the historian, such is the price—Ellison would suggest—of living in a democracy where the experiences of the people count for more than the authority of the trained expert. For jazz musicians and the music's ardent followers, jazz history has always been *their* personal history: their experience of playing, listening, dancing, debating, collecting, reminiscing. The "noisy lostness" that Ellison—a trumpeter before he became a writer—searched after in this essay was a "revolution in culture" that had transpired less than two decades earlier, in a place he knew well. Of such far-reaching language, hyper-condensed time frames, and personal memory was the "jazz tradition" made. Ellison's sense of the constructed, contingent, imposed nature of the "jazz tradition" came not least from his disappointment in seeing how little interest the Minton modernists seemed to have in the jazz history that came before them. In a letter to his friend Albert Murray, Ellison complained that the writing of "The Golden Age, Time Past" took "quite a lot of time running around and trying to talk to those screwed-up musicians, drinking beer so that I could listen to their miserable hard-bopping noise . . . and finally realizing that

I could write the piece without their help; for after all most of them simply know that they're dissatisfied and that they want fame and glory and to be themselves. . . ."[2]

The irony of Ellison's insistence that jazz still lingered in the age of folklore was that he was writing at a time when earnest efforts to tell the story of jazz—to insist that jazz had a history, that it was an important one that illuminated the larger history of America—had been one of the driving impulses of jazz discourse for at least a generation. We've already seen the historical impulse at work in John Hammond's "From Spirituals to Swing" concerts in 1938 and 1939, which chronicled the evolution of black American music from slavery to the New Deal. Winthrop Sargeant's *Jazz: Hot and Hybrid*, published in 1938, was the first U.S. book to apply the scrutiny of a professional music critic to jazz, describing chord structures, scale systems, and rhythmic patterns in a way that gave "hot jazz" meaning as a complex musical language rather than as a vague emotional state. Sargeant's book was the first to build a sustained argument about jazz as an American musical synthesis—a hybrid—of African and European musical elements. A year later came *Jazzmen*, a highly influential collection of essays that elegized New Orleans and Chicago early jazz in a rhetoric of heroism and nostalgia that anticipated the tone and spirit with which Ellison uncovered the mythic foundations of bebop in "The Golden Age, Time Past." At this same late 1930s juncture, Marshall Stearns interrupted *Down Beat*'s fan polemics with his series on the pre-1930s history of swing, setting himself on a course of scholarly research and networking that would lead to his series of jazz "roundtables" in the early 1950s and further blossom in his founding and stewardship of the Institute of Jazz Studies, his collaboration in the establishment of the Lenox School of Jazz, and his important historically oriented books *The Story of Jazz* (1956) and *Jazz Dance* (1964).[3]

Stearns was an important architect of the nonpartisan, consensus view of jazz history that became institutionalized in the 1950s in the Lenox School of Jazz, the Newport Jazz Festival, the State Department jazz tours, and new jazz magazines such as *Jazz Review*. This was a hard-won view, coming after the ferocious culture war of the 1940s that split the jazz community into modernist and traditionalist (also known as revivalist or, from the point of view of their modernist enemies, "moldy fig") camps.[4] This schism was rooted in attitudes toward jazz history, and it came at a time when musicians, critics, and listeners were looking both back and forward in time. As Dan Morgenstern has suggested, "One of the great paradoxes of jazz history is that the music's rich past was being rediscovered at the very same time when its present began to undergo its most radical change. While Dizzy Gillespie and Charlie Parker were jamming in Harlem, Bunk Johnson was being recorded in New Orleans."[5] Historicity was now a central feature of jazz criticism, with critics and aficionados defining themselves by whether they thought jazz was in decline or was still progressing forward.

In his acute analysis of 1940s jazz critical discourse, Bernard Gendron sets the beginning of the modernist-revivalist war in 1942, arguing that the later public debate over bebop, starting in 1946, was an extension of this earlier one that was focused on swing. In the early 1940s, the revivalists accused pro-swing critics like Leonard Feather and Barry Ulanov of "crass commercialism, faddism, and Eurocentrism." For their part, Feather and Ulanov—the "*Metronome* modernists"—attacked the revivalists for an "exclusionary purism" that romanticized the work of men who couldn't read or write music. In the late 1940s, the revivalists substituted bebop for swing as the focus of their antimodernist critique. "Like their swing forebears," Gendron writes, "bebop musicians were accused of fetishizing technique, of introducing excessive harmonic and rhythmic complications, and of being too mesmerized by the devices and concepts of European art music." Gendron likens this 1940s jazz culture war to "the centuries-old battle between ancients and moderns so endemic to Western culture."[6]

New Orleans trumpeter Willie "Bunk" Johnson and other mythic figures from jazz's past were resurrected and canonized by a collector's culture that through the 1940s and beyond shaded into an older-is-better preservationist ethos alongside the burgeoning Dixieland revival movement that captured the imaginations of many young white musicians and listeners. The key journals in this traditionalist camp were *Record Changer*, *The Jazz Record*, and *The Jazz Needle*; its bible was *Jazzmen*, and its manifesto was Rudi Blesh's *Shining Trumpets: A History of Jazz* (1946), which argued that jazz had hit its high classical moment in 1926 and had been on a tragic decline ever since. It was a controversial argument, deeply ahistorical in both its romantic vision of jazz's African retentions and its hysterical attack on swing, but nobody questioned that Blesh had set out to write a serious *history* of the music he defined as jazz. Barry Ulanov did the same in his 1952 *History of Jazz in America*, which countered Blesh's story of tragic decline with a pro-modernist evolutionary narrative, fleshing out the arguments Ulanov and Leonard Feather had made in *Metronome* throughout the 1940s against the traditionalists. Sidney Finkelstein, in *Jazz: A People's Music* (1947), also accused Blesh of a static ahistoricism by way of building his own Marxist model of jazz history rooted in the laboring practices of common people. Stearns's *The Story of Jazz* took a sweepingly ecumenical view of jazz history, linking the music's stylistic profusion—Stearns was the first to look seriously at Latin jazz in addition to boogie-woogie, bebop, cool, and other styles—to peculiarly American qualities of creative freedom and cultural hybridization.[7]

As I analyze these pioneering works of jazz history, several themes rise to the surface. First is jazz's history as a hidden, occluded history of the United States writ large—a "noisy lostness," as Ralph Ellison eloquently put it, at the heart of the nation's self-understanding. In this respect, each of these works deserves belated recognition for contributing to the study of the lives and cultural practices of American common people, a bottom-up focus the history profession did not widely adopt until the 1960s. These writers were not trained academic historians; they were art and literary critics, a lapsed art music composer, a cartoonist, and freelance writers of various persuasions who took on the study of jazz as an avocational interest. Yet in hindsight we can see this body of work as constituting a historiography of American culture that professional historians of the United States would do well to incorporate into their bibliographies. In particular, this body of work sought to uncover the African American foundations of American culture. "A land does not take its life and character from those who own its property, or who speak for it," wrote Sidney Finkelstein. "Just as American history, economic life, and civilization are to a considerable extent the creation of the Negro people, so American culture is to a considerable extent a creation of the Negro people."[8]

If the first generation of jazz histories reckoned with the African influence in American culture, they did so through competing conceptions of *how* and *to what extent* African cultural orientations and practices insinuated themselves into other cultural streams that were shaping American civilization. And so a second theme that emerges is the contact, interaction, and exchange between African and European cultures in the development of jazz. Embedded within this focus—crucial, in fact, to its status as an inquiry concerned with history—is a third recurrent theme: jazz as a cultural form and practice that develops within the context of larger historical narratives: migration, modernization, industrialization, and urbanization. The jazz historians I focus on here all grappled with the question of how to represent the transformations jazz had undergone in the first decades of the twentieth century in response to the economic, demographic, and cultural impact of the Great Migration of African Americans from the agricultural South to the industrial, urban North and Midwest; the Great Depression and the two World Wars; and the development of modern communication technologies (recording, radio, film) within the U.S. capitalist system. But these works were even more historically minded than that: each began its story of jazz in the years well before that word and the musical style it signified came into existence—each, that is, argued that the history of the music began long before the music itself was sounded, and that to understand the music one had to know something about the U.S. slave trade, plantation life and culture, the Civil War, Reconstruction, and the Jim Crow system. Writing at a time when jazz and American culture itself were changing in response to World War II and the cold war, suburbanization, the democratization of U.S. higher education, and the first stirrings of the modern civil rights movement, these writers sought not just to uncover the historical roots of jazz, but to use jazz as a means of better understanding American history and culture as a whole.

"An Old Testamentarian Lament"

In an introduction written for the 1985 reissue of the book *Jazzmen*, Nat Hentoff remembered being hit "so hard" by the 1939 first edition when he was fourteen that he "kept reading it for the rest of the year and for years thereafter." It was the first book Hentoff encountered that was about jazz, and the first book that "had the music in it." "There were passages that sang and others that sounded like a tailgate trombone," he wrote, and the book "unabashedly celebrated the romance of jazz." He came to think of the writers themselves as "figures of romance," especially co-editor Charles Edward Smith, who, as Hentoff later came to know him in the 1950s, "carried in his head so much jazz lore that it was like bumping into Homer at a bar."[9]

Smith's headpieces to each of the four sections of *Jazzmen* ("New Orleans," "Chicago," "New York," and "Hot Jazz Today") indeed sound like a tribal poet-singer declaiming a newfangled epic verse saturated with the rhythms and diction of ragtime and the blues. Smith commenced the lore cycle in "Callin' Our Children Home," a paean to an old New Orleans assumed to exist only in memory: "Don't look for the eagle on the Eagle Saloon. And don't look for Masonic Hall because it's a vacant lot. But listen hard some night, listen hard at the corner of Rampart and Perdido and you'll hear a whacky [sic] horn playing an uptown rag, way out and way off, filling the tune. That would be Kid Bolden, calling his children." In "Every Tub on Its Bottom," his evocation of 1920s Chicago, Smith breathed life into the legends connected with Bix Beiderbecke, the Austin High Gang, and Leon Rappolo ("how he leaned against a telephone pole, playing clarinet against the weird harmonies of the singing wires"). In "The World's Jazz Crazy," when Smith called out place names and images in a rolling cadence, readers could be forgiven for imagining a backing rhythm section and horn riffs:

> Drop a nickel in the slot and listen to the music of America. Jazz and the river. New Orleans to Natchez. St. Louis to Davenport. Tri-cities to Chicago. Rock Island to Roseland. Ragtime. Honky-tonk. Square set. Shag. Creole. Cajun. French quadrille. Buddy Bolden and Bix Beiderbecke. Slow blues. Deep Blues. Church Street Sobbin' Mamma Sweet Daddy. Aunt Hagar's Children. Had a nine pound hammer.
> Hold tight
> Hold tight
> The world's jazz crazy, Lawdy, so am I.[10]

Smith's was an American vernacular prose for *Jazzmen's* American story, an epic full of larger-than-life heroes and unforgettable places that cohered into a new national mythology. In locating the holy grail of jazz authenticity in New Orleans street parades, south-side Chicago saloons, and Harlem rent parties, Smith and his *Jazzmen* collaborators (Frederick Ramsey Jr., William Russell, E. Simms Campbell, Edward Nichols, Wilder Hobson, Otis Ferguson, Stephen Smith, and Roger Pryor Dodge) contributed to a new sense of the authentic American experience, an experience akin to those chronicled in 1930s urban proletarian literature and ethnographic journalism and pictured in one of the new Hollywood genres, the gangster film. To the American folkloric pantheon of Daniel Boone, Paul Bunyan, and John Henry were now added the gods and demigods of a new music—Buddy Bolden, Bunk Johnson, Joe "King" Oliver, Louis Armstrong, Leon Rappolo, Bessie Smith, Clara Smith, Bix Beiderbecke. No longer would the Wild West frontier stand alone as America's mythic place of adventure, not after *Jazzmen's* vivid etching of jazz's incubating sites—New Orleans's Storyville red-light district, Mississippi riverboats, Capone-controlled Chicago clubs, 52nd Street in New York—in all the glory of their racial and sexual taboo defiance.

Jazzmen featured intelligent musical analysis of lasting value, but the book's appeal beyond the hard-core jazz audience hinged on its qualities as an adventure story set in notably picturesque urban neighborhoods. Noting the "close correlation between political corruption and the development of hot jazz," William Russell argued that the jazz band was an urban institution that "flourished only in shady places of amusement which could support it, such as dance halls, houses of prostitution, gin mills, gambling joints, and other underworld spots."[11] Through Charles Edward Smith's anthropomorphic descriptions, the key cities in jazz's early development became characters in their own right: New Orleans was "a city with a hundred faces. The hard face for commerce and the soft face for making love"; Chicago "produced and was a big spender"; while New York "didn't spend. It bought and sold."[12] Readers of Nat Hentoff's generation—including the untold number of World War II servicemen who read the pocket Armed Services Edition— must have been stirred by *Jazzmen*'s evocations of a sporting life culture teeming with gamblers, pimps, prostitutes, card sharks, river roustabouts, and cutthroats. Amid its erudite discussions of polyphony, sonority, and glissandi, the book unveiled the rough-and-tumble, booze- and testosterone-soaked proving grounds of jazz's masculinist heroism. Buddy Bolden was "as immoderate in his appetite for women as for hard liquor and hot music." In his youth, Louis "the Roughneck from Rampart Street" Armstrong "used to swing some mean dukes." During Prohibition-era house party raids, Albert Ammons and Meade Lux Lewis hid on window ledges until the law finished its business, then climbed inside and "finished the unemptied jugs." The sports hero Babe Ruth comforted Bix Beiderbecke in his final days, because "Bix was a great ball fan, a great drinker, and a great guy."[13]

Perhaps because it all seemed too romantic and exciting to be true, co-editors Smith and Ramsey—then a young freelance writer, later an esteemed folklorist—took pains to underscore *Jazzmen*'s factuality. "One or another of the authors has interviewed every living jazz musician who could contribute factual material," announced their introduction, and in coming years both would publish articles in the music press vaunting their editorial rigor—fact-checking, personal on-site investigations, etc.—as a shining model of jazz research.[14] "The search for [jazz] data has been an arduous but interesting one," Smith and Ramsey described their tour of the key pilgrim stations, "taking us to the dives of Harlem, Chicago, and New Orleans, to the rice fields of Louisiana, to Storyville, the now legendary red-light district of New Orleans, to reform schools, even to the last stopping place of at least two jazz pioneers [Buddy Bolden and Freddie Keppard], a hospital for the insane." The book's aura of historical truth depended on its readers' faith in the memories of "forgotten and neglected" musicians who, like Bunk Johnson, "have had to forgo former glories, abandon music, drive a truck for $1.75 a day during the rice season, and starve the rest of the time."[15] Ramsey found Johnson working in a rice field in Iberia, Louisiana, and commenced a correspondence. In one epistolary passage used as the book's epigraph, Johnson enjoined the editors: "so you tell them that Bunk and King Bolden's Band was the first ones that started Jazz in the City or any place else. And now you are able to go now ahead with your book." Johnson's letters to Smith and Ramsey endowed *Jazzmen* with the status of jazz gospel among the traditionalists. One such, Ernest Borneman, described Johnson's voice as having "the dignity of an Old Testamentarian lament and the fierce authenticity of the Scottsboro story. It was the real thing."[16]

In 1943, Eugene Williams (then editor of *Jazz Information*), Rudi Blesh (then a San Francisco interior designer and art critic), William Russell (a seminal composer of modern percussion music who abandoned composition in the 1930s to focus on collecting recordings, instruments, and other memorabilia associated with traditional New Orleans jazz)[17] joined Ramsey in engineering Johnson's return to the bandstand. Outfitted by his patrons with a used trumpet and a new set of teeth, the hard-on-his-luck jazz veteran took to the stage and the recording studio in what was billed as an authentic representation of jazz's origins. Decca, Victor, and Blue Note recorded Johnson between 1943 and 1947. Russell and Charles Edward Smith also were centrally involved in various recording projects that brought Jelly Roll Morton back into the limelight in the late 1930s and early 1940s after the New Orleans pianist and composer had largely disappeared from public view. Morton—who was virtually absent from *Jazzmen*—would tell his own story with signature flair and colossal self-regard in a set of Library of Congress recordings made in 1938 with Alan Lomax.[18]

By using Bunk Johnson's voice—and not Morton's—as a kind of scriptural foundation, *Jazzmen* centered its narrative on the lineage of New Orleans trumpeters from Buddy Bolden to Freddie Keppard, Johnson, King Oliver, and finally Louis Armstrong. This enabled the book to canonize Armstrong as a product of the New Orleans tradition, to situate him among a group of elders, and in so doing to finesse a tricky ideological matter. For Louis Armstrong at this time was anything but "forgotten and neglected": he was a certified jazz star and Hollywood actor, a swing icon now playing in a style that was anathema to the purist code, a celebrity offering no resistance to the machinery of mass adulation. Even if it were true, as Ramsey's argument would have it, that Armstrong's Hot Five recording sessions in 1928 were "the inevitable reaction to a year of Harlem sophistication and Broadway artificiality," there was no denying Armstrong's willing embrace of his growing popularity.[19] Armstrong's fame and fortune was the stuff of rags-to-riches myth, a stock tale of individual heroism in the face of childhood hardship and deprivation. The challenge for *Jazzmen* was to embrace Armstrong's achievement while also honoring and keeping alive the legacy of his forebears. His genius, it had to be shown, had something to do with where he came from.

This was done by foregrounding the importance of Armstrong's apprenticeship with King Oliver, by suggesting specific stylistic affinities between Armstrong and his New Orleans forebears, and by arguing that Armstrong's stage persona was firmly rooted in New Orleans entertainment traditions. In Ramsey's essay on King Oliver and His Creole Jazz Band, Armstrong joins the band in Chicago as a "green-looking country boy" with a big sound but as yet undeveloped feel for the nuances of group playing. Oliver is the reigning trumpet king, having won his crown in a galvanizing display of blues blowing one night on a street outside Lala's Cabaret. But that was in the flush of his youth and now in Chicago he's "a band man, and a band man only" looking past his own glory. He recognizes Armstrong's huge gifts and nurtures his talent, providing especially important lessons in how to use melodic variation to achieve "intensity of expression." In 1924, Oliver humbly passes Armstrong the torch: "At 24, Louis could put the freshness and vigor of youth into his playing. Joe Oliver had been 24 in 1909. He realized this, and as there was no resentment in his nature, he was proud of his second cornetist."[20]

Jazzmen coupled this touching story of musical fathering with William Russell's discussion of Bunk Johnson's earlier influence on Armstrong during the youngster's barrel-housing days after leaving the Waif's Home at age fourteen. From his position on the "second-line" behind Johnson's Eagle Band, Armstrong sees how "Bunk made them cry on funeral marches with his beautiful, vibrant tone and the feeling he put into dirges." This feeling seeps into Armstrong's playing, feeding the "bigness and warmth of spirit" that come to mark the mature Armstrong's greatness. Bunk Johnson was also, Russell suggested, the source of Armstrong's unexcelled command of swing rhythm. "A lesson of inestimable importance which Louis absorbed more than anyone else," Russell wrote, "was the way Bunk had of hesitating, always a little behind the beat, a lazy yet most dynamic way of playing which is at the core of all hot jazz." Finally, in an effort to rebuff critics embarrassed by the hugely popular "Satchelmouth" stage mannerisms—the jive routines, facial contortions, and clowning—Russell argued that the New Orleans environment that produced Louis Armstrong was one in which "'good time' and 'to give satisfaction' were mottos," and "where 'everything goes' and 'pleasure is the watchword' set the tone of an evening."[21] The source of Armstrong's greatness as an artist, Russell implied, was his generosity of spirit as an entertainer.

This spotlighting of Armstrong's roots in the dual New Orleans traditions of funeral dirges and good-time dances and carnivals fed *Jazzmen*'s larger case for the populist authenticity of early jazz before an alleged decline into New York- and Hollywood-swathed "sophistication" and "artificiality." While the book didn't stage nearly as passionate or systematic a lamentation of jazz decadence in the age of the large swing orchestra as would Rudi Blesh in *Shining Trumpets*, its essays were peppered with anti–big band nuggets that had to have warmed the cockles of revivalist hearts. Ramsey, for instance, explained Bunk Johnson's decision to remain anonymously in the Deep South where he could "drive the blues down" as an understandable reluctance to avoid an orchestra business that "was becoming more and more 'sweet' as the axis of influence on popular taste was shifted to Hollywood." Ramsey celebrated the polyphonic improvisation of King Oliver's Creole Jazz Band as "almost a lost art, buried in the large dance orchestras of technically proficient readers who cling desperately to a written score."[22] Wilder Hobson's essay, "New York Turns On the Heat," carefully distinguished between the "warm spontaneity" of Fletcher Henderson's big band, which was to be embraced, and the "fetish with regard to precision" of most other swing orchestras, which was to be scorned. Duke Ellington was a tricky case for Hobson because of powerful critical voices—John Hammond and Roger Pryor Dodge, among others—claiming that the band had "lost the genuineness which characterized it in the late twenties" and had "become overly suave, elaborate, and virtuoso." Hobson deftly maneuvered out of the authenticity trap, however, arguing that Ellington was exceptional in maintaining fidelity to his folk sources *through* the instrument of the orchestra. "Jazz musicians are bound to be more and more experimental *orchestrally*," Hobson wrote, "and it is probably natural that some one organization should most vividly represent *all* the elements of this process in which a folk-music is gradually moving into general musical currents." Ellington and Ellington alone, Hobson suggested, had figured out how to use written scores and a large orchestra format in the service of jazz's "genuine" sources rather than in a vain effort to rise above them.[23]

Where this left the future of jazz was unclear. Ellington could not be the entirety of that future, and if the choice was between a thorough ascendancy of New York-centered symphonic swing and a revival of the New Orleans and Chicago small-band style—as *Jazzmen* implicitly suggested—the book came down emphatically in favor of the latter. Running throughout *Jazzmen*, in fact, was an assumption that New York, rather than being conducive to the organic creation of jazz, was much more a finishing school and a media/business platform for the music's national distribution. This was made explicit in Frederick Ramsey Jr.'s suggestion that Louis Armstrong's Hot Five recordings—made in the Okeh studios in Chicago in 1925—were "the inevitable reaction to a year of Harlem sophistication and Broadway artificiality." After his stint in the New York-based Fletcher Henderson orchestra in 1924, Ramsey suggested, Armstrong "just had to 'stretch-out,' and that meant with a five-piece barrel-house bunch." Ironically, given the canonical jazz masterwork status that the Hot Five and later Hot Seven records had already achieved by the late 1930s, Ramsey portrayed the recording dates as "never very serious affairs." Ramsey attributed the greatness of the records—"Potato Head Blues," "Muskrat Ramble," "Heebie Jeebies," "Hotter than That," "West End Blues," "Struttin' Some Barbecue," and the others—to the "height of informality" that obtained among Armstrong and fellow New

Orleans musicians Johnny Dodds, Kid Ory, Johnny St. Cyr, and the others, a casual bonhomie assumed not to be possible in the pressure-cooker conditions of New York show business.[24]

Otis Ferguson offered a more complex argument about New York's significance. While "there simply is no New York style," he asserted, the 1920s centralization of recording and radio studios, booking agencies, and publishing companies in the city had turned New York into a "microphone to the nation," making it necessary for promising musicians around the country to migrate there if they were to parlay their talents into lasting professional success. Ferguson didn't think this was a bad thing in and of itself, which seemed to put him at odds with those who harbored nostalgia for a romanticized jazz golden age when musicians didn't answer to booking agents, producers, and recording engineers. "If you forget what you've read and go back to some of the actual performances of the Heroic Days," Ferguson quipped, "you'll have to admit that the general background of clanging banjos and pumping pianos often wouldn't swing on a rope." No fan of symphonic jazz, Ferguson instead was making a case for small-group swing, a style he thought didn't achieve its classic form until cutting-edge recording and radio technologies helped bring about a streamlined "easy-ride quality that had been in the background all along, in the blues, in work songs, and the slower instrumental passages with feeling."

Here was an argument that could be seen as foreshadowing the jazz evolutionary narrative that Barry Ulanov, Leonard Feather, and others would construct in the years after World War II. (Ferguson died in the war, depriving jazz criticism of one of its most graceful stylists.)[25] But unlike these critics—and notwithstanding his acute insights into the relationship between jazz performance and modern technology—Ferguson still managed to evince a serious ambivalence about jazz's "progress" in the 1930s, an attitude that kept him in sync with *Jazzmen's* general line of argument. This ambivalence was of a piece with the widespread anti-commercialism we've already seen as being central to jazz discourse. In Ferguson's account, Red Nichols and his Five Pennies band—the ostensible focus of his essay—achieved a better sound (a "general ensemble feeling of drive") only after its immersion in New York's highly competitive environment. But no sooner did success come the band's way than Nichols "took the easy-money way," coasting on the band's reputation and dulling its creative edge.[26]

Ferguson's cautionary parable resonated with other moments in *Jazzmen* when New York figured as jazz's temptress, Faustian bargain, and site of tragedy. Edward J. Nichols, for example, attributed Bix Beiderbecke's descent into alcoholism to the increasingly commercial direction of Paul Whiteman's orchestra. The fatal blow came when the trumpeter and his bandmates were sent into a New York studio to record advertising jingles for a Lucky Strike-sponsored radio program. "Never a good reader, buried in the complicated scores demanded of the band, Bix began to lose his grip," Nichols lamented.[27] In a pathos-tinged Charles Edward Smith vignette, trombonist Jack Teagarden holes up in a Manhattan apartment hotel, musically bereft save for an occasional trip uptown to Harlem to hear Bessie Smith or sit in with Louis Armstrong, abandoned to his fellow down-and-out white musicians and their memories of better times in Chicago and New Orleans. It was then, pressed up against the wall of despair, that Teagarden found the theme for his twelve-bar blues, "Makin' Friends":

> I'd rather drink muddy water, Lord, sleep in a hollow log,
> I'd rather drink muddy water, Lord, sleep in a hollow log,
> Than to be up here in New York, treated like a dirty dog.[28]

Jazzmen was replete with similar examples of powerful cross-racial cultural exchanges and affinities, even as in its most politically progressive moments it reckoned honestly with the jazz world's own racism. Charles Edward Smith took the lead. He noted that black/white interaction in 1920s Chicago jazz could only take place in black neighborhood speakeasies and in the private homes of black musicians because the local chapter of the American Federation of Musicians remained segregated. Further, while Chicago jazz "was obviously a fusion of Negro and white influences, depending for its most significant qualities on the former, the musicians themselves were not always free of prejudice."[29] Smith's essay "White New Orleans" took aim at the "do-or-die 'Dixielanders' who claim that jazz came from the whites or the later 'Original Dixieland Jazz Band.'" The *real* original Dixieland band for Smith was not the Sicilian-dominated outfit led by Nick La Rocca, which had achieved fame in 1917 with its ballyhooed appearance at New York's Reisenweber's restaurant and its fast-selling Victor recordings of "Tiger Rag" and other New Orleans favorites, and which had regrouped in the late 1930s to make its claim as the inventors of jazz. Smith's true Dixieland originator was the unrecorded Jack Laine's Ragtime Band, which he credited with expanding white New Orleans dance culture, circa 1910, from tried-and-true quadrilles and polkas to "white imitations of Negro shags and trots." The secret to the Laine band's uptown black influence, Smith disclosed, was that it was in fact a racially mixed band: clarinetist Achille Baquet and trombonist Dave Perkins were "two light-skinned, blue-eyed Negroes" who were passing for white. Smith dated the end of the first period of Dixieland music to the moment when the white local took away Perkins's union card after he married a black woman.

Jim Crow was ever present, but it couldn't, in Smith's view, disguise the interracial, transcultural, class-defying nature of New Orleans jazz. This was not just a matter of a second-generation Sicilian like Leon Rappolo turning away from his father's concert training and, with other members of the white New Orleans Rhythm Kings, freshening their approach "with the discoveries of Negro improvisers" like King Oliver. It was also the way black and Creole musicians assimilated French opera, English and Continental folk songs, and a Caribbean Latin musical tradition that was already a polyglot mixture of Spanish, African, and Native American strains. "To ignore these influences, and the backgrounds from which they sprang" Smith wrote, "is to fail to grasp the significance of the music [New Orleans jazz] itself."[30]

Crucial to *Jazzmen's* account of cultural miscegenation was its brief but keen attention to the history and legacy of slavery. This was provided by the book's lone black contributor, the writer, cartoonist, and illustrator E. Simms Campbell, who discussed the blues as a product of slaves' desire for freedom. Campbell was deeply eloquent in his description of the blues: "To me they are filled with the deepest emotions of a race. They are songs of sorrow charged with satire, with that potent quality of ironic verse clothed in the raiment of the buffoon. They were more than releases, temporary releases, from servitude. The blues were the gateway to freedom for all American Negroes." Campbell's essay might have been exempt from Sidney Finkelstein's criticism that *Jazzmen* expressed "too poetic a nostalgia . . . about the life of the Negro people in the South." Yet Campbell was just as keen as several other of the book's contributors to stress the interracial dynamics at the heart of black music. Campbell explained the origin of the blues as an ironic consequence of blacks' negotiation of *both* white cruelty and white empathy: "One might as well be realistic about slavery. The South was as cruel as any Caesar to its slaves and many slaves were as vindictive as any Richelieu to their masters, but both sides have profited. Without pain and suffering there would have been no blues, and without an understanding white America there would have been no expression for them." This formulation defined the blues as an expressive form both black-centered *and* interracial, a form that both represented and spoke to a discrete black audience *and* that always carried within it a recognition of the white shadow over black America, and of the inevitability of black music's cross-racial commerce.[31]

"The Chant Rising from African Plains"

Utterly absent from *Jazzmen* was any serious engagement with Africa and African culture as root sources of blues and jazz. This opened up a space for the next major book-length work of jazz history, Rudi Blesh's *Shining Trumpets* (1946). The book evolved out of a series of lectures Blesh delivered at the San Francisco Museum of Art in the spring of 1943. Bunk Johnson appeared at the last lecture as a guest performer. That same season, Blesh—who at the time was writing a freelance jazz column for the *San Francisco Chronicle*—helped produce a concert at San Francisco's Geary Theater featuring Johnson, trumpeter Thomas "Mutt" Carey, trombonist Edward "Kid" Ory, and other noted New Orleans players. This major event in the revivalist movement was recorded by the Office of War Information and broadcast by short wave to American soldiers around the globe. Blesh moved to New York in 1944 and became jazz critic for the *New York Herald Tribune*. In 1946, Blesh, Harriet Janis, and Eugene Grossman established the Circle label, which set out to document continuities between African music, blues, and jazz and became best known for its "rediscovery" of blues singer Bertha "Chippie" Hill, New Orleans clarinetist Albert Nicholas, barrelhouse piano players Montana Taylor and Dan Burley, and several singers of the spirituals. Circle also issued on a series of 78-rpm discs the sessions Jelly Roll Morton recorded for the Library of Congress in 1938. Blesh conceived of his project as not just a revival but a revitalization, an effort both to search out and rescue from obscurity the great talents of the past and to "discover and encourage young players of promise."[32]

Blesh praised *Jazzmen* as the first book to offer "an authentic description of [jazz]'s New Orleans background" and as "a strong force in stimulating the jazz awakening," but disapproved of those sections—such as William Russell's enthusiasm for Louis Armstrong's showmanship and Wilder Hobson's espousal of Duke Ellington's development in the 1930s—that attempted "to reconcile the irreconcilable natures of jazz and swing." Blesh defined a jazz canon narrower and more peremptory than anything even John Hammond had dared to imagine: "To this day, with rare exceptions," Blesh asserted, "only New Orleans Negroes can play real jazz." Only New Orleans, with its "tumultuous echoes of dancing, shouting, and chanting in . . . Congo Square," retained a sufficiently palpable memory of Africa to ensure the music's purity in the face of modernity and commercialization. Real jazz, or the "hot concept," was a collectively improvised music employing "Negroid" qualities of rhythm (syncopation, polyrhythm, and what Blesh called "innerrhythm"), melodic structure (polyphony and heterophony, or a counterpoint of melodic variations), timbre (vocalized instrumental sounds tending toward growl or "dirty" tonalities), intonation (wide use of vibrato, glissandi, and other variations of pitch uncommon in European music), and tempo (moderate, to allow for clearly articulated part playing). Real jazz was a small-group music in which the trumpet or cornet played the melodic lead, the clarinet fell in with "liquid and piquantly sweet" antiphonal lines be-hind the lead phrases, and a trombone filled in the harmony with "pun-gent, rhythmically, expressive phrases" and propulsive glissandi. Real jazz was a collective music in which ensemble polyphony—the interweaving of melodic lines—was much more important than the improvised solo.[33]

Blesh's highly exacting schema of jazz authenticity attached itself to a rigorously precise narrative of historical decline. In a postscript written for the second edition of *Shining Trumpets* in 1958, Blesh corrected those who had come to refer to him as the man who wanted to take jazz back to 1928. "The date is not early enough," he complained. "I wanted to take it back to 1926, when it had reached its highest point and then stopped." In 1926, Jelly Roll Morton—"beyond doubt the most creative figure in jazz"—cut a series of records for Victor with a group that included Omer Simeon on clarinet, Kid Ory on trombone, and Johnny St. Cyr on guitar and banjo; in writing about one those records, "The Chant," Blesh seemed overcome by delirium: "Here is all that New Orleans polyphony means, much of what it can mean, pointed to swiftly by fingers that flash on clarinet and piano keys, on cornet valves! The sheer creative outpouring of communal song, like the chant rising from African plains, from Congo Square or from the sweltering, sunny cotton fields!" Thereafter, in Blesh's account, Morton fell victim to "the forces of money," as RCA gobbled up Victor and forced the great pianist to record "banal sentimental tunes." By 1926, Louis Armstrong had already cut the Blue Five records with Clarence Williams and the Hot Five records that Blesh deemed masterworks by virtue of their adherence to the collective polyphony ideal. By 1928, according to Blesh's declension narrative, Armstrong was flirting with apostasy by allowing pianist Earl "Fatha" Hines's non-blues, "sentimental" harmonies to infect "West End Blues," and, in using Don Redman on saxophone, breaking the rules of authentic jazz instrumentation. By 1930, in what Blesh construed as jazz's great tragedy, Armstrong had abandoned the New Orleans collective style by choosing to showcase his own individual virtuosity in the corrupt realm of commercial big-band swing.[34]

This emphasis on "the virtuosity of the group" over and against the in-dividual voice hinted at a vaguely left-wing perspective that Blesh never articulated explicitly, but that was readily identifiable as part of a Marxist discourse that circulated through the revivalist camp. The revivalists em-braced New Orleans jazz as an authentic folk expression of the U.S. prole-tariat, while denouncing swing as the homogenized cultural product of the U.S. bourgeois culture industry. As Bernard Gendron has pointed out, there was something disingenuous in the revivalists' use of the folk category for New Orleans jazz, a music that was recorded by commercial firms, played in nightclubs, publicized in newspapers and magazines, and—in the revivalists' own circle—consumed by a middle-class elite.[35] Certainly the market for traditional jazz was not nearly as large as the one swing developed in the 1930s and early 1940s, but it was a market all the same, occupying its own niche of the culture industry. Nevertheless, Blesh griped about a "commercial front" of magazines, record companies, radio and movie executives, and booking agencies engaged in a conspiracy against traditional jazz. At his most paranoid, Blesh characterized swing as a form of demagogic "mass autohypnosis."[36]

Blesh constructed an image of swing that figured the sound of the music, its channels of production and distribution, and its audience as a huge, ominous, fascistic machine. The big band was a "highly organized form of instrumental noise," a wall of "screaming brass and bleating reed riffs" and "drum blows." The riff band style—the conversation between brasses and reeds through extensive repetition of short rhythmic melodic phrases—was a purely mechanical, formulaic technique that smothered any opportunity for spontaneity among the musicians and instigated an "anarchic, orgiastic, dangerous excitement" in the audience. The very size of the swing big band made it incapable of handling complex rhythmic interplay: "A big sixteen-piece band cannot play—nor arrangements provide for—rhythms which are anything but simple compared with the complex polyrhythms of five men improvising freely." Written arrangements were ineffective: "No one has been able as yet to write the sort of free counterpoint which small bands improvise nor arrange for even the most gifted section to play it." Worse, written arrangements—along with instrumental training, precise intonation, clean articulation, and group polish—reified European standards at the expense of African cultural practices that Blesh argued were the primordial source of jazz.[37]

"African music is the key that unlocks the secrets of jazz," Blesh asserted. *Shining Trumpets* was the first book of jazz history informed by modern anthropological and ethnomusicological scholarship on Africa and the African diaspora, drawing heavily—though selectively—on Melville J. Herskovits's *The Myth of the Negro Past* (1941) and Richard Waterman's work on African rhythm to trace a transatlantic black music continuum. Blesh evinced a romantic, almost cosmic enthusiasm for Africa and African survivals that often strained his claims to academically sanctioned scientific discourse. We can attribute to Blesh's active imagination, and not just to the research files he consulted in Herskovits's office in the anthropology department at Northwestern University, this description of a southern black church service: "It is if these people were lifted bodily from a poor country church in Louisiana and deposited on an African plain or in an African forest, where long ago and in just this way, their ancestors had danced and chanted, not to Jesus, but to Ogun or to Shango." Equally fevered was Blesh's description of a Baby Dodds drum solo, whose polyrhythmic virtuosity he attributed to an unconscious, trance-like state of possession that supposedly gave the New Orleans drummer a direct line to the Dark Continent. Or, of the Golden Gate gospel quartet backing Leadbelly: "These singers are literally *sent* into an unconscious projection of their racial music which forms anew from a growing excitement that verges on trance," while Lead Belly was like an African tribal priest "using his powers in sanctioned ritual, dealing openly and directly with dark magic."[38]

Fully half of *Shining Trumpets* focused on jazz's prehistory, a black music lineage including West African choral singing and drumming; slave spirituals, work songs, ballads, and children's songs; and—especially—the blues. Recognizing that in early jazz "the Western *ingredients* are in a higher proportion than in earlier Afro-American music" (i.e., white brass band music and the various strains of French, Italian, Spanish, and Spanish-American music heard in New Orleans), Blesh centered his argument for jazz's African provenance on black music-making *methods* rooted in ancestral cultural practices. Perceived in the late 1940s as novel and highly speculative, the best of Blesh's analysis appears now as consistent with—if not a foundation for—some of the key conceptual developments in late twentieth-century black music scholarship. Blesh described African music's fundamentally communal nature, its central role in religious and social rituals. He detailed the primacy and complexity of rhythm and dance-centered aesthetics; the general percussive orientation to sound; the emphasis on improvisation, timbral variety, and call-and-response dynamics; the relative de-emphasis on harmony and fixed structure.[39]

"Western music is one of structure; African, one of free, continuous, creative energy," wrote Blesh in an acute formulation that foreshadowed Amiri Baraka's suggestion, seventeen years later in *Blues People* (1963), of a distinction between a Western focus on the *artifact* and an African focus on *expression*. Whereas Western music inclines toward an "architectural balance and satisfying structural completeness" based on a juxtaposition of forms (e.g., distinctive melodies, or the same melody expressed in a variety of keys or harmonizations), Blesh argued, African music favors a continuous flow of melodic and/or rhythmic voices arrayed in a pattern of repetition. This focus on cyclical, fluid, open-ended music making—a process of layering sonic textures and rhythms to express the "complete and exhaustive exposition of a particular mood"—bears marked resemblance to James Snead's influential concept of "repetition as a figure of black culture." Blesh described African-derived blues and jazz as "embodied in a ceaseless repetition like the human pulse." As elementally natural and infinite as the weather, they "neither have nor require formal beginning and end."[40]

Blesh anticipated both Baraka and Albert Murray (in his 1976 *Stomping the Blues*) in underscoring the fundamental vocal quality of blues and jazz instruments, a quality derived from the rich tonal variations in African speech and drumming. "Horns in jazz function *both as voices and as drums*," he wrote (italics in original). These were not trained artistic voices reaching for the conventionally beautiful but vernacular voices tuned to the elemental, the local, the everyday. "Listen to blues and real jazz not for the familiar harmonized music," Blesh wrote, "but for a conversation of people, all talking about the same thing, with statements and answers, questions, comments, exclamations, interjections, even asides, humorous or tragic, but all pertinent and to the point." To elaborate on this concept of blues and jazz as an extension of black vernacular speech, Blesh drew on studies of African American folklore by Herskovits, Alan Lomax, Dorothy Scarborough, Lydia Parrish, John H. Cox, and Newman White. He suggested that blacks tend to "use music as language and to employ speech in a circuitous and double-edged way." Black speech "is indirect and implicative as well as direct; its reference is many-faceted; it is universal as well as specific and, in these dualities, it is essentially poetic." Blesh traced this linguistic skill both to "the fertile and unflagging creativeness of the African" and, in the U.S. context, to the slavery experience, when concealment and double-voicing first used as strategic forms of communication for survival developed into their own vernacular art forms.[41]

Blesh was on less controversial ground in relating jazz and blues to traditions of black oral culture shaped by historical and political circumstances than he was in his assertions of Africans' racially innate rhythmic superiority, a biological-determinist position he knew to be at odds with post-Boasian anthropology. Why was it, Blesh asked, that white jazz musicians push the beat, while black musicians use the beat to pull the music along—the first approach creating a sense of hectic excitement, the second a sense of ease, assurance, and "natural ebullience." Why was it that Gene Krupa's drumming and Fred Astaire's tap dancing, despite their inspiriting black influences, seemed to be a "learned thing falling into repeated patterns, lacking to a marked degree the relaxation, the unpredictable nuance, and the expressive, improvisational inspiration of the Negro"? Blesh rejected current scientific theory that discounted racially inherited instincts and abilities. Environmental factors and cultural conditioning couldn't explain to Blesh why "in countless Negro churches, I have seen mere infants clap their hands or stand in pews dancing in rhythms that are simple but amazingly sharp and elastic." The simple answer for Blesh was that "Negroid rhythmic skill" was an innate "racial attribute."[42]

From a belief in inbred racial characteristics, it is a short distance to a belief in racial purity—with an allied faith in the possibility of a pure racial art—and from there to an anxiety about racial degeneration. This concern about "racial dilution" undergirded *Shining Trumpet's* narrative of decline, a cultural jeremiad that later would find an echo in Baraka's *Blues People*. Fueling the dilution and deracination of "unspoiled Negro art," according to Blesh, was African American weakness: It was the black man's "hyper-sensitivity to criticism," and "his pathetic and ill-founded desire to please the white" that led certain musicians to think they needed to "improve and refine" jazz. This misguided desire "led to a painful and superficial sophistication . . . to a deluge of the mere noise called swing, to a dozen forms of hybrid jazz, and to a spate of symphonized jazz and pseudo-jazz master-works." Echoing John Hammond, Blesh condemned Duke Ellington's suites and concert works as the worst travesty of "Europeanized Negro music." Ellington's "ridiculous and pretentious hybridizing," Blesh asserted, had deprived jazz of its "vestiges of hotness and African accent to become a variety of music thoroughly and solely in the western tradition."[43]

Blesh's tragic outlook embraced both racial and gender dimensions: jazz's loss of African purity was also its loss of masculine authority, its capitulation to the romantic and the sentimental. Real jazz, Blesh suggested, "is the lusty music of Negro men," a music that "externalizes the vitality and power of male procreativeness." This was not an acclamation of the "riotous living" in Storyville and other of early jazz's vice-district locales; *Shining Trumpets* did not follow *Jazzmen* in mythologizing jazz's relationship to bordellos, saloons, and a general spirit of dissipation. Blesh was advocating a more austere, astringent form of virility. Real jazz, he said, "is a lean and athletic music, unobsessed with romantic or commercial love. It shuns sentimentality and the languors of romantic desire. It demands monastic and arduous devotion from its practitioners, and when it deals with sex, does so frankly, without shame or furtiveness." Following Hammond, Roger Pryor Dodge, and other proponents of hot jazz purism, Blesh connected sentimentality and romance with "sweetness," a cloying, feminine quality negatively associated with salon and drawing-room music. Ellington had good company in the effete parlor culture Blesh equated with all jazz that didn't hew to his platonic masculinist ideal: trumpeters who had "assumed the languishing tones of the crooner"; "suave" and "devitalized" trombonists; clarinetists who couldn't match the "flashing, elastic whip-like quality" of Johnny Dodds's phrasing and instead were imitating the "drooping, decorative" phrasing of Artie Shaw and Benny Goodman; pianists Art Tatum and Teddy Wilson, purveyors of a "highly decadent . . . overornamented, decorative" pastiche of Delius and Debussy.[44]

Against Primitivism

In retrospect, the historical importance of *Shining Trumpets* rests less on the merits of its arguments than on its effects as a provocation, on the critical reactions generated by its bull-headed certitude, which themselves became the starting point for new arguments about jazz's past and future. Responses to the book left Blesh's masculinism unexamined, focusing instead on his argument for jazz as an African survival; his general theories of race and culture; and his approach to the question of historical change. The next two book-length works of jazz history published in the United States, Sidney Finkelstein's *Jazz: A People's Music* (1948) and Barry Ulanov's *A History of Jazz in America* (1952), explicitly defined their approaches as correctives to Blesh's Africanism and New Orleans absolutism, which they saw as backward-looking and racially condescending.

Finkelstein was a Marxist freelance critic of music, literature, and the arts who became active in the Communist Party U.S.A. (CPUSA) and served as one of the party's leading cultural theoreticians. The direction of his Marxism was diametrically opposite that of the jazz revivalists: deeply committed to the Western canon, he denounced attacks on "civilized" music as a misunderstanding of the populist foundation of all great art, and as its own philistine effort to circumscribe jazz's creative possibilities. Ulanov was a mainstream liberal, a professor of the interdisciplinary humanities, and—in his moonlighting gig as co-editor of *Metronome*—a well-known champion of modern jazz. His sprawling narrative history offered a compendium of jazz-related names, dates, and events whose very encyclopedic inclusivity—a chapter on singers, for instance, welcomed Frank Sinatra and June Christy into the jazz family—implicitly challenged narrow conceptions of jazz authenticity.

Finkelstein and Ulanov rejected Blesh's African survival thesis, taking special umbrage at his notion of an unconscious trance-state as the key to early jazz's ecstatic "hot" quality. Ulanov pooh-poohed jazz's African past as nothing more than a distant echo, one of many strands in the music's "elaborate compound of many folk strains." While praising Melville Herskovits for illuminating "the stubborn strength and beautiful variety of African culture," Ulanov worried that the Northwestern anthropologist's interpreters, with their "taste for and appreciation of the *recherche*," were unfortunately apt to confirm "the average man's impression of the Negro as a jungle-formed primitive whose basic expression is inevitably savage." Ulanov had no objection to the concept of primitive culture *per se* (he tended to use the term "primitive" as a synonym for "folk"), just with the idea that Africa alone was the source of jazz's basic practices. Culling a passage from André Gide's *Travels in the Congo* as an example of the Western exoticized gaze on Africa—Gide described women dancing to the beat of a tom-tom, using adjectives like "frenzied," "demoniac," and "lunatic"—Ulanov argued that "Africans have no monopoly on religious ecstasy or secular joy manifested rhythmically," citing the Italian tarantella, Spanish flamenco, Hungarian czardas, and Russian peasant and Cossack dances as examples of "frenzied folk dancing in Western culture." Ulanov likewise denounced as "unlettered nonsense" the suggestion by Blesh and other proponents of the jazz-as-African-survival paradigm that jazz melody and tonality—the common use of flatted thirds and sevenths (the so-called "blue notes"), pitch alterations, and glissandi—derived from conceptions outside of the Western diatonic tradition. "The basic chordal and melodic and rhythmic structure of the blues and of the jazz that has developed out of the blues is firmly within the orbit of Western folk music," he asserted, adding: "There is more of the sound of jazz in Middle-European gypsy fiddling than there is in a corps of African drummers."[45]

Ulanov attracted his own critics on the issue of African influence. John L. Fell accused Ulanov of a knee-jerk reaction against all anthropological investigation of African culture and of discounting the likelihood of *some* African influence on jazz melody, if not a full and unchanged survival. "The general proposition is that vestiges of African scale are evidenced only as they affect our European diatonic structure in performance," Fell suggested. "No one says that Jazz has African scales, pentatonic or otherwise." Orrin Keepnews lodged a similar criticism in a *Record Changer* review: "Since I know of no one who seriously advances any such total claim [of jazz's Africanism]—although I know of several who have worked to investigate and document the undeniable *partial* link between Africa and American jazz—I can only assume that Ulanov has built up this straw-man of an argument just to be able to knock it down." Keepnews and Charles Edward Smith—in a later *Record Changer* essay—found it odd that Ulanov would target Blesh's Afrophilism but neglect to directly engage *Jazzmen's* arguments for early jazz's inception as a U.S. urban, black-pioneered, multiracial art form.[46]

Though Finkelstein had avoided similar criticism by offering a more measured consideration of African influence than Ulanov's, his approach to the question was finally more devastating to those—especially Blesh—who saw Africa through the primitivist lens and defined jazz through images of racial mystique. "Jazz is not a 'primitive' music," Finkelstein argued, for the simple reason that "people are not 'primitive.'" Finkelstein was not a cultural relativist—he did not believe, with leading anthropologists of his time, in the equality of all cultures—but rather a Europhilic dialectical pragmatist who believed in "progress in human life, progress in respect to greater knowledge of the world, greater mastery over nature, greater potentialities of production and of human beings living better and more freely." Jazz, with its constant exploration, absorption, and mastery of new materials, its pragmatic openness to experience, was a quest for a better, creatively richer, freer life. Those who, in the name of "the noble simplicity of the 'primitive,'" would limit the scope of jazz's protean impulses, its urge to transform itself in response to changes in the world around it, were guilty of a kind of colonial exploitation. "If all cultures are equally good for themselves, why change?" Finkelstein asked rhetorically. Western bourgeois proponents of primitivism "show no rush to put on loincloths," but are "content to 'admire' other cultures from a comfortable perspective." Like "those who use colonial peoples for the most backbreaking labor at meager pay," these primitivists "find the preservation of old myths, customs, [and] ways of life . . . most useful to them." The most pernicious of these "old myths" for Finkelstein was the concept of race itself. "'Race,'" he wrote, "is an unscientific and meaningless term. The Negro people of America, in ancestry and physiology, are not a race. There is no special and limited 'music' of the Negro people. They have a right to know and use all music, making it their own, as they took over whatever music they needed in the past."[47]

In Finkelstein's pragmatist construction, the question of jazz's origins shifted from the idea of a primordial location and time that forever determined the character of the music to the idea of a continual process of reinvention. Jazz was constantly being re-originated "by men who regard a musical instrument as an extension of their hand, voice, and mind, [and] who regard music as a language with which they speak to their fellow human beings." In this respect jazz was kin to all "people's music," including the falsely labeled "classical" music of Bach, Handel, Purcell, Mozart, and Verdi. Before the music of these Europeans became canonized under the banner of elite fine art, these composers, like Jelly Roll Morton and Duke Ellington, approached music as a social art, as something that "should be made for people to use"—hence their delight "when their music was taken up and sung or danced to by people in the streets."

In conceptualizing Western music in terms of its social function, Finkelstein did not mean to diminish the role of the individual. Quite the contrary: like Ulanov, Finkelstein saw African music as a music of the group, Western music (even the folk music of the European peasant and working classes) as a music of interplay between the individual and the group. For instance, Finkelstein drew a sharp distinction between African drumming and jazz drumming. "For all of its intricacy of two or three rhythms at once," he wrote, African drumming "has a single-minded, compelling beat, aimed at fusing all listeners into one mind and one movement." In this respect African drumming, with its "hypnotic rhythm," was much closer in spirit to the military march than to jazz percussion. "Jazz drumming is much more modern, 'human' in the sense of never letting us forget that this is a new age in which the group is made up of more individual, thinking minds." In an assertion that surely failed to recognize the heterogeneity of African music, Finkelstein claimed that African music simply lacked the "surprise, the kidding, the serious-comic spirit" of jazz, as evidenced for him in the "elastic, human, and joyous character" of a New Orleans jazz march like "High Society."[48]

Working from distinct ideological positions, Finkelstein's and Ulanov's books together framed jazz history on radically different terms than did Blesh and the revivalists. The revivalists identified an ideal—an Aristotelian perfect form—which jazz had already discovered and which all subsequent jazz was obliged to recognize and reproduce. Finkelstein and Ulanov, in contrast, believed that change *itself* was one of jazz's essential properties and that the music had yet to reach its full potential. "Instead of seeing that jazz and American folk music have been continually changing," Finkelstein said, "to Blesh there was no change of importance up to the 1920s, and then a vast change which causes him to call all new jazz produced since, no matter how earnest its efforts to express new feelings and develop new techniques, a 'commercial conspiracy.'" Finkelstein believed that Blesh's Africanist paradigm locked him into a static view of jazz that failed to recognize how deeply the music was inscribed in the African American struggle for freedom and democracy. Jazz, Finkelstein argued, was "born not out of Africa but out of [African Americans'] struggles against slavery, and out of the part they took in every struggle for the progress of democracy from the War of Independence onward." Because of the enduring intensity of black resistance to slavery, exploitation, lynching, and disenfranchisement, and—crucially—because of its creators' location in urban environments where they absorbed a panoply of cultural influences, jazz was defined by "a tremendously rapid tempo of change" that set it apart from other folk cultures. Because African Americans *had* to change their social circumstances if they were to achieve their full humanity, their cultural expressions—especially music—contained an intrinsic urge to innovation. "Experiment and change," Finkelstein asserted, "are in the essence of jazz."[49]

Ulanov's jazz evolutionary narrative was less squarely embedded in the psychology and social and political history of black liberation. His was a more general optimistic liberal belief in cultural progress: for all of its seeming chaos and disorder, jazz was "always moving ahead in what for art is almost a straight line."[50] Exactly where jazz was headed, why it kept moving forward, what its final destination was, and how we would know it had arrived there were questions Ulanov did not engage in a systematic manner. But he left little doubt about his fundamental vanguardist sensibility, his belief in jazz's need for constant innovation. "The man who plays jazz is faced with several cruel alternatives," Ulanov wrote.

> He cannot in the future, unless he is intellectually slothful and emotionally spent, return to the kindergarten constructions of his New Orleans forebears, though he must pay his respects to them for yeoman service in building a craft with the crude implements at their disposal. If he is at all serious, he knows that the bop school, which first surged so brilliantly through the jungle of jazz weed, later began to grow its own branch of weed—heavy, clumsy, too often aromatic of the worst of weeds, and rotten at the roots. Rejecting these choices, the creative jazzman is left at the mercy of his own inspiration, his own groping after profundity, his solo intuition, and the rich tension he may feel when playing in a group.[51]

The revivalists were incensed—often apoplectically so—by the suggestion that New Orleans early jazz was important only as a precursor to later jazz, as they were by Ulanov's assertion that "until some of the later Ellington . . . Charlie Parker and Lennie Tristano, there was little if anything in jazz that could be called really profound."[52] Part of the problem was that Ulanov was quite slippery in defining profundity, and was no less so in defining the other two qualities he claimed to be essential to true art: freshness and skill. To understand the subjectivity of these terms as criteria of artistic evaluation, one need only recognize that Blesh and other revivalists attributed profundity, freshness, and skill to some the very same musical performances—Jelly Roll Morton's piano blues, for instance—Ulanov dismissed as shallow, mechanical, and clumsy.

Whatever specific, enduring insights Ulanov delivered in his support for the late 1940s and early 1950s jazz avant garde, we must see his critical sensibility as part of a larger trend in modernist literary and art criticism favoring complexity as a paramount aesthetic quality. Blesh, for his part, remained committed to an early twentieth-century modernism that foregrounded primitivism as an aesthetic model of profound simplicity that cut through the tangled, overwrought, dead weight of Victorian academicism. In Blesh's view, just as Matisse, Picasso, and Braque "discovered in the African mask the dynamic impulse" that regenerated the "moribund art" of Western painting, so jazz needed always to return to its own primitive sources, "which have always been the real elements of its modernness." Luckily for jazz, Blesh argued, "its Gabon masks are built in"—the blues being the best example of such a mask, "as though the plastic planes of ancient carved wood were transmuted into sound."[53] Ulanov, by contrast, regarded the blues as just one of the colors in the jazz musician's palate, and perhaps not the first one a postwar modernist should be expected to dip his brush into. It was Ulanov's assumption that modern jazz musicians were, like himself, intellectuals interested in cutting-edge developments in thought and culture. At a time when New Criticism mined literary texts for nuanced irony and layered complexity, when the leading art critics made sweeping philosophical claims for abstract expressionism, the very sturdiness and elemental simplicity of the blues—to some the key to its profundity—might seem sentimental and old-fashioned to a certain kind of vanguardist mind. Ulanov was not dissuaded from this mindset when his discussions with Charlie Parker and Lennie Tristano turned to the subjects of relativity and psychoanalysis.

Ulanov's jazz vanguardism carried an implicit art-for-art's-sake impulse propelled not just by high modernist dogma, but also by his liberal desire—stoked first by his college studies with Boas—to imagine a world not stuck in limiting, reactionary ideas about race. So strong was Ulanov's desire for a post-racial jazz discourse that *A History of Jazz in America* offered virtually no testimony about—as Orrin Keepnews said—"the whole pattern of abuse, social ostracism and prejudice that . . . jazz has always suffered—with particular emphasis, of course, on the key role that the Negro has played in jazz from the start."[54] While sharing Ulanov's conviction that race was a bankrupt concept on scientific and intellectual grounds, Finkelstein's *Jazz: A People's Music* put greater emphasis on the social and political effects of racism on jazz's historical development. More explicitly than Ulanov, Finkelstein tied his faith in jazz's progress to a sense of optimism about the historical decline of racist practices that excluded African Americans from the full range of educational and cultural opportunities. This optimism was rooted in the Marxist conception of a dialectical unfolding of history, as well as in a populist cosmopolitan aesthetic that favored the concert setting and symphonic forms as the proper provenance of a people's social music. New Orleans jazz, Finkelstein argued, "was a protest against the narrowness of semi-feudal, southern life, in the years before the first world war, using the idioms and forms given it by semi-feudal life." Jazz "had to break out of its New Orleans limitations," Finkelstein said, because of the "heightened consciousness of rights" blacks developed as they battled against a "jim-crowed life." There was an ironic consequence to this black freedom struggle: one measure of its success was the extent to which jazz, though created by African Americans in New Orleans, grew into a music that defied the boundaries of race and place, and in so doing ceased to become the sole property of black southerners. "In breaking out of New Orleans," Finklestein wrote, "jazz became a possession of all America; Negro and white; North and South; Eastern seaboard and Pacific coast."[55]

By Finkelstein's reckoning, the protest element of jazz shifted following the post–World War I migration of African Americans from the rural, semi-feudal plantation South to the urban, industrial North, Midwest, and West: "Modern jazz is a protest against monopoly control of music and the commodity-like exploitation of the musicians, a protest using the idioms and forms given it by commercial music." Finkelstein's anticommercialism was primarily an issue of political economy and social justice: the question was who controlled the means of musical production and distribution and thereby reaped the rewards of creative labor. When Blesh and the *Jazzmen* contributors fretted about the inimical effects of "big money," their concern was largely aesthetic: too much money corrupted the purity of the art. Finkelstein, by contrast, thought Louis Armstrong and Charlie Parker should make as much money as they could—and all the better if they made it by breathing life and creative subtlety into hackneyed Tin Pan Alley songs. This distinction between political economy and aesthetics went further: in Blesh's sweeping condemnation of post–New Orleans jazz, especially big-band swing, "commercialism" was synonymous with "sophistication" and "technique." These latter two terms were not included in Finkelstein's lexicon of opprobrium. Like Ulanov and later advocates of the Third Stream, Finkelstein welcomed the fusion of jazz and classical music. In his view, jazz critics who advocated a strict separation of these aesthetic spheres in the name of purity and authenticity were signing on to a system of class and racial exclusion. Black musicians especially "are kept out of [the concert world] not only by outright discrimination," Finkelstein wrote, "but by the roundabout discrimination which praises their 'folk art' and asks that they stay within their limits."[56]

Echoing Alain Locke, Finkelstein envisioned jazz as a symphonic music that expressed the democratic struggles of America's laboring people. Because jazz was the art that best represented "the peoples who together made America," it should grow into a "national culture" supported by government subsidies, performed not just by the leading professional bands but also by trained local orchestras in every community across the country. This would require the growth and institutionalization of a broad-based, nationwide jazz performance education system—the first such suggestion in the jazz literature. It would entail an expansion of the kinds of venues in which jazz was performed, in particular a move away from urban nightclubs where jazz had become, as Eddie Condon phrased it, "a poor man's art that only the rich can afford." Such changes were necessary, Finkelstein thought, not only to build a grassroots, democratic, participatory national jazz culture, but to counter the practical difficulties of the jazz life that he believed had prevented even the best professional bands from reaching their full potential. "If a band such as Ellington's or Basie's were made a national or local concern, given a steady, relaxed existence, removed from the terrible insecurity and homelessness that affects a band musician's life, and encouraged to develop its own music, the results would be astounding," Finkelstein wrote. He added (in an implicit rebuke of Blesh's declension narrative): "The story of jazz is not only the history of a great created music, but also the tragedy of a potentially great, never-created music."[57]

Though this vision of a "potentially great, never-created music" made clear that Finkelstein thought Duke Ellington had yet to do his best work, it was Ellington's aspiration—as a composer of great formal sophistication rendering in sound the heritage of U.S. common peoples—that Finkelstein hoped would become the aspiration of jazz writ large. In this respect Finkelstein was calling for jazz to become a nationalist cultural form, albeit one that avoided the "sentimental folksiness and longing for the 'good old past'" that he discerned in much nineteenth-century European concert music, with its "showy and shallow rhapsodies [and] fantasies." A better model, he thought, were the modern European composers Leos Janacek, Jan Sibelius, Bela Bartok, Ralph Vaughn Williams, Sergei Prokofiev, and Dmitri Shostakovich, and the American Charles Ives, whose work combined "the best of the symphonic and operatic tradition with the new traditions of folk music." Though Ellington had not yet "evolved enough of a new craft to match his new and exciting ideas"—Finkelstein thought *Black, Brown, and Beige* was "less moving than his dance music"—it was a sign of great hope that Ellington's music "sounds exactly like no music written in Europe or anywhere else," that "it speaks a language of its own," and that "it has been imitated, even by European composers, far more than it has imitated anybody."[58]

"No Brittle Egghead"

The evolutionary narratives of Ulanov and Finkelstein reflected a broader pattern in the thinking about jazz's past, present, and future—a pattern also evident in the ways that jazz critics and historians thought about their own endeavors. In 1952, *Record Changer* editor Orrin Keepnews, reflecting on the ten-year history of the journal, happily noted that "the most tremendous strides [have been] made towards actual, meaningful acceptance of the music by thinking Americans" since the early 1940s. Then came this stern caveat about the limits of jazz's newfound respectability:

> All the books, concert-hall appearances, and professors in the world aren't going to influence the people who just *know* that jazz is just a lot of raucous noise, that it is dirty, that it is played by a lot of hopped-up Negroes and white men low

enough to associate with them. It's sad but true that a fair number of people who gaped at the picture-magazine layouts on bop goatees and berets also happen to consider college professors pretty queer animals, too, and aren't going to be impressed if some of them find jazz worthy of serious study.[59]

Just one year later, after what was clearly a serious change of heart, a less cynical Keepnews introduced a special issue of *Record Changer* devoted to the founding of the Institute of Jazz Studies under the stewardship of Marshall Stearns. In an effort to show that jazz had indeed become an object of "serious study" by credentialed intellectuals, the issue reprinted transcripts of the seminars Stearns had organized in New York and Chicago in 1952 under the heading "Toward a Definition of Jazz."[60] That very title conveyed the positivistic objectivity fetish at work in these gatherings. At the New York seminar, anthropologist Stanley Diamond, ethnomusicologist Mieczyslaw Kolinsky, and Rudi Blesh got hung up on whether it was best to proceed toward a definition of jazz inductively or deductively.[61] At the Chicago seminar, anthropologist Alan Merriam, ethnomusicologist Richard Waterman, and linguist Lorenzo Turner engaged in this fussy exchange:

> Merriam: Well . . . we've divided the problem—and this is a simplification of course—into the study of the music itself and the study of its social impact. If, for example, you're going to study the music itself, you must have, to start out with, people who know jazz and people who know their own discipline. Now this is cross-disciplinary . . . . And at the same time you're going to have to concentrate on a factual, basic, musicological definition of jazz. Somewhere we've got to know what jazz is.
>
> Waterman: I don't think we need to be in too much of a hurry. If we're going to take the wide approach, it's better, at the present nebulous period, to wander around. We might come up with a definition quite different from the one we would have gone in with.
>
> Turner: To quote Louis Armstrong's famous statement: "Man, if you've got to ask what it is, you'll never get to know."
>
> Merriam: That's not fair; it's not right. It's a lovely statement, but I can't go with it.[62]

Pettifogging of this sort dominated the transcripts. Though photographs of the seminar participants helped break up the visual monotony of the print-heavy text, the pictures made Stearns's assembled group of "trained minds" look like an early 1950s meeting of the Atomic Energy Commission. The effect was to create an aura of solemn scholarly authority consistent with the post–World War II cult of the expert. If physicists could develop the bomb, scientific managers could run the military-industrial complex, and Freudian therapists could pinpoint the psychodynamics of the suburban family, then why—the tacit premise seemed to be—shouldn't a group of humanists and social scientists nail down a working definition of jazz, or at least reach the definitive conclusion that such a definition was not possible or desirable?

Postwar jazz discourse clearly had taken on academic overtones. Rudi Blesh's *Shining Trumpets* clocked in at more than four hundred pages, including appendices, discography, and musical transcriptions. With that book and his slimmer follow-up volume, *They All Played Ragtime* (1950), anchoring his curriculum vita, Blesh in 1956 began teaching a jazz history course at Queens College, CUNY. Marshall Stearns's *The Story of Jazz* came with a fifteen-page bibliography of jazz literature and a syllabus of the fifteen-lecture jazz history course Stearns taught in the adult division at New York University, with guest appearances by Blesh, Ralph Ellison, Barry Ulanov, John Hammond, Leonard Feather, and George Avakian. The fact that English professors Stearns and Barry Ulanov taught jazz history on a moonlighting basis in the NYU extension school, rather than as part of their regular curricular duties at Hunter and Barnard, showed that jazz was consigned to the margins of 1950s academia. But, as indicated by the title of Stearns's radio program—"Jazz Goes to College"—any suggested affiliation with scholarly authority was thought to bring jazz valuable cachet in the cultural marketplace.

Stearns was a scholar of medieval English known in jazz circles as the "horn-rimmed, clipped mustached apotheosis of The College Professor."[63] As the founder of the Institute of Jazz Studies and convener, starting in 1950, of a series of yearly seminars he called "Jazz Roundtables" that led to the creation of the Lenox School of Jazz, Stearns emerged as jazz's leading explicator, institution-builder, propagandist, and missionary. More than any of the critics writing in the post–World War II jazz press; more than Blesh, Ulanov, or Finkelstein; more, indeed, than any non-musician since John Hammond in the late 1930s, Stearns himself became a public icon of jazz's canonization. The *New Yorker* described Stearns as a man whose "mind is closely attuned to the disparate beats of Chaucer and Duke Ellington"; a spate of similar descriptions in other media notices cast Stearns as a minor oddity who was nevertheless an endearing symbol of jazz's mounting legitimacy.[64]

In the 1940s, during teaching stints at the University of Hawaii, Indiana University, and Cornell University, Stearns had become known on campus as much for his civil rights and jazz interests as for his lectures on Chaucer. At Indiana, as faculty advisor to the campus NAACP chapter, Stearns joined black and progressive white students in organizing resistance to the campus "KKK" (the white fraternity Kappa Kappa Kappa forces) and a university administration unwilling to challenge local Jim Crow customs.[65] As head of the Cornell Rhythm Club, Stearns organized concerts by Mary Lou Williams, Ethel Waters, Dizzy Gillespie, and Josh White. After winning a Guggenheim Foundation grant to write a history of jazz, Stearns moved to New York City to immerse himself in the contemporary jazz scene.

In 1951, *Negro Digest* published an essay by Robert Lucas on Stearns's jazz history class at NYU. A "tall, bespectacled professor" who "casually smokes while delivering lectures," Stearns was said to push aside his lectern at regular intervals to make way for a washboard player, a Dixieland combo, or a bop saxophonist. Stearns emphasized jazz"s "Negro origins" and scheduled guest lectures by Ralph Ellison, Charlie Parker, and other African American musicians and jazz experts who helped Stearns demonstrate that "the Negro people and the music they created cannot be separated." One student, following the example of Stearns and other white aficionados, had combed the city for out-of-print blues and jazz records, only to be urged by Ellison to consider that "by this time, the music is inside the people." Stearns and his guest lecturers encouraged the students to think broadly about jazz's cultural significance. An introductory survey of the class's attitudes toward jazz featured such leading questions as: "When you started listening to jazz, was your relationship with your parents good or bad?" and—revealing the assumption of a predominantly white audience—"Have you ever had Negroes in your home as guests?" Composed, as *Negro Digest* put it, of "a cross-section of Metropolis USA," Stearns's classroom was pictured as a model of a progressive, consensus-oriented social order. His students included "a lawyer, a psychiatrist, a booking agent from a big agency, a TV script writer, two girls living in a trailer camp in New Jersey, and three or four Negroes." Educated, curious, urbane, and nominally diverse, Stearns's audience was a microcosm of the postwar culture boom, a ballooning popular center hungry for cultivated leisure.[66]

Stearns calibrated his presentation of jazz history to fit the presumed middlebrow sensibility of a general audience. The publicity office of radio station WNEW, which broadcast Stearns's "Jazz Goes to College" program on Sunday afternoons, billed him as "a savant without being a pedant," an instructor who "approaches his subject with a stimulating enthusiasm which makes his scholarship in this field wholly palatable to the average dialer." The Columbia Lecture Bureau, which managed Stearns's Chautauqua-like speaking tours, advertised the professor as "no brittle egghead," but rather an "erudite and articulate" lecturer who "pushes his workshop along with informality, punctuating his theories and histories with recordings that vary as much as the antecedents of the music itself." At the National Gallery of Art, an audience of "white-haired old-ladies, serious-looking college-age intellectuals, Washington society leaders and at least two Congressmen" chortled delightedly as Stearns likened Bessie Smith to the Wife of Bath and referred to Jelly Roll Morton as the "Benvenuto Cellini of Jazz."[67]

Though a job teaching English at Hunter College materialized in the early 1950s, Stearns continued to devote himself first and foremost to his jazz research and evangelism. *The Story of Jazz*, which was translated into twelve languages and has remained in print by Oxford University Press since 1956, served as an international promotional tool for the Institute of Jazz Studies (IJS), exemplifying the style of interdisciplinary work Stearns thought the Institute should encourage and sponsor. No sooner had Stearns completed that book than he began to conduct interviews with the African American progenitors of American dance, leading to the publication, in 1964, of Marshall and Jean Stearns's *Jazz Dance: The Story of American Vernacular Dance*, the first book-length study of its subject and still a core text in the field of dance studies.

The linguist S. I. Hayakawa, a participant in several of Stearns's jazz roundtables, found it significant that Stearns had shifted from the study of literary texts to a more open-ended, interdisciplinary inquiry into the cultural meanings of jazz. Hayakawa interpreted the shift as an impatience with literary New Criticism's taut strictures:

> The fact that a man like Marshall Stearns, with his literary education, is so deeply interested [in] the meanings of jazz within our culture [is significant].... The prevailing literary styles are at present under the influence of T. S. Eliot and Allen Tate and other such people who go for an extreme degree of tightness of discipline and compression of statement. [This] prevailing literary climate is such as to discourage any kind of expansiveness, any kind of openness and warmth.... If you are expansive like Carl Sandburg, you just don't rate with the prevailing literary [authorities]. [Stearns understands that] a certain expansive and Dionysiac element is necessary in any kind of art.[68]

The eminent Yale art historian and pioneering Afro-Atlanticist Robert Farris Thompson, who served as an IJS research assistant in the late 1950s and considers himself a Stearns protégé, compared Stearns's approach to that of two leading critics of the next generation whom I'll introduce in chapter 4:

> Martin Williams would have loved to have turned jazz criticism into literary criticism. So would Whitney Balliett. They were trying to make it elegant. Marshall had already gone through the tenure struggle in the academic world; he had gone through the battle for "respectability," so now he wanted to get to something deeper and more visceral. He was really creolizing the discipline of jazz history,

starting with the methods of literary history, but reaching for a symphonic, all-embracing Wagnerian operatic quality.[69]

It makes sense that Thompson—a fiercely interdisciplinary scholar who has been described as "part anthropologist, part art critic, part musicologist, part student of religion and philosophy"—would have been inspired by Stearns.[70] For Stearns was bent on expanding the inquiry into jazz's history and culture using the disciplinary methods of anthropology, folklore, ethnomusicology, and American studies. Indeed, Stearns's IJS mission statement made the enterprise sound like a promising new American Studies department: "the basic subject of study here is American civilization—in its multiformed aspects—and such a great subject will and should consume many years of research. The rewards, however, will be great and should afford not only a key to the American character but also a lasting contribution to the understanding of American civilization."[71]

The original IJS was, quite literally, the 12,000-disc record and exhaustive jazz periodical collections in the study of Stearns's Greenwich Village apartment. In its infancy as much a jazz salon as formal research archive, the institute served as a parlor for musicians and connoisseurs to interact in a more deliberative, heedful manner than was customary in the bustling, slangy atmosphere of nightclub dressing-rooms. Yet the *bon vivant* sensibility of its founder ensured that the IJS was no grim scholarly tomb. "No one could give jazz parties like Marshall Stearns," recalled Robert Reisner, the Charlie Parker mythologizer whom Stearns hired as the IJS's first curator:

> Not big and brawling, they were selective affairs. An evening might be devoted to hearing records in which bass men were featured. He always gave you a chance to guess the man playing before revealing the title. Some of the cats who cut the sides would be there, and it was wild to hear one say, "Hey, did I do that? How did you get a hold of that disc? Don't hold it against me. I was too young when we did that disc."[72]

Robert Farris Thompson remembers the first time he visited "the sacred address," 108 Waverly Place:

> He showed me stuff that dazzled the hell out of me—like photographs from a famous party he threw when Dizzy Gillespie came, and while half of Dizzy's band was blaring away, somebody called the police. The cops showed up, but when they realized they were face to face with the *crème de la crème* of jazz, they started asking for autographs. Marshall served them champagne.[73]

When Thompson read Stearns's *The Story of Jazz* just before entering the military in 1956, he took special note of Stearns's chapter on Afro-Cuban music, the only such chapter in the book-length jazz histories of this period to give serious consideration to Latin musicians like Chano Pozo, Mario Bauza, Machito, Tito Puente, and Perez Prado. In 1958, while serving in the Historical Section of the Seventh U.S. Army, Thompson wrote to Stearns at the IJS, introducing himself as someone "writing a book on mambo, cha-cha-cha, rock-and-roll, and other jazz-related dances" and "the impact of these forms on Europe, Asia, and West Africa." While asserting that "the world conquest of jazz is an established fact," Thompson suggested it might be less well known "that jazz-related dances" like the mambo and the cha-cha-cha had also conquered all countries except poverty-stricken ones "like Nepal, where a friend writes the land is 'devoid of Cadillacs and mambo,' or Communist China, which, if we are to believe *Look* magazine, has banned mambo." For help in conducting his research, Thompson asked for addresses of "any tolerant, articulate jazz lover in the following cities who would be interested in discussing the mambo and rock-and-roll scene in his country with me." The cities Thompson listed were New Delhi, Bombay, Djakarta, Rangoon, Stockholm, Helsinki, Teheran, Karachi, Sydney, and Melbourne.[74]

This letter—one of hundreds in the IJS files dating to the late 1950s, from jazz fans in many different countries—played to several distinctive features of Stearns's approach to jazz. First was a preoccupation with jazz's international sweep and scope, which Stearns chronicled and celebrated in distinctly cold war–shaped ideological terms as the triumph of American interracial democracy. Notable among the consumers of Stearns's 1950s jazz writing were the U.S. State Department and the United States Information Agency (USIA), which employed Stearns as a lecturer on the international performance tours taken by jazz musicians as part of the foreign policy establishment's cold war cultural diplomacy. Stearns recounted his participation in this enterprise in *The Story of Jazz*:

> A sparkling new idea was tried in 1956 and worked out famously. Dizzy Gillespie and his orchestra (with the author as lecturer) were sent out on an eight-week tour of the Middle East by the United States government. They played in countries where no band had ever appeared. . . . The idea was to "win over the people," especially in those critical countries which Russia had been flooding with free talent. The friendly but free-wheeling band of sixteen musicians—four white and twelve colored—led many people to abandon their Communist-inspired notions of American democracy in the course of the concert. "This music," said the United States Ambassador to London, Mr. Donald Heath, "makes our job much easier."[75]

Despite his keen insights into what he called "the whole tangled skein of Negro-white relationships,"[76] Stearns proselytized jazz as an interracial brotherhood of peace and social harmony in a way that dovetailed with the consensus orientation of the policy establishment. In Stearns's sanguine account of the inaugural 1956 State Department jazz tour—which he discussed in more detail in a *Saturday Review* essay titled "Is Jazz Good Propaganda?"— Dizzy Gillespie and his band introduce Middle Eastern peoples to "the cheerful, informal, and generous side of life," the musicians serving dutifully as ambassadors of goodwill. Gillespie's flair for the comic becomes a diplomatic asset. Resplendently costumed in a Pakistani turban-headdress, performing duets with a flute-playing snake charmer, Gillespie—said Stearns—is a photogenic example of lighthearted cross-cultural exchange. The amiable Quincy Jones's gestures of friendship—buying an outfit of clothes for a sailor in the Pakistan navy, encouraging local musicians—exemplify the best tradition of American benevolence. Gillespie's band, with its diverse make-up and aura of success, models the best features of American society. A hotel chambermaid who "had been hammered with tales of the terrible fate of dark-skinned people in the United States," changes her mind after an encounter with Gillespie's wife, Lorraine. After baring her arm to note that she shared the same skin tone as Mrs. Gillespie, the chambermaid rifles her with questions: Was the band ordered to come and play? Were they paid? Was the female trombonist (Melba Liston) really a woman, or a man dressed like one? Were the white musicians in the orchestra really white, or were they black men who had whitened their faces with chalk? Relieved of her delusions by Mrs. Gillespie, the chambermaid promptly joins the ranks of the true believers. Now that the jazzmen looked to her "like a gang of wealthy capitalists," Stearns bragged, "her conversion to capitalism was complete."[77]

Stearns proved a very able propagandist, linking the global aspirations of cold-war liberalism to jazz's quest for cultural legitimacy on its home soil. "Jazz leads to disconcerting questions about who is really cultured," Stearns said by way of contrasting—as Sidney Finkelstein did earlier in *Jazz: A People's Music*—the free-swinging stride of the New Orleans march to the Prussian goose-step. Celebrating the blues as "real American history" that reflected "with unerring accuracy the salty humor, bittersweet philosophy, [and] hypocrisy-penetrating insight of a great minority group in the U.S.A.," Stearns appropriated the music, with its encoding of the black struggle for freedom and equality, as a nostrum for white middle-class tensions and apprehensions in the postwar "age of anxiety," and as a sop to intellectuals anguished over the conformist tendencies of mass society. "In a society of increasingly mass-produced, assembly-line entertainment, when every individual is treated like an empty pitcher to be filled from above, jazz retains something of the spirit of the handicrafts of yesteryear," Stearns wrote. "The print of the human spirit warms it. Deep down, jazz expresses the enforced and compassionate attitudes of a minority group and may well appeal to us [note, again, the presumption of a white audience] because we all have blue moods and, in a fundamental sense none of us is wholly free."[78]

Buffeted by cold war winds, Stearns's internationalist and consensus-building focus helped to dissolve—if not fully resolve—tensions between other jazz critics and historians. When Stearns brought Rudi Blesh and Barry Ulanov together in 1957 at the Lenox School of Jazz for a presentation on "Jazz and Its Correlation to the Arts," for example, the two downplayed their sharp doctrinal differences and instead stressed jazz's creative interaction with the worlds of contemporary visual art, theater, and film.[79] By this time Blesh had softened his dogmatic views on "real jazz," partly in recognition of a growing international audience that seemed to completely ignore the sectarian style wars of 1940s U.S. jazz criticism. "There is a lesson for us in the way the rest of the world accepts jazz—any and all jazz, from New Orleans to 'progressive,'" Blesh wrote in a postscript to the 1958 second edition of *Shining Trumpets*. "It becomes evident that the points of style over which we have endlessly argued are not comparably important elsewhere. What is important to people everywhere is the mere fact that a music like jazz can exist."[80] This was precisely the note that Stearns had sounded throughout the 1950s: what was important was jazz's fundamental identity as an American tradition, not the critical factionalism instigated by the music's stylistic variations. Oxford University Press editor Sheldon Meyer said that Stearns's book distinguished itself in the post–World War II jazz literature for "refusing to take sides" in jazz's culture wars.[81]

The Story of Jazz concretized a liberal consensus view of jazz history. By attenuating ideological differences within the music, Stearns's conception of jazz—as a symbol of freedom, democracy, and interracial communication—became that much more potent an ideological tool in the world at large. Eschewing both the purist conceptions of true jazz that had dominated jazz criticism up through the 1940s and the formalist models jazz had begun to inherit from his own field of literary criticism, Stearns settled instead on what Robert Farris Thompson calls a "creolizing" approach that traversed both disciplinary and national borders. While paying heed to the 1950s social science predilection for definitive answers ("we've got to know *what* jazz is"), Stearns cast as wide a net as he could imagine around his subject, taking pains to suggest its eternal and perhaps essential ontological slipperiness. Almost three hundred pages into *The Story of Jazz*—after sections on the African "prehistory"; the New Orleans synthesis of spirituals, work songs, blues, minstrelsy, and ragtime; the wide cultural ramifications of "The Jazz Age"; the profusion of styles from swing, to Dixieland, to bop, to Afro-Cuban, to cool—Stearns finally allowed that "we may define jazz *tentatively* [emphasis mine] as

> a semi-improvisational American music distinguished by an immediacy of communication, an expressiveness characteristic of the free use of the human voice, and a complex flowing rhythm; it is the result of a three-hundred-years' blending in the United States of the European and West African musical traditions; and its predominant components are European harmony, Euro-American melody, and African rhythm.[82]

Whatever the pros and cons of this definition from musicological and ethnomusicological perspectives, it had the ideological virtue—from the perspective of, say, the USIA—of positing the United States as the breeding ground of an art form with origins traceable to three-quarters of the globe. In this formulation, jazz stood as the universal cultural consensus.

One musicologist who did challenge the empirical and conceptual foundations of Stearns's definition was Lawrence Gushee. Among other forensic criticisms, Gushee questioned Stearns's use of the term "American music," saying that while jazz's "roots are American," the contemporary practice of the music "surely is not." He also quibbled with the phrase "immediacy of communication," arguing that this descriptor was "characteristic of many other musical styles."[83] Stearns wouldn't have disagreed with the latter point. In fact, in his contributions to the jazz roundtables, in his teaching at the Lenox School of Jazz, and in a series of essays he wrote for the *Saturday Review* in the late 1950s, Stearns demonstrated a catholic approach to American musical culture that made some of the same claims for gospel, rhythm-and-blues, rock'n'roll, and even musical comedy that he had been making for jazz. If anything, Stearns was caught between an older-style emphasis on "real jazz" and a newer ecumenism driven by the profusion of new and interesting popular music genres. "Near-jazz is better than no jazz," Stearns quipped in many of his lectures.[84]

As scrupulously evenhanded as Stearns strove to be in his musical appreciation and theorizing, however, there is no mistaking his burning passion for rhythm and dance. This was clearly evident in his enthusiasm for Afro-Cuban jazz. His writing on the form concentrated on the nuances of the clavé rhythm, and on the superior dancing skills demonstrated by Latin audiences in comparison to the kinesthetically challenged white audiences catered to by Xavier Cugat ("the Guy Lombardo of Latin music") and other "genteel orchestras at expensive nightclubs" that played "simplified tangos, rhumbas, congas, and sambas for society." Himself the scion of a Boston WASP family that hadn't put much stress on terpsichorean elegance, Stearns often played upon his audience's presumably low expectations for the rhythmic skill of a "horn-rimmed, clipped mustached apotheosis of The College Professor." Once, in Carlisle, Pennsylvania, in a lecture/performance with the Randy Weston Trio that illustrated affinities between traditional African rhythm and modern jazz, Stearns related his own experience taking lessons from master drummer Asadata Dafora: "It took me a whole month to do four with one hand and nine with the other. An African drummer does that 4-over-9 combination in his right hand alone."[85]

Stearns conceived of the African influence on jazz not—as Rudi Blesh tended to—as a mystical racial memory, but rather as an ongoing influence refreshed and regenerated by the still-unfolding history of Afro-Atlantic cultural exchange. Stearns took pains to observe this unfolding history first-hand. In 1953, under the guidance of folklorist Harold Courlander, Stearns took a field trip to Haiti. There he witnessed a voodoo ceremony led by a priest who, Stearns said, looked "so much like Charlie Parker that it made me uneasy."[86] Stearns also noted similarities between the "possessed" women dancers in the ceremony and the ecstatic behaviors he had observed on visits to Baptist revival meetings in South Carolina and Georgia. Those trips were undertaken at the prompting of Willis James, a professor at Spellman College in Atlanta who was at work on a study of African American folk music. Stearns pressed James for a systematic theory of jazz's evolution out of slave spirituals, work songs, ring shouts, and early country blues. Stearns was greatly indebted to James's 1955 *Phylon* essay, "The Romance of the Negro Folk Cry in America," for his understanding of black rhythmic and linguistic practices.[87]

Robert Farris Thompson remembers Stearns as a model of intercultural scholarship and interracial personal relations that he fears has been sacrificed to the postmodernist trends of the 1980s and 1990s:

> He knew so much about black traditions, so he was able to bring a relaxed, totally natural quality to his conversations across the race line. It was a revelation. It was the opposite of today's postmodern concept of the "other," with its thousands of spidery webs trapping us in self-consciousness, never allowing us to cross divides. Follow the implications of seeing culture as a "predicament" to the ultimate, and you might as well just slit your throat. Marshall would have none of that.

In 1966, shortly before Stearns died of a heart attack at age fifty-eight, Thompson sat in for his ailing mentor at the First World Black and African Festival of Arts and Culture in Dakar, Senegal. Thompson credits that event as the key formative experience in his career as a leading scholar of the

African diaspora. Another of the beneficiaries of Stearns's seminal efforts to map the global flow of black culture was the pianist and composer Randy Weston, who attended Stearns's Lenox workshops in the 1950s. Weston's interactions in Lenox with Stearns, Willis James, African master musician Babatunde Olatunji, and dancer Geoffrey Holder helped inspire his relocation to Africa in the 1960s, where he studied and collaborated with Gnawa and Jilala musicians. (I'll return to Stearns's Lenox jazz roundtables in chapter 5.)

"Singers of the Self and Historians of All Levels of American Experience"

How, then, to tell the story of jazz? And what do we learn from that story about the larger patterns of American culture, especially American attitudes toward its own history? With these questions in mind, let us return, finally, to the concise but powerfully suggestive jazz essays of Ralph Ellison.

In 1956, Ellison wrote to his friend Albert Murray: "If we don't tell the story [of jazz], the fay boys [the "ofay"—white—critics] will do to it what Stalin did to History."[88] This privately expressed concern didn't specify exactly how white critics were missing the story, and in his published writings Ellison only hinted—and slyly at that—at the problem. In 1958, in an essay on Charlie Christian in the *Saturday Review*, Ellison lamented that "while there is now a rather extensive history of discography and recording sessions, there is but the bare beginnings of historiography of jazz. We know much of jazz as entertainment, but a mere handful of clichés constitutes our knowledge of jazz as experience."[89] These words might have seemed puzzling to those who had slogged their way through *Jazzmen*, *Shining Trumpets*, *Jazz: A People's Music*, *A History of Jazz in America*, and *The Story of Jazz*. Others might have sensed self-deprecating irony in the fact that Ellison's stated impatience with the limitations of record reviewing came in his own review of an album of reissued recordings (Columbia's "The Charlie Christian Story"). But few readers of this review essay who knew the jazz literature could have missed the significance of Ellison's point. For here—and throughout the series of beautifully crafted jazz essays he wrote in the late 1950s for *Saturday Review* and *Esquire*—Ellison posed a challenge that has helped shape the canons of jazz writing ever since.

The heart of that challenge rests in the phrase "our knowledge of jazz as experience," especially in the word *experience*. In part this was a matter of the authority of personal experience. Many jazz writers developed close personal relationships with jazz musicians; indeed, as we'll see in coming chapters, some of the key critics who emerged in the 1950s—especially Nat Hentoff, Ralph Gleason, and Gene Lees—often wrote explicitly about their own intimate friendships with musicians as a means of illuminating the interracial dynamics of the jazz world. But Ellison's late 1950s jazz essays were singularly revealing as firsthand testimony to jazz's development within African American communities. In his review essay of the Charlie Christian reissues, and in another essay occasioned by Vanguard and Columbia reissues of Jimmy Rushing, both published in 1958 in the *Saturday Review*, Ellison reflected on his own upbringing in the Oklahoma City neighborhood that produced Christian, the pioneering electric guitarist who enjoyed a brief moment of fame with the Benny Goodman Sextet before succumbing to tuberculosis, and Rushing, the blues singer who came into prominence with the Count Basie orchestra. Ellison stressed how deeply the music penetrated to the core of the community's identity, not just as entertainment or art as conventionally conceived, but as a "total way of life." For Ellison, jazz and the public jazz dance were crucial *institutions* of community life, every bit as important as the church and the school. In his role as the official floor manager or "master-of-the-dance" at Slaughter's Hall, Jimmy Rushing was "the leader of a public rite." If jazz and blues "did not fit into the scheme of things" as defined by the church and the school, they "gave expression to attitudes which found no place in these and helped to give our lives some semblance of wholeness."[90]

"Total way of life" and "public rite" was the language of the Cambridge ritualist school, a group of critics whose style of literary exegesis employed anthropological and mythological conceptions of culture. Ellison scholar Robert O'Meally tells us that Ellison came to this school of criticism through Jessie Weston's *From Ritual to Romance*, which he had read while a student at Tuskegee Institute undergoing his "epiphanic literary discovery" of T. S. Eliot's *The Waste Land*. Through Weston, through the Cambridge School scholars Jane Ellen Harrison, Gilbert Murray, and James Frazer, and later through Kenneth Burke and Joseph Campbell, Ellison gained a sense of how myth and ritual "provide ways of understanding patterns of history and art."[91] Weston's study of Arthurian legend, the search for the Holy Grail, and the symbolism of the fisher king—all of which fundamentally informed Eliot's epic poem—instilled in Ellison a deep respect for the power of the culture-hero, a charismatic figure whose personality galvanizes the community and whose mastery of form and style distills, consolidates, and elevates the community's vernacular culture. In these essays on Christian and Rushing, and in later writing on Louis Armstrong and Duke Ellington, Ellison conceived of the jazz musician as a heroic figure whose art is forged in the crucible of local folk experience.

Especially alluring to Ellison, given what he felt was jazz's primary role in sustaining black Americans' hopes and dreams in the face of racist oppression and exclusion, was the notion of the Arthurian hero who slays the dragons of darkness. In Jimmy Rushing's "high and clear and poignantly lyrical voice," for example, Ellison heard "a value, an attitude about the world" that gave Oklahoma City east side blacks a vision beyond the circumscribed boundaries of segregation:

> We had a Negro church and a segregated school, a few lodges and fraternal organizations, and beyond these there was all the great white world. We were pushed off to what seemed to be the least desirable side of the city (but which some years later was found to contain one of the state's richest pools of oil), and our system of justice was based upon Texas law; yet there was an optimism within the Negro community and a sense of possibility which, despite our awareness of limitation (dramatized so brutally in the Tulsa riot of 1921), transcended all of this, and it was this rock-bottom sense of reality, coupled with our sense of the possibility of rising above it, which sounded in Rushing's voice.[92]

Jimmy Rushing's voice exemplified Ellison's notion of blues and jazz—the two were indissolubly linked for Ellison—as a language that mocked and subverted the limitations of both social aspiration and expressive meaning. Rushing's "romantic lyricism" suggested to Ellison something about the mysterious communicative power of the blues: "their ability to imply far more than they state outright, and their capacity to make the details of sex convey meanings which touch upon the metaphysical."[93] Rudi Blesh had suggested a similar way of thinking about the blues, emphasizing their roots in the "circuitous and double-edged," the "indirect and implicative" nature of black folk speech, and valorizing their virile, anti-sentimental sensibility. But where Blesh looked to Africa as the embryonic source for this communicative style, Ellison focused on the intercultural dynamics that Rushing and other Oklahoma City blacks shaped to their own ends. "Perhaps because he is more educated and came from a family already well on its rise into what is called the 'Negro middle class,' Jimmy has always shown a concern for the correctness of language, and out of the tension between the traditional folk pronunciation and his training in school, he has worked out a flexibility of pronunciation and a rhythmical agility with words which make us constantly aware of the meanings which shimmer just beyond the limits of the lyrics." These creative tensions, palpable in the African American experience that Ellison knew—tensions between the vernacular and the learned, the folk and the fine, the tragic and the comic, the joyous and the sorrowful, the said and the implied—endowed blues and jazz with their richly ironic affect. "The blues is an art of ambiguity," Ellison wrote, "an assertion of the irrepressibly human over all circumstance, whether created by others or by one's own human failings. They are the only consistent art in the United States which constantly remind us of our limitations while encouraging us to see how far we can actually go."[94]

Ellison's upbringing in Oklahoma, in the southwest territory that his and Charlie Christian's and Jimmy Rushing's forebears had come to "in search of a more human way of life," deeply grounded his argument for jazz's—especially the blues-based, hard-swinging jazz of Oklahoma City and Kansas City—mythological Americanness. Ellison said that Rushing's lyricism was "not of the Deep South, but of the Southwest: a romanticism native to the frontier, imposed on the violent rawness of a part of the nation which only thirteen years before Rushing's birth was still Indian territory."[95] Here was a socio-geographic paradigm of jazz history quite different from *Jazzmen*'s up-the-Mississippi-from-New Orleans narrative, Blesh's straight-out-of-Africa archetype, and the multiple-points-of-evolution models proffered by Finkelstein, Ulanov, and Stearns. Ellison's paradigm tapped into one of the most deeply ingrained myths in American culture: the Western frontier as a ritual space of existential identity. Ellison's southwestern frontier is a space where the very immanence of death made the struggle for survival all the more sacred and meaningful; a space where the forces of civilization and barbarism stood locked in endless battle; a space of the liminal and the experimental, of unfixed structures and uncertain boundaries and borders that called forth a sense of openness and possibility—and also the need for a fiercely disciplined pragmatism to wrest order out of chaos. Berndt Ostendorf has identified Ellison's southwestern territory background as the key to his cultural vision: "Ellison's sense of self, place, and time, as well as his particular cultural perspectives, are defined by the frontier paradigm, that transitional space with its options and its tensions between freedom and necessity, safety and danger, liberty and restraint, order and disorder."[96]

In his description of the Harlem club Minton's in "The Golden Age, Time Past," his famous essay about the early days of bebop, Ellison brought this paradigm into the urban sphere, linking jazz's avant-modernist experiments with the primal rituals of the frontier. In Ellison's imagination, the jazz jam session becomes a shootout at the OK Corral, the young musicians engaged in "ceaseless warfare for mastery and recognition." In this battle for the jazz player's "recognition of manhood," even "the greatest can never rest on their accomplishments, for, as with the fast guns of the Old West, there is always someone waiting in a jam session to blow him literally, not only down, but into shame and discouragement."[97] For Ellison, such warfare was the ritual core of the jazz experience, a baptism-of-fire initiation that took the place of more formal academic training:

> Here it is more meaningful to speak not of courses of study, of grades and degrees, but of apprenticeship, ordeals, initiation ceremonies, of rebirth. For after the jazzman has learned the fundamentals of his instrument and the traditional techniques of jazz—the intonations, the mute work, manipulation of timbre, the body of traditional styles—he must then "find himself," must be reborn, must find, as it were his soul. . . . He must achieve, in short, his self-determined identity.[98]

That identity was almost always figured as masculine, and Ellison harbored a very strong sense about the proper style of jazz masculinity. In one of the more striking details in "The Golden Age, Time Past," Ellison noted the "different physical build" of the bebop musicians, adding that "often they were quiet and of a reserve which contrasted sharply with the exuberant and outgoing lyricism of the older men."[99] As Robert O'Meally has recognized, this observation was central to Ellison's coolness toward bebop, his sense that the modernists had embraced a "decadent intellectualism" and air of despair at the expense of the older music's "vital physical immediacy" and life-affirming joy.[100] The "wholeness" Ellison perceived in Jimmy Rushing's lyrical voice and elegant physical amplitude was socially fecund: it birthed and nurtured its audience as a family. This was a maternal masculinism, a fertile, generative, life-giving force that nourished and protected the community. Bebop, by contrast, was characterized for Ellison by a tonal "thinness" and a self-conscious posture of alienation that set the musicians off against the community. The bebopper's rejection of the role of the entertainer—in particular their resentment toward Louis Armstrong in his most garrulous comic persona—consigned them, Ellison thought, to a desiccated, emotionally stunted state of being, robbing their sound and their physical ambience of the human warmth and generosity characteristic of the older jazz.

Ellison's critique of bebop connected to a larger narrative of cultural decline, a narrative that bore vestigial traces of Ellison's immersion in Marxism during his first years in Harlem in the 1930s. This narrative emerges clearly in "Harlem Is Nowhere," an essay Ellison wrote in 1948 but which first appeared in print in 1964 in the collection *Shadow and Act*. Ellison's essay describes the work of the Lafargue Psychiatric Clinic, an "underground extension of democracy" that provided "psychotherapy for the underprivileged." Ellison regarded the clinic as "one of Harlem's most important institutions," owing to the acute psychological stresses that addled many Harlem residents as they struggled to endure the harsh conditions of urban life in a country that still refused to accord them full rights. "Not quite citizens and yet Americans, full of the tensions of modern man but regarded as primitives, Negro Americans are in desperate search for an identity," he wrote. Ellison attributed the rising incidence of personality disorders in black urban neighborhoods to the rapid pace of change unleashed by the rise of the modern metropolis, an acceleration that was especially harsh on the bodies and psyches of a people whose survival mechanisms had been honed under the conditions of rural plantation slavery. "Historically," he wrote, "American Negroes are caught in a vast process of change that has swept them from slavery to the conditions of industrial man in a space of time so telescoped (a bare eighty-five years) that it is possible literally for them to step from feudalism into the vortex of industrialism simply by moving across the Mason-Dixon line." Ellison feared that the chaotic transformations of this migration had destroyed the "metaphysical wholeness" of the southern folk community. And one of the victims was jazz: "the lyrical ritual elements of folk jazz—that artistic projection of the only real individuality possible for [the black man] in the South, that embodiment of a superior democracy in which each individual cultivated his uniqueness and yet did not clash with his neighbors—have given way to the near-themeless technical virtuosity of bebop, a further triumph of technology over humanism."[101]

Such language would seem to have aligned Ellison with Rudi Blesh and other of the left-leaning 1940s jazz revivalists who disdained what they regarded as the technique fetish of modern jazz. But Ellison veered from the antimodernist ideology in several crucial respects. First, Ellison's writings showed no strong identification of jazz and blues (or of African American culture generally) with Africa, either in terms of racial memory (like Blesh at his most mystical) or in terms of cultural retention and diasporic diffusion (like Melville Herskovits, Blesh at his most ethnomusicological, and Marshall Stearns). The black folk heritage Ellison embraced was the blues culture of the South and southwest; unlike Stearns, he showed no interest in the Afro-Caribbean heritage or the various developments we now group under the rubric "Latin Jazz." Second, whereas the revivalists (Blesh in particular) defined real jazz as an African American music that was free of significant European influences, Ellison saw jazz as a synthesis of the black folk vernacular and the learned classical tradition. Countering the widespread perception of jazz musicians as musical primitives—a perception abetted by Blesh's assertions of black natural rhythm, and, earlier, by *Jazzmen's* canonization of Bunk Johnson and other unschooled New Orleans musicians—Ellison stressed the central role musical education played in the curricula of black schools. In describing Charlie Christian's musical education, Ellison noted the "two bodies of instrumental technique" that the young guitarist sought to master: "the one classic, widely recognized and 'correct,' and the other eclectic, partly unconscious and 'jazzy.' And it was the tension between these two bodies of technique which led to many of the technical discoveries of jazz."[102] To explain why Duke Ellington had made such a strong impression on him during his high school days in Oklahoma City, Ellison recalled that

> we were studying the classics then, working at harmony and the forms of symphonic music. And while we affirmed the voice of jazz and the blues despite all criticism from our teachers because they spoke to a large extent of what we felt of the life we lived most intimately, it was not until the discovery of Ellington that we had any hint that jazz possessed possibilities of a range of expressiveness comparable to that of classical European music.[103]

In this "Homage to Duke Ellington on His [Seventieth] Birthday," written in 1969, Ellison memorialized an Afro-classical aesthetic aspiration of the late 1920s and early 1930s more akin to Sidney Finkelstein and Barry Ulanov's evolutionary narratives than to Blesh's declension narrative. This underscores a third way in which Ellison diverged from the traditionalist/revivalist camp: Ellison strongly embraced swing, *even* the symphonic swing that Blesh and others despised. For Ellison, it was bebop—not swing—that introduced "near-themeless technical virtuosity." The "sophistication" demonstrated in particular by Duke Ellington and his band—the source of so much passionate rebuke from the revivalists—was something Ellison remembered as a bracing inspiration:

> And then Ellington and the great orchestra came to town; came with their uniforms, their sophistication, their skills and golden horns, their flights of controlled and disciplined fantasy; came with their art, their special sound, came with Ivy Anderson and Ethel Waters singing and dazzling the eye with their high-brown beauty and with the richness and bright feminine flair of their costumes, their promising manners. They were news from the great wide world, an example and a goal.[104]

Accenting this inspirational dimension of Ellison's jazz writing, Robert O'Meally suggests that "not only are jazz artists singers of the self and historians of all levels of American experience not recorded otherwise, but as leaders of the Saturday-night public dance they are joy-bell ringers, good-time rolling stewards of our national optimism."[105] This is the Ellison who celebrated jazz as an art created by a segregated and demeaned people, an art that then came to symbolize the cultural distinctiveness and aspirations of the entire nation. This is the Ellison who complained about Amiri Baraka's *Blues People* that the book lacked the "sense of excitement and surprise . . . of enslaved and politically weak men successfully imposing their values upon a powerful society through song and dance."[106] But O'Meally also notes the deeply tragic vision that pervades Ellison's jazz writings, the reckoning with calamity, oppression, and sorrow that give the writings their own blues character. "The blues," Ellison famously wrote in a 1945 essay on his mentor, Richard Wright, "is an impulse to keep the painful details and episodes of a brutal experience alive in one's aching consciousness, to finger its jagged grain, and to transcend it, not by the consolation of philosophy but by squeezing from it a near-tragic, near-comic lyricism."[107]

The blues lyricism of Ellison's jazz writings not only voiced "the painful details and episodes" of black experience; it also lamented American culture's predilection for destruction and wanton disregard for its own history. "We waste experience as we waste the forest," ran Ellison's jeremiad.[108] Where Marshall Stearns reveled in jazz's triumphal conquest of the world and imagined a future of unfettered creative ferment, Ellison balanced his celebration of the music with a mournful sense of what had been lost and forgotten in jazz's and American culture's headlong forward rush. While cold war propaganda used jazz as a symbol of freedom, Ellison said that jazz was what African Americans "had in place of freedom."[109] For Ellison, as William Maxwell has insightfully suggested, jazz was "the sound of political democracy denied."[110] In Ellison's jazz writing, we find neither the bourgeois assimilationist vilified by 1960s radical black nationalists, nor the wide-eyed American optimist celebrated by 1990s neoconservatives. We find instead a voice of deep ambivalence—a voice at once swinging in pulse with the onward-and-upward aspirations of his migratory people, and yet also rapt in elegy for the "noisy lostness" of the down-home communal experiences left behind.

If the Harlem club Minton's and other haunts were, as Ralph Ellison suggested, the "true academy" where the "continuing symposium of jazz" communicated the music's languages and traditions to new generations of musicians, the broader public's engagement with jazz in the years after World War II increasingly took on its own more conventional academic overtones. If jazz fan magazine discourse of the 1940s and 1950s remained as impulsive, melodramatic, and slangy as ever, now one could find on public library shelves—in *Shining Trumpets, Jazz: A People's Music, A History of Jazz in America*, and *The Story of Jazz*—jazz books written under the influence of mid-twentieth-century academic humanities and social science. Such signs of cultural capital were deemed significant because of still dominant public perceptions of jazz as the music of the whorehouse, the smoke-filled bar-room, and the lowdown café. Jazz critics fiercely battled those perceptions, both for the sake of the music's normalization in mainstream America and to assuage their own anxieties about being affiliated with a suspect, degraded culture. We turn in the next two chapters first to an overview of the gener-ation of American jazz critics who came of age in the 1950s, then to some of the important institutional developments in the "mainstreaming" of jazz during this period.

CHAPTER 4

Writer's Writers and Sensitive Cats

Mapping the New Jazz Criticism

Race, Culture, and Cold War Intellectuals

In a 1955 *Chicago Review* essay titled "Jazz and the Intellectuals: Somebody Goofed," Nat Hentoff, then the New York editor of *Down Beat*, excoriated American intellectuals for overlooking jazz "as a musical language and as a way of life." In their ignorance of "the pulsating ramifications of jazz and the jazz life," American intellectuals were guilty of perpetuating an insidious cultural racism. Hentoff's diatribe singled out Anatole Broyard's "too glib" essays in the *Partisan Review*, especially one from 1948 titled "A Portrait of the Hipster." In his romanticization of the jazzman as a connoisseur of street language, sex, drugs, and existential angst—a precursor of Norman Mailer's more famous 1957 *Dissent* essay "The White Negro"—Broyard demonstrated to Hentoff a typically shallow sensationalism that obscured jazz's artistic properties and cultural depth. "Few intellectuals," Hentoff charged, "have allowed themselves to become aware of the predominantly Negro contribution to American culture, apparently because of their inability to acknowledge this kind and range of American Negro creation in the arts." When *Time* finally decided to "recognize" jazz in 1955, Hentoff noted, it did so with a cover story on Dave Brubeck, who "was respectable enough for *Time* because he had studied with Milhaud, was a favorite among collegians—and was white." This was all the more lamentable given that *Time* had failed to eulogize Charlie Parker when he died that spring. "[T]he conception of an American Negro musical innovator of Parker's freshness, originality, and complex power," Hentoff wrote, "was quite beyond the knowledge or imagination of *Time*'s music editor—as it is beyond the ken of most American intellectuals, whether they work for Luce or write for the *Partisan Review*."[1]

The essay was both a noteworthy public jeremiad and an important manifesto: central to Hentoff's indictment of dominant American intellectuals was the idea that jazz critics and jazz musicians should be taken seriously at the highest levels. Hentoff's own experience told him that this was not the case. In 1950, shortly after taking his B.A. from Northeastern, Hentoff was covering jazz, sports, and politics for Boston radio station WMEX. That year, as a recipient of one of the first Fulbright fellowships, he set out for Paris to work on a comparative study of American and French literary modernism in the work of T. S. Eliot and Paul Valéry. The poetry treatise disappeared somewhere in the intoxicating haze of Parisian cineclubs, theaters, and jazz cafés. Returning home, Hentoff entered Harvard's graduate program in American Civilization, a leading institutional center of the upstart discipline of American studies. It was his intention to write a dissertation arguing for Duke Ellington as the "preeminent further extension of what F. O. Mathiessen had called the 'American Renaissance.'" This seemed a savvy and exciting plan: Mathiessen's New England-centric American literary canon was one of the foundations of the Harvard program, and though Hentoff's resumé showed that his cultural interests reached beyond the nineteenth-century Transcendentalists, by conceiving his jazz project in terms so conspicuously solicitous of Mathiessen's model, surely he would ensure that the proposal would receive a warm welcome.

Such, however, was not the case. Wandering through the stacks of Widener library one day early in his first term, Hentoff came upon one of his professors. After telling Hentoff how much he enjoyed his jazz radio show, the professor took issue with a seminar paper in which Hentoff had shown high regard for Phillis Wheatley, the late-eighteenth-century African American poet. "Would you be as enthralled with her verses if she were white?" the professor icily asked. He then suggested to Hentoff that perhaps the academy wasn't the best place to pursue an interest in jazz— perhaps he'd be better off sticking to radio and broadening his experience in the world "out there." The next week Hentoff withdrew from Harvard's American Civilization program.[2]

Nat Hentoff was neither the first nor the last to suffer Harvard's ivory tower snobbery, and the real significance of his truncated career as a graduate student lies instead in the assumptions and inclinations that he brought to the experience. Like Barry Ulanov, Rudi Blesh, Sidney Finkelstein, and Marshall Stearns, Hentoff had taken it for granted that jazz should anchor any serious reckoning with the history of "American civilization." In turn, he thought that the study of jazz required a serious reckoning with the history of U.S. race relations, along with honest and unfettered communication and interaction across the color line. This would not be easy in a society still riven by racial segregation, but that's what made it all the more necessary for intellectuals to undertake the challenge. As Hentoff soon found out, however, understanding jazz "as a musical language and as a way of life" was not a pressing matter for either Boston's Protestant old-guard intellectuals or for the New York–based cohort of Jewish intellectuals who would move from 1950s liberalism to post-1968 neoconservatism. But Hentoff and other of the more intellectually ambitious jazz critics knew that the story of jazz was a metaphor for modern America: its social pluralism, its bursting creative energy, and also, in the music's struggle for cultural legitimacy, its failure to come to terms with the racial underpinnings of its national culture. If European intellectuals had long celebrated jazz as America's own distinctive artistic creation, then why, with the country's postwar geopolitical and military dominance lending greater value to its homegrown cultural products, shouldn't American intellectuals do the same? Better yet, why shouldn't jazz develop its *own* intellectual infrastructure: its own institutions, journals, forums for debate, and methods of analysis and critique?

It was during the cold war years after World War II, as several scholars have argued, that American intellectuals became aware of themselves as a distinct social class and as agents of cultural, moral, and political leadership.[3] Postwar U.S. global military hegemony spawned a new scientific and technological elite, along with dramatic growth in the size and scope of the American higher education system and allied research institutions. While professionally trained scientists, engineers, and managers fine-tuned and rationalized a rapidly expanding and interlocking network of state, military, and corporate institutions, academics and cultural critics analyzed the strengths and weaknesses of the American system, exploring the tensions and problems of the new mass society. Cultural intellectuals concerned with art, music, and literature—university professors, museum curators, magazine journalists, and editors—benefited from the growth of an affluent middle class with the disposable income to enrich itself through upscale leisure and cultural consumption. The mass marketing of paperback novels, long-playing records, art prints, and movies enlarged the role of the critic as a cultural gatekeeper and interpreter. The most influential of these cultural intellectuals saw themselves as not merely consumer guides, but priestly agents of moral authority in an "age of anxiety" marked by the pervasive threat of nuclear annihilation, totalitarianism, bureaucratic standardization, and a conformist mass culture.

As Andrew Ross argues in *No Respect: Intellectuals and Popular Culture* (1989), cold war intellectuals considered it a matter of political and moral responsibility to nurture and defend a "serious" national culture, safeguarding it from the contaminating influence of political radicalism, sentimental populism, and an intellectually bankrupt mass culture.[4] David Hollinger has argued along similar lines that the group of postwar literary critics he calls "the keepers of the canon" (the New Critics R. P. Blackmur, Cleanth Brooks, John Crowe Ransom, Allen Tate, and the New York circle of literary critics led by Lionel Trilling) saw their mission as a humanistic defense against the assaults of science, technology, materialism, collectivist politics, and mass culture. By this account, these critics' common argument for art as autonomous and self-justifying, a realm of creative freedom insulated against the contingencies of politics, ideology, and history, was *itself* politically and socially motivated. If the United States had shouldered the military burden of power in the battle against fascism in the 1940s and then against communism in the 1950s, these intellectuals saw themselves as carrying an analogous responsibility to maintain an arsenal of aesthetic weapons in the battle to uphold cultural standards.[5]

Many of the scholarly histories of cold war–era U.S. intellectual life remain narrowly focused on the sectarian politics of anticommunism, failing to analyze in sufficient depth how race relations and racial politics shaped the intellectual climate of the period. A welcome exception is Harvey M. Teres's *Renewing the Left: Politics, Imagination, and the New York Intellectuals* (1996). Teres argues that a major failure of the intellectual leadership of the American Left in the 1950s and 1960s was "their Negro problem." The phrase cleverly appropriates the title of Norman Podhoretz's controversial 1963 *Commentary* essay, "My Negro Problem—and Ours." Frankly admitting his own deep ambivalence toward African Americans originating from a set of painful episodes in his youth, Podhoretz trenchantly noted the "curious phenomenon of white middle-class liberals with no personal experience of Negroes . . . discovering that their abstract commitment to the cause of Negro rights will not stand the test of a direct confrontation." For Podhoretz and other New York intellectuals, the prominent group of cold war–era cultural critics who wrote for the influential publications *Partisan Review, Politics, Dissent, Commentary*, and the *New York Review of Books*—a selective list of the circle would include Podhoretz, Nathan Glazer, Daniel P. Moynihan, Daniel Bell, Lionel Trilling, Mary McCarthy, Dwight McDonald, Irving Howe, Hannah Arendt, and Sidney Hook—"our Negro problem" was the nagging issue of how to overcome the historical legacy of slavery and Jim Crow segregation and bring about full African American inclusion in mainstream American economic and political life.[6]

Teres argues persuasively that the *real* problem for these intellectuals was how unwilling they were to engage in the kind of cross-racial cultural interaction that would inform and inspire their ostensible commitment to racial equality. Eager to appear concerned about the "problem" of race, they proffered detailed strategies and policies for combating the most obvious forms of discrimination. What they never allowed themselves to see, much less be tutored and transformed by, are what Ralph Ellison called the African American "concord of sensibilities": the full range of expressive styles and philosophical dispositions cultivated by blacks in their complicated social history as Americans. It is especially ironic but telling that a group with significant expertise in the areas of literature and culture remained largely blind and tone-deaf to developments in African American cultural expression. In refusing to embrace African Americans in their full humanity, these intellectuals failed to recognize how profoundly black culture had shaped the broader American culture and character.

Teres's powerful critique of the New York intellectuals makes the case of a Nat Hentoff an important alternative example of postwar cultural work. During these years Hentoff cultivated his skills as a warrior in the field of New York intellectual combat, acquiring a reputation as a kind of all-purpose heretic—an achievement he attributes to a combination of his Jewish heritage and the fact that he "came to know certain jazz musicians at so early an age that they, not unwittingly, were my chief rabbis for many years."[7] His is a political autobiography that defies the assumptions held by Norman Podhoretz and other of the mainly Jewish New York intellectuals. Far from suffering a "Negro problem," Hentoff attributed his fundamental ideological convictions to his formative experiences among black musicians. Hentoff claimed that his politics and his journalistic ethos grew out of his affinity for Duke Ellington's dictum to always remain a fierce individualist who is "beyond category," belonging to no school. When he wasn't reading *Down Beat* as a teenager in the early 1940s, Hentoff religiously imbibed George Seldes's four-page weekly sheet *In Fact: An Antidote for Falsehoods*, the first American publication devoted entirely to press criticism. Seldes, Hentoff later said, wrote with "a verve, an immediacy, a delight in risk-taking that reminded me of the jazz musicians I so respected and marveled at."[8] Hentoff found a similar spirit in *I. F. Stone's Weekly*, where Stone served up meticulously researched, sharply worded retorts to official government and mass media propaganda. Hentoff embraced these journalistic mentors as friends of the Bill of Rights and foes of ideological orthodoxy. A self-described liberal "Jewish atheist civil-libertarian, imperfect pacifist, [and later] committer of civil disobedience against the Vietnam War," Hentoff used his Old Testament beard and unstinting diligence as major assets in his various moral campaigns against the self-satisfied postwar liberal intelligentsia.[9]

The New Jazz Critics

As Teres suggests, it was in the realm of music "that we find examples of the kind of energetic, solicitous, and critical engagement with aspects of African American culture that allowed for mutual regard and influence."[10] Hentoff's example is amplified by other white jazz writers who came to prominence in the 1950s and influenced jazz discourse for decades thereafter. These include several, in addition to Hentoff, whom I'll introduce in this chapter and revisit in subsequent chapters: Martin Williams, Dan Morgenstern, Whitney Balliett, Ralph Gleason, Ira Gitler, and Gene Lees. To be sure, even as collectively these writers carried forward the racial liberalism of the prewar critics, the nature of their engagement with black culture and black people, and their sense of the importance of race, varied by individual. So too did their backgrounds, training, writing styles, politics, and general social and aesthetic philosophies. Hentoff, Williams, and Balliett were linked (along with Marshall Stearns) by affiliations with literary criticism, a field that enjoyed heightened prestige in the postwar academy as well as in public intellectual discourse. While Hentoff abandoned literary culture for more engaged political work, Williams and Balliett endeavored to make jazz criticism a branch of literary criticism—Williams through an academic approach modeled on the literary New Criticism he studied as an English graduate student at Columbia early in the 1950s, Balliett through a poetic style that itself aspired to the category of literature. The cool, poised, and genteel voices of these two WASP writers found powerful platforms: for Balliett, the *New Yorker* magazine, where he has been the regular, highly acclaimed jazz columnist since 1957; for Williams, the Smithsonian Institution, where after years of freelance writing he landed a position in 1972, and served as a head of several jazz programs until his death—at age sixty-eight—in 1992.

Balliett regarded social issues and racial politics as a distraction from what he took to be his primary duty of finding the right language to describe the music and the people who play it. Williams dismissed all talk of social context as an unfortunate Marxist intrusion and sublimated his considerable interest in race into a notion of the transcendence of art over race. Hentoff and Gleason, by contrast, thought about jazz as part of a larger set of social issues and concerns, civil rights and civil liberties preeminent among them. Hentoff, the Greenwich Village fixture, and Gleason, the suburban New York–born Irishman who became an icon of Berkeley and San Francisco, shared strong independent Left politics (anti-statist as much as anticommunist) and fierce activist commitments to the civil rights movement. Hentoff had a regular column in the *Village Voice*, Gleason one in the *San Francisco Chronicle* along with a weekly nationally syndicated jazz column. With their topical and fervent styles, these writers enjoyed wide popular acclaim beyond the jazz world. Hentoff joined the civil rights struggle in the late 1950s and raised money for the Student Non-Violent Coordinating Committee (SNCC), while Gleason was an important behind-the-scenes advisor to the leaders of the Berkeley Free Speech Movement. Such political commitment endeared these men to musicians and fans who involved themselves with struggles for social and economic justice, both in the jazz world and beyond. It also meant that these writers wrote less about jazz as they engaged with other cultural and political developments. Decades later, Hentoff would be known as much for his First Amendment advocacy as for his jazz expertise. Gleason, who was fifty-eight when he died of a heart attack in 1975, was eulogized not only as a jazz critic, but as the co-founder of *Rolling Stone* magazine, a Dutch uncle to the San Francisco rock counterculture, and a proud member of Richard Nixon's White House Enemies List.[11]

New Yorker Ira Gitler trained as a journalist at the University of Missouri, moved into publicity in a job with Prestige Records from 1950 to 1955, collaborated with Leonard Feather on several editions of *The Encyclopedia of Jazz*, and produced film scripts on jazz subjects for the USIA. With Hentoff, Gleason, Morgenstern, and Lees, his jazz press writing stressed personal intimacy with the musicians, an insider perspective, and a combination of biography, critical analysis, and advocacy. Gene Lees and Dan Morgenstern were newspaper journalists in the mid-1950s who then served as editors of jazz magazines late in the decade and into the1960s, highly challenging positions in these years given jazz's contentious cultural politics and the fragmentation of the jazz audience brought on by the youth culture revolution and ensuing generational and ideological cleavages. Both grew up outside the United States—Morgenstern in Denmark and Sweden, Lees in Canada—and, like Leonard Feather a generation earlier, first embraced American culture through their adolescent jazz enthusiasm and hero-worship of black musicians. As a European Jew fleeing the Nazis, Morgenstern had an especially acute sense of minority consciousness. As a boarding school student in Sweden he had been deeply moved by Richard Wright's *Black Boy* (1945) and Erskine Caldwell's lynching novel *Trouble in July* (1940), and one of the first books he read after arriving in the United States was the Swedish sociologist Gunnar Myrdal's landmark study of American race relations, *An American Dilemma* (1944).[12] Lees, in his1995 book *Cats of Any Color*, characterizes his early years as a reporter, first in Canada, then in the United States, as a "journey into difference," a ravenous hunger for ethnic variety marked by especially strong personal relations with blacks. He claims that growing up Canadian in the shadow of a dominant American culture left him "permanently sympathetic to the black-identity problem in the United States." The second black person he met in his life was the Canadian-born pianist Oscar Peterson. A barber had refused to cut Peterson's hair, and Lees, then a fledgling reporter at a small Canadian newspaper, was assigned the story.[13]

Lees and Morgenstern represent telling examples of the Left-to-center shift in cold war–era liberal politics. Lees, named after Eugene Debs, turned sharply against his parent's radicalism. Through the years, he has developed the view—the same one held by James Lincoln Collier, also the son of Leftist parents—that Leftist jazz writers from John Hammond to Hentoff and Gleason have "falsified" jazz history by exaggerating protest elements in the music and understating the American mainstream's acceptance of it.[14] Morgenstern—whose Polish-born Austrian father was an anti-Nazi journalist blacklisted by the Third Reich—grew up in a Scandinavian social democratic environment, supported Henry Wallace's Progressive party campaign in 1948, and flirted with early-1950s Leftist organizations. After attending Brandeis University in the mid-1950s (majoring in the History of Ideas, including classes with Irving Howe, Lewis Coser, and C. Wright Mills), he settled on a Left-leaning liberalism shared by Lees, Gitler, and many others in jazz circles, splitting the difference between the bedrock businessman's conservatism of a Stan Kenton and the pink-shaded dissent of a Dizzy Gillespie or Jon Hendricks. Since 1976, Morgenstern has been the director of the Institute of Jazz Studies, a leading jazz archivist and historian, a prolific annotator of reissue albums and CDs, and an important mentor to younger jazz critics and scholars. Lees, who has worked extensively as a lyricist, re-emerged as one of the most prolific jazz writers of the 1980s and 1990s.

These writers came of age at a time when jazz, as Orrin Keepnews has said, was prevalent if not popular. With rock'n'roll fast securing its niche as the music of adolescent rebellion, jazz—which had so ably filled that role in the 1920s and 1930s—was now respectable, even fashionable, among educated, adult professional elites. These writers carried the jazz crusade beyond the jazz trade press into the world of mass-market print and broadcast journalism, education, concert and festival promotion, and record production. They peddled freelance work to mainstream forums (the *New York Times, Esquire, Harper's, Saturday Review, Holiday*), alternative publications (the *Village Voice*), avant-garde journals (the *Evergreen Review*), and men's magazines (*Playboy, Nugget, Escapade, Cavalier, Rogue*). They hustled for liner-note commissions from major record labels like Columbia, Decca, and

RCA Victor as well as from smaller independents like Atlantic, Blue Note, Riverside, Prestige, and Contemporary. They did radio (Hentoff, Williams, and Gitler at WBAI in New York, Morgenstern at WBGO in Newark, Gleason at KHIP and KMPX in San Francisco) and television (Hentoff and Balliett as producers of the 1958 "Sound of Jazz" program on CBS, Gleason as producer and host of "Jazz Casual" on National Educational Television and as producer of documentaries on Duke Ellington and the Monterey Jazz Festival). They were centrally involved in the advent of jazz festivals: Hentoff as a friend and early supporter of Newport Jazz Festival producer George Wein; Gleason as a founder (with Jimmy Lyons) of the Monterey Jazz Festival. They promoted concerts, notably Morgenstern's "Jazz in the Garden" series at the Museum of Modern Art. They produced records: Hentoff as an A&R man at Contemporary, Verve, United Artists, and Candid; Gleason as a vice president of Fantasy Records. They taught jazz history courses. And they started their own jazz magazines: Hentoff and Williams's the *Jazz Review* (1958 to 1961) and Gleason's *Jazz: A Quarterly of American Music* (1957 to 1960).

This diligence can be ascribed in part to the relatively small, tightly interlocking nature of the jazz economy; in part to the modest remuneration that went with the work; and in part to the limitations of the established jazz trade press. When Gene Lees became editor of *Down Beat* in 1959, he discovered that "everyone who had worked [there] had left with a seething hatred of the magazine."[15] *Down Beat* owner John Mahar was notorious for his penury and for knowing or caring little about jazz or its audience. Lees, whose editorship lasted until 1961, several times threatened to quit when Mahar, worried about the magazine's sales in the South, forbade him to put photographs of black musicians on the cover. "I pointed out," Lees later wrote, "that thirty-four of the thirty-seven winners of the magazine's own popularity poll were black. To bar them from the cover, quite aside from any consideration of ethics or civil rights or history and the fact that black Americans had invented this music, was to exclude the people that our own readers most wanted to read about."[16] A telling irony of the situation was that Ted Williams, the *Down Beat* staff photographer who shot the covers, was one of the very few African Americans employed by the magazine. After serving as New York editor of *Down Beat* from 1953 to 1957, Nat Hentoff was fired after complaining to the publishers about the absence of blacks on the magazine's staff and for hiring a black secretary without his superiors' approval. "I think that the [jazz] magazines ought to try a recruiting campaign for more Negro writers and critics," Hentoff wrote in 1961, well before the term "affirmative action" entered public discourse. "I don't mean that a man or woman should be hired just because he is a Negro, but the law of averages should indicate that there *must* be more qualified Negro writers on jazz (and liner note writers) than are currently employed in those capacities."[17] Lees hired Barbara Gardner as a *Down Beat* contributing writer—the first black woman on a national jazz magazine. Dan Morgenstern, during a short stint as editor of *Metronome* in the early 1960s, worked with black writers LeRoi Jones (Amiri Baraka) and A. B. Spellman on some of their first published jazz pieces.[18]

Low staff morale and striking non-diversity notwithstanding, *Down Beat* maintained the largest readership of any jazz magazine. In the years during and after World War II the magazine dramatically increased its international reach, such that by 1957 it had subscribers in 75 countries. That year editor Jack Tracy reported that *Down Beat* counted more than 20,000 subscribers and 70,000 readers.[19] Through the 1960s and beyond the magazine capitalized on the growing high school and college student market. Advertisements for musical instruments targeted student musicians, while feature stories covered high school and college band competitions. Record company advertisements and record reviews together fed the burgeoning consumer market for jazz LPs. If jazz writers were to find a mass audience, their point of access was here amid the consumer discourse. Hentoff, Gleason, Williams, and Lees (along with Leonard Feather and Barry Ulanov) served at various times in the 1950s and 1960s as regular columnists in *Down Beat*; aside from the record reviews, profiles, and feature articles they otherwise published in the magazine, the column format provided a platform for armchair reflections on jazz and whatever else crossed their minds. Very often these reflections took the form of diatribes against the forces of commercialization.

Upstart alternative jazz magazines that pointedly eschewed *Down Beat's* commercialism all struggled for solvency, none building subscription lists of more than a few thousand. Set to fold after its December 1959 issue, *Metronome* won a reprieve when photography editor Herb Snitzer prevailed upon his wife's uncle, Robert Asen, to buy the defunct publication. Resuming operation with the June 1960 issue under the leadership of Snitzer, editor Dave Solomon, and art director Jerry Smokler, *Metronome* became, briefly, a hip, avant-garde publication that surrounded its jazz coverage with cutting-edge Beat literature (poems, a chapter from William Burroughs's *Naked Lunch*), politically charged cartoons, and other innovative visual material. Trouble came in July 1961 when a cover photograph of a Coney Island stripper raised the ire of high school librarians, five or six hundred of whom cancelled their subscriptions. Solomon was fired, Dan Morgenstern took over, and the magazine reverted to straight jazz coverage. But by the end of that year Asen, citing reverses in other of his business ventures, pulled his support, and the magazine ceased operation for good.[20]

Better Get It in Your Soul

In the late 1950s and early 1960s, the tension between critical and commercial discourses played itself out in jazz magazine coverage of "soul jazz" (also sometimes called "funk or "funky" jazz), a black roots-infused style marked by tuneful blues voicings, song titles displaying the speech inflections of black vernacular speech (e.g., Bobby Timmons's "Dis Heah" and "Dat Dere"), and a general ambience redolent of the down-home rhythms and spirit of the sanctified church. The emergence of the style—dated conventionally to the Horace Silver tunes "The Preacher" and "Doodlin'" on the 1955 Blue Note LP *Horace Silver and the Jazz Messengers*—coincided with epochal events in the modern civil rights movement, the 1954 *Brown v. Board of Education* decision and the Montgomery bus boycott. Ben Sidran has characterized the music as a watershed in black self-identity:

> The American Negro after 1954 . . . began to draw strength from the fact that the country's legal structure had, for the first time, publicly admitted the validity of the black man's cause and was prepared to make accommodations. For the first time in black American history, it seemed possible that history had turned in favor of even the poorest black and that he could do something to advance himself. "Soul" music . . . was one origin of a cultural self-improvement program and in insisting that the Negro had "roots" that were valuable rather than shameful, it was one of the most significant changes to have occurred with black psychology. "Soul" music was important not just as a musical idiom, but also as a black-defined, black-accepted means of actively involving the mass base of Negroes.[21]

Nat Hentoff has also stressed an economic motive in soul jazz: a reaction by black musicians against the popular vogue of West Coast jazz played by white musicians such as Chet Baker, Shorty Rogers, Dave Brubeck, and Shelly Manne. Writing in 1997, Hentoff described West Coast jazz as "well-mannered technically skilled music" that was "low in soul and high in pretensions," and rued that because of the popularity of this music among mainstream white listeners, these musicians "appeared in ads for colognes and other genteel merchandise in the fashion magazines." These advertisements, Hentoff noted, didn't include a single black face. "Cannonball and other [black] musicians were furious," Hentoff remembered. "Here were these white guys appropriating black music, stripping it of its soul, and making much more money than the deep swingers in the jazz capital of the world."[22]

But back in 1961, in a *Metronome* article about his experience as a record producer, Hentoff had this to say:

> One increasing problem I've found is that some jazzmen are so anxious to make records that will sell that they have to be dissuaded from using "commercial" material. I have vetoed, for example, some "soul" numbers which were brought to the date for no other reason than that "soul" music of a certain repetitive genre has been selling. Another leader had to be persuaded to do his own superior ballad compositions instead of certain warhorses with the sawdust coming through. "But," he protested, "is it safe to make an album of all originals?" Safe, hell. In the long run, it seems to me that the jazz album which is the strongest in material and the least compromising in the playing is the one that will last longest as an active part of the catalogue.[23]

At the time of the soul jazz movement, the passage suggests, Hentoff worried that its commercial appeal might undermine qualities of originality and individuality that he deemed integral to jazz art. By 1960, record companies had seized on soul as a marketing device, flooding jazz magazines with advertisements claiming their special prescience in advancing the genre. Prestige Records—in a full-page ad for LPs by Eddie "Lockjaw" Davis, Jack McDuff, Arnett Cobb, Gigi Gryce, Shirley Scott, and others—ran copy proclaiming that "Despite Opposition of Critics Prestige Gave Birth to Soul Jazz!"[24] Riverside Records took a more coy approach, perhaps a case of the company owner, former critic Orrin Keepnews, insinuating to savvy record buyers that his operation rose above the venal motives of his competitors. The top of the first page of the three-page ad carried a large banner announcing "Everybody's talking about SOUL but Riverside's got it!" Following a few punchy riffs on the tricky semantics of "funky," "earthy," and "down home," the copy reads: "It occurs to us that, *without our having particularly planned it that way*, large chunks of the RIVERSIDE catalogue offer an excellent practical definition of SOUL in its various aspects" (italics mine). In thus framing a commercial discourse for its product—the catalogue included LPs by Cannonball and Nat Adderley, Bobby Timmons, Blue Mitchell, and Johnny Griffin—Riverside tried to disavow any preordained mercenary motive; it could ride the trend, its integrity intact, not having engaged in anything so mendacious as a trend-setting campaign.

Ralph Gleason foreshadowed this kind of clever discourse when, in a 1957 *Down Beat* column, he likened soul jazz to the gimmickry of commercial advertising. "A good portion of the jazz on records released each month is shallow, superficial, ugly, and inartistic," he wrote. "We hear much about 'soul' in jazz. If 'soul' is anything, it is honesty and truth in emotion and how can you have this when you sit down and consciously strive for effect like an advertising agency copywriter selling the new look in autos?"[25] Gene Lees, in a 1960 *Down Beat* column, cast similar aspersions on the music, archly posing as a devotee of canonical high art not likely to be fooled by cultural counterfeits. "I am re-reading Northrop Frye's monumental study of Blake, *Fearful Symmetry*," Lees told his readers. "I wish all jazzmen and critics and admirers of the art would read it. . . . It makes so much of the current talk about 'soul' look as cheap and shallow as it is. It makes so much Gospelized playing look false. It makes so much of the current jazz aesthetic look as precious and pretentious as it is."[26] Other critics, in published interviews with musicians, framed their articles in such a way that the discussion of soul jazz could only address the issue of commercialization. Barbara Gardner, in a 1960 *Down Beat* article, registered the "torment" haunting pianist Bobby Timmons "because of the corruption and commercialism [in soul jazz] alongside sincere creation and accomplishment." "You can't take a thing like real soul and wrap it up in packages and sell it," Timmons said.[27] "Don't you think this funk thing is going a bit too far?" Leonard Feather asked Horace Silver in a 1961 piece for the British magazine *Melody Maker*. "I do think they are overdoing it a bit today," Silver responded, adding, "Maybe if all this 'soul music' sells records, that's good, but perhaps the record companies and some of the magazines are overdoing it. They are trying to hang on to a commercial gimmick." Silver warned that jazz needed to guard against what he saw happening in rock'n'roll, where the "pure kind, like Ray Charles," had been diluted. "I just hate to see people bastardizing this by making contrived, synthetic funk," Silver said. "That reminds me of rock'n'roll, in which so much of what you hear nowadays is synthetic, with these hill-billies trying to commercialize on it."[28]

Feather began his article belittling soul not so much for its commercial exploitation as for its ethnic folk provenance. "[O]wing some of its origins to the simple gospel music of the Negro churches," he said, "it represents a retrogression musically rather than an advance." Martin Williams articulated a more nuanced position in a 1958 essay titled "The Funky-Hard Bop Regression." Here too, though, the reigning assumption was that qualities of ethnic "authenticity" were valuable only so long as they served the more exalted purposes of high art. Williams praised the "return to the roots" impulse of Horace Silver and others for saving "both the emotional heart of jazz and its very substance from a preciocity, contrivance, and emptiness that certain tendencies in 'cool' jazz might have led to." But he warned that "a lot of what passes for 'funk' and 'soul' is more on the surface than in the depths." He found depth—and a resistance to the "regression" of his title— in the way Thelonious Monk, as a composer concerned with form rather than a wailing jazz musician *cum* preacher, had become a "great virtuoso of rhythm, meter, space, and time."[29]

Jazz was commerce, and jazz was art, but exactly where jazz should be positioned in relation to other cold war–era commercial culture and artistic discourses was a matter of some concern. *Jazz Review* publisher Hsio Wen Shih, in a 1961 column, fretted about jazz's cachet in two distinct but related discourses: the new, upscale men's magazines and Beat literature.[30] As Barbara Ehrenreich has suggested, what unites the *Playboy* bachelor and the Beats in 1950s American male culture is a shared disdain for the dowdy and repressed Organization Man, a thirst for more libidinally charged states of body and mind than those sanctioned in the bureaucratized establishments of business, education, and government.[31] Shih was running a publication whose editors, lapsed humanities graduate students Hentoff and Williams, set out to accomplish some of the same goals as the critics who were building the canon of Euro-American modernism in *Partisan Review, Kenyon Review, Hudson Review,* and other journals. Against this bookish backdrop of his magazine—but also with the grim knowledge that Hentoff and several other well-known jazz writers had been selling work to *Esquire* and *Playboy* at far better rates than those paid by his magazine or even by the commercial jazz magazines *Down Beat* and *Metronome*—Shih was concerned about where the dominant public image of jazz was headed. Was it a serious art deserving of dispassionate intellectual scrutiny, or simply "an accessory for sophisticated seduction like the sports car, the Italian tailoring, and the mixed drinks"? He wondered further, with evident unease, whether the "hip novelists" had gotten it right in representing jazz as "essentially orgiastic and therefore innately sexual, or that jazz and its milieu are the modern city equivalent of Huck Finn's Territory, 'the wild frontier of American nightlife,' as [John] Clellon Holmes called it."

On the basis of a sound article on the jazz avant garde in *Nugget*, unsigned but obviously to him the work of one of the established jazz writers, Shih allowed that the stroke magazines might be capable of sponsoring responsible jazz coverage. The really serious danger was an alliance between these magazines and the Beat writers outside of the oversight of legitimate jazz authority. Such was the case with a piece by Jack Kerouac in the December 1960 issue of *Escapade*, which Shih says was sent to him by Ira Gitler, who— one has to assume—had been perusing the magazine for reasons other than his interest in the latest jazz intelligence. Kerouac breathlessly enthused about a "parade of wailers who will make the New Wave Jazz pop," but was unable to spell their names correctly (pianist "Wintin Kelly"), match player to correct instrument (bass player Quincy Jones), or muster specifics about their playing style (Red Garland is "a strange thinker, actually.")

In general, the jazz writers I'm focusing on here were at pains to distance themselves from the Beat and "white Negro" discourses, eschewing both Kerouac's jazz-as-a-"heartbreaking grope" and Norman Mailer's jazz-as-"rage . . . joy, lust, languor, growl, cramp, pinch, scream, and . . . orgasm." On the one hand, writers such as Hentoff, Williams, Gleason, Balliett, and Morgenstern were convinced that jazz was a more sober and difficult craft, and that its players were a more temperate and dignified lot, than was portrayed in literature that foregrounded the music's visceral properties, spontaneity, and ecstatic states of feeling. On the other hand, these writers sought to code their own work as more "serious," to align themselves with what literary critic Seymour Krim called "the writer's writers" who derogated Kerouac's method—christened "spontaneous bop prosody" by Allen Ginsberg—as "non-stop gush."[32] The case for Kerouac and other Beat writers as richly learned in several artistic traditions, religions, philosophy, and emerging fields of psychology and anthropology, and as practitioners of an oral art form intimately related to jazz in its experimental approaches to rhythm, tone, and intersubjective communication—a case made most compellingly in recent years by American studies scholar Daniel Belgrad[33]—largely was one not taken up by jazz critics.

Ralph Gleason was one of the first to report on the jazz-poetry movement in San Francisco in the late 1950s, and the poet Lawrence Ferlinghetti later credited Gleason with being "the first and foremost critic" to see "the blue notes [and] the blue writing on the wall."[34] In a *Down Beat* column in May 1957, Gleason praised Ferlinghetti's poem "Autobiography" as "lyrically an opposite number of Charlie Parker and Dizzy Gillespie in that it has the same pleasure in the wording and rewording of popular phrases from the mass consciousness as they have had with the playing of bits and snatches of melodies from the mass memory."[35] But in November 1957, Gleason registered this complaint about the jazz-poetry movement: "Most of the poets are slumming. Jazz already has an audience and they don't. They're cashing in on the jazz audience but they won't learn anything about jazz or listen to it or try to allow the natural jazz rhythms they have to come out. Instead they are blithely wailing away with the same sort of thing that lost them their audience in the first place. . . . Not until a poet comes along who learns what jazz is all about and then writes poetry will there be any merger."[36] Nat Hentoff similarly attacked Norman Mailer's "The White Negro" for betraying an ignorance of jazz music, for propagating a fallacious image of the jazz musician, and for trafficking in racial stereotype. "[Mailer's] conception of the jazz musician, especially the Negro player, as the apotheosis of the purely existential 'hipster,' the Prometheus of orgasm," Hentoff wrote, "is not too far from the legend that 'all God's chillun got rhythm,' particularly the darker ones." Not only did very few jazzmen conform to Mailer's romanticized image of the hipster, Hentoff asserted, but reactions to the music on the part of the hipster/white Negro element in the jazz audience "are usually as superficial and unknowledgeable as those of the hungrily impressionable adolescents who watch Stan Kenton imitate the American eagle."[37]

Art, Intellect, and the Power of Love

The reference to adolescents was a signature gesture, emblematic of a new jazz writing that trumpeted its intellectual legitimacy by employing tropes of aging and maturation. According to the new gospel, the music and its audience had grown up: a fan culture driven by raw, undisciplined teenage enthusiasm had been supplanted by more sober and cerebral modes of adult appreciation. What Whitney Balliett derided as the "hot gassy prose, provincialism, inaccuracy, and condescension" of pre-1950s jazz writing now gave way, it was held, to a cooler, more measured sensibility.[38] In his introduction to a 1959 collection of critical essays for Oxford University Press pointedly titled *The Art of Jazz*, Martin Williams described the book as a "small but respectable body of criticism—the kind that only an art can inspire and that only an art deserves," a scholarly dossier, that is, that might help the American public view jazz as something other than "some sort of intriguing emotional outburst" or "strange branch of show biz that interests adolescents of all ages."[39] Too much jazz criticism, Williams complained in a 1958 *Down Beat* article on the role and training of the jazz critic, was public relations pablum or amateur journalism being palmed off as informed opinion, and this was incongruent with the high quality of the music. "We assure ourselves that jazz is an 'art,' and often proceed to talk about it as if it were a sporting event," he rued. Arguing that critical tools must be "trained, explored, disciplined, and tested like any other talent," Williams urged a stronger analytical approach to the music and more of an emphasis on content and meaning. "If I recommended that this training should begin with Plato, Aristotle, and Lucretius and end with Eliot, Tovey, and Jung," Williams asserted, "I would not be saying something academic or pretentious but merely stating the most ordinary commonplace of Western civilization as it exists."[40]

At the *Jazz Review*, Williams and Hentoff combined text-based analytical criticism (much of it by musicians, including Gunther Schuller, Dick Katz, Bill Crow, Cannonball Adderley, and Cecil Taylor) with interviews, biography, history, and social commentary. By making a case for a jazz tradition that transcended various schools and styles, the magazine claimed to be combating the internal sectarianism, sentimentalism, flippancy, and sensationalism that the editors said had promoted the decline in the quality of American jazz writing since the 1930s. "Basically what we were trying to do," Williams later said, "was to discuss jazz as if it were a music, an important music with an important heritage, and discuss jazz musicians as if they were creative people rather than public celebrities or colorful old characters."[41]

Just how to discuss jazz "as if it were a music" remained an open and vexed question. The *Jazz Review* offered one controversial example in an essay by Gunther Schuller, "Sonny Rollins and the Challenge of Thematic Improvisation," in the November 1958 issue. Using musical notations and terms like "tritone" and "major third," Schuller rendered an analysis of tenor saxophonist Sonny Rollins's recording "Blue Seven" that conceded nothing to the most laboriously close readings by the literary New Critics. Schuller's argument was that the musical rhetoric of "Blue Seven"—the grammar, syntax, and expressive style of the solos by Rollins and drummer Max Roach—represented a new threshold of "intellectual enlightenment" in jazz. Schuller exalted Rollins's skills as a "thematic" improviser who was pointing jazz beyond the shopworn theme-and-variations approach practiced by most swing and bop soloists. Overcoming its "humble beginnings," Schuller argued, jazz had undergone a "maturing" process that had "attracted interest in all strata of intellectual and creative activity." By purposely working to achieve thematic and structural unity in their solos, Rollins and Roach exemplified "the growing concern by an increasing number of jazz musicians for a certain degree of intellectuality." Just as in the new jazz criticism, with its more systematic methods and its containment of emotional excess and sentimentality, certain jazz musicians themselves—it went without saying that the "soul" players were not what Schuller had in mind—were now favoring "the power of reason and comprehension" over "purely intuitive emotional outpouring."[42]

We can see in Williams's and Schuller's invocations of jazz's "important heritage" and rational "enlightenment" a grasping for the aura of seriousness and cultural depth that Ross, Hollinger, and other scholars have diagnosed as central to cold war–era intellectual concerns. Central to this stance, I'm suggesting, was a desire to foreground a sense of masculinist authority in the new jazz criticism as well as in the more cerebral, less popular jazz. In both their rhetorical distancing of themselves from the swing-era fan culture of their own adolescence and their ambivalence about the "commercial" soul/funk music of the 1950s, these jazz critics invoked notions of high-art autonomy, rationality, and profundity to insulate jazz from the realm of mass culture, imagined as a space where putatively feminized, passive consumers were spoon-fed a diet of easily digestible pablum.[43] The *Jazz Review* buttressed these attitudes with flinty pronouncements on the jazz critic's responsibility to the causes of truth and objectivity. In one illuminating exchange in the magazine's letters section, Dan Morgenstern accused the editors of a "pseudo-Olympian, snobbish, and smugly omniscient" attitude. Miffed by what he deemed a bias against traditional jazz, alleging that dismissive reviews were threatening to undermine the careers of several aging swing musicians, Morgenstern paid tribute to the *Jazz Review*'s critical autonomy and integrity while at the same time issuing an appeal for a more humane, anti-intellectual approach:

> You have set yourselves up as the arbiters of standards in jazz criticism. You are uncommitted to advertisers and payola. You have prestige and ipso fact, authority. Your only business is jazz. Jazz is the *sine qua non* of your being. But you are becoming so concerned with problems of abstract critical and artistic ideals that you are rapidly losing sight of the essential fact in jazz: the living, breathing, working jazz musician who earns his daily bread by performing jazz music.[44]

Hentoff's response hinted at the unresolved nature of the jazz critic's role, at the tension between passion and reason, sentiment and judgment. "The effect of criticism on a musician's livelihood has absolutely no bearing on how a critic should function," Hentoff lectured Morgenstern. "[The critic] becomes patronizing to the musician and dishonest with himself and his audience if he allows non-musical considerations to affect his judgment." But Hentoff seemed cowed by the programmatic stiffness of his own words. Rather than soften his severe pronouncement, however, Hentoff tried to funnel and sift it through a pliable metaphor. "Too much of the past and a considerable amount of the present writing on jazz reflects a 'crush,' hardly a love affair," he wrote. "Certainly love must be part of any aspect of criticism," he conceded, "but infatuation is not love, and the more one understands what one loves, the more honest and giving that love is." Sentiment and ardor have their place in jazz appreciation, Hentoff allowed, but any emotion-saturated posture toward the music must be properly contained and channeled, lest it remain hopelessly mired in gushy adolescence. "You act like a servant to a girl, my friend," Hentoff admonished Morgenstern in tellingly gendered terms, "and she'll leave you for someone who can give her a stronger feeling of self-respect and of being realistically accepted—not served."[45] One can hardly imagine a more transparent image of jazz criticism as a chivalrous enterprise, gallantly squiring "lady jazz" into respectability.

This debate reveals something of the self-consciousness that pervaded the discourse, as critics wavered between postures of imperious critical authority, impassioned devotion, and selfless ministration. "To criticize any art form effectively postulates love," Ralph Gleason insisted. "If you do not love this art form with which you are occupying your days and nights there are only two other possible attitudes: neutrality or distaste. Either of these makes you a hatchet man or a ghoul. At the very best you can be an educated, intelligent cannibal living off the artistic carcass."[46] Several years after his tussle with the *Jazz Review*, Morgenstern reported on a discussion with a "well-known musician" who had been reading a great deal of jazz criticism in preparation for a brief stint as a disc jockey. "Most of these guys write as if they didn't really like jazz," the musician told Morgenstern. Such writing, Morgenstern speculated, was the product of a jazz critic's "status inferiority," his recognition that "jazz criticism is not a respected branch of contemporary writing," and his resulting tendency to "overcompensate by emphasizing in his work all the things that contribute to the respectability he craves for the music and for himself." It behooved jazz writers, Morgenstern admonished, "not to ride roughshod over the music and its practitioners in order to prove our own presumed intellectual superiority or to contemplate some abstract artistic ideal that has no relation to the problematic circumstances in which the creation of jazz takes place."[47]

Freed from the contained, disciplinary tightness that defined one side of the *Jazz Review* agenda, Hentoff's interaction with jazz musicians in this period took on many of the qualities that Morgenstern advocated. In 1957, for example, Hentoff and Whitney Balliett served as consultants for a CBS television program, "The Sound of Jazz," that featured musicians from the Count Basie band of the 1930s, including two, Lester Young and Billie Holiday, who were in poor health and nearing the end of their lives. The show's producer, Robert Herridge, a fierce advocate of "quality" programming whose projects included tele-dramas of works by Dostoyevsky, Joyce, Faulkner, and Melville, insisted on a *"Partisan Review* pure" approach: no set, no props, just the music. Billie Holiday bought a five-hundred-dollar gown just for the occasion, and when Herridge deemed it too ostentatious, it fell to Hentoff to tell Holiday she couldn't wear it. In the video of that program, a physically ravaged Lester Young, barely able to stand up straight, much less blow his saxophone with the controlled, understated intensity that was his trademark, takes a chorus on "Fine and Mellow." An equally wan, almost ghostlike Billie Holiday responds to her estranged friend's every note with a succession of facial maneuvers invoking the deepest feelings of affection. In later accounts of the episode, Hentoff came off as nostalgic and wistful:

> [Prez] blew the sparest, purest blues I had ever heard. Billie, smiling, nodding to the beat, looked into Prez's eyes and he into hers. She was looking back with

the gentlest of regrets of their past. Prez was remembering too. Whatever had blighted their relationship was forgotten in the communion of the music. Sitting in the control room I felt tears, and saw tears in the eyes of most of the others there. The rest of the program was all right, but this had been its climax—the empirical soul of jazz. . . . On the set, after the hour was over, Billie, pleased with the show, came over and kissed me. Lester was gone, somewhere in space.[48]

The tone of this passage—which I've assembled from accounts of the "Sound of Jazz" program in Hentoff's 1976 book *Jazz Is* and his 1986 memoir *Boston Boy*—noticeably breaks with the high modernist gravity that characterized so much of the jazz critical discourse of the late 1950s. In these later texts, Hentoff has abandoned the voice of the earnest intellectual and social crusader; once again, as in his youth, he speaks with a fan's enthusiasm and emotional commitment. The important implication here is that the figure of the jazz critic as a serious intellectual had special resonance in the late 1950s, and is best understood as arising in response to the cultural forces of that period.

An "insider" discourse, purposely made public, revealed the self-awareness behind this jazz-critic-as-intellectual construction. As if to pre-empt criticism's lofty pretensions, *Jazz Review* regularly published material that poked fun at the magazine's editors and other leading jazz critics. In one piece that ran under the mock-serious title "The Symposium," Joe Goldberg caricatured the voices of critics gathered together to discuss *cause célèbre* Ansel Jones, a fictionalized upstart trumpeter. Whitney Balliett is fussy, food-obsessed, and unable to keep his sentences under control: "In a typical solo he will start with a sort of agonized laziness, as if he were awakening from a dream caused by having eaten too much welsh rarebit the night before, and then, in about the third chorus, he will, in a series of short, splatting notes that give the effect of a catsup bottle hit once too often on its end, abruptly switch into a fast tempo that belies the furry bumbling that preceded it." Ralph Gleason is a self-important gadfly: "[Jones] shows a kind of courage I have only found in the poetry of Jon Hendricks and the humor of Lenny Bruce. And if you don't hear that parallel in the music, as well as overtones of Allen Ginsberg, Dylan Thomas, and Paul Klee, then your ears are stopped up by prejudice, and I don't want to have anything to do with you." Gene Lees is an insecure elitist desperate to prove how tight he is with musicians: "I'm not as friendly with Ansel Jones as I am with Quincy and some of the other guys, but some of the things they play remind me of tunes I've heard in my extensive collection of Hindemith and Stravinsky records." Martin Williams is an insufferable pedant: "It is impossible to write about the music of Ansel Jones without using the word 'artist.' His compositions are five-strained rondos with the fourth strain omitted (ABACAE) and, in using this approach he might seem to incorporate the form that had previously been notable in only the work of, say, a Jelly Roll Morton, a Duke Ellington, a John Lewis, a Thelonious Monk." Nat Hentoff can't resist expressing outrage at American social conditions: "As the plane crossed the Mason-Dixon line"—Hentoff is on his way to Texas to check out Jones's home town—"I noticed that certain of the passengers had been given containers with a large 'N' stenciled on them. Is this the America of Dwight McDonald?"[49]

Williams's and Hentoff's decision to publish Goldberg's spoof hints at a spirit of writerly bonhomie, a healthy willingness to air out and loosen up the discourse. But it suggests something more: the anxiety and ambivalence that lurked beneath the surface of their assertive public voices. For Hentoff, this stemmed from a recognition of the jazz musician's—especially the black jazz musician's—keen sense of accomplishment and self-possession. He wrote in *The Jazz Life:*

> The jazzman, particularly the Negro, is proud of what he has developed by himself. Because of the huge emotional investment he has made in his music, the jazz musician generally respects only the opinions of other musicians who have also worked out their problems and styles by themselves and does not always respect theirs. In addition, the Negro player frequently does not believe that the critics—nearly all of whom are white—have paid the emotional 'dues' he has been assessed from the time he was born. Therefore, he reasons, not always with justice, how can the critics possibly understand his message, which is so much more than the notes he plays?[50]

Williams was famous for his imperious manner and donnish conceits, yet he was also obsessed with his limitations as a jazz writer. He deferred to Gunther Schuller's musicological authority and envied Whitney Balliett's reputation as a superior stylist. Though less vocal than Hentoff in the 1950s in decrying the paucity of black jazz writers, Williams in subsequent years championed the work of LeRoi Jones (before his turn to black nationalism), A. B. Spellman, Albert Murray, Hollie West, and Stanley Crouch. He was acutely aware of musicians' skepticism about jazz criticism. "I've often considered writing a column dedicated to the proposition that musicians are the only qualified critics," Williams wrote in a *Down Beat* column in the 1960s. After first citing Miles Davis and Gil Evans as especially discerning and articulate critics, Williams then told a story meant to show how criticism operates internally in jazz musician discourse. In the story, Art Tatum takes Billy Taylor to hear an old blues piano player. The bluesman, Old Joe, is having a very rough night: "He couldn't stumble through a blues chorus without making a major mistake." Taylor assumes that Tatum was disappointed in Old Joe's performance and found nothing in it of value to his own playing. But then one afternoon Tatum invites Taylor over to hear him play. Taylor listens intently as Tatum stretches out on a 12-bar blues. When Tatum uses a "deft and beautiful bass movement," Taylor indicates his delight and asks the master where he learned the figure. "That's Old Joe's riff," Tatum says, "that's the one he uses."

The lesson of the story for Williams?

> A good jazz critic certainly does need to be musical. And a great jazz critic will probably be a musician, just as most great critics of poetry have been poets. But he will have to be critical, in the strict sense of the word, and all musicians aren't critical. But a truly great critic will also need—without being sentimental or indulgent about it—some of the understanding and largess that Art Tatum had for Old Joe.[51]

The Born Pedagogue

Behind this folksy anecdote was a formidable theory: Williams believed that the primary force acting on the jazz musician was the legacy—the tradition—of jazz *itself*. In an unmistakable echoing of T. S. Eliot's classic essay "Tradition and the Individual Talent," Williams maintained that "the jazz musician is a part of what an academician might call an 'historical process,' and he knows it and takes his place in it as an individual."[52] Williams began his career as a jazz critic in the early 1950s while studying English literature and literary criticism at Columbia. "I had the guidance of literary critics, whom I respected," Williams later recalled. "I was really drawn to literary criticism. I was [particularly] influenced by the New Critics. They were talking about a novel as if it were a novel, a poem as if it were a poem, a play as if it were a play."[53] New Criticism was the doctrine forged in England in the 1920s by I. A. Richards, F. R. Leavis, and Eliot, in which the art work—usually, for the New Critics, a poem—was seen as a self-contained, self-sufficient object, and criticism was the investigation of how the work resolves its formal tensions to achieve structural coherence. By the late 1940s university-based literary critics (the keepers of the canon), imperially confident of the objective, timeless, authoritative quality of their evaluations, thought themselves to be identifying precisely those works of literature that compelled the serious attention of educated people. Leavis, for example, was telling his Harvard students that a scholarly study of modern English literature required the reading of Austen, Eliot, James, and Conrad but not of Fielding, Thackeray, Dickens, Joyce, or Woolf. And if a student had the audacity to question this reading list, Leavis, armed with the formidable scholarly ammunition of his treatise *The Great Tradition*, was prepared to fire off as many rounds of Leavisite literary principle as it would take to win consent on his choices.[54]

For Williams, this approach seemed germane not just to literature but also to jazz. Just as Nat Hentoff's Fulbright-sponsored studies in modernist poetry disappeared in the Paris night, so Williams's academic work in English literature fizzled in the ferment of New York's 1950s jazz scene. In 1953, fully in thrall to jazz but fearful of his parents' reaction were he to drop out of graduate school, Williams started writing freelance reviews for the *Record Changer* while continuing to teach and work toward his Ph.D. In these reviews, Williams began applying his graduate school training to canon-building efforts already underway in the field of jazz criticism. Central to Williams's New Critical approach was the notion of the art work as a seamless and nonfungible whole, with virtually every detail playing an essential and unchangeable role. In a 1956 review of a Jelly Roll Morton reissue, Williams was aghast that the first few bars of "Mamie's Blues" had been excised from the original recording. He likened this "amputation" to "leaving out the first few lines of a finely wrought sonnet."[55]

Like the literary critics he admired, Williams's inclination was, as David Hollinger says of the keepers of the literary canon, to "simply be committed to texts."[56] Williams's immense and precise knowledge of the history of recorded jazz—the canon of jazz texts—was the envy of many critics and musicians. At the 1958 summer session of the Lenox School of Jazz, Williams attended Marshall Stearns's seminar on jazz history and, with the rest of the class, took a listening examination asking for identification of the personnel and dates of ten recordings, with brief discussion of each record's style and artistic significance. A typical exam was the one turned in by a Lenox faculty member—a composer of some note—who missed three of the identifications outright; marshaled only the vaguest recognition of three others; supplied marginally correct information on the four others; and declined to offer any stylistic analysis. Williams went a perfect ten for ten on the identifications, provided extensive and precise discographical information, and offered incisive commentaries such as the following:

(On James P. Johnson's piano roll of "The Charleston"): Gives lie to all clichés about stride monotony. Those trills toward end of choruses before verse interpolated sound faked on roll. This roll is *definitely* transcribed too fast. Fine rhythmic variety—*the* point of the performance.

(On a Lennie Tristano cut): Mostly fatuous piano doodlings to me—a man swimming around under water with his eyes shut. . . . No melodic or rhythmic imagination. . . . All harmonic but not arpeggios—pseudo-melodies. Bauer (not a jazzman, I think) on guitar pleasant and empty. Typical suspended ending—off into nothing (but from nothing and through nothing too).

(On a Charlie Parker record with Cuban percussionist Machito): Marshall, I'm sorry but this kind of thing is (temporarily) abandoned. Didn't work. Alto rhythmic conception (unlike Dizzy's) owes nothing to this kind of rhythm. It's a mambo with the usual mambo tricks and rather mechanically played by the band.[57]

Here, perhaps even more clearly than in his published criticism, we see what Gary Giddins meant when he described Williams as "a born pedagogue who seemed obsessed with locating masterpieces, pinpointing their significance, and demonstrating precisely what made them tick."[58] He did so with an austere prose style and an intensity of purpose that sometimes grated. He made enemies, who retaliated by painting him as a scourge. "I'd feel happier about Williams's pedestal if he could ever be caught tapping his foot on it, or smiling," wrote Willis Conover, describing Williams's critical tools as "a dissector's blade, an intricate system for pigeonholing the parts, and a sophomoric pretense of Olympian detachment."[59]

Whitney Balliett called Williams "the American counterpart of the French jazz *philosophe* André Hodeir," and it was in the composer Hodeir's *Jazz: Its Evolution and Essence*—published in this country in 1956 after appearing in France in 1954 as *Hommes et problèmes du jazz* (1954)—that Williams found his model.[60] Hodeir's book gathered under one cover a periodization of jazz history, a canon of jazz performances, a technical vocabulary for discussing the music, and a theory of the music's aesthetic essences. The book's form *itself* struck Williams as an illuminating act of criticism: an introductory suggestion of jazz's place in contemporary culture (which, to Williams's liking, argued that the music must be seen as a development within the framework of Western music, not as a separate development); an outline of the evolution of jazz keyed to transcendent individual achievements (Armstrong's Hot Fives, Ellington's "Concerto for Cootie," Charlie Parker's Savoy recordings, and Miles Davis's "Birth of the Cool" records); and a discussion of the essential characteristics of jazz. Some American jazz writers found the book rarified and laborious. Balliett called it a "dry and difficult semi-musicological study" suffering from a "hyper-intensity that leads M. Hodeir into the hushed zones of French theoretical criticism," while Dan Morgenstern lampooned Hodeir as "the great white father of current criticism" who, "in the best French intellectual tradition," was trying to teach Americans how to see jazz as a "Serious Art Form."[61] A few suggested that Hodeir's remoteness from the American scene and his Eurocentric assumptions led him to misunderstand the music's fundamental properties. These critics—notably Balliett and Billy Taylor—took particular exception to Hodeir's argument that improvisation and the blues are not essential to jazz.[62]

Williams embraced Hodeir's book as the first work of jazz criticism to argue unequivocally that "people make the music change," not technology, geography, or abstract social forces. He was more receptive to Hodeir than other American critics in part because the French composer represented for him a highbrow sensibility he thought jazz criticism could use, but equally because he found Hodeir's systematic approach enticing. He was won over by Hodeir's argument that Charlie Parker had deeply enriched and replenished jazz by burrowing deep into the organic roots of the music, particularly in regard to rhythm, at the same time that he was crafting improvisations out of the harmonic and melodic languages of European music. In the late 1950s, when Ornette Coleman took the advances of Charlie Parker a step further—subverting conventional chord structures, bar lines, and ways of fingering and blowing a saxophone—Williams insisted that Coleman too was working within the implicit resources of jazz, especially in his deep feeling for the blues. This reckoning with the avant garde came at the same time that Williams was writing monographs on King Oliver and Jelly Roll Morton. He insisted on seeing jazz whole.[63]

In the early to mid-1960s, Williams wrote a series of essays on individual jazz musicians (all black save for Bix Beiderbecke) for the *Evergreen Review* that later, collected, became his masterwork, *The Jazz Tradition*, published by Oxford University Press in 1970. In 1992, Oxford editor Sheldon Meyer—the leading jazz book editor of his time—characterized *TJT* as "the most influential book written about jazz in the last twenty years."[64] The book served as a blueprint for the canon of jazz records that came to assume semi-official status in Williams's selections for *The Smithsonian Collection of Classic Jazz* multi-disc LP set, first released in 1973. Formalizing his *idée fixe* of a coherent tradition, Williams argued for two basic thrusts in the evolution of jazz: first, all key stylistic innovations in the music result from changes in rhythmic conception (e.g., "We may say that Armstrong's rhythms are based on a quarter-note. Parker's idea of rhythm is based on an eighth-note"); and, second, jazz history breaks down into alternating periods of innovation and consolidation (e.g., Ellington's and other swing bands ordered and institutionalized the Promethean innovations of Armstrong; after 1940s bebop challenged and tested jazz's basic musical language, Thelonious Monk, John Lewis, and Sonny Rollins set about "establishing some sort of synthesis within the idiom").[65] Williams grounded his insights in close and repeated listening; he later described his research methodology as a matter of scrutinizing a well-chosen stack of records.[66] Musician testimony appears only incidentally, and the book makes no claims as a social history of the jazz life. In a philosophical aside, Williams assails sociological treatments of jazz (all of which he labels "Marxist") as reductive and obtuse. "Art does not reflect society and environment and consciousness," he wrote, "so much as it tells us what environment and society and consciousness do not know."[67] This was in spite of Williams's passionate feelings about race: "Jazz is the music of a people who have been told by their circumstances that they are unworthy," he says at the end of *The Jazz Tradition*, "[a]nd in jazz these people discover their own worthiness."[68]

Some reviewers took issue with Williams's method and tone. "His writing gave me the strange feeling that to him such legendary jazzmen as [Johnny] Dodds, Jelly Roll [Morton] or Charlie Parker mean no more than an entry in a record catalogue or prized and rare records in his collection," complained journalist Jackie Kendrick. "[T]he book reads like the lines of a *magister* in a Renaissance theoretical dialogue," carped musicologist Frank Tirro. "Can a tradition be covered in sixteen individuals?" asked Duke Ellington's nephew, Michael James. Leonard Feather questioned Williams's use of the royal "we" and an overall tone of omniscience that led to "sententious generalizations." "A statement such as: 'Johnny Hodges can play the blues; Benny Carter not' may come as a shock to those of us who treasure our Benny Carter blues records," Feather wrote. Dan Morgenstern praised Williams's musical interpretations but criticized his "ambiguous attitude towards the jazz environment." Williams "underestimates the jazz audience," Morgenstern reckoned, "putting 'fans' in quotes and otherwise adopting an elitist attitude." Morgenstern found it "baffling" that Williams did not reflect on the paradox, "inseparable from the jazz tradition," of serious playing and listening oftentimes taking place in a "barroom atmosphere." Such was "the price the serious jazz critic has to pay," Morgenstern concluded, for working "in an atmosphere considerably more rarified than that in which the artist lives and creates."[69]

The idea that Williams's approach gave short shrift to the gritty (or even prosaic) social realities of jazz experience would blossom through the next several decades, even as *The Jazz Tradition* and *The Smithsonian Collection* accrued more power and presence in jazz criticism and education. In 1992, an influential article by musicologist Gary Tomlinson singled out Williams's work as constituting a "monological canon"—Tomlinson noted that four major jazz college textbooks used *The Smithsonian Collection* as a companion—that preempted the "search for jazz meanings *behind* the music, in the life-shapes that gave rise to it and that continue to sustain it."[70] Foreshadowing this scholarly assessment were the cavils of Conover and others concerning Williams's mandarin posture and the bludgeoning that his high-art purism took in the culture wars of the 1960s. But these important interrogations of Williams can't erase the fact and scope of his influence. In 1970, Lawrence Kart provided a clue as to why Williams would loom so large: "It may seem like a simple thing to direct the reader to Morton's 'Dead Man Blues,' Ellington's 'Blue Serge,' or Monk's 'Criss Cross,'" he wrote, "but if one is unfamiliar with such works (and many earnest apprentices may be) this guidance is invaluable." Testifying to the larger impact of Williams's career, Kart added, "Speaking personally, I could not begin to enumerate the times during the past decade and a half when Williams's writing led me to music that I came to know and love."[71]

For budding younger critics, Williams was much more than a consumer guide; he provided a map through the thickets of jazz's recorded history and a model for discussing the music in precise but non-technical language. "Although never as influential with a mass readership as Leonard Feather, Nat Hentoff, or Whitney Balliett," Francis Davis wrote in 1987, "Williams has long been the critic from whom others in the field take their cues." Davis calls Williams "the most perceptive critic ever to write about jazz."[72] At the Smithsonian, in 1974 and 1975, Williams created a fellowship program in jazz criticism, with a faculty that included Albert Murray, David Baker, Dan Morgenstern, and Jaki Byard. Among the student fellows were some of the most important voices to emerge in jazz criticism in the post-1975 period: Gary Giddins, Stanley Crouch, Bob Blumenthal, J. R. Taylor, Peter Keepnews. "We all recognized Martin's abiding influence," Giddins later wrote. "We were a generation in part formed by him, able to quote him chapter and verse."[73] A new edition of *The Jazz Tradition* in 1983 carried a back-cover blurb from Morgenstern hailing Williams as "the most distinguished critic America has produced." The most recent edition, from 1993, has an introduction by musicologist Richard Crawford, in which he calls *TJT* "one of the great books in American music history."

In a 1989 interview, Williams reflected on his career and legacy:

> It took until J. R. Taylor and Gary Giddins's generation [before] I had any credibility as a critic. Except for people like Nat and Whitney, who did like me. Whitney doesn't like my writing, he never has. He likes my ideas. Most of the writers on jazz who were my contemporaries or older thought I didn't know how to write. George Frazier once tried to give me lessons in how to write. I told him I wasn't trying to write that kind of criticism. They'd say 'Does

Martin Williams really like jazz?' because I wasn't brimming over with the kind of adolescent enthusiasms that they were used to. I hoped I was trying to say something a little bit more substantial. But I was probably so damned full of myself and so egotistical that I was insufferable to them—let's throw that in.[74]

The Sound of Surprise

Whitney Balliett aspired "to be a famous literary critic" when he was hired by *New Yorker* editor William Shawn after his graduation from Cornell in 1951.[75] Balliett worked first at the magazine as a "collator," the person who tracked the work of fact-checkers, copy-editors, and the legal department and collated articles into master proofs. A drummer—a great admirer of Sid Catlett—Balliett had long been a jazz enthusiast. In the mid-1950s he began to place jazz essays with *Atlantic Monthly* and the *Saturday Review*. Shawn offered him a regular *New Yorker* jazz column in 1957 (he continued to write news items, book and theater reviews, and unsigned Talk of the Town pieces until Shawn retired in the 1980s). Balliett prized the *New Yorker* as a "writer's magazine," a place to rub shoulders with the likes of A. J. Liebling, Edmund Wilson, E. B. White, Janet Flanner, and Joseph Mitchell. This fast literary company not only enhanced Balliett's development as a prose stylist; it provided cachet in his incarnation as a jazz writer. As the one jazz writer who enjoyed mainstream legitimacy merely by virtue of his platform, Balliett boldly seized the opportunity to move jazz writing beyond the generic boundaries of record reviewing and infracritical debate.

In Otis Ferguson, George Frazier, and Richard Boyer, jazz had attracted some very skillful writers. But only Balliett could describe trumpeter Red Allen's face as a "study in bassett melancholy" and Jo Jones's physique as "resembl[ing] a tightly packed cigar," or say that "Jimmy Rushing, the suave, blimp-sized blues shouter, has always sounded as if he were wearing spats and morning coat and had just had a good laugh," or deride the pretentious Stan Kenton band's "glistening limousines of sound that, in the end, tended only to stifle whatever potentialities for jazz there were on hand." Only Balliett's eye for detail could produce this memorable picture of Pee Wee Russell—

> Thin and tallish, he has a parenthesis-like stoop, spidery fingers, and a long, wry, gentle face governed by a generous, wandering nose. When he plays, this already striking facial arrangement, which is overlaid with an endless grille of wrinkles and furrows, becomes knotted into unbelievable grimaces of pain, as if the music were pulling unbearably tight an inner drawstring.[76]

—or this one of drummer Ed Blackwell:

> No matter what tempo he is playing, he sits behind his drums—his dark glasses
> halfway down his nose, his elbows loose, his shoulders rounded, his hands
> hayforks—as if he were ambling down a country road.[77]

When Leonard Feather said that Balliett "may well be the most gifted writer
ever to bring jazz into print," he meant to imply that Balliett's literary virtuosity itself contributed significantly to the polishing of jazz's public image.
In a 1992 essay paying tribute to his critical forebears, Gary Giddins admitted to an initial impatience with Balliett's "metaphorical overdrive," but also
deemed Balliett "a miraculous writer" of whom "it has been said that you
can read him even if you don't care for jazz."[78]

Unlike John Hammond, Nat Hentoff, and Ralph Gleason, Balliett was
not on a mission to save America's soul. "At its best," Robert Warshow
said caustically but insightfully about the *New Yorker* in the post–World
War II years, "[it] provides the intelligent and cultured college graduate
with the most comfortable and least compromising attitude he can assume
toward capitalist society without being forced into actual conflict. It rejects
the vulgarity and inhumanity of the public world of politics and business
and provincial morality, and it sets up in opposition to this a private and
pseudo-aristocratic world of good humor, intelligence, and good taste."[79]
When Balliett had an axe to grind, his tools were irony and humor. He argued
implicitly that the case for jazz should be made in the quality of refinement
and discernment with which one approached it: the highest compliment one
could pay the music, and the most effective way to enhance its appeal with
the general public, was to write about it with grace and elegance. "Until the
past five or so years," he wrote in a 1956 essay explaining why so much jazz
writing of the past was intemperate and overzealous, "jazz has been widely
regarded in this country as a kind of queer Victorian aunt who laces her
tea, belches at the wrong moment, and uses improper amounts of rouge."[80]
At a time when jazz's increased presence in festivals, at colleges, and in the
mass media made it possible for critics like Marshall Stearns, Hentoff, and
Gleason to become public spokesmen for the music, Balliett chose to let his
jazz writing speak for itself. Endowed with the *New Yorker's* cultural capital
and true to his own self-effacing temperament, Balliett set out, as he put it,
to "breathe on some of the aesthetic mysteries of the music."[81]

Balliett developed a mastery of the prose portrait that discussed a musician's style as a function of personality and character. Not until the 1960s
did Balliett regularly conduct interviews with musicians and quote them
in his pieces. Before that, in a concern likely influenced by New Critical

orthodoxy, Balliett worried that the interviewing process might cloud his critical judgment.[82] Ben Yagoda, in his recent history of the *New Yorker*, suggests that in the turn to using his informant's voices, Balliett may have been following the example of Joseph Mitchell, the magazine's most revered reporter. Mitchell's technique, and later Balliett's, was to splice together discrete quotations, creating what appears in the published essay as a long, uninterrupted monologue.[83] Particularly in these biographical profiles, but sometimes also in reviews and critical pieces, Balliett worked against benighted images of jazz as a deviant subculture, even as he looked for the quirks and idiosyncrasies that gave each musician a stamp of individuality. He preferred not to make an issue of race, rarely mentioning a musician's racial identity, and, if commenting on the jazz world's racial sociology, doing so as a deeply embedded aside. No propagandist for color-blindness, Balliett simply didn't find the topic compelling in and of itself. Yet, ironically, often it was Balliett's writing alone that recorded black culture and experience in the nation's most distinguished magazine. Especially in the early years of his tenure at the magazine, as Yagoda has pointed out, African Americans were hardly ever represented in *New Yorker*, and when they were, "one got the sense that the writer was an ornithologist studying an odd species."[84] This cannot fairly be said of Balliett's respectful treatment of Duke Ellington, Teddy Wilson, Ornette Coleman, and many others.

Unlike Martin Williams, Balliett did not rest his case on close readings of isolated records and performances. As Gary Giddins has argued, when Balliett set about describing Pee Wee Russell's sound—"In the lowest register, which he seems increasingly to prefer, he gets a hushed, edgeless sound. In the middle range, his tone becomes more explicit, suggesting soft, highly polished wood"—he was describing the "mythical ur-Russell performance," not any *actual* Russell performance. Balliett brusquely dismissed annual critic's polls and short lists of greatest jazz moments or "desert island" records, deriding those exercises as typical of the vulgarity and triviality of a fan-centered discourse the serious jazz writer must transcend. But he felt equally that the serious jazz writer shouldn't take his subject *too* seriously. The concept of a masterpiece, the breastplate of Williams's critical armor, violated Balliett's sense of the music's uniqueness. "Unhappily," Balliett complained, "most admirers of jazz still appear to be governed either by a short-winded faddism that selects its youthful heroes on a kind of musician-of-the-month basis or by an academic approach that sets up in bronze and stone musicians who haven't played a fresh, honest note in fifteen years."[85] Jazz, Balliett wrote in the introduction to his first collection, *The Sound of Surprise* (1959), is a "highly personal, lightweight form—like poetry it is an art of surprise—that, shaken down, amounts to the blues, some unique vocal and instrumental sounds, and the limited, elusive genius of improvisation. At best, these can provide an intense, sometimes profound emotional satisfaction, which is altogether different—largely because of sheer mathematical proportions—from that induced by the design and mass of, say, Berlioz's 'Requiem.'"[86]

Like Williams, Balliett eschewed technical musicological terminology, approaching jazz criticism instead as a literary form aimed at the educated general reader. "I had a teacher once who told me that if you're going to be a critic the first thing you have to do is *describe* what it is you're criticizing," Balliett said in a recent interview. Music in general, and jazz in particular, posed an especially difficult challenge:

> Music is not easy to write about. It's not there. You can't see it, or smell it, or touch it. It's amorphous. As a result, I've used a lot of metaphor. It's the only way I know how to do it. If you're going to be a good critic you need to excite the reader. You have to make the reader hear the music. You're not going to be excited by a notation of a Pee Wee Russell solo. Because it's almost impossible to notate jazz. You can't get the sound of the instrument. You can't get the placement of the notes, whether they're a little ahead of the beat, or behind it. So I try to describe solos, try to describe how a musician sounds.[87]

One way to grasp Balliett's method is by way of a comparison. Here's a sample from Gunther Schuller's aforementioned *Jazz Review* essay on Sonny Rollins's "Blue Seven":

> The chord structure underlying the entire piece is that of the blues in B flat. The primary notes of the theme (D, A flat, E) which, taken by themselves, make up the essential notes of an E-seventh chord thus reveal themselves as performing a double function: the D is the third of B flat and at the same time the seventh of E; the A is the seventh of B flat an also (enharmonically as G sharp) the third of E; the E is the flatted fifth of B flat and the tonic of E. The result is that the three notes create a bitonal complex of notes in which the "blue notes" predominate.[88]

The same month that Schuller's essay appeared in the *Jazz Review*, Balliett reported in the *New Yorker* on a Rollins performance at Carnegie Hall. Balliett also credited Rollins with developing an important new approach to extended improvisation, but with markedly different tone and texture:

> [Rollins] is an improviser who, at the outset of just about every tune, invents a slight variation (rather than the shards of the melody) as a theme, which he turns over, pokes, pulls, slaps, throws into the air, and then restates. He also

has developed a sly, comic approach by frequently intoning his variations in a slightly bleary, sidling way, falling away from each note as if it were slippery.[89]

Schuller's discourse presumed a specialized audience of musically literate jazz intellectuals, musicians and aficionados for whom a scientifically precise discussion of Rollins's tonality served as evidence of jazz's status as a serious art. Balliett assumed that his *New Yorker* readers wanted to feel themselves more sensually connected to jazz's creative moments. His efforts to link musical style to defining character traits—to craft the image of a distinctive performance persona—worked better for readers who lacked strong convictions about a given musician's work or who had little interest in either abstract theory or historical genealogy. If you flatly disagreed with Balliett's assessment of a musician, or if you were looking for a methodical historical argument, Balliett's stylistic flair might seem more puzzling than illuminating. When Balliett criticized drummer Max Roach for an "aggravating monotone," but then, in the same review, called him a "first-rate technician" and admitted to being "absorbed" by his "precision and authority," the reader might have been unclear exactly where to stand on Max Roach—even while thrilling to Balliett's unexcelled portrait of a drummer at work.[90] "Balliett the stylist and Balliett the critic often appear to be two men," Giddins says. "The former dazzles you with a description of Cecil Taylor at work that is more vivid than any photograph, but the latter offers little about the value, historical place, or emotional impact of Taylor's music."[91]

Balliett fiercely defended himself against the oft-repeated charge that he was a mere impressionist, a literary interloper poaching jazz for its poetic possibilities but always maintaining a sense of cool detachment from his subjects. In a sharp exchange in the *Jazz Review* in 1959, Balliett abandoned his customary reticence to defend himself against what he characterized as an unfair and provincial-minded attack on his work. The British critic Max Harrison, in a review of *The Sound of Surprise*, had accused Balliett of pandering to a "non-jazz audience" with prose that drew attention away from the musicians and the music. Balliett admitted to approaching jazz with a writer's concerns, but denied that this removed him from the jazz world: "[Harrison] states that the 'picturesqueness' of my style, which uses a good deal of metaphor and in which, God forbid, there are even some attempts at humor, is a result of having to sugar coat my materials because I am writing for a non-jazz audience—a non-jazz audience, I guess, that includes such self-revealed readers as Charlie Mingus, Dizzy Gillespie, Pee Wee Russell, John Lewis, Marian McPartland, Rex Stewart, Tony Scott, and more." If musicians read him, Balliett implied, it was because they could see themselves and their creative process in his writing. The things that made jazz special and unique—its quicksilver sounds of surprise that eluded musical notation—called for a fresh, fluid, sensuously attuned language and a sense of timing. "My style," Balliett protested, "is—rather than being merely confectionary—a serious attempt to *describe* the music, to make the reader *hear* what jazz is." And this required the jazz writer to be no less imaginative and inventive than the jazz musician:

> If Mr. Harrison does not hear the "port and velvet" in Gil Evans's orchestrations, I can't help him. If he can't see the difference between a "crablike run" run and a "grapeshot" run, then he doesn't know the difference between a crab and grapeshot, which must be a handicap. As to the "curious" verbs I have "devised"—"blat," "whump," and "thunk." "Blat" is, of course in Webster's, "whump" is an old American colloquialism, and "thunk" is an onomatopoetic invention meant to describe a sound otherwise indescribable—a linguistic process that, if outlawed, would soon reduce the English language to the level of Mr. Harrison's prose.

Balliett's detractors in the late 1950s argued, in effect, that Balliett the stylist trumped Balliett the critic. Saxophonist Julian "Cannonball" Adderley and composer George Russell, occasional contributors to jazz magazines, suggested that Balliett's writerly concerns overshadowed his interest in jazz. Russell questioned Balliett's commitment to serious critical explication: "[Balliett] writes very much to the image of the *New Yorker*. It seems his most important consideration." Adderley concurred: "[Balliett's] most important consideration is writing; what is written [about] is not of importance."[92] Latter-day critics have accused Balliett of being overly precious. Bruce Tucker, for instance, characterized Balliett's collection *Jelly Roll, Jabbo, and Fats: 19 Portraits in Jazz* (1983) as a study of "garrulous older gents under a patina of polite prose."[93] Jon Hendricks begs to differ, defending Balliett's writing as a tribute to the music. "I would never criticize Balliett for caring about the words. It has beauty, a lot of beauty. He's a great writer, and for him to apply that talent to jazz has been a real boost."[94]

Sensitive Cats

The writers I've introduced in this chapter came of age at a time when "individuality" was both a buzzword and a mandate, an antidote to the "conformity" of cold war mass society. But it was also a time when many musicians embraced middle-class lifestyles, and black musicians—along with other black Americans—struggled for equal and full participation in all arenas of American life. Ralph Gleason was fond of saying that the modern jazz musician was a "poet in the supermarket" of American life, an artist who creates among the rabble, an "impermanent audience of casual friends and fans" that typified sociologist David Riesman's notion of the "lonely crowd."[95] Yet, at the same time, Gleason reveled in the warmth and openness of the jazz community, maintained friendships with Gillespie, Duke Ellington, John Lewis, Miles Davis, Carmen McRae, Jon Hendricks, and others, and proudly claimed that it was jazz musicians who showed him how to live. "Dizzy is one of the very few completely *free* men I have ever known. . . . [He] is simply himself at all times and under all circumstances," Gleason wrote.[96]

On Gleason's pioneering television series "Jazz Casual," which ran on National Educational Television from 1960 to 1968, the very ambience seems to express the longings and contradictions in its producer's jazz vision. The soundstage is stripped-down, functionalist, with technicians milling about—a "casual" space conducive to the musicians' ease and comfort, sealed off from the glare of supermarket mass society. In one corner stands a more conventional "set," obvious as such to the viewer because one of the cameras looks behind it, revealing its frame. This set evokes the fake-brick-paneled living room of a late 1950s ranch house, with host Gleason—usually clad in a cardigan sweater, sometimes smoking his pipe, always looking like a latter-day Oliver Wendell Holmes—lingering insouciantly on the edge. Between numbers, Gleason and the headline musician repair to a couple of designer chairs and chat amiably about the music and life in general.[97] The social dynamic here turns on a subtle tension. The critic and the musician share the same bourgeois habitus, but they're different, and it's this difference that the critic is at pains to capture and convey. If Gillespie couldn't be the "colorful old character" that Martin Williams cautioned against as the condescension of an earlier jazz discourse, he could still be—must be—*interesting*.

For the writers I've introduced in this chapter, the challenge of representing the jazz musician was made more difficult by the heightened expectations they brought to their craft, as well as by the demands made on them by musicians who were themselves undergoing processes of self-discovery and self-definition. Among serious musicians and writers, this amounted to an expectation of reciprocity. Gunther Schuller's analysis of Sonny Rollins's "Blue Seven" may have read like an academic exercise, but it grew out of his interactions with Rollins and other musicians, and Rollins read it as a statement about *him*, not as the harbinger of a new mode of jazz criticism. "I read all the magazines when they were writing about me," Rollins told Joe Goldberg in an interview in 1961, then two years into a self-imposed exile from the public stage. "I began to worry about things I shouldn't have. People said that I did a certain kind of thing and I began to believe them, and by the time I figured out how I did it, I was unable to achieve the effect any more."[98] Rollins assured Goldberg that he would not read what he said about him in his book *Jazz Masters of the 50s*. But, significantly, he jumped at the opportunity to talk to Goldberg. Like other modern jazz musicians struggling to articulate a creative vision and negotiate the marketplace, Rollins knew that a sympathetic critic could help. Partly, of course, this was a matter of necessity: through reviews, liner notes, profiles, reportage, record production and concert promotion, the critics had the power to shape the musician's public image, a situation many musicians resented. Still, a musician might well embrace a critic as an ally—if only in private. "Thanks for your kind words," Charles Mingus wrote to Whitney Balliett after a review in the *New Yorker* in 1957. "I'll try to continue to justify them and, who knows, maybe even improve."[99]

Mingus also went the other way. Miffed by something Gene Lees wrote in *Down Beat*, Mingus (by Lees's account) called the writer on the phone, raged and screamed "You're a dirty white motherfucker!" and hung up. He then called back several times, each time starting with a mild-voiced apology, but ending in another obscenity-laced assault.[100] The exercise suggested not just Mingus's famous tendency to oscillate between a menacing posture and a tender desire for reconciliation, but a sense that it was his obligation to perform the role of the angry black musician calling out the misguided white critic. Indeed, in public, Mingus seemed to be competing with Miles Davis to deliver the most lacerating, racially righteous attacks on white critics. Mingus's autobiography *Beneath the Underdog*, published in 1971 but begun in the late 1950s, bristles with rage against a jazz industry figured as a diabolical white supremacist conspiracy. In one symbolically crucial scene, Mingus imagines himself and other black jazz icons (Coleman Hawkins, Roy Eldridge, Art Tatum, Charlie Parker, Dizzy Gillespie) gathered together, jiving and backslapping and presumably ready to get down to the business of making authentic jazz. The good feeling abounds until an intrusive specter suddenly looms up. It's that most horrible of interlopers—a group of white critics. "Man, that's a lot of talent, don't you dig it?" Mingus says facetiously. With wry humor, he assigns the critics places on the bandstand:

> I see Leonard Feather, he's a piano player. There's Bill Coss and Gene Lees— they sing, I heard. Barry Ulanov must play drums or something, dig, with that *Metronome* beat. Martin Williams can play everything. I can tell by the way he writes. Put Marshall Stearns on bass and let Whitney Balliett score and John Wilson conduct. Let all them other young up-and-coming critics dance. How would you like to review that schitt [*sic*] for the *Amsterdam News*?[101]

But even as *Beneath the Underdog* careens from one psychoanalytically induced fantasy to the next, and as Mingus fulminates against the commercialism and racism of the jazz world and America itself, a jazz writer suddenly appears as a benign, even redemptive figure. Mingus goes to Boston for a gig. "And in Boston," Mingus narrates in the third-person confessional mode that dominates the book,

> you meet a very sensitive cat named Nat Hentoff who interviews you on his radio show and turned out to be one of the few white guys you could really talk to in your life. Afterwards you get in the habit of writing him from time to time when you're feeling the pain in the middle of the night and the larger questions that seem to have no answers loom up before your eyes but Hentoff always digs the meaning of the question, and replies. . . .[102]

Mingus reproduces a set of letters he exchanged with Hentoff, including one from New York's Bellevue mental hospital: "Dear Nat, bulletin from Bellevue. I've seen this point in my life coming and I need to know someone human understands, not mechanical men paid to listen and trained to react—a *machine* fed the same information could come up with just as good an analysis of my problems."[103] Hentoff's letters modulate between a friendly intimacy ("Charlie, this is what I think: love, the difficulties of real communication, the reason for wanting to have a reason for staying alive, these have concerned me too ever since I can remember") and a what's-the-meaning-of-it-all? gravity ("for me a man's meaning, the reason he has to keep on living is that were he to live thousands of years he would never fulfill all his possibilities, never communicate or create all he is capable of").[104]

Publicly, Hentoff touted Mingus as a brutally honest man living in an insidiously dishonest age. In a liner note for Mingus's 1957 Atlantic LP *The Clown*, Hentoff likened Mingus to William Butler Yeats's Crazy Jane, a character who in Hentoff's reading "felt beneath the 'sanity' of conformity." In this, the so-called age of conformity, Hentoff leaned on high literary authority to mythologize Mingus's instability, to endow it with the weight of prophecy. "There's more enterprise in walking naked," Yeats said. "Mingus tries harder than anyone I know to walk naked," Hentoff riffed off of Yeats, and it is indeed a naked Mingus on display in Hentoff's writing. In other places, Hentoff described Mingus's personality and music as "irrepressibly spontaneous," "constantly probing," "stormily individual and restless," "expansively romantic." Though steeped in black church music, thoroughly trained in both jazz and classical music, and above all "the most astonishing virtuouso on the double bass that jazz has ever known," Mingus's creative force, Hentoff suggested, came not just from his training or his black roots but from his tumultuous personality and protean intellect. Mingus was a "thorough-going autodidact" who, in response to being ignored by his racist white grade school teachers, "struggled on his own with Freud's *Introduction to Psychoanalysis*." In Hentoff's reckoning, even Mingus's stormy and unstable love life ("it has taken Mingus a couple of marriages to learn that he has first to be able to live with himself") was a source of creative fecundity, a sign of his unflinching commitment to his art.[105]

Miles and the Critics

Mingus was deeply complicit in these constructions of his image as a man of rage and combativeness, tenderness and sensitivity. Other musicians were able to use critics to their own ends. The best example is Miles Davis in his relationships with the few critics (Gleason, Feather, and Hentoff) he saw as exceptions to the racist norm. These critics he challenged, provoked, titillated, humiliated—and used to secure the cachet and cultural capital he needed to triumph in the white-dominated marketplace. Part of this effort included establishing *himself* as a highly articulate critic, able to offer acute and strongly opinionated assessments of other jazz musicians. In 1955, for instance, Davis was trying to regain his perch at the top of the jazz world after a lackluster period marred by his struggle with heroin addiction. His performance with Thelonious Monk at the Newport Jazz Festival that summer garnered rave reviews, and a new contract with Columbia Records promised better distribution than the smaller Prestige label had been able to give him. That fall, Davis gave Hentoff—then the New York editor of *Down Beat*—an interview in which he spoke enthusiastically about his new band members, Sonny Rollins, Red Garland, Paul Chambers, and Philly Joe Jones. He also surveyed the current jazz scene and offered some pointed opinions: Saxophonist Jimmy Giuffre and drummer Shelly Manne can really play, but in general the West Coast music "gets pretty monotonous even if it's skillfully done." Dave Brubeck has wonderful harmonic ideas, but has no sense of touch and can't swing. Saxophonist Lee Konitz does swing, but relies a bit too much on off-center 7- or 11-note phrases. Richie Powell plays too much comp piano behind Max Roach and Clifford Brown. Charles Mingus's composition "The Mingus Fingers" performed with Lionel Hampton is "one of the best big band records I ever heard," but some of the pieces Mingus and Teo Macero have written for small groups "are like tired modern pictures." Singer Billy Eckstine "needs somebody like Sinatra . . . to tell him what kind of tunes to sing and what kind of background to use." The best drummers are Max

Roach, Kenny Clarke, Philly Joe Jones, Art Blakey, and Roy Haynes, though Haynes "has almost destroyed himself working with Sarah [Vaughan]."[106]

At the *Jazz Review*, one of Hentoff's ideas was to hatch a better version of the "Blindfold Test" Leonard Feather had started in the 1940s in *Metronome* and then carried over to *Down Beat*. Calling Feather's tests "adventures in skeet shooting," Hentoff aimed to create a more relaxed and mutually enriching atmosphere by identifying the recordings beforehand, transcribing the musicians' reactions, and encouraging them to elaborate on stories about the jazz life. The plan was to engage Miles Davis in a series of these encounters to be published over the course of several issues. Hentoff ended up with only one session, but that one, published in the December 1958 *Jazz Review* under the title "An Afternoon with Miles Davis," turned out to be a classic in the history of jazz letters. The interview airs a few of Davis's trademark acid dissections ("Oscar [Peterson] makes me sick because he copies everybody. He even had to *learn* how to play the blues. Everybody knows that if you flat a third, you're going to get a blues sound. He learned that and runs it into the ground worse than Billy Taylor . . . ") and dyspeptic asides ("I usually don't buy jazz records. They make me tired and depressed"), but the dominant tone is one of reverence and deep feeling for the accomplishments of his forebears and the innovations of his contemporaries.

Part of the editorial mission of the *Jazz Review*, recall, was to make the case for a jazz "tradition" that transcended any one particular style. Davis did just this here, and with an understated elegance and feeling for the humanity of the music only rarely found in the work of the best critics themselves. Responding to a Bessie Smith record, Davis said, "She affects me the way Leadbelly did, the way some of Paul Laurence Dunbar's poetry did. I read him once and I almost cried. The Negro Southern speech." On Louis Armstrong's "Potato Head Blues": "You know you can't play anything on a horn that Louis hasn't played—I mean even modern." On Coleman Hawkins: "I learned how to play ballads from Coleman Hawkins. He plays all the chords and you can still hear the ballad." On Ahmad Jamal: "Listen to the way Jamal uses space. He lets it go so you can feel the rhythm section and the rhythm section can feel you." On Thelonious Monk: "A main influence he has been through the years has to do with giving musicians more freedom. They feel that if Monk can do what he does, they can. Monk has been using space for a long time." On the future of jazz: "I think a movement in jazz is beginning away from the conventional string of chords, and a return to emphasis on melodic rather than harmonic variation. There will be fewer chords but infinite possibilities as to what to do with them."[107]

These interviews don't square very easily with the unambiguous, summary dismissal of white critics that Davis delivered to Amiri Baraka in their interview for a *New York Times Magazine* profile in 1985. "I don't pay no attention to these white critics about my music," Davis said. "Be like somebody from Europe coming criticizing Chinese music. They don't know about that. I've lived what I've played."[108] Jazz lore is filled with stories about Miles Davis giving writers his backside (though trombonist-turned-writer Mike Zwerin, who as a wet-behind-the-ears college student in 1948 was tapped by Davis to play in the Birth of the Cool band, says that later when he interviewed Davis "he always greeted me with a hug"). Many of these are stories that writers willingly tell about themselves, as if a blunt rebuke by Davis were a masochistic hazing ritual required to maintain good standing in the jazz critic fraternity. Ralph Gleason may have been one of the few writers Davis trusted, but this didn't preclude him from confirming that he too had been firmly put in his place. Gleason wrote in his liner notes to the Columbia LP of Davis's live date at the Blackhawk club in San Francisco in 1961: "Once [Miles] told me that he had been past my house that afternoon en route to Dave Brubeck's. 'Why didn't you stop in?' I asked in a stereotyped social response. 'What for?' he answered with shattering frankness." In 1969, Martin Williams went to the Columbia studios in New York to watch a recording session on which the young guitarist George Benson joined Davis and his celebrated 1960s quintet with saxophonist Wayne Shorter, pianist Herbie Hancock, bassist Ron Carter, and drummer Tony Williams. In his article on the session for *Stereo Review*, Williams portrayed Davis as a careful craftsman, intensely attentive to musical details, but also adroitly working the room with a stream of dialogue by turns friendly, humorous, and wickedly sardonic. Williams himself became implicated: producer Teo Macero told Davis that Williams liked a take of one of his solos that the trumpeter himself found dissatisfying. "What the——has Martin got to do with it?" Davis sneered.[109]

In truth, however, Davis's relationships with critics, both black and white, were cunningly personal, usually selfish, sometimes cruel, and always full of intrigue. For all of his shyness, his wariness of people taking up his time, his defensiveness and bluntness, it's remarkable how intimate he could become with those writers he invited into his home and his life. This intimacy comes through in the language and feeling of *Miles: The Autobiography,* his as-told-to memoir written with the black poet Quincy Troupe. But it also surfaced in the 1950s and 1960s with the white writers Hentoff, Feather, and Gleason. When the "New Journalism"—with its emphasis on visual detail and the subjective presence of the writer—worked its way into popular music criticism in the late 1960s, Davis proved to be an alluring subject. Rock writer Stephen Davis, interviewing Davis in 1973, was astonished when Davis, to show the effects of thirty years of playing the horn, took the writer's hand and guided his fingertip over his scarred lip. Profiles of Miles Davis in this period dwelled on the private details of a life that seem scripted by the Playboy Advisor. Dan Morgenstern wrote in *Down Beat* in 1970 that he found Davis's bedroom "so groovy that if it were mine, I might never leave it." Morgenstern went on to detail his experience watching Davis work out at Bobby Gleason's gym and having Davis drive him around Manhattan in his new Lamborghini. When physical problems and a nasty cocaine habit overtook Davis in the late 1970s and early 1980s, some of these scenes played out as bad pornography. Writer Eric Nisenson, by his own account, found himself in a kind of "indentured servitude," servicing Davis's drug needs and witnessing first-hand his appalling violence against women. Eventually, Nisenson reports, Davis "cut me off very sharply," and his hopes of being the co-writer of Davis's autobiography vanished. Deeply hurt, Nisenson tried to assuage himself with the knowledge that "sooner or later Miles did this to almost everyone close to him; for some reason I thought that I was the exception."[110]

Coda

In February 1961, in Davis's apartment on West 77th Street in New York, a group of jazz musicians reveled in a mock-revenge fantasy. Under a table-turning "press conference in reverse" contrived by publicist Pete Long, Nat Hentoff, Ira Gitler, John Wilson, Martin Williams, Stanley Dance, Robert Reisner, and Dan Morgenstern submitted themselves to a post–cocktail party interrogation by Cannonball Adderley, Gerry Mulligan, J. J. Johnson, Philly Joe Jones, Horace Silver, Billy Taylor, and Gil Evans. As host, Davis cut an understated, slightly mysterious profile. Press coverage of the event said very little about the famous trumpeter and bandleader himself, focusing instead on the stylish ambience of his upscale dwelling. New York *Post* reporter Gene Grove took note of the "walnut coffee tables" in Davis's "white-walled, book-lined living room," while Morgenstern's dispatch in *Metronome* mentioned the chauffeured Rolls Royce lurking on the street in front of the apartment, a special touch that Davis—well known to favor Italian sports cars—had leased out for the occasion.[111]

As if applying his less-is-more musical credo in his approach to hospitality, Davis confined his participation in the hour-long inquisition to a few concise interjections—and not one of them laced with the creative obscenity that was as much his signature as the vibrato-free sound he seduced out of his horn. Cannonball Adderley assumed the role of moderator, leading with a question that affably but piercingly hoist the writers on their own petards: "What is Jazz?" the stumper that musicians had been fed for years, often to their bafflement. ("If you have to ask, you'll never know," ran Louis Armstrong's classic retort). After Hentoff spent a few minutes dissembling, Davis mumbled something under his breath and walked out of the room. Horace Silver jumped in with a question that had the musicians and onlookers licking their chops: "What qualification does a jazz critic need?" Hentoff, still reeling from the first question, confessed, "anybody can be a jazz critic. The standards are very low."

The ever-earnest Martin Williams tried to defend the craft, arguing that not everyone who writes about jazz qualifies as a "real" critic. Hentoff agreed, saying that while there are a number of Europeans with the requisite musical knowledge, here in the United States there were only a handful, notably Williams and Gunther Schuller. Just then Davis reappeared and said that he'd be willing to include Hentoff himself on that list, but only if Hentoff acknowledged the debt he owed to his questioners. "Now Nat, when did he become a critic?" Davis asked. "You remember, J. J.," he said, turning to trombonist J. J. Johnson. "We gave Nat his first gig."[112]

It wasn't enough to bash the intellectuals, Hentoff learned: the serious jazz writer had to *get with* the musicians.

Bluesman John Lee Hooker audits a lecture by Marshall Stearns at the 1952 "jazz roundtable" in Lenox, Massachusetts. (Photo by Clemens Kalischer. Used by permission of the photographer.)

CHAPTER 5

Swinging in a High-Class Groove

Mainstreaming Jazz in Lenox and Newport

The Jazz Mainstream

In a photograph of a lecture by Marshall Stearns in Lenox, Massachusetts in 1952, a pensive John Lee Hooker listens as Stearns explicates a blackboard chart labeled "The Blues." The chart maps a historical evolution from primordial marches, hymns, ring shouts, reel jigs, and jug bands through to what is coded as a post-1920 jazz "Main Stream." Though Stearns's presentation was primarily concerned with jazz's prehistory, his terminology presaged jazz criticism's future. The term he used as shorthand for the history of jazz itself—the jazz "main stream"—soon saturated 1950s jazz commentary, serving as the basis of canon-building efforts by Stearns, Ralph Ellison, Nat Hentoff, Orrin Keepnews, Whitney Balliett, Martin Williams, Dan Morgenstern, Gunther Schuller, and Stanley Dance. In part an effort to heal the fundamentalist-modernist divide of the 1940s and to consolidate under one rubric a stylistic panoply ranging from prewar Dixieland and swing to postwar bop and cool, the trope of the mainstream also served, as Ronald Radano argues, to "shape jazz into an analogue of the European musical heritage."[1] Signifying stylistic unity and "an agreement on what jazz really was," the jazz mainstream connoted a "seamless, organic continuum," a process in which incremental expressions of individual talent reinforced the sense of a collective history.

As Burton Peretti has suggested, mainstream jazz "was not the middle-of-the-road popular music the term suggests, but rather the jazz [the critics] valued most."[2] In 1953, in his first published jazz article, Whitney Balliett assured lingering anti-modernists that bebop had been "absorbed into the main stream of jazz." Swing bands like the Count Basie and Harry James orchestras, he said, "have written bop figures, bop harmonies, and bop rhythms into their arrangements," and "their soloists will, nine out of ten times, use bop phrasing."[3] Later in the decade, British emigré critic Stanley Dance, well known for his dislike of bebop, wrote a series of essays outlining the contours of a "jazz mainstream" that originated with the Armstrong Hot Five and Seven recordings of the late 1920s and took full shape with the Basie, Ellington, and Goodman small group recordings of the 1930s. For Dance, jazz was synonymous with traditional notions of "swing"; his concept of the jazz mainstream favored the rejuvenated Basie and Ellington bands of the 1950s but eschewed the post-bop avant garde.[4] Hentoff, Williams, and Schuller were more ecumenical; in the *Jazz Review* and elsewhere, these critics made the case for John Coltrane, Charles Mingus, Ornette Coleman, and other late 1950s innovators as part of a coherent jazz tradition stretching back to the 1920s.

"Jazz has always had a tradition," John Clellon Holmes wrote in 1959, "but until recently jazzmen and their followers have seldom respected it or understood it. The history of jazz until the last few years has been pretty drearily the history of warring cliques and clashing styles and cries of heresy." In contrast to this messy heterodoxy of the jazz past, "today jazz is in the midst of a delighted rediscovery of its sources and of its continuity," a continuity based on the recognition of a jazz "mainstream," defined in vague terms by Holmes as "the essential melodic and rhythmic element which is jazz itself."[5] In 1964, when Ralph Ellison published his acclaimed collection *Shadow and Act*, he titled the music section "Sound and the Mainstream," arguing that the merging of classical and vernacular traditions in the work of Jimmy Rushing, Charlie Christian, Mahalia Jackson, and Charlie Parker was a singular achievement of American culture.

The emergence of a consensus history of jazz that conformed to high-culture notions of stylistic order and continuity—jazz's "end of ideology"—went hand in hand with popular media constructions of jazz's centrality in the mainstream of American life. Shorn of subversive associations with racial and bohemian subcultures, jazz could be made to fit nicely in the "vital center" of American culture. Noting jazz's appeal to everyone from "a pneumatic drill operator to a little old grandma knitting in a rocking chair," the *New York Post* claimed that one did not have to be a "rootless drifter of the Beat generation," a "boozer," or a "weedhead" to appreciate "America's only true native art." Contrasting jazz with "such popular lunacies as rock and roll," the *Post* counted among the jazz listening public "doctors, lawyers, housewives, and even Congressmen."[6] In Boston, the popularity of WBUR jazz disc jockey Father Norman O'Connor, a snowy-haired Paulist priest, was said to owe "less to his knowledge of jazz, which is not prodigious, than to the remarkable fact that a clergyman should be interested in jazz at all."[7]

By Holmes's reckoning, the jazz audience was no longer just the "ten dozen stubborn record collectors . . . mumbling matrix numbers over their drinks" he remembered from the 1930s, nor "the wan and embattled faces I got to know so well along the bar in the Three Deuces" during the war years; the jazz fan was now "a poet in San Francisco, a farm hand in Iowa, an ad man on Madison Avenue, a hipster in Detroit, a student in New Hampshire . . . [and] the vast multitude in twenty other countries that finds, most clearly in jazz, evidence of the American Dream."[8] *Variety* approvingly noted that in John Foster Dulles's State Department "the hipsters have virtually been given striped pants and sent overseas as ambassadors of good will."[9] *Good Housekeeping* characterized jazz musicians as "no longer murky characters with short beards and berets on their heads, or hopped-up fellows who sleep all day and crawl forth at 4 A.M.," likening jazz's transformation in the public mind to "the boy with dirty hands whom you wouldn't let into your house" becoming one with "clean hands . . . found in the concert halls, the music conservatories, and by way of respectable and carefully produced LP records, in the nicest living rooms."[10]

The "dirty hands" metaphor, an allusion to the red-scare linkage of blackness and bop with communism,[11] typified a common practice of casting jazz's new mainstream respectability in images of catharsis and purification. Holmes contrasted the "Dark Age" of jazz's association with "the night side of life" to the 1950s Golden Age of LPs and concert halls. In a liner note to a Modern Jazz Quartet album recorded in Lenox, jazz critic John Wilson wrote, "It's a long trip from dingy backroom dives in New Orleans to a sun-bathed, verdant hillside in the Berkshire Mountains of Western Massachusetts but jazz has made the journey." Music historian Henry Pleasants described this "journey" in language that joined the term "mainstream" to images of purification and imperialism. "Jazz," Pleasants wrote, "may be thought of as a current that bubbled forth from a spring in the slums of New Orleans to become the mainstream of the twentieth century. In less than fifty years it has flooded the United States and the rest of the world."[12]

Jazz's global reach was expanded and consolidated in these cold war years through a series of foreign jazz tours sponsored by the U.S. State Department and through Voice of America jazz radio programming that broadcast over the Iron Curtain, behind the Great Wall, and around numerous corners untouched by more traditional forms of diplomacy and propaganda. At home, two institutions emerged in the 1950s as important symbols and powerful agents of the mainstreaming of jazz. In 1954, the Newport Jazz Festival opened to great fanfare, ballyhooed by its energetic founders as the American equivalent of the Athenian and Elizabethan theaters and the Italian opera: a grand event celebrating a popular art form indigenous to the nation. Alongside the emergence of the jazz festival (dozens followed Newport in the 1950s, hundreds in the ensuing decades) came the beginnings of formal jazz education, with curricula that stressed both performance ability and historical knowledge. Beginning in 1950, at a Lenox, Massachusetts country inn owned by Stephanie and Philip Barber, Marshall Stearns hosted a series of yearly seminars called "Jazz Roundtables," at which academics and musicians debated the origins, definition, and cultural meaning of jazz. From 1957 to 1960, Stearns and several other academics and jazz critics joined a group of jazz musicians led by Modern Jazz Quartet pianist and composer John Lewis to form the faculty of the School of Jazz, a first-of-its-kind institution aimed at establishing an academic basis for the study of jazz performance, theory, and history.

In Newport and Lenox, whose spectacular Gilded Age cottages had fallen into disrepair as global travel, the income tax, and ever-rising maintenance costs undermined aristocratic lifestyles, jazz symbolized the refining impulses of an educated, curious, urbane, and diverse audience. Jazz's cultural capital accrued by virtue of its association with northeastern social elites, its propaganda value as a form of interracial "democratic" public culture, and its symbolic status as a serious American "art" legitimated by intellectuals and jazz critics who seized upon it as a bulwark against a perceived threat of mass-entertainment youth culture, especially rock'n'roll. For many of the new breed of jazz musicians who considered themselves at least as cultured as the audiences they performed for, the well-manicured New England landscape represented a welcome change from the hurly-burly pace of the customary jazz life. Jazz musicians of the 1950s thought of themselves as educated artists and as contributors to an important American tradition.

In legend, jazz always is played in brothels, speakeasies, gin joints, chicken shacks, and other roguish locales where, in point of fact, the music very often found a sustaining if not consistently rewarding environment. But for the last fifty years, it has been much more common for jazz master performance, as well as jazz apprenticeship, to take place in a concert hall, at a festival, or at a school. Traditionally, a jazz event was an occasion of joy, physical expressiveness, and telepathic communication between musicians and audiences; if jazz maintains these qualities, it does so increasingly in venues whose architectural style and social ambience were designed for the performance and teaching of European concert music. The precedents for jazz as a concert art date to James Reese Europe's Clef Club performances in Carnegie Hall from 1912 to 1914, and include such famous events as Paul Whiteman's 1925 Town Hall concert, Benny Goodman's 1938 Carnegie Hall concert, and the "Spirituals to Swing" concerts at Carnegie Hall in 1938 and 1939. The latter, a program of African American vernacular musics organized by John Hammond, carried the banner for the Popular Front social movement. So too did the first Jazz at the Philharmonic concert in Los Angeles in 1944, organized by Norman Granz as a benefit for seventeen young Chicanos convicted of murder in the Sleepy Lagoon case. Granz, a former MGM film editor, was, in the words of Whitney Balliett, "a jazz fan and a strong liberal [who] decided that jazz should be listened to in the pleasantest surroundings by the largest possible number of people of all races, creeds, and colors."[13]

In 1945, Granz applied the "Jazz at the Philharmonic" name to a traveling concert series with a loosely organized ensemble of star performers, including Dizzy Gillespie, Charlie Parker, Roy Eldridge, Lester Young, Coleman Hawkins, Ben Webster, Stan Getz, and Oscar Peterson. By the 1950s, JATP had grown into a 150-performance-a-year series that spanned the globe, with concerts in Europe, Japan, and Australia. Granz was also a record producer, and in that capacity, as both a pioneer of live recording and a tireless studio tinkerer, he (along with George Avakian at Columbia) was responsible for using the LP as a tool for turning a few jazz musicians into mass-market popular stars. Profiling Granz in the *Saturday Review* in 1954, Balliett estimated that "perhaps 50 percent of all the jazz records produced last year came from Granz factories." "To at least half a million potential customers around the world," Balliett quipped, "Granz may well be doing for jazz what another prestidigitator, P. T. Barnum, did for midgets."[14]

JATP disbanded in 1967, then resumed for a few years in the 1970s; the concert series and Norman Granz continue to reach jazz audiences through CD reissues of recordings Granz made for his Clef and Verve labels and their subsidiaries.[15] George Wein, another jazz entrepreneur/producer who got his start in the post–World War II period, continues to promote and package the music for mass audiences into the first years of the twenty-first century. Wein is best known as the founder of the Newport Jazz Festival. Though not the first jazz festival—it was preceded in 1948 by the Nice Jazz Festival, a traditional program organized by Hugues Panassié that featured Louis Armstrong's All Stars, and by the Festival International de Jazz (known commonly as the Paris Jazz Fair), organized by Charles Delauney and featuring American bebop musicians—Newport quickly established it-self as the largest and most famous event of its kind. By the end of the 1950s the $20,000 two-day inaugural festival in 1954 seemed dilettantish. In 1959 the festival spent $265,692 to employ forty-three groups and individuals in a variety of activities, including tours of the United States and eight foreign countries.[16]

Granz and Wein's ventures were not always profitable—Wein found fi-nancial security only in the 1970s after securing corporate sponsorship—but they were emphatically commercial operations responding to shifts in the economics of entertainment during and after World War II. In broad terms, the festival and concert movement in these years was part of jazz's struggle to find its niche in a world of suburbanization; changing patterns of middle-class leisure and tourism predicated on the automobile, the tele-vision, the private one-family home, and the summer vacation; and the rise of the university as a center of American cultural life. Jazz was born and nurtured in the city—in black and multi-ethnic neighborhoods, in ur-ban public schools, and in the commercial sphere of dance halls, clubs, and electronic media outlets. Jazz continued through the 1950s and 1960s to feed on urban energy (particularly the soul jazz movement), but now much of the audience and the resources for jazz were shifting to other locations.[17]

World War II veterans on the G.I. Bill flocked to U.S. colleges and uni-versities, and as those institutions fattened up on cold war educational in-vestments, they developed a cultural infrastructure—art studios, concert halls, film editing facilities, etc.—to service the interests of both students and the surrounding middle-class populations. As Alice Goldfarb Marquis has noted, in the 1950s and 1960s "colleges discovered music's charms as student entertainment and also as a rich source of cash for student orga-nizations." Student musician numbers grew so markedly that music trade publications (*Down Beat* and *Billboard* in particular) targeted the college market with advertisements for musical instruments, talent agencies, and record labels. A 1966 *Billboard* poll showed that, despite the mass popular-ity of rock'n'roll and folk music among middle-class youth, Dave Brubeck, Miles Davis, Gerry Mulligan, Stan Kenton, Duke Ellington, and the Modern Jazz Quartet were among students' favorite performers. *Variety* reported that same year that colleges were the most lucrative music venue in the United States, with some jazz groups pulling down as much as $30,000 per appearance.[18]

While jazz concerts proved lucrative for musicians and student organi-zations alike, jazz music education remained marginal or even absent in college and university curricula, and hence also in secondary school programs staffed by graduates of these higher education institutions. Marshall Stearns was able to attract an ethnomusicologist like Richard Waterman to his jazz roundtables, and to count on his support for his Institute of Jazz Studies, in part because this was a maverick scholar working on the edges of the academy. The situation was not radically different at the century's end. In a 1995 book, ethnomusicologist Bruno Nettl lamented the "determinedly uni-musical" focus of midwestern university music schools, whose purpose he described as the "study and propagation of the Central classical music." In 1956, North Texas State became the first college in the world to establish a jazz major—but camouflaged it in the college catalog as "dance band." The nation's most prestigious university music departments continued to teach the elite western European canon to the almost total exclusion of other musical traditions. The situation was no different at traditional black colleges; at Howard University, for example, it was not until the 1970s, in response to student protests, that jazz and other black music genres were introduced into the curriculum.[19]

The 1960s cultural revolution was a boon to jazz education, both in the United States and abroad. In 1998, the International Association of Jazz Educators held its twenty-fifth annual convention for seven thousand jazz educators, musicians, and business people from thirty-five countries. "Jazz education is a big part of the future," said Bill McFarlin, the association's executive director. "I don't think it's a replacement for the European classical education—you don't throw out the Dutch masters for modernism—but music programs that don't have a jazz component suffer now in terms of student enrollment." Billy Taylor reflected: "In 1958, Stan Kenton and I were invited to lecture at the Music Educators National Conference about the advisability of teaching jazz. They were exceptionally patronizing. 'Jazz in school?' they said, patting us on the head. Forty years later Wynton Marsalis and I are on the board of advisers. They really see the strides we've made, and strides the international community has made. Go to Cuba, or Japan, or Europe, and you see how it's become part of the pedagogy."[20]

"Doctor Billy Taylor"—Taylor holds a Ph.D. in music from the University of Massachusetts, has taught and written widely, and holds sixteen honorary degrees—has served as a proselytizer and, owing to his professorial demeanor, a popular symbol of jazz education since the late 1950s. Many other top-rank jazz performers who came of age in the 1950s and 1960s (David Baker, Archie Shepp, Anthony Braxton, Reggie Workman, Sam Gill, and others) have held teaching posts and have been instrumental in the

institutional development of jazz performance studies. Jazz studies flourished over the last two decades of the century at many universities and at
music schools as different as Berklee and the New England Conservatory
But it was the faculty of the Lenox School of Jazz in the late 1950s (Marshall
Stearns, John Lewis, George Russell, Gunther Schuller, Dizzy Gillespie, Max
Roach, William Russo, and Jimmy Giuffre among them) who pioneered a
model of jazz education that combined history, theory, composition, and
improvisation.

As I narrate the story of jazz in Newport and Lenox in the 1950s, I want
to highlight several intersecting themes and storylines that underscore the
complex cultural politics of jazz in this period of mainstreaming. The first
theme is the effort on the part of the festival's and the school's promoters and
supporters, drawing on the cultural capital, material resources, and physical
beauty of Newport and Lenox, to endow jazz with new images of respectability and aesthetic worth and to trumpet the music as a uniquely American
cultural product. Contributing to this effort—sometimes in alliance with
local producers, sometimes not—were the national and international media, some representing jazz for the very first time, and an assortment of
artists, intellectuals, and critics. A second theme is the construction of a jazz
canon (or "tradition") in the programming and personnel of the two institutions, the debates and tensions behind this construction, and the ways it
reflected larger patterns in American culture of the period. A related storyline focuses on the vexed relations between Newport's producers and a few
influential jazz critics who had supported the festival in its first years but
turned against it as the festival grew in size and began to feature popular acts
that transgressed the critics' notions of jazz authenticity and purism. This
storyline also considers how jazz musicians interacted with the producers
and the critics/intellectuals in shaping this construct of the jazz tradition
and in negotiating their positions at the festival and the school. Shadowing
this storyline is the theme of racial politics—specifically, the experience of
black jazz musicians, intellectuals, and fans who embraced the Newport
and Lenox mission, enjoyed the interracial bonhomie at these gatherings,
but who continued to struggle for equality and a true pluralist ideal. While
allied with jazz's white patrons in seeking to capitalize on the opportunities
represented by jazz's new status as a serious American art, these African
Americans simultaneously asserted jazz's significance as a crucible of black
cultural memory, agency, and autonomy and looked for ways to increase
their economic control over the music.

Even as jazz was being evangelized as a force of racial harmony and bourgeois normalcy, the mainstreaming of its image was racially rigged: in the

1950s American popular mind, jazz was represented not by Lee Morgan's jamming at black neighborhood bars, but by Dave Brubeck's concerts at white colleges, genteel affairs attended by lots of earnest students in plaid shirts and khakis. Yet the 1950s was also, in Gerald Early's phrase, the "age of the cultural crossover," a time when African American writers, performing artists, and athletes cut high profiles in mainstream public life.[21] Gwendolyn Brooks, Ralph Ellison, James Baldwin, and Lorraine Hansberry exerted a black presence in literary circles. Sidney Poitier and Dorothy Dandridge became Hollywood film stars. Nat King Cole, who joined Frank Sinatra in refashioning swing into a sophisticated, adult-oriented popular music, broke into network television with a middle-of-the-road variety show (albeit a short-lived one, owing to advertising sponsors' fear of offending southern audiences). Jackie Robinson, who integrated Major League Baseball in 1947 and proceeded to parry racist taunts with disciplined fury and heroic poise, chose the most dramatic moments of the Brooklyn Dodger season to audaciously demonstrate his patented steal of home plate. Willie Mays, Hank Aaron, and the 1952 Olympic heavyweight boxing champion, Floyd Patterson, redefined canons of athleticism, combining power with ineffable grace and élan. Miles Davis began to show up regularly on lists of the "best dressed men in America."

This effulgence of black dignity, elegance, and intellect did not so much assimilate the white mainstream as transform it, press claims against it, and urge it into a fuller recognition of both its inadequacies and its potencies. *Down Beat* reported that a "well-dressed young Negro" at a Dave Brubeck performance grew so impatient with the rowdy white teenagers behind him chanting "go man, go!" that he finally turned and admonished them, "Have some respect, won't you please?"[22] The implication was that traditional notions of cultural hierarchy had been overturned: now it fell to the Negroes to civilize the whites. The same dynamic obtained at the Lenox School of Jazz, where an international student body received instruction from a predominantly black faculty. Early suggests that the 1950s "was the coming of age, the maturity of the black bourgeois consciousness as an urge to change, and paradoxically, to challenge the white racist mind, [to] purify the American democratic vision. [T]he 50's taught us that there could be no democratic consciousness without realization of the black and, further, that there could be no democratic impulse without a recognition of black consciousness as an essential mode in the national character." In this sense, Early suggests, the Modern Jazz Quartet's donning of tuxedos and dabbling in fugue forms was part of the same cultural vector as the implementation of the 1954 *Brown* decision, the emergence of Martin Luther King Jr., the sit-down demonstrations, and even the resurgence of Pan-Africanism.

A Jazz Salon

In all [my time writing about jazz], with all the extraordinary experiences I've had listening to the music and talking to the musicians, a phenomenon unto itself was the time I spent at Music Inn. I learned so much during those days and nights that I have been mining that information ever since.

—Nat Hentoff

There was a night when Lee Konitz, Sonny Rollins and I sat in my room, after Sonny's concert, discussing at length whether it would be possible for musicians to critique one another, since we were all reasonably secure in our worlds . . . [the] vote was 2-1, Lee losing. There was a day when Percy [Heath] came by my workshop and explained how the afterbeat made the downbeat possible, a lesson I have been using in practice and in teaching ever since.

—Bob Brookmeyer

It was a time of revelation, discourse, and just plain happiness.

—Jimmy and Juanita Giuffre[23]

In 1950, a young couple from New York named Stephanie and Philip Barber purchased a cluster of buildings (barn, potting shed, icehouse, and stables) on the former summer estate of the Countess de Heredia in Lenox, Massachusetts. The estate was a short walk from Tanglewood, since 1938 the center of a classical music school and summer festival hosted by the Boston Symphony Orchestra. Weary of urban professional life and pining "for things that couldn't be found in New York . . . [things like] fresh air and freedom, rugged individualism, beauty, trees and time and place for friends," the Barbers had "searched everywhere and decided that Berkshire County was the most pleasant place to live a civilized life in the United States." Home in the past to sculptor Daniel Chester French and writers William Cullen Bryant, Herman Melville, Nathaniel Hawthorne, and Edith Wharton, the Berkshire cultural scene now featured summer performing arts programming led by Tanglewood, the Jacob's Pillow dance festival, and the Williamstown and Stockbridge theater festivals. This venerable arts tradition inspired the Barbers, who christened their property the Music Inn and hosted presentations of American folk music organized by Alan Lomax and a jazz seminar run by Marshall Stearns.[24]

Stearns's "stimulating, briskly argumentative" roundtables operated as an "antiphonal chorus," as a festival publicist dubbed it, with Pete Seeger, Eubie Blake, Mahalia Jackson, John Lee Hooker, Brownie McGhee, Tony Scott, Wilber de Paris, Dizzy Gillespie, and Billy Taylor trading fours with Stearns, Nat Hentoff, Richard Waterman, Henry Cowell, folklorist Willis James, newspaper editor and blues pianist Dan Burley, poet/critics Langston Hughes and Sterling Brown, semanticist S. I. Hayakawa, literary critic Stanley Edgar Hyman, and American studies professor Tremaine McDowell. "With surprising consistency," Stearns reported, "the musicians become articulate and the professors practical." The hallmark of the 1950s Lenox jazz roundtables was the construction of jazz as a network of traceable genealogies and transgenerational alliances. Stearns's blackboard charts of the jazz "main stream" sprang to life when the artists on hand demonstrated the validity of the connections it proposed. Modern pianist Ralph Sutton "discovered parallels to his own playing in the ragtime of Eubie Blake." Jazz dancers Al Minns and Leon James "found their own steps in a [Haitian] voodoo dance." Spelman College folklorist Willis James noted basic stylistic resemblances between modern bebop and traditional field hollers, street cries, and work songs. Langston Hughes characterized jazz as "a great big sea" that "washes up all kinds of shells and spume and waves with a steady old-beat, or off-beat." Mahalia Jackson defied religious proscription by singing the blues. Charles Mingus exclaimed, "Hey, I've got roots!" after a performance by stride pianist Willie "The Lion" Smith. Later in the decade when the roundtables grew into the School of Jazz, Stearns's required jazz history course highlighted these continuities, illustrating for his students and auditors that "jazz has a usable past." Free jazz pioneer Ornette Coleman, who took the class, credited Stearns with helping him come to an appreciation of Louis Armstrong and Jelly Roll Morton. A session one Lenox summer on the history of jazz rhythm moved from a demonstration of early jazz piano by Sammy Price, who started playing professionally in 1914, to a drumming demonstration by bebopper Max Roach.[25]

In 1955, when the Barbers launched an annual concert series in the Berkshire Music Barn, an editorial in the *Berkshire Eagle* beamed, "Performers such as Dizzy Gillespie and Thelonious Monk, Einsteins of bop, will certainly add a fourth dimension to the sylvan glades of Lenox." "[I]t is only right," the *Eagle* claimed, "that this type of music should gravitate to Berkshire County where it will be treated with the dignity and care it deserves. The social upstarts at Newport were a little forward in presenting the festival of jazz. They should stick to their tennis and quiet dinner parties in the summer and leave the important cultural events to us."[26] In summer evening and weekend matinee concerts throughout the late 1950s, the Music Inn featured The Modern Jazz Quartet, Thelonious Monk, Dizzy Gillespie, Louis Armstrong, Oscar Peterson, Dave Brubeck, Sonny Rollins, Ahmad Jamal, Randy Weston, Duke Ellington, Dinah Washington, Mahalia Jackson, and folk performers Harry Belafonte and Pete Seeger. "I will never forget singing at Music Inn back in the days of the Blacklist," Seeger recently wrote to Stephanie Barber. "I call them 'the frightened Fifties.'"[27] If the po-litical climate was frightening for all on the Left, the social climate could be especially tricky for black musicians visiting the lily-white Berkshires, no matter the "dignity and care" their music received. "Black people were not popular in New England," recalls Stephanie Barber. "In the early days, when we overflowed our own capacity we had problems finding beds at local inns for artists who happened to be black. People in the village did not approve of what we were doing. But in good New England fashion, they believed we had the right to do it."[28]

In 1956, the Modern Jazz Quartet (pianist John Lewis, vibraharpist Milt Jackson, bassist Percy Heath, and drummer Connie Kay) served as Music Inn's "jazz group in residence." The original MJQ had morphed out of the rhythm section of Dizzy Gillespie's big band into a quartet led by Jackson, with Ray Brown on bass and Kenny Clarke on drums. As The Milt Jackson Quartet, the group recorded several albums of standards and originals based on popular chord progressions, and was best known for Jackson's soul-ful, blues-saturated improvisations. Recently Lewis had assumed the upper hand and had shifted the group's focus to his own compositions—"Django," "Vendome," "Concorde," and others—and to collaborations with the Beaux Arts Trio and the Stuttgart Symphony. Lewis was an educated, cosmopoli-tan man who exuded an aura of learning and authority. A graduate of the University of New Mexico who had studied both anthropology and music, a student and then teacher at the Manhattan School of Music even as he was working with Dizzy Gillespie and Charlie Parker, Lewis was schooled in European music and culture as much as in blues and jazz. With Gunther Schuller, he was a founder of the Jazz and Classical Music Society and, in his work as a composer, a pioneer of the "Third Stream" merging of blues feeling and language with the formal devices and architecture of European music. Mirroring Lewis's interest in fugues and baroque counterpoint was a pointed courtliness of style. "Carefully tailored and a gourmet," Nat Hentoff described Lewis, "he has been known to fly to London from New York for a few days rest walking around the city." Lewis imbued the MJQ with these values. "Impeccably attired, with the bearing, manner, and appearance of gentlemen in the employ of Schweppes beverages," wrote Joe Goldberg, " its members play some of the most respectable music ever to be called jazz."[29]

This gentility was admired and emulated by some other musicians, espe-cially those at Lenox. "I still remember," says trombonist Bob Brookmeyer, "the sense of pride and honor I had being around the MJQ, whose individual members I secretly lionized, not only for their music but for the way they car-ried themselves, the way they talked and dressed and reacted to the world—I wished deeply that someday I would have the dignity and composure I was observing."[30] Other musicians scoffed at what they construed as posturing. "I don't go with this bringing 'dignity' to jazz," Miles Davis told Hentoff. "The way [the MJQ] bring[s] 'dignity' to jazz in their formal clothes and the way they bow is like Ray Robinson bringing dignity to boxing by fighting in a tuxedo."[31] At the level of performance, the MJQ embodied the tensions between jazz's folk sources and its high art aspirations—between Milt Jackson's blues and church-inspired blowing and John Lewis's scholastic formalism. This tension is well captured in an incident at an MJQ concert described by Don DeMichael and quoted by Joe Goldberg in *Jazz Masters of the Fifties*:

> The concert's finale was given over to a several-part composition written by Lewis, who announced and explained each part. Before the third section, as he was explaining his attractive, but complex, piece of work, a man in the first row shouted, "Bag's Groove!" Lewis recoiled as if a bucket of ice water had been thrown in his face. He replied with dignity, "We'll play *that* later. And now, in this third section. . . . " When the man had shouted, Jackson threw his head back and laughed a silent laugh.[32]

In Lenox, Lewis found an opportunity to exercise his pedagogical impulse. In 1956, as the MJQ worked closely with Stearns on the roundtable discussions, Lewis, as John Wilson reported, "was disturbed that this exchange of such a wide range of jazz knowledge should be so ephemeral. He urged the Barbers to give it some form of continued existence so that both established jazzmen and youngsters just getting started could benefit from it." Lewis's intention, he later said, was "to heal the musical misunderstanding between the older masters of jazz and the younger jazz innovators." He thought a jazz summer school at Music Inn could be "a special way to pass on the traditions, the history, and the theoretical language of jazz music."[33] In 1957, the Barbers bought Wheatleigh, a grand mansion on the original estate, giving them room to expand the summer programming. In August of that year came the inaugural three-week session of the School of Jazz. Over the next four summers, 155 students from the United States, Europe, Africa, Brazil, and Turkey enrolled. Scholarship subsidies came from the Schaefer Brewing Company, Atlantic Records, United Artists Films, Broadcast Music Incorporated, Associated Booking Corporation, Norman Granz, George Wein, and Elaine and Louis Lorillard. Graduates include Ornette Coleman, Don Cherry, David Baker, Arif Mardin, Ran Blake, John Eckert, Don Ellis, Peter Farmer, Vera Auer, Don Heckman, Joe Hunt, Chuck Israels, Steve Kuhn, Gary McFarland, and Larry Ridley.[34]

The school advertised itself as "the first effort to present jazz as a creative and vital art form which can be presented and taught as other art forms are taught, in a serious and vital relationship between the student and the creating artist."[35] *Down Beat* reported that "in all the classes and lectures and ensembles there was a soberness and dignity of demeanor that was encouraging."[36] Cultural critic Eric Larabee claimed that he had "seldom encountered such an exhilarating atmosphere. Once the students get over the shock of finding themselves performing side by side with their idols, the greats of jazz, they seem to achieve a state of full-throttle serenity in which nothing can stop them."[37] One student marveled at the quality of the school's teaching, pointing out that "it is very unusual for students of European classical music to study with the top rank *players*, rather than *teachers*, until they are at a very advanced stage. A school such as this, which has at least five players who are by and large unexcelled on their instruments (Ray Brown, Dizzy Gillespie, Milt Jackson, Oscar Peterson, and Max Roach) and three top writers (Bill Russo, John Lewis, and Jimmy Giuffre) is almost unknown to European music."[38]

In addition to courses in history, composition, and small-ensemble playing, each student was required to take at least two private instrumental lessons a week. Student pianist Ron Riddle described the intensity Dizzy Gillespie brought to his ensemble class in the summer of 1957:

> Once, in the middle of a chorus of "Indiana-in-F," Mr. Gillespie suddenly stopped playing and gave me a piercing look. "NEVER play that chord!" he said. Then he parked his incredible horn and took a seat at the piano. What followed was an amazingly lucid 15-minute lecture-demonstration on the use of diminished chords, altered and unaltered. Originally, he had intended to show the virtue of using an E-flat augmented 11th chord in bar 24, but his remarks lengthened into an enlightening discourse on harmonic theory, with many illustrative examples (quite a pianist, Dizzy Gillespie). Surprises like this were by no means infrequent and the students in this group (four of us) also received valuable suggestions from Percy Heath and Connie Kay.[39]

Gillespie characterized the atmosphere in Lenox as "just ideal for modern jazz, [a place] where musicians didn't have to compete with customers ordering drinks and were not pushed around musically to satisfy commercial demands." He found the school "creative and therapeutic, notably for the faculty, many of whom felt the grind of being on the road, rushing from one club to another. Yard [Gillespie's deceased friend Charlie Parker] would have enjoyed it if he had lived."[40] Many musicians of the period criticized the working conditions of jazz nightclubs, especially modernists who were experimenting with longer forms and experimental sonorities incongruent with a traditional saloon atmosphere.[41] In an article titled "What's Wrong with the Clubs," Kenneth Rexroth complained that club owners, agents, "cheap record companies," bartenders, and cocktail waitresses all "bear a singular resemblance to the people who prey on boxers." The stigma of underworld association was out of step with jazz's push for respectability. The musician who "works hard, studying piano or trumpet, gaining scholarships, living in a poor flat in a Negro ghetto, perhaps helped by a mother who works as a domestic, is about as far from the underworld, black or white, as could be."[42]

Rexroth's conflation of black and white jazz musicians overlooked significant class and regional differences. In the class of 1959 at the Lenox School of Jazz, for instance, one of the Atlantic Records scholarship students was black alto saxophonist Ornette Coleman, who grew up in a working-class family in Fort Worth, Texas, and cut his musical teeth in southwestern honky-tonk bars before moving to Los Angeles, where he lived in Skid Row hotels and studied musical theory while working as an elevator operator.[43] Several of his white classmates who were subsidized by the Schaefer Brewing Company Intercollegiate Scholarship, by contrast, were Ivy Leaguers.[44] Martin Williams dismissed some of the Ivy Leaguers as "dabblers" who were "buying their way into a world they may secretly think they should feel superior to."[45] But the school quickly weeded out these dabblers, as well as "teach me the changes and just let me wail" triflers, by treating jazz as a language whose mastery required formal education. Gunther Schuller—who inherited Marshall Stearns's jazz history class at Lenox and there began the series of analytical close readings of recorded jazz history that would later form the basis of his books *Early Jazz* (1968) and *The Swing Era* (1989)[46]— considered the school of "inestimable importance" for countering the "old saw that 'jazz can't be taught' or 'too much knowledge will inhibit you, man.'" The attitude that it was "shamefully 'unhip' to study seriously" was dangerously outmoded, Schuller argued, at a time when jazz was becoming more sophisticated and technically demanding.[47]

The teaching function and salon-like atmosphere provided an occasion for the faculty and visitors from the larger jazz community to sustain and develop their own projects. "It was really in some respects like being on shipboard," reminisced Nat Hentoff, "because there were really no delimitations as to hours or place, in terms of when you could talk to musicians and when they could talk to each other. It was a continuous flow, extraordinarily relaxed."[48] William Russo, who had studied with Lennie Tristano in the 1940s and became chief arranger for the Stan Kenton orchestra in the early 1950s, used his composition course to test out the ideas he was formulating for his book, *Jazz: Composition and Orchestration*. Jimmy Giuffre used a teaching residence for his trio with guitarist Jim Hall and trombonist Bob Brookmeyer to continue work in what he called "blues-based folk jazz"; after working with the MJQ and absorbing Ornette Coleman, Giuffre hatched a quiet free jazz idiom in a new Jimmy Giuffre 3 unit with pianist Paul Bley and bassist Steve Swallow. Dave Brubeck remembers a lecture on African American field hollers by Dr. Willis James, in which James demonstrated a holler in five-four-time. Brubeck was exploring time signatures not used much in jazz—"Take Five," a five-four tune on his album *Time Out* would become a hit—and he appreciated it when James praised the Brubeck quartet for experimenting with African rhythms. "That was my big moment of glory," Brubeck says. Part of Brubeck's next album, *Time Further Out*, was written at Music Inn.[49] Also written at Music Inn was Randy Weston's "Berkshire Blues," a meditative blues inspired by the serenity of the surrounding landscape. "The Berkshires is a very beautiful place," Weston told critic Ira Gitler. "[I wanted] to write a piece about the Berkshires . . . because I spent so much time up there. Usually at night, I used to take a walk, and breathe the air, look at the trees, and just sort of get with the place itself. Somehow I [got] a musical message."[50]

Weston, a Brooklyn native, had been playing in New York and studying with Thelonious Monk in the late 1940s. In the early 1950s, uncertain of his musical future and wanting to get away from New York, Weston took a job as a cook at a private school in Lenox which was serving as a summer camp for elderly refugees from central Europe. Most of the refugees were artists, and they encouraged Weston to perform for them. Rejuvenated by their enthusiastic reception, Weston wandered over to the Music Inn and put himself in the mix. With support from the Barbers and Marshall Stearns (whose seminars in the early years were short on modern jazz), Weston formed a trio with bassist Sam Gill and drummer Willie Jones. Weston met Riverside records president Bill Grauer, who had a summer home down the road from Music Inn, and became, with a 1954 recording of Cole Porter songs, Riverside's first post-bop player. He also worked for Riverside in the shipping department. Though never a School of Jazz faculty member or student, Weston spent eight straight summers at Music Inn refining his writing skills and piano technique, listening to the Boston Symphony Orchestra, and soaking up information on pan-African musical and cultural traditions. Weston developed a strong interest in African music and, with his collaborator-arranger, Melba Liston, began to write pieces ("Little Niles," "Bantu Suite," "Uhuru Afrika") with African themes. He made two trips to Africa in the early 1960s sponsored by the State Department and the American Society of African Culture, then later lived in Morocco, studying and collaborating with Gnawa and Jilala musicians. Weston's interest in the music of the African diaspora started with his upbringing—his Panamanian father introduced him to West Indian calypso—but it was at Lenox that the interest crystallized and pointed him toward Africa. "I got a lot of my inspiration for African music by being at Music Inn, meeting people like [dancer] Geoffrey Holder, Babatunde Olatunji, Langston Hughes, and Dr. Willis James," Weston recalls. "They were all explaining the African-American experience in a global perspective, which was unusual at the time."[51]

Lenox brought other musical horizons into focus. Composer and theorist George Russell, who taught at the school from 1958 to 1960, had published his landmark conceptual breakthrough *The Lydian Chromatic Concept of Tonal Organization* in 1953. Heralded by John Lewis as "the most profound theoretical contribution to come from jazz," Russell's theory pointed the way to modal improvisation based on scales rather than on chord changes, a breakthrough that undergirded the famous work of Miles Davis (through his pianist, Russell acolyte Bill Evans) and John Coltrane in the late 1950s and early 1960s. Russell, who got his start playing drums in Benny Carter's big band in 1943, had been composing large-ensemble works—including "Cubano Be, Cubana Bop" for Dizzy Gillespie's orchestra—since the late 1940s. He was part of an avant-garde clique (including Davis, Lewis, Charlie Parker, Gerry Mulligan, and Lee Konitz) that plotted the jazz future from composer/arranger Gil Evans's basement apartment in midtown Manhattan. His 1956 RCA record *The Jazz Workshop,* a collection of his compositions that used modality, African-influenced rhythms, and changing tempos, confounded critics such as Whitney Balliett, who said it "comes dangerously close to a highly skilled travesty of jazz that might have been cooked up, in anger and condescension, by someone who despised the music." *Contra* Balliett, Eric Nisenson has suggested more recently that the album's modality, ostinatos, and guitar vamps presaged the jazz-rock fusion of the late 1960s and the 1970s; indeed, Russell's experiments in new meters and complex textures, sometimes woven through use of electronics, sounded futuristic, even as his theoretical work reached for the ancient foundations of organized sound.[52]

At once ahead of his time and a searcher for timeless, cross-cultural truths, Russell was a scientist of sound whose research, in its purest form, resisted popularization and mainstream approbation. His glory came first in the application of his ideas by Davis, Coltrane, and others, and later with the international acclaim accorded his big band, The Living Time Orchestra, and recognition at the highest levels of his status as a major American composer. But in the 1950s, when Russell had to support himself by working the counter at Macy's department store, the Lenox School of Jazz provided an important opportunity to fine-tune and teach his theoretical concepts. Two Lenox students, Don Ellis and David Baker, became members of the George Russell Sextet, which recorded and performed in the early 1960s. Gunther

Schuller, writing in the *Jazz Review*, cited a Lenox jam session led by Ellis and Baker as "symptomatic of a trend to overthrow the tyranny of the 4/4 meter." Ellis, said Schuller, "has listened to and understood the music of Webern, Stockhausen, Cage and others of the avant-garde"; those influences, coupled with Baker's "bi-rhythmic approach," in which a soloist plays at a different tempo from the rhythm section, resulted in a "magnificent atonal collective improvisation, which gave a glimpse of the kind of freedom jazz will undoubtedly someday achieve."[53]

Just what constitutes "freedom" in jazz was, and remains, a deeply contested issue. For Schuller it meant "Third Stream" music that combined the improvisation and emotional power of jazz with the formal architecture of European classical music. A musical polymath, Schuller had already crisscrossed these boundaries as a performer, playing principal horn in the Cincinnati Symphony at age seventeen and the Metropolitan Opera at nineteen, at the same time he was exploring the New York bebop scene and performing and recording with Miles Davis, Dizzy Gillespie, and John Lewis. He would go on to become a major force in the music world as president of the New England Conservatory of Music and artistic director of the Tanglewood Berkshire Music Center, operator of several recording and publishing companies, composer of more than 160 works in a variety of genres, and a prolific writer on a number of topics in music history, aesthetics, and education. At Lenox, with his ties to both Tanglewood and Music Inn, Schuller was an important exemplar and liaison for those musicians with interests in modern composition and various experimental hybrid musics; later, for example, he would hire George Russell, Jimmy Giuffre, and Ran Blake to the faculty of the New England Conservatory. Blake, as chairman of the conservatory's Department of Third Stream Studies since the early 1970s, has broadened the multiple-stream concept far beyond Schuller's original notion of a jazz/classical alliance, exploring ethnic and folk musics in particular. One of the department's most notable products has been the Klezmer Conservatory Band, the Yiddishe revival ensemble that has included such non-Jewish musicians as Don Byron and Ingrid Monson.[54]

To some Lenox participants in the 1950s, however, Schuller's notion of "freedom" in jazz appeared somewhat limited and self-serving. One musician cynically characterized "Third Stream" as "a term invented to get work for Gunther Schuller." Milt Jackson, who played Schuller's *Concertino for Jazz Quartet and Orchestra* with the MJQ and the Stuttgart Symphony, said, "I don't want to run him down, because he's an excellent composer, but he's not writing jazz—he's not from the jazz environment." What constituted real jazz for Jackson was not strictly a matter of racial pedigree, nor did he think that immersion in "the jazz environment" necessarily produced good jazz: as skeptical as he was of Schuller, he was openly critical of Ornette Coleman's radical experiments in the name of "free jazz"—experiments encouraged and nurtured in Lenox by John Lewis and Percy Heath, among others.[55]

Among the critics on hand in Lenox, Martin Williams took a special interest in Coleman and set about evangelizing on his behalf. In "A Letter from Lenox, Massachusetts" published in the *Jazz Review* in 1959, Williams waxed rapturous: "When he stood up to take a solo on the blues with the big band on the first day of school, I was taken. It was as if he had opened up something in one's soul and opened up the way for jazz to grow. His music makes a new sensibility for one's ears and heart and mind, all the while including the most fundamental things in jazz." Williams boldly announced that "what Ornette Coleman is doing on alto will affect the whole character of jazz music profoundly and pervasively." Williams's letter, and his ensuing role as a supporter and confidant of Coleman's as acid criticism rained down on his radical innovations, served as a fitting coda to the Lenox School of Jazz and its role in shaping both jazz education and the jazz avant garde. Over the next two years—until both the school and the *Jazz Review* folded in 1961— Williams and co-editor Nat Hentoff provided a forum for Gunther Schuller, George Russell, Don Heckman, and others to explain the new music and agitate for its inclusion in constructions of a jazz mainstream tradition.

Compelling as these efforts proved in intellectual terms, however, they swam against a new, powerful tide in the American cultural mainstream: the emergence of a middle-class youth culture that favored the participatory simplicity of folk music and rock'n'roll over the abstract complexities of avant-garde jazz. An augury of this shift came in 1961 with a change of ownership at Music Inn and new programming that in subsequent years included Joan Baez, Bob Dylan, the Byrds, Janis Ian, Mary Travers, Richie Havens, Arlo Guthrie, the Allmann Brothers, Bonnie Raitt, Carly Simon, and James Taylor.[56] A similar story was unfolding across New England in that other old-money bastion of Newport.

Hipsters, Bluebloods, Rebels, and Hooligans

> I have two criteria. I used to have three. I program the music I love, and I program the music that sells. I used to also do music that would give me credibility with the critics. I've given up on the third.
>
> George Wein, in a 1997 interview about his career as a jazz producer[57]

"We could make Newport the jazz center of the world," George Wein excitedly told the *New Yorker*'s Lillian Ross, in town to cover the first Newport

Jazz Festival in 1954. "What Salzburg is to Mozart! What Bayreuth is to Wagner! What Tanglewood is to classical music! That's what we could make Newport be to jazz!" Underwriting Wein's grand vision was $20,000 from Louis and Elaine Lorillard, he a great-grandson of the founder of a tobacco fortune, she a Madison Avenue fashion illustrator before marrying into the Newport gentry. In the winter of 1954 Elaine Lorillard had commuted once a week from Newport to attend Wein's jazz history course at Boston University. Since her marriage in 1946, Elaine had found Newport "a town living more or less in the brave elegance of the past." In 1879 Louis Lorillard's grandfather, Pierre, had been a founder of the Casino, site of the United States's first lawn tennis championships. Louis remembered from his boyhood years summer concerts at the Casino featuring musicians that maestro Theophilus Wendt borrowed from the New York Philharmonic and from the Philadelphia, Cleveland, and Boston symphony orchestras. He also remembered the fashionable soirées where Rudy Vallee and Artie Shaw made their Newport debuts, and the glittering nights at the Newport beach dance pavilion jitterbugging to the swinging big band rhythms of Mal Hallet, Cab Calloway, Chick Webb, and Glen Gray. Newport's music scene quieted when a hurricane destroyed the pavilion in 1938 and the war brought a general downturn in local cultural activity. In 1953, in emulation of the successful Tanglewood festival in the Berkshires, the Lorillards brought the New York Philharmonic to Newport for a series of summer concerts. Disappointed by sparse attendance, Elaine and Louis nevertheless felt emboldened to make their mark as young movers and shakers. At the intermission of one of the Philharmonic concerts, John Maxon, curator of the Rhode Island School of Design museum, put the bug in Mrs. Lorillard's ear: a big-time jazz festival, in Newport, right here at the Casino.[58]

The Lorillards lost face with the starchiest of their blueblood neighbors—Louis encountered cold shoulders and arched eyebrows at his men's club—but it didn't take long for Newport burghers to see that jazz was freshly minted cultural capital, a homegrown cosmopolitan form more vibrant than faded Euro-gentility. One document that dramatizes this cultural transformation is the 1956 movie *High Society,* a musical comedy that signifies on the plot changes of *The Philadelphia Story*. Bing Crosby plays a well-heeled Newport slacker named Dexter, a jazz buff inspired by Louis Lorillard's efforts to sell the local bluebloods on jazz. In a famous scene, Crosby's Dexter cuts into a society ball waltz to introduce Louis Armstrong and his band, which to this point in the film has provided background music for the romantic contretemps between Dexter and his fiancée, played by Grace Kelly. Crosby and Armstrong launch into an extraordinary rendition of "Now You Has Jazz." Crosby, in brilliant voice, easily relieves the audience of its elitist prejudices. But the really memorable performance is Armstrong's. Constrained by a Hollywood formula in which the black musician serves to authenticate a white star's knowing hipness—Armstrong plays similar roles opposite Danny Kaye in *A Song Is Born* (1948) and Paul Newman in *Paris Blues* (1961)—Armstrong deftly unmasks the film's neo-minstrel scheme, purloining Crosby's crystalline vocal lines into a glare of hot trumpet and signature rasp-scat.[59]

The real-life festival itself was no less exciting and colorful. On the inaugural weekend of July 16 and 17, 1954, Newport's narrow streets thronged, *Time* reported, "with loud-shirted bookie types from Broadway, young intellectuals in need of haircuts, crew-cut Ivy Leaguers, sailors, Harlem girls with extravagant hairdos, and high school girls in shorts. They were cats. From as far away as Kansas they had come to hear a two-day monster jazz festival." Fourteen thousand attended the Saturday and Sunday evening concerts at the Newport Casino (in a band shell designed by Hsio Wen Shih, the architect, acoustic designer, and erudite jazz buff who later served as publisher of the *Jazz Review*). The *New Yorker* noted that on Saturday afternoon, "an elderly lady wearing a large white hat and carrying a white lace parasol" beetled about in an agitated search for the "jazz-music lecture." She was one of an estimated one thousand who attended a panel discussion on "The Place of Jazz in American Culture," modeled after Marshall Stearns's Lenox jazz roundtables. The panel—moderated by the "jazz priest" Father Norman O'Connor, with presentations by Stearns; Alan Merriam, an anthropology professor at Northwestern University; Henry Cowell, a composer and music professor at the Peabody Institute; and Willis James, folklorist and ethnomusicology professor at Spelman College—symbolized jazz's rising legitimacy among intellectuals. Local newspaper notices from the *Sacramento Bee* to the *Roanoke Times* testified to the festival's national scope. Such was the rapture of the European press that when Wein arrived in France on a business trip that fall, French jazz enthusiasts received him as *un homme formidable*.[60]

Wein had established his reputation as a savvy and musically literate jazz impresario at his Boston jazz nightclubs, Storyville and Mahogany Hall. The son of Boston's best-known plastic surgeon, Wein saw his own premedical studies founder in the late 1940s when his love for jazz and his budding entrepreneurial skills came together to point him toward a new career. As a pianist, Wein had played traditional jazz behind trumpeter Max Kaminsky at the Ken Club and clarinetist Edmond Hall at the Savoy. He became a promoter when he formed a combo called "George Wein's Danceable Jazz Featuring Edmond Hall" and toured the New England college circuit. In 1950, Wein launched Storyville on $5,000 cobbled together from his G.I. benefits and a loan from his mother. The suggestion to name the club after the legendary jazz and red-light district of New Orleans came from Wein's friend Nat Hentoff, at the time host of a popular jazz radio program in Boston and an aspiring jazz writer. "We grew up together and we hung out together at the Savoy," Wein said recently. "Nat introduced me to my wife [Joyce Wein]. I was playing the music, but he knew more about the history. I'd listen to his radio program, hear Bessie Smith for the first time—that sort of thing." Hentoff wrote the notes for the first concert Wein produced in Boston, at Jordan Hall, and he wrote a narrative script for the first Newport Jazz Festival—a condensed history of jazz—that was read by master of ceremonies Stan Kenton.[61]

In a profile of Wein in *Esquire* in 1955, George Frazier told a story about one night at Storyville when Wein still served as house pianist. Drummer Jo Jones, known both for his good-natured disposition and for his rhythmic perfectionism, found Wein's block chords and comping technique unforgivably clumsy. "George, you gotta make up your mind whether you want to run a night club or play piano. I'm sorry man, but I just can't use you," Jones told him, then cashiered him off the bandstand in what is surely one of the high points in the history of jazz labor-management relations. In the same *Esquire* profile, Frazier quoted Wein as saying that "the worst enemies of jazz are often the musicians themselves"—an argument for the Newport festival's "respectability-by-osmosis" uplift strategy. Some musicians found this attitude patronizing. Worried that Dizzy Gillespie's comic stage antics might profane the solemn rites of the opening night concert, Wein asked the trumpeter to affect a more serious pose. "In my most snobbish manner I decided to ask Dizzy to cut the clowning and just concentrate on his music," Wein contritely wrote in a 1956 *Playboy* article about the festival. "Seeing his goateed jaw drop several inches once I had made my suggestion was one of the most painful experiences of my life. I really hit him below the belt and I think it wrecked the entire festival for him." Offended by Wein's heavy-handed gesture, Gillespie redoubled his merry-andrewish efforts. Wearing a wrinkled brown suit and brandishing his signature vertical-belled trumpet, Gillespie paused in his performance, took the mike, and in a tone of mocking gravity, introduced the members of his band—to each other. Upon resuming, Gillespie pulled a small camera out of his pocket and spent the rest of the set photographing members of the press.[62]

In planning for the Newport festival, Wein traded on his reputation as, in Frazier's words, "one of the very few night-club operators who is liked and trusted by musicians of violently conflicting schools of jazz." While his own tastes ran to early jazz and swing, Wein had hired Mingus, Charlie Parker, Max Roach, and other bebop players to play at Storyville. "We want to throw modern, swing, and Dixieland together—even have the guys playing them together," Wein wrote, describing his Newport programming philosophy. "As long as there's a common beat, every guy can play solo his own style. One big happy family." Wein's "one big happy family" was a more sentimental, middlebrow version of what jazz critics had begun to call the jazz tradition or the jazz mainstream. The inaugural concerts began with a front line of Eddie Condon's Dixieland associates backed by the swing rhythm section of drummer Jo Jones and bassist Milt Hinton. The Modern Jazz Quartet, Dizzy Gillespie Quintet, and Gerry Mulligan Quartet shared a section with Billie Holiday. A tribute to Count Basie was followed by Gillespie and the George Shearing Quintet. Lennie Tristano and Lee Konitz segued into the Gene Krupa Trio. Stan Kenton—whom Wein had enlisted as master of ceremonies after Duke Ellington was unable to re-schedule another engagement—led a closing-night jam session involving all the artists.[63]

Newport festival programs and publicity campaigns featured chamber-of-commerce–style rhetoric about "the great Newport doctrine of helping new people and new ideas." This publicity linked the 1950s canonization of jazz to a Newport legacy of social, intellectual, and artistic reform. Dizzy Gillespie and John Lewis joined a pageant of freedom-seekers stretching back to the Vikings who found shelter in Newport waters two centuries before Columbus, the proprietors of the tall sailing ships that carved out global trade routes (no mention, of course, of the triangle trade in African slaves), and the patriots of 1776. "Tonight Newport went back to its beginning," intoned society columnist Cleveland Amory at a party at the Lorillards' after the inaugural concert. "Back to the time when it hummed with artists, writers, schoolteachers, ministers, and freedom." Institute of Jazz Studies director Marshall Stearns, in a festival program essay titled "Jazz Comes of Age" that foreshadowed his role as a consultant for the State Department tours, credited the music's global popularity to an anti-totalitarian ethos that "transcend[s] rules and regulations" and "offers a common ground on which the conflicting claims of the individual and the group may be resolved."[64]

Stearns was a respected scholar, while Amory's faith in the Newport crusade to "prove that jazz deserved something better than smoke-filled dives and zoot-suited patrons" might have struck a chord with jazz modernists looking for a reprieve from the hurly-burly jazz life. All the same, boosterish claims about Newport's noble history and jazz's democratic ideology gave little solace to black musicians and fans who were turned away at Newport's Viking Hotel. A 1955 *Time* dispatch on the second festival, reporting that "cats, hipsters, vipers, and even a few moldy figs swarmed the stately mansions of Newport," told one side of the story; *Ebony*'s coverage, noting that pianist Billy Taylor had been refused service at a hotel bar, told another. In other cases, racial insensitivities registered more subtly as screwball-comedy–style faux pas. At the post-concert party at the Lorillards', Lillian Ross reported in the *New Yorker*, a local old-line matron boasted to Modern Jazz Quartet bassist Percy Heath about "the old, lush days of Newport" when "every house had a large staff of liveried servants."[65]

Concerns about racist incidents in Newport dominated the festival board of directors' meeting in 1955. Leonard Feather and Barry Ulanov, citing incidents of racial discrimination at the Viking Hotel and other local establishments, made a motion to move the festival out of Newport. They also called for a loud publicity campaign shaming the town's burghers for their affront to the democratic principles enshrined in the music. As editors of *Metronome* in the 1940s, Feather and Ulanov were known not just as supporters of bebop but also as liberals with a foursquare commitment to racial equality. John Hammond, however, remained the jazz critic most identified with this issue. Hammond, whose Vanderbilt forbears were the bulwark of the Newport aristocracy, had an especially strong interest in the fate of jazz and race relations in Newport. Long engaged in a drama of class treason, Hammond now reveled in seeing his commitment to jazz and black causes delivered on the doorsteps of his family. Responding to Feather and Ulanov's motion, Hammond said:

> I think the fact that the . . . jazz festival was held in Newport, the most unlikely place, is essential. I think that if we had tried to have this festival any place else we would find that 80% of our publicity from the past and our good will would be dissipated . . . I think many of us who are on this advisory committee have been fighting for jazz for a long time. We have no particular love for Newport— I less than almost anybody here [what] with family, relatives and forebears all coming from Newport. It is a kind of society and a kind of life [that I] abhor. Yet in one sense of the word we have brought democracy to Newport, which was that last place in the world where it could have been expected to be found in America.[66]

The festival stayed in Newport and its advisory board continued to be dominated by white liberals. The inclusion of black members on the board— musicians Louis Armstrong and Duke Ellington, novelist and critic Ralph Ellison, and *Ebony* magazine editor Alan Morrison—symbolized the pluralist aspirations of the enterprise. Through the mid-1950s, a significant number of black writers, intellectuals, college students, and middle-class vacationers (many from nearby Martha's Vineyard) attended the festival. Ellison, Willis James, Langston Hughes, James Baldwin, and Sterling Brown participated in the panel discussions. Civil rights activist Julian Bond remembers the festival as an important social event for his circle of college friends in the late

1950s. In the New York *Amsterdam News* and other black newspapers, festival coverage ran not just in the entertainment section, but also in the social pages, where it exemplified the cultivated leisure of the black bourgeoisie.

Amsterdam News reporter Melvin Tapley, covering the 1957 festival, challenged black middle-class leaders to throw more support behind jazz. "I only wish that some of our people with the loot," Tapley wrote, "our doctors, lawyers, and business executives . . . would establish some sort of preservation society, like the Newport nabobs, for our own artists before our cultural bank account is overdrawn and squandered by the 'Great White Father' promoters." Langston Hughes sounded the same note in a private letter to Arna Bontemps. Noting that "half of cullud Harlem" was in Newport for the 1958 festival (and singling out for praise a jazz dance seminar led by Marshall Stearns and S. I. Hayakawa's lecture on the blues with a demonstration by singer Jimmy Rushing), Hughes wrote that "Cullud ought to be in on some of this jazz PROMOTING instead of just the playing." This desire for greater black control of cultural production was something Hughes and others had advocated for years and would continue to pursue in years to come. But this didn't prevent Hughes from strategically embracing the mission of the Newport sponsors. "For giving jazz its golden crown at Newport," Hughes wrote in the New York *Post* in 1963, "the Lorillards themselves deserve a crown." Writing in the public forum of a mainstream newspaper column during a time of increasing civil rights agitation, Hughes celebrated the Newport festival as a shining example of racial equality: "From its beginnings the board of the Newport Jazz Festival insisted that the Festival be completely democratic and interracial. Audiences, performers and (after a few early adjustments) all Newport hotels, restaurants and places of public accommodation were happily integrated without regard to race, color, age, sex or previous conditions of unhepness."[67]

Emboldened by such optimism, Newport's sponsors looked beyond the summer festival to spread the gospel of jazz as a "universal" art. In 1955, Louis Lorillard initiated talks with the State Department about the possibility of using the Newport festival as a tool of cultural diplomacy in Europe. John Hammond, who thought Rhode Island Democratic senator Theodore Green lacked sufficient clout, encouraged the Lorillards instead to cultivate Harlem congressman Adam Clayton Powell. Powell proved a key player in Congress in securing funds for Dizzy Gillespie's tour of the Middle East in 1956, which initiated the series of international tours by jazz musicians during Eisenhower's second term and beyond. The Newport Jazz Festival proved to be a launching ground into the cold war internationalist bureaucracy. In the 1960s, Elaine Lorillard became a consultant to the Citizen's Exchange Corps; with Billy Taylor as her advisor, she traveled to Moscow to propose artist exchange programs. Newport Festival advisory committee members Leonard Feather and Willis Conover became Voice of America disc jockeys, spinning jazz records for audiences all over the globe. Visiting Moscow and Leningrad in the early 1960s, Feather's introduction to the Russians invariably invoked the response, "Ah, yes! Jazz Club USA," the result of a brisk trade in bootlegged copies of his early 1950s Voice of America broadcasts. In 1955, Conover, a successful Washington disc jockey who served as a master of ceremonies at Newport, took over the VOA reins with his "Music USA" show, which lasted until the mid-1990s. *Look* magazine asserted in a 1962 profile that Conover "may be the world's favorite American." In 1985 *Reader's Digest* was less equivocal, headlining its Conover profile "The World's Favorite American" and celebrating the disc jockey as the leading herald of the music that "mocks authoritarian impulses" by giving "politically repressed listeners . . . a heady whiff of freedom." In an interview in the early 1990s, Conover took great pains to suggest that his work had no political agenda; that he could not have survived the alternation of Republican and Democratic administrations if he were grinding some partisan ideological axe; that he was simply in the business of promoting great American music. After recounting some stories about his warm reception in eastern Europe, he then wondered out loud, "you know, maybe I really *did* have something to do with the failure of Communism."[68]

Clearly, the effort to propagandize jazz as a universal art had gotten far beyond the Newport festival promoters' strained analogies with freedom-seeking Vikings and the emancipatory impact of colonial-era mercantilism. Gillespie, for his part, was proud of his efforts at Lenox and Newport and on State Department tours to, as he put it, "establish a proper place in U.S. society and in the world for our music." "Yardbird [Gillespie's deceased friend, Charlie Parker] became a martyr for our music," he said, "and I became a reformer." With his goatee and horn-rimmed glasses and his jocular stage presence, Gillespie could give reform a very amiable face. At the same time, Gillespie's notion of reform pulsed with a strong sense of history and an uncompromising commitment to racial justice. Told that he would have to be briefed by the State Department before going abroad to perform, Gillespie sharply responded, "I've got three hundred years of briefing. I know what they've done to us, and I'm not going to make any excuses." Later he wrote in his memoir, "I sort of liked the idea of representing America, but I wasn't going to apologize for the racist policies of America."[69]

Like Langston Hughes, musicians well understood the social significance and influence of the Newport Jazz Festival. In 1956, the Duke Ellington orchestra was mired in a slump, its low ratings in fan polls and struggle for steady work a sad sign of the decline of the swing band movement Ellington had pioneered in the 1930s. Sensing an opportunity to recapture the public imagination by premiering a new piece at that year's festival, Ellington composed "The Newport Suite." While the festival opened on Thursday night, Ellington was scheduled for Saturday night and remained in New York until that day. George Wein was at an after-concert party at the Lorillards' late Thursday night when he was summoned to the phone for a call from Ellington. "I don't know how the hell he knew where I was. But he was clearly very excited. He said, 'What's happening up there? What's the mood?' I told him we were all waiting for him, looking forward to Saturday night. I asked him what he was going to do. He said 'I thought we'd do the medley ["Newport Festival Suite"] and maybe some other stuff. I said to him: 'Edward, here I am working my fingers to the bone to perpetuate the genius that is Ellington and I'm not getting any cooperation from you. You better come in here swinging.'"[70]

The good feeling behind this mock jousting dissipated a bit on Saturday night. When four of Ellington's musicians were late, Wein decided to run other acts while waiting for the missing players. The players soon arrived, but the band had to wait for three hours to take the stage. An irritated Ellington groused to Wein, "What are we—the animal act, the acrobats?" Finally, the clock nearing midnight, the band opened with "The Newport Festival Suite," followed by "Diminuendo and Crescendo in Blue," two medium tempo blues Ellington had written in 1937 spliced together with a "wailing interval" by tenor saxophonist Paul Gonsalves.

Ellington kicked off "Diminuendo and Crescendo in Blue" with four un-remarkable introductory choruses. As drummer Sam Woodyard and bassist Jimmy Woode dug a deep groove and the horns leaned hard into their ex-uberant ensemble choruses, Ellington started verbally exhorting the band, shouting out "Uh-huh! Come on! Yeah!" Jo Jones, who earlier in the evening had backed up pianist Teddy Wilson and was now standing in a runway below the left front of the stage, joined Ellington in pushing the band harder, hollering encouragement and rhythmically swatting the edge of the stage with a rolled-up copy of the *Christian Science Monitor*.

Gonsalves stood and launched into his solo. Three choruses in, a platinum blonde in one of the front boxes broke loose from her escort and started spinning wildly, whirling-dervish-like, around the field. Ten choruses in, half the audience was jitterbugging in the aisles, the other half standing on their seats, cheering and clapping with mounting fervor. As the crowd energy surged and a possessed Gonsalves shut his eyes and pressed on, Wein and the local police grew agitated, fearful that a riot might break out. Wein and one of the officers tried to signal to Ellington to stop. In the heat of the moment, Ellington shook his finger at Wein and shouted, "Don't be rude to the artists."

Gonsalves's Olympian twenty-seven-chorus solo subsequently has entered jazz legend as an endlessly fetishized performance: in aficionado circles, there are people who can provide you the matrix number of a 1951 studio recording of "Diminuendo and Crescendo in Blue" in which Gonsalves took only *twenty-six* choruses. The Columbia recording of the entire Newport Ellington set, *Ellington at Newport,* went on to become Ellington's best-selling LP. A cover story in *Time* magazine called Ellington's Newport performance the "big news . . . that the whole jazz world had hoped to hear: [that] the Ellington band was once again the most exciting thing in the business."[71]

The story of this galvanic performance usually figures as a kind of stock scene of jazz scripture connoting nothing less than the resurrection of the messiah. Those less given to hagiography might interpret the event as a triumph of African-American performative culture, an eruption of spontaneous jam-session–styled energy trumping the containment strategies of the jazz establishment. Yet one might also discern in Ellington's wry rebuke of George Wein the practiced gesture of a celebrity with a well-earned position of influence among national media elites, a savvy operator who knew how to work with promoters like Wein to advance his own interests. It wasn't just Ellington who discovered the career-enhancing possibilities of a Newport appearance. The year before, Miles Davis, after a five-year struggle with heroin addiction, had ended a conspicuous absence from the jazz world with a triumphant appearance at Newport with Thelonious Monk. On the strength of glowing reviews of the performance, Davis was able to secure a lucrative recording contract with Columbia. Along with recording deals, musicians profited from Newport media exposure that projected a new kind of image of the jazz musician to the broad American public. In a foreshadowing of the sartorial image-making campaigns for the jazz "young lions" of recent years, fashion editors from *Vogue, Esquire, Ebony,* and *Playboy* descended on Newport in July, embracing jazz musicians as exemplars of bourgeois style. A 1955 *Vogue* photo spread on the second Newport festival featured John Lewis, described as a "well-adjusted Othello"; Charles Mingus, "a handsome, solid-looking man . . . with a deep, brooding voice"; Dave Brubeck, "an amiable-faced young man with a great wide-jawed grin and black-rimmed spectacles"; and Count Basie, pictured seated a grand piano suavely ornamented by "two cool blue notes," a pair of young and pretty white New York women outfitted in satin evening dresses.[72]

A new conjunction of jazz, advertising, and modernist visual aesthetics appeared with the feature documentary film *Jazz on a Summer's Day.* Shot at the 1958 Newport festival and released to high praise at international film festivals in 1960, the film was produced and directed by Bert Stern, a successful New York advertising photographer venturing into moviemaking for the first time. Stern, according to critic Jerry Tallmer, had no more knowledge of jazz than Robert Oppenheimer. What he did have, however, was a sense of Newport as a landscape for a new jazz aesthetic. "Too many movies have given jazz an association with violence, narcotics, electric chairs, and murder," Stern explained. "We tried to show the form and beauty of jazz by various devices, such as wave and water effects, children playing, and reflections." Featuring a cinematographic purity of color reported to have "knocked every New York critic out of his seat," Stern's film interweaves festival performances with shots of a racially integrated audience, several dowagers in rococo dress surveying the strange Newport scene, a rooming house roof party, a Dixieland combo of Yale men spiriting through town in a Jazz Age roadster, a solitary young woman on a morning walk of the beach. Tallmer praised the documentary as a "rambling free-form mood poem" that captured the "eternal bold youth of everything," the "ordinary uncomplicated joyousness of sitting around and getting beautifully muzzy on beer as these guys blow these horns through the bright midday and the long afternoon and the soft enfolding evening of a rich little green little seaside town . . . far out of this world."[73]

Stern's artistic sensibility confounded the film's music director, George Avakian, who felt that on-site fussing over camera angles and post-production sleight of hand detracted from the film's value as a musical document. Indeed, the music in the film often functions as background for Stern's highly stylized vignettes. Throughout Anita O'Day's hyper-cool mannerist introduction to "Sweet Georgia Brown," the camera lingers on a woman in the audience deeply immersed in a paperback copy of *Camille* and a female photographer trying to keep her hat on as she focuses her lens. Thelonious Monk takes the stage and delineates a spare, pointillist sketch out of the head of "Blue Monk," providing the segue for a montage of the America's Cup yacht trials being held in Newport Bay. The languorous tempo of Louis Armstrong's "Up the Lazy River" is underscored by a recurring close-up of a man in the audience snapping his fingers just a shade behind the beat.[74]

Jazz on a Summer's Day is full of artifice: the yacht trials actually took place later in the summer, the audience shots were reconstructed in a New York studio over the winter. But the film's very quality of self-conscious artiness was itself a telling point, a symptom of jazz's association with the rarified discourses of modern art. One of the revealing subtexts of the film is the contrast it draws between Armstrong's old-time image of the good-natured entertainer and the modern jazz musicians' preferred image of a serious, non-accomodating artist. The film historian Donald Bogle has argued that to young blacks coming of age in the 1950s, Armstrong's glowing musicianship provided little inoculation against the embarrassment of his Uncle Tom–like eye-popping, shucking and jiving, and too-friendly banter with white co-stars. Unfairly and with little appreciation of his gift for subversive mimicry, jazz purists often winced at the Sambo inflections of Armstrong's comic persona. In 1958, when Leonard Feather ran a reader-response survey in *Down Beat*, to the question "What was the worst thing that happened to jazz in the last year?" the most common response was Louis Armstrong's appearance at the Newport Jazz Festival. Even so staunch an Armstrong partisan as Ralph Ellison lamented—in a letter to Albert Murray—that at the 1957 festival Armstrong "was wearing his ass instead of his genius." In *Jazz on a Summer's Day*'s footage of the 1958 festival, Armstrong is shown mugging with Voice of America disk jockey Willis Conover, the festival master of ceremonies, before performing "Up the Lazy River" and his perennial "Rocking Chair" vocal duet with Jack Teagarden. Though the audience appears to love the broadly grinning Satchmo, the filmed performance offers no window into Armstrong's complex psyche—no hint, for instance, of the burden he was carrying for having boldly defied his friend and manager, Joe Glaser, by speaking out against Arkansas governor Orval Faubus during the 1957 school desegregation crisis. That sort of image—of the jazz artist with a complicated inner life—is reserved for the modernists. A long passage in the film that captures Chico Hamilton and his sidemen in rehearsal is lit in a film-noirish chiaroscuro, much like Blue Note album cover photographs of the period—an image that suggested deep emotion, anxiety, and searching intensity. When Conover introduces Thelonious Monk, he archly describes the pianist as a kind of existentialist misanthrope:[75]

> [And now], one of the complete originals of music. A man who lives his music, a man who thinks his music, and it's possible to say he lives and thinks of little else. We can't describe him exactly as daring, because he is unconcerned with any opposition to his music. He concerns himself with such elements as the quarter-tone, which he doesn't find in our Western scale, so he'll strike two adjacent keys on the piano to imply the missing note between. Ladies and gentlemen, Thelonious Monk.

To his credit, George Wein programmed post-bebop players and even the late 1950s avant garde—Monk, Chico Hamilton, Cecil Taylor, Max Roach, Charles Mingus, Jimmy Giuffre—despite his own retro tastes, audience diffidence, and a hammering in the general press. Harold Schoenberg, the *New*

York Times's classical music critic, panned the modernists at the 1955 festival (Lee Konitz, the Modern Jazz Quartet, Miles Davis, Charles Mingus) as "dissonant, tight, overintellectual, and nonmelodic," preferring the "earthy and low-down . . . anti-intellectual" fare of Louis Armstrong and Jimmy Rushing. Roger Maren, writing in *The Reporter* that same year, also preferred the "rarely pretentious" traditionalists to modern players who "often give the impression that they are members of a metaphysical cult rather than simply entertainers." Maren found the whole Newport scene too serious. Expecting to find a raucous crowd shouting "go, man, go," he was disappointed to encounter an atmosphere "resembling Tanglewood's or Salzburg's"; a festival program and souvenir booklet whose typography "echoed the experimental art of the 1920s"; a "professor [Stearns] comparing Bessie Smith to the Wife of Bath"; and song titles like "Epistrophy" and "Fugetta." "The word 'semantic' was used so many times at the Festival with so many odd meanings," Maren complained, "that it took on a new semantic value." In 1958, gospel singer Mahalia Jackson raised similar concerns about the festival's more cerebral dimensions. After listening to a panel discussion on "Jazz and American Life" involving Ralph Ellison, Langston Hughes, Marshall Stearns, Sterling Brown, and S. I. Hayakawa, Jackson said, "There's been too much analysin' here and not enough heart."[76]

Nat Hentoff and Whitney Balliett condemned Maren in a pair of blistering letters-to-the-editor that linked their writerly agendas to the fate of the embattled jazz modernists. Balliett's letter to *The Reporter* diagnosed a malignant symmetry in Maren's Newport analysis: Maren's dismissal of Charles Mingus's aspirations as a jazz composer, Balliett noted, came just two paragraphs before he "takes jazz critics to task for using terms like 'counterpoint,' 'atonality,' and 'polytonality.'" At issue here—as ever in jazz criticism—was the question of what constitutes real jazz, whether the latest stylistic developments were authentically rooted in the already canonized tradition, and what kind of environment and performing posture were appropriate for the music's presentation. When Wein caught promoter's fever, enlarging the festival each year and aiming to pull in the burgeoning rock'n'roll youth audience, he became a ripe target for the critics' purist righteousness. Balliett started turning on Wein in 1956, decrying a "fat hand of bigness" that had begun to strangle the festival in 1955 after it moved from the Casino to Freebody Park, a municipal baseball facility where in later years crowds of 20,000 and up would convene. Richard Gehman excoriated the festival management for treating jazz as a "huge supermarket" set up for the benefit of a "vast and generally tasteless public." Dan Morgenstern characterized jazz festivals as "three-ring circuses, crass commercial supermarkets of jazz, cold and uninspired variety shows, and unseemly mixtures of pretentiousness and sham." Wein's old friend Nat Hentoff rued that Newport had become "a money-grubbing enterprise of the same category as any giant midway staffed with shell games, taffy candy, freak shows and thrill rides."[77]

In his liner notes for the LP *Ellington at Newport*, Columbia Records producer George Avakian took pains to suggest that the audience's behavior during "Diminuendo and Crescendo in Blue," while impassioned, was "no rock'n'roll reaction." The allusion called to mind the epidemic of highly publicized disruptions at rock'n'roll concerts that season, including a flare-up in September 1956 at a Fats Domino concert at a Newport naval base that resulted in the hospitalization of a dozen servicemen both black and white. Avakian's language linked the rhetoric of cold war domestic containment to jazz's mounting high-culture pretensions. "Despite the unbridled enthusiasm [during Ellington's performance]," he wrote, "there was a controlled, clean quality to the crowd."[78]

Clean or not, the Newport audience from 1957 on encountered a regular diet of acts that jazz critics and purists took as a personal affront, a challenge to their canon-forming endeavors. Whatever one might think about the Four Freshmen, the Kingston Trio, Pat Suzuki, and Eartha Kitt, the indictment ran, they did not belong at a festival that had originally defined itself by its curatorial embrace of the *jazz* tradition. Of the critics, interestingly, it was the old lions John Hammond and Marshall Stearns who encouraged a pluralist outreach to the new popular music. Hammond prevailed on Wein to present Chuck Berry at the 1958 festival, backed by members of a Count Basie reunion band. This half-way covenant between Kansas City 4/4 swing and backbeat-driven rock'n'roll appears in *Jazz on a Summer's Day* footage to confound the musicians and not quite jell into a compelling rhythmic groove. Many in the audience, however, found Berry's rocking guitar and patented duckwalk reason enough to get on their feet and dance, which they continued to do when Mahalia Jackson's infectious gospel beat capped off the concert. Avakian, who was also Jackson's producer at the time and who thought the dancing a sacrilege against the gospel matriarch's religious purity, was highly displeased.[79]

So was Melvin Tapley of the New York *Amsterdam News*; he criticized both the Newport impresarios and Jackson herself for "desecrat[ing] music born of our religious beliefs." Ralph Ellison, for his part, was less concerned with a bleeding of the line between the sacred and the secular than with preserving the "authentic" character of Jackson's gospel music. In a 1958 *Saturday Review* essay on Jackson, Ellison lamented the singer's appearance at the 1957 Newport Festival singing the "Come Sunday" movement of Duke Ellington's *Black, Brown, and Beige Suite*. Calling the performance "a most unfortunate marriage and an error of taste," Ellison contrasted Ellington's "impression" of a Sunday service with the "real thing"—Jackson's performance at Newport's Afro-American Episcopal Church on Sunday morning, much more effectively evoking "the shared community of experience" that defines the black church. Ellison was even more censorious in a letter to Albert Murray, carping not only about Louis Armstrong's embarrassing performance but also about an appearance by "that creep Eartha Kitt and some non-jazz dancers." "The whole circus sounds as though it was rather limp," Ellison reported. "I guess you can't throw too many musicians and hep cats manque together too many times and have it come out listenable."[80]

These pleas for purity—whether the white critics' anti-commercialism or black critics' briefs for authentic black culture—were thrown up against a rising juggernaut. By the end of the 1950s, the audience for Newport Jazz Festival productions was estimated at more than a quarter million people. The fact that the festival was running a financial loss every year made Wein all the more contemptuous of his critics. Wein claimed that the problem with adverse notices by critics was not so much that it soured public reaction to the festival, but that it made artists leery of performing there, fearful that the critics would be harder on them at Newport than they were in reviewing their performances in clubs. But Wein was also critical of the artists themselves for demanding fees double and triple what they were receiving for club dates. "The original concept at Newport was to give *all* of jazz as big an audience as possible. That is not going to happen. Now the big artists are taking all the money. We are spending more than ever before and getting less."[81] Unable to see how his own growth-oriented policy contributed to setting the trap that he now found himself in, Wein complained that his increasing overhead costs (publicity, staff, year-round organizational work) made it necessary for him to tilt his programming toward recognizable stars.

Shaken by attacks on its increasingly commercial orientation, the festival board of directors tried mounting a counter-assault on jazz critics. In 1958, the board distributed a letter to magazine editors defending the festival for bringing jazz to a bigger public and accusing the critics of elitism:

> Do Gehman, Balliett, and Hentoff typify an alarming trend in jazz criticism today?—are they the foremost spokesmen for that element which is dismayed by popular success for what they consider (privately or subconsciously) to be the proper concern only of "experts"? Thus, while on the one hand they lament the American neglect of its own native music, they deliberately foster contempt for those who would make it accessible to the public.[82]

The older critics cut Wein more slack than the younger ones. In an incestuous dispute among Boston comrades, George Frazier defended Wein against Hentoff, calling the younger critic "nothing if not naive." Frazier wrote: "To indict the Newport Jazz Festival, as [Hentoff] did . . . because funny hats were sold on the premises is rather like belittling the beauty of a Mickey Mantle homerun because baseball caps are sold at Yankee Stadium."[83] Leonard Feather defended Wein's approach as one that enlarged the jazz audience and thereby helped the musicians. In a *mea culpa*, Feather compared the critics' attacks on Newport to those visited on Dave Brubeck when he achieved "staggering heights of popular acclaim . . . to which some of us peevishly felt our own pet groups were more justly entitled." Inherent in the critics' craft, he felt, was a resistance to "majority opinion." And while critics have every right to their idealism, they must also recognize how "unrealistic" their preferences might be in the practical realm. "If Wein were to turn over the operation of the Newport Festival to one of his critics, and if the latter were to run it entirely according to his own predilections," Feather wrote, "I have little doubt that the festival would be a colossal financial flop."[84]

These issues came to a head in 1960. At the festival on the 4th of July weekend that year, thousands of white youths described by *Life* magazine as "more interested in cold beer than in hot jazz" spilled from the jazz concerts into Newport's downtown, attacking policemen, kicking in store windows, and manhandling the town's residents and visitors. Press reports noted that many of the drunken rioters screamed racial epithets while rampaging through town. State police used billy clubs and tear gas to stem the riot, then called on the Marines for help in restoring order. When the air cleared, more than 200 of the marauders found themselves in local jails, while more than 50 of their victims required medical attention. One witness told the Providence *Journal*: "I've experienced fear twice in my life. Once was in combat during World War II; the other was Saturday night in Newport." Scheduled to end on Sunday night, the festival was ordered shut down on Sunday afternoon by the Newport city council. The last act was a program of blues narrated by Langston Hughes. Anticipating the city council's action, Hughes penned a set of lyrics on a Western Union sheet. He handed them to Otis Spann, who sang them slowly as the crowd quietly departed:

> It's a gloomy day at Newport,
> It's a gloomy, gloomy day.
> It's a gloomy day at Newport.
> It's a gloomy, gloomy day.
> It's a gloomy day at Newport,
> The music's going away.[85]

Among a rash of press reports on the riot, one commentator blamed the allure of Newport, a "resort area which hold[s] a fascination for the square collegian who wants to ball without running the risk of mom and dad stumbling across his prostrate form on somebody's lawn." Mordantly noting the contrast between the Newport gentry "in the front row with their Martini shakers" and the youngsters "squatting in the back, their heads between their knees, upchucking their beer," journalist Murray Kempton wondered, "Was ever anything in America at once so fashionable and so squalid?" To many who had embraced Newport as jazz's City on a Hill, a sterling model of New England brahmin philanthropy, more disconcerting than the spectacle of loutish yahoos profaning the festival was the rioters' identity. These were not switchblade-wielding rebels without a cause, nor pot-head beatniks in overalls. These "young hooligan herrenvolk of the Eastern seaboard," as *Village Voice* jazz critic Robert Reisner dubbed the rioters, were students from the elite colleges, fraternity brothers on a fast track to the corporate boardroom. "You could tell the students from Harvard and Yale," wagged one man on the street. "They were throwing only *imported* beer bottles."[86]

Hooliganism wasn't the only turbulence that swept through the 1960 festival. That same weekend, a group of musicians led by Charles Mingus and Max Roach, aggrieved by festival management techniques and programming policies, organized an alternative or "rebel" festival in another part of town. Claiming that the main festival reeked of Jim Crow, finding its supporters' embrace of jazz suffocating rather than liberating, the rebels literally constructed their own bandstand, printed their own handbills, and erected tents on their own guerrilla concert site. Seizing the rhetoric and imagery of the *Salon des Réfusés*, the rebel festival fancied itself a virtuous self-governing republic of artists pitted against a corrupt empire of profiteering booking agents, promoters, and hoteliers.

The *Voice*'s Reisner deemed it "a case of getting back to the jazz truth," a matter of artists "renew[ing] their creative faculties by embracing poverty." Max Roach characterized the event as an effort to "prove that the musician can produce, present, and participate [by and for] himself"—an idea that Mingus and Roach had enacted earlier in the 1950s through owning and managing their own label, Debut Records. Proceeds collected in a noncoercive passing of the hat established a fund for fighting economic injustices plaguing musicians, such as onerous cabaret card laws and unemployment taxes. A correspondent from *Time*, struck by the political significance of the rebellion, unsuccessfully lobbied his editors to get his dispatch in the magazine's national affairs section rather than the music section. "This is an extension of the sit-ins," he told them. "[It's] a sit-out."[87]

Contra Langston Hughes's sunny account of Newport equality, Nat Hentoff asserted that Jim Crow was still a problem in Newport, citing the complaints of several black musicians who claimed to have been turned away from motels in 1959 and 1960. Hentoff grew exasperated at what he regarded as the festival's unconscionable refusal to address this problem head-on. "The lame automatic response by Festival officials to criticism of Jim Crow in Newport was, 'Well there'd be Jim Crow anywhere we went. Besides, our musical director is married to a Negro,'" he complained. What Hentoff did not mention in this account—published first in 1960 in *Commonweal* and then in 1961 in his book *The Jazz Life*—is that he himself had introduced George Wein to the black woman who became his wife, back when the two men were on better terms.[88]

What this points to is that at a time when jazz was being exported around the globe and trumpeted as the world's first universal art, the fact is that the jazz world itself was a small one, small enough that personal relationships really mattered. One of the musicians who'd had trouble getting a motel room was Charles Mingus. Acutely sensitivity to racism, Mingus interpreted this snubbing as part of the same Jim Crow arrangement under which the festival payed him less than Benny Goodman. (According a report in the Providence *Daily Bulletin*, Mingus had agreed to appear at the 1960 festival for $700, but later asked for $5000 after discovering that Benny Goodman had been paid $7500 for his appearance at the 1958 festival. Wein pointed out that Goodman had played an entire evening's program and had to pay a 17-man band plus singer Jimmy Rushing.) Mingus was notorious for ripping into jazz critics, but he was on good terms with Hentoff, who not only had been writing supportively about Mingus but, as an artists-and-repertory producer, had been recording him for the Candid label. When Mingus enlisted Hentoff's help in securing a location for the alternative festival, Hentoff turned to Elaine Lorillard, who was recently divorced from Louis, had been voted off of the festival board of directors, and was very receptive to the idea of protesting the venality and treachery of the main festival. She introduced Hentoff and Mingus to Nicholas Cannarozzi, owner of the Cliff Walk Manor, a seaside establishment that proved very congenial to the protesters' purposes.[89]

The rebel festival included one pick-up group led by swing-era titans Coleman Hawkins and Jo Jones and another by the hard bop trumpeter Kenny Dorham, Max Roach's quintet, the Charles Mingus Jazz Workshop, and the Ornette Coleman Quartet. Throughout the weekend the groups and players reshuffled into different combos. The program ran from Thursday through Monday, outlasting the main festival. Hentoff in *Commonweal*, Whitney Balliett in the *New Yorker*, and Robert Reisner in the *Village Voice* all sang the praises of the music and the setting. Balliett described the event as a "pure and simple . . . virtually handmade . . . wind-driven affair" that served as a perfect antidote to the main festival's "notorious mastadon ways." Hentoff noted that Jo Jones had also broken with George Wein because he thought the main festival was giving short shrift to the young modern players. "The big festival forgot about the music," Jones said, "but these little kiddies—he pointed to several modernists on the stand—have got to have a chance to be heard. That's one reason we did this." Balliett's review implied that the congenial ambience of the event inspired some of the musicians' best playing to date. A spontaneous grouping of Mingus, Roach, Dorham, Julian Priester (Roach's trombonist), and Coleman, he wrote, "provoked Mingus into one of the best solos he has ever played." Summing up the weekend, Balliett wrote: "The Thursday concert at Cliff Walk Manor had an attendance of ten. By Sunday hundreds were on hand. Throughout there was a catching bonhomie between all present, and this, together with Roach's effortless emceeing, gave the event an unfailing smoothness and graciousness. Best of all, there wasn't an impresario in sight."[90]

The sorting out of what happened in Newport in 1960 hinged on the juxtaposition of the two local events—the youth riot and the musicians' rebellion—within a framework that was defined by the larger social revolution unfolding in U.S. culture. Hentoff invoked the moral authority of the civil rights movement in coupling his condemnation of the riot with his support for the rebellion. He noted that none of the many black college students in town for the festival had joined the rioting: they had seen the efficacy of nonviolent direct action during the southern sit-ins, and besides, the rioters seemed bereft of a cause or commitment any higher than their own freedom. A *New York Herald-Tribune* editorial made this case by putting the Newport riot into a broader political and global context:

> In capitals around the world, desperately earnest students lately have been demonstrating, often rioting, for causes. Some of these have been good causes, some bad; it is as if a contagion of violent fervor were overleaping national boundaries and spreading from university to university. But these young Americans [the Newport rioters] had no cause. They were rioting for nothing but the perverse pleasure of violence. Theirs was a hedonism gone wild, and an irresponsible animal self-indulgence that reflects discredit on their generation.[91]

At a time when the spirit of "freedom" inspired bold new directions in jazz as well as bracing political activism in domestic civil rights and international anticolonialism campaigns, here were the most privileged white kids in the world asserting their freedom to turn a serious cultural event into a frat-house debauch. Tempting as it might be to read the riot as entirely a case of racial backlash—to argue, that is, that the rioters were acting primarily out of resentment toward the Newport festival's aura of liberal interracialism and its spotlighting of black cultural excellence—the facts suggest a slightly more tempered interpretation. A similar if less convulsive disturbance, very likely involving some of the same New England college students, had broken out at a Kingston Trio concert a year earlier at the Music Inn in Lenox, Massachusetts. Preppie hooliganism, it seemed, was all the rage, a cultural tremor whose reverberations could drown out dulcet three-part harmony just as easily as down-home twelve-bar blues.[92]

Still, the sound of racial epithets in the Newport air gave this particular riot special resonance. For Hentoff and others invested in the hope that jazz should rise above America rather than capitulate to its worst impulses, this sound was of a piece with the general deterioration of the festival in recent years—years, for these observers, in which the high artistry of jazz and the noble righteousness of the civil rights cause stood as indictments of both mass culture decay and social quiescence. Along these lines, Hentoff's friend Murray Kempton characterized Newport 1960 in terms that linked highbrow purism with social justice: "Jazz has [become] so vogued and Kerouacked as to be unheard . . . and nowhere [is] its presentation more nauseating than at Newport. But whenever either a musician or a sensitive observer complain[s] about these conditions, Newport's sponsors answer in tones of personal righteousness that sound like the letter Woolworth's sends people who want to know why a Negro can't get a cup of coffee at its lunch counter."[93]

Such clamors of outrage packed resonance precisely because of the jazz press's uneven response to both the civil rights movement and the jazz avant garde. Both *Down Beat* and *Metronome* took pains to defend the Newport promoters, casting the youth riot and the musicians' rebellion as twinned acts of heedless irresponsibility. Gene Lees, then editor of *Down Beat*, voiced the most intemperate version of this position. Lees made much of a rumor that Mingus had threatened to kill George Wein and throw acid in the face of Louis Lorillard—a literalist misreading of Mingus's Theater of the Absurd-ish agitprop that fueled Lees's argument that the musicians' rebellion was nothing more than a sideshow for self-pitying malcontents. In Lees's view, Mingus was an angry man "whose career has known many frustrations," while the musicians who joined him in the rebellion "had reputations as men with problems—eccentrics, to be kind about it." Lees also attacked Hentoff as "a some time jazz writer and full-time opponent of almost everything."[94]

The rebel festival was a bold protest against a self-congratulatory lib-eralism that framed the music as a "cause" whose "acceptance" was more important than the fortunes and feelings of the musicians themselves. In challenging jazz's racially structured power relations, the event foreshadowed the black freedom movement's turn to more assertive demands for cultural and economic autonomy. The rebels' initiative for self-determination intersected with and was crucially inspired by domestic civil rights and international anticolonial freedom struggles, pan-Africanism, and African American cultural traditions. These jazz musicians were not pushing for racial separatism, but rather for greater influence and control over the making of the music, its public dissemination, and its use as a symbol of American culture. "Race" was operating at Newport in 1960 in more nuanced ways, and on more levels, than a straightforward cultural resistance model will enable us to see. The alternative festival reached out to Newport's cosmopolitan, multiracial contingent of intellectuals and middle-class jazz consumers and connoisseurs, while showing great skill in appropriating for its own purposes the artistic discourse of critics like Hentoff and Balliett. That discourse was permeated with a cold war intellectual distrust of youth culture, an anxiety that in this case focused on transgressions of taste and decorum among the white audience. In going to such great lengths to condemn the riot, jazz critics and purists exposed the fiction of a unified American cultural mainstream. In doing so, they resisted the mass popularization of jazz, elevating artistic values over unchecked audience growth.

George Wein, skilled promoter that he was, continued to search for new formulas, new audiences, and new rhetoric—even if the search took him beyond the boundaries he had helped to erect around the term "jazz." In 1959 Wein organized a folk music festival the weekend after the jazz festival featuring such performers as the Ward Gospel Singers, the Abyssinian Choir, bluegrass banjoist Earl Scruggs, bluesman Robert Pete Williams, and an angelic-voiced singer by the name of Joan Baez, who had been playing for students in Harvard Square. As Robert Cantwell notes, by the late 1950s it was clear that the audience at Newport now "was not the summer elite but their sons and daughters, a new campus bohemia searching for a community, a politics, and forms of personal identity consonant with a developing mood of contempt for the commercial establishment."[95] That folk music was itself a construct of the commercial establishment was a point that was easily overlooked: it was the appearance of authenticity that mattered, and by that measure jazz's very success at cracking bourgeois codes in the early years of Newport was held against it. The folk revival audience had no use for the hooligan element at the 1960 jazz festival, and though it could sympathize on ideological grounds with the aims and methods of the alternative festival rebels, in general it found their music too difficult, too arty, too removed from any discernible set of "roots." Bob Dylan going electric at the 1965

Newport Folk Festival was a betrayal; Ornette Coleman's arcane theory of harmelodics was merely incomprehensible.

"Jazz doesn't belong to Nat Hentoff and Whitney Balliett; it belongs to the world," George Wein said recently in a discussion of his battles with critics in the early years of the Newport Jazz Festival. "I thought that if I could bring more people into Newport to hear the music, maybe some of them would become real jazz fans. I'm really no different than the critics. We both have ideals about the music. I've always been concerned about getting respect for the music. But I did know one thing: if the world outside of the small jazz community didn't get exposure to the music, it was going to be a minuscule thing." Guided by this rationale, Wein is not only unapologetic about programming non-jazz music at jazz festivals; he sees this approach as necessary to the economic viability of both the festivals and jazz itself. "The direction that jazz festivals have taken started that night [in Newport in 1958] with Chuck Berry," he said. "You go to festivals all over Europe and you hear all kinds of music. Without that variety, there wouldn't be jazz festivals. A festival doesn't exist without people. Even though something may be non-profit, as the first seven years of Newport were, it doesn't mean there are limitless funds to keep it going. The necessity to maintain a level of bottom-line success is always there."[96]

Chastened by the events of 1960, George Wein stayed away from Newport in 1961. He returned in 1962 with a festival called "Newport '62: The Meaning of Jazz" and with a new organizational structure that cut out the advisory board and the nonprofit corporation headed by Louis Lorillard. Newport became the fountainhead of an international production empire that Wein has built with his company, Festival Productions, Inc. Wein moved the Newport festival to New York in 1972, rechristening it the Kool Jazz Festival and later the JVC Jazz Festival as his corporate sponsorship shifted. In the 1950s and 1960s, Wein produced Thelonious Monk (among others) in hundreds of concerts in Europe, Asia, and Australia. Since the 1970s, he has produced the Boston Globe Jazz and Heritage Festival, the Grand Parade du Jazz Nice, the Copenhagen Jazz Festival, and the Playboy Jazz Festival. Wein tried during the early 1960s to start a festival in New Orleans but came up against local segregation laws and customs: the mayor felt the festival would cost him politically when it became known that Wein was married to a black woman. Emboldened by the 1960s civil rights movement, Wein persisted and in 1970 formed an association with New Orleans producer Quint Davis, who had been running a small local festival. Together they launched the New Orleans Jazz and Heritage Festival, a two-week spring extravaganza featuring jazz, blues, reggae, zydeco, and other ethnic world musics. Wein also markets black ethnic heritage through the Toyohashi (Japan) Black Heritage Festival (started in 1985) and the Essence Music Festival (started in 1994). As founder of the New York Jazz Repertory Company and the Carnegie Hall Jazz Band, Wein played a pioneering role in the jazz repertory movement that also includes the Smithsonian and Lincoln Center programs. It was George Wein, working with record company executives Nesuhi Ertegun and Bruce Lundvall, who produced (and named) the 1982 "Young Lions Concert" that helped launch Wynton Marsalis.[97]

In 1988 a young impresario named Michael Dorf launched What Is Jazz?, an alternative, avant-oriented festival centered at the Knitting Factory, then a ramshackle joint on the edge of the punk-chic East Village. In programming, attitude, and ambience, What Is Jazz? was a guerrilla war against Wein's regime and concept; it was also a symbol of the level of cultural capital that jazz has accrued in recent decades, due in no small measure to Wein's efforts. By the 1990s, with Wein's JVC festival and the new Lincoln Center jazz program focused on mainstream audience development, a space had opened up for an edgier programming strategy aimed at hip, moneyed New York yuppies. This is the cultural turf Dorf has exploited with an eclectic, postmodern mix of avant-garde and mainstream jazz, world music, and progressive rock. Critic Gene Santoro has suggested that despite their differences of age and taste, Wein and Dorf have much in common: they're "both smart, short, Jewish, from well-off backgrounds, balding, pragmatic, driven, obviously ambitious and able to translate entrepreneurial dreams about sound into reality." In 1989 and 1990 the two forged a tentative alliance, with Wein bringing a few of Dorf's Knitting Factory programs uptown to Carnegie and Avery Fisher Halls. Poor ticket sales cemented Wein's faith in the status quo, and he pulled out of the deal. But Wein has big musical ears and savvy promotional instincts, and in recent years he has absorbed some of the acts that Dorf nurtured at the Knitting Factory. Dorf, for his part, took notes on Wein's modus operandi, learning some lessons about how to pitch jazz in the corporate marketplace—valuable lessons at a time when jazz continues to gain cachet with upscale consumers.[98]

Throughout his long career, Wein has struggled with the perception of the producer as an enemy of the musician. He readily admits to instances of friction, but he takes pride in the friendly rapport he enjoys with most musicians he has worked with over the years. "I can't think of one of the older musicians who's still around who I'm not friendly with," he said. "There's the recognition that we're on the same team, fighting the good fight. But it takes a few years to establish that. There's a point in the relationship—most of them, anyway—where I gain their trust. Before I gain their trust there are many problems. After I gain their trust they're with me for the rest of their life. Miles [Davis] was with me until the day he died. [Thelonious] Monk was with me, [Charles] Mingus was with me. And I can name others. You gain their trust. I never gained Sarah Vaughan's trust even though I worked with her for many, many years. I should have, I always treated her well, but she always thought I paid Ella [Fitzgerald] more money than I did her."[99]

Challenging both Gene Lees's and Nat Hentoff's accounts of the convulsive events of 1960, Wein claims to have been sympathetic to the rebels' cause and only laments that the riot stole their thunder. He attributes the riot in small part to his festival's effort to attract a younger audience, but in the main to the town's greediness in enacting liquor licensing policies that encouraged the high school and college students to booze up. "If we didn't have the riot," Wein said, "the rebel festival would have meant more than it did. It would have been incorporated into the main festival the same way [later] I incorporated the Knitting Factory into the JVC festival. I always thought that way." Wein thinks Lees's 1960 account, with its emphasis on Mingus's menacing posture, missed the real story. "Mingus might have cussed me out in public," Wein said, "but we were good friends and we understood each other. I was a P.R. person, and Charlie was too. Charlie and Max saw a chance to grab a lot of publicity—don't forget that they had a record deal for the rebel festival—and they grabbed it. They were smart. It was a smart maneuver. I *never* rejected it or was upset about it." Nat Hentoff is skeptical: "To the best of my knowledge George didn't try to block the rebel festival, but he certainly didn't support it." Whatever the truth of Wein's thinking about the Newport rebels in 1960, it is notable that when Wein came back to Newport in 1962, his festival program included Charles Mingus and Max Roach. Mingus was even one of the speakers on a panel discussion of "The Economics of the Jazz Community." And in the days leading up to the festival, Mingus's band and George Wein's band played together at the Cliff Walk Manor.[100]

It was a small world. Circulating within this small world, however, were all the forces that were transforming American culture. Jazz had brought hipsters and bluebloods together in Newport in the late 1950s. It had attracted intellectuals, fashion editors, and filmmakers, all fascinated by the music and its players. In 1960, the rebels and the hooligans delivered something else: a foreshadowing of things to come both in the jazz world and beyond, a preview of both the purposeful grass-roots organizing work and the terrifying disorder that would compete for attention in the national imagination during the most turbulent decade of the century.

Finally, there was the music. Charles Mingus, Max Roach, and the other rebels were not *just* registering their impatience with a patronage arrangement they deemed condescending or unjust; they were trying to find a serious audience for an artistically adventurous and intellectually challenging music. It was for this reason, in fact, that Mingus and Roach insisted that their effort was less a rebellion than a vindication of Newport's original mission. Surveying the scene at the Sunday afternoon concert at the Cliff Walk Manor in 1960, gratified by the audience's attention and enjoying the sound of jazz cushioned by the ocean waves, Mingus mused, "This is what jazz at Newport was supposed to be."[101]

CHAPTER 6

The Shock of the New

Black Freedom, the Counterculture, and 1960s Jazz Criticism

Freedom Now

On the cover of his 1958 Riverside album *Freedom Suite*, tenor saxophonist Sonny Rollins appears in bare-chested profile, a beacon of pride and determination. Rollins's iconic pose, reminiscent of Paul Robeson's Emperor Jones in muscular vigor and defiant spirit, projects an aura quite different from the arty, film noir-ish Blue Note covers of the period. Unlike the typical Blue Note design, a nocturnal fantasy set in a smoky nightclub, with sweating jazz artists bearing down hard on their instruments,[1] the photograph on this Riverside album shows Rollins erect and stately, a warrior ready to do battle. Complementing this powerful visual image is an eloquent back-cover epigram from W. E. B. Du Bois:

> America is deeply rooted in Negro culture: its colloquialisms, its humor, its music. How ironic that the Negro, who more than any other people can claim America's culture as his own, is being persecuted and repressed, that the Negro, who has exemplified the humanities in his very existence, is being rewarded with inhumanity.[2]

In his liner notes to the original issue of *Freedom Suite*, Riverside producer Orrin Keepnews strains to interpret Rollins's image and sentiments within the conceptual framework of the jazz mainstream. Keepnews notes the album's careful balance between the old and the new: one side of the album an interpretation of pop standards and waltzes, the other an innovative nineteen-minute composition—the title suite—based on a single melodic figure, developed and improvised upon in such a way as to convey an overall "unity of expression." Appearing in the same season as Gunther Schuller's *Jazz Review* essay exalting Rollins's skills as a "thematic" improvisor, Keepnews's notes portray Rollins's musicianship as a progressive development within the context of the jazz tradition rather than a willfully avant-gardist experiment. Just as he was at pains to deny *Freedom Suite*'s aesthetic radicalism, so Keepnews acknowledges but studiously downplays the political implications of the album's title, cover photograph, and artist's statement. The use of the word "freedom," he argues, should be understood more as an expression of artistic individuality than as a cry of social protest or as an allusion to jazz's creative procedures. "['Freedom Suite'] is not a piece *about* Emmitt Till, or Little Rock, or Harlem, or the peculiar election laws of Georgia or Louisiana, no more than it is *about* the artistic freedom of jazz," Keepnews contends. "But it *is* concerned with all such things, as they are observed by this musician and as they react—emotionally and intellectually—upon him."[3]

After Riverside went bankrupt in 1964, ABC Records bought the rights to its catalog and began to reissue selected items. When Rollins's *Freedom Suite* was reissued in 1968, it came with a new set of liner notes by Frank Kofsky, a white writer known to readers of the jazz press as an ardent champion of black cultural nationalism. Kofsky was a professional historian, a Marxist student of U.S. foreign policy who years later would publish a study of the birth of the cold war military-industrial complex alleging that the Truman administration manufactured the war scare of 1948 at the urging of aircraft industry leaders. Before undertaking to lay bare the cynical machinations of the U.S. foreign policy establishment, Kofsky had sharpened his New Left radical critique in a series of acerbic writings that attacked the liberal assumptions of what he called the jazz "Establishment critical fraternity."[4] In Kofsky's Marxist model, white jazz critics functioned as "active ideologists" of a racist ruling class, intellectual apologists for jazz's colonial economy. "Linked to the white ownership of the jazz business by ties of economics, race, and social outlook," he wrote, "the jazz critic has had as a major, if not *the* major task, the obscuring of the actual social relations that prevail within jazz society."[5] Those social relations, in Kofsky's analysis, mirrored the relations governing U.S. imperialism. Jazz club owners were "cockroach capitalists" whose wariness of Cecil Taylor, John Coltrane, Albert Ayler, and other representatives of the "jazz revolution" reflected the same attitude that stood behind white resistance to black equality and the suppression of social revolution in Vietnam.[6]

In a blaze of polemical heat, Kofsky's liner notes for the *Freedom Suite* reissue album accuse Keepnews of censoring and denuding Rollins's intended message of cultural and political militance. The album, Kofsky argues, is unequivocally "a statement of [Rollins's] pride in the heritage of being born black," and as such, evidence of strong proto-black nationalist sentiment in late 1950s jazz that anticipated and informed the radical political movement of the 1960s. *Freedom Suite* is one of many composition titles from that period that "affirmed the unique worth of blackness," along with Rollins's "Airegin" (Nigeria spelled backwards), John Coltrane's "Dahomey Dance" and "Africa," and Randy Weston's "Uhuru Afrika (Freedom Africa)." To ignore the significance of these symbols of international black solidarity, Kofsky charges, is to suffer the illusion that jazz was a universal "Utopia where distinctions of social class and 'race' no longer are a matter for concern."

The disjunction between these two packagings of *Freedom Suite* provides a snapshot view of one key aspect of the war among critics over the "jazz revolution" of the late 1950s and early 1960s. As we have seen, jazz had been a hothouse of fractious politics and warring stylistic ideologies going back to the 1930s. But the 1960s stands out as a period of especially intense politicization and fervent debate overshadowed by the larger political and social events convulsing U.S. society, especially the struggle for freedom embodied in the African American civil rights and black nationalist campaigns of the period. The shock of the new in this period was about more than aesthetics and taste: it was about the new politics of black assertion in the public sphere, the politics of racial presence and voice in what continued to be a white-dominated critical and commercial establishment.

The musical revolution of the late 1950s and early 1960s, as John Szwed observes, was really a case of "multiple revolutions," a period in which "we can first see jazz moving into a state of permanent diversity." Szwed suggests 1959—the year of Miles Davis's *Kind of Blue*, John Coltrane's *Giant Steps*, and Ornette Coleman's *The Shape of Jazz to Come*—as a watershed moment in which "jazz ceased to follow an evolutionary handbook," the linear path outlined by theorists of the jazz mainstream.[7] Over the next several years, jazz would fracture into a plurality of styles that challenged such received notions of jazz musicianship as centered tonality, a regular beat and tempo, bar divisions, conventional chorus structure, and improvisation based on chord changes. At stake was nothing less than the definition of the art form. This was evident in the controversy that commenced in 1961 when

Down Beat critic John Tynan pinned the label "anti-jazz" on John Coltrane and Eric Dolphy, using words such as "gobbledegook" and "nonsense" to describe the sound produced by the two saxophonists and claiming that the Coltrane quintet failed to "swing."[8] Coltrane's tone had always been an object of critical fascination—in the 1950s Ira Gitler had coined the term "sheets of sound" to describe his densely layered effusions—but over time, as Coltrane and his acolytes experimented with far extremes of pitch and dissonance, much of the interest turned sour. The British poet and jazz critic Philip Larkin, who found most jazz after Charlie Parker merely ugly, singled out Coltrane as being "ugly on purpose."[9] This captured a widespread feeling among critics and listeners that the post-1959 avant garde was an assault on the traditional jazz audience, a willful effort to deny listeners the pleasure of recognizable melody and rhythm. One story has it that after avant-garde tenor player Archie Shepp came off stage following a performance full of honks, squeals, and bleats, he told pained auditor Johnny Griffin that he was expressing what it felt like to be a black man in America. "I know it's hard," said Griffin, a black saxophonist who was no enemy of the modernist vanguard, having played with Thelonious Monk, "but why do you have to take it out on the music?"[10] For others, there was great beauty in the ostensible ugliness. Amiri Baraka in particular heard in the music a new paradigm of aesthetic value that required new modes of listening and engagement.

Just as hard bop stalwart Sonny Rollins wrestled to absorb the influence of Ornette Coleman and John Coltrane, so several of the established critics understood that these and other insurgent voices called for a new revision of a jazz canon that had only just recently made room for bebop. But the new dispensation came with provisos and conditions and, as always in canon formation, a premium on distinguishing the real from the ersatz, the authentic geniuses from the hack imitators. Whitney Balliett, for instance, championed Coleman and Cecil Taylor (the subject of his first *New Yorker* column in 1957) for an "honest ferocity that is new in jazz and perhaps in any music," while at the same time lamenting that because many of the "new-thing" musicians play too loudly, too long, and with little evident attention to their fellow musicians, the new music at its worst "is long-winded, dull, and almost physically abrasive."[11] Dan Morgenstern struck a similar chord in a review of "The October Revolution in Jazz," a four-day event in 1964 in New York organized by trumpeter-composer Bill Dixon to showcase the avant garde (participants among the twenty-odd acts included Jimmy Giuffre, Sun Ra, Paul Bley, Charles Moffatt, Milford Graves, John Tchicai, and Roswell Rudd). Morgenstern drew a distinction between the "new thing," which he characterized as "a form of 20th-century 'art music,'" and "that unique blend

of popular and 'true' art that has been (and is, and will be) jazz as we know it."
He found that the new music was "frequently capable of producing moments
of rare beauty" and was "infused with an underlying romantic yearning
for joy, acceptance, and that indefinable something called 'freedom,'" but
that it was also "often exasperatingly diffuse, verbose, undisciplined and
chaotic." He warned of the danger of the avant garde lapsing into "musical
charlatanism and incoherence" if an "aura of uncritical acceptance" prevailed
among "the young and easily swayed."[12]

This ambivalence about "freedom" in the new music—were musicians
skilled and responsible enough to use it? was it serving jazz itself rather
than a personal indulgence?—was a defining feature of the mainstream critical discourse. It was this ambivalence that fed Martin Williams's conviction
that Ornette Coleman was a more important figure than John Coltrane in
the development of the modal concept. The scalar or pedal-point modality
that Coltrane introduced in his classic quartet's best-selling 1960 recording
of "My Favorite Things," and then further explored in the quartet's 1961
recordings "Impressions" and "Chasin' the Trane," represented a turn to a
linear, horizontal style of improvising from a player who had just recently,
in the title piece of his *Giant Steps* recording, bobsledded with breathtaking
vertical virtuosity through a dense harmonic maze. These modal performances were hugely influential on younger musicians, immediately so in
jazz and, in a few years, also with rock groups like the Byrds and the Animals. To Williams's ear, these performances were skilled, sincere, full of
"authentic emotion"—and boring. He deemed Coleman the more "orderly"
player, finding his use of modality and microtones "developmental and se-
quential," whereas Coltrane's was "repetitive and incantatory." "One man's
incantation is another man's monotony," Williams wrote. He recognized the
bracing effect Coltrane had on his listeners—calling *Ascension* "at the same
time a contemporary jazz performance and a communal rite"—but was
uneasy about the changes in Coltrane's music that brought him this new
impassioned audience, speculating that these changes "may have been signs
of personal indecision or frustration."[13]

Implicit in these evaluations by Balliett, Morgenstern, and Williams was
an anxiety about political overtones associated with the new music, whether
black nationalist, more broadly countercultural (including dabblings in non-
Western cultures), or even simply personal. This concern separated these
critics not only from the Marxist academic Frank Kofsky, but also from one
of their own, Nat Hentoff. The new politics surfaced in a forum in *Down Beat*
in 1962 prompted by Ira Gitler's controversial review of a record by black
singer Abbey Lincoln. Lincoln at this time was emerging as a stirring symbol
of strong black womanhood, outspoken in her commitment to the freedom

struggle. A few years earlier Lincoln (née Anna Marie Wooldridge) had undergone an image makeover from sultry cabaret chanteuse (with album covers invoking an ebony Julie London) to jazz singer, a transformation influenced by her romantic relationship with—and later marriage to—drummer Max Roach. Orrin Keepnews of Riverside Records signed her to a contract in 1957, put her in the studio with Roach, Sonny Rollins, Kenny Dorham, Paul Chambers, and other top-drawer instrumentalists, and set about trying to market Lincoln as the new Billie Holiday. Hentoff, for one, was not won over, saying of Lincoln's second Riverside release, *It's Magic* (1958), that she "does not swing," that her tone is "hard," her phrasing "gratuitously angular," and that "jazz may not be her line" after all.[14] Two years later, radicalized in part by his own association with Roach (see the discussion of the Newport rebel festival in chapter 5), Hentoff was far less concerned about Lincoln's ability to swing. As producer of the landmark 1960 Candid LP *We Insist!: Max Roach's Freedom Now Suite*, Hentoff recorded Lincoln (in "Protest," the album's most famous cut) abandoning any pretense to tonality or phrasing, delivering herself of a piercing scream. "In the scream," the scholar and critic Farah Jasmine Griffin writes, "I can hear the beaten slave women, the mourning black wife or mother, the victim of domestic abuse and the rage and anger of contemporary black Americans."[15]

In February 1961, Lincoln recorded the Candid LP *Straight Ahead*, again under Hentoff's artists-and-repertory supervision. The liner notes made much of Lincoln's feeling that she had recently found her voice as a singer out of a "renewed and urgent pride in herself as a Negro." Ira Gitler made clear in his review that he did not like Lincoln's singing style. But rather than register this judgment in aesthetic terms and restrict himself to the cultural artifact at hand, Gitler mounted a full-throated attack against what he rued as jazz's alleged new turn to racial "propaganda." Tendentiously labeling Lincoln a "professional Negro," Gitler dismissed her record as a lame statement about "the slowness in the arrival of equal rights for the Negro," a cause he claimed to support but deemed inappropriate as the subject matter for a jazz record. Evidently unconcerned that his review might be construed as being guilty of the same charge that he was leveling against Lincoln, Gitler launched into a highly politicized *ad hominem*:

> I don't say that Miss Lincoln is not sincere in her racial attitude, but I do think she is misguided and naive. For instance, according to the [liner] notes, she is president of the Cultural Association for Women of African Heritage and attends other meetings to hear African nationalists speak. She is involved in African nationalism without realizing that the African Negro doesn't give a fig for the American Negro, especially if they are not blackly authentic.... Pride

in one's heritage is one thing, but we don't need the Elijah Muhammad type thinking in jazz.[16]

As historian Kevin Gaines argues, Gitler's polemic betrayed an ignorance of cultural and political solidarity between black Africans and African Americans based on the mutuality of their struggles for self-determination.[17] Gitler's statement makes clear that the cold war–era canonization of jazz's "universality" was often premised on a very narrow, parochial view of the political universe. When Lincoln and Max Roach fiercely protested, *Down Beat* empaneled the two of them, along with Gitler, Hentoff, and several other musicians and critics, for a discussion of "Racial Prejudice in Jazz." Lincoln contested Gitler's premise that art must be apolitical, arguing that "all art must be propaganda; all art must have an attitude; all art must reflect the times you live in." *Down Beat* editor Don DeMichael, endorsing Gitler's original charge that when Lincoln sang about the trials of poverty "you get the impression that it is only about Negro poverty," urged Lincoln to consider that current social struggles are "not for just one race but for all men." Hentoff rose to Lincoln's defense with an impassioned argument about the need to concentrate singularly on the struggle for black rights and equality:

> I don't think it's realistic for the American Negro right now to expend any energy, or any significant amount of energy, toward working for "all of mankind." There's just so much that has to be done right now [for black Americans]....And it seems to me...that it's also unrealistic not to expect a period of catharsis for the American Negro—a period where all the rage and bitterness and anger and torment has to get out. I think it's very healthy that it gets out in the music and in writing and in all those areas. To expect the American Negro to say okay, we've got it or are about to get it, and then suddenly forget everything that has gone before is akin to expecting Jews to immediately forgive...the Germans. It's just not possible.[18]

Hentoff elaborated on this theme in his 1964 book *The New Equality*, warning that white society was obliged to suffer "the compressed accumulation of Negro anguish" as part of the process of achieving interracial understanding. Gloria Oden, a black writer who reviewed the book in *Down Beat*, called this notion "masochistic," arguing that blacks had plenty enough to do for themselves without also having to provide therapeutic comfort to the white community. "The white majority will have to purge itself of guilt the best way it can without looking to the Negro to do it for him," she wrote.[19]

White Critics and the New Black Music

In 1963, the first issues of *Jazz* magazine—published by Bob Thiele and Pauline Rivelli, and edited by Dan Morgenstern—featured the masthead inscription "Jazz and freedom go hand in hand—Thelonious Monk," a sentiment buttressed by editorial statements that pushed a cold war liberal consensus line positing jazz as a crucial element in John Kennedy's campaign for an anti-communist New Frontier. An editorial in the second issue announced the publisher's decision to send free copies of the magazine to jazz fans in Eastern Europe—"[our] small contribution to the cause of peace and freedom." Jazz, according to the editorial, was a key to "a peaceful solution to the problem of co-existence." As "the first universal art" and as a symbol of "the creative union of all races and creeds," jazz was "one of the best and cleanest weapons in the battle for a brighter world."[20] The membership of *Jazz's* "International Advisory Council" apotheosized the idea of a nonpartisan, pan-generational, global jazz consensus. The American liberal Marshall Stearns joined forces with the French conservative Hugues Panassié and the British Marxist Francis Newton (Eric Hobsbawm). The new guard of American jazz criticism (Martin Williams, Nat Hentoff, Gunther Schuller) met the old (Charles Edward Smith and John Simon). Duke Ellington and John Coltrane symbolized continuity and good will between different generations of musicians. Ernest Borneman, UNESCO's director of cinematography, and Tom Scanlan, a reporter for *Army Times*, provided links to the official bureaucracies of internationalism. There was even a clergyman (the "jazz priest" Father Norman O'Connor), perhaps to balance off the agnosticism and atheism known to be strong in jazz criticism circles.

By 1965, these signs of unity had all but disappeared under a blizzard of dissension brought on in large measure by the provocations of ubiquitous contributor Frank Kofsky.[21] On the international front, Kofsky attacked Willis Conover's USIA jazz broadcasts as cold war propaganda, arguing that for Conover to play jazz records without commenting on the racial discord in U.S. society was to implicitly endorse capitalist social relations and perforce to engage in psychological warfare against socialist movements.[22] On the domestic front, he worked to "expose"—a word he borrowed from the 1930s Left—a reactionary bourgeois conspiracy against black nationalist influence in jazz, focusing especially on hostile, ambivalent, or even just grudging critical responses to John Coltrane and his acolytes. He intensified the assault on *Down Beat*, targeting white critics (Leonard Feather, Martin Williams, Dan Morgenstern, Michael Zwerin) who themselves may have criticized the magazine's anti-black bias, but who in continuing to write for the magazine were complicit, by Kofsky's logic, in its defense of the white supremacist status quo.[23] He shined a censorious light on conflicts of interest inherent in critics' cozy relationships with record companies, focusing in particular on liner note commissions. Kofsky took special, cynical glee in noting that in 1961 Leonard Feather had endorsed John Tynan's "anti-jazz" diatribe against Coltrane and Eric Dolphy, but within a few years was writing liner notes for the LPs of these and other avant-garde musicians.[24]

Of the well-known white American jazz critics, only Ralph Gleason— embraced for his "materialist understanding of the political economy of jazz" and his success at pressuring San Francisco musicians' union locals to desegregate—was exempted from Kofsky's blanket condemnation of jazz criticism as an insidious force of "social control."[25] During the 1960s, Nat Hentoff eluded the sustained censure that Kofsky visited on Feather, Ira Gitler, and Martin Williams. But in his 1997 book *Black Music, White Business*, Kofsky retrospectively attacks Hentoff as a traitor to his own convictions for not undertaking Kofsky's project, a no-holds-barred analysis of the racist political economy of jazz. He describes Hentoff as "someone in profound conflict over whether to be faithful to his professed socialist politics at the risk of alienating his friends and associates in the white business institutions of jazz, or whether to maintain these relationships even at the cost of biting his tongue."[26]

To Kofsky, either you were completely with the black nationalist revolution, or you were against it. Under such an unyielding standard, even Hentoff's muckraking exhortations might seem timid, or even counterrevolutionary. Hentoff implored college students to agitate for visiting professorships for struggling avant-garde musicians, nominating Cecil Taylor as "Visiting Professor of Where It's At." He criticized New York's new Lincoln Center arts complex for ignoring the cultural lives of the blacks and Puerto Ricans in its own neighborhood on the Upper West Side, and he admonished normally cutting-edge record executives Bob Thiele, Alfred Lion, and Nesuhi Ertegun for not recording Taylor, Abbey Lincoln, and other pioneers of the new jazz. In 1966, in a diatribe against the National Endowment for the Arts for its neglect of all but the most conventional jazz, Hentoff seethed, "A country that's going to bring peace to Vietnam even if it has to kill everybody there to do it simply isn't ready to listen to what Betty Carter and Jaki Byard have to say."[27] The sentiment and syntax could have been mistaken for Kofsky himself; yet this evidently was an example of the rhetoric Kofsky had in mind when he later upbraided Hentoff for "invoking a wealth of radical sounding phrases while . . . committing himself to nothing more than a collection of high-flown but completely abstract and vacuous generalizations."[28]

Other critics made no secret of their discomfort with the new politicization of jazz. Leonard Feather, whose color-blind ethos was at odds with the decade's foregrounding of racial awareness, was as offended by black musicians' "militance"—at one point he accused Archie Shepp of being a straight-out racist—as by new strains of White Negro-ism in the critical corps. "We are going through a period of unparalleled agony in our society, with hatred mounting on either side of an ever-higher racial fence," Feather lamented, "while white critics try to outrace one another in a sort of 'Tom-Uncle' attempt to show a more-militant-than-thou face to black musicians."[29] Dan Morgenstern objected to the "black pride" overtones of a Jazz and People's Movement appearance on the Dick Cavett TV show in 1970. Five musicians (Cecil Taylor, Freddie Hubbard, Billy Harper, Andrew Cyrille, and Lee Morgan) seized this rare opportunity to articulate for a national audience a common cause between contemporary jazz and the social struggle of the black masses. Morgenstern found the performance as "tedious" as "the rhetoric of libbies, yippies, and assorted other factions clamoring for attention." Hippies at least are not "uptight," mused Morgenstern, whereas these musicians were "tense and tight and unswinging as the music should never want to be." The argument here was that the very existence of jazz was evidence enough of the "vast, revolutionary potential of America," a potential brought to fruition in the pleasurable interracialism of the swing-centered mainstream; for jazz now to be associated with the voicing of racial grievances was a travesty of the tradition.[30]

Martin Williams also turned to tradition, often less to castigate black polemicists than to invoke a secret miscegenated cultural history that it was the responsibility of ignorant whites to discover and embrace. "Is it any wonder that some Negroes see a conspiracy afoot—a conspiracy to write them and their contributions out of the cultural history of the United States?" Williams asked. "How many Americans know where tap dancing comes from? How many proud middle-western parents know where all that strutting and baton tossing and twirling come from? (And what would they think if they *did* know?)"[31] This turn to history and a composite American identity, whatever its astuteness and even profundity, could be read in the overheated context of the 1960s culture wars as a clever strategy for trumping the provocateurs at their own game—as if to say: When we get past the shrill jeremiads of Frank Kofsky and Archie Shepp, we'll still have a lot of work to do in figuring out who we really are. For Williams, that process had to be about artistic integrity and individualism rather than political cause-making. Presuming on his close relationship with Ornette Coleman, Williams claimed to understand better than others why, for a period in the mid-1960s, Coleman did not perform in the United States. Williams claimed it was not true, as widely alleged, that Coleman had no offers, or that he was boycotting U.S. venues because he wasn't being paid enough (though

Coleman *did* feel he was underpaid); the real reason was not "anyone's business." But Williams knew that Coleman "was annoyed when pursued by would-be artists who staged 'happenings' and who seemed to feel his music somehow belonged in their deliberately disorganized events," and was "annoyed by the black supremacists of various persuasions who have pursued him."[32]

The notion of the artist who lives in a politics-free zone, uncontaminated by pressures and interests extrinsic to his individual creative vision, was very dear to Williams. In a 1968 *Down Beat* column, he applied it to a pointed comparison between Norman Mailer and Sonny Rollins, each the subject of a recent documentary film. Williams said he shared Mailer's opposition to the Vietnam War—the film covered Mailer's antiwar activism as described in his book *Armies of the Night*—but felt that Mailer's mode of expression embarrassed and undermined his position. "He was snobbish, arrogant, sneering, self-righteous, patronizing, boorish. In short, he was himself all the things he professes to abhor and fear in American foreign policy." How so very different from Sonny Rollins, Williams suggested, "a man of dignity and beauty" who does not "blame others or blame the world for faults or shortcomings that are his own." Pictured in the film woodshedding on the Williamsburg Bridge and visiting a Harlem grade school's music class, Rollins represented for Williams the paragon of "a man and an individual" who truly knew himself and whose quiet humility was a mark of his high character. "I would guess that there are few evils abroad in the world that Sonny Rollins would make worse by contaminating them with his own," Williams wrote.[33]

There's no reason to doubt that musicians like Coleman and Rollins appreciated a critic like Martin Williams who stood up for their artistic autonomy; he did even more for Coleman, going so far in hyping him to New York record producers, club owners, and taste-makers that he came under attack by some musicians and anti-Coleman critics, one calling him a "king-maker" guilty of "artificial promotion."[34] This gave Williams the power to speak on behalf of Coleman within the critical discourse. But it didn't give him a monopoly of access to, or exclusive understanding of, Ornette Coleman's "true" beliefs or self-perceptions. "Whatever Coleman believes on the subject of race is his own belief, is something he has discovered through observations, feeling, and thinking and not something someone has told him he ought to believe," Williams wrote in one sentence, and then followed it immediately with three more that tried to spin Coleman in the direction of Williams's own race-transcending, universal humanism: "when [Coleman] says 'music is for our feelings,' he means it. *Our* feelings. And all of them."[35] The point isn't that Williams was misrepresenting Coleman—who said many things that suggested a desire to reach beyond the limiting framework of race—but that he was representing only one part of Coleman's complex belief system and wasn't recognizing how his *own* racial identity may have shaped what Coleman said to him. Consider how differently Coleman came off when speaking to black writer A. B. Spellman, for his book *Four Lives in the Bebop Business* (1966):

> I think black people in America have a superior sense when it comes to expressing their own convictions through music. Most whites tend to think it's below their dignity to just show suffering and just show any other meaning that has to do with feeling and not with technique or analysis or whatever you call it. And this to me is why the black man has developed in the field of music that the white man calls jazz. And basically I think that word, the sense of that word, is used to describe music that the white man feels is really inferior.[36]

—or to the black drummer Arthur Taylor, in a 1969 interview for his book *Notes and Tones: Musician to Musician Interviews* (1977):

> I grew up in a white society with white rules and a white philosophy, but I grew up with a black conscience. My consciousness of myself as a black man makes me realize that unless I can be integrated into white society and its values, I can't achieve the wealth they have created. They have created a society where any unknown white person can put something on the market and become successful. I don't see why a black person can't do that. They have to control what you do first, then give it to you like welfare.[37]

Testimony such as this speaks to a wider range of feeling, experience, and consciousness than Williams and other white critics brought to their discussion of Coleman and other black musicians. My point here is not so much to favor one interpretive angle over another, but rather to recognize the complexity of the relationship between music, race, and social positioning, and how especially difficult it was in the heat of the 1960s jazz wars for commentators to see more broadly than the lens of their ideologies would permit. Frank Kofsky serves as a conspicuous case in point. Owing to his reverence for Malcolm X, his understanding of international anticolonialist movements, and his reading of the emergent 1960s historiography of African American experience (citations to C. Vann Woodward, Leon Litwack, and others dot his essays), Kofsky *was* better equipped than the mainstream white critics he attacked to ascertain important connections between the black freedom struggle and the 1960s jazz avant garde. He was right that musicians like Archie Shepp, Max Roach, Abbey Lincoln,

Bill Dixon, Marion Brown, and Cecil Taylor were inspired by African independence, domestic civil rights protests, resistance to the Vietnam War, and their own struggle for artistic survival in what he called the "jazz club-narcotics-alcohol-mobster-ghetto milieu." At a time when musicians were organizing benefit concerts for SNCC, Kofsky's claim that the new music represented "Negro disaffiliation from the American consensus" was hardly the wild-eyed absurdity that some of his critics charged. Kofsky grasped more clearly than the mainstream critics the importance of Africa and Asia as cultural influences in the new music.

But as incisive as Kofsky's analysis could be, often it sagged under the weight of a dogmatic and rigid ideological purity. The corollary to Kofsky's contempt for mainstream white critics was his condescension toward black musicians who didn't pass a litmus test of black nationalist revolutionary zeal. Why would trumpeters Kenny Dorham and Freddie Hubbard go on record in *Down Beat* expressing skepticism about the avant garde? Not, according to Kofsky, because of an honest feeling about the music, but because they felt threatened economically—an argument hard to square with Kofsky's justified plaint that the more radicalized musicians were hard pressed to find work. And so Dorham, in Kofsky's characterization, was a "nice, safe, domesticated neobopper" and Hubbard a timid milksop who "doesn't want to be considered *too* unconventional by his mates." Kofsky's way of marking a 1966 SNCC benefit as a landmark in the jazz revolution was to cast it as a moment of reincarnation for its organizer, saxophonist Jackie McLean. Prior to this event, Kofsky brazenly wrote, McLean had a reputation as "another one of the Establishment's good niggers in jazz."[38]

When he wasn't Uncle Tom–baiting alleged enemies of the revolution, Kofsky was trying to canonize its leaders as Marxist saints—John Coltrane, Ornette Coleman, and Cecil Taylor being, for him, "the Lenin, Trotsky, and Luxemburg of the new wave in jazz."[39] Rarely was John Coltrane's near-mythical serenity so evident as when, in an interview with Kofsky in 1966, he maintained perfect composure in the face of questioning that at times resembled a Moscow show trial. In the transcript that was first published in *Jazz* shortly after Coltrane's death in 1967, Kofsky keeps pushing Coltrane to confirm that his music is pro-Malcolm and anti-Vietnam War and that he disdains white audiences and white club owners. Coltrane parries the assault with statements like "this music is an expression of higher ideals" and with a call for "brotherhood." Coltrane's heart is clearly with Kofsky—and Kofsky tells us that after the interview Coltrane was curious to hear about his politics—but he says at one point in the interview: "you can't ram philosophies down anybody's throat . . . the music is enough!"[40] These hardly seem the words of an insurrectionist; if they were voiced by someone

Kofsky hadn't yet embraced as his personal God, one suspects, he might have tagged them as soft-headed pap.

Coltrane's words speak, in fact, to an aesthetic that he was nurturing in the years before his death that refused to be defined by a particular social agenda: call it the aesthetic of *transcendence*. By 1964, in his album *A Love Supreme*, Coltrane's music had become a form of rapture with *his* God, an effort to capture in sound the feeling of intense spiritual awakening. In both the depth of its personal meaning and the boldness of its religious theme, *A Love Supreme* makes Kofsky's dogmas seem very limiting indeed. The same may be said of mainstream critics who, if they came this far with Coltrane, did so in part to protect him from what they regarded as spurious political appropriations. Martin Williams, for instance, in framing his ambivalent response to Coltrane's direction after 1961, insisted that the music was always a private quest: "Like all true artists [Coltrane] spoke of matters of the spirit, not of society and politics," he wrote.[41] As Phil Watson has implied in a sharp attack on Kofsky from a cultural Marxist perspective, the complicated nature of artistic mediation—the relationship between art and "reality"—will never be fully apprehended in a debate between two fetishized positions: in this case, between Kofsky's externalized political critique and Williams's inner-directed aesthetic individualism.[42]

Amiri Baraka's Bohemian Blues

The pioneer and preeminent symbol of the 1960s black cultural revolution was the poet, editor, and critic Amiri Baraka (LeRoi Jones). By and large, the Baraka who has been both memorialized and scorned is the black nationalist of the mid- to late 1960s, the firebrand proselytizer of the black aesthetic, the dazzling "geniu[s] of performance and chameleon register-shifting," as literary critic Houston Baker Jr. has remembered him.[43] In this period Baraka joined such political figures as Malcolm X, Eldridge Cleaver, Stokely Carmichael, and Huey Newton in giving black power a distinctive masculinist intonation. Like Norman Mailer and other celebrity intellectual outlaws, Baraka embodied the convulsive, spontaneous, and violent impulses of the 1960s. Obscured in this telescoping of Baraka's image, however, is the crucial point that Baraka, as Gerald Early has perceptively argued, was not a product of the 1960s, but "an intellectual child of the fifties."[44]

Born in 1934 in Newark, New Jersey, Baraka grew up in a middle-class family, his father a postal supervisor, his Tuskegee-alumna mother a social worker. At Howard University in the early 1950s, Baraka studied black literature and folklore with Sterling Brown and sociology with E. Franklin

Frazier. Frazier's book *The Black Bourgeoisie* (1947) provided intellectual cover for Baraka's caustic judgment of Howard as a "sick" institution that "makes most Negroes who go there turn out bourgeois conservatives." After dropping out of Howard in 1954, Baraka served in the Air Force for two and a half years, much of it spent reading broadly in the Western literary and philosophical canon, a practice condemned by his superiors. During basic training, a foot-locker inspection that turned up a volume of T. S. Eliot's poetry won Baraka a day of hard labor. Less than a year into his permanent assignment with the Strategic Air Command in Puerto Rico, Baraka was given a dishonorable discharge for subscribing to subversive literature—the *Partisan Review*.[45]

As Baraka recounts in *The Autobiography of LeRoi Jones/Amiri Baraka*, his self-tutorial during his Air Force years led him "into the world of Quattrocento, vers libre, avant-garde, surrealism and dada, New Criticism, cubism, art nouveau, objectivism, 'Prufrock,' ambiguity, art music, rococo, shoe and non-shoe, [and] Highbrow vs. Middlebrow."[46] Werner Sollors has written that the bohemian Baraka's "first form of protest against the middle class was an aesthetic rebellion, formulated as an indictment, not of racism, capitalism, or the Cold War, but of middle-brow taste."[47] This protest was waged on the turf of literary politics, and in the very journal that had symbolized Baraka's rebellion against the military establishment. In a reply to Norman Podhoretz's "Know-Nothing Bohemians" in the *Partisan Review* in 1958, Baraka defined the Beats as "less a movement than a reaction" against "*New Yorker* suburban intellectual types of the late '40s and early '50s," and against "fifteen years of sterile, unreadable magazine poetry." Characterizing his own Beat affiliation as aesthetic commitment rather than racial estrangement, Baraka wrote that "the Negro Bohemian's flight from Harlem is not a flight from the world of color but the flight of any would-be Bohemian from . . . the provinciality, philistinism and moral hypocrisy of American life."[48] Baraka's poems and social essays in this period were startling: spring-loaded, razor-sharp, humorous, lacerating, prophetic, they called out the trite, the false, the philistine, and the hypocritical in American culture. His main target was the middle class—the white one that dominated American politics and culture, and the black one from which he had emerged and never tired of savaging for what he regarded as a feeble grasping for respectability through slavish mimicry of the decadent white mainstream.

William J. Harris has perceptively written that "Amiri Baraka is a Manichean: he has always divided the world up into good guys and bad guys and he has always imagined himself as being some kind of poetic Lone Ranger fighting for truth and justice."[49] The ridicule of stuffed-shirt squares would remain a key weapon in Baraka's arsenal, but under the influence of the black freedom struggle of the 1960s, his antibourgeois opposition moved on to the stage of politics and increasingly became reframed as a racial antagonism. During a writer's trip to Cuba in 1960, Baraka was denounced by Latino revolutionaries as a "cowardly bourgeois individualist" for speaking of his poetry in apolitical terms as a "cultivation of my soul." The visit—detailed in "Cuba Libre," an audacious essay in the *Evergreen Review*—was a turning point for Baraka, alerting him to the racial dynamics of the international anticolonial movement, reinforcing his revulsion toward U.S. imperialism, and quickening his resolve to use his talents in a more activist fashion. As whites in the South turned to tear gas, cattle prods, attack dogs, water hoses, bombs, and firearms, Baraka dissented from Martin Luther King's campaign of nonviolent moral suasion and sided with Malcolm X and other radicals in calling for more militant forms of black action.[50]

Baraka entered the world of jazz criticism at the same time, and in the same place, that he pursued romance across the color line. The year was 1957, and the place was the offices of the *Record Changer*, the bible of traditional jazz collectors. Hettie Cohen, a Jewish girl from Long Island, was the subscription manager; LeRoi Jones was the shipping manager, hired on the strength of his diligence and typing proficiency. "[S]mall and wiry, with a widow's peak that sharpened his close-cut hair, and a mustache and goatee to match," Hettie describes him in her memoir *How I Became Hettie Jones*, "a combination of rakish triangles" that was "set back, made reticent, by a button-down shirt, Clark's shoes," all of it adding up to a "Brooks Brothers' look."[51] Baraka's stint at the fig rag *Record Changer*, cataloguing wooden milk crates full of old 78-rpm records in crumbling sleeves, significantly informed his development as a music writer. Hettie Jones remembers the office as no musty archive of dead history, but rather a seminar room crackling with informal but passionate jazz chatter:

> People dropped in all the time, flung their coats on the shipping table, and sat down to talk. Work stopped; on went the phonograph, and then came the illustrated lecture—snatches of solos, bridges, riffs, played over and over. The first critic I got to know was tall, grinning, gracious Martin Williams, subsequently director of the Smithsonian Jazz program, who was always natty and slick, in a belted raincoat, like a private eye with a baby face. He and Dick [Hadlock, then *Record Changer* editor] were the first white men I met who didn't make me feel uneasy. One day Martin arrived with a handsome young man with Boston broad *a*'s and a dark, affirmative beard, a friend of his named Nat Hentoff, who sat on Dick's messy desk all afternoon, swinging his legs and yelling "But you *can't* say that! . . . He and Martin would soon publish a magazine of their

own, *The Jazz Review*. To them there was no one "real jazz," because like all arts it was subject to change without notice, and their objective, in writing of it, was less to debate its absolute form than to consider it part of a wider arena. They called it a uniquely American art form, thus predicting a new approach to black culture, as well as an even more significant economics: live people require live money—*you dig.*[52]

Baraka says in his autobiography that the job at the *Record Changer* enabled him "to meet many of the Ivy-trained slick young white critics who were just coming into the open (some of the older ones as well) and got a chance to peep close up on the development of the species." Being around these people made Baraka's "desire to know and write more about the music bloom." He explains that this job—and another one later with a private record trader—"were like graduate school," providing crucial training in the formal, recorded history of the music:

> Every day I came to the [*Changer*] I had to go through stacks of records looking for the ones ordered in the auction. I studied bands and players from different periods, labels, and trends. I got to know the key personalities in the different periods of jazz, I began to understand when and how the music changed. Later I would do my own deeper research to find out *why* it changed, which remains to me the most important question.[53]

Baraka "learned a great deal not only from [*Record Changer* editor] Dick [Hadlock] but from the many types who wandered through," especially Martin Williams:

> Martin and I became pretty good friends, though we had our differences about the music. But Martin was not a fig, he did have a scholar's regard for the traditional but at the same time he was very much into the contemporary music. He dug Monk, which brought us closer, since Monk was my main man. Martin was also one of the first persons I knew who dug and hipped me to Ornette Coleman when he blew into town a little while later. And one of the best magazines about the music, the short-lived *Jazz Review*, which was edited by Martin, remains one the hippest magazines ever to appear.[54]

After discovering, among other factors bridging their ethnic differences, that her love for sweet watermelon was matched by LeRoi's frequent yearning for a good sour pickle, Hettie Cohen became Hettie Jones. LeRoi and Hettie Jones's household soon became a major venue of the new downtown bohemia: a work space for their magazine, *Yugen: a new consciousness in arts and letters*, a play space for such vivid illustrations of the new consciousness as a nude, lotus-positioned, mantra-chanting Allen Ginsberg. Ginsberg, in a 1988 interview, recalled the heady, multi-arts, intergenerational spirit of that time:

> I met Langston Hughes at LeRoi Jones's party one night when Ornette Coleman was playing music and everyone was dancing. That's the only time I met Langston Hughes. In '59 or '60. A great touching moment in history. When Black Mountain, Beatniks, the Abstract Expressionists, the freedom jazz, the Harlem Renaissance, all met in one room.[55]

The marriage would produce two children (the writer Lisa Jones and the art historian Kellie Jones). But when LeRoi Jones in the mid-1960s became, as Amiri Baraka, prophet of the black arts movement, Hettie Jones became, as a victim of Baraka's suddenly urgent pursuit of racial purity, his abandoned white wife. In Hettie Jones's memoir, the early relationship is brave, passionate, and beautifully enriched by their mutual commitment to literature and jazz. Baraka, in his autobiography, is far less generous, referring to his ex-wife as "some kind of classic bohemian accouterment."[56] Casting the relationship in sociological terms as an emblem of the Eurocentric cosmopolitanism he then craved, Baraka counts himself among

> perhaps a whole generation or two of black intellectuals, who, seeing segregation and discrimination as the worst enemy, sought a more open contact with the world. And certainly, those taught that Europe was the source of intellectual life and measure could have that understanding shaped in some specific social context into a liaison or affair or long-term relationship with whites, a romantic connection. This was one of the advertised characteristics of the bohemia I came into.[57]

The Village's cheap rents, coffeehouses, bars, and galleries offered a tentative but shaky refuge from dominant American racism and philistinism. "Living in Greenwich Village . . . perhaps the most highly 'integrated community' in the United States," Baraka later recalled, "I felt free to move and think as I wanted to, but I was nevertheless constantly running into the northern liberal bohemian varieties of racism and national oppression and tried to deal with it as I could."[58] The East Village proved more progressive and emerged as a center of the black avant garde. A kind of downtown Harlem Renaissance arose on the Lower East Side, with the Umbra writer's collective, *Freedomways* magazine, La MaMa Experimental Theater, and the Negro Ensemble Company foreshadowing the full flowering of the Black

Arts Movement uptown in Harlem later in the decade.[59] Black writers and
artists on the Lower East Side in these years included David Henderson, Ish-
mael Reed, A. B. Spellman, Tom Dent, Calvin Hernton, Lorenzo Thomas,
Brenda Walcott, Sarah Wright, Emilio Cruz, Ted Joans, Bob Kaufman, and
Bob Thompson, and such "new thing" jazz musicians as Ornette Coleman,
Don Cherry, Cecil Taylor, Albert Ayler, Archie Shepp, Marion Brown, and
Sonny Murray. The sound of the new jazz was, literally, in the air of the
Jones's Cooper Square neighborhood, as Hettie Jones lyrically observes:

> the trumpeter Don Cherry would announce his arrival by playing a wooden
> flute, so clear it broke through the traffic noise. The acoustics of Cooper Square
> augmented every music: if it was warm weather when Archie [Shepp's] groups
> played, they'd open his studio windows and let the sound ricochet off the
> factories and repeat a millisecond later on the tenement wall on Fifth Street.
> The Five Spot was only a stone's throw away. Roi was always hanging out the
> window. The casual proximity to his life of his chosen frame of reference, the
> source of so many images, made him deeply happy.[60]

Baraka's first jazz writing, a piece on saxophonist Buddy Tate, was published in 1959 in Hentoff and Martin Williams's *Jazz Review*, and by the early
1960s he was also appearing in *Down Beat*, in *Metronome*, and in jazz LP liner
notes. His liner for *Coltrane Live at Birdland* opens with one of the acerbic,
paradoxical images characteristic of the new sensibility that Baraka brought
to jazz letters: "One of the most baffling things about America is that despite
its essentially vile profile, so much beauty continues to exist here." Coltrane's
music, Baraka deadpans, "is one of the reasons suicide seems so boring."
Brashly defying the strictures of New Critical formalism and the pleasantries
of middlebrow journalism, Baraka turned jazz writing into a performance,
an intense drama of sound, feeling, and movement. Here he is describing
Elvin Jones's drumming: "The long tag of 'Afro-Blue,' with Elvin thrashing
and cursing beneath Trane's line is unbelievable. Beautiful has nothing to do
with it, but it is. (I got up and danced while writing these notes, screaming
at Elvin to cool it)." The words "thrashing and cursing" ride the pulse of the
music and endow it with human personality; Elvin Jones is a percussion
warrior, waging battle in sound. The terse dismissal, then fleet embrace, of
the concept of the "beautiful" pithily captures Baraka's ambivalent posture
toward the Western art tradition; he'll accept the category, but insists on
defining it on his own terms. No sooner does he invoke the vocabulary of
classic criticism, however, than Baraka redirects attention to his own body
and voice—he puts himself back on the stage, dancing and screaming, one
with the music.[61]

For Stanley Crouch, then a student in Los Angeles, Baraka's writing was an exhilarating discovery:

> I had discovered Jones as an essayist in the liner notes of *Coltrane Live at Birdland*, which was the first time I had seen that kind of poetic sensibility brought to the discussion of jazz. It was as new to me as the way Coltrane and his band were reinventing the 4/4 swing, blues, ballads, and Afro-Hispanic rhythms that are the four elements essential to jazz. Jones was then influenced by [William Carlos] Williams, [Ezra] Pound, and Charles Olson but had done the same thing with them that Baldwin had with Henry James. His was the first Negro voice that sailed to the center of my taste by combining the spunk and the raw horrors of the sidewalk with the library, then shooting for an elegant manhandling of the form.[62]

Baraka was developing this new black critical voice for the new black music while still immersed in an interracial jazz writer's milieu. Years later, Baraka would underline his disgust with the reactionary racial politics of the Reagan era by looking back fondly on his jazz writing experience in the late 1950s and early 1960s:

> Many of the white critics of the period, like Martin Williams, Larry Gushee, Frank Kofsky, Nat Hentoff, Frank Driggs, Ross Russell, were ready and able to go beyond surface interviews, gee-whiz-ism, and commercial puff pieces, to deal with intriguing aspects of the music technically, historically, aesthetically, and socially. The *Jazz Review* had a great deal of input from the musicians themselves. *Metronome* took up some of the burning social questions related to the music and its principal players. And there were quite a few black writers who left their mark on the development of an all-around American critical standard, such as Larry Neal, A. B. Spellman, James T. Stewart, and, a little later, Ron Welburn and Holly West.[63]

That Baraka would continue to praise certain white critics even after his turn to black cultural nationalism must be borne in mind when considering his 1963 *Down Beat* essay, "Jazz and the White Critic." Often read retrospectively as a proto-nationalist call for racial exclusion, the essay in its own time was instead a challenge to jazz writers of all backgrounds to reckon with the lived experience of black Americans and to consider how this experience had been embedded in the notes, tones, and rhythms of the music. Identifying *class* privilege as the key stumbling block, Baraka dissected the middlebrow attitudes he thought had prevented the white jazz writers of the 1930s and 1940s from understanding the fundamental emotional and psychological motivations of the black jazz musician. "Reading a great deal of old jazz criticism," Baraka wrote, "is usually like boning up on the social and cultural malaise that characterizes and delineates the bourgeois philistine in America." Most white jazz critics "began as hobbyists or boyishly brash members of the American petit bourgeoisie," Baraka asserted, and they tended to write about the music as an act of *appreciation*, rather than as an effort at understanding the cultural conditions of black Americans that produced the music; they approached the music as an object or artifact unrelated to society, history, and the lives of the musicians and listeners. Each note of music "*means something*; and the something is, regardless of its stylistic considerations, part of the black psyche as it dictates the various forms of black culture." The task was to "set up standards of judgment and aesthetic excellence that depend on our native knowledge and understanding of the underlying philosophies and local cultural referents that produced blues and jazz in order to produce valid critical writing or commentary about it."[64]

Blues People

By the time he published *Blues People* in 1963, Baraka's work had come to embody a racialized version of existential hip. In this book, Baraka's recuperation of African culture as the core of African American identity was a brief for racial solidarity that anticipated the black nationalist agenda.[65] But it was also a modernist gesture redolent of the mass culture critique formulated by 1950s Left intellectuals. In popular works like David Riesman's *The Lonely Crowd* (1950), William Whyte's *The Organization Man* (1956), John Kenneth Galbraith's *The Affluent Society*, and Vance Packard's *The Hidden Persuaders* (1957), and in influential little magazine fare like the *Partisan Review*'s 1952 symposium "Our Country and Our Culture," Dwight McDonald's "Masscult & Midcult," and Norman Mailer's "The White Negro," leading social critics agonized over soul-deadening conformity, mindless materialism, and cultural sterility in postwar America. It seemed to these critics that America's triumph in World War II and emergence as a military and economic superpower had delivered nothing better than prefabricated ranch houses, packaged food, tailfins, specious advertising, and lifeless corporate bureaucracies. Baraka's voracious reading in the 1950s—he admits to stealing books from the *Partisan Review* offices when Hettie worked there—exposed him to these laments. Writing in 1959 of Ellison's *Invisible Man*, Baraka suggested that while the book superficially addressed a "Negro theme," it was actually more concerned with the "horrifying portrait of a man faced with the loss of his identity through the weird swinishness of American society." *Blues People*, a racially inflected modern American jeremiad, abounds in references to "vague, featureless Americans," "the sinister vapidity of American culture," and the "shoddy cornucopia of popular American culture." In an echoing of Mailer's "White Negro"—but without that essay's stereotyped equation of black culture with lack of inhibition and sexual prowess—Baraka insisted in *Blues People* that "Negro-ness . . . is the only strength left to American culture."[66]

If the status and fate of this "Negro-ness"—where it comes from, who has it, who has lost it, who wants it, how it expresses itself in sound and attitude—is the central question of *Blues People*, the book always defines black music by its relationship to white culture. The full title of the book—*Blues People: Negro Music in White America*—provides an important clue: Baraka was interested in jazz's position at the seam between black and white culture, its status as a black-centered object of both white intellectual fascination and commercial commodification. While coining a perspective recognizably distinct from those of Hentoff, Williams, Ellison, Feather, Stearns, Balliett, and Morgenstern, the Baraka of the early 1960s worked within the same general intellectual framework as these critics. Baraka sharply challenged the critical establishment, to be sure, but in doing so he embraced several of its fundamental purposes: establishing jazz's centrality in American national culture, honing tools of historical analysis and textual criticism, guarding the music against the contaminating influence of mass culture. The challenge that Baraka took on in the early years of his jazz writing was to pull black music out of the triumphalist American ideology while still keeping it at the center of the national narrative.

Here was a young black writer, just now gaining the spotlight of literary celebrity, loudly defaming the whole black literary tradition, pointing to black music as the only source of authentic black consciousness and culture. In 1962, in "The Myth of Negro Literature," an address delivered to the American Society for African Culture, Baraka rued the "almost agonizing mediocrity" of black literature. Citing Phillis Wheatley's "pleasant imitations of 18th century English poetry" and the "embarrassing and inverted paternalism of Charles Chestnutt and his 'refined Afro-American heroes,'" Baraka attributed this alleged mediocrity to black literature's pursuit of middle-class cultivation, its investment in "culture" at the expense of truth. "Negro music alone," he said, "because it drew its strengths and beauties out of the depth of the black man's soul, and because to a large extent its traditions could be carried on by the lowest classes of Negroes, has been able to survive the constant and willful dilutions of the black middle class."[67] *Blues People* redoubled this attack on the class-striving assimilationist ethic, tracing its origins to slave-era "house Negroes, who spent their lives finding new facets of white culture that they could imitate," deaf to the black voices that filled southern nights with hollers and chants, exiled from the bracing communal energy of the ring shout. This undermining of racial authenticity took modern form during the Harlem Renaissance, Baraka argued, when the deracinated New Negro tried to "climb on to the bandwagon of mainstream American life," while would-be urban realists "attempted to glorify the lives of the black masses, but only succeeded in making their lives seem *exotic* as literary themes."[68]

As Rudi Blesh and Marshall Stearns had done before him, Baraka's cultural argument elaborated on some of the central claims of Melville J. Herskovits's *The Myth of the Negro Past* (1941), which argued for direct continuities between African and black American culture, particularly in the religious sphere. Following Herskovits's emphasis on the survival of a communal, holistic ethos in African-based American slave religious practice, Baraka in *Blues People* contrasted the "functional," expressive nature of African music with the "artistic," artifactual focus of European music: "It was, and is, inconceivable in the African culture to make a separation between music, dancing, song, the artifact, and a man's life or his worship of his gods. *Expression* issued from life, and *was* beauty."[69] Citing the call-and-response patterns and kinetic dynamism in pre-emancipation spirituals and praise singing, Baraka underlined the African cultural orientation of the slave community. Essential to that orientation throughout black music history, and integral to Baraka's notion of a "blues people," is the black oral tradition, the sound and feeling of the voice present even in purely instrumental music. "Blues-playing is the closest imitation of the human voice of any music I've heard; the vocal effects that jazz musicians have delighted in from Bunk Johnson to Ornette Coleman are evidence of this," Baraka wrote. According to Lorenzo Thomas, the saxophonist and composer Marion Brown, a "running buddy" of Baraka's in Lower East Side artistic circles, influenced Baraka with his "ability to identify by ear the African tribal and African American geographical origins of specific Rhythm & Blues and jazz motifs."[70]

"The black man came from Africa, not Howard University," Baraka asserted in one of the lines that Joe Goldberg may have had in mind when he wrote, in the *Saturday Review,* that *Blues People* has "wit on nearly every page, and Jones has the rare faculty of making a point seem obvious after he has made it."[71] But if Africa was the primordial source of black culture, what happened when Africans became Americans? What happened when these African Americans adjusted to the changes wrought by industrialization, migration, and urbanization? What came of American Negritude when the "pure African songs" and "pure African dances" in Congo Square mixed with French and Spanish military marches, Protestant hymns, Scots-Irish jigs and reels? When Delta blues met French Creole parlor ballads and Tin

Pan Alley ditties? When swing and boogie-woogie moved into the concert hall? When post–World War II modernists entered the academy? Baraka was alert to these changes; his whole point was that the music had adjusted and evolved as the "blues people" responded to social, political, and technological shifts. But Baraka also insisted that "blues people" were forever marked by their original American condition of slavery and their second-class citizenship as ostensibly "free" people in the postbellum period. "Negro music and Negro life in America were always the result of a reaction to, an adaptation of, whatever American Negroes were given or could secure for themselves," Baraka wrote. "The idea of ever becoming 'Americans' in the complete social sense of that word would never have been understood by the Negro slaves."[72] Hence this tragic irony: blues and jazz are American, insofar as they were created in circumstances unique to America, but their creators will never achieve full American citizenship. "Bessie Smith was not an American," Baraka asserted, "though the experience she relates could hardly have existed outside of America; she was a Negro."[73]

The logic of this position, paradoxically, forced Baraka to acknowledge interracial contact as the defining feature of a music he wanted to claim as an emblem of racial authenticity. One of the more fascinating features of *Blues People*, in fact, is Baraka's serious reckoning with white interest in black music, and his honest (though rueful) recognition of black interest in white performance (including his own listening to Stan Kenton and Dave Brubeck while a student at Howard University).[74] Part of the significance of jazz, he wrote, is that "it was a music capable of reflecting not only the Negro and a black America but a white America as well."[75] He credited some early white jazz players—Bix Beiderbecke in particular, but also Nick La Rocca and his Original Dixieland Jazz Band—with a regard for black culture that transcended mere imitation and minstrel caricature (qualities that he *did* ascribe to the Dixieland revival movement of the 1940s and 1950s). These serious white jazz musicians, with their sincere desire "to play the music because they thought it emotionally and intellectually fulfilling," served "to place the Negro's culture and Negro society in a position of intelligent regard it had never enjoyed before."[76] But whereas for black musicians jazz was a refinement of expressive practices organic to black culture, for white players the music was a *learned* art that separated them from their native culture. In Baraka's archetypal example, Bix Beiderbecke, a middle-class white man from Iowa with a musical palette influenced by Stravinsky and Debussy, turned to jazz in a "conscious or unconscious disapproval of the sacraments of his culture"; Louis Armstrong, by contrast, a poor black man from New Orleans who came by his musical taste in the streets, became "an honored priest of his culture" who "was not *rebelling* against anything with his music." But because of America's devaluation of black culture, Louis Armstrong needed Bix Beiderbecke for a certain kind of "official" validation. "Afro-American music did not become a completely American expression until the white man could play it!" Baraka said. Jazz provided a "common cultural ground" for whites who used black culture as a critique of mainstream America and for blacks who needed recognition from that mainstream if they were to become recognized as American artists.[77]

Baraka's sociology becomes an index to style: Beiderbecke plays with "impressionistic lyricism," while Armstrong's "brassy, broad, and aggressively dramatic" tone draws its expressive power from the vocal blues tradition. This assumption of a correspondence between social class and sound became a tricky matter when Baraka considered the swing era and its aftermath, when many black musicians also approached jazz as a learned art that required some measure of formal training. Noting the number of major black big-band performers who went to college—Fletcher Henderson, Benny Carter, Duke Ellington, Coleman Hawkins, Jimmie Lunceford, Sy Oliver, Don Redmen—Baraka suggested that "the older *lowdown* forms of blues" were no longer as "direct" an influence on swing as on earlier jazz. Big-band jazz brought the professionalization of the black musician, a greater influence of American popular music, and arranging techniques that drew on certain formal European traditions. In an argument that separated him from Ralph Ellison, Albert Murray, and a great many African Americans who passionately listened and danced to this music, Baraka claimed that big-band jazz "developed [into] a music that had almost nothing to do with blues" and "had very little to do with black America, though it is certainly where it had come from."[78]

This concern for blues authenticity colored Baraka's perception of even some of his own favorite postwar music. Baraka strained to keep Miles Davis tucked inside his concept of an authentic black aesthetic, but Davis kept pushing against the boundaries. "For all his commitment to the blues," Baraka wrote, "[Davis] often seems to predicate his playing on the fabrication of some discernable object. And in this he seems closer to Bix Beiderbecke than Louis Armstrong."[79] Baraka esteemed John Lewis as "one of the most moving blues players in jazz" and credited the Modern Jazz Quartet with "some of the most exciting jazz of the last few years," but he disparaged Lewis's efforts to combine classical music and jazz as one of the "frightening examples of what the *final* dilution of Afro-American musical tradition might be."[80] Many thought it was the free jazz avant garde, in its dalliances with Third Stream fusion and European modern music, that augured just such a final dilution. Baraka disagreed, arguing that though Cecil Taylor and Ornette Coleman "know the music of Anton Webern and are responsible to it intellectually," their emotional and philosophical attitudes ensured that they remained deep "blues people" however much their music might challenge and confound traditional blues form.[81]

It was in fact *attitude*, more than sound—or, better, attitude as a signature of sound—that seemed to be the key to Baraka's code of blues purity. "[Charlie] Parker's modern placement of blues is as classic as any Negro's and at least as expressive as Bessie Smith's," Baraka wrote. What had changed with bebop was "the address, the stance, the attitude."[82] Bebop's "willfully harsh, *anti-assimilationist* sound" registered its meaning through the musicians' extramusical postures of defiance and sovereignty. "Musicians like Charlie Parker, Thelonious Monk, and Dizzy Gillespie were all quoted as saying, 'I don't care if you listen to my music or not,'" Baraka wrote, adding, "This attitude must have mystified the speakeasy-Charleston-Cotton Club set of white Americans."[83] The white "cool" musicians of the 1950s might on the surface have sounded like Miles Davis, but they lacked the "fluency of attitude or stance" characteristic of black cool, a posture of detachment and stoicism born of the "repression of suffering" used as a psychological mechanism for negotiating white oppression and dominance.[84]

It wasn't just pale white imitations of blackness under scrutiny here; Baraka's highly exacting, even elitist nose for authenticity sniffed out black counterfeits as well. Hazel Scott came in for a beating for the "pitiful spectacle" of her performance of Grieg's *Concerto in A Minor* at Café Society and the "modern minstrelsy" of her "concert boogie-woogie."[85] Baraka embraced rhythm and blues as a black working-class form, but cringed at the fake burlesque of its more histrionic performers: "One gets the idea that a man who falls down on his back screaming is doing so, even though he might be genuinely moved to do so, more from a sense of performance than from an unalterable emotional requirement."[86] *Blues People's* most sustained critique of black musicians came with Baraka's discussion of the hard bop/soul jazz movement of the late 1950s. It was here that Baraka's modernist avant-garde investment in "making it new" became clearest. He regarded hard bop's turn to gospel and traditional blues as a "debilitation of the most impressive ideas to come out of bebop," a retrogressive stylistic effect with no "serious commitment to expression or emotional profundity." Hearing no fresh rhythmic or melodic ideas in the music, Baraka pronounced it a clichéd revivalist venture, "a black version of American middlebrowism." And "merely calling tunes *Dis Heah* or dropping g's from titles is not going to make the music more compelling," he sniped.[87]

The publication of *Blues People* immediately sharpened debate about the relationship between black music, black cultural identity, and the larger

American mainstream. In a review for the New York *Herald Tribune*, Nat Hentoff framed *Blues People*'s publication as a watershed in black music scholarship, American cultural criticism, and black-white relations, praising the book as "the first attempt to place the entire continuum of the black man's music in this country in the context of his cultural history as an American."[88] Hentoff held up *Blues People* as a powerful rebuke to Nathan Glazer and Daniel Moynihan's recent book, *Beyond the Melting Pot*, which asserted that "the Negro is only an American and nothing else. He has no values and culture to guard and protect." On the contrary, Hentoff wrote,

> [Baraka/Jones] indicates convincingly that the Negro, particularly in his music, has created ways of expression that are at the same time, "only American," but also fundamentally Negro. By relating that musical culture to Negro attitudes, the changing stances which infused and shaped the music, LeRoi Jones has also contributed importantly to an understanding of the core of the current alienation of those American Negroes who, after equality has been achieved, will persist in criticizing American society.

Calling Baraka "a critic of American society for many other reasons besides its attempted brutalization of Negroes," Hentoff noted that like "more and more of the younger Negro intellectuals," Baraka "watches sardonically as 'the American Negro is being asked to defend the American system as energetically as the American white man.'" Underlining Baraka's pummeling attack on "the Negro middle class which have continually tried to abandon such elements of their heritage as the blues and other 'Negroid' ways of expression," Hentoff noted that for Baraka traditional blues and the "assertively Negro-based jazz" of bebop and the post-bebop avant garde represent a crucial separation from the mainstream of American society.

Ralph Ellison's famous critique of *Blues People*—published in the *New York Review of Books* in 1964—is best known for its classic signifying parry: "The tremendous burden of sociology which Jones would place upon this music is enough to give even the blues the blues."[89] Ellison would have none of Baraka's alienation, and he gave the back of his hand to the idea that blues and jazz were anything *but* the mainstream of American culture. Where Baraka saw black music as a defiance of the dominant white culture, Ellison refused to accept a view of American culture that ceded dominance to whites and that remained blind to the interconnectedness of the races:

> any viable theory of Negro American culture obligates us to fashion a more adequate theory of American culture as a whole. The heel bone is, after all, connected through its various linkages, to the head bone. Attempt a serious

evaluation of our national morality and up jumps the so-called Negro problem. Attempt to discuss jazz as a hermetic expression of Negro sensibility and immediately we must consider what the "mainstream" of American music really is.[90]

Ellison's position offered little help in understanding why whites remained so willfully blind to their cultural Negro-ness, so resistant to residential and educational integration, and so wary of political equality. Ellison ignored the legacy of black music's appropriation by the white-controlled music business and the ways in which resentment of this control sparked black musicians' efforts to reappropriate and revitalize their music. And when Ellison said, "today nothing succeeds like a rebellion (which Jones as a 'beat' poet should know) and while a few boppers went to Europe to escape, or become Muslims, others took the usual tours for the State Department," he leaned toward the untenable position that rebellion is *necessarily* a stance, which made him as guilty as Baraka of imposing a narrow limit on the meaning of art.[91] But Ellison's point was that Baraka's obsession with white power, his fear that whites were getting more out of the music than blacks, made it impossible for him to appreciate how much pleasure and how much of a sense of life-affirming accomplishment African Americans took from their own music.

Ellison and Baraka parted company on several levels. On the first level, their difference turns on the relationship between black and white in the crucible of American culture. Ellison (with Albert Murray) affirmatively celebrates American culture as a triumph of miscegenation in which blacks and whites engage in a tussle of "antagonistic cooperation" that helps them bring out the best in each other. Baraka, by contrast, grimly sees the dynamic of American culture as black resistance against white corruption, a rearguard action made necessary by the American culture industry's seemingly inexhaustible capacity for appropriation and debasement. Ellison incisively underscores the pessimism inherent in Baraka's argument: if Baraka was right that black culture had been denuded of its authenticity, stripped of its essential properties, by its commodification in the American entertainment industry, then the "blues people" of twentieth-century urban America were trapped in a defensive, reactive posture, fatally consigned to having their cultural expression predetermined by forces beyond their control. In that case, Bessie Smith's blues and Charlie Parker's bop—which, however compelling as human expressions, were also cultural commodities produced and distributed under the aegis of American capitalism—would have to be recognized not as unadulterated, authentic African American creativity, not as the expression of a discrete black aesthetic, but as the manifestation of a debased *American* culture. Ellison argued that Baraka's "version of the blues lacks a sense of the excitement and surprise of men living in the world—of enslaved and politically weak men successfully imposing their values upon a powerful society through song and dance."[92] For Ellison and Murray, the key is not American capitalism's negative capacity to co-opt and balkanize black music, but American pluralism's positive capacity to absorb it and be transformed by it.

The second level of difference has to do with matters of generational experience and personal taste. Where Ellison came of age in the 1930s and remained a swing man for the rest of his life, Baraka first came to jazz in the late 1940s and claims bebop and free jazz as his creative and spiritual touchstones. If Baraka's career has been defined by its metamorphoses, from Beat to black nationalist to Marxist and beyond, it was in bebop that as a teenager he first glimpsed the power and mystery of transformation. As he explains in his autobiography, after hearing bebop "I wanted to go to some other kinds of places, and usually by myself. Not because I suddenly felt estranged from people . . . [b]ut because BeBop, 'The Music,' had got into me and was growing in me and making me hear and see things. I began to want things. I didn't even know what."[93] Having grown up with bebop, Baraka very much wanted this music to be seen as the key threshold in black-white relations, as a cultural fault line marking the distinction between slavery and freedom. Among other things, this enabled Baraka, at the very moment when he was emerging as a prophetic figure in black arts and letters, to claim a personal history that coincided with a liberationist thrust in the black arts.

Baraka and the New Blackness

In the jazz press and among jazz musicians and aficionados, it was Baraka's position as scribe of the 1960s avant garde and black nationalist partisan that made him a lightning rod of cultural combat. When Baraka elaborated on his hard bop critique in a caustic review of Art Blakey's Jazz Messengers in *Jazz* magazine, a reader from Philadelphia named Ben Page took him to task:

> When Jones first appeared, being a Negro writer and all, I was very happy indeed and had hoped that he might develop his capacities and evolve into perhaps the first major Negro jazz critic. But instead he has merely found a forum for

his "new thing" type vernacular (which might explain his preoccupation with "new thing" musicians).

Page took exception to Baraka's sarcastic tone:

> he really did it when he referred to the effusive Art Blakey as "Massa Blakey." If I were Art I'd have to *speak* to him about *that*. Or better yet, I'd give him a nice fat shunk in his unbaptized mouth, *ala Mingus*. Jones should be happy he is a Negro when doing something like that; otherwise he would be open to very, very many and sundry racial charges none of which I care to mention here.[94]

As it happens, Baraka did have occasion to trade blows with Mingus. As he tells the story in his autobiography, one night he was standing outside the Five Spot rapping with some friends when Mingus came by. Baraka offered a friendly greeting, but Mingus started talking "some off-the-wall stuff, most of which I didn't even get with." Mingus then pushed and slapped Baraka, unaware he was dealing not with some timid, effete writer—as Baraka is at great pains to emphasize—but a street-tested tough guy:

> Mingus starts this spew of profanity, saying something like "you goddam punk," and I could hear that it had something to do with something I'd written, that I was sympathetic with the avant-garde musicians, or something like that. But this time when he came forward, I went into my Newark Sugar Ray stick and run, jab and duck, and started popping him side his fat head. . . .
>
> Mingus stops, then he puts out his hand to shake. He says, "I'm sorry. I made a mistake. I was wrong." I guess he meant because he thought he could just slap me and walk away, having chastised some jive intellectual. But I'd ducked and dodged around some much meaner with they hands mf's than Charlie Mingus.[95]

The "jive intellectual" tag speaks to an anxiety—here manifested as a perceived threat to his manhood—that Baraka and other writers suffered as they contemplated the deep expressive power of the music. Baraka tells another story in his autobiography that reveals something of his soul-searching. Albert Ayler had showed up at his house and was asking Baraka about his writing on "the Music":

> He asked me did I think it was about *me*? He said, "You think it's about you?" I did and didn't know what he meant. In some ways, I guess, I did think it was about me. Albert meant it was really about Spirit and Energy.

When Baraka goes on to describe Ayler's playing, you can feel him straining for a vernacular linguistic effect that matches the visceral, physical power of the music:

> Albert, we found out quickly, could play his ass off. He had a sound, alone, unlike anyone else's. It tore through you, broad, jagged like something out of nature. Some critics said his sound was primitive. Shit, it was before that! It was a big massive sound and wail. The crying, shouting moan of black spirituals and God music. . . . Albert was *mad*. His playing was like some primordial frenzy that the world secretly used for energy.[96]

Like other jazz writers, Baraka suffered musicians' accusations that he was ill-equipped and opportunistic. 'Baraka?" Cecil Taylor responded to a query by Gerald Early, "Oh, he never knew what he was talking about when he discussed my music."[97] Trumpeter and composer Bill Dixon, in a letter to *Down Beat* in 1964, complained that Baraka's jazz writing "too obviously smacks of a kind of 'in-group' superiority generally and rightly associated with pseudo-intellectuals." Dixon questioned whether Baraka wrote on jazz "because he loves the music and wants to help it and its practitioners, knows the music and feels he has something to say, or if he feels that by stirring up 'controversies' his name will become synonymous with those he constantly champions, thereby creating a niche in the world of jazz for himself."[98]

In truth, free jazz would have been controversial with or without Baraka's imprimatur, simply because the sound of the music was so irksome to a broad swath of the jazz audience. What gave Baraka's jazz writing an extra whiff of polemical heat in the mid-1960s was his increasing assertiveness on racial issues combined with the fact that the white cultural establishment was now taking serious notice of him. The success of his poetry collection *The Dead Lecturer* and his off-Broadway plays *Dutchman* and *The Toilet* yielded fellowships, awards, and teaching engagements. As one observer noted, "In 1965, LeRoi Jones was a young, black, literary lion . . . the more he attacked white society, the more white society patronized him."[99] But the tumultuous events of the early 1960s—black uprisings in the cities; the murder of four black girls in a church bombing in Birmingham, Alabama; and then, even more decisively, the assassination of Malcolm X in February 1965—prompted more and more zealous attacks and an abrupt severing of interracial contacts in his personal life. In a forum on race held at the Village Vanguard, Baraka and Archie Shepp attacked their Jewish friend Larry Rivers, the painter and saxophonist, as an "enemy," while Baraka derided the slain Jewish civil rights activists Andrew Goodman and Michael Schwerner as "artifacts" and "paintings on the wall."[100] In 1965, Baraka left his wife, Hettie, and their two daughters and moved to Harlem. A man who leaves his family usually has something to hide, but Baraka's move to Harlem was less an act of guilty concealment than of highly publicized cultural and political commitment. In joining forces with Larry Neal, Askia Touré, and other insurgent black intellectuals in launching the Black Arts Movement with the opening of the Black Arts Repertory/Theater School, Baraka's mission was to take up where Malcolm X had left off, using culture to guide the black masses further along the path to liberation, self-consciousness, and autonomy.[101]

Baraka threw himself headlong into the work of building networks and institutions in the black community that would, as Larry Neal described the purpose of the Black Arts Movement, "speak to the spiritual and cultural needs of black people." Not incidentally, this cultural work signaled a key shift in Baraka's relationship to jazz and in his approach to writing about the music. Where earlier—even in his sharp critiques of white critics—Baraka had engaged "my more serious colleagues" in analytical debates about Western concepts of art and criticism, now he was a people's intellectual, a revolutionary voice heralding a new expressive mode for a new black identity. As Baraka aligned himself with the community-oriented goals and methods of the black power movement, drenched his writing and public performances in the rhythms and tonalities of the black urban vernacular, and hoisted himself up as an arbiter of black authenticity, his quest for what Werner Sollors has called a "populist modernism" involved a tricky effort to reconcile collective political imperatives with the individual aesthetic freedom he prized as both a poet and a champion of the jazz avant garde.[102]

After 1965, Baraka dug deeper into the performative, spoken-word idiom he had pioneered in his *Coltrane Live at Birdland* liner notes. Now the writing became so charged with feeling, so bardic, its apparent purpose less to reason and persuade readers than to sweep them up in a tribal, cosmic energy wave:

> Listening to [drummer] Sonny Murray, you can hear the primal needs of the new music . . . from ghastly moans of spirit, let out full to the heroic marchspirituals and priestly celebrations of new blackness.[103]

> Marion Brown was rising with Pharoah. It was a mad body-dissolving music . . . rose and stayed there . . . ecstasy of understanding then, evolution. The feeling such men make is of the consciousness of evolution, the *will* of the universe.[104]

ALBERT AYLER thinks that everything is everything. All the peace. All the motion. That he is a vessel from which energy is issued, issues. He thinks (or maybe he doesn't think) that he is not even here. Not even here enough to be talked about as Albert, except we *are* biological egos (we Think). Separate. Sometimes unfeeling of each other (thing) but Music joins us. Feeling. Art. Whatever produces a common correspondent for existence.[105]

The historian Eric Porter has astutely argued that when Baraka's nationalist project focused on jazz, the emphasis was less on protest politics and polemics than on a romantic notion of spiritual liberation and transcendence through a new black consciousness. In a panel discussion in 1965 on "Jazz and Revolutionary Black Nationalism," Baraka, drawing on the philosophical work of Frantz Fanon, outlined a conception of blackness that connected the biological with the ontological, the black body with a unique black metaphysics. "It goes back to the body," Baraka argued, "your organs hanging in that black space have a life of their own, and they predict your attitudes and predict your life." This physical essence, Baraka claimed, was the basis of "a new species, a new sensibility, a new attitude" that most clearly manifested itself in the spirit and energy of the music.[106]

The literary critic Philip Brian Harper argues that Baraka and other black nationalist poets conceived a rhetorical strategy in which they were "heard" by whites and then "overheard" by blacks, as the poets ventured to impress each other and the larger black community with demonstrations of their righteous blackness.[107] Baraka employed this strategy not just in his poetry, but in all his public utterances, becoming a master of incendiary anti-white rhetoric. His blacker-than-thou posture not only put a torch to the Martin Luther King–led civil rights movement vision of an interracial beloved community, but also cordoned off black culture as a blacks-only space, a culture whites did not have the biological and mental equipment to feel and perceive. At the 1965 jazz and black nationalism panel, Baraka asserted that whites could never understand the music of Archie Shepp, Ornette Coleman, or Albert Ayler. When Frank Kofsky protested that *he* could hear the "revolutionary consciousness" in this music, Baraka replied that the difference between a white listener like Kofsky and a black musician like Shepp was "the difference between a man watching someone having an orgasm and someone having an orgasm."[108]

Not surprisingly, what most of the white jazz audience now heard in Baraka, as well as in the music of Shepp and Ayler and other avant-garde players, was the sound of racial exclusion. In an interview with Baraka published in *Down Beat* in 1965, Archie Shepp spoke at length about his personal background and his playing with Cecil Taylor, and then, striking a more general note, offered these words about the responsibility of the black artist:

> The Negro musician is a reflection of the Negro people as a social phenomenon. His purpose ought to be to liberate America aesthetically and socially from its inhumanity. The inhumanity of the white American to the black American as well as the inhumanity of the white American to the white American is not basic to America and can be exorcised, gotten out. I think the Negro people through the force of their struggles are the only hope of saving America, the political or cultural America.[109]

Here was a cultural critique that echoed American exceptionalist ideology and held out hope for important reform. But because Baraka framed the remarks in racial terms ("Archie expressed the weight of black in his thinking, which is also, of course, in his playing"), some *Down Beat* readers heard only racial hostility. Joyce Derksen from Ontario, Canada, wrote to say "I love jazz, but I get the feeling that I am being put down because I am white." Jerry Guild of Brooklyn characterized the Shepp piece as a "venom-filled thrust from [Baraka]'s dagger of hate." "It has become apparent that the small success Jones received for his plays makes him feel that in whatever field he treads, he must hate the white man," Guild wrote. Jazz, he said, "has no place for these feelings."[110]

In 1967, in a *Down Beat* review of Baraka's *Black Music*, a collection of his jazz essays, sketches, reviews, and liner notes since 1961, Thomas Conrad praised Baraka's writing skills and knowledge of the music, but found "disturbing" what he described as the "racist" turn in Baraka's writing after 1965. Conrad noted that the pre-1965 essays in *Black Music* had good things to say about the white avant-garde musicians Charlie Haden, Roswell Rudd, Steve Lacy, Scott LaFaro, Buell Neidlinger, and even the more traditional Jim Hall. But in the post-1965 pieces Conrad thought Baraka had gone out of his way to disparage Albert Ayler's white cellist, Joel Freedman, and the white free players Burton Greene and Frank Smith. "I have not called Jones a 'racist' without acknowledging the *general* validity of many of his claims," Conrad wrote, continuing:

> Certainly there have been relatively few great white jazz musicians. Certainly much in the society whites have created is sick—perhaps even sick unto death. Certainly one could cite many examples of whites who have gotten rich by offering for sale a slick, watered-down version of the music of a black innovator who has remained in obscurity. But to conclude, therefore, as Jones does, that

any white musician who draws on black sources for his music is (a) an inferior artist and (b) a mercenary usurper is to close one's eyes to the whole truth.[111]

Baraka frankly admits in his autobiography that during his Black Arts period in Harlem, he and other black radicals who had moved uptown from Greenwich Village were consumed with anxiety about their interracial relationships and as a result were given to fanatical demonstrations of racial purity. "We hated white people so publicly," he says, "because we had been so publicly tied up with them before."[112] But this was only one facet of the nationalist revolutionary program, and not the most challenging one when it came to theorizing jazz's position in the black community. While white readers and writers in the jazz trade press focused almost entirely on Baraka's anti-white rhetoric, among black artists and intellectuals a more important consideration was the relationship between the avant garde and the black masses. If the idea of a black nationalist arts program was to bring about race-based cultural unity and economic self-sufficiency, what would be the role of the new jazz, so fiercely complex and often esoteric, and to this point dependent on white-owned magazines, record companies (Impulse, Prestige, Fantasy, Atlantic, Blue Note), and downtown night clubs and coffeehouses (the Five Spot, the Half Note, Slug's, The White Whale, the Playhouse Coffee Shop, the Avital and Metro Cafes)? How would artists who had traded on a mystique of hipness and social alienation in cultivating their predominantly white audiences now answer to the black mass audience's demands for social relevance and intense emotional bonding? A. B. Spellman recognized that it was soul music, not the jazz avant garde, that had popular currency in the black community:

> The reality is that it was Greenwich Village which heard the evolution of the New, not Harlem. The man standing in line for the Otis Redding show at the Apollo almost certainly never heard of tenor saxophonist Albert Ayler, and wouldn't have the fuzziest idea of what he was doing if he did hear him.[113]

Baraka began to engage this issue in 1965, fretting that the Rolling Stones and other English rock bands sometimes seemed more plugged in to the black blues tradition than did the jazz avant garde, and counseling jazz musicians to seize some of the populist energy of black rhythm and blues and soul:

> All the young players now should make sure they are listening to the Supremes, Dionne Warwick, Martha and the Vandellas, The Impressions, Mary Wells, James Brown, Major Lance, Marvin Gaye, Four Tops, Bobby Bland, etc. just to

see where contemporary blues is; all the really nasty ideas are right there, and these young players are still connected with that reality, whether they understand why or not. Otherwise, jazz, no matter the intellectual bias, moved too far away from its meaningful sources and resources is weakened and becomes, little by little, just the music of another emerging middle class.[114]

Baraka says in his autobiography that during this period "I had a new ear for black music." Though still a "jazz freak, " he felt rhythm and blues gathering "special significance and meaning." Martha and the Vandellas' "Dancing in the Streets" became "our national anthem," reflecting the "rising tide of people's struggles" by capturing the grass-roots energy of black urban communities. Baraka and his Black Arts friends took to the dance floor, learning the popular new steps. "We did the Philly Dog and the Boston Monkey, whirling and being as revolutionary in our dancing as we were in our own thoughts." Getting his groove on became an important marker of racial authority, especially after a rival for power in the black nationalist movement spread word that Baraka "danced like a white boy." "I used to dance pretty well back home [as a teenager in Newark]," Baraka writes in the autobiography, "but when I heard that, I figured maybe my living downtown had cooled my cool. Ruined my rhythms."[115]

Baraka's anxieties about white influence and concerns about divisions of taste, style, and cultural identification in the black community came together in his 1966 essay "The Changing Same (R&B and New Black Music)." Like a free jazz solo he wanted not merely to describe but to imitate, Baraka's essay is a long, intense performance, full of new vernacular voicings and a sweeping epic vision. The point of the essay is to evangelize the coming of a "unity music" that combines virtually the entire panoply of black musical expression into a new "social spiritualism." Where earlier Baraka had ridiculed the black church as a tool of white power, here he adopted a funky avant-Baptist sermonizing idiom to call for a black music communalism that dissolves the border between sacred and secular and transcends social divisions and stylistic differences. Reversing his earlier dismissal of the 1950s funk-groove-soul revival, Baraka now praised Horace Silver and Ray Charles for using gospel influence to "'rescue' the music from the icebox of cool jazz." The avant garde and rhythm and blues, he wrote, "are the same family looking at different things. Or looking at things differently." The difference between the avant garde and "what the cat on the block digs" is a difference in the level of self-consciousness, not in fundamental emotional and physical reality. Surface stylistic differences between James Brown, John Coltrane, the Supremes, and Albert Ayler were insignificant compared to the platonic blackness they shared. As ever, Baraka defined what this racial identity is by what it is not: blackness for him is something that is lacking in whiteness, an emotional and spiritual authenticity—almost invariably masculine in his imagination—that blacks see whites desperately seeking but never achieving. The black in James Brown is the dose of male hormones and mystical soul that a latter-day minstrel performer like Mick Jagger would need to be James Brown.[116]

In 1967, in his magisterial study *The Crisis of the Black Intellectual*, Harold Cruse rued that Baraka, after the success of *Blues People*, did not take the next step of founding a black jazz publication and a jazz institute in Harlem. "The problem here is that despite *Blues People*, the white jazz critics are still deciding the status and fortune of Negro jazzmen," Cruse wrote.[117] In fact, Baraka did make gestures in the direction of institution-building and community outreach. In Harlem, the Black Arts initiative—aided by government and mainstream foundation monies—included the Jazzmobile, a jerry-rigged truck and banquet table stage that delivered the new jazz to the people. John Coltrane, Pharoah Sanders, Albert Ayler, Archie Shepp, Sun Ra, Cecil Taylor, and other black players—integrated groups were discouraged and boycotted—became part of a floating street-corner multi-arts festival that filled Harlem with music, dance, poetry, and painting. "People danced in the street to Sun Ra and cheered Ayler and Shepp and Cecil and Jackie McLean and the others," Baraka remembers, scorning the idea that the new music was inaccessible.[118]

Later, after moving back to Newark, Baraka, with Larry Neal and A. B. Spellman, launched *The Cricket* (1968-69), after the music gossip newspaper published in New Orleans by Buddy Bolden. In its visually ascetic, mimeographed pages, *The Cricket* resonated with the same aura of spartan revolutionary spirit, city street authenticity, and interartistic collaboration as the Jazzmobile and neighborhood festivals. An editorial in the first issue proclaimed the editors' desire to "bring all Black Art back into the community, putting it at the core of the developing black consciousness." Poetry and drama intermingled with record reviews and black nationalist polemic ("we are saying to the world that no longer will we as Black Men allow the white sensibility to dominate our lives"). Musician-writer-activists Sun Ra and Milford Graves spun verse and prose; poet-essayists Baraka, Spellman, Neal, James T. Stewart, Sonia Sanchez, Don L. Lee, Clyde Halisi, and Stanley Crouch (ensconced in his high nationalist period in Los Angeles) tried to capture the pulse and attitude of the new music while trumpeting black power and condemning white racism. "We wanted an art that was as black as our music," Baraka recalled. "A blues poetry (à la Langston and Sterling); a jazz poetry; a funky verse full of exploding antiracist weapons. A bebop and new music poetry that would scream and taunt and rhythm-attack the enemy into submission."[119]

The Cricket lasted just four issues before falling casualty to the demanding political agenda it championed. "We had gotten so deeply immersed in the political aspect of it [Black Nationalism] that really the kind of edifying things like *The Cricket* were let slip," Baraka told interviewer Christopher Funkhouser in 2000. "We left that to concentrate on public education and the school systems. These were correct decisions to a certain extent, but to let go of the cultural work to the extent that we did was an error."[120] A few years later, in the mid-1970s, Ron Welburn, James T. Stewart, and Roger Riggins launched *The Grackle: Improvised Music in Transition*, hoping to revive something of the activist spirit and cross-arts energy of *The Cricket*. While noting that these two publications provided an important forum for black musicians and poets, Lorenzo Thomas laments their failure to develop a "more rigorous standard of critical inquiry among African American jazz critics." He cites a particularly egregious example of slack writing in a purported review of an Archie Shepp record in *The Cricket* ("Listening to this album. Makes me tired. Its jive. Shepp hasn't, lost his, soul. Yet. . . . ") and notes that Welburn, in a letter to the contributors of *The Grackle*, called for a turn away from "superficial sociology to serious musicological and socio-aesthetic matters about particular artists and periods."[121]

These calls for critical standards by Welburn and Thomas are important insofar as they prove that it hasn't been only the Ellisonian wing of African American jazz letters (and particularly the standards-obsessed troika of Albert Murray, the post-nationalist Stanley Crouch, and Wynton Marsalis) that has employed this rhetoric. But it is also true that Baraka, Larry Neal, Al Young, Sonia Sanchez, June Jordan, Eugene Redmond, Welburn and Thomas themselves, and other Black Arts poets had elevated poetry and performance *above* criticism, or at their best, had figured out how to embed criticism *in* poetry and performance, to communicate meaning, perspective, and memory in dialects, rhythms, and intonations drawn from the lived experience of the black masses. Literary critic Houston Baker writes:

> The days of the Black Arts Movement were heady, full of experimental concept, institutions, dogmas, and nationalistic arbiters of taste . . . [but] it is never, of course, the doctrines that survive or become important for any revolutionary artistic movement. It is the creativity, the personalities of the artists themselves, the actual works they produce that energize the lives and imaginations of audiences and followers and fellow artists for years to come. Jazz poetry, blues poetry, vernacular signifying in the arts of America were at their highest order of achievement during the Black Arts Movement.[122]

Since the 1960s, Baraka's influence in jazz letters has not been limited to the debates about his criticism: it flourishes through his work as a jazz-mad romantic artist. In 1965 Baraka recorded his poem "Black Dada Nihilismus" on the record *New York Art Quartet*, and in the late 1970s and early 1980s he performed a series of jazz poetry collaborations with a new generation of avant-garde musicians including David Murray, Arthur Blythe, Henry Threadgill, Fred Hopkins, and Steve McCall. In the liner notes for *New Music—New Poetry*, his 1981 record with tenor saxophonist Murray and drummer Steve McCall, Baraka observes that "Black poetry in the main . . . means to show its musical origins. Just as Blues is, on one level, a verse form, so Black poetry begins as music running into words." In poetry-jazz songs like "In the Tradition," "The Last Revolutionary," "Class Struggle in Music," and "Against Bourgeois Art," Baraka thrashes and curses capitalism, racism, and America.[123]

By the end of the 1960s, those afternoons at the *Record Changer* with Hettie Cohen, Nat Hentoff, and Martin Williams were but a distant memory. The clean Afro-Edwardian Brooks Brothers look had given way to a righteous African dashiki; the "middle-class kid from Newark"—as Williams insisted on remembering Baraka[124]—had gone from bohemian to black nationalist to Muslim to Marxist political guerrilla. As these transformations unfolded, Baraka moved further and further away from the models of jazz criticism he had both absorbed and critiqued in the early 1960s. If "Jazz and the White Critic" was a manifesto and *Blues People* a larger historical argument for a jazz criticism more attuned to black experience, the deeper black aesthetic poetics of "The Changing Same" pointed toward an engagement with music that defied and transcended the boundaries of traditional jazz criticism altogether. It is that Amiri Baraka—the one who sensed that the musicians were ahead of the critics in expressing the contradictions and conflicts of the age, the one who fervently hoped that the galvanizing beauty of John Coltrane's playing might erase the nation's "essentially vile profile"— who remains the most challenging figure in 1960s jazz letters.

The Wall of Sound

In 1971, Ron Welburn, a poet of African American and Native American heritage recently graduated from Lincoln University, published an essay titled "The Black Aesthetic Imperative." Welburn's sweeping essay—which appeared in *The Black Aesthetic*, the canonical Black Arts Movement collection edited by Charles Gayle Jr.—was black nationalist catnip, an emphatic declaration of jazz and 1960s soul music's revolutionary power. "More than any other kind of black artist," Welburn wrote, "the musician creates his own and his people's soul essence, his own negritude. He can also do more damage to the oppressor's image of himself than heavily armed urban guerillas." Dripping with Baraka's influence but endowed with its own formidable rhetorical lucidity, Welburn's essay linked the late 1950s soul/funk movement and the 1960s "new black music" of Coltrane, Coleman, and Sun Ra to a larger Afro-Asian cultural force that had "moved into the heart and soul of the universe" and thus had avoided the spiritual, cultural, and moral decay of Western civilization. In terms that echoed the early twentieth-century primitivist critique of Western industrial culture, Welburn propagandized black music's superior human qualities of vocal and bodily expressiveness against the soul-deadening techniques of Euro-American culture. While positing that "black music in the 1970s must incorporate a world of non-white musics if black people in America hold the key to the world's survival," Welburn emphasized the crucial importance of protecting black culture from polluting contact with white culture. Piggybacking on the jeremiads central to the critical stances of Alain Locke and Baraka, Welburn warned of the danger inherent in black music's mass commercial popularity, its proneness to "vampirish" white appropriation. "We cannot afford to allow our music to remain a surrogate for white American psychosexual illusions," he exhorted. Welburn first targeted white saxophonist Stan Getz and his early 1960s bossa nova vogue, which he claimed "killed off the down-home, earthy musical dominance" of the soul/funk jazz movement and "was popular long enough to let whites straighten themselves out psychologically." But the nationalist cultural imperative of a pristine, purified black music aesthetic had become especially acute in the late 1960s with the huge commercial ascendancy of rock music, characterized by Welburn (in terms reminiscent of Rudi Blesh's anxieties over big-band swing) as a hyper-technological, quasi-fascist phenomenon:

> White rock is a technology, not a real music. It is an affectation, not a felt experience. It is parasitic, not symbiotic, to black culture and life-styles. It has a quasi-aesthetic. Ralph Nader's Raiders are worried that American (white) youth will do damage to their nervous systems with this music-technology; at least he and [Amiri] Baraka would agree that the white race might die out.[125]

In a 1997 interview with Charley Gerard, Welburn—now an English professor at the University of Massachusetts—reflected on his 1971 essay in light of his subsequent experience as a music listener, critic, editor, poet, and academic. Though no longer satisfied by "the old nationalistic arguments about jazz and race," Welburn clung to the idea of jazz as—"no matter who plays it"—"an African-American expression or mode that develops out of a particular mindset or cultural response." Years of research and experience in the jazz world—editing *The Grackle*, staff work at the Institute of Jazz Studies, writing a doctoral dissertation on jazz criticism up to 1940[126]—had convinced Welburn that jazz was an international phenomenon involving "peoples who represent various cultural backgrounds, people of color and Native Americans." While maintaining his critique of the white-dominated commercial culture industry, Welburn rued his earlier "lashing out at white musicians" as a "self-serving if not altogether superficial" tactic. But Welburn held strong in his condemnation of rock music as a technological assault on jazz's spiritual and aesthetic values:

> One of the things that I noticed in *Down Beat* [during the 1960s] was what Jim Stewart called a "retooling." You no longer saw advertisements for acoustic instruments. You saw advertisements for guitars and electrical instruments. There was that insistent metallic wall of sound that seemed to be encroaching and replacing the jazz sound. . . . That sound that Jimi Hendrix helped create, that wall of metal, I found irritating, and I still do. And my son [Eliot] likes to listen to it! It's more the sound than the musicians [that disturbed me]. I felt that the regrouping that needed to take place in black musical communities was to stay away from that sound, because I though that sound was dangerous. . . . I could see certain musical groups and musical sounds coming into jazz and just ruining it.[127]

Ironically, for all of the ideological and tonal differences that separated the black nationalists and the white liberals in 1960s jazz criticism, on this point—an anxiety about rock's commercial, technological, and sonic encroachment on jazz—the two camps found considerable common ground. As always, the jazz magazines targeted the youth and college markets; but now, while the student crowd embraced rock, Motown, and soul as their generation's defining music, the established jazz critics, now middle-aged and older, struggled to reconcile themselves to the new cultural forces.

Scuffling for media bandwidth was a perennial struggle of the jazz critic, but business-mandated shifts in the jazz magazine world in the 1960s made it especially difficult for critics who had come up at a time when writing about Louis Armstrong or Fletcher Henderson wasn't considered a dusty antiquarian pursuit. After leaving *Metronome* in 1963, Dan Morgenstern moved on to the editorship of *Jazz*, owned by Bob Thiele, at that time the very successful producer of John Coltrane and others at Impulse Records. In lieu of a regular salary, Morgenstern was promised liner note commissions for Impulse. Dubious about the magazine's thinly veiled connections to the record label (evident in the perceptible tilt of advertising space and record reviews), Morgenstern grew even more uneasy when he suspected that Thiele was using him to groom assistant editor Pauline Rivelli, Thiele's girlfriend, to take over the magazine. Morgenstern left *Jazz* in 1964, just as Frank Kofsky was beginning to surface in the magazine's pages as the *bête noir* of the jazz criticism establishment. Under Rivelli, the magazine soon changed its name to *Jazz & Pop* and aggressively pursued the growing rock audience. Morgenstern moved over to *Down Beat*, assuming the editor's chair in 1967, at a time when pressure from the ownership and the business office—now buttering its bread with advertisements for electric guitars and amplifiers—forced him also to shift editorial coverage in the direction of the youth rock market.[128] He did so on terms that made clear his primary loyalty to jazz and his belief that jazz was the superior aesthetic expression. In an editor's note in June 1967, Morgenstern told *Down Beat* readers that the "growing sophistication" of rock, and the fact that many "many of the most gifted rock musicians are now showing an increasing awareness of jazz," mandated that the magazine expand its coverage to include "musically valid aspects of the rock scene." He assured readers that *Down Beat's* rock coverage would be "stimulating, informative, and always concerned with encouraging high musical standards."[129]

While *Down Beat* courted the rock generation with electric guitar advertisements and Jefferson Airplane covers (February 5, 1970), the older jazz critics patrolled the contemporary musical scene for transgressions against jazz's purportedly elevated musical standards. In April 1970, Leonard Feather tried to explain how Herbie Mann could have five of the twenty top-selling "jazz" albums in the country. Feather seemed to admire Mann's effort to fuse gospel, bossa nova, blues, and R&B, even if it meant using a rock rhythm section anchored by a Fender electric bass—at least he wasn't playing middle-of-the-road jazz covers of Beatles tunes, as Count Basie had done in a way Feather found embarrassing. Mann, he said, "has an uncannily astute ear for what his audiences want, an intelligent awareness of how best to surround himself with capable and inspired musicians, a very sharply honed business sense, the ability to help establish trends as well as the willingness to follow them; and, let us not forget, a not inconsiderable talent as a flutist and composer." This concept of "talent" was, by implication, grounded in a jazz aesthetic that assumed an autonomous artistic vision, one that somehow remained uncontaminated by commercial influences even as it shrewdly calculated how to negotiate the commercial sphere. Like the most commercially successful albums of the 1950s, Mann's recordings were "musically valid," Feather argued, because they expressed the musician's "own instincts" rather than capitulating to the dictates of record producers and marketers.[130]

Feather employed similar logic in responding to a *Jet* magazine column that complained about Miles Davis appearing as a warm-up act for "Johnny-come-lately white rock groups" in arena-style concert billings. Feather was sanguine about the crossover success of Davis's electrified *Bitches Brew* LP—less out of admiration for Davis's new sound, it seemed, than for his excitement over the racial boundary-crossing nature of Davis's new band and new audience. For Davis to appear at the Hollywood Bowl in front of a predominantly rock-oriented crowd should be "a cause for rejoicing," Feather urged. "It's a Barnum and Bailey world," he wrote, "a world in which Jimi Hendrix, The Who, The Guess Who and The God Knows Who are playing at giant bowls and forums with close to 20,000 capacity, earning staggering five-figure nightly fees, while Freddie Hubbard, Gary Burton, the MJQ, Bill Evans, Dizzy Gillespie and a hundred other jazz giants never get to see the inside of such places, let alone top the bill there."[131]

Feather argued that rock and its audience should be seen as an economic opportunity for jazz rather than as a political threat or an illegitimate appropriation of African American culture. That a jazz icon like Miles Davis would court rock's larger audience was "a matter of rock outgrossing jazz, not white demoting black." By contrast, Martin Williams was much more deeply invested in a notion of black musical authenticity assumed to be inherent in the best of jazz and blues but rarely found in rock. Williams guardedly welcomed the Beatles, praising their songwriting ability but denigrating their "somewhat effeminate hairdos" and criticizing their performance style as a "strident imitation of American Negro blues singing."[132] The Liverpool lads at least dodged the full censure Williams heaped on the Rolling Stones and "many of our U.S. folkniks," whose "unpainted blackface" he found "painful and embarrassing."[133] Williams's attitude toward the rock audience and 1960s youth culture ranged from archly condescending to openly contemptuous. It also manifested a certain unmistakable gendering pattern that coded authentic jazz and blues as serious and masculine, rock as hysterical and feminine. Baffled by the spectacle of young girls screaming at Beatles concerts, Williams claimed to have consulted a Jungian analyst on the matter (were the Beatles a "collective archetype" that triggered the girls' "hypnotic bacchanal," he asked?), only to find the specialist as perplexed as himself. In the imperious tone that often characterized his *Down Beat* column "The Bystander," Williams proclaimed it a matter of serious intellectual business to discover "what is going on in the soul of a generation that must scream constantly through a performance, blocking out any possibility of even hearing what they are presumably there to hear."[134]

Just as Williams lamented Amiri Baraka's political turn to black nationalism in Harlem and Newark as a sacrilege against the memory of the budding jazz critic LeRoi Jones he had known in late 1950s Greenwich Village, so he upbraided white jazz critics who seemed to have been seduced by rock and the 1960s counterculture in a way that compromised their commitment to jazz. In one instance, Williams targeted Michael Zwerin's *Village Voice* column, in which—as Williams read it—the critic/musician Zwerin habitually complained about jazz being mocked and underappreciated, but then turned around and raved about rock and the looming utopian possibilities of a jazz/rock amalgam. "[I]f [Zwerin] tells us anything more about how wonderful the Byrds are, or how he was there when the latest rock idol got busted by the cops, or how they don't make hedonist jazz musicians like they used to," Williams seethed, "then I guess he should expect to have a few people sneer at jazz in his presence."[135] Williams found rich irony in the putatively progressive racial impulse at work in the radicalized white critics' embrace of rock. In a veiled reference likely directed at Frank Kofsky and other *Jazz & Pop* contributors, Williams called it "very interesting that a couple of commentators who are militantly Crow-Jim about jazz avidly embrace white rock groups, and are absolutely thrilled to discover an integrated, black and white rock band."[136]

"Don't Define It, Dig It"

Among the older established white jazz critics, only the San Francisco–based Ralph Gleason immersed himself in the 1960s youth movement and embraced rock as a salutary cultural movement. "[J]azz began by accusing the symphony and conservatory players of refusing to listen to them," Gleason wrote in *Jazz & Pop* in 1967. "Now the jazz musicians, or at least a regrettable majority of them, are not opening their ears to the worthwhile music coming from the new generation." Open-minded jazz musicians surely should recognize that what the Grateful Dead plays "is really jazz," Gleason argued, "even though the sound of the guitars at first inhibits you from saying that."[137] In his *San Francisco Chronicle* column, and in his work as a disc jockey at KHIP and KMPX, a vice president of Fantasy/Prestige Records, and an advisor to the Monterey Jazz Festival, Gleason pushed hard against the generic boundaries of jazz, rock, blues, and rhythm-and-blues. Gleason became especially important as a bridge figure between the jazz and rock worlds as co-founder—with acolyte Jann Wenner—of *Rolling Stone* in 1967. As Robert Draper documents in his fascinating history of the magazine, the "floppy-haired, acid-dropping" Wenner might never have gotten his colossally successful enterprise off the ground without the imprimatur of the "graying and bespectacled" Gleason, whose relationships with printers, broadcasters, record companies, and key musicians like Bob Dylan and John Lennon gave *Rolling Stone* a competitive edge in the emerging underground press. In the impetuous Wenner—a rock-obsessed Berkeley student when Gleason met him at a psychedelic dance party at San Francisco's Longshoreman's Hall in 1965—Gleason recalled something of his own college years in New York in the late 1930s, when he launched his jazz writing career in the pages of the *Columbia Spectator* and then, after getting kicked out of school, founded the traditionalist sheet *Jazz Information*. Though soon repulsed by Wenner's megalomania and financial chicanery, Gleason clung to his *Rolling Stone* column "Perspectives" as a direct line to the Love Generation throughout the late 1960s and early 1970s.[138]

When Gleason died following a heart attack in 1975, some of the most venerable jazz critics hailed his big ears and open-mindedness. "He was the first of any of us jazz critics to acknowledge that a new wind was blowing . . . [that] for the reality of what's happening today, we must go to rock," Leonard Feather wrote. "He probably had as great an influence on younger generations as any writer of our times," John Hammond claimed in a eulogy that underscored not only Gleason's "uncanny ear" for new trends in music but also his role as a "fiercely effective fighter" for racial justice and civil liberties.[139] By this time, Gleason's influence extended through but also beyond the jazz world—as evidenced in a *Rolling Stone* tribute section with testimony from Feather, Hammond, Milt Gabler, Studs Terkel, Nat Hentoff, Carmen McRae, Dizzy Gillespie, Frank Sinatra, John Lewis, Miles Davis (writing succinctly "GIVE ME BACK my friend"), Al Aronowitz, Ken Kesey, Lawrence Ferlinghetti, Jerry Garcia, John Lennon, Paul Simon, Robbie Robertson, Mike Bloomfield, and Greil Marcus, among others.[140] During the mid-1960s, when San Francisco and Haight-Ashbury became synonymous with the counterculture, Ralph and Jean Gleason's home on 2835 Ashby Avenue in Berkeley provided sanctuary for a motley crowd of Free Speech Movement and antiwar students, street philosophers, aspiring artists and writers, and soon-to-be-famous musicians (the Grateful Dead, Jefferson Airplane, Big Brother and the Holding Company, and others) associated with San Francisco's psychedelic movement. In his popular *Chronicle* column, Gleason used a slangy prose full of phrases like "groovy" and "freaky far-outness" to preach resistance to established authority, back renegade movements (he was a leader of the Dizzy Gillespie for President drafts), and spotlight Bay Area protests, be-ins, love-ins, and assorted other "happenings."

Like LeRoi Jones/Amiri Baraka, Gleason's dissenting spirit had been forged in the 1950s, in his absorption of the Left intellectual mass culture critique of postwar American conformity. He was quite fond of quoting radical social critics C. Wright Mills and Paul Goodman on the atomization, soul-lessness, and absurdity of American institutions. Gleason became one of the most influential propagandists of Joseph Heller's landmark 1961 novel, fre-quently calling 1960s youth "the Catch-22 generation." Also very much like Jones/Baraka, Gleason moved from a late 1950s/early 1960s quasi-scholarly posture to a self-consciously hip one meant to connect more decisively with the communal ethos and participatory, experiential impulses of readers who considered themselves active agents of radical cultural transformation. In 1957, Gleason launched *Jazz: A Quarterly of American Music*, which, in its short tenure, shared the gentlemanly tone and little-magazine earnestness of Hentoff and Williams's *Jazz Review*. A decade later, Gleason's credo—much cited by his rock critic apostles—had become: "Don't define it, dig it." This meant—again, as with the post–*Blues People* Baraka—the cultivation of a new prose style, in Gleason's case one redolent with spacy Age of Aquarius wonderment. "This music is. This music is new. This music is new music and it hits me like an electric shock, and the word 'electric' is interesting because the music is to some degree electric music either by virtue of what you can do with tapes and by the process by which it is preserved on tape or by the use of electricity in the actual making of the sounds themselves"—so went Gleason's freaky far-out liner note to Miles Davis's *Bitches Brew*.[141]

The Grateful Dead's Jerry Garcia described Gleason as "the perpetual newspaper hippie. You could see him at all the scenes, always enthusias-tic. . . . He finally transcended talking about the music and that got to be the coolest thing about him, got to be his riff later on—not to talk about the music but about the event. He liked to see people having a good time."[142] Gleason might have seemed hopelessly faddish when he enthused about a San Francisco club's pairing of the Dizzy Gillespie Quintet and the Jefferson Airplane on the same bill (and then noted how "groovy" Gillespie's comic banter was, and that the Airplane was loud but no louder than Count Basie), or when he pushed the *San Francisco Chronicle* to editorialize for the reopen-ing of city ballrooms for psychedelic dances.[143] But the larger vision was actually nostalgic—a reprise of the aging jazz fan's bygone youth dancing the night away at the Savoy. For Gleason, rock presented an opportunity to complete the unfinished cultural work of the Swing Era: to use black rhythm and style to cool out and syncopate an uptight, neurotic white na-tion. In one of his early *Rolling Stone* columns, titled "A Power to Change the World," Gleason rhapsodized about the increasing rhythmic finesse of main-stream audiences: "[W]hite audiences today can keep time. They don't clap as well as a James Brown audience in the ghetto, but they clap a thousand times better than their parents did."[144] Like Baraka and the black national-ists, Gleason was a romantic with a utopian vision of a social and spiritual revolution sparked by musical prophets but ultimately realized by "the people." But Gleason's people—mainly white countercultural youth, a subculture, as sociologist Kenneth Keniston noted, of the larger postwar white middle class "that takes for granted the technology and the economy necessary to provide its own material base—a high standard of living, psychochemistry, cars, films, electronics, and an enormously prolonged education"[145]— were the very people black nationalists like Baraka and Welburn thought to be the problem with America, not its salvation.

Such were the fractures of American culture in the 1960s, and of jazz criticism itself, which began the decade embroiled in partisan debates over the relationship between free jazz, the black freedom movement, and the cold war, and ended it trying to make sense of jazz's fate in the wake of the British Invasion, the ascendancy of rock, Black Power, and the counterculture. At the start of the decade, the figure of the skinny-black-tie-wearing jazz critic was part of the background scenery of the hip avant garde. As the decade progressed, the established critics risked becoming curios, guardians of the sacred relics, propagandists of the lost cause. No matter that Martin Williams could say "I dig Aretha Franklin," if in the same *Down Beat* column he curtly dismissed Bob Dylan as a faux poet who "knows a lot about *other* people's faults."[146] This was a man proudly out of sync with the countercultural zeitgeist, which might be said as well of Whitney Balliett. Amiri Baraka was his own zeitgeist. Others—Nat Hentoff, John Hammond, Leonard Feather, Dan Morgenstern—searched for a rapprochement with the new forces. Ralph Gleason gave himself over to them—kept "bathing himself in the fountain of youth," Al Aronowitz said—which made him an avuncular prophet to the Love Generation, but then something of a curious vestige when that generation moved on. "While the children of the sixties had grown up and come to terms with the System," Robert Draper writes of Gleason's last, difficult years at *Rolling Stone* in the early 1970s, "there was Old Man Gleason, his hair now grown out like LBJ's in his final days, murmuring 'groovy,' stranded in a depleted era."[147]

If Gleason's infatuation with the new was a sunburst of 1960s modernism—"A new beauty," he continued in his rapture over Miles Davis's electrification. "This is new and right now it has the edge of newness and that snapping fire you sense when you go out there from the spaceship where nobody has ever been before"—it was also a sentimental reaction to aging, memory, and loss. "Ralph wrote a lot of obituaries," said Greil Marcus in his Gleason obituary.[148] Rhapsodizing Davis's electro-psychedelia on the same days that he was eulogizing Louis Armstrong, Duke Ellington, John Coltrane, and Albert Ayler, Gleason personified the dilemma that jazz criticism itself had been wrestling over since the music's canonization had begun in the late 1930s: how to reconcile the music's ceaseless forward-moving energy with its equally strong impulse to commemorate and celebrate its history and tradition. Gleason's posthumously published collection of jazz writings—*Celebrating the Duke and Louis, Bessie, Carmen, Miles, Dizzy and Other Heroes*—is richly emblematic: the jazz critic who (along with Amiri Baraka) flexed hardest to shape the contours of the 1960s cutting edge, left behind a document whose very title announced itself as a gesture of utterly conventional, age-old memorialization. Such is the cultural work of canonization—even, or perhaps especially, at a time of exciting and bewildering newness.

How and what and who to remember? How to give shape and order and meaning to the memories? How to recover and make sense of the "noisy lostness"? How to make the past knowable and useful? How to carry on into the future? These were abiding questions for jazz's canonizers going back to *Jazzmen* and the Lenox "roundtables," and they remained abiding questions—even if framed in new ways and answered in new rhetorics—in the pages of *Blues People* and *Rolling Stone*.

In my final two chapters, I delve more deeply into jazz criticism's discourses of memorialization—first, in the protracted effort by one critic to come to terms with the life and career of one legendary musician; second, in the jazz culture wars of the 1980s and 1990s.

CHAPTER 7

Race-ing the Bird

Ross Russell's Obsessive Pursuit of Charlie Parker

What's hard is to circle about him and not lose your distance, like a good satellite, like a good critic.

—Julio Cortázar, "The Pursuer"

Recording Bird

In "The Pursuer," a short story by the Argentine writer Julio Cortázar, a Parisian jazz critic named Bruno obsesses over his relationship with the genius musician Johnny Carter, whose unparalleled musical exploits are matched by equally extraordinary acts of personal dissolution. Bruno, the narrator, considers himself Johnny's friend. He has written a well-received biography of Johnny that has enhanced the saxophonist's reputation with the Parisian intelligentsia. He has also made a habit of intervening to save Johnny from bouts of highly erratic, irresponsible behavior. Forever protesting his own innocence and forbearance, Bruno seemingly earns his cultural capital by cleaning up the mess of Johnny's childish bohemian lifestyle. Yet, as literary critic Doris Sommer has brilliantly argued, the very language of "The Pursuer" reveals Bruno's uneasiness and paralyzing self-doubt. As a matter of established convention, Bruno the intellectual is expected to impose order and stable meaning on the discordant life and work of his artistic subject. But throughout the story Johnny's "disarming lucidity"—his superior intelligence and technical appreciation of his own work—continually stokes Bruno's anxiety about his purpose and identity as a critic.[1]

299

The details of the story plainly reveal Johnny as a literary stand-in for the legendary bebop alto saxophonist Charlie Parker, to whom Cortázar in fact dedicates the story *in memoriam*. Parker died in 1955 at the age of thirty-four. He was canonized immediately by a legion of cult worshipers, including Greenwich Village hipsters who festooned New York subways and building walls with the graffiti tag, "Bird Lives!" Many likened Parker to the poet Dylan Thomas, who had died a year earlier under circumstances similarly hospitable to the romantic myth of the tragic artist. Cortázar encourages this affiliation by using as an epigram a line he attributes to Thomas, "Oh make me a mask," and then by having Johnny mouth these words at the moment of his death. Like Parker himself, whose death certificate fixed the age of his heroin- and alcohol-saturated corpse at fifty-three, Johnny is a man of many masks, a chameleon-like character who constantly eludes the pursuit of critics and coroners alike. The problem with his biography, Johnny tells Bruno, is that "what you forgot to put in is me."[2]

If Cortázar's Bruno is right to say that Johnny's (Bird's) true biography is in his records, then all the more reason to be fascinated by the story of the relationship between Charlie Parker himself and his first real-life biographer, Ross Russell (1909–2000). Driven by a feeling for Parker that he characterized as "an obsessive thing [that] was almost like a disease,"[3] Russell wrote first *The Sound* (1961), a novel whose protagonist is based on Parker, and then *Bird Lives!* (1973), a full-length Parker biography. When Martin Williams, one of several confidants privy to the soul-searching that Parker had elicited from his biographer, congratulated Russell on the publication of *Bird Lives!*, he observed: "It's as though *The Sound* had to be got out of the way . . . for you to reach the inner layers of your own being and Parker's."[4]

Russell's literary and critical/historical representations of Charlie Parker bear the traces of a complicated personal relationship dating to the 1940s, when Russell owned Dial Records, one of the small independent labels that first recorded Parker playing with small groups in the new bebop style.[5] Russell, who launched the Dial record company in 1945 as an adjunct to his retail record store in Hollywood, was the producer of seven recording sessions with Parker in 1946 and 1947. Parker also recorded for Savoy Records from 1944 to 1948, and cut sides for Norman Granz's Clef, Mercury, and Verve labels from 1946 to 1954. But, as Edward Komara has suggested, because of their more limited distribution and high quality of technical craftsmanship, Parker's Dial sides—including versions of "Ornithology," "Yardbird Suite," "A Night in Tunisia," "Max Making Wax," "Dexterity," and "Drifting on a Reed"—held special interest for record collectors and musicians.[6]

The significance of Parker's Dial sessions was never, however, simply a matter of commodity exchange: several of them, by virtue of the extraordinary circumstances of their unfolding, immediately became part of Bird mythology, grist for the legend mill that shaped perceptions of Parker in both life and death. Parker's very first recording for Dial, "Moose the Mooche," cut in Los Angeles in March 1946, was a tribute to his local heroin connection, Emry "Moose the Mooche" Byrd, a Central Avenue paraplegic pusher who made his way around jazz clubs in a wheelchair. The Moose mooched the profits from this recording and several others from Parker's first Dial session: Parker, it seems, had signed over his rights to Byrd, an agreement Russell learned of in a letter postmarked from San Quentin Prison.[7]

At his second Dial recording session in July 1946, Parker, malnourished, pumped with alcohol and inferior-quality narcotics, and depressed over recent public attacks on his music, was in the throes of a mental breakdown. In a surreal episode that for Miles Davis and Howard McGhee constituted the very definition of exploitation, Russell insisted on continuing with the session in spite of Parker's obvious distress. The brother of Russell's business partner, a psychiatrist, supplied Parker with an emergency dose of phenobarbital. Russell literally propped Parker up to the recording mike, holding him in place from behind as Parker played. Later that night, Parker snapped: after twice appearing in his hotel lobby in just his socks and then setting fire to his room, Parker wrestled with blackjack-wielding policemen before being cuffed and muscled off to the psychopathic ward of the east L.A. county jail. When McGhee and Russell found him there ten days later, Parker was slated to go to a maximum-security prison for the criminally insane. Russell's intercession helped move him instead to the Camarillo State Hospital, where he spent six months before being released into Russell's custody in January 1947.[8]

The wrenching, anguished version of "Lover Man" that came of the July 1946 Dial session has been called Parker's most poetic statement on record, while the tunes Parker recorded in a February 1947 Dial session after his Camarillo release—"Relaxin' at Camarillo," "Cheers," "Stupendous," and "Carvin' the Bird"—have struck many listeners as his most joyous and optimistic. Parker himself was incensed that Russell released "Lover Man," feeling that the record caught him playing beneath his abilities. He also accused Russell of committing him to Camarillo as leverage to force him to renew his breached contract. Russell has said very little about his decision to release "Lover Man." Writer Elliott Grennard witnessed the recording session and claimed that Russell decided to release the record after Grennard's short story, "Sparrow's Last Jump," inspired by the session, was published in *Harper's* in May 1947. In a New York night club in December 1954, in a last brush with Parker just months before the saxophonist's death, Russell was warned that Parker was carrying a gun and threatening to shoot him, and that it would be in everyone's best interest if he left the premises.[9]

While some musicians have claimed that Russell was a "money-grubbing record company executive intent on exploiting the musicians under his contract," the jazz historian Ted Gioia has argued that Russell's financial investment in bebop was a "godsend" to L.A. boppers like Teddy Edwards, Wardell Gray, and Dexter Gordon.[10] Gioia contends that it was the absence of Dial—Russell moved the company to New York in 1947 and dissolved it in 1954—and other independent companies recording and marketing the harder bop style that cleared the way for the cool sound more popular with white musicians and audiences to secure West Coast dominance by the mid-1950s. Whatever effect Russell's Dial recordings had in shaping the jazz marketplace, however, it was inevitable that Russell himself would loom as a symbol of the jazz establishment, the white-dominated class of club owners, record company executives, union officials, personnel managers, and booking agents. For black musicians in particular, Russell was easily targeted as The Man—a designation that subjected him to an uneasiness and vulnerability beyond that which Cortázar ascribes to his fictional critic-biographer, Bruno. Miles Davis slandered Russell as "a jive motherfucker who I never did get along with because he was nothing but a leech, who didn't never do nothing but suck off Bird like he was a vampire."[11]

Russell's anxiety over this image was no less acute when he turned to the task of representing Parker in words rather than on wax. "Since you are a writer yourself, as well as a musician, and knew Bird," Russell wrote to the composer and performer David Amram in 1969, shortly after Amram had published a memoir and Russell was starting serious work on *Bird Lives!*, "you well appreciate the complexity of the job of trying to do an honest biography of Bird, especially for a person like myself who is white, middle-class, and whose relations with Bird were colored by the inevitable entrepreneur–creative artist relationship."[12]

Parker was by all accounts a supremely difficult person—in Ralph Ellison's judgment, "one whose friends had no need for an enemy, and whose enemies had no difficulty in justifying their hate."[13] Davis, bitter over having been constantly harangued for drug fix money and made to watch Parker receive sexual favors, remembered Parker as "a great and genius musician . . . [but] also one of the slimiest and greediest motherfuckers who ever lived in this world."[14] When Russell lamented to Amram "the persistent image my memory holds of Bird as a willful psychopath,"[15] his concern was not the faithfulness of his memory, but whether his recollections would be perceived as tainted by the nature of his relationship with Parker. Russell hoped that by adopting the pose of the dispassionate critic and historian he would distance himself from the stereotype of the parasitic music industry operator and the ingratiating White Negro. Among cold war–era liberal jazz critics, in fact, Russell was known not as a hipster but as an important pioneer of a self-consciously elevated, analytical and historical style of jazz writing. In 1948 and 1949, in the midst of the scorched-earth debates over bebop, Russell stepped back from the sectarian battle lines and wrote a series of acclaimed articles for *Record Changer* tracing connections between bebop and earlier jazz traditions, focusing particularly on the line of stylistic descent from Lester Young to Parker.[16] Russell's evolutionary framework strongly influenced those critics (Whitney Balliett, Nat Hentoff, Martin Williams, Dan Morgenstern) I discussed earlier as the theorists and tribunes of a jazz "mainstream."

Between *The Sound* and *Bird Lives!* Russell published the highly regarded *Jazz Style in Kansas City and the Southwest* (1971), which has become a staple of jazz history courses.[17] Even in his fiction, Russell could show a fine, subtle touch in describing the nuances of jazz performance:

> Hassan's ride cymbal began to vibrate, pumping its shimmering sound across the bandstand. He was playing six notes to the bar, And-One-TWO, And-Three-FOUR, but the notes seemed to run together so that the big cymbal, with light splashing off its gentle coolie-hat curves, had a musical pulse of its own.[18]

The *New Yorker*'s Balliett embraced Russell as a model of the "coolheaded professional critic"; Hentoff and Williams, both of whom credited Russell with helping them overcome an initial distaste for bebop, solicited contributions from him for the *Jazz Review*; Williams urged Russell to join him in writing for the *Evergreen Review* because "they need someone besides me and the beatniks."[19] These ascendant critics (all born in the late 1920s) claimed Russell (born in 1909) as a father figure of the jazz critical fraternity. He was certainly a colorful figure for this role. In the late 1950s, while these thirty-something urbane men were making their way in the world of New York middlebrow cultural journalism, Russell, pushing sixty, embittered from his record company experience, was running a golf course outside of Worcester, Massachusetts and dabbling in the Canadian stock market. Returning to California in the 1960s, Russell eked out a living writing publicity for a motor speedway, selling pictures and reviews to jazz magazines, and teaching jazz history in adult education programs. His unpublished fiction from the period includes soft-core pornography (one pulp story titled "The Girl Who Liked Muscles" details erotic goings-on between a call girl and a boxer), stories about dope smuggling, motorcycle racing, and dune buggy culture, and a book-length thriller featuring an assassination attempt on a character patterned after Herbert Marcuse.[20] Hearing that one of Russell's late-1960s adjunct teaching gigs was at the University of California at San Diego, Martin Williams wrote him, "Just wait until Ronald Reagan finds out about *you!*"[21]

Despite the esteem for his jazz criticism, in other words, Russell was no New Critical man of letters, and his eccentric interests defied the reigning image of the postwar jazz intellectual as aspiring sophisticate. Unbeknownst to the New York critics, in fact, Russell had cut his writing teeth covering sports for a California local newspaper and penning crime and sex thrillers for pulp magazines from 1936 to 1941. Russell spent years working on an unpublished biography of Raymond Chandler, convinced of his superior understanding of both the poetics of pulp and the southern California of Chandler's imagination.[22] In the 1970s, discussing the crafting of his novel *The Sound* and his in-progress Parker biography with English-professor-turned-popular-culture-critic Albert Goldman, Russell emphasized his enduring affinity with the *Black Mask* school of pulp writing, which he described as a graphic, visually oriented approach in which the writer's point of view is epitomized in the taut interplay of character, setting, and situation.[23] *The Sound*, originally titled "The Hipsters," can be read as an updating of the overlapping hard-boiled and film-noir genres, shifting focus from the Depression-era gangster and private dick to the late-1940s jazz milieu that Russell knew well.

Russell's friendship with Goldman—to whom *Bird Lives!* was dedicated for Goldman's "unselfish dedication in getting me straightened out"[24]— unmasked parts of Russell's sensibility not evident in his more detached, professional intercourse with Balliett, Hentoff, and Williams. Before achieving notoriety for his sex-and-drug-saturated pathographies—to use the term coined by Joyce Carol Oates—of Lenny Bruce, Elvis Presley, and John Lennon, Goldman collected his 1960s freelance pieces for *Life, The New Leader, The New Republic, The New York Times,* and *Newsweek* into a 1971 volume extravagantly titled *Freakshow: The Rocksoulbluesjazzsickjewblackhumorpoppsych Gig and Other Scenes from the Counter-Culture.* A former literature professor at Columbia fond of quoting Goethe in the original German, Goldman (1927–1994) rode the pulse of the 1960s out of the academy on a frantic quest for experience that joined intellectual edginess to surging popular culture energies. Self-described as "a nice silvering Jewish college professor with a hard-on for authentic black culture,"[25] Goldman toiled in freelance purgatory in the late 1960s and early 1970s, exploring Bruce's jazz-inspired scatology, the history of the American cannabis trade, Brazilian carnival, and the birth of disco, before hitting pay dirt with his best-selling biographies of white rock icons.

Russell's correspondence with Goldman brims with talk of race and sex, themes entirely absent from his correspondence with his jazz critic admirers. "In many ways we're blood brothers," Russell wrote to Goldman.[26] It was to Goldman that Russell joked about being an "unreconstructed post-pioneer stock WASP."[27] It was to Goldman that Russell vented his anger over being cut out of his father's will for marrying a black West Indian woman he had met while recording calypso music in the early 1950s.[28] To avenge that and other familial grievances, Russell joked with Goldman that he has considered writing "a long novel about my asshole WASP relatives."[29] Add Russell's interracial marriage to his jazz-world experience, and he defines the outer reaches of class and race rebellion for his generation of World War II Anglo Americans. And yet, in the 1970s, Russell embraced Goldman, a generation younger and by virtue of his Jewishness already situated in ambivalent racial territory, as a cosmopolitan antidote to his WASP provincialism. "Let's face it," Russell told Goldman, "if I had never gotten into black culture and Jewish-American culture I'd still be sitting at the sports desk of a paper in Glendale, California and the most unenlightened shit that ever lived."[30]

Goaded by Goldman and nursing his own ambivalent reaction to the black cultural ascendancy of the 1960s, Russell's anxieties over his whiteness spilled over into an increasingly strained, even vindictive vision of blackness. Russell wrote in the acknowledgments to the 1973 publication of *Bird Lives!*: "Of course it is absurd that the biography of one of the great figures of Afro-American music has been written by a white man, and a middle-class, western, establishment-educated white man at that, but no black writer or scholar has come forward to write about one of his own great culture heroes."[31] The liberal paternalism of this public statement at least has the ring of piety: not so the cruder sentiments Russell expressed in his private correspondence, which often bristles with racial backlash resentment. In a letter to the sister of Linda Kuehl, a white woman writer of Russell's and Goldman's acquaintance who died of mysterious causes while researching a biography of Billie Holiday, Russell wrote: "You wonder if writing about the jazz life and trying to enter the jazz world is the kiss of death. And why the slovenly mal-educated arrogant black writers have to leave the job of writing about their culture heroes to the ofays."[32] Given his ferocious disdain for the work of even canonized black writers, it is hard to imagine who Russell thought might measure up to the task. Russell insistently degraded the work of James Baldwin, Ralph Ellison, and "the guy who wrote *Native Son*," favoring as a more authentic brand of black writing the ghetto primitivism of Robert Beck, a.k.a. Iceberg Slim, the pimp-turned-1960s-blaxploitation-novelist who authored such classics as *Pimp: The Story of My Life*, *The Naked Soul of Iceberg Slim*, and *Trick Baby: The Story of a White Negro*.[33]

These knotty attitudes about racial difference and representation reverberated from but also stimulated Russell's obsessive engagement with Charlie Parker, shaping the production and the reception of his novel *The Sound* and biography *Bird Lives!*. *Bird Lives!* is well known to jazz scholars but has been out of general circulation since the mid-1970s, when the widow of Russell's former friend and fellow Bird chronicler, Robert Reisner, initiated copyright infringement litigation that forced Russell to forfeit all of his royalties and his publisher to take the book out of print.[34] As if to underscore the burden that Charlie Parker imposed on those who would deign to represent him in words, Russell turned around and threatened to sue Nat Hentoff for allegedly lifting passages out of *Bird Lives!* in the essay Hentoff wrote on Parker in his 1976 book *Jazz Is*.[35] For Russell, chasing the Bird was an obsession that became a nightmare, a psychological burden he sublimated into years of writing, only to have the fruit of his efforts wither on a vine of bitter resentment. The later legal contretemps aside, Russell knew earlier on, at the time of *The Sound*'s publication, that he had courted serious controversy by engaging Charlie Parker as a vexing social subject rather than as a bloodless object of musical analysis—and one who fascinates but, in the manner of Cortázar's Johnny Carter, also makes claims on his interpreters.

Writing Charlie Parker into history has proved to be a difficult task. During his lifetime, Parker was given short shrift in the jazz press and either completely neglected or tortuously misrepresented in the mainstream media.[36] The black press was no better: the African American writer John A. Williams has noted that the severest criticism levied against Parker at the time he was committed to Camarillo came from "the pretentious Negro press of Los Angeles."[37] Few newspapers of any kind ran an obituary for Parker, and several that did failed to list his proper name, burying him as "Yardbird Parker." *Life* published a big story on bebop at the height of Parker's career but failed to mention him, concentrating instead on cabalistic subcultural emblems such as Dizzy Gillespie's secret handshake. In his one surviving television appearance, Parker, billed second to trumpeter Gillespie, stares down Earl Wilson, the ingratiating emcee who spouts platitudes about jazz's color- and creed-blindness before asking if the musicians have anything to say before they play. "They say that music speaks louder than words, so we'd rather voice our opinion that way," Parker says through gritted teeth. The fact that Gillespie garnered more mainstream recognition than Parker might suggest that Parker's marginality was more a function of his artistic persona than of his race. Black musicians like Gillespie skilled in the role of the comic entertainer better fit both the racial codes and the leisure desires that prevailed among most white and black Americans in the 1940s and 1950s. The drummer Art Blakey said that Parker held no special meaning for black people because "they never heard of him."[38] Blakey, who often lectured his audiences on jazz's orphan status in its own family, was exaggerating for effect. But it is surely significant that the group that gave Parker his strongest public embrace, the "beatniks," did so as a countercultural impulse of rebellion against the hypocrisies and banalities of American society. Ralph Ellison argued that these educated, white, middle-class youth seized on Parker as a "thrice alienated" figure—as a black man, a drug addict, and an artist of the avant garde—in fellowship with their own struggles for creativity and meaning in a culture of mass conformity plagued by the threat of nuclear annihilation.[39]

Ellison's observation that the dominant image of Charlie Parker was as a "white" hero underscores the racial crossover dynamics at work in most Bird mytho-biography. Nat Hentoff suggests in *Jazz Is* that "more than any critic or biographer, it would more likely be a novelist, a black novelist, who might eventually illuminate those parts of the cold inner darkness that finally took over all of Bird."[40] But when Hentoff endorsed the 1988 film *Bird* in a very friendly interview with director Clint Eastwood, he implicitly validated Eastwood's claim to an authenticity based on having grown up in Oakland, California "around this kind of music" and thus knowing the "black experience . . . as well as any white person around."[41] The sternest critics of *Bird* were unimpressed with Eastwood's feel for black culture. Stanley Crouch panned the film as an exercise in "crude hipster mythology" that removed Parker from the "bittersweet intricacies of African American life." "[Eastwood's *Bird* is] just a colored man with a saxophone, a white girlfriend, and a drug problem," Crouch wrote. "When he dies you are almost relieved."[42]

If Crouch's critique of Eastwood's film provides a brief glimpse into the stakes involved in racing after (and race-ing) Charlie Parker, an analysis of the racial politics attending the writing and the reception of Ross Russell's *The Sound* and *Bird Lives!* provides a full view.

Pulp Addiction

The Sound, a largely forgotten and neglected jazz novel, was published by E. P. Dutton in 1961. It is not the cloth Dutton first edition, however, but the 1962 MacFadden paperback, with all of its pulp novel trimmings, that most effectively conveys the novel's bid for singular authenticity in the depiction of the jazz life. "Of the few novels that have seen the jazz world from the inside,

The Sound is unique," screams the promotional pitch on the paperback's back cover. Promising such picaresque features of "the real jazz world" as "the tawdry grime of quick love in a nightclub dressing room" and "the grip, the choking stranglehold of heroin on a trumpeter who is a national hero," the novel leads the reader to expect a "convincing" and "honest" story that "pounds to an absorbing finish."[43]

Writers often distance themselves from the mercenary promotional rhetoric with which publishers adorn their work, but in the case of *The Sound* one is struck by a strong affinity between the tabloid-style back cover and the contents of the novel itself. The novel is full of juicy narrative hooks; cheap thrills; countless incidents of "quick love" marked by varying degrees of tawdriness; luridly precise descriptions of narcotics trade and usage; terse and idiomatic popular culture details intensifying the novel's sense of contemporaneity; carefully etched cityscapes suggesting, in the manner of Dashiell Hammett, Raymond Chandler, and Edward Hopper, the inner emotional lives of their inhabitants.

Knowledgeable readers of *The Sound* immediately recognized it as a *roman à clef*, the trumpeter character Red Travers a stand-in for Charlie Parker. Travers is a musical genius of Mozartian heft, the "High Priest of the New Sounds,"[44] a heroic but tragic romantic artist who singlehandedly turns the jazz world on its head, simultaneously becoming increasingly consumed by his own excesses and ultimately destroying himself. To Bernie Rich, the white, middle-class, masters-degree-holding pianist who serves as *The Sound*'s third-person narrator, Travers embodies the "Negro core of jazz,"[45] a holy grail of emotional, existential truth. Steeped in the ancient blues, but now a "heedless Pied Piper adrift in the carnival of postwar confusion,"[46] Travers played like "he had a grudge against the world."[47] Despite his misanthropy, however, he's an orgiastic cult hero to a national horde of hipsters, a man of Rabelaisian appetites, consuming food, drugs, and sex in epic, almost mythical proportions. Living only for these appetites and for his music, he is childish, rude, dishonest, and paranoid. He is "fiercely possessive" of his sexual partners, whom he mounts with "empowering virile odor and primitive genital force."[48] Flamboyantly generous one moment, sinister and violent the next, Travers compels from his tribal followers a mixture of hero worship, morbid fascination, and horror.

He's smart—devilishly so. In spontaneous protest of an Italian club owner's rapacity, he improvises a medley of Italian folk songs and opera arias, fracturing their familiar forms with hyper-fast bop tempi and chord progressions. But he's also out of control: he follows this brilliant satire by urinating in the club's telephone booth. His intelligence is that of the street-smart pimp: he has the wiles and cunning to survive the day, but has no vision of the future, much less an understanding of his artistic importance and potential place in history. He treats record sessions and club dates not as cultural work, but as sources of quick cash to feed his habit.

In private correspondence with Russell about *The Sound*, Martin Williams registered skepticism about the Red Travers character, which he simply assumed to be inspired by Russell's relationship with Charlie Parker. Williams had been introduced to bebop in Los Angeles during a World War II stint in the navy, and he was a frequent visitor to Russell's record store. The two men respected each other's critical intelligence, and Russell had solicited Williams's opinion about the novel. In a critique that Russell found penetrating, Williams wondered whether the novel's structuring as a melodrama had led Russell to render moralistic judgments about his character's basic humanity, and in so doing had made it impossible for the reader to grasp Travers's (Parker's) complexity and greatness. By employing the melodramatic form, Williams argued, Russell narrowed the terms by which the Travers/Parker character could be assessed: he could only be either a good man or a bad one. Counting himself lucky never to have met Parker, Williams hinted that Russell's vexed personal relationship with Bird had clouded his efforts. *The Sound* was too much like a detective story, Williams contended, "where the whole point is to find the guilty one and point the finger, and it is always somebody else. In life it is never really somebody else, but everybody."[49] Russell wrote back protesting his own innocence, and defending his choice of the melodramatic literary mode:

> In trying to cast the material of Bird's life and Bird's time, I was struck by its own melodramatic qualities. What else was his life, considered as a series of biographical events . . . than a melodrama? [How] else can you evaluate Lover Man, Camarillo State Hospital, pissing on the floor of a night club, disembarking from a stopped train in the middle of a desert to look for a doctor and a fix, drinking iodine, and winding up on a slab in a morgue?[50]

Albert Goldman was more sanguine about *The Sound*, calling it in a published review "a slightly disguised but essentially faithful portrait of . . . the greatest embodiment of the jazz life, Charlie Parker." Esteeming the novel as "a courageous piece of work," Goldman credited Russell with "a love for his subject . . . so great that he can admit all the evil, all the coarseness, all the egotistical violence of Parker and yet make us admire the extraordinary strength and truth of his genius."[51] Leonard Feather, well known as an early critical supporter of bebop and as an intimate of Parker's, also recognized Bird in Red Travers, but his assessment of the character and of Russell's novel was just the opposite of Goldman's. Despite crediting Russell with having "been more a part of the [jazz] scene than any previous writer" and for a "very well-developed awareness of the struggle between art and business," Feather took umbrage at *The Sound*'s "dreadful clichés and stock characterizations," its "farrago of pseudo-philosophical reflections and wildly exaggerated hip talk," and the "tiresome inevitability of [its] link between jazz and narcotics." Feather's judgment was withering: "Charlie Parker," he wrote, "understood more about Ross Russell than Ross Russell understood about Parker."[52] Feather preferred to remember Bird "when he had the drugs under control and was able to lead the life of the square, driving to Coney Island for hot dogs and beer, charming my [British] father by assuming his best upper class accent and making eloquent small talk."[53]

As Feather notes, *The Sound* revels in the postwar vernacular of jazz musicians and their ardent followers. Russell's Menckenite interest in an authentic American language directs his ear to the hip argots of sexual desire and racial negotiation. One of his male characters describes another's sexual ineptitude as putting him "on the Jersey side of the snatch play."[54] His ultra-hip white female protagonist declares herself "a queer for spades." She has big eyes for Red Travers even though he's "one stud that just can't tog up"[55]— i.e., not a good dresser. A hipster lamenting an instance of southern bigotry says, "Like somebody got to straighten them peckerheads on the corn pone side of the black and white split."[56] The black drummer Hassan, who has hipped himself to "the Mohammedan thing," wearing soft leather slippers, learning a smattering of Arabic, and carrying around English translations of the Koran and Omar Khayyam's *The Rubaiyat* ("The craziest, dad. The original jive! Old Omar really laid down a righteous spiel!"[57]), discovers the advantages this mask holds for dealing with Jim Crow:

> Like, I'd walk up to some big fat-assed cracker policemans and fold my hands inside my sleeves and bow and ask him directions, like where the A-rab consulate was located. . . . Yes, daddy, this rig makes it every time below the line.[58]

Leonard Feather's dismissal of *The Sound* singles out Hassan's voice as especially affected—"a heavily caricatured combination of Wingy Manone, Babs Gonzales, and the first edition of Cab Calloway's *Jive Dictionary*." In retrospect, Russell's rhetorical strategies are less interesting for the degree of their authenticity, their fidelity to a "real" jazz world and its argot, than they are as evidence of Russell's self-positioning as a figure of ethnographic and critical white intellectual authority. One cannot help but notice, on this count, the heterosexist and racial anxieties coursing through the novel, nor the way in which exoticized Others are brought on stage to allay these anxieties to permit some sort of narrative resolution. Raymond Chandler hyped *his* virility, for example, by describing an effeminate male character as speaking softly "in the manner of a sultan suggesting a silk noose for a harem lady whose tricks had gone stale."[59] Russell, for his part, makes the drug peddler of *The Sound* a homosexual with campy orientalist touches: named Fat Girl (and loosely modeled after the bebop trumpeter Fats Navarro), the character has "large, liquid eyes that swam under beautifully modeled lids and lashes," reminiscent of an "eastern idol."[60] When the oversexed black trumpeter invites the libidinally challenged white pianist to "go three in the feathers," the "chick" who is "hip to the play" is a Puerto Rican exotic dancer. "I mean these Spic women really give you something in the feathers," Red says to Bernie.[61]

In a rhetorical maneuver elevating the tough-minded masculinity of the jazz critic/expert over the soft-boiled femininity of the jazz fan, Russell describes the hipster cabals in jazz clubs as sharing "the same figure-S postures, the same inscrutable faces, bright eyes, and soft-wristed feminine gestures."[62] Such gender coding of jazz authority may partially account for the overwhelmingly positive reception *The Sound* enjoyed among the leading white jazz critics, excepting Feather and Williams. Given their anxieties about their own intellectual legitimacy and their progressive liberal efforts to propagandize the middle-class "normality" of the jazz musician, these late-1950s jazz critics might have been expected to condemn the foregrounding of kinky sex and hard drugs in Russell's depiction of the jazz life. Significantly, however, with the exception of Feather's heated pan and Williams's exacting but friendly rebuke, the major jazz critics pronounced Russell's novel not just a success but something of a landmark statement. Nat Hentoff called *The Sound* "the first real jazz novel."[63] Ralph Gleason's review in the *San Francisco Chronicle* said that "Ross Russell has written one of the very few fictional treatments of the jazz world that has validity." In a review in the *Village Voice* that he admitted was hard to write because of his jealousy, Robert Reisner declared *The Sound* "the finest novel ever written about jazz."[64]

Interestingly, the mainstream press, habitually denounced by the critics for pushing a jazz-junk-sex line, appeared in its reception of *The Sound* to have fully adopted the critic's jazz-as-good-works missionary posture. Deeming the book "not for libraries," the *Library Journal* charged Russell with harming jazz and "abet[ing] the squares by perpetuating a stereotype of the musician as ignorant, amoral, and dope-destroyed." The reviewer found Russell's descriptions of club dates and jam sessions "occasionally believable," but characterized the "constant 'all-reet, daddy-o' dialogue" as "tiresome and embarrassing, and pervaded by anachronistic 1961 beatnikese."[65] A notice in the *Saturday Review* satirically suggested that "*The Sound* has the ring of the real jazz world, which to most of us is as foreign as Timbuktu and, from the way the author portrays its inhabitants, just as exotic."[66] A *Newsweek* review titled "Jazz and Junkies" absolved Russell on the junk theme ("Beethoven had his red wine and cirrhosis of the liver; the late jazz master Charlie Parker had his drugs") but lamented the "revolting clichés of hipster talk ('Like, solos from another planet, man! Dig!')."[67] The reviewer for a West Virginia newspaper, perhaps swayed by Leonard Feather's concerns, wondered when "someone is going to have the inspiration to write a novel about a jazz musician who doesn't drink and dope himself to death."[68]

Robert Reisner and several other jazz critics defended Russell against these attacks. Warning of the dangers of a distorting overcompensation in the vogue for "clean" jazz books, Dan Morgenstern wrote that "if jazz is an art, and surely it is, it is pure folly and a particularly nasty species of Comstockery to pretend that jazz artists live and act like choir boys. That should not be construed to mean that all jazz musicians are drug addicts, lechers, and notorious characters . . . but that's not Russell's contention either." "Plain folks made poor subjects for novels," Morgenstern suggested, "and the particular era of jazz which Russell deals with here was not notable for sweetness and light."[69] Whitney Balliett, underscoring the authority of Russell's experience as a jazz impresario, said that Russell "makes it plain that the world of jazz is populated largely by clean-living middle-class Negroes"; in the case of Travers-Parker, however, Russell was dealing with an "atypical human being . . . whose profession is all but incidental."[70]

Though Balliett felt that Travers "eventually overpowers Russell," forcing him to end the book with "a clap of melodrama," he esteemed *The Sound* as "an accomplished *critical novel*" and "an even better *novel*." Given that it was Balliett who earlier had demeaned the "hot gassy prose" of the fan magazines that dominated American jazz commentary from the 1930s down through the war years,[71] he might have been expected to decry the steam rising off of *The Sound*'s more lurid passages. On the contrary, however, Balliett (in judgments later blurbed on the inside front cover of the MacFadden paperback) found Russell's prose as "plain as a dishrag, never . . . getting between his material and the reader," and his rendering of several scenes and characters "indelible," especially noting the "monstrous homosexual drug peddler" Fat Girl.

Clearly, Russell had touched a nerve with the jazz critical fraternity. Reisner suggested a subtext:

> No one could have written the book except Mr. Russell and perhaps a few other ofays who found themselves pioneering proselytizers of an unappreciated art created by embittered and exploited Negroes. Some of these white middlemen in the [1940s] were talented men in certain other areas, but because they were

so affected by what they heard, they pushed their own personalities into the background and touted jazz, carrying the monkey of inferiority on their back in the form of always knowing it was the Negro who created the music. It was . . . a psychic immolation on the cross of jazz.[72]

Reisner, who produced a series of Charlie Parker performances in 1953 and 1954 at a downtown New York club called The Open Door, was the Village hipster of the jazz critical establishment, a man who liked to say that he based his life on the holy trinity of sex, jazz, and psychoanalysis.[73] Where Balliett wrote with cosmopolitan sophistication in the New Yorker, Hentoff and Williams sought Partisan Review–level credibility in the Jazz Review, and Morgenstern tried to elevate the discourse of the fan magazines Down Beat and Metronome, Reisner fit jazz into the alternative cultural format of the Village Voice and relished placing freelance pieces in Playboy and the more specialized stroke books Nugget and Cavalier. He was convinced that "art is a form of sublimation and is created by neurotics and compulsion-ridden people, not by the happy, nine-to-five family man."[74] Reisner's purpose in putting together his 1962 collection of oral testimonies, Bird: The Legend of Charlie Parker, was to show Bird as the supreme icon of hipsterism, an anarchic, amoral spirit, overcivilized to the point of decadence. The suit that Reisner's widow brought against Russell on the grounds that Bird Lives! plagiarized from interviews in Reisner's book was petty and craven. It was also based on an underlying truth: Reisner and Russell were mining the same psychosexual-racial ore of Bird mythology.

While other critics were not of the intellectual temperament to hang themselves in "psychic immolation" on the "cross of jazz," martyrs to the cause of guilt-ridden white privilege, what is notable in their response to The Sound is an avoidance of the book's full reckoning with racial politics, an avoidance so conspicuous as to invite speculation of subconscious anxieties. Feather and other critics may have disagreed over Russell's depiction of a Charlie Parker–like character, but they were united in assuming that their main responsibility in passing judgment on The Sound was to assess Russell's handling of this character. But what is much more interesting about the book, and what the book's narrative strategy in fact highlights, is the drama of the pianist Bernie Rich's anguished struggle with his whiteness: his feelings of sexual and artistic inadequacy, his castrating sense that for all of his assets—masters workshops with Schoenberg, compositional and arrangement skills that ensure steady employment with a Kenton-like big band, a Greenwich Village apartment with a small Steinway grand and state-of-the-art hi-fi equipment—he nevertheless finds himself taking coital seconds on the shopworn blonde groupie with whom he has bonded in common worship of a black junkie. Son of a doctor, Bernie often finds Red's world "as remote from his own experience as the witch doctor's art lies from the practice of clinical medicine."[75] But when Bernie, chasing some of Red's magic, turns to heroin and needs Red's guidance on shooting up, he's struck by the thought, while watching Red neatly tap a vein, that this ghetto god would have made a good doctor. Whitney Balliett was being optimistic, if not obtuse, when he said that "Russell miraculously makes the white reader see himself with the black man's eyes."[76] For what *The Sound* actually does is make the white reader see himself through the eyes of a white man facing his own benighted vision of blackness.[77]

Bernie learns something about the new jazz: he overcomes some of his Brubeckish earnestness and becomes a solid "feed pianist," a good chord man clearing the runway under Red's virtuosic flights. But what he really learns is that jazz "was still the language of the Negro, the Negro's gift to culture." And it's his conceit—as it was the conceit of many white jazz critics—that "the Negro still didn't understand that he had made [this gift]."[78] Hung up on this aesthetic and intellectual asymmetry, Bernie defaults to a position of white safety and power. When he takes a pass on the *ménage à trois* proposed by Red, he backslides into squareness, but also, in the logic of the narrative, saves his life. At the end of the novel, in what Russell describes as a "show of Latin melodramatics," the dancer pulls "the old Spanish streetwalker's trick."[79] Feigning affection, she asks for a goodbye kiss—Red is headed to France, where an incurably Afrophiliac Parisian critic has arranged some concert dates. With catlike swiftness (if not a clear motive) she pulls a knife and slashes him from temple to chin. After Red chases her through the streets of Spanish Harlem, disarms her and plunges the knife into her stomach, a cop shoots Red and watches him die. In an epilogue saturated with knowing irony, Bernie is comfortably ensconced as the musical director of a Hollywood studio, laying tracks for a B-movie about an up-from-the-ghetto jazz musician. "Originally the kid had been colored," Russell writes, "but it hadn't taken them long to make him white."[80] It's a pulp-fiction ending, but one with a twist. The cop, significantly, is a black man, one of the first on the Harlem force, hired with precisely this sort of incident in mind. Who, after all, could "raise the ugly cry of race prejudice," the narrator cynically suggests, in a case of one black killing another?[81]

And who's to blame, really, when a musician doesn't understand—as Travers in an earlier scene apparently doesn't, and as Russell badly needed to believe Charlie Parker didn't—that when it comes to making music, "the cream of the thing isn't the cash in hand—it's the [royalty] revenue over the years"?[82] It is difficult not to conclude that the subtext of Russell's novel is an implicit but unmistakable plea for absolution from the charge of racial exploitation in his own dealings with Parker. The political economy Russell sets up in *The Sound* accurately reflects the racial colonialism of the actual postwar jazz world: Red Travers and the other black musicians control the expression of the "Negro core of jazz" while performing on the bandstand, but every other aspect of the *sound's* fate as creative property—its codification and commodification as notated and recorded *music*—is controlled by whites.

Despite his trenchant critique of Hollywood's deracination of black jazz, Russell is complacent about this racial division of labor in the jazz community itself; indeed, he naturalizes and romanticizes this division, suggesting that to have things otherwise would be to undermine the roles that blacks and whites have chosen for themselves. Hence, as a matter of principle, he has Red Travers eschewing the act of writing down his music. "If you got the music inside, why, you don't need no notes set down on papers, by somebody else, you got your own, and they're better," he says.[83] When Bernie "inadvertently" steals one of Red's unwritten compositions—inadvertent because it is only in hindsight that he realizes how thoroughly Red's musical ideas have colonized his mind—he voluntarily gives Red the composer's credit and suggests that the two form a writing partnership. "You have a fortune kicking around in your head but it isn't worth a dime until somebody helps you mine it," Bernie tells Red.[84] But when Red's erratic work habits undermine the partnership, Bernie concludes that it was futile to challenge the natural order of things. A paragon of white paternalism, Bernie is sure he knows what's best for his black friends: he's concerned about Red's well-being, but in the manner of one whose job it is to be concerned.

The "Existential Hero Par Excellence"

Following *The Sound's* publication, Russell's concern for Charlie Parker's legacy came to be equated with concern for his own fate in the marketplace and in the literary court of opinion. When he wrote Albert Goldman to thank him for his positive review of *The Sound*, Russell also complained that the book "has been an outstanding flop," garnering disappointingly little attention outside of jazz circles. The hardcover version sold only 3,200 copies, the paperback rights netted Russell only $1,400, and Warner Brothers and United Artists had nixed his screenplay pitches. Some of Russell's readers, echoing his friendly jazz critic reviewers, told him that *The Sound* was the best jazz novel ever written. One, Safford Chamberlain, went so far as to suggest a comparison with *Moby Dick*, the jazz world representing for Russell "the same sort of comprehensive metaphor that whaling presented for Melville."

The literary establishment showed no inclination to make room for Russell in their canon, however. Irked by this snubbing, Russell used Goldman to vent his opinion that American letters had succumbed to the "growing pressures of Madison Avenue, television, bad American movies, and the whole discount-house mass consumer." This anticommercial rant was quite odd coming from a former pulp writer who was angling for his own movie contract. But Russell had a receptive correspondent in Albert Goldman, who was frantically trying to carve out a living peddling his professorial capital in the world of mass-market journalism.[85]

Russell and Goldman were drawn together even more strongly by their shared preoccupation with Charlie Parker, their kindred devotion to an underappreciated cultural hero. Over the better part of the next two decades, Russell and Goldman engaged in a fascinating correspondence touching on jazz and the ascendancy of black culture, the exigencies of freelance writing, and their mutual professional and personal struggles. In the 1960s and early 1970s, the correspondence hummed with optimism: Russell was working on a biography of Charlie Parker, Goldman on his biography of Lenny Bruce (Parker's "verbal counterpart," said Russell), and together the two figured that they had cornered the market on post–World War II hipsterism.

For Goldman, Charlie Parker's death signified both the end of jazz as a creative process and the lost possibility of a genuinely meaningful alternative culture. In his review of *The Sound*, Goldman questioned the jazz critical establishment's reigning assumptions about Parker's significance. Morgenstern, Hentoff, and Balliett defended Russell's treatment of the Travers/Parker character on the grounds of its historical accuracy but made clear their desire for a jazz world freed of its associations with drugs and deviance. Goldman, by contrast, argued that the whole point of bebop was to fashion "a defiant new way of life" that enshrined irony, mockery, and underground ritual as coping mechanisms against cultural despair. "Recent criticism has struggled vainly to dissociate the jazz life from the art of jazz," Goldman wrote;

> We have been told again and again that dope has nothing to do with music; that the anti-social behavior of jazz musicians is merely an accident of their race or class; that the fiercely self-destructive dives of such great jazzmen as Charlie Parker are merely regrettable instances of psychic infirmity associated with artistic ability. What modern criticism has failed to recognize—or more accurately, what it fitfully recognizes and uneasily rejects—is the essential connection between a kind of being or vision and a style of art.[86]

That kind of being and style of art had been consummated, Goldman argued in a series of writings in the early 1960s, in the symbiotic relation between

Parker's "violent and erratic personality" and his unexcelled improvisational abilities. Convinced that "in jazz . . . suffering and greatness [are] inseparable,"[87] Goldman claimed that Bird "had inside him a bottomless well of frustration, particularly oral frustration, the kind that leads to overeating, alcoholism, and drug addiction"[88]—and also to dizzying levels of creativity. Comparing Parker to Beethoven in his "passionate commitment to naked self-expression,"[89] Goldman portrayed Parker as the greatest Romantic artist in American music history. According to Goldman, Parker's only true heir was the bebop pianist Bud Powell, who was crippled by bouts of psychosis, and who had "Parker's power, anger, and defiance and [was] infected with the same racial virus that embittered Bird's life."[90]

In his analysis of the ambivalent racial attitudes of the Reconstruction-era collectors of slave songs, Ronald Radano argues that these pioneering white American folklorists were guided by German romanticist ideology in their search for a primordial "folk" expression.[91] These codifiers and celebrants of black folk culture came out of New England abolitionist families and were engaged in a project of progressive racial reform. But they were also beholden to the privileges of a racialized social order, and in Radano's sharp reading, even as they exalted black difference they were also seeking to contain it. Albert Goldman's writings about black music a century later during the civil rights movement—the "second Reconstruction"—express some of the same "paradoxical moods of praise and reproach, desire and disgust" that Radano has identified in the slave song collector's attitudes toward the music of the recently emancipated slaves. Goldman's "hard-on for authentic black culture" made black pain an enabling condition of white pleasure: by the mid-1960s, when jazzmen like Archie Shepp and Miles Davis were adopting aggressively defiant public stances, Goldman took to delivering jazz postmortems in a shrill tone of disgust:

> About the time I started listening to rock in the mid-Sixties, I stopped listening to jazz. I was fed up with the bad vibes, the arrogance, hostility, and craziness of the jazz scene. Guys getting knifed to death at the pimp bar in Birdland. Hysterical Jewish managers right out of the old Berlin cabarets. Arrogant spades sticking it up every white man's ass.[92]

Goldman's construction of Parker as primitive genius was part of a larger nostalgic idealization of the 1940s as a summa moment of jazz authenticity, a modernist synthesis in which jazz's folk materials were taken to their logical artistic ends. Acknowledging the brilliance of Parker's advanced harmonic concepts, Goldman nevertheless prized the saxophonist's connection to his "native soil." If Parker's abstract shapings did not directly reproduce the "whole rich rhetoric of Negro speech"—the anthropomorphic growls, drawls, shouts, and squeals that early jazz horn players and Parker himself in his Kansas City days employed in an effort to foreground black oral and kinetic expressiveness—those vernacular resources, Goldman argued, were always implicit in his creative imagination. "Bird was a Bartok who sublimated a potent folk essence without losing any of its pungency," Goldman suggested.[93]

But by the time of Parker's death in 1955, by Goldman's reckoning, jazz had already begun succumbing to impure influences. Goldman's writing about post-1955 jazz takes on a starkly gendered vocabulary, with jazz authenticity coded in a language of overt masculinity, jazz fakery in a feminized vocabulary of wily make-believe and deception. Defining real jazz as "hot, existential get-it-off music," Goldman counted the Third Stream movement's jazz concertos an especially galling travesty: he described the Modern Jazz Quartet under John Lewis as drifting "away from jazz toward the Frenchified, faggotized art music that has always been the black jazzman's idea of 'class.'"[94] Charlie Parker's own late-career experiments with string-and-woodwind orchestras and talk of studying composition were for Goldman musical blunders "strongly motivated by a naive craving for extramusical status."[95] Free jazz was a matter of black jazz musicians "whoring after strange European and Oriental gods."[96] The very fact that the term "soul" became a buzzword with some late-1950s hard-bop musicians signified for Goldman how little real soul these musicians actually had. The ultimate sign of jazz's fatal feminization, however, was the ascendancy of Miles Davis. "Miles was a soul man," Goldman wrote, "a sound, a black Bogey. He was also an insufferable prick. Posturing onstage in his shades, continental suits and bantyweight boxer's physique, he played the role of the jazz genius."[97] But he wasn't, by Goldman's lights, a real jazz genius like Charlie Parker. Davis was a poseur, a mime, "jazz's Marcel Marceau"; when Miles played with Parker in the 1940s, "his role," Goldman wrote, "was that of femme foil to Bird's aggressively thrusting horn."[98]

The terms on which Goldman lionizes Parker and denigrates Davis—a pattern that Russell duplicates—reveal a quite narrow, static notion of postwar black masculinity. Krin Gabbard argues that Miles Davis was the progenitor of a "post-phallic" trumpet style that has been influential in shaping a nuanced bourgeois image of black masculinity purposely distinct from black working-class traditions of male boisterousness evident in early jazz, urban rhythm and blues, and more recently rap and hip-hop.[99] Among post-1960 black male intellectuals prominent in challenging the historically white-dominated institution of jazz criticism for control of the public meaning of jazz, Miles Davis has reigned as a sovereign symbol of stylish masculinity, restless creativity, and black power. From Amiri Baraka ("I wanted to be that hip, that whatever it was I felt you were. I wanted to be that. All my life."[100]) to Quincy Troupe ("he was clean as a broke dick dog, a ladies' man and didn't take shit off no one . . . the legendary slick man of impeccable style and class, he of the kiss-my-ass attitude and stance, the black Romeo"[101]) to Greg Tate ("Miles Davis *is* the black aesthetic . . . the objectified projection of our darkest desires, a model for any black artist who wants to thoroughly interpenetrate Western domains of power and knowledge with Africanizing authority"),[102] the pattern is clear. Goldman's divergence from these constructions of authentic black manhood in his valorization of Parker as the dominant signifier of jazz-inspired black masculinity derives from a debatable interpretation of bebop's cultural dynamics.

Bebop traded heavily on imitative parody and developed a glossary of stylized mannerisms that went far beyond the figure of the assertively virile horn. The very theatricality of bebop performance called attention to itself *as* a performance, a display. In so doing, bebop's male performers positioned themselves as objects of the spectatorial gaze, a position many scholars have argued is normatively assigned in Western aesthetic traditions to the feminine pole of the gender continuum. It was trumpeter Dizzy Gillespie, not Parker, who was most closely identified with those extramusical elements of bebop's subcultural style—berets, secret handshakes, jive talk—that fueled the mainstream media's depiction of the music as a weird cultish spectacle. Parker, in fact, is said to have condemned Gillespie's foppish stage antics and media-friendly posture as Uncle Tommish.[103] Intriguingly, for reasons that are never made fully clear in their published jazz criticism or their private correspondence, Goldman and Russell both thought that Gillespie's role in bebop's musical development had been overestimated by other critics.[104] Goldman's and Russell's rebukes of Davis and Gillespie might be explained as an anxiety over the trumpeters' feminized mass-culture gestures threatening to castrate Parker's masculine autonomous high art.

It needs immediately to be emphasized that these gender categories— which echo Theodor Adorno's tendentious dismissal of American popular music and Andreas Huyssen's characterization of a modernist "great divide" between masculinized high art and feminized mass culture[105]—reflect a European intellectual tradition that may make less sense in the context of African American, or even popular American, musical performance and reception. Gabbard—influenced by Steven Cohan's analysis of Fred Astaire's masculine spectacle—offers as an example of African American performative masculinity the pelvic thrusts that were part of Gillespie's stage presentation in the 1940s and 1950s, suggesting that Gillespie might have been offering a wry commentary on received notions (i.e., phallic power) of black masculine sexuality.[106] It is important to note that no black writer of the postwar or post-1960 generations has stigmatized Gillespie as an Uncle Tom. On the contrary, Gillespie is often celebrated as his jazz generation's master of the black vernacular art of "signifying," and as such, the shrewd vindicator of Louis Armstrong's persona of the comic entertainer. On this view, Armstrong's mugging and Gillespie's jiving were not instances of Tomming, but of an artfully subversive mimicry that ingeniously critiqued the racist attitudes of their culture industry sponsors.

The way gender plays differently in white and black jazz discourse points to more fundamental differences of representation across the color line. As Jon Panish perceptively observes, white and black writers of the 1950s and early 1960s tended to articulate divergent fictional images of Charlie Parker.[107] White writers, seeking to universalize Parker's condition, emphasized his travails as an artist living in a conformist philistine society. Black writers, on the other hand, tended to focus on his struggles as a black man living in a racist society. In Jack Kerouac's *The Subterraneans* (1958) and *Mexico City Blues* (1959), Parker appears as a solemn, suffering martyr resigned to his social victimization, apotheosizing in performance into a Buddha-like symbol of kindness and love.[108] By contrast, in James Baldwin's short story "Sonny's Blues" (1957), the character Sonny, a bebop pianist who embraces Charlie Parker as his hero, is a defiant man, embittered by racism, purveyor of music that brims with explosive rage.[109] Amiri Baraka's 1964 play *The Dutchman* goes even further in using Parker as the symbol of righteous black anger and violence. Bitterly denouncing whites' appropriation of Parker as *their* culture hero, Baraka has one of his characters say: "Charlie Parker? Charlie Parker? All the hip white boys scream for Bird. And Bird saying 'Up your ass, feeble-minded ofay! Up your ass.' And they sit there talking about the tortured genius of Charlie Parker. Bird would've played not a note of music if he just walked up to East Sixty-seventh Street and killed the first ten white people he saw. Not a note!"[110]

It is not that white writers discounted violence and aggression as central animating forces in postwar black jazz. But, as Panish argues, whereas for Baldwin and Baraka the figure of the angry black jazzman represented the *collective* desires and historical grievances of the black community, white writers who seized on jazz as a symbol of resistance and nonconformity elevated the concerns of the *individual*. In Baldwin's "Sonny's Blues," Sonny's older brother, a schoolteacher who harbors all the traditional black middle-class suspicions about jazz, experiences an epiphany when he finally goes to hear his brother play. The music both stirs his memories of a painful past and liberates him from the oppressive burden of those memories: the modern jazz he has blamed for his brother's heroin habit has become the agent, through its evocation of racial memory, of his own spiritual transcendence. The concept of jazz as black cultural memory—in particular as a mode of socialization into African American manhood—is conspicuously absent from the work of white Beat and Leftist writers of the period. In their critique of American cold war ideology and dominant white middle-class culture, these writers embraced jazz as a hallmark of "personal freedom," grafting African American rebellion onto their own programs of political and cultural dissent. The most famous example was Norman Mailer's 1957 essay, "The White Negro: Superficial Reflections on the Hipster." A landmark of 1950s dissidence considered by some a crucial harbinger of 1960s countercultural attitudes, Mailer's essay spoke to the existential angst of whites who felt alienated in Eisenhowerian America. As an antidote to the "psychic havoc of the concentration camps and the bomb" as well as the dehumanization of the suburbs and the Organization Man ethic, Mailer urged white identification with black hipsters, whom he imagined as id-centered hedonists living for drug-induced kicks and other Dionysian pleasures available only outside the inhibiting strictures of totalitarian U.S. civilization. Mailer's white Negro countered the absurdities and conformities of post–World War II America through an insistent focus on the body, especially its circuits of sexual energy. For Mailer, the search for meaning in an insane world leads to the viscera and the genitals; the prescribed existential response to the horrors of Auschwitz and Hiroshima and the monstrous banality of Leavittown is a good orgasm. And jazz, in Mailer's formulation, is orgasm: "it is the music of orgasm, good orgasm and bad," it is the art form of "instantaneous existential states" that communicates by saying, "'I feel this, and now you do too.'"[111]

Mailer has been roundly criticized for his narrow, self-serving reading of black culture, particularly his implicit stereotyping of the black jazz musician, whom others chose to see not as an id-dominated night crawler, but as an ego-resolved middle-class professional struggling with mastery of an exacting craft.[112] Mailer's fantasy of the black man as a purely instinctual creature serves as the leading example of white writers, in Panish's words, "distort[ing] African American rebellion to meet their own psychological, political, and cultural needs."[113] Paramount among these needs is the consolidation of a sense of masculine identity relevant to the cultural moment. Eric Lott has said that Mailer's essay "codifies the renegade ethic of [white] male sexuality conceived out of and projected onto black men."[114] Mailer's imaginary black man facing "a life of constant humiliation or ever-threatening danger" who has learned to follow "the need of his body" becomes through cross-racial projection the white man's equipment for living in the nuclear world. Lott, in his book *Love and Theft*, has shown how nineteenth-century American white working-class men looked to black slaves for affective structures of feeling missing from the disciplining structures of industrialization.[115] Albert Goldman's appropriation of Charlie Parker, a more informed gesture of jazz consumption than Mailer's high-wire act of intellectual minstrelsy, turns on an updated, post–World War II version of the ideal black other: not the grinning, dancing darky but the angry primitive savant.

Most of the Goldman/Russell correspondence took place before Goldman published his Elvis Presley and John Lennon biographies in the 1980s. Many critics panned these books for their bitter view of a world gone mad, their relentlessly lurid depiction of the vices, weaknesses, and neuroses of their subjects.[116] The Goldman of the late 1960s and early 1970s certainly shows signs of the misanthropy later attributed to him by his critics. His was emphatically not the style of radical engagement that Tom Wolfe, in *The Electric Kool-Aid Acid Test*, attributed to hip-Leftist circles—intellectuals who "were always hung up with the feeling that they weren't coming to terms with real life," who felt that "real life belonged to all those funky spades and prize fighters and bull fighters and dock workers and grape pickers and wet backs."[117] Unlike Hunter Thompson, Goldman's was not the story of the straight journalist "going native," embracing the outlaw culture he was writing about. Thompson, in *Hell's Angels: A Strange and Terrible Saga*, wrote approvingly of an aging middle-class car dealer who "broke down under the strain of respectability and answered the call of his genes," chucking career and family for the super-masculine delirium of the motorcycle trade.[118] This served as a blueprint for Thompson himself, who reveled in the role of counterculture icon given to ever more outrageous send-ups of middle-class morality. Goldman, by contrast, veered strangely between Maileresque psychosexual mythology and a modern Solomonic persona in which he fancied himself a bulwark of morality and wisdom holding the line against a rising tide of mindless deviance. At bottom, however, Goldman clung tenaciously to his Romantic faith in the genius rebel, the individual artist-hero who lives in defiance of cultural norms. The virulence of his attacks on Elvis Presley and John Lennon tapped the same root as the intensity of his commitment to the legends of Charlie Parker and Lenny Bruce. Presley and Lennon represented for Goldman the monstrous excesses of celebrity culture: their transgressions revealed nothing so much as an infantile need for attention. Parker and Bruce, by contrast, personified the best possibilities of an ethnically charged, anti-establishment culture: they were authentic outsiders whose trespasses were meaningfully liberating, even if ultimately tragic. Bruce's manner, language, and attitude exemplified the struggles of Brooklyn Italian and Jewish "sidewalk types" of the World War II generation. His hip, cynical humor captured the foibles of men facing their own weaknesses and limitations: it was the humor of self-hatred, sexual failure, alienation, and suppressed violence.[119] Parker transported similar resonances across the color line. "The dominant note [of your biography]," Goldman counseled Russell, "should be that Bird was the one and only man to totally embody the myth of the jazz age—the real jazz age not the literary one in the 1920s."

> Bird was the Existential Hero par excellence. Once you've said that, you can spell it out in terms of the racing-off-the-top lifestyle, the wild, way-out music, the drugs, the sex, gourmandising and boozing, the subcultural uppercuts; the haute culture flirtations. The angry black and the humorously detached hipster. . . . What you should avoid is that crap about "from the honky-tonks of Kansas City to the. . . ." That's the old sentimental nostalgia of the Hollywood jazz film.[120]

Goldman's antisentimental but highly idealized vision of Parker turned on an existentialist coupling of sex and violence. "Short of murder," wrote John Clellon Holmes in one expression of this notion, "sex might be said to be the ultimate existential act. The participant swings perilously back and forth over the abyss of absolute Merging on the one hand and absolute Contingency on the other."[121] Goldman imagined Parker as permanently suspended over this abyss. On Russell's behalf, he interviewed Dr. Robert Freymann, the personal physician of the Baroness Pannonica Koeningswarter and the man who pronounced Parker dead of stomach ulcers and lobar pneumonia at the baroness's apartment in the Stanhope Hotel. Goldman's purpose was to "extract more data" from the doctor. The "data" he was after—but didn't get—was confirmation of a suspicion he and Russell nurtured: that the true immediate cause of Parker's death was a heart seizure suffered while engaged in sex with the baroness.[122]

Failing to nail down this perfect existentialist ending didn't dissuade Goldman from pushing for other Maileresque details. Arguing that "the myth [of Bird] counts for as much or more than the man," Goldman urged Russell to use the perhaps apocryphal story of Parker having once killed a man. Whether true or not, Goldman reasoned, the story had become part of the underground legend of Bird, and hence part of the real story of Parker's cultural meaning.[123] Goldman similarly implored Russell to depict Parker's sexual exploits and drug consumption in mythical terms: it was his job as biographer not to confirm the truth but to fire the imagination, not to fix the boundaries of actuality but to trace the parameters of possibility. "I feel that for such a great cocksman your treatment of [Parker's] sex life is disappointing," Goldman wrote in critiquing a preliminary draft of the manuscript. "How about the faggot angle? You told me that Bird was intimate with [singer] Earl Coleman. [*The Sound*] has him suggesting that another man get in the sack with him and two other chicks. Please make sure you're not copping out in this area. It's a very important theme."[124]

Russell took a pass on the "faggot angle," which seems in any case to have been a fleeting interest on Goldman's part; it foreshadowed a theme he would pursue with voyeuristic fervor in his Elvis Presley and John Lennon biographies, but it was anomalous in the context of his establishment of Bird as hero. More typical of Goldman's masculinist orthodoxy was his response upon hearing that a Hollywood producer interested in *Bird Lives!* was envisioning black comedian Richard Pryor in the lead role: "Pryor [is] a good candidate to play some other clown," Goldman chuckled, "but [he's] a ridiculous choice for a real stud like Bird."[125] Russell also failed to adopt Goldman's Bird-as-cold-blooded-killer existential theme. But Russell's focus on Parker's sexuality, drug usage, and eating habits clearly show the influence of Goldman's pathographic excesses. *Bird Lives!* veers from Russell's lucid documentary social history (what Goldman denigrated as the "crap about 'from the honky-tonks of Kansas City to the . . .'") to a New Journalism–style immersion in Parker's profligate lifestyle. As Siva Vaidhyanathan observes, Russell speaks in several different authorial voices: the New Journalist, or as Goldman called it, the "journalistic fiction" mode, using invented dialogue and status details to give the reader a sense of occupying the same social space as the characters; the academic historian, relating the "facts" of Parker's past uncovered through documentary research and oral interviews; and the memoirist or participant-observer, detailing the author's own interaction with his subject.[126] In the book's acknowledgments Russell claims that his research "has led to interesting adventures and discoveries in areas rapidly becoming forbidden to the white man."[127] Russell told David Amram that *The Sound*'s Red Travers reflects "the persistent image my memory holds of Bird as a willful psychopath, at least insofar as his social behavior was concerned." But Russell claimed that subsequent discussions with black musicians "have helped fill in the far broader canvas" of Parker's personality—especially "Bird's very deep interest in trying to become, in a cultural sense, a citizen of the world, to enjoy the classical things in the common heritage of the educated man, in so far as we can know him in America."[128]

Russell did in fact interview many black musicians for *Bird Lives!*, but none of them play as large a role in the book as the white trumpeter Red Rodney. Rodney, a diminutive, red-headed, freckle-faced Jewish hipster who became a Parker sideman and devotee, is certainly a fascinating character. In an episode in *Bird Lives!* that also figured prominently in the Clint Eastwood film *Bird*, Parker crafts an ingenious solution to the problem of employ-ing Rodney in his otherwise all-black band when it tours the South, where integrated bands ran afoul of local Jim Crow customs. "We'll bill Rodney as Albino Red," Parker says. "I'll have him sing the blues every set."[129] An entertaining, richly ironic send-up of American racial codes, to be sure. But when Stanley Crouch undertook research on his own Parker biography in the early 1980s, he could not find any witnesses to confirm that the southern tour ever took place, raising suspicion as to whether Rodney had fabricated the whole "Albino Red" story.[130] *Bird Lives!* does offer evidence of Parker's as-piration to become a "citizen of the world"—or at least to signify on the role of the cosmopolitan sophisticate, such as Parker greeting Jean Paul Sartre, "I'm glad to meet you, Mr. Sartre. I like your playing very much"[131]—but the book gives infinitely more weight to Parker's larger-than-life derelictions. In a chapter titled "A Queer Night in Brussels," Russell details Parker and Rodney's adventures scoring simon pure heroin from a Belgian pharma-cist. While less sensationalistic than the sustained junkie pornography in Goldman's Lenny Bruce biography, Russell's purplish account obscures from view the significance that Parker himself attached to his European tours: the immense gratification he felt from being honored as a world-class artist.

As an example of Russell's "interesting adventures and discoveries" on his journey into the jazz heart of darkness, consider the following:

> As a cocksman Charlie was much in demand. His sexual energy seemed to flow from the same spring as his music and with comparable force. Years of saxophone playing and the demands on his tongue and lips had given him a tremendous oral effect. One night at the Three Deuces he spotted a beautiful model that excited him and that he wanted. Finishing the set, he went directly to her table and, ignoring the party there, pulled up a chair at her side. Without preamble or introduction, he asked in an eager, charged voice, "Are you going to let me suck your pussy tonight?" The girl blushed deeply; but when the club closed she left with Charlie, not her own escort.[132]

Just how Russell came to know specific details about Parker's sexual habits is not clear. Did he witness this encounter? Or is it, as is more likely, a story he was told by one of his musician or jazz-world informants? Not being so informed, readers are left to submit to the authority of Russell's implied omniscience. But Russell seems himself uncertain of that authority. While clearly showing the influence of Goldman's pop-Freudian speculations and scatological vocabulary, the passage also hints at confusion on Russell's part about how to incorporate Goldman's agenda. It seems curious, for instance, that Russell would have the great "cocksman" so brashly advertise his oral talents. It is worth noting, in fact, that throughout *Bird Lives!* it is not Parker's phallus but his oral skills—erotic, epicurean, musical, verbal—that figure as the touchstone of his manhood. In the book's opening "obbligato," Russell introduces Parker in the dressing room at Billy Berg's with a corporal description: "His body is strong and solid, the body of a workman, a stevedore, or a teamster."[133] But he's not working, he's eating—eating "working-man style," scoffing huge mouthfuls of food and drink. Russell dwells on the prodigiousness of Parker's intake: not one but two of Berg's deluxe Mexican dinners, the *Comida Conquistador*, washed down with three Tecate beers, followed by glassfuls of Gordon's gin. Parker's fetishized mouth—port of superhuman consumption on the one hand, fountain of erotic pleasure and magical sound on the other—is also a source of linguistic versatility. Russell's Parker impresses Benedetti with both his hip argot ("Hey Dean, dig this crazy Mex stuff!") and the affected upper-class voice with which he tells the waiter that he expects the management to cover his dinner tab: "It is customary in the eastern states to extend these courtesies to the artist," Bird announces with just the right dash of stilted mockery.[134]

While casually tossing off bon mots and surfeiting himself gastronomically, Parker bids the compliant Dean Benedetti to pull out his Selmer E-flat alto. Benedetti, a former sax player, notices that Parker is using a number five Rico reed, the stiffest reed made. It's the reed that produces the biggest sound, but it requires massive blowing power and a strong embouchure. Parker challenges Benedetti to try it. Despite years of training which included chewing on towels to strengthen his jaws, Benedetti can barely produce a sound. The slight squeal he forces out of the horn, Russell writes in a tellingly gendered phrase, was "a kind of muted hysteria." If this feminized description weren't obvious enough, Russell makes explicit what's at stake in this blowing contest: it was, he writes, "a test of manhood [Benedetti] had wished to avoid."[135] Russell has Benedetti ascribe his inability to blow with Bird entirely to racial difference. "As he sees it," the passage continues in an awkward narrative fissure, "the fault is that he was born white, an ofay, lacking the power and special knowledge of the black players who dominate jazz. He has missed out on their culture."

Just how Parker's oral prowess relates to black culture—or how an aspiring White Negro like Benedetti might bring his chops up to speed through acquisition of special knowledge—is never explained. More broadly, one of the subtexts of *Bird Lives!* is Russell's struggle to find a larger cultural matrix for Parker's black masculinity, to find some footing for this mythically tragic, rebellious, phallic "Existential Hero" on the ground of everyday black social relations. Independent of Goldman's encouragement, echoing the media buzz generated by the 1965 "Moynihan Report" on the alleged pathologies of the black family,[136] Russell called heightened attention to aspects of Parker's upbringing he thought might explain the problems Parker experienced as an adult. Parker's father left the household when Charlie was still in grade school and his mother manifested traits of the stereotypical strong black woman, facts Russell hypes into a highly questionable if predictable psychological interpretation. "In the protective, permissive, matrifocal soil of the reorganized household," Russell asserts, "Charlie's personality developed like an exotic flower."[137] Russell amplifies this psychological syndrome into a kernel of black jazz history. In a thumbnail sketch of Thelonious Monk, Russell refers to the bebop pianist's "devoted, doting, permissive mother, that recurrent tragic heroine in the biographies of so many jazzmen."[138] This racialized variant of Philip Wylie's "momism" thesis begs serious skepticism: taking Russell on his own terms, if Parker and Monk were victims of suffocating maternal overprotection, why did they (not to mention other jazzmen) develop such divergent personality profiles and favor such different forms of behavior?[139] But Russell is confident making broad generalizations about black culture and using them to interpret individual psychology. Hence he can suggest that Parker's self-destructiveness derived from the gender balance of power in the black community:

> It was the black women who survived and kept his race solvent. The men were either failures, doomed from the start, like his father, or hustlers. The men were expendable, as Charlie felt that his own vital force and talent would in the end prove expendable.[140]

If such a notion has any validity—and it is interesting to note that Stanley Crouch shares Russell's sense that Parker's relationship with his mother strongly influenced both his creative urges and his social dysfunctions[141]—it strains under the weight of evidence found in Russell's own book. For in its most valuable sections, *Bird Lives!* offers a vivid account of the hearty and sustaining masculine ethos of the 1930s Kansas City black jazz community where Parker cut his musical teeth. Russell portrays Kansas City's "vigorous grassroots musical culture"[142] as both challenging and nurturing—as, in effect, a healthy family environment where Parker was able to develop a sense of self. Jam sessions at the Reno Club, sponsored by the small-time gangsters who thrived under the frontier-style Pendergast government, served as Homeric "trials of manhood." Parker took his lumps, most famously the time he put himself prematurely in the very fast company of Count Basie sidemen. Parker botched an impetuous effort to switch keys and passing chords in the middle of a solo on "I Got Rhythm," losing sense of his place in the music and—sin of sins—falling behind the beat. Rhythm patriarch

Jo Jones proceeded to ritualistically shame Parker, first falling silent on the drums, then pulling a cymbal off its stand and flinging it across the bandstand, where it crashed at Parker's feet. Russell tells the story in a way that underlines its significance as a rite of passage. Parker's precocious musical intelligence did not absolve him from the requirement of submitting to the exacting standards of apprenticeship in the jazz guild. Like craft workers defining their citizenship through fraternal socialization around a special set of skills, Parker's identity—his manhood—was tied to the hard-won knowledge he gained after the Reno Club hazing through a period of intense "woodshedding." Several months in the Ozark Mountains playing along with Lester Young records brought him to a mastery of the fingering and phrasing techniques he needed to articulate his revolutionary ideas.

Parker, Russell asserts, was no "'natural-born genius, somehow sprung full-loined from the brow of a modern Jupiter, divinely inspired and beyond logical explanation." He was instead "the last of a breed of jazzmen apprenticed at an early age, styled in emulation of great master players, tempered in the rough-and-tumble school of the jam session."[143] In his correspondence with Goldman and others Russell made much of his discovery, gained through interviews with Parker's fellow musicians, that when Parker reached New York in the early 1940s he was one of the most thoroughly trained musicians in jazz. "I figure he had at least 20,000 hours in on the saxophone, counting bandwork and rehearsals, but not jamming or woodshedding," he wrote to Rudi Blesh.[144] It was an important discovery, a revealing insight into the communal processes that help create the superior individual artist. But Russell was unable to reconcile the implications of this discovery—its suggestion that Parker's cultural grounding gave him a sense of artistic citizenship that in turn provided a stable social identity—with his Goldman-inspired voyeuristic tendencies.

Throughout *Bird Lives!*, Russell's worthwhile insights into the ethics of work and responsibility and the transmission of masculine identity within the community of black jazz musicians get lost as he trips over himself trying to hold Parker up as the "existential hero par excellence" who informs and encourages the attitudes and behaviors of his white hipster followers. Goldman's suggestion to base the biography on the interaction of "the angry black" and "the humorously detached hipster" proves unwieldy: the angry black keeps unhumorously whipping the detached hipster. To give the "existential hero par excellence" contemporary cachet, Russell seized on the trope of the angry black, that bogeyman of post–civil rights era racial discourse. Parker becomes not the dutiful apprentice to his Kansas City musical ancestors, but the "first angry black man of music"[145]— the Eldridge Cleaver of the 1940s entertainment world. Moving beyond

Louis Armstrong's "archaic minstrelsy" and Lester Young's "bittersweet romanticism," Russell argues, Parker's music "cried of love, rage, and black power."[146] Russell cites Hampton Hawes as saying that Parker talked to musicians "about things I wasn't to read until years later in books by Malcolm X and [Eldridge] Cleaver."[147] Though avowedly nonpolitical, Parker, Russell claims, was a forerunner of such "militant" figures as Martin Luther King Jr., Malcolm X, Eldridge Cleaver, Angela Davis, and Shirley Chisholm.[148] Russell's notion of militancy was very flexible, it seems. But clearly it is the Eldridge Cleaver of *Soul on Ice*, the avatar of black revolutionary manhood, who lurks in the shadow of a passage such as this:

> Contrasted with the young white hipsters, who were seeking emancipation from the multiple hangups of a post-Victorian background, and in many cases, desperately striving to become "white Negroes," Charlie was a sexual revolutionary. He was not above making sexual conquests for the sake of scoring, or, in the case of white targets, asserting his mastery and black male force.[149]

In *The Sound*, Red Travers's sexual athleticism both fuels and mocks White Negro aspirations. In the novel's histrionic denouement, Travers (Parker) dies for his sins, while Bernie, the chastened hipster, lives on in Hollywood comfort and banality. Between 1961 and 1973, the publication dates for his novel and then his biography, Russell discovers that the phrase "Bird Lives!" has undergone a cultural shift: originally the tag of late-1950s Greenwich Village white hipster graffiti artists, by the late 1960s it has gained cachet as an emblem of black culture hero worship. If Bird lives, then so too does a heritage of heroic black artistic achievement and political resistance to the white establishment.

Russell's take on Parker as a black power hero appears to have been informed less by Goldman than by the 1960s work of black writers Baraka and A. B. Spellman, both of whom Russell includes in a selected bibliography at the end of *Bird Lives!* Russell there says that "LeRoi Jones [Baraka] raises more questions than he answers, but is penetrating and provocative," but he doesn't elaborate. Russell had no personal relationship with these black writers, but he did conduct an amicable correspondence with Frank Kofsky. Russell lamented Kofsky's tendency to engage in ad hominem attack, but professed sympathy with part of Kofsky's anti-establishment agenda—the part that celebrated militant black resistance to the white racism of the jazz world. In a move owing as much to Baraka, Spellman, and Kofsky as to Goldman, Russell wholly adopted for *Bird Lives!* the theme of the exploited underclass black artist rebelling against the philistine white power structure. In *The Sound*, Red Travers urinates in a jazz club telephone booth because he is a dissolute junkie who has lost control of himself. In *Bird Lives!* Charlie Parker urinates in a telephone booth because he is an angry black man striking a blow against the forces of oppression. In Russell's telling of the story, Parker comes out of the booth laughing and offering no explanation or apology: he has donned the mask of the agitprop revolutionary. Russell asks, "Was he urinating on the public, on Billy Shaw [Parker's white manager], Dizzy Gillespie [Parker's more audience-friendly bebop associate], or the operator of the Argyle Lounge [the Chicago club where Parker was performing]?"[150] The implicit answer is all three, and the suggestion is that this kind of episode made Parker a "genuine culture hero" for urban blacks of his generation.

Russell, Parker, and the Politics of Racial Representation

Since the 1960s white jazz critics have had to position themselves in relationship not *just* to black cultural production, but also in relationship to black intellectual and critical authority. In the case of such a well-established and influential white interpreter of black culture as Ross Russell, the choice was to engage or resist, to work with or against, the emergence of the black critical voice. To ignore this voice was no longer a choice, as it had been even for Russell himself earlier in his career. It was in this vein that Russell, early in his correspondence with Goldman, ventured the following:

> It seems to me the biggest cultural issue of the present time is the resurgence of black culture (combined with politics) and the welcome situation that black people are now interested in it. Lot going on in the avant garde (Cecil [Taylor], [Archie] Shepp, [Albert] Ayler) but many critical problems. Leroi [Amiri Baraka] has done the best writing so far but I don't believe these answers are complete.[151]

Echoing the missionary conceit of white collectors and critics of blues and jazz dating to the 1920s, Russell sincerely believed that part of what he was doing was helping black people understand black culture. Russell's pitch to a publisher for the Parker biography makes this clear:

> I need a publisher who isn't afraid of a big book and who will keep it in print and take advantage of sales to university libraries, collectors, intellectuals, musicians, and the rising generation of black people who are interested in Afro-American culture.[152]

But Russell's deeply ambivalent and even contradictory attitudes toward black culture and male heterosexuality complicated his role as a contributor to black cultural enlightenment. These ambivalences and contradictions stand out in the correspondence between Russell and Goldman. Consider the following Goldman letter from 1978, a decisive rebuke of "the culture of the ghetto"—or, more precisely, a *mea culpa* excoriating white middle-class slummers for their blindness to the corrosive effects ghetto culture could have if not properly contained:

> I'm into a whole new thing about the counter-culture these days. I call it: the counter-culture is the criminal culture. My line is that we all began by admiring the culture of the ghetto and believing that it would make a good counter-balance to our own uptight middle-class world. Now that the ghetto is triumphant in our culture, we are beginning to see that it doesn't stop just with ghetto sounds and ghetto clothes and ghetto speech patterns. When you get as deep into the ghetto as this country has gotten, everybody ends up a hustler, a pimp or a whore. America has been ghettoized from top to bottom. The squarest people are into the craziest scams and schemes. I meet guys at cocktail parties in this town who come from the finest families and work in the most prestigious institutions and they're talking about buying a whole kilo of coke and cutting it up for profit. . . . [I]t's time we changed our tune and started telling the world that black is not only beautiful but bullshit. We've paid our dues; now it's time to kick ass.[153]

Just two days after this seething backlash rant, Goldman wrote in a more contemplative vein about the "dialectic" nature of interracial exchange:

> I was deeply impressed by what you said about middle-class whites with a hard-on for the counter-cultural blacks. Your piano player in *The Sound* sort of gets blown away by the hurtling action of the hero. Where should he have wound up if he had been a more skeptical, resistant, and intellectually powerful personality? *Zwei seelen wohnen in meinem Brust*—two souls dwell in my breast, Goethe makes Faust proclaim. And there we mark one of the great commencement points of modern culture. We are all so divided in our minds, so torn between competing claims, so ambivalent in our feelings and actions. Afro-America is one word but two worlds; those of us who are responsive to both worlds have a heavy burden to bear. I would never shirk the conflict but I am always fighting to resolve it or transcend it or at least trace it out with its dialectic—clear and forceful. Perhaps that was why I was always drawn towards you and your writings: you had been there before me.[154]

Prompting these letters was the mysterious death of Linda Kuehl, an acquaintance of both Russell and Goldman who had been researching a biography of Billie Holiday. Russell and Goldman were negotiating with Kuehl's family to gain control of Kuehl's unfinished manuscript, convinced that only they could do it justice. Russell and Goldman knew that Kuehl had collected a rich archive of primary materials on Holiday, from court records to handwritten shopping lists, and had interviewed dozens of people who had known Holiday, including former lovers, doctors, and narcotics agents.[155] On the basis of a series of letters Kuehl had sent him, Russell judged her a "pedestrian" writer: compared to us, he told Goldman, Kuehl lacked "the kind of imagination that plays against the chains of words and supplies wit, irony, contrast, metaphor, even hyperbole." Russell speculated, more ominously, that Kuehl might also have fatally lacked the skills needed to negotiate the dark underworld she had plumbed in her effort to find the authentic Billie Holiday. He was especially concerned about a scary encounter she reported having with the blaxploitation writer Robert Beck. As much as he admired Beck's street-slang prose, Russell shuddered to think what might have befallen Kuehl once she stepped into the former pimp's perilous milieu. "She's a good girl, or was, from a nice middle-class family, with a good education," Russell reflected, but "this is a strange, forbidding world to enter, even in daylight hours."[156]

Russell's description of Keuhl as a "good girl" with a "good education" from a "nice" family hints at the avuncular, protective impulses of a white man tacitly steeped in the ideology of Victorian pure womanhood.[157] Goldman was far less sentimental: "OK, she cut into some mean old spades in the course of her work," he wrote in dismissal of Russell's fanciful conjectures about the cause of Kuehl's death, "but what could she have revealed that they feared so much they killed her?"[158] Goldman did, however, take Russell's point about the dangers inherent in this kind of work. Just then engaged in writing a magazine series on the history of illegal narcotics in the United States, Goldman claimed that his investigative reporting had put his life at risk. "My own recent experiences working with the dope smugglers," he wrote, "has made me acutely conscious of how us nice white middle-class intellectual types can follow our fantasies way into the fatal darkness."

The tone of these exchanges tellingly illuminates Russell and Goldman's efforts to define their own authorial identities, to revel in the creative possibilities available to "us nice white middle-class intellectual types" if only "we" don't get hung up on Faustian psychological conflicts or endanger ourselves by getting stuck in the black "ghetto." In searching for an authentic "black" Charlie Parker, Russell redoubled the sense of his own whiteness, a cultural identity figured simultaneously as absence (of whatever properties made jazz a "black man's game")[159] and entitlement (as a certified and celebrated "critic"—not just chronicler—of jazz experience). Goldman and Russell constantly reminded each other that their authority as interpreters of black culture rested with their strengths as writers, as imaginative and skilled stylists and clear-headed thinkers. "You have a great gift for *epitomizing* the jazz world, delivering it in a series of flashes, which would make any other biographer die of envy," Goldman wrote Russell.[160] "[The] reason I read and reread your books so much [is] that they have the archetypical quality that I strive for myself . . . the ultimate type of comprehension and criticism."[161] Goldman and Russell were fond of crediting each other with skills they found lacking in other writers: gifts for narrative construction and vivid language conjoined with critical insight, the ability to bring experience to life but also to keep enough distance from the material to maintain an analytical edge. Where should the white piano player in *The Sound* have ended up if he were more skeptical, resistant, and intellectually powerful, Goldman asks rhetorically? Certainly not wrestling with his own drug habit: the idea is to siphon off the artistic energies of the hipster demimonde, not mimic its self-destructive behaviors. Cokeheads at Wall Street cocktail parties should be used as racy material for cultural jeremiads, Goldman implied, not as models for one's own identity.

The authorial stance of *Bird Lives!* hinges, then, on a fragile ethnographic balance: to be *in* the world of black music or "ghetto culture," but not *of* it. This stance was consistent with Russell's desire to be received as a hard-minded critic and historian rather than as a hipster or White Negro. But Russell's effort to speak for Parker's meaning among African Americans further confounded an authorial role that was already complicated by his tangled personal relationship with Parker. For Russell to bring off his argument about Parker as black power revolutionary, two conditions would have to be met. First, Russell would have to dissociate *himself* from the white jazz establishment, the ostensibly parasitic class of club owners, record company executives, union officials, and personnel managers. For Parker to be, as Russell claimed he was, "the first jazz musician who carried the battle to the enemy,"[162] there had to be a clear picture of who that enemy was. Only by raising the specter of institutional racism could Russell confer any validity on his image of Parker as a pioneering militant. But only by exempting himself from the charge of racial exploitation could Russell deliver a convincing indictment of the music industry in general. Second, Russell would have to seriously explore whether blacks of Parker's generation did indeed embrace him as a symbol of their aspirations for political and social change—not just as a brilliant artist, if that. Hampton Hawes's suggestive testimony aside, the claim for Parker as an influential black political thinker and activist symbol is a debatable one, especially if it is true, as Russell otherwise was wont to argue, that bebop was a contentious avant-garde development that struggled for popular acceptance.

The reviews of *Bird Lives!* by white writers tended to focus on the first point rather than the second, and in general came down favorably for Russell. Apparently accepting at face value Russell's description of his dealings with Parker during the Dial years, most reviewers framed their remarks with praise for Russell's efforts as a record producer two and a half decades earlier. Ralph Gleason criticized Russell for dwelling too much on sex and drugs, but set an overwhelmingly positive tone for his review by paying tribute to Russell's Dial sessions. "Whatever else may be said about those records," Gleason wrote, "regardless of whether or not Bird or those close to him felt they were representative and righteous, our culture is richer for their having been made." Nominating *Bird Lives!* as "one of the very few jazz books that deserve to be called literature," Grover Sales asserted that since Russell "has paid unusual dues," he was able to tell readers "what it meant for oppressed minorities—blacks, artists, junkies." Richard Locke wrote in the *New York Times* that Russell "never moralizes" and is "pleasingly modest and candid about his own dealings with Parker." Stanley Dance wrote in *Jazz Journal* that "[Russell's] own important association with the saxophonist, described with dignity and modesty, establishes his authority." *Newsweek's* Arthur Cooper agreed, writing that "it is hard to think of a white writer better qualified than Ross Russell for the difficult job of writing a biography of Charlie Parker."[163]

White commentators, in other words, read *Bird Lives!* primarily as a parable of integration—as the story of two individuals confronting each other across the color line. *Their* issue was whether a single white man could understand a single black man. Notable reviews by African American writers eschewed this individualist and integrationist framework and instead judged the book for its treatment of the *group* history and culture of African Americans. Hollie West, then a staff writer for the *Washington Post*, called on his own experience and memory to rebut Russell's claim that Parker was a social leader for post–World War II blacks. West recalled that when he was a high school student in the early 1950s in a small Oklahoma town, his school band director pointed to Parker as a model of "technical excellence." But Russell's claim that Parker was a forerunner of the black political activists of the 1960s was "malarkey," West contended. Russell's knowledge of black life being limited to jazz, he was simply unable to imagine black social and political leadership outside of that world. Russell claimed that "the only place for the black man before World War II was music"—an astonishing statement revealing colossal ignorance of African American history. Just in the mid-1940s, West pointed out, "there were A. Philip Randolph, Adam Clayton Powell, Mary McLeod Bethune, Walter White, James Nabrit, and Roscoe Dungee, all of whom were making a significant social and political impact." Russell's understanding of black culture was as partial and unenlightened as Norman Mailer's and the Beats'; what Russell could not see, West powerfully argued, was that Charlie Parker "represented an extreme for blacks as well as whites."[164]

In a front-page piece in the *New York Times Book Review*, black novelist and critic Ishmael Reed praised Russell's thorough research on the jazz milieu but attacked several of his interpretive angles. Targeting Russell's black matriarchy argument, Reed caustically wrote, "Parker was black and so we read the familiar story of the devoted mother, struggling to make ends meet as a charwoman and domestic, and the runaway father (a phantom figure in much of black writing who, one hopes, will someday be accorded equal time to tell his side of the story)." Reed likewise summarily dismantled Russell's argument for Parker as a revolutionary social and political figure. The connection drawn in *Bird Lives!* between Parker and 1960s black radicals "loses me completely," Reed wrote. Russell's characterization of Parker's episode of public urination as a revolutionary act struck Reed as "way off the beam." Even within the social network of the jazz world, Reed argued, Parker should not be viewed as a *sui generis* or exceptional figure. To demean Louis Armstrong's music as "archaic minstrelsy" is to deny the transgenerational power of the black musical tradition; it is to use Parker in the 1970s as a pawn in the outdated sectarian wars that attended the white critical reception of bebop in the 1940s. The sharpest edge of Reed's critique cut into Russell's white liberal assumptions. Even after placing due blame on the puritanical, inhumane laws that reinforced Parker's drug habit, ultimately the act of shooting heroin was "his choice and his responsibility." By blaming Parker's drug problems entirely on social oppression, rather than on Parker's own poor choices, Russell denied Parker's agency as a free individual and mistakenly imputed to black culture traits that were Parker's alone.[165]

If Charlie Parker's character flaws should not be interpreted as an index on black culture writ large, how then to read Charlie Parker's surpassing artistic achievements as the sign of black distinction? In his sharp rejoinder to the white hipster and white jazz critic/historian constructions of bebop, the African American poet and critic Lorenzo Thomas forcefully argues that Parker and his associates should be understood "as more clearly part of an African-American cultural continuum than as an unexpectedly avant-garde 'artistic rebellion.'"[166] Thomas contends that the "racial pride" evinced in bebop was the logical extension of the desire for artistic recognition and self-determination that had been articulated in the work of such Harlem Renaissance writers as Alain Locke and Maud Cuney Hare. "The aesthetic made explicit by the Bebop pioneers was not entirely new," Thomas writes, "it was the fruit of four decades of African-American intellectual debate."[167] Thomas's implicit call for addressing bebop as an expression of black *intellectual* life represents a healthy alternative to the romantic primitivism that dominates the white imagining of a figure like Charlie Parker. But the issue of how to represent Charlie Parker as a *man* remains a challenge and a puzzle. Thomas seems to acknowledge as much in his moving poem "Historiography," each stanza of which moves from a meditation on Parker's cerebral quest to an abrupt reckoning with his demons:

> According to my records, there was something
> More. There was space. Seeking. And mind
> Bringing African control on the corny times
> of the tunes he would play. There was Space

> And the Sun and the Stars he saw in his head
> In the sky on the street and the ceilings
> Of nightclubs and Lounges as we sought to
> Actually lounge trapped in the dull asylum

> Of our own enslavements. But Bird *was* a junkie.[168]

Ultimately, the vexations of representing Charlie Parker point to a larger syndrome in American culture that exceeds the boundaries of jazz writing and the larger intellectual discourse of which it is a part. The anthropologist J. Lorand Matory laments that "both the academy and the public communications media have left an analytic void between two copiously discussed dimensions of African-American life—the deprivation and dysfunctionality of the ghetto, on the one hand, and the extraordinary power of Black artistic and political movements, on the other."[169] Ross Russell's Charlie Parker brings this schizophrenic representational pattern to bear on a single individual: a ghetto junkie on the one hand; the premier artist and political revolutionary of his time on the other. So engrossed in this construction was Russell that when Chan (Richardson Woods) Parker, the last of Charlie Parker's four wives (and the only one who was white), solicited Russell's editorial counsel on the writing of her memoir *Life in E-Flat*, Russell tried to nudge her away from her memory of Parker as a sentimental family man with an "extreme conservative side"[170] toward the "existential hero par excellence" of his and Albert Goldman's conception. "[T]he centerpiece of

[your] book," Russell wrote Chan in language reminiscent of his own letters from Goldman, should be

> what it is like to live with a genius, to struggle to keep him on an even keel and capable of continuing as a creative artist in a hostile society. Ups and downs. Triumphs and disasters. Pads and retreats. Dope and alcohol. Suicide attempt. Hospitals. Booking agents. Personal managers. Other chicks. The whole rich, compelling, often tragic, and of course ultimately tragic scene. This ends with his death. . . . It's got to be great stuff, Chan. You lived that life. You were closer than anyone to a man whom some consider the greatest of all jazz musicians, perhaps the greatest musical mind produced in America. What's more, if there was ever a perfect woman for Bird, that woman was you, because you, alone of all those close to him, knew what it was like to be a creative artist in America and immensely gifted and black, and burdened with the unshakable garments of the Kansas City ghetto. You tried. In a way you failed, because nobody could have succeeded with Bird over the long pull. But in another way you won.[171]

Chan certainly won in at least one sense: Clint Eastwood's film *Bird* leans even more heavily on her point of view than does Russell's *Bird Lives!* Stanley Crouch pointed this out by way of attacking *Bird* for trafficking in a "melodramatic notion of suffering" and for depicting black life as "an incredible house of pain."[172] Crouch's critique is penetrating: Eastwood's movie dramatizes the "Lover Man" recording session and Parker's junkie struggles but conveys little of the transcendent communal spirit that bound Parker's fellow musicians and friends to him despite his monstrous behavior. Perhaps most significant about Crouch's blistering attack on Eastwood is his assertion of the importance of black women in Parker's life: "There is something distasteful about the film's general slighting of black women, not least in light of Parker's friendships and working relationships with women such as Mary Lou Williams, Sarah Vaughan, and Ella Fitzgerald."[173] Given jazz criticism's tendency to function as a staging ground for male-bonding ritual (whether Russell and Goldman's "blood brothers" affinity, or Baraka, Troupe, and Tate's circling of the wagons around the memory of Miles Davis), Crouch's concern about the erasure of black women from jazz history is certainly well-founded. But one wonders whether Crouch's and others' efforts to rectify this problem do not inadvertently reinforce it by representing women primarily or exclusively in the context of their relationships to canonized male heroes.

Chan Parker's memoir is instructive in this regard. Though she was married first to Charlie Parker and then later to the saxophonist Phil Woods, the book is manifestly *her* story—the story of a woman who came from a show business family (her father was a producer of vaudeville shows, her mother a Ziegfield dancer) and made her own mark as a dancer, writer, arts patron, horticulturalist, and farmer, all while cultivating a rewarding domestic life in households in Greenwich Village, rural Pennsylvania, and the French countryside. Her story of her experience as a young jazz fan in the 1930s and 1940s flatly contradicts Russell's portrait, in both *The Sound* and *Bird Lives!*, of a jazz culture and allied hipster demimonde that was almost exclusively male, with woman serving only as sexual objects. "My lovers were plentiful and easy to come by," Chan Parker writes; "however, they took second place to the music."

> I never had a lover who was a musician I couldn't respect. The music was my consuming need. It occupied me totally and was the most important thing in my life. My buddies and I ran from club to session to rehearsal. We shared our records and learned all the solos of our bebop heroes. We were witnessing, as well as participating in, a musical revolution.[174]

Chan Parker is honest about Charlie Parker's drug problems while resisting the hyberbole urged on her by Russell. She tells charming stories about their romance but offers nothing about his sexual techniques. Many of her descriptions of Charlie Parker make laughable Russell's effort to hype him into an avatar of black power. "Bird strived for normalcy and was happiest when . . . he had a band with bad violinists. They were all white and legitimate. I would come to find this aspect of his personality innocent and touching," she writes. The music he preferred listening to was "square": "He bought records of Kay Kyser's 'Slow Boat to China,' which he played often, and Mario Lanza singing "Be My Love," which he would imitate, singing in an exaggerated, fractured tenor." He loved spending time in the East European bars in their East Village neighborhood, "chatting with the old men, learning Russian phrases, talking politics, eating piroshki." Chan muses: "His rapport with ordinary people led me to believe that he would have been happier had he been born white and untalented."[175]

It seems the truth about Charlie Parker is not just in his records, as Julio Cortázar's Bruno pleads, but also in his wives' memories. What we are supposed to conclude from these memories is unclear, however. Beyond Ross Russell's Charlie Parker, that strange cipher born of pulp fiction, jazz criticism, *The Naked Soul of Iceberg Slim*, *Soul on Ice*, Albert Goldman's tortured existentialism, and the Moynihan Report, the man who lived in the space between the overdetermined discourses of black pain and black artistic grandeur remains a mystery. The Bird races on ahead of his race-ing, confounding his pursuers.

CHAPTER 8

Tangled Up in Blues

The New Jazz Renaissance and Its Discontents

The "Marble Bust" Era

Grappling with the mystery, complexity, and roiling messiness of Charlie Parker has been a preoccupation and signature gesture for two of this generation's most influential and eloquent jazz critics—Stanley Crouch, who remains devotedly at work on the Charlie Parker biography he began to research in 1982; and Gary Giddins, who in 1987 published the book *Celebrating Bird: The Triumph of Charlie Parker* and directed a film documentary of the same name.

"WHAT ELSE CAN I TALK ABOUT BUT MY SICKNESS," screams the Bird figured in Crouch's poem "Up on the Spoon," a harrowing portrait of Parker's drug addiction and despair published in Crouch's verse collection *Ain't No Ambulances for No Niggahs Tonight*. This was 1972, when Crouch was still in the grip of a 1960s radical black nationalist sensibility he would later zealously renounce, casting himself as the youthful, deluded victim of a cult movement led by Amiri Baraka. In his 1980s move to a democratic classicist position shaped by new mentors Ralph Ellison and Albert Murray, Crouch has become an evangelist for the view that jazz's triumphant Americanness resides in an African Americanness that confronts pathos and tragedy with wit, satire, and elegance. Parker's gargantuan dissipations don't easily fit the "heroic individuality" Crouch finds in the best exemplars of the American tradition; he fits rather the "anarchic individuality represented by Billy the Kid and the various bad boys our society has had crushes on for over a century."[1] In his blistering review of the film *Bird*, Crouch attacked Clint Eastwood for representing Parker as the "caged coon" of "crude hipster mythology" rather than as the "perfect metaphor for the turmoil that exists in this democratic nation."[2]

Gary Giddins writes in the introduction to *Celebrating Bird* that "the one irreducible fact of his existence is [Parker's] genius, which will not cater to the routine explanations of psychologists, sociologists, anthropologists, or musicologists."[3] Encouraged by Crouch ("Stanley made all of his research available to me so I could 'get it right'"), Giddins conducted extensive interviews with Parker's childhood sweetheart and first wife, Rebecca Davis Parker, who, he says, "convinced me that she knew the story I wanted to tell." Giddins says he chose to concentrate on Rebecca's perspective because Ross Russell had completely ignored it in favor of Chan Richardson Woods's perspective when he wrote *Bird Lives!*, a book Giddins claims "is often more *roman à clef* than biography."[4]

The story Giddins tells is one that aims to rescue Parker from Russell's pulp-blaxploitation sensationalism by figuring him as a kind of American artist-hero. Giddins uses a concept of heroism much influenced by Albert Murray, while steering clear of Murray and Ralph Ellison's sense of Parker as a tragic figure. Giddins's Parker is "the autodidactic country boy from Kansas City who brought modernism to jazz," a bluesman first and foremost who marries the swinging spirit and vernacular flavor of the territories to the cosmopolitan *savoir faire* of New York—a formulation that might be used to describe the Alabamian Murray and Oklahoman Ellison's own artistic arcs. Parker's "triumph" unfolds on several levels: He masterminds bebop's postwar revolution, while always remaining part of the evolutionary web spun during his apprenticeship in the 1930s swing of Lester Young, Roy Eldridge, Teddy Wilson, and Jo Jones. He "could not be cowed by the insanity of white supremacism," and he persists with his innovations in the face of "contempt, neglect, mindless worship . . . [and] a nexus of commercial interests that sought to market his music as passing jive." He achieves his "hipster sainthood" by "transcending, in word if not in deed, a full measure of Augustinian vices." Though Parker dies at thirty-four, his music lives on—indeed, "his life is what his music overcame. And overcomes."[5]

Crouch and Giddins are prominent voices in Ken Burns's epic film history of jazz, a canonization effort in which mostly male, mostly black heroes (Parker, John Coltrane, Miles Davis, Jelly Roll Morton, Count Basie, Duke Ellington, and especially Louis Armstrong) lead jazz to a grand triumph of American idealism. Burns's is a deeply romantic story of African American artist-heroes vindicating the most hallowed American values—freedom, democracy, individualism—against the country's equally entrenched traditions of bigotry, philistinism, and commercialism. After nineteen-plus hours of diligent marble carving, Burns's *Jazz* unveils a new Mount Rushmore, a pantheon headed by Louis Armstrong, America's Shakespeare; Duke Ellington, its urbane ambassador; and Charlie Parker, its rebel outlaw. While breathless encomia to the genius of these and other black masters establish jazz as an African American classicism, the film also depicts the jazz world as a place of noble interracialism. *New York Times* jazz critic Ben Ratliff humorously summarizes this storyline:

> Original Dixieland Jazz Band cause popular craze with noisy, caricatured approximation of black jazz: icky, shameful. Bix Beiderbecke and Louis Armstrong develop a mutual love for each other: wonderful. Young Dave Brubeck encounters black old man with slavery brand: a lifelong commitment to antiracism is born. Miles Davis hires Bill Evans, defends the right to play with musicians of any race: the Defiant Ones![6]

As several critics of the film have argued, Burns misses a ripe opportunity to trumpet jazz as a triumph of miscegenation—and of the universalism that might better sustain its classicizing rhetoric—in his excision of post-1969 fusion, avant-garde, funk, Latin, and European styles that have been played by musicians of many ethnic groups all over the world. Instead, the film limits its vision of jazz's future to the neoclassical school headed by Marsalis—who figures in the film as both jazz's authoritative spokesperson and its latest artist-hero—and to his would-be acolytes, described by Ratliff as "high school kids reading freshly transcribed Ellington charts commissioned by Jazz at Lincoln Center."

Throughout the 1990s, Stanley Crouch whetted the jazz world's appetite by presenting pieces of his Charlie Parker biography-in-progress as part of the cultural enrichment activities for the Lincoln Center jazz program, where he—in league with Albert Murray and artistic director Marsalis—has exercised a much-publicized and hugely controversial influence. Since the mid-1980s, Marsalis's rising stardom has been intimately tied to the influence and visibility of Crouch and Murray, whose books *The Hero and the Blues* (1973) and *Stomping the Blues* (1976) probe the existential profundities of the blues and promulgate an exacting aesthetic agenda for blues and jazz musicians, artists, and writers. Sitting at Murray's knee in the master's Harlem lyceum, apprentice Marsalis gleaned a passing familiarity with the Western classics and an avowed, almost theological commitment to a "vernacular imperative" that canonizes the blues-based swing of Armstrong, Ellington, and Basie. Meanwhile, Crouch manned the ramparts to strafe the ground of recent jazz, clearing the way for Marsalis's ascent. An early battle cry came in 1986 in a paper delivered at a meeting of the National Jazz Service Organization:

> At this point, after many years of avant-garde frauds and sell-outs to the rock-and-roll god of fusion, we are lucky to see a growing number of young musicians, most of them black, who are committing themselves to jazz. Wynton Marsalis has been an extraordinary catalyst in this resurgence of interest among young musicians in jazz, but he is only an indication of what is now taking place. Every few months, another young man or woman, black or white, arrives in New York expressing the ambition to swing and to meet the artistic standards set by the music's greatest practitioners. This is something that all of us who believe in jazz must be grateful for, because the vast majority of those who were considered avant-garde twenty years ago represented the first generation in the history of the art who were incapable of meeting the technical standards set by their predecessors.[7]

In recent years, as the mainstream media has rapturously celebrated Marsalis's achievements, a crucial factor in his canonization has been the notion that he is the virtual personification of a post-1980 jazz renaissance that was inspired and blueprinted by Murray's and Crouch's writings. Marsalis's 1989 release *The Majesty of the Blues* includes a Crouch sermon called "Premature Autopsies," read by Reverend Jeremiah Wright Jr., an arch stem-winder on the moral superiority of the blues and swing tradition and its importance as a bulwark against forces of cultural decay in America.[8] Marsalis's Pulitzer Prize–winning, three-hour oratorio *Blood on the Fields*, from 1995, is a programmatic work about the tragedy of American slavery and the nobility of the African American quest for freedom. Not far beneath the surface of this grand narrative, as several commentators have noted, is a parable about Marsalis's own redemption and salvation—his discovery, at the hands of his mentors Murray and Crouch, of the "majesty of the blues," after an early-career obsession with modal and harmonically complex forms that might have led him in a different direction.[9]

The widespread popular image of Marsalis as jazz's savior hinges on a particular reading of what happened to jazz in the early 1970s.[10] This was a time when the major record companies chased crossover gold with electronic fusion, while many of the music's key figures expatriated to Europe, sought sanctuary in university teaching positions, or hustled gigs in studios and pit bands. For some, it was the deaths of John Coltrane (1967), Louis Armstrong (1971), and Duke Ellington (1974) that best symbolized the passing of jazz's golden era; for others—Crouch among them—it was Miles Davis's abdication of Oxford shirts and wing-tips in favor of psychedelic tunics and clogs.

This was also a time when the critics who had come of age in the 1950s arguing for a "jazz tradition" were translating their visions into projects that ordered and canonized the jazz past. Martin Williams, now at the Smithsonian, was converting his book *The Jazz Tradition* (1970) into *The Smithsonian Collection of Classic Jazz*, which fast became the audio foundation for many college jazz history courses. Gunther Schuller, with his book *Early Jazz* (1968) and his strong footing in the orchestral world, was spearheading the jazz repertory movement. The focus of these efforts, an extension of the late 1950s New Criticism–influenced approach, was to document and analyze an archive of musical texts—recordings that could be listened to and studied, written scores that could be performed—that were held to represent an empirically knowable artistic tradition. For his study *Early Jazz*, Schuller claimed to have listened to "virtually every record made, from the advent of jazz through the early 1930s." He also transcribed improvised passages from the recordings, creating notated musical examples amenable to performance and stylistic analysis.[11]

So, at the very time that the intellectual foundations for jazz history and education were being firmed up, the working conditions for living, breathing jazz musicians were at an all-time low. There was also the sense among some older critics that John Coltrane's late-career explorations into soundscapes far removed from his bebop roots, Ornette Coleman's orchestral and harmelodic innovations, and various other avant-garde developments (many now unfolding primarily in Europe) signaled the end of the "jazz tradition" or the "jazz mainstream" as those concepts had been defined since the 1950s. Younger critics like Gary Giddins, who were initiated into the 1960s avant garde at the same time that they were learning about the jazz canon through these older critics, thought differently. Giddins, whose "Weather Bird" column began in 1973, succeeded earlier *Voice* jazz commentary by Robert Reisner and Michael Zwerin. Giddins spearheaded a new generation of critics that included J. R. Taylor, Howard Mandel, Francis Davis (contributing to the *Voice* and later the *Atlantic Monthly* from Philadelphia), and Bob Blumenthal (writing for Boston's alternative weekly, the *Phoenix*). These writers had followed jazz's contorted responses to the rock juggernaut as college students in the 1960s. Now they were inheriting the jazz-crit mantle from Williams, Ira Gitler, Gene Lees, Dan Morgenstern (soon to become director of the Institute of Jazz Studies at Rutgers/Newark), and Whitney Balliett (still covering jazz for the *New Yorker*). In the first years of his "Weather Bird" column—which appeared cheek-by-jowl with the *Voice*'s more ample coverage of punk, disco, funk, glam-rock, and other diffusions of 1970s pop—Giddins gamely stepped into the breach that was early 1970s acoustic jazz.

Giddins's first professional jazz writings were performance and record reviews commissioned by Dan Morgenstern for *Down Beat*, and he knew Martin Williams's essays from *The Jazz Tradition* "chapter and verse." Having absorbed the gospel of his critic forebears, but keen on new music they might not especially care for, he was passionately intent on helping jazz navigate its way toward a bright future.[12] This was no easy task, especially given rock's popular hegemony at this time. In one of his early columns, Giddins, who grew up on classical and early rock'n'roll in the 1950s, lamented rock's 1960s development in lines that might have been written by Martin Williams just a few years earlier:

> Rock pretended to be subversive but was too completely acculturated to make itself felt as anything more than nose-thumbing. All of its outward manifestations, from layered hair to plaster castings to transvestism, have been less subversive than decadent—temporary aberrations cheerfully played up by the big media. Alice Cooper is perfectly at home on Hollywood Squares. Louis Armstrong, not to mention Charlie Parker and Cecil Taylor, operate on the outside. Americans recognize him as an extraordinary entertainer (which he was) but not as an innovator of genius.[13]

Complaining that "creative jazz is largely an invisible art relegated to the fringes of society by the national state of mind," Giddins tried to explain why it was that so much jazz criticism was "paranoid, bitter, and esoteric":

> The knowledge of jazz can be as poisonous as it is pleasurable, for it isolates us, adapts us into its own impossible state of being. My frustration with jazz was clarified for me one evening when a gathering of friends was listening to famous and obscure recordings by Lester Young. We were getting high on each solo, marveling anew at the man's genius, his sad-eyed wisdom and sardonic cleverness, the depths of his melodic capacity, as sobering and prophetic as Mozart's. At the height of our celebration, someone asked: "Hey, how many people know about this? How many of us are there in this whole country who *hear* Lester Young?" The consensus was: a few thousand.

This early sounding of a theme that has resonated throughout Giddins's jazz writing career had particular poignancy at a time when even certified jazz masters like Sonny Rollins, John Lewis, and Bill Evans were dabbling in electronic fusion and cutting records clearly not aimed at the mainstream jazz audience they had commanded in the 1950s and early 1960s. But unlike Stanley Crouch, who later dismissed this period as a jazz black hole and portrayed the Marsalis-led "young lion" phenomenon of the 1980s as jazz's resurrection, Giddins felt jazz's renaissance stirring up in the mid-1970s. In a recent recollection of the era, Giddins says that the "compromise and despair" of the Nixon/Ford years began to lift in New York in "the banner year of 1975," when "jazz once again raised its head as an uncompromising art," and

> a wave of major musicians who had been riding out the storm away from the limelight regenerated their careers, among them James Moody, Hank Jones, Tommy Flanagan, Dexter Gordon, John Carter, Don Pullen, Art Pepper, Cecil Taylor, Johnny Griffin, Red Rodney, Phil Woods, Frank Morgan, Jimmy Rowles, Jackie McLean, and Benny Carter. The young and not-so-young (but little known) musicians from the West and Midwest who turned up in New York as members of collectives, cooperatives, or rehearsal bands included Lester Bowie, Muhal Richards Abrams, Henry Threadgill, Sirone, Roscoe Mitchell, Leroy Jenkins, Fred Hopkins, Steve McCall, Julius Hemphill, Oliver Lake, Jerome Cooper, Leo Smith, Anthony Braxton, Hamiett Bluiett, David Murray, Arthur Blythe, James Newton, Marty Erlich, James Blood Ulmer, Shannon Jackson, and many more. They eschewed the mainstream (or vice versa) and transformed New York's jazz scene, organizing concerts, producing records, and gentrifying low-rent lofts into performance venues.

The irony is that Crouch himself was a key figure in the West Coast migration that fertilized the mid-1970s New York jazz resurgence. Reared in Los Angeles, Stanley Crouch began his career as a West Coast cultural nationalist polymath. He wrote poetry and plays, acted in the Studio Watts Company, taught at the Claremont Colleges, and played drums in free jazz combos. When he moved to New York from Los Angeles in 1975, he holed up in a Bowery loft and presented musicians like Henry Threadgill, Butch Morris, Bobby Bradford, James Newton, Arthur Blythe, and David Murray, the last four members of a Crouch-led L.A. band called Black Music Infinity.

Both Crouch and Giddins eloquently chronicled the ensuing "loft era" in New York, on their way to becoming major figures in American cultural criticism. Crouch's pungent political analysis and molten prose evocations of American turmoil, rendered in a mountain of essays (through the 1980s primarily for the *Village Voice* and subsequently for *The New Republic* and the *New York Daily News*) and an ambitious novel (*Don't the Moon Look Lonesome: A Novel in Blues and Swing* [2000]), have earned him consistent notice in the world of letters, while his colorful truculence, gutbucket sagacity, and mack-daddy/egghead persona have translated into PBS and C-SPAN media celebrity. Giddins, though not nearly as public an intellectual as Crouch, is widely regarded as the most eminent jazz critic of the last quarter century and as a distinguished cultural historian of the American arts and literature.

In 1986, Giddins formed the American Jazz Orchestra, a repertory ensemble led by John Lewis that performed works by Duke Ellington, Billy Strayhorn, Benny Carter, Charles Mingus, and other jazz composers. Each of his essay collections and his biographies of Louis Armstrong, Charlie Parker, and Bing Crosby have garnered breathless praise from jazz and non-jazz figures alike.[14] His National Book Critics Circle Award–winning *Visions of Jazz: The First Century* (1998) comes festooned with accolades from mandarin literary critic Harold Bloom ("invariably eloquent and illuminating"), nonfiction author and editor Daniel Okrent ("No American writer has ever written better about music"), and novelist Rick Moody ("To say that Gary Giddins is a great jazz critic is no more useful than saying Ruskin wrote well about art or that Johnson was a darned good lexicographer. Giddins is an essayist and thinker capable of astonishing erudition, insight, and sensitivity . . . [and he's] a breathtaking stylist").

The eclectic range of Giddins's *Visions of Jazz* (not just canonical figures but also precursors like Al Jolson, Irving Berlin, and W. C. Handy; fellow-travelers like Spike Jones and Rosemary Clooney; and post-1970 innovators like Marty Erlich, Joe Lovano, and Charles Gayle), its attention to musical detail, and its vision of jazz evolution as labyrinthine rather than linear ("the King Oliver begat Louis Armstrong rendition") make the book a much more inclusive representation of jazz history than was Ken Burns's documentary. Despite his own contributions to that film's genius-besotted discourse— and his tireless efforts to lobby the Pulitzer, Kennedy Center, and other big-time awards committees on behalf of major but underappreciated jazz musicians—Giddins is well aware of the problems with a "marble-bust" conception of jazz and with narrow jazz ideologies that would seal the music off from the surrounding culture:

> Unlike Ellington, who reveled in diversity and abhorred restrictions, the guardians of musical morality are appalled by such latitude (Sartre's phrase, "to freedom condemned," comes to mind) and mean to cleanse jazz of impurities transmitted through contact with European classics, American pop, new music, and other mongrel breeds. But this is merely what Walter Benjamin called "processing of data in the Fascist sense." If jazz ceases to interact with the musical world around it, will inbreeding bring it down? What's to become of a music that once epitomized play and is now flaunted as culture with a capital K?[15]

Giddins's vision of jazz is an Ellison-like assertion of American individualism ("Buddy Tate once identified the first task of a jazz musician as the fulfillment of an individual sound, an observation that virtually defines the gap between the American jazz aesthetic, on the one hand, and the standards of European fiat and African communalism on the other") and democratic triumph ("The one truth about jazz of which I am certain is that it incarnates liberty, often with a perversely proud intransigence, merging with every-thing and borrowing anything, yet ultimately riding alone").[16] Yet, in his willingness to follow the music through all of its stylistic permutations, ab-sorptions, subversions, and even its decadence, Giddins ironically has been more Ellisonian than Ralph Ellison himself—who largely disdained jazz's de-velopments after swing—and the Ellison friends and acolytes who've been much given to delivering fiats on what jazz is and what it is not.

Albert Murray's Stomp

One of those Ellison friends is Albert Murray, whom Giddins—in his own spirit of jazz-like fluidity—credits as one of his major influences, along with Morgenstern, Williams, Dwight McDonald, Edmund Wilson, and Aldous Huxley. "I was lucky enough to count Al as a friend when I was young, and I can't overstate his impact on my thinking and writing," Giddins says. "He introduced me to Constance Rourke, Susanne Langer, John Kouwenhoven, and Thomas Mann's incomparable Doctor Faustus. Albert was my graduate school."[17] Similarly, not long after his move to New York in the 1970s, Crouch rejected his cult-nat and bohemian past and converted to the gospel of Murray and Ellison, whose company he had begun to keep in Harlem. In 1995 Crouch wrote that his affiliation with Murray and Ellison had given him "a Southern and Southwestern one-two punch that flattened all of my former involvements with black nationalism and liberated me from the influence of LeRoi Jones, whose work I once copied as assiduously as Sonny Stitt did Charlie Parker's."[18]

Murray and Ellison had both graduated from Tuskegee in the 1930s but hadn't become close friends until crossing paths in New York during the war years; Ellison was serving in the Merchant Marine while Murray was beginning a twenty-year military career in the U.S. Army Air Corps and Air Force. They bonded as Tuskegee men with high literary ambition, stoked by a shared enthusiasm for the French existentialist André Malraux and by a willingness, Murray has recalled, to "accept the challenge of William Faulkner's complex literary image of the South."[19] While serving from 1955 to 1958 as a plans and operations specialist based in Morocco, Murray lec-tured on jazz at the American consulate in Casablanca and kept up on jazz, literature, and the civil rights movement in his correspondence and visits with Ellison, who spent 1957 and 1958 at the American Academy in Rome. Riffing choruses across the Mediterranean, the two Tuskegee men lyrically evoked the language and experience of their Southern and Southwestern roots, even while donning the mantle of cosmopolitan men of letters.[20] Reflecting on Ellison's canonical *Invisible Man* (1952) and his own trilogy, *Train Whistle Guitar* (1974), *The Spyglass Tree* (1991), and *The Seven League Boots* (1995), Murray grandly states: "Yes, it would be the likes of him from the Oklahoma Territory and me from the Deep South, the grandchildren of slaves freed by the Civil War, betrayed by Reconstruction and upstaged by steerage immigrants, it would be us who would strive in our stories to provide American literature with representative anecdotes, definitive episodes, and mythic profiles that would add up to a truly comprehensive and universally appealing American epic."[21]

After retiring from the Air Force with the rank of major in 1962, Murray moved his family to Harlem and began to establish his reputation as a polymath, writer, and raconteur who salted his deep learning with crackling Southern wit. The courtly Ellison, now under attack for a refusal of political engagement that young black radicals (including Baraka) deemed straight-up Uncle Tom, maintained his mandarin distance from public life. The more combative Murray took to the ramparts, forging his reputation as an acerbic critic of 1960s black cultural nationalists, whose dismissal of the Western tradition he deemed barbaric and whose guerrilla tactics he found embarrassingly inept. In Murray's view, the nationalists sacrificed culture on the altar of politics, trading the enduring universal significance of art for the cheap thrills of political polemic. Murray became known for an abiding, almost religious faith in the power of art—which, following Malraux, Kenneth Burke, and others, he conceived as enabling myth, or as Burke put it, "equipment for living."

In *The Omni-Americans: Black Experience and American Culture* (1970), a collection of essays written during the late 1960s, Murray rages against social science treatments of black culture, especially Daniel Moynihan's controversial 1965 report on the black family, labeling such work "the folklore of white supremacy and the fakelore of black pathology." He rejects the separatist thrust of black power ideology, arguing that blacks are the truest, most representative Americans and should accept nothing less than the entire national experience as the basis of their identity. Following Ellison, he espouses the resilience and suppleness of black life—its "elastic individuality . . . esthetic receptivity, and its unique blend of warmth, sensitivity, nonsense, vitality, and elegance"—as an antidote to the black rage that in those years found its most eloquent spokesman in James Baldwin. He turns the tables on Jewish intellectuals who condescendingly anguished over blacks' fitness for assimilation, pointedly asking, "Is Norman Podhoretz more assimilated than Count Basie?" Henry Louis Gates Jr., who read *The Omni-Americans* while a Yale student "majoring in history but pursuing extracurricular studies in how to be black," has ironically suggested that Murray was "the ultimate black nationalist" in "declaring the entire harvest board of American civilization to be his birthright."[22]

Building on John Kouwenhoven's theory that a distinctive American culture had been forged out of the interaction of vernacular and classical traditions, Murray in *The Omni-Americans* posits jazz as the ultimate refinement of the "Negro idiom" within the frame of a European-centered concept of civilization. "Europe," for Murray, embodies a classical aesthetic that sponsors and legitimizes, but is also transformed by, creative interaction with emergent vernacular styles. Heavily influenced by Constance Rourke's seminal American studies writings, in which the antebellum Yankee, the frontiersman, and the Negro serve as archetypes of the national character, Murray mythologizes the black jazz musician as the modal twentieth-century American, the quintessential modern, the successor to the English gentleman as a globally emulated model of cultural style.[23]

Murray extended and systematized these views in *Stomping the Blues* (1976), which has subsequently become canonized alongside Amiri Baraka's *Blues People* as one of the most influential statements on black music and American culture. A passing glance at the two books reveals their distinct approaches. Baraka's book begins with these measured, scholarly words: "I am trying in this book, by means of analogy and some attention to historical example, to establish certain conclusions about a particular segment of American society." This feels bookish and highbrow compared to *Stomping the Blues*, which seduces its reader with a feast of visual culture, a photograph gallery of musicians, dancers, dance halls, church meetings, parades, parties, movie stills, record labels, and publicity posters. Murray's prose sits among images of swing bands regally turned out in three-piece suits and two-tone shoes; Duke Ellington in tails and top hat; Bessie Smith in high plumage and a drop-waisted flapper gown; Lester Young brandishing his tenor saxophone at his trademark high-elbow tilt; Louis Armstrong in razor-edge-creased, striped seersucker pants posing alongside the baseball team he sponsored in New Orleans; dancers in full swirl at the Savoy ballroom; parishioners in their Sunday best milling and gossiping outside a Southern Baptist church. The opening paragraph, rendered with the easeful, earthy intimacy of a down-home preacher, invokes the blue "devils," the ghostlike agents of "botheration" that blues music stomps away:

> Sometimes you forget all about them in spite of yourself, but all too often the very first thing you realize when you wake up is that they are there again, settling in like bad weather, hovering like plague-bearing insects, swarming precisely

as if they were indeed blue demons dispatched on their mission of harassment by none other than the Chief Red Devil of all Devils himself; and yet perhaps as often as not it is also as if they squat obscene and vulturelike, waiting and watching you and preening themselves at the same time, their long rubbery necks writhing as if floating.[24]

Through such imagery, Murray lays out the elemental, material, physiological, and psychological underpinning of blues music. In a short dissertation on "railroad onomatopoeia," Murray connects the industrial lyricism of "locomotive talk"—"the sound of steam-driven railroad trains as heard by blacks on farms, in work camps, and on the outskirts of southern towns"—to the train whistle–inspired, bell-like piano chords and other railroad sounds called out by Count Basie and Duke Ellington, answered by horn ensembles and rhythm sections that imitate the blue-steel sonority and pumping motion of an express train. In an aside explaining the enthusiasm for baseball among blues musicians, Murray points to the way that particular sport encourages "rituals of elegant endeavor" and hinges on "perseverance in unfavorable circumstances." Like the blues, the culture of baseball evinces an underlying pragmatic attitude: "Not only are there bad times as well as good times, but even during the best of seasons when your team wins more games than its opponents, most of its efforts end in failure."[25]

Baraka's "blues people"—black musicians and audiences—use music to grind the axe of political critique. Murray's concept of the blues is more primordial and mythic: music as purification ritual, a cleansing of the body, the home, the village, and the nation of evil spirits big and small. Murray's blues musician is a hero in the mode of classic tragedy, akin, he tells us, to the hero/king of *Oedipus Rex* who battles the curse that hangs over the city/state of Thebes, the knight errant in T. S. Eliot's *The Waste Land* who comes into a region suffering under the blight of the bewitched Fisher King, the young prince of Shakespeare's *Hamlet* charged by the ghost of his late father with ridding Denmark of the evil forces that bedevil it. By confronting adversity with an unshakeable spirit of affirmation, a will to survive, these heroes literally save their communities. More importantly, in the very process of performing their transformations these heroes develop a vernacular style— an aesthetic of speech, dress, movement, body attitude—that represents the finest distillation of the community's values.[26]

The range of Murray's literary references is part and parcel of his purpose: while speaking in the voice of a black insider, his point is to underline how the blues functions as a cultural universal, the "product of the most complicated sensibility in the modern world." Polemicizing against writers who read defeat and victimization into blues lyrics' descriptions of back-breaking labor, infidelity, and social dislocation, Murray defines the blues tradition, as Stanley Crouch has put it, as one of "confrontation more often than lamentation." In that tradition, ragtime and barrelhouse piano players confront the challenge of entertaining an extremely discerning clientele, an audience that expects, along with "all the good barbecue and fried chicken, seafood, and all the whiskey and all the cigars and cigarettes and shaving lotions and hair pomade and perfume and powder," to dance the whole night long. Young trumpet and saxophone players confront the rigorous demands of their craft, trying to establish their identity by spinning a fresh two-chorus variation on a theme that has been worked over for years by the very best players of the instrument. The "dynamics of confrontation," a phrase Murray borrows from Kenneth Burke, is by definition a communal process that binds performers and their audiences together in a shared cultural experience, using art to wrest order, meaning, and style out of the chaos of life:

> when the Negro musician or dancer swings the blues, he is fulfilling the same fundamental existential requirement that determines the mission of the poet, the priest, and the medicine man. He is making an affirmative and hence exemplary and heroic response to that which André Malraux describes as *la condition humaine*. Extemporizing in response to the exigencies of the situation in which he finds himself, he is confronting, acknowledging, and contending with the infernal absurdities and ever-impending frustrations inherent in the nature of all existence by *playing with the possibilities that are also there*. Thus does man the player become man the stylizer and by the same token the humanizer of chaos; and thus does play become ritual, ceremony, and art; and thus also does the dance-beat improvisation of experience in the blues idiom become survival technique, esthetic equipment for living, and a central element in the dynamics of U.S. Negro life style.[27]

For those jazz critics trained in literary studies, deeply invested in the idea of jazz as universal art, certain of the music's social and political significance but wary of Baraka's black nationalism and Marxism, *Stomping the Blues* came to serve as a way to affirm jazz's black cultural roots while steering clear of 1960s radical ideology. In remarks that became back-cover blurbs for later editions of Murray's book, Gary Giddins heaps praise on *Stomping the Blues* for its "discussion of the basic aesthetic values of blues music, how those values embody ritual responses to life, and the manner in which they originated in American black communities and were stylized by individual geniuses into an art of universal import." Martin Williams calls the book "by far the most stimulating interpretation of the meaning of jazz in African-American life," while Stanley Crouch anoints it as "the most eloquent book ever written about African-American music." Such plaudits could only be understood as carrying an implicit rebuke of Baraka, especially the Baraka who in the mid-1960s began to insist on the pure blackness of black music, a property theorized and historically delineated in *Blues People* but now brandished as the unique and exclusive cachet of black people's art and culture.

The differences between Murray and Baraka are also matters of generational experience and personal taste. Baraka first came to jazz in the late 1940s and claims bebop and free jazz as his creative and spiritual touchstones. If Baraka's career has been defined by its metamorphoses, from Beat to black nationalist to Marxist and beyond, it was in bebop that as a teenager he first glimpsed the power and mystery of transformation. As he explains in *The Autobiography of LeRoi Jones/Amiri Baraka*, after hearing bebop "I wanted to go to some other kinds of places, and usually by myself. Not because I suddenly felt estranged from people . . . [b]ut because BeBop, 'The Music,' had got into me and was growing in me and making me hear and see things. I began to want things. I didn't even know what." This restless intellect, combined with his political commitments, led Baraka in the 1960s to link gospel, soul, and rhythm and blues with jazz in a construction he called "the changing same." In the black church–influenced sounds of black popular idioms, coupled with the spiritual questing and cult-like following of John Coltrane's 1960s music, Baraka found the makings of a zenith in black communal expression, with black people united in a common articulation of their collective, historical identity.[28]

Murray, who came of age in the swing era and regards Louis Armstrong and Duke Ellington as epic American heroes, sees bebop and free jazz as adulterations of the true jazz tradition. Like Ralph Ellison, Murray is an ardent and passionate champion of American individualism, freedom, and cultural fluidity—except when it comes to post-1940s jazz. John Coltrane, a culture hero to black artists and intellectuals of Baraka's generation, is for Murray an afterthought, "not part of the mythic conversation." In *Stomping the Blues*, he credits Charlie Parker's "dazzling innovations" as "a primal source of the so-called bop movement," but is careful to locate a so-called *real* Parker in the incubus of the 1930s Kansas City swing bands where Parker developed "blues-idiom musicianship, brilliant conception, and authentic passion." These qualities of authenticity are to be distinguished from "the clichés of most of his hypnotized imitators," the "undanceable European concert-oriented pretentiousness that has been perpetrated by self-styled disciples while using his name in vain."

One such example is Miles Davis in his large ensemble works of the late 1940s and 1950s. "To me," Baraka has said of "Venus de Milo" and "Move," from Davis's 1949 *Birth of the Cool* session with a sixteen-piece interracial band, "that was where the definition of 'high art' began." For Murray, this session and Davis's later collaborations with the white arranger/composer Gil Evans were cases of misguided miscegenation. Writing to Ralph Ellison in 1959 about the Davis/Evans recordings *Miles Ahead* and *Porgy and Bess*, Murray says: "It's nice and pleasant but other than that all I can hear is a bunch of studio musicians playing decadent exercises in orchestration based on Ellington's old pastel period. It is incredible to me that anybody seriously interested in jazz would rave about *Miles Ahead* and pan or pass up [Ellington's 1957 record] *Such Sweet Thunder*." *Stomping the Blues*, like Baraka's *Blues People* and notion of the "changing same," is a brief for the essential unity of "authentic" black music; but where Baraka was radically shaped by the new black music styles of the 1950s and 1960s, Murray was largely deaf to these developments. In an age when James Brown, Aretha Franklin, and Otis Redding defined soul for millions of listeners, Murray insisted on the "unsurpassed soulfulness" of Johnny Hodges. "Both soul and rock make free use of idiomatic devices borrowed from blues musicians," he asserted, "but the so-called funky atmosphere they generate is charged with sentimentality rather than earthiness."[29]

Changing Sames

These views assumed a mesmeric power for Stanley Crouch, a product of the black power and soul generation yet one who, like Murray and Ellison, rejects black separatism and argues for African American culture as a vital stream of Western civilization. Crouch came into his own as a trenchant essayist at the height of the 1980s culture wars, when his columns at the *Village Voice* fueled that paper's bonfire of democratic turmoil. At the *Voice*, Crouch did battle with a younger generation of New Black Aesthetic proponents, feminists, and gay rights advocates whom he accused of engaging in a "mirror-licking of ethnic nationalism and condescending self-regard" that he deemed a desecration of the noble purity of the civil rights movement. Crouch's infamously pugnacious style of intellectual combat spilled from his prose—always redolent with pugilistic imagery—to the *Voice* office floor, where his fistic assaults on fellow staff members eventually got him fired from the paper. This wasn't before Crouch's feisty vernacular had helped make the paper's jazz and pop music section, edited by rock critic Robert Christgau, a lively forum for some of New York's edgiest cultural journalism.

In "Body and Soul," an extraordinary essay published in the *Voice* in 1983, Crouch reports on his trip to that year's Umbria Jazz Festival in Perugia, Italy.

Crouch is not content merely to review the festival performances by Dizzy Gillespie, Freddie Hubbard, Jackie McLean, George Coleman, and other distinguished jazz players; instead, he uses the whole of Italian history, from the Etruscans to the Red Brigade, as the backdrop for an imaginative history of African American culture and as the foundation for a comparison between jazz and the Italian Renaissance. The musical genius of African American slaves, their ability to breathe life into stiff Protestant hymns, is posited as a cultural reference point serving the same function as the mastery of perspective in early Renaissance painting, The best of the black preaching tradition is credited with having ascended to the level of epic poetry on the order of Dante. Louis Armstrong's seminality—his pioneering ideas about "the relationship between artistic consciousness and the body," his discovery for jazz of the power of the individual voice, his fixing of a balance between the functional and the decorative—is likened to Giotto's influence on Da Vinci and Michelangelo. The "sullen gravity, majesty, and defiance" of Charlie Parker's saxophone is adduced as evidence—no less compelling than Piero della Francesca's *The Flagellation of Christ*—that "only in the transcendence of the difficult can we know the intricate riches and terrors of the human soul." Photographs seen in Perugia shop windows of Armstrong, Parker, Duke Ellington, Lester Young, Jo Jones, and Thelonious Monk elicit reference to Kenneth Clarke's description of the men in a Masaccio paiting: "They have the air of contained vitality and confidence that one often sees in the founding fathers of a civilization."

In Italy, Crouch suggests, the truly cultured understand that jazz is to late modern civilization what the Renaissance was to early modern civilization, and so audiences there expect jazz musicians to uphold the high standards of great art and to resist the seductions of the trendy, the faux-hip, and the adolescent. Crouch is thrilled that the Perugia audience boos Dizzy Gillespie for playing funk rather than bebop. "In Italy, we feel if a musician is great, he should be great," an unnamed local tells Crouch. "In America, it may be necessary for Miles Davis or Sonny Rollins to play rock and roll—or perhaps it is less painful to act young than wise. Here we feel sad or angry when a great man will abandon wisdom for ignorance. . . . Why should they travel this far to put on a silly mask?" Crouch hears something similar from pianist Harold Mabern: "The reason cats come over here and have a good time is that they hear the truth. These people want the best that they can get. They don't let this [black] skin scare them into some other stuff. They want the real deal."[30]

The "real" jazz Crouch touted in a kind of new moldy-fig classicism was blues-based and hard-swinging in the traditions of Armstrong, Ellington, Basie, Parker, Monk, Clifford Brown, Sonny Rollins, and 1950s and early

1960s Miles Davis and John Coltrane. In a much-discussed essay following the publication of Miles Davis's autobiography in 1989, Crouch savaged Davis for his late-1960s turn toward rock rhythms, electric instrumentation, and radical chic fashion. Davis, he said, had "turned butt to the beautiful in order to genuflect before the commercial," and in his 1980s comeback performances "blurts forth a sound so decadent that it can no longer disguise the shriveling of its maker's soul." Crouch also challenged conventional opinion about Davis's place in the jazz canon, arguing that Clifford Brown—with "his extraordinary technique, his large sound, his unlimited swing, and his heroic combination of melancholy and grandeur [which] brought an Armstrong-like bravura to the bebop trumpet"—has been a more important influence on trumpeters from Donald Byrd, Lee Morgan, Booker Little, and Freddie Hubbard down to Wynton Marsalis. Echoing Albert Murray, Crouch dismissed Gil Evans's arrangements on *Miles Ahead*, *Porgy and Bess*, and *Sketches of Spain* as sounding "like high-level television music," damning proof that Davis "could be taken in by pastel versions of European colors."[31]

For Crouch, the decadence of Miles Davis, fusion, and the avant garde was not just the abandonment of blues and swing, but the apostasy against traditional codes of authentic black manhood. One of the many firestorms Crouch has ignited in the New York jazz world came in 1982 when he outed avant-garde pianist Cecil Taylor as gay, suggesting that this sexual orientation explained why Taylor couldn't swing. (Taylor later recorded a percussion-and-verse diatribe against Crouch.)[32] Taylor was likely one of those Crouch had in mind when, in an earlier *Voice* essay, he railed against "jazz musicians so studied in bohemian ways that they wear their hair like dirty pipe cleaners or step on bandstands looking as though they just came in from the Men's Shelter—and yet have to figure out why their audience is almost totally white." Even before Wynton Marsalis, Roy Hargrove, Christian McBride, Cyrus Chestnut, and other "young lions" became almost as well known for their fine tailoring as for their music, Crouch had promulgated a dress code for proper jazz masculinity. "Three years ago or so," he wrote in his liner notes for the World Saxophone Quartet's *Revue* in 1980,

> the World Saxophone Quartet played two shows in Manhattan opposite Art Ensemble of Chicago, and the sidewalk score was WSQ-2, AEC-0. As usual, most of the jazz press missed the point, interpreting the tuxedo and gleaming shoes worn by each player as some sort of superficial commentary or parodic assault, when any examination of bandstand dress by black American musicians prior to the influence of rock and roll will reveal aristocratic modes of dress, sometimes given even deeper idiomatic turn by the presence of those banjos in the laps of the proud musicians seated in rows behind a smiling James Reese Europe.[33]

The *Voice* at this time was a forum for a vibrant chorus of black voices that recalled the Harlem Renaissance in its colorful spray of alliances, conflicts, and vendettas. In counterpoint to Crouch's neoclassical, early-DuBoisian bourgeois vision were the countercultural, black feminist voice of Thulani Davis and the soul/funk/hip-hop–inflected New Black Aesthetic voices of Lisa Jones, Greg Tate, Barry Michael Cooper, Harry Allen, and Nelson George. Greg Tate, who started filing pieces with the *Voice* in 1980 from his hometown of Washington, D.C., offered a particularly illuminating contrast with Crouch when it came to jazz commentary. After his early 1980s move to New York, Tate emerged as a hip-hop–era black bohemian with an encyclopedic command of modern and postmodern literature, art, and music. His was a fiercely original voice, a hip new hi-low urban vernacular that combined street slang, Continental cultural theory, and science fiction ("A sort of teenage mutant b-boy cadence," Henry Louis Gates Jr. called it).

"Is jazz as we know it dead?" Tate asked in response to Crouch's sermon "Premature Autopsies" on Wynton Marsalis's *The Majesty of the Blues*.

> When the Art Ensemble of Chicago popped the question in 1970 they took it for a joke, a setup for Lester Bowie's arch retort, "That depends on what you know." Back then jazz could stand a little mock irony. It was to laugh a few years later when saxophonist Billy Harper said all this talk about jazz being on the way out was tantamount to saying the black man was on the way out. Would that he'd foretold hiphop, the new black machismo, so he'd know that our nuts would be safe again for democracy. Nowadays the discussion done got grim. You got muhfukahs so hyped on a jazz is dead kick idea they want to be the first on the block to deliver the last rites and shit. . . . It doesn't take a genius to know that things ain't what they used to be in jazz, when innovation was the music's stock-in-trade. If you want the cutting edge of formal experimentation and progressive thought in black music you're listening to hiphop, house, and black rock. Yet, in the immortal words of Frank Zappa, jazz isn't dead, it just smells funny. And if these young (35 and under) black jazz musicians would tune into our avant-pop culture for instruction and inspiration, their music might not sound so stale and juiceless by comparison. Keeping one ear to the street and the other to the academy was good enough for Edward Kennedy Ellington. Therefore it ought to be good enough for these antediluvian whippersnappers.[34]

Born in 1957, a generation younger than Crouch (b. 1945), Tate's path into jazz came through the avant garde (Coltrane, Archie Shepp, Cecil Taylor, Anthony Braxton, Sun Ra, Bill Dixon, et al.) and the 1970s jazz/funk/Afropop synthesis in Miles Davis, Fela Kuti, Pharoah Sanders, Norman Connors, Lonnie Liston Smith, and others. Instead of reading the jazz canon forward from Armstrong to Coltrane, Tate *started* with the 1960s avant garde—an avant garde which, as Amiri Baraka noted at the time, often showed more interest in jazz's deep past (early jazz polyphony, for instance) than did the jazz mainstream. The avant garde served Tate as a "master guide"

> through which I toured and understood all subsequent and successive jazz history, from Ellington to Miles's black-noise Afro-futurist *Agharta* band. Ellington, already great, became more great once understood as a precursor to the large ensemble works of Ra, Abrams, Braxton, Threadgill, and Murray. Parker, already dope, became an immeasurable figure for his impact on Ornette, Jimmy Lyons, Roscoe Mitchell, and James Spaulding. The same applied to Ben Webster for his impact on Archie Shepp and Paul Gonsalves for his impact on David Murray.[35]

While Martin Williams's *Smithsonian Collection of Classic Jazz*, the jazz repertory movement, and the neoclassical young lions looked at the avant garde as a terminal point in jazz's evolution, Tate was among those critics (Giddins, Francis Davis, Gene Santoro, John Szwed, Bob Blumenthal, John Litweiler, Howard Mandel, and others) who saw it as a new beginning—what Szwed has called a "permanent avant-garde," with Ornette Coleman, Cecil Taylor, Anthony Braxton, Jack De Johnette, Charlie Haden, Henry Threadgill, Roscoe Mitchell, Julius Hemphill, David Murray, Oliver Lake, Marty Erlich, William Parker, and others continuing their explorations through the 1980s and 1990s, and with new waves of post-millennium maverick experimentation coming from musicians like Matthew Shipp, Dave Douglas, Greg Osby, Kenny Garrett, Don Byron, Jason Moran, Uri Caine, John Zorn, and Vijay Iyer.

Tate's grounding in a polyglot 1970s musical spectrum (fusion, funk, punk, heavy metal, soul) gave him a kaleidoscopic view of jazz that was fluid and open-ended, disturbing orderly notions of a jazz canon and a jazz tradition. Where it was an article of faith among jazz purists that fusion was a creative dead end, Tate considered how the form connected with developments outside the jazz mainstream. In a recent retrospective look, he notes that fusion "inspired some of the most influential African American musicians of the late 1970s and '80s in the form of Bad Brains, Prince, Funkadelic, and Living Colour," and was a refuge for "so many great black guitar players frozen out of the rock'n'roll dream by an apartheid-oriented radio/recording industry."[36]

Tate is a founding member of the Black Rock Coalition, the author of *Midnight Lightning: Jimi Hendrix and the Black Experience* (2003), and founder/writer/guitarist/producer of Burnt Sugar, which he describes as a neo-tribal "Gotham-based ensemble of African-Americans, South Asians,

Middle-Easterners, Oregonians, Minnesotans, Ohioans and Europeans." In striving to be not original, but aboriginal, Burnt Sugar advertises itself as "a contemporary version of Miles Davis's Bitches Brew Band, exploring the connective tissue binding jazz, rock, funk, twentieth-century composition, and African music in a lyrical, seductive, exploratory, and improvisational manner."[37] Tate foreshadowed this creative venture with a series of essays in 1983 celebrating Miles Davis's electric music as a watershed of "revolutionary aesthetics" and "visionary beauty."[38] He embraced *Bitches Brew* as an "orchestral marvel" that fuses "James Brown's antiphonal riffing against a metaphoric based drone with Sly [Stone]'s minimalist polyrhythmic melodies and Jimi [Hendrix]'s concept of painting pictures with ordered successions of electronic sounds." The double album is also "an act of comic blasphemy" on rank with "Richard Pryor's Preacher routines or with certain African genesis myths in playing prankster with God's tongue by dragging the heavens back into the province of the vernacular—namely the streets." Those streets are "a place of mystery and romance," and because "Miles knows them and their music inside out, it's not surprising that the melodies on *Bitches Brew* croon, sway, and reveal themselves like those of such balladeers as Smokey Robinson, Marvin Gaye, Curtis Mayfield, and Stevie Wonder."[39]

Tate's vision was a 1980s updating of Amiri Baraka's "changing same" concept, a black-music unity of sound and spirit. Davis's *Agharta* (1975), Tate said, "remains the closest anyone has yet come to seeing Baraka's prophecy of black populist modernism made manifesto."[40] *Dark Magus* (1974) "tracks as a surrealist collage of the crossroads where African rites and urban Afro-American means converge," a site also delineated in the black visual art of Romare Bearden, Bettye Saar, and David Hammons, and in the poetry of Jayne Cortez.[41] Tate posed a radical challenge to the Crouch/Murray concept of black authenticity, seeing the blues as a cultural force much larger than just the twelve-bar form with dotted eighth-note rhythm. Miles Davis uniquely captured this transformative blues power in trading the conventions of mainstream jazz for the fresher, more dynamically charismatic feeling of 1970s funk:

> I think Miles left post-bop modernism for the funk because he was bored fiddling with quantum mechanics and just wanted to play the blues again. The blues impulse is charismatic because of its sexual energies, but as a ritual process, a rite of passage, the blues are alluring because they make the act of confession a means of publicly redeeming your soul, as Mass does for Catholics and as speaking in tongues does for those in the holy-roller church. As an art form the blues are seductive because they give soulfulness and simplicity the same constructivist value harmonic complexity has in European symphonic music

and bebop. This is what makes the blues the most difficult music to perform convincingly, because not only do you have to convert its clichés into your own style, but you've also got to mean every note since the only thing more tired than some tired blues is some fake funk—and that's because when you come looking for the Holy Ghost and find nothing but some lame hypocrites thumping on the back-beat in the name of The One, well your soul do get weary. . . . Proof that Miles funk wasn't fake, wasn't the fetish work of a clone, is the fact that all the real funkateers I know dig Miles as much as they do some P-Funk, and that's because the feeling in Miles's funk is just as for real while the schizzy musical fusions are maybe twice as surreal.[42]

Tate's writing has approached jazz from the perspective of an avant-populist black critic concerned with the music's role in a larger Afro-diasporic cultural aesthetics. Other critics have worked similarly toward fresh understandings of jazz's place in a more capacious and inclusive concept of American musical culture. Since the 1970s, Francis Davis has written beautifully crafted reviews and profiles of jazz musicians old and young, from swing traditionalists, classic pop singers, and aging beboppers to the neo-classicists, from the 1960s "new thing" to the 1990s downtown avant-garde scene.[43] Davis is especially adept at puncturing holes in these categories, showing how musicians move deftly between styles and scenes in defiance of the expectations of critics and fans alike. He's also a connoisseur of the jazz "Missing Person—the great player who drops out of sight." In a striking essay on the "White-Anglo-Saxon-Pythagorean" trombonist Roswell Rudd, Davis tracks down this former stalwart of the 1960s avant garde playing in the early 1990s in a show band in a Borscht Belt resort. Formerly known for "his sprung time and his knack for locating dissonances between positions on his slide," techniques plied in his co-leadership of the free jazz ensemble The New York Art Quartet and as a sideman with Archie Shepp and Carla Bley, Rudd was now singing "Beer Barrel Polka" and knocking out Burt Bacharach and Broadway show covers. Davis frames his discovery of Rudd not as a nostalgic pining for the good old days of the free jazz revolution, but as an appreciation of how a middle-aged musician has come from the heady days of vanguardism to the prosaic struggle to keep up his craft. "In some ways he's a better musician now than he was before," Davis writes.[44]

Like Davis, Howard Mandel and Gene Santoro have covered an eclectic range of turn-of-the-millennium jazz mainstreamers, traditionalists, and vanguardists, while also exploring cutting-edge developments in related and overlapping styles, from post-1970s black urban popular music to Jewish klezmer and other recombinant idioms hatched on the downtown New York scene. Santoro, in his regular music column for *The Nation*, has ranged over jazz, blues, rock, alternative, hip-hop, reggae, salsa, and other popular musics, painting a gorgeous mosaic of American sonic multiculturalism and sharply illuminating the challenges and triumphs of musical craft and vision in a manner worthy of his models, Robert Palmer and Gary Giddins.[45] Will Friedwald has worked brilliantly on an equally large canvas, one that has often been obscured in jazz criticism: the Great American Songbook from Tin Pan Alley forward, and the art and craft of pop and jazz vocals as practiced by everyone from Billie Holiday, Ella Fitzgerald, Sarah Vaughan, Carmen McRae, Frank Sinatra, Tony Bennett, Peggy Lee, Joe Williams, Abbey Lincoln, and Nancy Wilson down to Cassandra Wilson, Dianne Reeves, Kevin Mahogany, Jane Monheit, Diana Krall, and Paula West.[46]

Canon Fodder

These leading contemporary critics have given us a vision of recent U.S. jazz that is manifestly multiracial, inter-ethnic, and intercultural. In 1993, Francis Davis noted a trend that appeared to be reversing jazz's traditional racial division of labor:

> Something peculiar is happening in jazz, an art music in which innovation has always been regarded as the young black man's burden. We assume that a wave of like-minded young brothers will arrive right on schedule, every ten years or so, to shake things up the way that Bird and Diz did way back when. So what are we to make of a generation of reverent black classicists embracing as its modest goal the preservation of jazz *as we know it*? Or that so much of today's boldest and most piquant improvised (or semi-improvised) music is being made by a radical fringe of men and women in their late thirties or forties, a disproportionate number of whom are Europeans or white Americans?[47]

Davis's formulation at that time included black American musicians like Wynton Marsalis, Nicholas Payton, Marcus Roberts, Terence Blanchard, James Carter, and Joshua Redman; white American musicians like Joe Lovano, Allen Lowe, John Zorn, Bill Frisell, and Uri Caine; and European musicians like Willem Breuker, Hans Bennink, Pierre Dorge, and older stalwarts Bengt Hallberg and Peter Brotzman. Ten years later, the broad-stroke argument applies equally well to a jazz organization chart that would include one line for the Lincoln Center Jazz Orchestra's young black musicians Wes Anderson, Eric Lewis, Victor Goines, André Hayward, and Herlin Riley; another for white U.S. avant-players like Myra Melford, Dave Douglas, Jim Black, Matt Manieri, Ethan Iverson, and Tim Berne (connecting to the pre-1960s innovations of figures like Lennie Tristano, Jimmy Giuffre, and Shelley Manne); a third for international musicians like Tanya Kalmanovitch (Canada), Ronan Guilfoyle (Ireland), and Aldo Romano (Italy). To fill up the canvas of the early twenty-first-century jazz world, the chart would also need a line for living titans like Sonny Rollins, Max Roach, Abbey Lincoln, Johnny Griffin, Cecil Taylor, Ornette Coleman, Lee Konitz, Hank Jones, Phil Woods, and Tommy Flanagan; another for repertory orchestras and non–Lincoln Center traditionalists like Scott Hamilton, Bob Wilber, and Kenny Davern; another connecting the 1960s avant garde with the continuing creative output of black vanguardists like Anthony Braxton, David Murray, Oliver Lake, Odean Pope, George Lewis, William Parker, Hamid Drake, Charles Gayle, Matthew Shipp, and the East Indian–American pianist Vijay Iyer; a line for vocalists like Cassandra Wilson and Jane Monheit; a very fat and long line for Latin jazz players like Jerry Gonzalez, Andy Gonzalez, Steve Turre, Eddie Palmieri, Arturo Sandoval, Hilton Ruiz, Ray Vega, Dave Valentin, and Chucho Valdes. And still this overflowing chart wouldn't begin to map the diversity—stylistic, geographic, and ethnic—of contemporary jazz.

For all of its creative profusion, in the United States jazz remains a distinctly subcultural phenomenon, with sales consistently below 5 percent of the recorded music consumer market. To the extent that jazz has captured the American public imagination in recent years, it is largely through the celebrity cult of Wynton Marsalis. And if the average American has registered anything about jazz criticism in recent years, it's been the controversy over the Lincoln Center jazz program—its framing of jazz aesthetics and history via the black-centric Americanist vision of Stanley Crouch and Albert Murray; its construction of a canon of jazz masters emphasizing the African American blues and swing traditions; hiring practices alleged by some to constitute Crow Jim discrimination against white musicians; imperial dominance over the mainstream media representation of jazz (e.g., Ken Burns's PBS documentary) and over material resources for jazz's institutional development (e.g., the program's lavish new home at Columbus Circle financed by the City of New York, major foundation grants, and extensive corporate underwriting).

The strongest critics of the Murray/Crouch jazz model have included Richard Sudhalter, author of *Lost Chords: White Musicians and Their Contributions to Jazz, 1915–1945* (1999); James Lincoln Collier, the prolific author of many books on jazz, including highly controversial biographies of Louis Armstrong and Duke Ellington; Terry Teachout, a music, drama, dance, and film critic who contributes to *Commentary*, the *Wall Street Journal*, the *New York Times*, and the *Washington Post*; the veteran jazz writer Gene Lees; Eric

Nisenson, author of *Blue: The Murder of Jazz* (1997); and the British jazz critic Stuart Nicholson (*The Observer* and *BBC Music Magazine*), author of *Jazz: The 1980s Resurgence* (1995) and biographies of Billie Holiday, Ella Fitzgerald, and Duke Ellington. All of these critics target Albert Murray's *Stomping the Blues* as the pernicious *Ur*-text of the Lincoln Center canon. Nisenson and Nicholson largely endorse the notion of a black-dominated jazz history but think white American musicians like Bill Evans, Stan Getz, Paul Desmond, and Jim Hall, and the best European jazz musicians, have been given short shrift. Sudhalter, Collier, Lees, and Teachout allege a deeper historical revisionism. They claim that a hegemonic liberal jazz historiography, buttressed by post-1960s multicultural ideology, has inflated the reputations of black musicians and devalued the contributions of white ones, including Bix Beiderbecke, Jack Teagarden, Frank Trumbauer, Benny Goodman, Artie Shaw, Dave Tough, Red Norvo, Pee Wee Russell, and Bud Freeman. Sudhalter says that the "black creationist canon" he sees institutionalized at Lincoln Center is an example of the sort of "noble lie" that Plato has Socrates tell Glaucon in *The Republic* in an effort to effect a worthy goal—in this case, to grant "American blacks—particularly urban, high-risk black youth—the worthiest of birthrights, a lineage brimming with estimable role models."[48]

If the black-dominated jazz canon is a "noble lie," the liars have had to work very hard to make it stick. As I show in the early chapters of this book, it took the intensely ardent advocacy of liberal critics like John Hammond, Leonard Feather, Marshall Stearns, and Barry Ulanov to establish the artistic importance of Louis Armstrong, Duke Ellington, Count Basie, Charlie Parker, and Dizzy Gillespie, given the greater popularity of their white counterparts (achieved in no small part because of their unearned advantages in the Jim Crow music industry) and deep-seated racist beliefs that undermined the very concept of black artistry. Postwar critics who were racial liberals continued to combat overt Jim Crow—including Gene Lees's battle with the owners of *Down Beat* to have black musicians pictured on the magazine's cover. This included the fight against whitewashed nostalgic memories of the swing era. In 1970, Time-Life Records released a multi-album project called "The Swing Era," with studio groups recreating the sounds of the 1930s and 1940s. In a blistering review, Martin Williams criticized not just the musicianship of the "largely lily-white studio bands," but the project's skewed history of swing. He asked: "Why was Fletcher Henderson, who forged this music and directly or indirectly made everyone's style, assigned to the back of the book (I almost said the back of the bus), with a comforting photo of a record date where he used a white trumpeter?" Williams continued in a vein that sheds light on why his subsequent *Smithsonian Collection of*

Classic Jazz looks more like the Lincoln Center canon than like a soundtrack to Sudhalter's *Lost Chords*:

> The buyers of these albums don't need to be told that there were some good white jazz musicians, that some of them were drawn to the music because it expressed their deepest feelings and that some of them were able to play it even with excellence. . . . [T]he buyers of these records need to be reminded that by far the greatest creativity in this music belongs to black men. And if the buyer already knows that, then maybe he needs to be encouraged to think about it. He needs to be reminded that those white jitterbugs on the cover of these albums are after all undertaking a dance originated by black Americans, and he might ask himself why he himself found dancing so wonderful and so expressive of himself as a young man in the 1930s. . . . He does not so much need to be told that [Tommy] Dorsey got "Marie" from Doc Wheeler as to ask why a white man's version of a black man's irreverent interpretation of an Irving Berlin waltz could become an enormous hit, sell millions of records, and move and instruct millions of people.[49]

Martin Williams was no special pleader; nor was Ralph Ellison, who in 1958 wrote to Albert Murray about his participation on a panel at that summer's Newport Jazz Festival:

> [O]ne of the critic-composers interrupted some remark I made concerning the relationship between Negro dance audiences and jazz bands, to say that he didn't believe that Jazz was connected with the life of any racial group in this country—but when one of his numbers was played by the International Youth Band, a Swedish boy stood up and tried to play Bubber Miley on a trumpet and the voicing was something copied from Duke. I really don't have much patience anymore, Albert, and I didn't bite my tongue in telling this guy where he came from and who his daddy was—who his *black* daddy was. I don't fight the race problem in matters of culture but anyone should know the source of their tradition before they start shooting off their mouth about where jazz comes from.[50]

Wynton Marsalis's vision of the Lincoln Center jazz program reflects a backlog of critical work that had to strain hard to put a black face on jazz *at all*, much less put blacks in control of the jazz story. This kind of long historical view—coupled with a wide-frame perspective on what it means to be the first black jazz musician with power over a major cultural institution—is necessary for fairly assessing Marsalis's performance. A young man of great talent and ambition gains power, engages in some old-fashioned cronyism, and shows a touch of megalomania; to hype this into a case of reverse racism, as was done in particular by Collier, Lees, and Teachout, smacks of its own racial obsession and double-standard-ism. As Scott DeVeaux points out, charges of arrogance, conservative programming, and high-handed management were also leveled at Rudolf Bing when the Metropolitan Opera came to Lincoln Center in the mid-1960s.[51] Nobody framed these charges as a case of white racial tribalism, just as today there is no public outrage over the overwhelmingly white racial composition of the Met, the New York Philharmonic, and the other organizations under the Lincoln Center umbrella.

If the canonization of black jazz came as the result of a liberal conspiracy, a politically correct compensation for racist exclusion, it would not have been the case that so many of the greatest white musicians started out by imitating blacks and soaking themselves in black culture, before going on to find their own distinctive voices. The critics of the Lincoln Center jazz program who condemn Albert Murray's *Stomping the Blues* do so for Murray's exclusive focus on black musicians, pinpointing for special opprobrium a photograph caption in which Murray refers to white musicians as members of jazz's "third line—following behind (in the manner of a New Orleans street parade) the "first line" of master musicians, and a "second line" of "dancing-and prancing fans and protégés."[52] This opportunistic reading of Murray narrows the focus entirely to the matter of identity politics, completely avoiding the substance of Murray's larger argument about the culture of blues and jazz—its ritualistic elements, its spirit of celebration, its dynamic link between the Saturday night secular dance and the Sunday morning sacred church service. These critics evidently have not read enough of Murray to know that he has celebrated certain white jazz players for evincing a feeling for black culture that often eludes white writers. In a biting review of William Styron's *Confessions of Nat Turner*, Murray wrote:

> seldom do white authors develop an empathy for blackness equal to that of Negro-oriented white jazzmen, whose music makes it appear that being closely interrelated with Negroes is the most natural thing in the world. Unlike the white writer, who rarely endows black people with drama and heroic aspirations that in any way approach his own, the white jazzman eagerly embraces certain Negroes not only as kindred spirits but also as ancestral figures indispensable to his sense of purpose as well as his feeling for romance, sophistication, and elegance.[53]

Murray's focus on the dynamics of interracial cultural interaction makes him uneasy with talk of racial theft and economic exploitation. Benny Goodman may have reigned as the "king of swing" while "playing with all these chittlin'-eatin', pork-chop-eatin' Negroes who need that stuff to play the blues,"

Murray ruminated in a 1997 interview with Sanford Pinsker, "[but] the point is that what they're doing is bigger than all that. It's the dynamics I'm talking about, the impact [swing] made on the American sensibility. Which is why I get so tired of people who point out that Goodman made more money . . . because that's not the issue. The issue is the universality of the music, which is nothing if not a Negro idiom."[54]

When Murray defines jazz as a "Negro idiom" he does not mean that it is not "American" music—he means that it is *more* American than any other music, black culture being, to his way of thinking, the most inclusive form of American culture. It's relatively easy to attack Murray and Stanley Crouch for slighting white musicians—especially Crouch, whose attacks in 2003 on Dave Douglas, characterizing the white trumpeter as the darling of a white-controlled, Francis Davis–led "jazz critical establishment," revealed a delusional non-recognition of his own establishment power and a transparent defensiveness perhaps occasioned by Wynton Marsalis's struggles after being dropped by Columbia Records in 2001.[55] A more powerful way to critique the Murray/Crouch jazz aesthetic is to show how it fails to live up to the promises of Murray's concept of an "incontestably mulatto" Omni-America, even in its treatment of the black heroes it canonizes. One can agree with Richard Sudhalter that the story of jazz is, as he puts it, "a picaresque tale of cooperation, mutual admiration, cross-fertilization, comings-together and driftings-apart—all *despite*, rather than because of, the segregation of the larger society"—and yet not see this, as Sudhalter does, simply as a matter of adding more white faces to the canon. Greg Tate's criticism does not remove Miles Davis from the canon, nor does it seek to canonize Davis's many white collaborators; instead, it seeks to challenge a jazz canon that imposes narrow definitions on blues authenticity, rhythmic structure, sonic texture, modes of technology, and codes of appearance.

Very often those who criticize the Lincoln Center jazz program on racial grounds end up reproducing and reinforcing the narrow race-bound aesthetics that govern the program. Take Eric Nisenson's book *Blue: The Murder of Jazz* as an example. In the book's early pages Nisenson waxes passionate about jazz as a crucible of freedom, of individual expression, and of a universal appeal and significance that breaks down racial barriers. He excoriates Lincoln Center for imposing a constructed "tradition" on the music ("the only real tradition in jazz has been no tradition at all," he asserts) and registers discomfort with what he calls the "Great Man" theory of jazz history. These are perfectly reasonable intellectual notions, fully deserving of a serious airing, and one reads on expecting the elaboration of a fresh way of thinking about the jazz past. But instead what one reads is a thoroughly conventional thumbnail sketch of jazz history, a familiar canon of the great men of jazz with their styles parsed out into lines of influence, a museum gallery of heroes replete with labels bearing—as in Ken Burns's film—the increasingly overworked word "genius." Most curious, given the rev-up polemic against Crouch and Murray, is that when Nisenson takes to chiseling his own marble busts, his brief is premised on a set of criteria that sound remarkably similar to the prescriptions of authenticity found in *Stomping the Blues* and in Crouch's essays. We are told that late in his career Chet Baker's trumpet playing took on "emotional depth . . . dark beauty and melancholy yearning," that his singing had a "ragged eloquence." These qualities are said to distinguish his work from the general run of cool jazz, which Nisenson—implicitly invoking Murray and Crouch's critique of the movement—was incorrectly denigrated for being "lighthearted and convey[ing] nothing but pastel emotion."[56]

But if jazz really is about unfettered freedom and individual expression, one might ask, why should "pastel emotion" be any more or less appropriate than any other kind of emotion as an object of musical expression? Nisenson's defense of Chet Baker and cool jazz argues this music *did* have qualities conventionally associated with the blues and swing. Where does that leave music that wants to call itself jazz but challenges, subverts, or eschews conventional definitions of blues and swing? This was the crux of the matter in the contretemps over Crouch's diatribe against white critics in 2003. Crouch suggested that critics like Francis Davis see "jazz that is based on swing and blues as the enemy and, therefore, lif[t] up someone like, say, Dave Douglas as an antidote to too much authority from the dark side of the tracks." In a distinct echo of Amiri Baraka's 1963 essay "Jazz and the White Critic," Crouch accused white critics of promoting white musicians and European music—in question was a Douglas performance drawing on Balkan polyrhythms—in order "to make themselves feel more comfortable about evaluating an art form in which they feel substantially alienated."[57] Adam Shatz, writing in *The Nation*, came to Davis's defense, calling him a "gifted critic" who "has sung the praises of countless black musicians," just "not the ones in Crouch's Rolodex." But Shatz endorsed the central plank of Crouch's platform against white critics:

> The search for the great white hope is as much a tradition in jazz as it is in boxing. (The romance of black authenticity, in which writers white and black are both complicit, is another.) And Crouch's depiction of white jazz critics tracks with my own experience. The typical jazz critic is a white man in his 50s who feels underappreciated by the publishing world, a state of affairs he mistakenly blames on jazz's marginality—or on more prominent critics like Crouch—rather than on the quality of his prose.[58]

Crouch goes even further, bootlegging the writer Tom Piazza's argument that many white jazz writers "suffer from intense inferiority feelings in front of the musicians they write about. This results in a vacillation between an exaggerated hero-worship of musicians and an exaggerated sense of betrayal when the musicians don't meet their needs."[59] This generalization is flatly belied by Francis Davis, Gary Giddins, Bob Blumenthal, Howard Mandel, and other white critics in their writing on such black musicians as David Murray, Henry Threadgill, Lester Bowie, Odean Pope, Sonny Sharrock, James "Blood" Ulmer, Joshua Redman, and even Wynton Marsalis. Moreover, it's a generalization whose psychosexual reductiveness recalls nothing so much as 1960s black nationalist rhetoric defaming the masculinity of white men in the presence of ostensibly super-virile black men. "We cannot afford to allow our music to remain a surrogate for white American psychosexual illusions," wrote Ron Welburn in 1971, by way of attacking Stan Getz and early 1960s bossa nova for "kill[ing] off the down-home, earthy musical dominance" of black jazz.[60] So, similarly, does Stanley Crouch, in 2003, characterize Dave Douglas as "white, blond, short, and from the upper middle class," a musician who "knows the modernist language and does 'projects'" and who "provides the same thing that at a certain point so-called 'West Coast Jazz' provided, which is a rebellion against the Negro."[61] Here is an aspect of patriarchal nationalism that Crouch has never shed despite his passionate denunciations of Amiri Baraka, just as his incendiary critiques of rap music can't conceal his own macho gangster pose in the literary world.

Can Stanley Crouch's new black nationalism be reconciled with the Omni-American vision of Albert Murray or with his own eloquent rhetoric about "the decoy of race"? Only by hewing to a strict constructionist interpretation of blues and swing musicianship that stands in contrast to the often freewheeling, loose-limbed rhythms and multi-hued tonalities of Murray's and Crouch's own writing. Under such an interpretation, white musicians like Stan Getz, Gerry Mulligan, Joe Lovano, and Bill Charlap might qualify as American masters, but a black musician like the saxophonist, composer, and theoretician Anthony Braxton gets pegged as an alien. If Duke Ellington was beyond category, then what to make of Braxton, a "jazz" musician who identifies himself as a disciple of John Cage and a soulmate of European modernists like Schoenberg, Webern, Boulez, and Stockhausen, yet also traces his lineage to pop artists like Chuck Berry, Elvis Presley, and Frankie Lymon; white jazzmen like Paul Desmond, Lee Konitz, Dave Brubeck, and Lennie Tristano; black jazzmen like Ellington, John Coltrane, Eric Dolphy, and Cecil Taylor; and to both gospel music and the military marches he played as the first black member of the Fifth Army Band. Nothing but a fluid, open-ended, ravenously Omni-American concept of black culture will account for the intellectual vision of a musician who has counted mysticism, astrology, numerology, Scientology, and Afrocentrism among his enabling worldviews, and whose boyhood infatuation with science fiction and NASA combined with vocational training in reading electrical wiring schematics informed his later use of diagrammatic picture titles in place of song titles.[62]

A similar iconoclasm informs the musicianship of the African American pianist/composer Matthew Shipp, who gives his work such titles as *Symbol Systems*, *Multiplication Table*, and *Critical Mass*, reads transcendental philosophers like Emanuel Swedenborg in his spare time, and considers himself "possibly the leading twelfth-century-Christian-mystic jazzman below 14th Street." One might think that such egg-heady interests would recommend Shipp to Crouch as a brainy exemplar in the battle against the anti-intellectualism of black youth culture. But like the "down" but delinquent black teenager telling the studious one that he's acting white, Crouch demeans Shipp's "European music" and—at an awards dinner in 1999—barely avoids physically assaulting Shipp because "there wasn't going to be any great glory for me in putting my foot in his ass."[63]

Coda

As the war among jazz critics continues, jazz musicians make their own way, often crossing the boundaries the critics have erected. Ben Ratliff, a jazz and rock critic for the *New York Times* since 1996, says of the Murray/Crouch/Marsalis orthodoxy that "a lot of practicing musicians can take it or leave it." He also says, however, that "a lot of this Marsalis-as-narrow-minded-tyrant talk is starting to seem dated. For a putative blues chauvinist, Wynton is deeper into European and South American music than a lot of our loft-era warriors who concern themselves with multiculturalism and tapping into the future."[64]

Ratliff—who took a cultural criticism class with Gary Giddins when he was a Columbia undergraduate, later filled in for Giddins at the *Village Voice* when Giddins went on sabbatical, and soon was recruited as a stringer for the *Times* by Peter Watrous and Jon Pareles—is one of the ten critics who conduct a dialogue in *The Future of Jazz* (2002), a book reminiscent of the "jazz roundtables" hosted by Marshall Stearns in the early 1950s. The book serves implicitly as a powerful critique of the Lincoln Center jazz program and Ken Burns's *Jazz*, most importantly by showing how both the music and the criticism of recent years have raised fundamental questions about what jazz really is. John Szwed discussed how the avant garde has been important not just for its experiments in sound, but as a query into the nature of art and cultural expression:

> What's always amazed me about the harshest critics of free jazz is their willingness to dismiss the music without serious consideration of its assumptions and aspirations. Instead of treating it as a problematic, they see it as a problem, a threat of some kind, and dismiss it with glib comments about "craft," "professionalism," "tradition," and the lack of swing. Why not consider a few of the questions that free jazz raises: Is there such a thing as pure creativity? How many restraints can you remove and still have music? How artificial and unnecessary are artistic boundaries and cultural constraints? What is swing? How distinctive and "ethnic" must jazz be still to retain its identity? Is identity necessary? How is it possible for several people to play together and not limit each other's invention and creativity? What are the limits of invention? Creativity? Of music?[65]

Other contributors suggest that it's not just free jazz that has challenged orthodox jazz ideologies. Coursing through the book is a serious reckoning with jazz's role in transforming concepts of race, nation, and culture. K. Leander Williams, a staff writer for *TimeOut New York* and contributor to the *Village Voice*, *Rolling Stone*, *Vibe*, and *Artforum*, recognizes the power of a jazz "master narrative" that tells the story of ex-slaves and melting-pot immigrants introducing a "user-friendly modernism" to the world; but he insists on a new "millennial cosmopolitanism" that tracks how the rest of the world (Europe, Africa, Asia, South America) makes its own uses of jazz. Stuart Nicholson seizes on this theme to hype the jazz coming out of Scandinavia, Germany, and England (which he suggests has been better recognized by Chicago musicians than by New York ones). Jim Macnie, managing editor of VH1.com, notes how the new cultural globalism, in the form of South Asian, Balkan, East European Jewish, and even Afro-Celtic flavorings, has infused the downtown New York avant garde. A chorus of voices proclaim the music of Cuba, Puerto Rico, Brazil, and other locales in the greater Americas to be the vernacular womb nourishing the future of jazz. Will Friedwald suggests that the true ethnic and regional diversity of U.S. jazz has yet to be fully understood, pointing to the heavy Italian presence in early New Orleans jazz and the hillbilly-jazz of Hank Garland and Bob Wills's western swing. All agree that the future of jazz—and a richer understanding of its past—eludes or explodes the traditional black-white racial binarism that dominates American cultural discourse. "As an Afrocentrically romantic African American patrimonist, I do miss the days when jazz was a predominantly and dominantly African American thing," Greg

Tate rues, adding that he recognizes "that a music few African Americans under the age of forty-five listen to belongs to whoever shows it love, no matter where it might have originated."[66]

The jazz renaissance of the 1980s and 1990s was part of a larger reckoning with American history and culture in the wake of the social, political, and intellectual convulsions of the 1960s. In the academy, the traditional Anglo-European canon has been challenged, critiqued, and revised by a generation of scholars—many of them people of color—inspired by the civil rights and ethnic consciousness movements of the 1960s and 1970s. The late- and post-baby boom middle class educated under this new regime has at least been made aware of America's tragic racial history and of the heroic struggles that people of color and their white allies have engaged in to force the country to live up to its democratic ideals. Jazz is a crucial and powerful player in this chastened and transformed American narrative, and it is no coincidence that the music's symbolic capital has spiked with the ascendancy of multiculturalism as both an ideology and an agenda.

Forty years after Ralph Ellison, in his majestic essay "Golden Age, Time Past," sought to extract from jazz's "noisy lostness" some sense of a communal history, the construction of a jazz usable past has become a central preoccupation of American culture. Jazz's heavy symbolic burden in the American imagination ("America's only indigenous art form," "African-American classical music") is today abundantly evident across both academic and popular fields of representation. Duke Ellington figures in our cultural landscape as both an artistic legacy and a growth industry. Strains of "Harlem Air Shaft" and "Mood Indigo" linger, invisible and unnamed but palpable and resonant, between the lines of Toni Morrison's novel *Jazz*, while the Smithsonian Institution receives the largest grant in its history to house an archive for Ellington scholars and to organize exhibitions of Ellingtonia for the American public. Major museum retrospectives on the careers of Romare Bearden and Jean-Michel Basquiat figure jazz as a cultural resource and aesthetic template for African American visual art. Jazz history classes are among the most heavily subscribed in many American colleges and universities. In that alleged wasteland of American television, nourishing cultural oases such as PBS and Bravo offer a steady diet of programs that document the lives of Louis Armstrong, Billie Holiday, Thelonious Monk, and John Coltrane and show contemporary musicians paying homage to these masters.

How interesting, then, that though jazz has been canonized in many of the ways that several generations of jazz critics hoped it would be, jazz criticism remains marked—as this chapter shows—by as much or more dissension than ever. That dissension is in part the age-old sectarian spirit that has both fueled and hobbled jazz discourse since the 1930s. But it might also be the byproduct of a rich historical moment in which jazz criticism and academic jazz studies have been especially incisive, searching, and challenging. The questions and issues that have riven jazz criticism over the last twenty years—on matters of race, culture, aesthetics, history, and power—are knotty and difficult. They constitute a dissonant "noise" that is a necessary antidote to the emptily pious jazz hero-worship that threatens to reduce a fiercely complex music to feel-good Muzak. Jazz and its history are full of dislocations, heresy, iconoclasm, and stupendous feats of imagination. Jazz criticism should be no less gloriously messy.

Change of the Century

I count myself among those aggrieved by the Lincoln Center jazz program's denigration of the post-1958 avant garde, its exclusion of late John Coltrane, electric Miles Davis, the Art Ensemble of Chicago, Jack De Johnette's Special Edition, Keith Jarrett, Jan Garbarek, and others, for the selfish reason that this was the first music I heard that called itself jazz, when it did. It was *this* music that led me to Louis Armstrong, Duke Ellington, Charlie Parker, Thelonious Monk, and other of the figures canonized by Lincoln Center and its Ken Burns promotional film. But it's also for this very reason—the fact that as a curious but untutored listener in the 1970s I had to work hard to find my way to Armstrong's Hot Fives and Sevens—that I appreciate the value of a well-heeled repertory program and educational initiative that conserves and disseminates the legacy of these artists, and of a film that artfully weaves striking visual imagery into a romantic storyline aimed at a mass audience.

Jazz is a big story—or rather, it's a big collection of a lot of different stories. I've tried to tell some of these stories in my teaching of American studies in a variety of U.S. colleges and universities over the last fifteen years, mostly in classrooms filled with young Generation X and Y Americans, sometimes in summer seminars for European and Asian teachers of English and American studies. My foreign students almost invariably know the basic narrative of jazz history before I set about introducing it to them; some even possess a mastery of discographical minutia that would further threaten the already fragile masculinity of several of my jazz nerd male friends. Once, in one of these seminars, when I dropped the needle on a recording of Count

Basie's "Jumping at the Woodside," preparing to explain the band's call-and-response riffing as an example of the black orality that suffuses classic swing, the Japanese auditors whispered frantically among themselves. After the class, the student who spoke the best English told me that he and his colleagues were comparing notes on the recording date and session personnel, there being some confusion over the identity of the second trumpeter. Practically none of my American students—white, black, Latino, Asian—have ever heard of Count Basie, and they hold only the fuzziest notions of Louis Armstrong and Duke Ellington. Many of these students have found the Burns film an eye-opening revelation about men they now embrace as American heroes. They've been receptive to my criticism of the film for its scant attention to women, but utterly unmoved by my complaints about its historical shortsightedness and American chauvinism.

I hope I've convinced at least some of these students to read Gary Giddins and Stanley Crouch, the jazz critics most prominently featured in Burns's film, and the other writers who first inspired my interest in the craft of jazz criticism when I was a college student. Or maybe they'll find more to connect with in the work of Gene Santoro, Greg Tate, Peter Watrous, Ben Ratliff, Jim Mcnie, and K. Leander Williams, younger contemporary critics who write about jazz along with hip-hop, alternative rock, Afropop, salsa, reggae, and other musics that turn-of-the-millennium global capitalism and digital technology have made so readily consumable.[1] Perhaps the hippest students—though they might not seem so to their classmates for a few years—will tuck into Giddins's biographical/critical study of Bing Crosby, David Hajdu's of Billy Strayhorn, or Will Friedwald's of Frank Sinatra.[2]

If more of my students and other Americans were to acquaint themselves with the history of jazz criticism, then hopefully Francis Davis, as he tells us in the introduction to one of his books of collected essays, won't ever again have to endure being at a party and finding that "the people to whom I'm introduced have no idea what they're supposed to say to me when I tell them I make my living writing about jazz."[3] All those words and stories circulating about jazz, lo these many years, evidently provide no inoculation against—as Davis puts it—"the alienation that one is likely to feel as a result of one's advocacy of jazz." Pious clichés about "America's classical music" and "America's only indigenous art form" notwithstanding, old-fashioned boosterism has always been fundamental to the rhetoric of U.S. jazz criticism—that, and a certain self-pitying pathos that goes with working so hard to try to make people care about something they're *supposed* to care about. But there's ambivalence even about this effort. "Perhaps because it elicits concentrated emotional and carnal responses, music often makes us pietists and hypocrites," Gary Giddins has written. "Having experienced great music, we are torn between promulgating it and protecting it from the great unwashed."[4]

In the late 1980s and early 1990s, Giddins was riding high—in jazz-crit terms—with his influential *Village Voice* column, his role as founder and artistic director of the American Jazz Orchestra, and his biography/film documentaries of Louis Armstrong and Charlie Parker. Nevertheless, in the yearly *Village Voice Jazz Supplements* he edited during that period, Giddins struck tones of lonely—albeit faintly ironic—lament:

> *Jazz Styles of the Obscure and Neglected* (June 1988): All jazz musicians are underrated. The greater they are, the more lamentable the neglect. What musician is more misunderstood by his countrymen than Louis Armstrong?

> *Jazz Obsessions* (August 1990): We all have personal favorites that the rest of the world stubbornly ignores. We know we are right and everyone else is wrong, but that's small comfort when the world goes on being wrong. Eventually, of course, Bach finds his Mendelssohn, *Moby Dick* is beached in the classroom, and Van Gogh's "Sunflowers" exceeds the national debt. Meanwhile it's scuffle, scuffle, scuffle.[5]

Throughout the previous decade, my reading of Giddins, Crouch, Francis Davis, Howard Mandel, and Bob Blumenthal had led me back to the earlier work of some of their still-active predecessors, especially Whitney Balliett, Martin Williams, Dan Morgenstern, Orrin Keepnews, Gene Lees, Ira Gitler, Ralph Gleason, Nat Hentoff, and Amiri Baraka.[6] It has taken me quite some time to untangle the dynamics of influence, affiliation, and antagonism between these writers, but immediately perceptible was a basic generational cleavage. The essays the older critics had written in the 1950s and the early 1960s, while seasoned with the tart querulousness that has flavored U.S. jazz criticism since the 1930s, hummed with a steady optimism buoyed by jazz's internal creative fecundity and external impact on broader American culture, manifest in everything from the Newport Jazz Festival to the Black Arts Movement. These critics could argue about the merits of this or that musician, the pros and cons of this or that stylistic development, the ups and downs of this or that political shading in the music, without pausing to question whether jazz was still alive and growing and culturally relevant. This was in pointed contrast to the younger critics, whose frequent need to ask whether jazz was dead or dying—or to protest otherwise—made clear that the role of the jazz critic had become in large part that of a guardian of the sacred relics, propagandist of a noble cause that was in imminent danger of becoming a lost cause. That they carried out this mission with so much verve, passion, and commitment had much to do with my first becoming a jazz fan, and then, as an American studies graduate student, undertaking to study the cultural history behind the music.

Later, I came to understand that part of what energized both the Eisenhower/Kennedy-era critics and the Carter/Reagan-era critics was a desire to counter the currents of tragedy and nostalgia that run deeply throughout the history of jazz criticism. From the 1930s through the 1950s, critics like Roger Pryor Dodge, Rudi Blesh, and William Russell argued that real jazz had died, and the only question was whether this had happened when Louis Armstrong went to New York and became a star soloist, when Duke Ellington abandoned "jungle music," or when the big bands attracted a mass audience of jitterbugging teenagers. When Charlie Parker, Dizzy Gillespie, and their bebop revolutionary co-conspirators revved up jazz's rhythmic and harmonic intensity and demanded to be called artists, many critics pined for the more pleasurably melodic, more evenly cadenced jazz—and the more publicly cheerful jazz musicians—of the past. This included the WASP patrician John Hammond, the swing era's most powerful evangelist/entrepreneur, who thought the modern sounds too arty and serious, as well as the African American writer Ralph Ellison, who heard in much of bebop a cold, intellectual abstractness that he felt undermined the warmth and genial humanity of the traditional black community. The trend continued in the early 1960s when certain critics—briefly including Leonard Feather, who'd been hip to jazz's incessant style morphings since the 1930s—assailed John Coltrane and Eric Dolphy for playing what they called "anti-jazz."

The buoyancy of Balliett et al. had much to do with their sense—much abetted by the thoughtful musicians of the day—that jazz was finally achieving its due measure of intellectual and cultural legitimacy. And this had much to do with cold war–era assumptions about race, class, and culture—literally, what the words "art," "artist," "culture," "intellectual," and "critic" had come to mean in the discourses of high modernism that now adorned jazz's public image in an age of jazz schools and festivals, college concert bookings, a burgeoning LP trade, and serious jazz journals such as the *Jazz Review*. Jazz now had an aura of "cool" leisure-class intellectualism and suburban chic far removed from its historic association with the "hot" (read black and lower-class) commercial urbanism of clubs and dance halls. Cool jazz, the music blowing in from the West Coast, was something these critics for the most part disdained. But their own critical style was coolly cerebral compared to the "hot gassy prose"—as Balliett put it—of their predecessors.[7] The figure of the skinny-black-tie-wearing jazz critic became part of the background scenery of the avant garde. Amiri Baraka could later so persuasively malign this scene because earlier, as LeRoi Jones, he had been an important part of it. And Martin Williams, though politically and temperamentally out of touch with the black power overtones of late 1960s jazz, could still consider himself a part of the avant-garde jazz world because earlier, as a champion of Ornette Coleman, Eric Dolphy and others, he had helped to create it.

This sense of a knit-together jazz family, however dysfunctional and faction-ridden, came undone in the late 1960s, with the ascendancy of rock and a youth culture that largely rejected jazz as timeworn and culturally obsolete. There had been premonitions of this impending generation gap in the 1950s, when early rock'n'roll captured an interracial teenager market, and films like *Blackboard Jungle* and *Jailhouse Rock* made fun of jazz and the adults who liked it. But the important difference is that in the 1950s it was still possible for adult culture to seem exciting and cutting-edge. As Gary Giddins has written, "jazz had come to embody the sleek, affluent, postwar adult world. It was original New Frontier, not just smart and hip but also socially adventurous, patriotic, and incredibly sexy. Everybody said so, from Lenny Bruce to Jack Kerouac to Norman Mailer to Steve Allen to Leonard Bernstein to James Baldwin to Hugh Hefner to Peter Gunn."[8] The youth counterculture, black power, and various other radical movements of the 1960s owe a great deal of their energy and edge to New Frontier hip (including its overtly masculinist pulse, as the *Playboy* bachelor gave way to the blaxploitation macho dude), but in the heated dialectics of that decade, cold war cool came to be seen as fustily bourgeois and reactionary. Having first read and become smitten with 1950s and early 1960s Williams, Hentoff, Balliett, Morgenstern, et al., it pained me to see them, in the mid-to-late-1960s jazz press, subjected to merciless, incendiary attacks by Frank Kofsky and other New Left–influenced critics, even as my own politics were closer to the 1960s radicals than to the cold war liberals.

I think it pained Giddins, Stanley Crouch (less so in the 1960s than later), Francis Davis, Howard Mandel, and Bob Blumenthal even more. They were all themselves, to one degree or another, touched by the new politics and cultural impulses of the 1960s, yet they were also highly literate and concerned about the craft of writing, and they could well appreciate their predecessors' efforts to elevate jazz criticism into a venerable field of arts and cultural commentary. Plus, their ears were too big and their enthusiasms too catholic to cater to the forces of political or sonic correctness. Davis and Giddins have kidded each other about who was the bigger fan of Bobby Darin in his Copacabana days, even as Davis tells us what a galvanic experience it was to be seated inches away from Cecil Taylor at his piano, "close enough to be hit by his sweat," while Giddins recounts his epiphany upon first hearing John Coltrane's eighty-chorus "existential yawp" on the 1963 live recording of "Chasin' the Trane."[9] In a narration of his musical coming of age in Chicago during the 1960s, Howard Mandel remembers going with his parents to a suburban shopping mall to hear Duke Ellington, Count Basie, Woody Herman, and Stan Getz; then to Soldier Field to hear John Coltrane and Archie Shepp; then out to the Ann Arbor Blues Festival to hear Son House, Lightnin' Hopkins, Sleepy John Estes, John Lee Hooker, and others. He counts as his "soul-changing experience" his weekend-night forays to Hyde Park, the neighborhood surrounding the University of Chicago, to absorb the "head-changing music" of the AACM (Association for the Advancement of Creative Musicians), but then wonders if the effect was all that different from when, during the same period, he took in concerts by the Jefferson Airplane, Vanilla Fudge, Jimi Hendrix, Cream, the Doors, and other rock/pop acts.[10]

Mandel's broad-minded, ardent spirit of discovery has continued in the thirty-odd years since. It suffuses his recent book *Future Jazz* (1999), a collection of profiles and interviews with members of the AACM, the Black Rock Coalition, David Murray, Wynton Marsalis, George Benson, John McLaughlin, Joe Lovano, Cassandra Wilson, John Zorn, and many others. His message is that jazz is not dead, but that its future depends on its own spirit of discovery and mutual dialogue with rock, soul, funk, blues, gospel, Latin, and other global ethnic and popular musics. Francis Davis, for all his palpable melancholy, sends a similar message in his book, *Bebop and Nothingness* (1996), when he spotlights Don Byron's klezmer jazz and John Zorn's Knitting Factory eclecticism, and notes the enthusiasm among heavy metal fans for the late free jazz guitarist Sonny Sharrock.[11] Bob Blumenthal now works as a consultant to the record label started by Branford Marsalis, the Marsalis brother who has toured with Sting and not made a point of disavowing his love for funk and intelligent pop. Gary Giddins's magisterial *Visions of Jazz: The First Century* (1998) offers a heterodox jazz history that runs from precursors like Bert Williams and Al Jolson to contemporary musicians like Don Byron, James Carter, Geri Allen, Joshua Redman, and Matthew Shipp—Giddins is a master of the career profile—and that recognizes jazz's historic affiliations and cross-fertilizations with popular entertainment from Tin Pan Alley down to rock and funk ("Thirty years from now, it will be a rare jazz expert who fails to value the relevance of James Brown or Jimi Hendrix").[12]

Stanley Crouch is the conspicuous dissenter from this pluralist trend. Crouch's rise to prominence as a public intellectual has floated on the rhetorical flair of his attacks on youth culture from 1960s rock to post-1980 hip-hop, and on various strains of 1960s and 1970s cultural and political insurgency.[13] Working with the novelist and critic Albert Murray as a consultant to the Lincoln Center jazz program, Crouch has promulgated an aesthetic philosophy of jazz centered on traditional notions of blues tonality, swing rhythm, acoustic instrumentation, and bourgeois deportment. To jazz has fallen the task—according to this vision—of demonstrating the intellectual and creative excellence of African Americans while at the same time vindicating the doctrine of American exceptionalism for the arts. Indeed, the claims that Jazz at Lincoln Center makes for itself mark one of the extraordinary turnarounds in American cultural history. In the 1920s, jazz's legion detractors scorned the music as the sound of barbarism, a threat to the very foundations of Western civilization. Today, Lincoln Center's propaganda would have us believe that it is jazz, and only jazz, that is keeping the barbarians at the gates. These are not, however, just village elders spouting a doctrine of discipline and responsibility; at its most audacious, the Lincoln Center jazz program proposes a concept of American cultural identity that challenges the assumed opposition between American and African American cultural nationalism. "Today," Albert Murray says, "America's only possible hope is that the Negroes might save us. We've got Louis, Duke, Count, and Ralph [Ellison], and now we're trying to do it with Wynton and Stanley. That's all we are—just a bunch of Negroes *trying* to save America."[14]

This audacious vision has attracted a huge amount of criticism, some finding it racially exclusionary because it allegedly excises whites from jazz, others because of its limited view of black culture and the constraints it would put on any artist (black or not) who tries to play black music.[15] More broadly, some thoughtful observers ask whether jazz's canonization as an American art in the institutions of high culture—a process, this book aims to show, that didn't begin with the Lincoln Center jazz program and Ken Burns's PBS documentary, but goes back at least to the 1930s—is itself inimical to the health and well-being of jazz music. Ben Ratliff, the young jazz critic for the *New York Times*, suggests that "race expresses itself most succinctly through vernacular culture, and jazz has almost left vernacular culture entirely . . . in its lack of popular support, its too-vaunted reputation, its recent character as a mostly educational entity, it's much closer to museum-vitrine culture than robust, mass-produced, nation-defining flotsam."[16]

This is another way of saying that jazz no longer provides the central rhythmic pulse for U.S. culture—a fact that led Peter Watrous, Ratliff's predecessor in the *Times's* jazz critic seat, to abandon jazz for Latin and Brazilian music:

> Here's why I'm not so interested [in jazz] anymore: I like rhythm, and, as I got older, I liked rhythm more and more and was drawn to rhythm genius. I like Saturday night celebration, I like the dance floor, I like women and men mingling, and sweating together, and the sweet humidity of sex and the glories of movement, and while it's fine to spend an evening once in a while in the

company of mostly white males, it's not something I can live with too much. I got bored. I moved into the world of Cuban swing, and Puerto Rican swing and Brazilian swing, into the glories of new-world mulattoism, where music and look and movement all add up to the idea of, yes, swing, personal groove, the way of maintaining elegance in the face of all the stupid oppressions, big and little, that fuck up the day.[17]

Watrous colorfully pinpoints a perennial issue: the intellectual remove of jazz criticism and much of modern jazz from the body-centered, dance-oriented sensualism of popular music. In doing so, he recalls the scene I painted in chapter 1, when I introduced John Hammond and Leonard Feather together in 1935, on a night crawl through Harlem, standing on the floor of the Savoy Ballroom, *not* dancing, doing all they could not to get caught up in the sensual pleasure of the scene—two white men without dates, neither catting nor slumming, ardently pursuing a romance less favored by Eros than by Aristotle: they would be judges, dissectors, and evangelists of Art.

Is it really the case that the tradition of jazz criticism from Hammond and Feather on down—from the trench work of record reviewing to the glory of instituting a jazz canon in a major cultural institution—is a threat to jazz itself? Some critics themselves think so. "I rarely hear any jazz musicians involved in the huffing and puffing that embitters those in the superstructure," says Watrous. "They're dedicated, like most jazz musicians have always been, to learning, playing, and making a living in a manner in which they feel comfortable."[18] Stuart Nicholson worries that "the unexpected rise in the importance of the 'jazz tradition' over the last twenty years" has sapped the music's energy, creating "an American jazz mainstream that has evolved into a touchstone of craft rather than creativity, a place where like-minded musicians gather to sharpen their skills to impress other musicians, a celebration of American cultural achievement rather than a steadily evolving, developing, growing art form."[19]

Such views are too simple. Sometimes the creative output and livelihood of key musicians have been crucially abetted by the work of critics—John Hammond's patronage of Count Basie and Benny Goodman; Nat Hentoff's and Martin Williams's hyping of Charles Mingus, Ornette Coleman, and Thelonious Monk; Amiri Baraka's scribing of the 1960s "new thing"; Gary Giddins's numerous interventions on behalf of loft-jazz warriors and aging masters; Albert Murray and Stanley Crouch's coddling of the 1980s neoclassicists. When Marshall Stearns and other critics helped construct the concept of the "jazz mainstream" and had it implemented at the Newport Jazz Festival and the Lenox School of Jazz, they provided important opportunities not just for a celebration of the jazz past, but for the hatching of creative visions for the jazz future. Such efforts were crucial for another reason: they made jazz part of a larger cultural discourse, and they secured its place in the American narrative.

Today, even as jazz moves further from the center of mass culture, it more firmly secures its hold on the American imagination, and critics, white and black, fall on the mythic themes of American literature and history to explain its import. "Perhaps the best way to convey the effect that jazz has had on my life," writes the white jazz critic and biographer Eric Nisenson, "is to say that I, like many white jazz fans, often felt quite a bit like that ultimate icon of American culture, Huckleberry Finn, floating on the currents of the great American river with the black slave Jim, both of us finally, ecstatically, free, lighting out for new territories."[20] "Among them," the black critic Stanley Crouch rambles lyrically about his time in the company of black jazz musicians,

> I know again the barbershops and the pool halls, the big family dinners and the counterpoint of whist and domino games, the back porches and the locker rooms, the street corners and the church parking lots where I had learned so much while tested against the gruff friendship and gallows wit that have come, sometimes as slowly as the proverbial molasses in January, all the way from those slave cabins where the partying and the singing went on late into the night, puzzling old Thomas Jefferson, who knew his human property had to meet their mules and their labors in the dawn morning, to grunt and sweat until dusk.[21]

It's a long way from those slave cabins to the cosmopolitan élan of a Duke Ellington or Miles Davis. The black jazz musician, says anthropologist and jazz historian John Szwed, was "the first truly nonmechanical metaphor for the twentieth century"—successor to the English Gentleman as a globally emulated model of sartorial and verbal style.[22] Because jazz demands that musicians find their own sound and stamp their performances with a singular individuality, those who succeed in the music tend to be distinctive, singular individuals. Their distinctiveness—of experience, vision, and personality; of adornment, comportment, and speech—is an endless source of fascination not just for poets, novelists, photographers, and filmmakers, but also for the kind of jazz critic who sees the craft as its own form of literature. One such critic, Francis Davis, says that he tries "to crowd even those pieces that begin as record reviews with what Dwight McDonald, in his essay on Hemingway, described as 'the subject matter of the novel: character, social setting, politics, money matters, human relations, all the prose of life.'"[23]

Even as a genre of literature, jazz criticism faces a formidable challenge in trying to capture the voice, thinking, and presence of the musician. Since the 1970s, the typical Whitney Balliett byline in the *New Yorker* has been a profile featuring extensive musician testimony—sometimes up to three-quarters of the column—framed by personal background and scene-setting details implying intimacy with the musicians and access to their private lives. A 1990 profile of Dizzy Gillespie, to take an example, recounts conversation between Balliett and Gillepsie over dinner at a venerable French restaurant in Manhattan. Balliett sets the scene by describing Gillespie devouring a plate of haute cuisine frogs' legs with the same relish he brings to a basket of roadside-stand fried chicken. The trumpeter discourses on subjects ranging from Charlie Parker to the art of improvisation to a racist snubbing at the hands of a white barber in his hometown of Cheraw, South Carolina. "No one talks like Gillespie," Balliett says. "His voice is potatoey, burred, edgeless. His consonants and vowels are indistinguishable, a gumbo. His laughter barks." But it's hard to pick up these resonances in Balliett's transcription of Gillespie's words. On the page, Gillespie's voice ("Later, I got a letter from Cheraw asking me if I would mind if they put up a sign on the outskirts saying Dizzy Gillespie was born there. I said I would mind—it would embarrass me if someone I knew came through and wanted a haircut and couldn't get it. But later I relented.") sounds more like a decorous *New Yorker* "Talk of the Town" correspondent than a soulful Southern raconteur.[24] Still, our sense of Gillespie is much fuller, and in general Balliett's interviews have crucially enriched and deepened our understanding of the lives jazz musicians lead.[25]

Another strategy takes the relation between writer and subject a step further, with the writer inserting himself as a central character in the life of the musician. This is the approach employed by Gene Lees in a series of books published in the 1980s and 1990s, drawing mostly on relationships forged in the 1950s and 1960s. The Canadian-born Lees was the editor of *Down Beat* from 1959 to 1961; in 1981 he began to publish "Gene Lees' Jazzletter," a private monthly sheaf of essays circulated among several hundred of Lees's jazz world associates. An accomplished lyricist and arranger, Lees is also a skilled storyteller, and the stories he tells revolve around his intimate interactions with other musicians. When Lees takes the reader to pianist Hank Jones's upstate New York home, he describes the passing landscape on the drive there. When he meets Billy Taylor in a hotel room, he notes the quality of the housekeeping. When he paints the scene at Jim & Andy's tavern on 48th Street in Manhattan—a musicians' hangout in the 1960s—he tells us who said what, who drank what, and what was playing on the jukebox and the television. Lees reveals Taylor's pride and wonder at the salary pulled down by his daughter, a Yale graduate and Washington, D.C.

attorney. He recounts the grief he shared with Gerry Mulligan when their close friend, actress Judy Holliday, passed away. He scotches the suggestion of a sexual relationship between Dave Brubeck and Paul Desmond, assuring readers of Brubeck's "unshaken lifetime devotion" to his wife Iola, extolling Desmond as "a womanizer who doted on beautiful girls," and puzzling over the "extraordinary rarity of homosexuality in jazz."[26]

Lees presumes to know such things because he has, in fact, been deeply entangled in the personal lives of some of his subjects. This was especially true of his relationship with pianist Bill Evans. Lees first heard Evans on the Riverside album *Everybody Digs Bill Evans* in 1959, shortly after he took over at *Down Beat*. Astonished by the intense privacy of the music, Lees wrote to Evans saying that the album "sounded like love letters written to the world from some prison of the heart." He put Evans on the *Down Beat* cover and talked him up, amplifying the buzz that surrounded Evans for his central role in the epic 1960 Miles Davis LP *Kind of Blue*. In 1962, Lees introduced Evans to his romantic partner of the time, talent manager Helen Keane, who became Evans's manager and, later, producer. In a profile published in his 1988 book *Meet Me at Jim & Andy's*, Lees movingly recalls how he, Keane, Orrin Keepnews, and Creed Taylor struggled with Evans's heroin addiction. Far from judging Evans, Lees offers only empathy and understanding "for this extraordinarily intelligent and sensitive man." In a striking vignette, Lees, in the hospital recovering from knee surgery, needs morphine to dull his pain. As Evans sits at his side, Lees feels "the warmth of the drug spread through my body and the pain dissolv[e] in it." Looking at Evans, Lees says, "I felt that I truly understood him."[27]

Lees says he began writing his profiles because he "grew tired of reading that jazz musicians are inarticulate men," seeing them instead as "mostly gentle men and women, sensitive and cultivated, and very middle-class." Lees insists that jazz musicians "don't consider themselves outcasts," even as he celebrates them as people of "exaggerated individuality."[28] But he makes them seem very much alike in one respect (aside from his presumption of their heterosexuality, which might be offensive to musicians who are openly homosexual, or humorous to those who are secretly so): they enjoy talking and listening to Gene Lees. Much unlike Balliett, who in the 1970s stopped using the "I" in his writing, Lees keeps himself in the middle of the dialogue, often noting his subjects' assent to his opinions. His conception of jazz is utterly personal, a matter of consensus among friends. To dismiss as myth the notion that black bebop musicians tried to shame white players off the bandstand, he invokes his friendship with Dizzy Gillespie: "It was not in the great and glorious heart of Dizzy Gillespie to do something so mean," he says.[29] Lees excludes from his inner circle anyone who violates what he regards as jazz's cherished integrationist values, the ones exemplified in his own story of a white man who finds his life's purpose among black men—much like the white musicians he thinks have been written out of jazz history.

I've learned a lot and taken much pleasure from Lees's writing, and I'm being more snippish toward him than I'd care to. My point is to raise as a critical issue—to analyze rather than sentimentalize—uncomplicated notions of jazz as an oasis of interracial harmony in an otherwise racist society. For while I agree with Lees, Eric Nisenson, Richard Sudhalter, and others who argue that the jazz world has been a place where "cats of any color" have worked together in a spirit of mutual respect, affection, and sometimes even love, I think it's crucially important to examine the racial dynamics of status and power—both personal and institutional—that have inevitably shaped these relationships. The interracial intimacies, affinities, and alliances forged by Lees and many other critics and musicians are an important achievement, in some respects as culturally compelling as the music's own polyglot synthesis of Africa, Europe, the Caribbean, and the Americas. But while personal friendships and individual virtue can help dissolve the color line, they can't quite as easily dismantle the power of systemic, institutional racism in a culture that was founded on white supremacy.

Jazz criticism remains dominated by white voices. Throughout the 1960s and 1970s, a sprinkling of black writers (Baraka, Barbara Gardner, Gloria Oden, Brent Staples, Lofton Emenari, Roger Riggins, and a few others) appeared in *Down Beat*; the one black editor at the magazine during this period was Bill Quinn, who worked with chief editor Dan Morgenstern in the late 1960s. In the late 1960s and 1970s, Hollie West introduced jazz along with other aspects of black culture to the *Washington Post*, which until then had almost completely ignored the cultural life of Washington, D.C.'s dominant ethnic group. Socially aware, jazz-minded newspaper writers of any ethnic background know that any coverage the music receives might be the only positive news about African Americans in their papers. Jim Macnie, now the managing editor of VH1.com, says that "Part of the reason I started to write about jazz was the fact that McCoy Tyner gigged in Providence back in the late 1970s and the daily paper didn't make a peep before or after. Yet the headlines around that time kept harping on a string of breakings-and-enterings in a low-income, predominantly black neighborhood."[30]

In recent years, the ubiquitous cultural power of hip-hop—piggybacking on the black mass popularity of 1960s soul and 1970s funk—has heightened the challenge for black jazz writers who are trying to reach a black audience. "Blacks create and move on. Whites document and then recycle. In the history of popular music, these truths are self-evident"—so says the prolific black popular music critic Nelson George, and to the extent that he's right, he pinpoints the problem for black jazz critics at a time when hip-hop has super-accelerated the create-and-move-on syndrome, while most young black jazz musicians have adopted a curatorial, document-and-recycle approach.[31] It falls to Gene Seymour, Willard Jenkins, Sharony Andrews Green, K. Leander Williams, Greg Tate, and other contemporary black writers—and all writers with a black audience—to make the case for jazz as an authentic part of black cultural identity, rather than an unhip whiteface burlesque, at a time when major black media institutions (Black Entertainment Television, *Ebony*, *Essence*, the vast enterprises headed up by moguls Russell Simmons and Sean "Puffy" Combs) pay jazz little or no mind.

Greg Tate, perhaps the most brilliant critic of the generation that came of age in the 1980s, has articulated a postmodern, polystylistic aesthetic that links jazz with hip-hop, rock, science fiction, and African diasporic postcolonial literature, visual art, and cinema. But he wonders if jazz has now completely severed its connection to the black vernacular womb that nurtured it into existence:

> As the cultural ground has shifted under the feet of jazz's pro-black advocates over the last couple of decades, the defense of jazz as a Black Thing has largely been quieted by the realization that, like rock'n'roll, it is a black thing that few African Americans give a damn about. The fate of jazz has become so much the province of white scholars, critics, and fans as to drag the subject from the ironic to the sublimely ridiculous. . . . The overriding question is whether American jazz has a vital, creative future if none of the next generation of inner-city African Americans are encouraged to bring the wit, ingenuity, and rhythmic acuity of their hip-hop surround into the field.[32]

Does jazz have to be connected to inner-city African American youth culture? Jazz musicians in Europe, Asia, and Burlington, Vermont certainly hope not. Does jazz have to be male- and heterosexual-dominated? Female and gay musicians certainly hope not. Is jazz fated to remain overwhelmingly "the province of white scholars, critics, and fans"? Scholars, critics, and fans of color certainly hope not. These are just a few of the questions licking at jazz as it embarks on its second century.

Jazz was born in the street parades and sporting houses of early twentieth-century New Orleans; nurtured in the rent parties, speakeasies, and dance halls of 1920s and 1930s Chicago, New York, St. Louis, Washington, Baltimore, and Boston; seasoned in the corner saloons and barber shops of Philadelphia, Detroit, and Los Angeles in the 1940s and 1950s; and refined in the concert halls, conservatories, and universities of post–World War

II cultural capitals the world over. At each stage, jazz critics have been on the scene—sometimes in the guise of a&r men, concert producers, personal managers, or lecturers. At each stage, musicians have fought for greater control over their music and its messages, while audiences have angled for more and more unfiltered access to the music. Today, jazz musicians in college and university academic posts—not nearly enough of them—shape a growing number of jazz performance programs. Interdisciplinary jazz studies initiatives, such as the Center for Jazz Studies at Columbia University, bring musicians together with scholars looking at jazz through the lenses of history, art history, literature, cultural studies, anthropology, and philosophy. Especially resourceful musicians like Oliver Lake and Matthew Shipp record and distribute their own music and keep fans abreast of their musical, literary, and philosophical interests on impressive websites. Patricia Parker and her husband, the bassist and bandleader William Parker, run the Vision Jazz Festival in New York's East Village, a yearly gathering of avant-garde musicians, poets, dancers, and visual artists around themes of spirituality and progressive politics.

All of this vibrant cultural and educational activity—some of it touched by the hip-hop influence Tate deems indispensable, some of it not—absorbs, reframes, and extends work undertaken by jazz critics since the 1930s. Indeed, the ultimate value and vindication of those critics is that their work lives on in the music and its allied institutions and discourses. Jazz criticism, as such, is bigger than the jazz critic; it is nothing less than the rowdy conversation that gives jazz its incisive edge in shaping the contours of America and New World modernity. Jazz criticism is the noise—the auditory dissonance—that gives the music cultural meaning. May the noise forever clamor, and may we listen and learn.

Introduction

1. The story is told in Bill Crow, *Jazz Anecdotes* (Cambridge: Oxford University Press, 1990), 328.

2. Roger Pryor Dodge, "Consider the Critics," in *Jazzmen: The Story of Hot Jazz Told in the Lives of the Men Who Created It,* ed. Frederick Ramsey Jr. and Charles Edward Smith (1939; New York: Limelight, 1985), 301.

3. Whitney Balliett, "Dixie in the Library," *Saturday Review,* October 30, 1954, 54.

4. Ken Burns, *Jazz: A Film by Ken Burns* (The Jazz Film Project, Inc., DD4721). For a sampling of critical reactions to the film, see Krin Gabbard, "Ken Burns's 'Jazz': Beautiful Music, but Missing a Beat," *Chronicle of Higher Education,* December 15, 2000, B18–B19; Keith Jarrett, "'Jazz': 40 Years Missing," *New York Times,* January 21, 2001, section 2, 4; Ronald Radano, "Myth Today: The Color of Ken Burns' Jazz," *Black Renaissance* 3, no. 3 (2001): 43–54; Ben Ratliff, "Fixing, for Now, the Image of Jazz," *New York Times,* January 21, 2001, section 2, 1; Alan Stanbridge, "Burns, Baby, Burns: Jazz History as a Contested Cultural Site," *The Source: Challenging Jazz Criticism* 1 (2004): 81–99. The "funeral procession" quip belongs to Peter Watrous, in *The Future of Jazz,* ed. Yuval Taylor (Chicago: A Capella Books, 2002), 204. The characterization of neoclassicism as "musical necrophilia" is by Stuart Nicholson, in *The Future of Jazz,* 126.

5. For more about my college years, see my essay "Nearer, My God, to Thee," in *Some of My Best Friends: Essays on Interracial Friendships,* ed. Emily Bernard (New York: HarperCollins/Amistad, 2004), 32–53.

6. Gary Giddins's essays from this period are collected in *Riding on a Blue Note: A Jazz Chronicle* (New York: Oxford University Press, 1981); *Rhythm-a-ning: Jazz Tradition and Innovation in the 1980s* (New York: Oxford University Press, 1985); and *Faces in the Crowd: Players and Writers* (New York: Oxford University Press, 1992). Stanley Crouch's essays of the period are collected in *Notes of a Hanging Judge: Essays and Reviews,*

1979–1988 (New York: Oxford University Press, 1990); *The All-American Skin Game; or, The Decay of Race; The Long and Short of It, 1990–1994* (New York: Pantheon, 1995); *Always in Pursuit: Fresh American Perspectives, 1995–1997* (New York: Pantheon, 1998). Francis Davis's essays are in *In the Moment: Jazz in the 1980s* (New York: Oxford University Press, 1986); *Outcats: Jazz Composers, Instrumentalists, and Singers* (New York: Oxford University Press, 1990); and *Bebop and Nothingness: Jazz and Pop at the End of the Century* (New York: Schirmer, 1996). Howard Mandel's work is collected in *Future Jazz* (New York: Oxford University Press, 1999). Bob Blumenthal's essays have appeared in the *Boston Phoenix, Boston Globe, The Village Voice, The Atlantic Monthly, Rolling Stone, Down Beat,* and *Jazz Times.*

7. Ted Gioia, in *The Future of Jazz*, 192, 196.

8. Miles Davis (with Quincy Troupe), *Miles: The Autobiography* (New York: Simon and Schuster, 1989). Stanley Crouch notes similarities between passages in *Miles* and in Jack Chambers, *Milestones* (1983, 1984; New York: Da Capo, 1998), calling it "parasitic paraphrasing," in his essay "On the Corner: The Sellout of Miles Davis," in *The All-American Skin Game*, 184.

9. Nat Hentoff, *The Jazz Life* (New York: Da Capo, 1975), 251.

10. For a particularly excellent study of African American musicians as critical intellectuals, see Eric Porter, *What Is This Thing Called Jazz? African American Musicians as Artists, Critics, and Activists* (Berkeley: University of California Press, 2002).

11. Geoff Dyer, *But Beautiful: A Book about Jazz* (New York: North Point Press, 1996), vii–viii, 183–91.

12. Dyer, *But Beautiful*, 196–97.

13. Dan Morgenstern, "A Critical Matter," *Down Beat*, January 9, 1969, 14.

14. Martin Williams, "The Bystander," *Down Beat*, August 29, 1963, 33.

15. Morgenstern, "A Critical Matter," 14.

16. Amiri Baraka, "Homage to Miles Davis," in *The Miles Davis Companion: Four Decades of Commentary,* ed. Gary Carner (New York: Schirmer, 1996), 41.

17. I refer here to Langston Hughes's poem "House in the World," in *The Collected Poems of Langston Hughes,* ed. Arnold Rampersad and David Roessel (New York: Alfred A. Knopf, 1998): 138.

> I'm looking for a house
> In the world
> Where the white shadows
> Will not fall.
> *There is no such house,*
> *Dark brothers,*
> *No such house*
> *At all.*

18. Emily Bernard, "A Familiar Strangeness: The Spectre of Whiteness in the Harlem Renaissance and the Black Arts Movement," in *New Thoughts on the Black Arts*

Movement, ed. Margo Natalie Crawford and Lisa Gail Collins (New Brunswick, N.J.: Rutgers University Press, 2005).

19. Ishmael Reed, "Introduction," in *The Ishmael Reader* (New York: Basic Books, 2000), xvi.

20. Billy Taylor, "Negroes Don't Know Anything about Jazz," *Duke* (August 1957), reprinted in Dom Cerulli, Burt Korall, and Mort Nasatir, eds., *The Jazz Word* (New York: Ballantine, 1959), 43. *Duke,* a short-lived black men's magazine modeled after *Playboy,* was founded by Dan Burley, a blues pianist, writer, and editor for the *Chicago Defender,* the *New York Amsterdam News,* and the Johnson Publishing Co. (publisher of *Jet* and other magazines aimed at the African American mass market).

21. Scott DeVeaux, "Constructing the Jazz Tradition: Jazz Historiography," *Black American Literature Forum,* fall 1991, 553.

22. A bibliography of this work includes (but should not be limited to): Gary Carner, ed., "Literature of Jazz," Special Issue of *Black American Literature Forum* (fall 1991); Brent Hayes Edwards, Farah Jasmine Griffin, and Maria Damon, eds., "Jazz Poetics: A Special Issue," *Callaloo* (winter 2002); Scott DeVeaux, *The Birth of Bebop: A Social and Musical History* (Berkeley: University of California Press, 1997); Gerald Early, ed., *Miles Davis and American Culture* (St. Louis: Missouri Historical Society Press, 2001); Lewis Erenberg, *Swingin' the Dream: Big Band Jazz and the Rebirth of American Culture* (Chicago: University of Chicago Press, 1998); Krin Gabbard, *Jammin' at the Margins: Jazz and the American Cinema* (Chicago: University of Chicago Press, 1996); Krin Gabbard, ed., *Jazz among the Discourses* (Durham, N.C.: Duke University Press, 1993); Krin Gabbard, ed., *Representing Jazz* (Durham, N.C.: Duke University Press, 1993); Bernard Gendron, *Between Montmartre and the Mudd Club: Popular Music and the Avant-Garde* (Chicago: University of Chicago Press, 2002); Ted Gioia, *Imperfect Art: Reflections on Jazz and Culture* (New York: Oxford University Press, 1988); Ted Gioia, *West Coast Jazz: Jazz in California, 1945–1960* (New York: Oxford University Press, 1992); Farah Jasmine Griffin, *If You Can't Be Free, Be a Mystery: In Search of Billie Holiday* (Glencoe, Ill.: The Free Press, 2001); William Howland Kenney, *Chicago Jazz: A Cultural History, 1904–1930* (New York: Oxford University Press, 1993); Graham Lock, *Blutopia: Visions of the Future and Revisions of the Past in the Work of Sun Ra, Duke Ellington, and Anthony Braxton* (Durham, N.C.: Duke University Press, 1999); Paul Lopes, *The Rise of a Jazz Art World* (Cambridge: Cambridge University Press, 2002); Ingrid Monson, *Saying Something: Jazz Improvisation and Group Interaction* (Chicago: University of Chicago Press, 1996); Kathy J. Ogren, *The Jazz Revolution: Twenties America and the Meaning of Jazz* (New York: Oxford University Press, 1989); Robert O'Meally, *Lady Day: The Many Faces of Billie Holiday* (New York: Arcade Publishing, 1991); Robert O'Meally, ed., *The Jazz Cadence of American Culture* (New York: Columbia University Press, 1998); Robert O'Meally, Brent Hayes Edwards, and Farah Jasmine Griffin, eds., *Uptown Conversation: The New Jazz Studies* (New York: Columbia University Press, 2004); Jon Panish, *The Color of Jazz: Race and Representation in Postwar American Culture* (Jackson: University Press of Mississippi, 1997); Burton W. Peretti, *The Creation of Jazz: Music, Race, and Culture in Urban America* (Champaign: University of Illinois Press, 1992); Burton W. Peretti, *Jazz in American Culture* (Chicago: Ivan R. Dee, 1997); Porter, *What Is This Thing Called Jazz?;* Ronald M. Radano, *New Musical Figurations: Anthony Braxton's Cultural Critique* (Chicago: University of Chicago Press, 1993); Guthrie P. Ramsey Jr., *Black*

Cultures from Bebop to Hip Hop (Berkeley: University of California Press, 2003); Scott Saul, *Freedom Is, Freedom Ain't: Jazz and the Making of the Sixties* (Cambridge: Harvard University Press, 2003); David Stowe, *Swing Changes: Big Band Jazz in New Deal America* (Cambridge: Harvard University Press, 1994); John F. Szwed, *Space Is the Place: The Life and Times of Sun Ra* (New York: Pantheon, 1997); John F. Szwed, *So What: The Life of Miles Davis* (New York: Simon and Schuster, 2002); Mark Tucker, *Ellington: The Early Years* (Champaign: University of Illinois Press, 1991); Mark Tucker, *The Duke Ellington Reader* (New York: Oxford University Press, 1993); Sherri Tucker, *Swing Shift: "All-Girl Bands" of the 1940s* (Durham, N.C.: Duke University Press, 2000); Walter Van De Leur, *Something to Live For: The Music of Billy Strayhorn* (New York: Oxford University Press, 2002); Penny M. Von Eschen, *Satchmo Blows Up the World: Jazz Ambassadors Play the Cold War* (Cambridge: Harvard University Press, 2004).

23. For a gesture in this direction, see the essays in Eric Weisbard, ed., *This Is Pop: In Search of the Elusive at Experience Music Project* (Cambridge: Harvard University Press, 2004). Gene Santoro's *Highway 61 Revisited: The Tangled Roots of American Jazz, Blues, Folk, Rock, and Country Music* (New York: Oxford University Press, 2004); and Francis Davis's *The History of the Blues* (New York: Hyperion, 1995) show contemporary jazz/pop critics taking interesting historical approaches to American vernacular musics.

24. The unrepresented include Dave Dexter, Franklin S. Driggs, Albert McCarthy, William Grossman, Bill Coss, Dom Cerulli, Dick Katz, Don Heckman, Richard Hadlock, Bill Crow, Jack Tracy, Don Gold, Burt Korall, John McDonough, Tom Stites, Tom Piazza, and Kevin Whitehead. The underrepresented: Stanley Dance, Helen Oakley Dance, Ira Gitler, John S. Wilson, Joe Goldberg, Michael Zwerin, J. R.Taylor, and Lawrence Kart, among others.

25. James Lincoln Collier, *The Reception of Jazz in America: A New View* (New York: Brooklyn Institute for Studies in American Music, 1988) and *Jazz: The American Theme Song* (New York: Oxford University Press, 1993).

26. Among today's many excellent European jazz journals are *Musica Jazz*, an Italian journal edited by Maurizio Franco, and *The Source: Challenging Jazz Criticism*, a UK journal edited by Tony Whyton.

27. John Szwed, in *The Future of Jazz*, 156–57.

28. Dirk Sutro, *Jazz for Dummies* (Foster City, Cal.: International Data Group Books, 1998); Alan Axelrod, *The Complete Idiot's Guide to Jazz* (New York: Alpha/Macmillan, 1999).

29. See John Storm Roberts, *Latin Jazz: The First of the Fusions, 1880s to Today* (New York: Schirmer, 1999); Ned Sublette, *Cuba and Its Music: From the First Drums to the Mambo* (Chicago: Chicago Review Press, 2004); Max Salazar, *Mambo Kingdom: Latin Music in New York* (New York: Schirmer, 2003); Ruth Glasser, *My Music Is My Flag: Puerto Rican Musicians and Their New York Communities, 1917–1940* (Berkeley: University of California Press, 1995).

30. Matthew Fry Jacobson, *Whiteness of a Different Color: European Immigrants and the Alchemy of Race* (Cambridge: Harvard University Press, 1998); Jennifer Guglielmo and Salvatore Salerno, eds., *Are Italians White? How Race Is Made in America* (New York: Routledge, 2003); Bruce Boyd Raeburn, "Jazz and the Italian Connection," *The Jazz Archivist* (Newsletter of the William Ransom Hogan Jazz Archive), May 1991.

31. Sharony Andrews Green, personal communication with author, February 2002.

32. Valerie Wilmer, *As Serious as Your Life: The Story of the New Jazz* (1977; Westport, Conn.: Lawrence Hill and Company, 1980; Sharony Andrews Green, *Grant Green: Rediscovering the Forgotten Genius of Jazz Guitar* (San Francisco: Miller Freeman Books, 1999).

Chapter 1

1. Leonard Feather, *The Jazz Years: Eyewitness to an Era* (New York: Da Capo, 1987), 5–26.

2. Ibid., 16.

3. Ernst-Alexandre Ansermet, "Bechet and Jazz Visit Europe, 1919," English translation by Walter Schaap, reprinted in *Frontiers of Jazz,* ed. Ralph de Toledano (1947; Gretna, La.: Pelican/Gretna 1994), 110. On the U.S. culture war over jazz in the 1920s, see Neil Leonard, *Jazz and the White Americans: The Acceptance of a New Art Form* (Chicago: University of Chicago Press, 1962); Kathy Ogren, *The Jazz Revolution: Twenties America and the Meaning of Jazz* (New York: Oxford University Press, 1987); and McDonald Smith Moore, *Yankee Blues: Musical Culture and American Identity* (Bloomington: Indiana University Press, 1985).

4. Richard O. Boyer, "The Hot Bach" (1944), in *The Duke Ellington Reader*, ed. Mark Tucker (New York: Oxford University Press, 1993), 216.

5. Phyllis Rose, *Jazz Cleopatra: Josephine Baker in Her Time* (New York: Random House, 1989), 24.

6. Boyer, "Hot Bach," 215.

7. De Toledano, *Frontiers of Jazz*, 111.

8. Feather, *The Jazz Years*, 7–18.

9. Ibid., 18–22, 32–38. *Metronome* introduced Feather in its March 1936 issue as "the great English musical authority, Leonard G. Feather" (15).

10. Gary Giddins, "Leonard Feather: 1914–1994," *Village Voice.* Available online at www.leonardfeather.com/feather_obituary.html.

11. John Hammond, with Irving Townsend, *John Hammond on Record* (New York: Ridge Press, 1977): 326–27.

12. Leonard Feather, "Feather's Nest," *Down Beat*, August 27, 1964, 42–43.

13. Dan Morgenstern, remarks made in response to my paper "Duke Ellington, John Hammond, and the 'Lost Cause,'" at The Third Annual Duke Ellington Society Conference, The Institute of Jazz Studies, Newark, New Jersey, November 2, 2002.

14. David Stowe, *Swing Changes: Big Band Jazz and New Deal America* (Cambridge: Harvard University Press, 1994), 56.

15. Feather, *The Jazz Years*, 5 ("the forced attitudes . . ."), 48–49 (relationship with Vivian Dandridge).

16. Feather, *The Jazz Years*, 7.

17. Hammond and Townsend, *John Hammond on Record,* 77–87, 187–201. For excellent portraits of Hammond, see Lewis Erenberg, *Swingin' the Dream: Big Band Jazz and the Rebirth of American Culture* (Chicago: University of Chicago Press, 1998),

120–49; Paul Allen Anderson, *Deep River: Music and Memory in Harlem Renaissance Thought* (Durham, N.C.: Duke University Press, 2001), 219–47; and Stowe, *Swing Changes*, 54–64.

18. Erenberg, *Swingin' the Dream*, 124; Hammond and Townsend, *Hammond On Record*, 35.

19. Stowe, *Swing Changes*, 57.

20. Irving Kolodin, "Number One Swing Man," *Harper's*, September 1939.

21. Kevin Mumford, *Interzones: Black/White Sex Districts in Chicago and New York in the Early Twentieth Century* (New York: Columbia University Press, 1997), 155 ("all-white leisure zone") and 143 ("the cultural equivalent . . . "). Mumford's chapter titled "Slumming: Appropriating the Margins for Pleasure" (133–56) is a brilliantly incisive discussion of the phenomenon.

22. See, for instance, Ann Douglas, *Terrible Honesty: Mongrel Manhattan in the 1920s* (New York: Farrar, Strauss and Giroux, 1995); and Rose, *Jazz Cleopatra*.

23. W. E. B. Du Bois, "Criteria of Negro Art," *Crisis* 32 (October 1926). On Du Bois, see Arnold Rampersad, *The Art and Imagination of W. E. B. Du Bois* (Cambridge: Harvard University Press, 1968); David Levering Lewis, *W. E. B. Du Bois: Biography of a Race, 1868–1919* (New York: Henry Holt, 1993) and *W. E. B. Du Bois: The Fight for Equality, 1919–1963* (New York: Henry Holt, 2000); and Anderson, *Deep River*, 13–58. On the Harlem Renaissance generally, see Anderson, *Deep River*; Douglas, *Terrible Honesty*; Nathan Irvin Huggins, *Harlem Renaissance* (New York: Oxford University Press, 1971); David Levering Lewis, *When Harlem Was in Vogue* (New York: Vintage, 1979); Cary Wintz, *Black Culture and the Harlem Renaissance* (Houston, Tex.: Rice University Press, 1988); and George Hutchinson, *The Harlem Renaissance in Black and White* (Cambridge: Harvard University Press, 1995).

24. Langston Hughes, "The Negro Artist and the Racial Mountain," *Nation*, June 23, 1926, 692–94.

25. *Fire!!* 1, no. 1 (November 1926). This was the only issue of the journal. It was reprinted in 1982 by the Fire!! Press, Elizabeth, New Jersey.

26. Carl Van Vechten, "The Folksongs of the American Negro," *Vanity Fair*, July 1925, 40, 78, 84; "The Black Blues," *Vanity Fair*, February 1926, 57, 86; "Negro 'Blues' Singers," *Vanity Fair*, March 1926, 67, 106, 108.

27. These two examples of Van Vechten's popular reputation are cited in Mumford, *Interzones*, 144. The history book cited is Lloyd Morris, *Incredible New York: High Life and Low Life of the Last Hundred Years* (New York: Random House, 1951). On Van Vechten generally, see Bruce Kellner, *Carl Van Vechten and the Irreverent Decades* (Norman: University of Oklahoma Press, 1968); and three works by Emily Bernard—"What He Did for the Race: Carl Van Vechten and the Harlem Renaissance," *Soundings* 80, no. 4 (winter 1997): 531–42; *Black Anxiety, White Influence: Carl Van Vechten and the Harlem Renaissance* (Ph.D. dissertation, Yale University, 1998); and *Remember Me to Harlem: The Letters of Langston Hughes and Carl Van Vechten* (New York: Alfred A. Knopf, 2001).

28. Bernard, *Remember Me to Harlem*, xiv.

29. Quoted by Bernard, "What He Did for the Race," 531.

30. Bernard, *Remember Me to Harlem*, xv.

31. For a summary of these responses, see Bernard, *Remember Me to Harlem*, 532–34. Bernard argues that efforts "to downplay and even erase Van Vechten's role in the Harlem Renaissance reflect a widespread critical anxiety about white influence on black culture, which presumes that relationships between whites and blacks only benefit whites and always leave blacks compromised."

32. Ostensibly the story of a thwarted love affair between a Harlem librarian and an aspiring writer, Van Vechten's novel gave an insider's detailed portrait of Harlem life, using street vernacular, and paying special, even obsessive attention to sexuality and vice. Du Bois, writing in *The Crisis*, damned the novel as "an affront to the hospitality of black folk and to the intelligence of white" (W. E. B. Du Bois, review of *Nigger Heaven*, *The Crisis*, December 26, 1926, 81–82). In *The Messenger*, J. A. Rogers dismissed the book as "smut." Underlying these attacks was a concern that the commercial success of the book might encourage other writers to capitalize on salacious treatments of black life; for years after, book reviews in *The Crisis* invoked *Nigger Heaven* as the textbook example of an unacceptable representation of African American subject matter. The black press's denunciations of Van Vechten's novel diminished his status as a privileged insider. But Van Vechten still had friends in Harlem. Even they—James Weldon Johnson and Langston Hughes, for example—wouldn't defend the book's title or praise its literary merit. As Emily Bernard skillfully shows, however, Hughes and the other rebellious writers of the *Fire!!* school used the controversy over *Nigger Heaven* for their own purposes, framing the debate as an issue of artistic freedom—*their* freedom to write about sex, vice, and the colorful lives of "low-down Negroes" without being accused of betraying the race (Bernard, "What He Did for the Race," 535).

33. Mumford, *Interzones*, 149.

34. Mumford, *Interzones*, 145; Bernard, *Remember Me to Harlem*.

35. Mezz Mezzrow and Bernard Wolfe, *Really the Blues* (1946; New York: Citadel Underground, 1990). For a brilliant analysis of Mezzrow, see Gayle Wald, *Crossing the Line: Racial Passing in Twentieth-Century U.S. Literature and Culture* (Durham, N.C.: Duke University Press, 2000), 53–81.

36. Hammond and Townsend, *Hammond on Record*, 106.

37. Feather, *The Jazz Years*, 27–31.

38. Leonard Feather, "The Politics of Jazz," *New Republic*, December 16, 1985, 6. Feather was responding to a *New Republic* article by James Lincoln Collier titled "The Faking of Jazz" [*New Republic*, November 18, 1985, 33–40]. In that article (and later in his monograph, *The Reception of Jazz in America: A New View* [New York: Institute for Studies in American Music, 1988]), Collier makes the argument that the leading American jazz critics of the 1930s and 1940s were Communist dupes who created a myth of American hostility toward jazz in order to make the establishment look bad. I take on these and other of Collier's dubious arguments in my essay "Jazz Criticism: Its Development and Ideologies," *Black American Literature Forum* (fall 1991): 449–523.

39. Charles Edward Smith, "Class Content of Jazz Music," *Daily Worker*, October 21, 1933, 7.

40. Erenberg, *Swingin' the Dream*, 130.

41. John Hammond, quoted in "Interview with John Hammond," in Ronald G. Welburn, *American Jazz Criticism, 1914–1940* (Ph.D. dissertation, New York University, 1983), 214. Cited by Anderson, *Deep River*, 236.

42. James Smethurst, *The New Red Negro: The Literary Left and African American Poetry, 1930–1946* (New York: Oxford University Press, 1999), 30. On the 1930s folklorists more generally, see Benjamin Filene, *Romancing the Folk: Public Memory & American Roots Music* (Chapel Hill: University of North Carolina Press, 2000), especially 47–75. On folk music and Leftist politics, see Robert Cantwell, *When We Were Good: The Folk Revival* (Cambridge: Harvard University Press, 1996); and Robbie Lieberman, *My Song Is My Weapon: People's Songs, American Communism, and the Politics of Culture, 1930–1950* (Champaign: University of Illinois Press, 1989).

43. Smethurst, *The New Red Negro*: 49, 93–116, 137–41. On Zora Neale Hurston's construction of the black folk, see Hazel Carby, "The Politics of Fiction, Anthropology and the Folk: Zora Neale Hurston," in *New Essays on "Their Eyes Were Watching God,"* ed. Michael Awkward (Cambridge and New York: Cambridge University Press, 1990); and Anderson, *Deep River*, 197–213.

44. Stowe, *Swing Changes*, 94–140.

45. On the Popular Front and jazz, see Michael Denning, *The Cultural Front: The Laboring of American Culture in the Twentieth Century* (London: Verso, 1996), 328–38; Erenberg, *Swingin' the Dream*, 120–49; and Stowe, *Swing Changes*, 50–93.

46. Dave Dexter Jr., "Los Angeles Hot Fans Flayed for Hammond Attack," *Down Beat*, July 15, 1940, 6.

47. Anderson, *Deep River*, 229; Erenberg, *Swingin' the Dream*, 126–27; Benny Goodman and Irving Kolodin, *The Kingdom of Swing* (1939; New York: Frederick Ungar, 1961;), 129, 133, 157; Hammond and Townsend, *Hammond on Record*, 127–48.

48. For a discussion of Hammond's 1933 recordings of Holiday and Bessie Smith, see Robert O'Meally, *Lady Day: The Many Faces of Billie Holiday* (New York: Arcade, 1991), 59–61. Chris Albertson notes that Hammond thought the Bessie Smith sides—"Do Your Duty," "Gimme a Pigfoot," "Down in the Dumps," and "Take Me for a Buggy Ride"—were inferior to her best material from the 1920s, largely because the band he assembled "lacked the special qualities essential to good accompanists." Evidently Smith requested that it not be a blues session. Chris Albertson, *Bessie* (1972; New Haven, Conn.: Yale University Press, 2003), 228.

49. Albertson, *Bessie*, 224–25.

50. Ibid., 215–26.

51. John Hammond, "Did Bessie Smith Bleed to Death While Waiting for Medical Aid?" *Down Beat*, November 1937, 3.

52. O'Meally, *Lady Day*, 109–15.

53. Erenberg, *Swingin' the Dream*, 128.

54. Hammond and Townsend, *Hammond on Record*, 165–70.

55. John Hammond, "Kansas City a Hot-Bed for Fine Swing Musicians," *Down Beat*, September 1936, 1, 9.

56. John Hammond, "Basie Makes Chi Debut—Field's Flops in N.Y. 'Satchelmo's' Book Reveals Boastful Artist," *Down Beat*, November 1936, 3. This and the previous citations are made by Anderson, *Deep River*, 241.

57. John Hammond (Henry Johnson), "Jim Crow Blues," *New Masses*, December 13, 1938, 27; Hammond and Townsend, *Hammond on Record*, 171.

58. Albertson, *Bessie,* 284, 287.

59. Billie Holiday with William Dufty, *Lady Sings the Blues* (1956; London and New York: Penguin, 1992), 74.

60. Holiday and Dufty, *Lady Sings the Blues*, 60–61; O'Meally, *Lady Day*, 125.

61. Jones, quoted in Donald Clarke, *Wishing on the Moon* (New York: Viking Press, 1994), 69. Clarke accepts Jones's version and says, "As far as we can ever reach a conclusion, it certainly looks as though Hammond meddled between Basie and Billie and helped to wreck what must have been one of the era's great partnerships" (70). Paul Allen Anderson quotes and implicitly endorses this conclusion in *Deep River*, 242. Robert O'Meally advances a different view. First, he notes that Willard Alexander, writing in *Down Beat* in September 1938, argued that Basie (and Alexander) had wanted to fire Holiday even earlier, because of her "distinctly wrong attitude towards her work," but Hammond had pushed for keeping her. While not categorically endorsing this version, O'Meally wants to suggest that Hammond might not have played the heavy in forcing a rupture between Holiday and Basie. The best explanation, in his view, is that the collaboration "ceased to make sense" economically. He writes: "Because Basie and Holiday had contracts with different record companies, they could not make records together. Basie always said simply that she was becoming a star on her own and had begun to get offers that he could not begin to match. He said she had left with his blessing" (O'Meally, *Lady Day*, 126). Hammond himself denied responsibility for the firing and clearly would have preferred O'Meally's version. Whatever the truth about this particular case, what's not disputable is the resentment that some musicians harbored toward Hammond. "If you dare to criticize him," trumpeter Rex Stewart told Chris Albertson, "John Hammond will go out of his way to prevent you from working" (Albertson, *Bessie*, xiv).

62. Dorothy Chamberlain and Robert Wilson, eds., *The Otis Ferguson Reader* (Highland Park, Ill.: December Press, 1982), 102. Cited by Stowe, *Swing Changes*, 60.

63. B. H. Haggin, "Music," *Nation*, October 14, 1939, 420.

64. Duke Ellington, "Situation between the Critics and Musicians is Laughable—Duke Ellington," *Down Beat* (April 1939): 4, 9. This article was one of a series that Ellington published in *Down Beat* in 1939 that are reprinted in Tucker, *The Duke Ellington Reader*, 132–40.

65. *Down Beat*, May 1939, 10.

66. The "From Spirituals to Swing" concerts of 1938 and 1939 were recorded and later released on the Vanguard label in 1959 as a double LP. They were reissued by Vanguard in a two-CD format in 1987, then in a three-CD format in 1999.

67. Anderson, *Deep River*, 225.

68. Howard Taubman, "Negro Music Given at Carnegie Hall," *New York Times*, December 24, 1938, reprinted in *The Black Perspective in Music* 2 (1974): 207–8; "Boogie-Woogie," *New Yorker* (December 31, 1938): 13.

69. Anderson, *Deep River*, 235.

70. Gerald Early, "Pomp and Circumstance: The Story of Jazz in High Places," in *The Jazz Cadence of American Culture*, ed. Robert O'Meally (New York: Columbia University Press, 1998), 393–430.

71. Ibid., 409.

72. Anderson, *Deep River*, 235.

73. Alain Locke, *The Negro and His Music* (1936; New York: Arno Press, 1969). For a thorough and brilliant discussion of Locke's music criticism and larger cultural theory, see Anderson, *Deep River*, 113–66.

74. See the collection of Roger Pryor Dodge writings edited by his son, Pryor Dodge (with a keen and helpful introduction by Dan Morgenstern), *Hot Jazz and Jazz Dance: Roger Pryor Dodge Collected Writings, 1929 to 1964* (New York: Oxford University Press, 1995). "Whiteman-Gershwin faddism" and "white-collar meddling," along with my paragraph's final quotation, are drawn from the essay "Consider the Critics," 44–74, originally published in the book *Jazzmen* in 1939. "Virile non-emasculated," "primitive innate musical instinct," and "continuous flow of musical thought" come from the essay "Negro Jazz," 3–8, originally published in London's *The Dancing Times* in 1929. Dodge elaborates on early Ellington in the essay "Harpsichords and Jazz Trumpets," 12–26, originally published in *Hound & Horn* in 1934.

75. Early, "Pomp and Circumstance," 424.

76. Hammond and Townsend, *Hammond on Record*, 200.

77. James Dugan and John Hammond, "The Music Nobody Knows," program notes to "From Spirituals to Swing" (December 23, 1938), reprinted in *The Black Perspective in Music* 2 (1974): 196–207.

78. "Between Ourselves," *New Masses*, November 15, 1938, 2; cited by Anderson, *Deep River*, 239.

79. "Boogie-Woogie," *New Yorker*, December 31, 1938, 13; Anderson, *Deep River*, 239–40.

80. Mark Tucker, *Ellington: The Early Years* (Champaign: University of Illinois Press, 1991), 3–28; Constance McLaughlin Green, *Washington: Capital City, 1879–1950* (Princeton, N.J.: Princeton University Press, 1963), vii–viii. For an eloquent discussion of Ellington in relationship to Washington, D.C., see also Albert Murray, "Storiella Americana: Duke Ellington, the Culture of Washington, D.C. and the Blues as Representative Anecdote," *Conjunctions* 16 (summer 1991): 209–19.

81. Edward Kennedy Ellington, *Music Is My Mistress* (New York: Doubleday, 1973), 17.

82. Arthur A. Schomburg, "The Negro Digs Up His Past," in *The New Negro*, ed. Alain Locke (1922; New York: Albert & Charles Boni, Inc., 1925), 231.

83. Gerald Early, "Pomp and Circumstance: The Story of Jazz in High Places," in *The Jazz Cadence of American Culture*, ed. Robert O'Meally (New York: Columbia University Press, 1998), 413–14; Anderson, *Deep River*, 104.

84. Anderson, *Deep River*, 265.

85. John Hammond, "The Tragedy of Duke Ellington, the 'Black Prince' of Jazz," *Down Beat*, November 1935, 1, 6, reprinted in Tucker, *The Duke Ellington Reader*, 119–20.

86. Duke Ellington, "Duke Says Swing Is Stagnant," *Down Beat*, February 1939, 2, 16–17, reprinted in Tucker, *The Duke Ellington Reader*, 135.

87. As Krin Gabbard has detailed, Ellington's ambitions in this direction were well represented in his feature role in the nine-minute short film *Symphony in Black*, released in 1935. *Symphony in Black* was a hymn to Ellington's aspirations as a serious composer, starting with the high-art connotations of the title and including carefully edited shots

showing the master at work in the "Duke Ellington Studio" writing out music on score paper, then leading his orchestra in performance in a stately concert hall with both the musicians and the all-white audience clad in formal attire. Throughout the film, these scenes of Ellington in the process of composing and of the orchestra in performance are intercut with a series of dramatizations of episodes in black life. Four vignettes unfold in tandem with a musical score that references different idioms of black music. The opening segment ("The Laborers"), showing heavily muscled black men loading bales on a riverboat and stoking a blast furnace, features a work song theme. The second section is a melodramatic rendering of a love triangle, with Billie Holiday, in her first film appearance, singing a blues. The third section, called "A Hymn of Prayer," dramatizes the death of a child, using a musical theme drawn from the spirituals to commemorate black religious piety. The final section ("Harlem Rhythm") is a joyous celebration of uptown nightlife, with "Snake Hips" Tucker and four chorus girls sensuously dancing to the Ellington orchestra's swinging jazz. Krin Gabbard, *Jammin' at the Margins: Jazz and the American Cinema* (Chicago: University of Chicago Press, 1996), 172–76.

88. On World War II–era pluralist ideology and African American culture, see Barbara Dianne Savage, *Broadcasting Freedom: Radio, War, and the Politics of Race* (Chapel Hill: University of North Carolina Press, 1999); and Lauren Sklaroff, *Ambivalent Inclusion: The State, Race, and Official Culture, 1930–1950* (Ph.D. dissertation, University of Virginia, 2003).

89. Ellington's original conception for the work included two movements, titled "Africa" and "Slaveship." Ellington historian John Hasse suggests that Ellington may have dropped those two movements because of "his innate patriotism and a desire, especially during wartime, to emphasize positive aspects of American pluralism." John Edward Hasse, *Beyond Category: The Life and Genius of Duke Ellington* (New York: Da Capo, 1993), 261.

90. Irving Kolodin, "Notes on the Program" (Duke Ellington and His Orchestra, Carnegie Hall, January 23, 1943), reprinted in Tucker, *The Duke Ellington Reader*, 161–64.

91. John Hammond, "Is the Duke Deserting Jazz?" *Jazz*, May 1943, 15, reprinted in Tucker, *The Duke Ellington Reader*, 171–73.

92. Bob Thiele, "The Case of Jazz Music," *Jazz*, July 1943, 19–20, reprinted in Tucker, *The Duke Ellington Reader*, 175–78.

93. Dodge, *Hot Jazz and Hot Dance*, 349–50.

94. Leonard Feather, [a rebuttal of Hammond], *Jazz*, May 1943, 14.

95. Stowe, *Swing Changes*, 50–51.

96. Tellingly, in Ellington's *Music Is My Mistress*, a memoir largely organized as a series of reminiscences about musicians and music business people, one of the very few sustained discussions of a set of performances comes in the section titled "Jump for Joy Extension." Ellington had placed great hopes in *Jump for Joy*, and he was deeply disappointed when the show closed after just a three-month run at Los Angeles's Mayan Theater and then failed to secure backing for a Broadway run. At the urging of his agent, William Morris Jr., Ellington returned to the writing of a long composition that he hoped would salvage and augment the "feeling of responsibility that *Jump for Joy* had aroused." Ellington, *Music Is My Mistress*, 175–85. For discussion of *Jump for Joy* as part

of Popular Front musical theater, see Denning, *The Cultural Front*, 309–19; and Erenberg, *Swingin' the Dream*, 144–49.

97. Hammond and Townsend, *Hammond on Record*, 209; Denning, *The Cultural Front*, 325.

98. Hammond and Townsend, *Hammond on Record*, 136–37.

99. Leonard Feather, *The Book of Jazz* (1957; New York: Horizon, 1965), 47.

100. Ibid., 39.

101. Ibid., 52–53.

102. Ibid., 41.

103. Feather, *The Jazz Years*, 30.

104. This episode is discussed by Ernest Borneman in "The Jazz Cult [Part Two]: War among the Critics," *Harper's*, March 1947, 69. I return to Borneman, Feather, and Ulanov in chapter 3.

105. Leonard Feather, "Wanted: A White Mammy," *Negro Digest*, November 1945, 45–47. The title captured the column's spirit of a jocular racial revenge fantasy. Feather would have his fictional black professional hire an "ofay maid" and tell his friends: "Why, I have nothing against white people. Why, we've even had a dear old white [mammy] in our house for years and I just don't know *what* we'd do without her!"

Chapter 2

1. E. J. Hobsbawm, *The Jazz Scene* (1959; New York: Pantheon, 1993), xiii–xv.

2. Krin Gabbard, *Black Magic: White Hollywood and African American Culture* (New Brunswick, N.J.: Rutgers University Press, 2004), 203.

3. Hobsbawm, *The Jazz Scene*, xv.

4. Ibid., 199.

5. Ibid., xvii.

6. Gabbard suggests that "like all homosocial activities, a serious devotion to collecting may even hinder a man from acquiring the regular company of a sympathetic woman, and not just because so many record collectors end up with the unkempt look of the nerd." To go with the hangdog look that comes from too much time spent in attics and basements poring over matrix numbers, the stereotypical record collector struggles—according to Gabbard and other scholars writing under the influence of Lacanian psychoanalytic theory—with anxieties over the completeness of his masculine inventory. On this theory, the completist mode of collecting—trying to accumulate the entirety of a particular artist's recorded output, for instance—is the displacement of an anxiety over the wholeness of the body (and of the psychosexual emotional balance that goes with it) within a symbolic order: "the man whose collection is complete has no gaps and thus no anxieties about what is not there. The serial collector seeks plenitude, the warding off of castration" (Gabbard, *Black Magic*, 200).

7. *Blackboard Jungle*. Dir. Richard Brooks. Metro-Goldwyn-Mayer, 1955.

8. *Ghost World*. Dir. Terry Zwigoff. Metro-Goldwyn-Mayer/United Artists, 2000.

9. Gabbard, *Black Magic*, 224.

10. Ibid., 212.

11. Nat Hentoff, *Boston Boy* (New York: Alfred A. Knopf, 1983), 59, and interview with author, October 21, 1992.

12. John Gennari interview with Nat Hentoff, October 21, 1992.

13. George Frazier, "Swing Critics," *Jazz Hot* (July 1936): 3.

14. George Frazier, "Martha Tilton Stinks," *Down Beat* (November 1938): 1.

15. George Frazier, "'Boston Remains as Dull and Stupid as Ever,'" *Down Beat* (February 1937): 2, 4.

16. Cited in Charles Fountain, *Another Man's Poison: The Life and Writing of Columnist George Frazier* (Chester, Conn.: Globe Pequot Press, 1984), 138.

17. Ibid., 139.

18. Ibid., 79.

19. George Frazier, "Crosby Band 'My Pet,' but Dissipates Talent," *Down Beat* (August 15, 1941): 8.

20. Hentoff, *Boston Boy*, 128.

21. Ibid., 128.

22. Bryant Dupre interview with Martin Williams, February 28, 1989. This interview is also the source of the other quoted phrases in this paragraph.

23. Ibid. In the interview Williams, after delivering the quoted line, says, "I should have said to her: 'You ought to know.'"

24. Ibid.

25. This description draws from J. C. Thomas's discussion of the early 1950s Philadelphia jazz and R&B scene in *Chasin' the Trane: The Music and Mystique of John Coltrane* (New York: Da Capo, 1976), 55–58.

26. From "It had to do . . . " to "arrogant, uppity" comes from Dupre's interview with Williams, February 28, 1989. The remainder of the quotation, from "[When I] saw Bird's combo . . . ," is from a conversation Williams had with Gene Santoro, which Santoro cited in his column in *The Nation* on November 11, 1991.

27. Most of this passage is taken verbatim from the Dupre interview with Williams. The phrase "one aesthetic whole" and the line "I think it was then that I was first in touch with the essential miracle of the music" are from Williams's brief mention of this incident at the end of his chapter on Bechet in *The Jazz Tradition* (New York: Oxford University Press, 1993 [1970]), 47.

28. Fredric Jameson, "'In the Destructive Element Immerse': Hans Jurgen Syberberg and Cultural Revolution," *October* 17 (summer 1981): 113.

29. Ralph Gleason, *Celebrating the Duke* (New York: Da Capo, 1995 [1975]), 64.

30. "United Hot Clubs of America Get Going," *Metronome* (December 1935).

31. Fountain, *Another Man's Poison*, 51.

32. John Gennari interview with George Avakian, September 20, 1992.

33. Transcript of Marshall Stearns interview with Sheldon Harris, 1961; found in box labeled "Stearns" at Institute of Jazz Studies, Newark, New Jersey.

34. Neil Leonard, *Jazz and the White Americans* (Chicago: University of Chicago Press, 1983), 138; Dave Dexter Jr., "They All Know Milt Gabler," *Down Beat* (April 15, 1940): 12.

35. Bryant Dupre interview with Walter Schaap, May 17, 1992.

36. Stearns interview with Harris.

37. This passage comes from a transcript of the responses made by jazz critics to a set of questions posed by Ken Williamson in the volume he edited titled *This Is Jazz* (London: Newnes, 1960), 250.

38. Ibid.

39. Gleason, *Celebrating the Duke*, 64–65.

40. My discussion of Schaap in the next several paragraphs is drawn from Bryant Dupre's interview with him on May 17, 1992.

41. Charles Delauney, *New Hot Discography: The Standard Directory of Recorded Jazz*, ed. Walter E. Schaap and George Avakian (New York: Criterion, 1948). A key breakthrough in this research came when Schaap gained access to the files of the American Federation of Musicians. With the recording ban in the early 1940s, the AFM began paying royalties on previously produced records into a musicians' pension fund, the receipts for which constituted a de facto discography of those records.

42. Ralph de Toledano's papers are at the Hoover Institution at Stanford University. The "Correspondence, 1949–1971" and "Writings, 1940–1970" files are a good place to start for an overview of his career. For a sampling of his voluminous published writings, see *Nixon* (New York: Henry Holt, 1956); *Seeds of Treason: The True Story of the Chambers-Hiss Tragedy* (Boston and Los Angeles: Americanist Library 1956, 1962); *J. Edgar Hoover: The Man in His Times* (New Rochelle, N.Y.: Arlington House, 1973); and *Notes from The Underground: The Whitaker Chambers-Ralph de Toledano Letters, 1949–1960* (Indianapolis: Regnery, 1997). De Toledano's syndicated column continues to appear in such conservative outlets as *The Federal Observer* and *Insight on the News*. See Kenneth R. Weinstein, "Rise of the Judeo-Cons," *Azure* (autumn 1999), for discussion of de Toledano's flirtation with Catholicism under the evangelical hand of William F. Buckley Jr. Weinstein writes that de Toledano—a Moroccan-born Sephardic Jew—"stopped short of conversion out of respect for his Sephardi forebears who had suffered at the hands of the Inquisition." De Toledano contributes music essays to the *National Review*. At the 2002 meeting of The Philadelphia Society, a forum for conservative intellectuals, he delivered a paper titled "American Music: Classical, Popular, and Jazz," in which he characterized the Ken Burns PBS jazz series as "reversely racist" in allegedly claiming that "jazz is strictly African-American in derivation." He wrote, "When the Swing Era broke upon us in the mid-1930s, I was one of a group of young critics, many of us still in college, who tried to define the music in which Benny Goodman, Artie Shaw, Louis Armstrong, Duke Ellington, and many others were playing—and to dig back to the roots." He goes on to present a portrait of the multiracial origins of jazz not so very different from Burns's in its praise of both "great innovators" like Jelly Roll Morton and Duke Ellington and great white musicians like Bix Beiderbecke, Jack Teagarden, and Benny Goodman. "It was recognized as America's contribution to a music not lost in atonality and hyper-intellectualism," its "beat and its song" having been drowned out by "the meanderings of bop and eventually the obscenities of rap" (Cleveland Regional Meeting of The Philadelphia Society, September 21, 2002, www:townhall.com/phillyssoc/toledano.htm).

43. Ralph de Toledano, ed., *Frontiers of Jazz* (New York: Pelican/Gretna 1994 [1947]), xii.

44. Mary Cummings, "Traveling on Unbeaten Paths," *Columbia College Today* (May 2001), www.college.columbia.edu/cct/may01

45. De Toledano reports this in the Class of 1938 Notes in *Columbia College Today* (November 2001).

46. Cummings, "Traveling on Unbeaten Paths."

47. Edward Rice, *The Man in the Sycamore Tree: The Good Times and Hard Life of Thomas Merton* (New York: Harcourt, 1985 [1970]). Ralph de Toledano, "Correspondence Courses," *Jester* (December 1935): 20; "Greyhound Rococco," *Jester* (February 1936): 22.

48. Barry Ulanov, "The Swing of Man," *Jester* (January 1936): 12.

49. Barry Ulanov, "In the Groove," *Jester* (September 1936): 11.

50. Barry Ulanov, untitled essay, *Jester* (October 1936).

51. For this overview of Barry Ulanov's career, I've used an obituary essay published in the *Barnard Campus News* (September 10, 2001) as well as information from an interview I conducted with Ulanov at the Union Theological Seminary in New York on December 13, 1994 (notes and transcript in author's possession).

52. All quotations in the foregoing three paragraphs are from John Gennari interview with Barry Ulanov, December 13, 1994.

53. Bob White, letter to the editor, *The New Republic* (February 12, 1940): 215.

54. Bob White, "'Stir' Haircut Plus Sneer at Goodman Equals a 'Critic,'" *Down Beat* (August 1, 1940): 9.

55. Bryant Dupre interview with George T. Simon, August 16, 1988.

56. "Impressions in Wax," *Metronome* (July 1937): 24.

57. "Impressions in Wax," *Metronome* (December 1936): 23.

58. "Impressions in Wax," *Metronome* (November 1937): 24.

59. Gary Giddins, *Faces in the Crowd* (New York: Oxford University Press, 1992), 120. The Goodman quote, from Benny Goodman with Richard Gehman, "That Old Gang of Mine," *Collier's* (August 20, 1956): 28, is cited by Erenberg (*Swingin' the Dream*, 4) whose account of the event has informed mine.

60. Stanley Dance, letter to editor, *Down Beat* (January 15, 1940).

61. John Gennari interview with George Avakian, September 20, 1992.

62. "Who's Who in the Critics Row," *Down Beat* (November 15, 1940): 2.

63. George Avakian, "Where Is Jazz Going?" *Down Beat* (September 1939): 9.

64. T. W. Adorno, "Perennial Fashion—Jazz," in Stephen Eric Bronner and Douglas MacKay Kellner, eds., *Critical Theory and Society: A Reader* (New York: Routledge, 1989), 205–6.

65. I take the *Down Beat* estimate from Charles Fountain, *Another Man's Poison*, 50. The *Metronome* figure is cited in Dave Dexter, *Jazz Cavalcade: The Inside Story of Jazz* (New York: Criterion, 1946). Dexter places *Down Beat's* readership at 50,000 as well. Fountain's figure seems more reliable. My research hasn't turned up an authoritative record of *Down Beat's* readership in the period, but I have considerable anecdotal evidence suggesting that *Down Beat* had a higher profile than *Metronome* until the early 1940s, when *Metronome's* All-Star concerts, featuring the winners of the magazine's reader's poll, boosted its popularity. *Metronome* remained New York–centered in its

editorial operation after its transformation into a swing magazine in the middle of the 1930s; its coverage of jazz over the next couple of decades was manifestly New York-centric. *Down Beat* was based in Chicago but used correspondents from all around the country in the late 1930s and ran many articles on popular musical developments in what it referred to as the "Corn Belt." David W. Stowe is on the mark in deploring the "urban chauvinism" of *Down Beat*'s coverage of so-called "corn" music in his article "Jazz in the West: Cultural Frontier and Region During the Era," *Western History Quarterly* (February 1992): 64.

66. "The Nation's New Radio Stars," *Metronome* (May 1935): 12.

67. Albert Heink Sendrey, letter to editor, *Metronome* (January 1937): 13.

68. George Simon, *The Big Bands* (New York: Macmillan, 1971 [1967]), 11.

69. "Who's Who in the Critics Row," *Down Beat* (November 15, 1940): 2.

70. "Chloroform 'Jeeter Bugs,' says Panassié," *Metronome* (November 1938): 44.

71. Milton Gabler, "Jazz, Critics, and This Book," Preface to *Frontiers of Jazz*, ed. Ralph de Toledano, vii.

72. See Dexter, "They All Know Milt Gabler," 12.

73. Ron Welburn interview with Russell Sanjek, February 11, 1982 (transcript in appendix to Welburn, "American Jazz Criticism, 1900–1940," Ph.D. dissertation, New York University, 1983).

74. Ibid.

75. Scott DeVeaux makes a similar argument about 1940s jazz polemics in his article, "Constructing the Jazz Tradition: Jazz Historiography," *Black American Literature Forum* (fall 1991): 537.

76. Ernest Borneman, "The Jazz Cult [part two]: War among the Critics," *Harper's* (March 1947).

77. If we think of jazz primarily in terms of the music's recorded history, then the United Hot Clubs and Milt Gabler's Commodore label and retail operation clearly overshadowed the Hot Record Society in terms of lasting presence in the jazz market. Gabler's Commodore label became a sanctuary for record projects holding little promise of a major financial return, often involving musicians who were otherwise, or at other times, commercially successful—a strategy through which Commodore netted, for instance, Billie Holiday's classic "Strange Fruit" recording. Much more important than a scorecard tabulation of the winners and losers in the critical wars of the 1930s, however, is a recognition of the connections between first-generation jazz criticism, the emerging market for jazz records, the shaping of audience tastes, and the advent of a jazz canon.

78. Hobsbawm, *The Jazz Scene*, 243–45. Hobsbawm explains that the European record companies turned to the critics for selections of U.S. imports and of European recording dates for American musicians. Because of Europe's comparatively laissez-faire intellectual property laws—coupled with the difficulties U.S. companies had in policing their copyrights internationally—the European critics were able to pick and choose from the recorded archive with a freedom not available to U.S.-based critics.

79. Here, according to the results of the *Down Beat* reader's poll, are the top ten swing bands of 1936, 1938, and 1939. In parentheses is the number of votes received by each band.

1936: Benny Goodman (3,534); Casa Loma (2,102); Jimmie Lunceford (744); Fletcher Henderson (705); Duke Ellington (645); Mal Hallett (605); Tommy Dorsey (231); Bob Crosby (183); Jimmy Dorsey (172); Chick Webb (158). *Down Beat* (October 1937): 8.

1938: Artie Shaw (2,535); Benny Goodman (2,497); Bob Crosby (1,486); Count Basie (889); Jimmy Dorsey (714); Tommy Dorsey (676); Casa Loma (618); Duke Ellington (461); Jimmie Lunceford (401); Gene Krupa (304). *Down Beat* (January 1939): 16.

1939: Benny Goodman (5,251); Glenn Miller (3,211); Bob Crosby (2,139); Artie Shaw (2,116); Count Basie (1,774); Duke Ellington (1,087); Jimmy Dorsey (992); Gene Krupa (945); Jan Savitt (931); Charlie Barnet (719). *Down Beat* (January 1, 1940): 12.

What is most revealing about these poll results apropos of the question of the relative popularity of white and black bands is not the predictable white dominance of the top spots, but the dramatic drop-off in votes between the top two positions and the rest of the field. Thus, while the third, fourth, and fifth place finishes by the Jimmie Lunceford, Fletcher Henderson, and Duke Ellington bands in 1936 at first suggests a strong showing for black swing bands, on closer inspection one realizes that these three bands *together* amassed fewer votes than the Casa Loma band. Duke Ellington is consistently in the top ten, but he never polled even a fifth of the votes that Benny Goodman did.

80. Here are the *Metronome* Musician's Hall of Fame inductees from February 1936 to August 1937: Red Norvo (2/36); Glen Miller (3/36); Toots Mondello (4/36); Anthony Rocco (5/36); Bunny Berrigan (6/36); Eddie Miller (7/36); Jimmy Dorsey (8/36), Teddy Wilson (9/36); Charlie Spivak (10/36); Artie Bernstein (11/36); Jack Teagarden (12/36); Sonny Dorham (2/37); Dave Tough (6/37); Casper Reardon (8/37).

81. In March 1936 Simon criticized Fletcher Henderson's band for being out of tune. In September 1936, Simon wrote that Jimmie Lunceford's saxes were out of tune. When Simon wrote, in 1937, that the Count Basie band played out of tune, John Hammond was furious. In a November 19, 1980 interview with Ron Welburn, Simon says of this incident: "John would never forgive me, though Bill [Basie] told me I was absolutely right because he changed some of the musicians after I wrote the article." In a later interview with Bryant Dupre (August 16, 1988), Simon reiterated the story, adding a new detail. The reason for the black bands' intonation and pitch problems, Simon said, was that "black musicians couldn't afford good horns."

82. *Metronome* (November 1936): 7–9.

83. "Panassié's All-Star Band Not So Bad," *Metronome* (December 1938): 16.

84. Ibid., 16.

85. *Amsterdam News* (April 8, 1939): 20.

86. The closing of the Savoy is well covered in Ken Burns's PBS jazz series, episode seven, "Dedicated to Chaos."

87. Edward Pessen, "The Kingdom of Swing: New York City in the Late 1930s," *New York History* (July 1989): 277.

88. David W. Stowe, *Swing Changes: Big Band Jazz in New Deal America* (Cambridge: Harvard University Press, 1994); Michael Denning, *The Cultural Front: The Laboring of American Culture in the Twentieth Century* (New York: Verso, 1997), especially 319–62;

Lewis Erenberg, *Swingin' the Dream: Big Band Jazz and the Rebirth of American Culture* (Chicago: University of Chicago Press, 1998).

89. Welburn interview with Sanjek.

90. See the interesting footnote on race records and the politics of jazz criticism in Albert Murray, *Stomping the Blues* (New York: Vintage Books, 1976), 50.

91. Lizabeth Cohen, *Making a New Deal: Industrial Workers in Chicago, 1919–1939* (New York: Cambridge University Press, 1990), 156

92. Frank Marshall Davis, *Livin' the Blues: Memoirs of a Black Journalist and Poet,* ed. John Edgar Tidwell (Madison: University of Wisconsin Press, 1992), 44–45. Davis also discusses his involvement with Black Patti Records, a short-lived Paramount race record spin-off named after the opera singer Sissieretta ("Black Patti") Jones. An editorial footnote indicates that the first twenty of the label's fifty-five issues were advertised in May 1927, but that trading appears to have ceased only four months later (357). Davis says he was to be part of a male choir of "native Africans" cutting a Black Patti record of African tribal, hunting, and fertility songs and war chants, but that the morning the group assembled for the recording session, they were told that Black Patti had gone bankrupt (118–19).

93. Marshall Stearns, *The Story of Jazz* (New York: Oxford University Press, 1956): 168.

94. Welburn interview with Sanjek.

95. Duke Ellington, "'Situation between the Critics and Musicians Is Laughable,'— Ellington," *Down Beat* (April 1939): 4, 9, 33.

96. John Gennari interview with Timuel Black, May 11, 1993.

97. *Down Beat* ran the "Is Benny Goodman's Head Swollen?" editorial in February 1937, motivated by "universal expressions of dislike for Benny among musicians, bookers, publishers, and other band leaders in New York." None of the Goodman detractors are quoted by name, but the piece does quote John Hammond as saying that Benny's enemies are also his own, suggesting the possibility that the whole thing was a Hammond-engineered publicity stunt. If so, it succeeded beyond its original intentions. *Metronome* ran a piece in April 1937 titled "'Benny; Swelled Head? Nix!' Say New York Boys," in which various musicians and industry professionals testify that Benny remains the same swell fellow he's always been.

98. The catalyzing article was R. Whitney Becker's "Disc Collectors Are Jerks," *Down Beat* (January 15, 1940). It was followed by a Dave Dexter Jr. piece in the February 15, 1940 issue of *Down Beat* with the headline "Record Collectors Rise Up to Razz Ideas of Whitney Becker, Who Calls 'Em Jerks," and the subhead "Protests Pour in from Three Nations!" Among the fan responses to the Becker piece quoted by Dexter was a letter from a Henry Miller, of Juarez, Mexico, calling Becker "a real ick" and inviting him south of the border for a "puss punching duel with no holds barred."

99. Benny Carter, "Do Critics Really Know What It's All About?" *Metronome* (May 1937): 17.

100. *Down Beat* (June 15, 1941): 21.

101. In addition to those of his writings we've already looked at, Hammond also published in *Down Beat* articles with titles like "Predicted Race Riot Fades as Dallas

Applauds Quartet" (October 1937): 1, 4, detailing the successes of the Goodman band, in this case in challenging the color line in the Deep South.

102. Stearns mentions this correspondence (with no further elaboration) in the 1961 Stearns-Harris interview cited above, a transcript of which I located at the Institute of Jazz Studies. I am not aware if this interview was ever published. Unfortunately, I was not able to find any of the letters themselves, nor have I been able to find out any information about Harrison Smith.

103. Marshall Stearns, "The History of 'Swing-Music,'" *Down Beat* (January 1937): 6.

104. "Chicago," *Metronome* (September 1936): 4.

105. Stearns, "The History of 'Swing-Music,'" 6.

106. Ellington, "Situation between the Critics and Musicians Is Laughable."

107. Benny Carter, "Do Critics Really Know What It's All About?" 17.

108. Gennari interview with Black.

109. Ron Welburn interview with Billy Rowe, March 17, 1981 (appendix, "American Jazz Criticism").

110. Ibid.

111. Frank Marshall Davis letter to Ron Welburn, August 31, 1982 (appendix, "American Jazz Criticism").

112. In an article such as "Should Negro Musicians Play in White Bands?" *Down Beat* (October 15, 1939), attention is drawn to the fact that the advent of mixed bands made it possible that black musicians could be taking jobs away from white musicians. But what is significant is how peremptorily this issue is dismissed, and how the discussion moves almost immediately to the question of musical style.

113. Leonard Feather letter to Ron Welburn, dated June 11, 1981 (appendix, "American Jazz Criticism").

114. Ron Welburn interview with John Hammond, June 3, 1980 (appendix, "American Jazz Criticism").

115. Dan Burley, "And What of Our Songwriters?" *New Amsterdam News* (September 9, 1939): 6.

116. A good example was Chase's column of May 20, 1939 (21), in which he instructs his readers on how to mount a campaign to pressure NBC.

117. Welburn interview with Hammond.

118. Davis letter to Welburn.

119. Davis, *Livin' the Blues*, 97.

120. Ibid., 136.

121. Ibid.

122. Ibid., 236–37.

123. Frank Marshall Davis, "No Secret—Best White Bands Copy Negroes," *Down Beat* (June 1938): 5.

124. Davis, *Livin' the Blues*, 286.

125. Ibid.

126. Ibid., 290.

127. Ibid.

128. Ibid., 284.

129. Ibid., 235.

130. Bernard Gendron, "'Moldy Figs' and Modernists: Jazz at War (1942–1946)," in *Jazz among the Discourses*, ed. Krin Gabbard (Durham, N.C.: Duke University Press, 1995), 31–56.

131. Davis, *Livin' the Blues*, 284–85.

132. Ibid., 284.

133. Ibid., 238.

134. Quoted in Studs Terkel, *"The Good War": An Oral History of World War II* (New York: Ballantine, 1984), 277.

135. "French Bury Jazz Discs Underground," *Down Beat* (November 1, 1939).

136. Charles Delauney, "Delauney in Trenches, Writes 'Jazz Not American,'" trans. Walter Schaap, *Down Beat* (May 1, 1940): 6.

137. Ibid.

138. For this quick sketch of this fascinating story I've relied on Ernest Borneman's article "The Jazz Cult (Part II. War Among the Critics)," *Harper's* (February 1947): 270–71, and on Marshall Stearns's discussion of the episode in *The Story of Jazz*, 285–86. Schultz-Kohn, who became Germany's leading jazz critic, is discussed at length in Michael H. Kater, *Different Drummers: Jazz in the Culture of Nazi Germany* (New York: Oxford University Press, 1992), especially 70–101.

139. This was a special edition of the book edited by Frederick Ramsey Jr. and Charles Edward Smith, and published by Harcourt, Brace, and Jovanovich in 1939. These Armed Services editions were supervised by a group called the Council on Books in Wartime.

Chapter 3

1. Eric Hobsbawm and Terence Ranger, *The Invention of Tradition* (Cambridge: Harvard University Press, 1983).

2. *Trading Twelves: The Selected Letters of Ralph Ellison and Albert Murray*, ed. Albert Murray and John F. Callahan (New York: Modern Library, 2000), 193.

3. Winthrop Sargeant, *Jazz: Hot and Hybrid* (New York: Da Capo, 1975 [E.P. Dutton, 1946, 1938]); Frederick Ramsey Jr. and Charles Edward Smith, eds., *Jazzmen: The Story of Hot Jazz Told in the Lives of the Men Who Created It* (New York: Limelight, 1985 [Harcourt Brace Jovanovich, 1939]); Marshall Stearns, *The Story of Jazz* (New York: Oxford University Press, 1956); *Jazz Dance: The Story of American Vernacular Dance* (New York: Schirmer, 1964).

4. According to Leonard Feather, one of the modernists given to using the term "moldy figs" as an epithet, the term originated with Sam Platt, a naval officer who had written to *Esquire* in June 1945 complaining about the self-righteousness of the traditionalists (Feather, *The Jazz Years: Eyewitness to an Era* [New York: Da Capo, 1987], 88).

5. Dan Morgenstern, "Introduction," in *Hot Jazz and Hot Dance: Roger Pryor Dodge Collected Writings, 1929 to 1964* (New York: Oxford University Press, 1995), vi.

6. Bernard Gendron, "Moldy Figs and Modernists," in *Between Montmartre and the Mudd Club: Popular Music and the Avant-Garde* (Chicago: University of Chicago Press, 2002), 121–41, quotations on 123, 139.

7. Rudi Blesh, *Shining Trumpets: A History of Jazz* (New York: Da Capo, 1976 [Knopf, 1958, 1946]); Barry Ulanov, *A History of Jazz in America* (New York: Da Capo, 1972 [1952]); Sidney Finkelstein, *Jazz: A People's Music* (1948; New York: International Publishers, 1988).

8. Finkelstein, *Jazz: A People's Music*, 15.

9. Nat Hentoff, "Foreword," in Ramsey and Smith, eds., *Jazzmen*, xi.

10. Each of the three quotations is from the section headpieces written by Charles Edward Smith in *Jazzmen*: "Don't look for the eagle . . . ," 4; "how he leaned . . . ," 98; "Drop a nickel . . . ," 248.

11. William Russell, "Boogie Woogie," in *Jazzmen*, 202.

12. Smith, *Jazzmen*, 3, 209.

13. *Jazzmen*, 13, 122, 190, 159.

14. Ramsey and Smith, *Jazzmen*, xv; Charles Edward Smith, "It's Tough Trying to Run Down Jazz Facts," *Down Beat* (January 1, 1940); Frederick Ramsey Jr., "What Shall We Do with Jazz," *High Fidelity* (April 1956).

15. *Jazzmen*, xiii.

16. Ernest Borneman, "The Jazz Cult (Part II. War among the Critics)," *Harper's*, March 1947, 266. Whether Johnson really was "the real thing" became a controversy that raged throughout the 1940s and 1950s in the pages of *Record Changer*, the traditionalist collector's magazine. The bickering quieted until 1978, when Donald M. Marquis, in his book *In Search of Buddy Bolden: First Man of Jazz* (Baton Rouge: Louisiana State University Press, 1978), forensically dismantled Bunk Johnson's self-authored legend, starting with Johnson's claim that he had played with Bolden. William Russell's posthumously published *New Orleans Style* (1994) is conspicuously silent on Marquis's revision, and in 1990 Russell recycled the original Johnson mythology in his liner notes to a series of CD reissues of his traditional jazz catalogue, American Music. Gary Giddins dissects these matters in *Visions of Jazz: The First Century* (New York: Oxford University Press, 1998), 59–62.

17. William Russell (1905–1992) amassed a major collection of jazz recordings, instruments, periodicals, photographs, and artifacts. The collection is housed at the Williams Research Center of The Historic New Orleans Collection, in New Orleans. In 1958, Russell became the first curator of the William Ransom Hogan Jazz Archive at Tulane University in New Orleans. Russell's percussion pieces from the 1930s—characterized by some critics as equal if not superior to the more celebrated work of John Cage, Henry Cowell, and Lou Harrison—are collected on the CD *Made in America: The Complete Works of William Russell*.

18. Alan Lomax, *Mister Jelly Roll: The Fortunes of Jelly Roll Morton, New Orleans Creole and "Inventor of Jazz"* (New York: Pantheon, 1993 [1950]). For an excellent recent biography of Morton, see Phil Pastras, *Dead Man Blues: Jelly Roll Morton Way Out West* (Berkeley: University of California, 2001).

19. William Russell, "Louis Armstrong," in *Jazzmen*, 130.

20. Frederick Ramsey Jr., "King Oliver and His Creole Jazz Band," in *Jazzmen*, 59–91, quotations on 71, 74.

21. William Russell, "Louis Armstrong," in *Jazzmen*, 119–42, quotations on 123, 139, 126, 130.

22. Ramsey, "King Oliver and His Creole Jazz Band," in *Jazzmen*, 85, 71.

23. Wilder Hobson, "New York Turns on the Heat," in *Jazzmen*, 213–20, quotation on 218.

24. Ramsey, "King Oliver and His Creole Jazz Band," in *Jazzmen*, 130–32.

25. Otis Ferguson's small oeuvre of jazz writing—about thirty-five essays, most published in *The New Republic*, where he also wrote about film—have been lauded by Whitney Balliett and others as a model for literate jazz writing. See Whitney Balliett, *Goodbyes and Other Messages* (New York: Oxford University Press, 1991), 57–61. Nat Hentoff dissented from this view in a response to Dan Morgenstern's claim that Ferguson "was a better writer than any the *Jazz Review* [the magazine edited by Hentoff and Martin Williams] has yet to come up with." Hentoff wrote back: "I do not agree that Ferguson was quite the remarkable prose stylist he is claimed to have been. He was often brilliantly evocative, but he was also often sentimental and, unwittingly, patronizing to the musicians." *Jazz Review* (March/April 1960): 4.

26. Otis Ferguson, "The Five Pennies," in *Jazzmen*, 221–42, quotations on 222, 222, 230, 231, 232.

27. Edward J. Nichols, "Bix Beiderbecke," in *Jazzmen*, 143–60, quotation on 158.

28. Smith, *Jazzmen*, 212.

29. Charles Edward Smith, "The Austin High School Gang," in *Jazzmen*, 161–82, quotations on 171, 179–80.

30. Charles Edward Smith, "White New Orleans," in *Jazzmen*, 39–58, quotations on 42, 57.

31. E. Simms Campbell, "Blues," in *Jazzmen*, 101–18; quotations on 104, 105. Finkelstein, *Jazz: A People's Music*, 3.

32. Blesh, *Shining Trumpets*, 185, 337.

33. Ibid., 324, 178, 18–23.

34. Ibid., 346, 135, 247, 244, 258–59.

35. Gendron, *Between Montmartre and the Mudd Club*, 130.

36. Blesh, *Shining Trumpets*, 241, 288, 290.

37. Ibid., 290, 278.

38. Ibid., 25, 75, 40, 87.

39. Ibid., 188, 25–47.

40. Ibid., 31, 101. James Snead, "Repetition as a Figure of Black Culture" (1984), reprinted in O'Meally, *The Jazz Cadence,* 62–81.

41. Blesh, *Shining Trumpets*, 63, 45.

42. Ibid., 207, 89, 88.

43. Ibid., 38, 14, 134, 259.

44. Ibid., 134, 200, 266, 320.

45. Ulanov, *A History of Jazz in America*, 9–13.

46. Fell, "Coolin' Off Ulanov," 11; Orrin Keepnews, "Barry's Clambake," *Record Changer* (April 1952): 5; Charles Edward Smith, "The Fog in the Fig Tree," *Record Changer* (March 1953): 3–5, 8.

47. Finkelstein, *Jazz: A People's Music*, 16, 104.

48. Ibid., 7–8, 27–28.

49. Ibid., 4, 176, 53, 111.

50. Ulanov, *A History of Jazz in America*, 4.

51. Ibid., 347–48.

52. Ibid., 339.

53. Blesh, *Shining Trumpets*, 377–78.

54. Keepnews, "Barry's Clambake," 6.

55. Finkelstein, *Jazz: A People's Music*, 150, 90–91.

56. Ibid., 150, 168.

57. Ibid., 105, 141, 137.

58. Ibid., 170, 163, 127.

59. Orrin Keepnews, "Jazz and America," *Record Changer* (August–September 1952): 32.

60. *Record Changer* (July–August 1953), "Special Issue: The Institute of Jazz Studies."

61. Ibid., 9.

62. Ibid., 14.

63. J. R. Goddard, "The Night Groundhog was King of the Gate," *Village Voice* (November 26, 1954).

64. "The Jazz Hoot," *New Yorker* (April 1, 1950); Richard Gehman, "The Jazz Scholar," *New York Herald-Tribune* (May 9, 1954): section 7.

65. Marshall Stearns, "Jim Crow at College," *Tomorrow* (February 1947): 5–10.

66. Robert Lucas, "Jazz Goes to College," *Negro Digest* (August 1951): 45–49.

67. I have culled these descriptions of Stearns and his lectures from a press kit titled "Columbia Lecture Bureau Leaflet" [IJS, box marked "Stearns"].

68. "Special Issue: The Institute of Jazz Studies," 15.

69. Robert Farris Thompson interview with John Gennari, June 3, 1999.

70. This description is drawn from a *New York Times Book Review* essay on Thompson that appeared as a blurb on the paperback edition of Thompson's *Flash of the Spirit: African and Afro-American Art and Philosophy* (New York: Vintage Books, 1984 [1983]).

71. Marshall Stearns, typewritten memo titled "By Way of Summary," undated [IJS, box marked "Stearns"].

72. Robert Reisner, "Reminiscences of Marshall Stearns," *Journal of Jazz Studies* (October 1973).

73. Robert Farris Thompson interview with John Gennari, June 3, 1999.

74. Robert Farris Thompson, letter to Institute of Jazz Studies, dated April 28, 1958 [IJS, box marked "Stearns"].

75. Stearns, *The Story of Jazz*, 295. Stearns's anticommunism had been firmly in evidence earlier in the decade. "American jazz circled the world in 30 years, and the Communists are *still* trying," he wrote in 1951, arguing that since "a totalitarian can't understand mobility or relaxation . . . of course [he] doesn't grasp jazz." "Reds Can't Comprehend Jazz, So Put It Down," *Down Beat* (March 23, 1951).

76. Stearns, *The Story of Jazz*, 315.

77. Marshall Stearns, "Is Jazz Good Propaganda? The Dizzy Gillespie Tour," *Saturday Review* (July 14, 1956): 28–31.

78. The "salty humor" quote is from Stearns's program notes for "A Concert in Blue," Cornell University, November 8, 1946. The other quotes in this paragraph are from Stearns, *The Story of Jazz*, 305, 307. The line "none of us is wholly free" was first used by Blesh, in *Shining Trumpets*, 148.

79. "Evening Event Schedule, School of Jazz, 1957" and Stearns's handwritten notes [IJS vertical file "Lenox"]. Blesh and Ulanov had always been on cordial terms in spite of their contrasting views. But their earlier public appearances together—such as a 1947 radio "battle of the bands" waged between a traditionalist band selected by Blesh and a modernist one selected by Ulanov—had been expressly designed to showcase their differences (Ulanov, *A History of Jazz in America*, 68–69).

80. Blesh, *Shining Trumpets*, 360.

81. Sheldon Meyer interview with John Gennari, July 16, 1992. Meyer had just joined the publishing house when Stearns's book was going to press. In the ensuing forty years, Meyer shepherded a number of the most important jazz books published in the U.S. and British markets.

82. Stearns, *The Story of Jazz*, 282.

83. Larry Gushee, "A Reconsideration [book review of *The Story of Jazz*]," *Jazz: A Quarterly of Music* 5 (winter 1960): 57–66. Gushee found wanting Stearns's explanations of harmony, melody, and rhythm as manifested in jazz and classical music, and took special exception to Stearns's suggestion that the only complex feature of African music was its rhythm:

> I suspect that the African Negro has been turned into the noble savage somewhere in [Stearns's] network of hypotheses. Contrary to what the overly intellectual non-jazz lover may think, the rhythms of the noble savage are really *complex*. What chagrin our civilized square must feel when he finds that the complexity which he prizes so highly in the melody and harmony of music he loves best, is also cultivated in African music—but in the very area where he has had to be content with stodgy minuets and the like. I'm sure Professor Stearns did not intend his ideas on jazz rhythm to be taken as a version of "The Black Man's Revenge"; but I think his exceptionally strong emphasis on African rhythm coupled with the way in which "classical" music and certain kinds of jazz are treated can't help but create such an impression.

84. Stearns's contributions to *Saturday Review*'s "Perspectives in Jazz" series included: "Breaking the Rhythm Barrier" (December 28, 1957: 35), on a cluster of recent Afro-Cuban recordings; "Make a Joyous Noise unto the Lord" (January 25, 1958: 47), on gospel; "Rock'n'Roll: Its Cause and Cure" (March 15, 1958: 47), on the good things about black rhythm-and-blues artists Ray Charles, Fats Domino, Little Richard, Joe Turner, Ruth Brown, and La Vern Baker, and the "relatively innocuous" nature of Elvis Presley's "muscular spasms," given that "the undulations of a genius named 'Snake Hips' Tucker at the Cotton Club in the late Twenties would have made Presley look like Rebecca of Sunnybrook Farms"; "Those Everlasting Blues" (March 29, 1958: 40), on a number of blues-oriented recent jazz records; and "How Square Is Musical Comedy" (April 26, 1958: 58–59), on jazz versions of 1950s musical comedies, such as The Tony Scott Quintet's *South Pacific Jazz* (ABC-Paramount 235), The Chico Hamilton Quintet's *South Pacific* (Pacific Jazz 1238), and André Previn and Shelly Manne's *My Fair Lady*,

Lil' Abner, and *Pal Joey* (Contemporary 3527, 3533, 3543). Stearns's "near-jazz is better than no jazz" comes from my interview with Robert Farris Thompson.

85. "Columbia Lecture Bureau Leaflet."

86. Stearns, *The Story of Jazz,* 24.

87. Willis Laurence James, "The Romance of the Negro Folk Cry in America," *Phylon* XVI/1 (1955): 15–30. Letter from Willis James to Marshall Stearns, dated August 13, 1951 [IJS, box marked "Stearns"].

88. Ralph Ellison letter to Albert Murray, April 1, 1956; *Trading Twelves*, 121.

89. Ralph Ellison, "The Charlie Christian Story," *Saturday Review* (May 17, 1958), reprinted in O'Meally, *Living with Music,* 34–42, quotation on 39.

90. Ralph Ellison, "Remembering Jimmy," *Saturday Review* (July 12, 1958), reprinted in O'Meally, *Living with Music,* 43–49, quotation on 46.

91. Robert O'Meally, "Jazz Shapes: Introduction," in *Living With Music,* xiv.

92. Ellison, "Remembering Jimmy," 44–45.

93. Ibid., 48.

94. Ibid.

95. Ibid., 47.

96. Berndt Ostendorf, "Anthropology, Modernism, and Jazz," in Robert O'Meally, ed., *New Essays on Invisible Man* (New York: Cambridge University Press, 1988), 95–118, quotation on 99.

97. Ellison, "The Golden Age, Time Past," 61.

98. Ibid., 60–61.

99. Ibid., 63.

100. O'Meally, "Jazz Shapes: Introduction," xxvii.

101. Ralph Ellison, "Harlem Is Nowhere," in *Shadow and Act* (New York: Random House, 1964), 294–302, quotations on 297, 296, 300.

102. Ellison, "The Charlie Christian Story," 41.

103. Ralph Ellison, "Homage to Duke Ellington on His Birthday," in O'Meally, *Living with Music,* 77–86, quotation on 80–81.

104. Ibid., 81.

105. O'Meally, "Jazz Shapes: Introduction," xx.

106. Ralph Ellison, "Blues People," in O'Meally, *Living with Music,* 120–32, quotation on 130.

107. Ralph Ellison, "Richard Wright's Blues," in *Shadow and Act*, 77–94, quotation on 78.

108. Ellison, "The Golden Age, Time Past," 54.

109. Ellison, "Blues People," 129.

110. William J. Maxwell, "In Place of Freedom: Ralph Ellison's Jazz Democracy," unpublished conference paper, quoted by permission of author.

Chapter 4

1. Nat Hentoff, "Jazz and the Intellectuals: Somebody Goofed," *Chicago Review* 9, no. 3 (fall 1955): 111. The Anatole Broyard reference is in retrospect all the more intriguing in light of Henry Louis Gates Jr.'s "outing" of Broyard as a black man who

passed for white. See Gates, *Thirteen Ways of Looking at a Black Man* (New York: Random House, 1997).

2. Nat Hentoff, *Boston Boy* (New York: Alfred A. Knopf, 1983), 162–65.

3. For overviews of and arguments about the cultural authority of American intellectuals after World War II, see Richard H. Pells, *The Liberal Mind in a Conservative Age: American Intellectuals in the 1940s and 1950s* (New York: Harper and Row, 1985); Andrew Ross, *No Respect: Intellectuals and Popular Culture* (New York: Routledge, 1989); Neil Jumonville, *Critical Crossings: The New York Intellectuals in Postwar America* (Berkeley: University of California Press, 1991); Harvey M. Teres, *Renewing the Left: Politics, Imagination, and the New York Intellectuals* (New York: Oxford University Press, 1996); Alan M. Wald, *The New York Intellectuals: The Rise and Decline of the Anti-Stalinist Left from the 1930s to the 1980s* (Chapel Hill: University of North Carolina Press, 1987); and David Hollinger's *In the American Province: Studies in the History and Historiography of Ideas* (Bloomington: Indiana University Press, 1985), chapter 5, "The Canon and Its Keepers: Modernism and Mid-Twentieth-Century American Intellectuals," 74–91.

4. Ross, *No Respect*, 42–64.

5. Hollinger, *In the American Province*, 74–91.

6. Teres, *Renewing the Left*, 204–29; Norman Podhoretz, "My Negro Problem—and Ours," *Commentary* (February 1963): 98.

7. Hentoff, *Boston Boy*, 3.

8. Nat Hentoff, *Speaking Freely: A Memoir* (New York: Alfred A. Knopf, 1997), 69.

9. Ibid., 5.

10. Teres, *Renewing the Left*, 208.

11. Hentoff discusses his New York-based activism in *Speaking Freely*. Gleason's prominence in San Francisco protest politics is celebrated in the testimonials included in "Ralph J. Gleason in Perspective," *Rolling Stone* (July 17, 1975): 39–49.

12. The biographical information on Dan Morgenstern in this paragraph and the next is drawn from interviews Morgenstern gave to Bryant Dupre and Eve Zanni, December 11, 1989, February 13, 1990, and June 13, 1990. The tapes are available at The Institute of Jazz Studies.

13. Gene Lees, *Cats of Any Color: Jazz, Black and White* (New York: Da Capo, 2001 [1995]), 4, 9.

14. Ibid., 5–6; Gene Lees, *Meet Me at Jim & Andy's: Jazz Musicians and Their World* (New York: Oxford University Press, 1988), 25–44.

15. Gene Lees, "Down Beat Days," *Gene Lees Jazzletter* (February 15, 1982): 3.

16. Lees, *Meet Me at Jim & Andy's*, xv.

17. Hentoff gives this account of his *Down Beat* firing in *Speaking Freely*, 45. A supporting contemporaneous source is his article "Going Out on the Street," *Metronome* (July 1961): 24–25.

18. Janet Sommer, "Dan Morgenstern Interview," www.allaboutjazz.com/journalists, 4.

19. Jack Tracy, [untitled editor's note], *Down Beat* (June 17, 1957): 5.

20. Sommer, "Dan Morgenstern Interview," 5–6.

21. Ben Sidran, *Black Talk* (New York: Holt, Rinehart, and Winston, 1971), 125.

22. Hentoff, *Speaking Freely*, 41–42.

23. Nat Hentoff, "The Other Side of the Record," *Metronome* (May 1961): 12.

24. The advertisement appeared in *Down Beat* (September 1, 1960).

25. Ralph Gleason, "Perspectives," *Down Beat* (January 23, 1957): 38.

26. Gene Lees, "Afterthoughts," *Down Beat* (December 22, 1960): 64.

27. Barbara Gardner, "Timmons in a Tempest," *Down Beat* (November 24, 1960): 14.

28. Leonard Feather, "Horace Silver Talks to Leonard Feather about Funk Fever," *Melody Maker* (January 28, 1961): 5.

29. Martin Williams, "The Funky-Hard Bop Regression," in *The Art of Jazz*, ed. Martin Williams (New York: Collier-Macmillan, 1964), 233–37.

30. Hsio Wen Shih, "Jazz in Print," *Jazz Review* (January 1961): 33–34. Shih, the son of a Chinese diplomat, was an MIT-educated architect, jazz writer, publisher of the *Jazz Review*, and, briefly, a partner of brothers Iggy and Joe Termini in the management of the Five Spot, the famous Lower East Side jazz club (Martin Williams, "A Night at the Five Spot," *Down Beat* [February 13, 1964]: 24). In 1961, Shih married the jazz harpist Daphne Hellman. As reported in obituaries for Hellman after her death in 2002, Shih walked out of their New York brownstone one day in 1965 and disappeared. ("Daphne Hellman, 86," *Provincetown Banner*, August 15, 2002). His fate remains enshrouded in mystery. A fine example of Shih's considerable musical perceptivity and writing skill is his liner note for the Afro-Cuban record *Palo Congo* (Blue Note BLP-1561, 1957).

31. Barbara Ehrenreich, *The Hearts of Men: American Dreams and the Flight from Commitment* (New York: Anchor Press/Doubleday, 1983), 42–67.

32. See the chapter "What Rough Beats?" in Dan Wakefield's *New York in the 50s* (Boston: Houghton Mifflin, 1992), 160–94. The "writer's writers" Wakefield says he regarded as exemplary were James Baldwin, William Styron, J. D. Salinger, and Carson McCullers.

33. Daniel Belgrad, *The Culture of Spontaneity: Improvisation and the Arts in Postwar America* (Chicago: University of Chicago Press, 1998), 179–222.

34. "Ralph Gleason in Perspective," *Rolling Stone* (July 17, 1975): 39–49.

35. Ralph Gleason, "Perspectives," *Down Beat* (May 2, 1957): 32.

36. Ralph Gleason, "Perspectives," *Down Beat* (November 14, 1957): 20.

37. Nat Hentoff, "A Brief Note on the Romance of 'The White Negro,'" in *The Jazz Life*, 138–42.

38. Whitney Balliett, *The Sound of Surprise* (New York: E. P. Dutton, 1959), 14.

39. Williams, *The Art of Jazz*, i.

40. Martin Williams, "Criticism: The Path of the Jazz Critic," *Down Beat* (August 21, 1958): 11, 42.

41. Martin Williams, "Introduction," in *Jazz Panorama*, ed. Martin Williams (New York: Collier-Macmillan, 1964), 8.

42. Gunther Schuller, "Sonny Rollins and the Challenge of Thematic Imrovisation," *Jazz Review* (November 1958), reprinted in Schuller, *The Musical Worlds of Gunther Schuller* (New York: Oxford University Press, 1986), 94.

43. See Peter Stallybrass and Allon White, *The Politics and Poetics of Transgression* (Ithaca, N.Y.: Cornell University Press, 1986) for a compelling theory of the symbolic

association between the "grotesque" female, maternal body and the degraded realm of popular culture, with consumers figured as helpless children wet-nursing at the breast of mass commercial institutions. Janice Radway brilliantly deploys this theory in *A Feeling for Books: The Book-of-the-Month Club, Literary Taste, and Middle-Class Desire* (Chapel Hilll: University of North Carolina Press, 1997), 210–12.

44. Dan Morgenstern, "Letters," *Jazz Review* (March–April 1960): 3–4.

45. Nat Hentoff, "Letters," *Jazz Review* (March–April, 1960): 4.

46. Ralph Gleason, *Celebrating the Duke (and Louis, Bessie, Billie, Bird, Carmen, Miles, Dizzy and Other Heroes)* (New York: Da Capo, 1995 [Little, Brown, 1975]), 200.

47. Dan Morgenstern, "Musings of a Jazz Critic," *Down Beat* (January 12, 1967): 22.

48. From beginning of quote up to "On the set": Nat Hentoff, *Jazz Is* (New York: Ridge Press, 1976), 50; from "On the set" end of quote: Hentoff, *Boston Boy*, 128. Much of this language reappears in Hentoff's recent recollection of the event in *Speaking Freely*, 54–68.

49. Joe Goldberg, "The Symposium," in *Jazz Panorama*, 294.

50. Hentoff, *The Jazz Life*, 251.

51. Martin Williams, *Down Beat* (September 19, 1968): 14.

52. Williams, "Introduction," in *Jazz Panorama*, 8.

53. Martin Williams interview with Bryant Dupre, February 18, 1989.

54. This description of F. R. Leavis at Harvard borrows from John Updike's testimony in "The Virtues of Playing Cricket on the Village Green," *New Yorker* (July 30, 1990): 85–89.

55. Williams, "Records Noted," *Record Changer* 14, no. 7 (1956).

56. Hollinger, *In the American Province,* 92.

57. I found these exams in one of the boxes at the Institute of Jazz Studies labeled "Marshall Stearns." This particular box contains notes and other materials Stearns used during his work at the Lenox School of Jazz.

58. Gary Giddins, *Faces in the Crowd* (New York: Oxford University Press, 1992), 257.

59. Willis Conover, "Query on a Critic," *Saturday Review* (July 25, 1964): 6.

60. Martin Williams interview with Bryant Dupre, February 18, 1989.

61. Whitney Balliett, *Collected Works: A Journal of Jazz, 1954–2000* (New York: St. Martin's Press, 2000), 13; Dan Morgenstern, "Hodeir's Party," *Jazz* (February 1963): 15.

62. Balliett and Leonard Feather organized a debate about Hodeir's book in which these views were given voice. Hodeir's response to his critics appears in chapter 6 of his later book *Toward Jazz*, trans. Noel Burch (New York: Grove Press, 1962).

63. André Hodeir, *Jazz: Its Evolution and Essence* (New York: Grove Press, 1979 [1956]), 99–116; Martin Williams, *The Jazz Tradition* (New York: Oxford University Press, 1983 [1970]), 3–10, 135–54.

64. Sheldon Meyer, speaking at Williams's memorial service at Mount Vernon, Virginia, April 18, 1992.

65. Williams, *The Jazz Tradition*, 141, 184.

66. Martin Williams interview with Bryant Dupre, February 18, 1989.

67. Williams, *The Jazz Tradition*, 251.

68. Ibid., 256.

69. Jackie Kendrick,[untitled book review], *Esher News and Advertiser* (September 17, 1970): 23; Frank Tirro, "Book Review," *Notes* (December 1970): 34; Michael James, [untitled book review], *Jazz Monthly* (December 1970): 7; Dan Morgenstern, "Books," *Down Beat* (October 15, 1970): 30.

70. Gary Tomlinson, "Cultural Dialogics and Jazz: A White Historian Signifies," *Black Music Research Journal* 11, no. 2 (fall 1991): 245–49.

71. Lawrence Kart, "Books," *American Record Guide* (May 1970): 777.

72. Francis Davis, "Struggling with Some Barbeque," *Village Voice* (July 21, 1987): 80.

73. Gary Giddins, "Setting the Standard: Martin Williams, 1924–1992," *Village Voice* (April 28, 1992): 67.

74. Martin Williams interview with Bryant Dupre, February 28, 1989.

75. Whitney Balliett interview with John Gennari, July 29, 1996.

76. Balliett, *Collected Works*, 76. The quoted phrases from the previous paragraph are from the same collection.

77. Ibid., 612.

78. Giddins, *Faces in the Crowd*, 261.

79. Robert Warshow, *The Immediate Experience* (Garden City, N.Y.: Doubleday, 1962), 105.

80. Balliett, *Collected Works*, 10.

81. Balliett, *The Sound of Surprise*, x.

82. Whitney Balliett interview with John Gennari, July 29, 1996.

83. Ben Yagoda, *The New Yorker and the World It Made* (New York: Scribner's, 2000), 401.

84. Yagoda, *About Town*, 316.

85. Balliett, *Collected Works*, 31.

86. Balliett, *The Sound of Surprise*, ix.

87. Whitney Balliett interview with John Gennari, July 29, 1996.

88. Gunther Schuller, "Sonny Rollins and the Challenge of Thematic Improvisation," *The Jazz Review* (November 1958), reprinted in Schuller, *Musings* (New York: Oxford University Press, 1986), 88–89.

89. Balliett, *The Sound of Surprise*, 189.

90. Balliett, *Collected Works*, 79.

91. Giddins, *Faces in the Crowd*, 262.

92. *Down Beat* (June 18, 1964): 17, 39.

93. Bruce Tucker, "Living Metaphors: Recent Black Music Biography," *Black Music Research Journal* (1983): 64–65.

94. Jon Hendricks interview with John Gennari, June 9, 2000.

95. Gleason, *Celebrating the Duke*, 135.

96. Ibid., 99.

97. A number of the original episodes of the "Jazz Casual" series are available on Rhino Home Video. The Dizzy Gillespie Quintet appeared on the show in 1961.

98. Joe Goldberg, *Jazz Masters of the Fifties* (1965; New York: Da Capo, 1983): 102.

99. Balliett quotes from Mingus's letter to him in an endnote in *Collected Works*, 74.

100. Lees, *Jim & Andy's*, xii.

101. Charles Mingus, *Beneath the Underdog* (New York: Random House, 1971), 294.

102. Mingus, *Beneath the Underdog*, 325.

103. Mingus, *Beneath the Underdog*, 340.

104. Ibid., 325–26.

105. These phrases appear in Hentoff's essay on Mingus in *The Jazz Life*, 157–69.

106. Nat Hentoff interview with Miles Davis, *Down Beat* (November 2, 1955), reprinted in Gary Carner, ed., *The Miles Davis Companion: Four Decades of Commentary* (New York: Schirmer Books, 1996), 58–64.

107. Nat Hentoff, "An Afternoon with Miles Davis," *Jazz Review* (December 1958), reprinted in Carner, *The Miles Davis Companion*, 86–92.

108. Amiri Baraka, "Homage to Miles Davis," reprinted in Carner, *The Miles Davis Companion*, 50.

109. Mike Zwerin, liner notes for *The Complete Birth of the Cool* (Capitol Records, 1998); Ralph Gleason, "At the Blackhawk," reprinted in Carner, *The Miles Davis Companion*, 84; Martin Williams, *Jazz Masters in Transition: 1957–1969* (New York: Da Capo, 1970), 276.

110. Stephen Davis, "My Ego Only Needs a Good Rhythm Section," *The Real Paper* (March 21, 1973), reprinted in Carner, *The Miles Davis Companion*, 161; Dan Morgenstern, "Miles in Motion," *Down Beat* (September 3, 1970), reprinted in Carner, *The Miles Davis Companion*, 113; Eric Nisensen, "Hangin' Out with Daffy Davis," introduction to *'Round about Midnight: A Portrait of Miles Davis*, reprinted in Carner, *The Miles Davis Companion*, 172–84.

111. Dan Morgenstern, "Sippin' at Miles' or a Press Conference in Reverse," *Metronome* (May 1961): 8, 46; Gene Grove, "Jazz: The Authors Meet the Critics," *New York Post* (February 21, 1961).

112. In my recreation of the "press conference in reverse," the dialogue quoted comes from Dan Morgenstern's account of the event in his 1961 *Metronome* dispatch. Nat Hentoff vouched for the accuracy of Morgenstern's account in a telephone discussion with me in April 2000.

Chapter 5

1. Ronald Radano, *New Musical Figurations: Anthony Braxton's Cultural Critique* (Chicago: University of Chicago Press, 1993), 14–16. My discussion of the jazz "mainstream" is deeply indebted to Radano's subtle insights.

2. Burton Peretti, *Jazz in American Culture* (Chicago: Ivan R. Dee, 1997), 107.

3. Whitney Balliett, "Jazz Today," *Atlantic Monthly*, November 1953, 80.

4. Stanley Dance, "The Main-Stream Jazz War," *Melody Maker*, April 16, 1955; "No Checking Mainstream," *Jazz Journal*, August 1959; "Far Out in the Mainstream," *Jazz Journal*, October 1957.

5. John Clellon Holmes, "The Golden Age/Time Present," *Esquire*, January 1959, 100–101.

6. Don Nelson, "Cool but Not Crazy," *New York Post*, July 27, 1958.

7. George Frazier, "Blue Notes and Blue Stockings," *Esquire*, August 1955, 56.

8. Holmes, "The Golden Age/Time Present," 101.

9. Mike Gross, "Jazz's New 'Commercial' Beat," *Variety*, January 7, 1959.

10. Georg Marek, "From the Dive to the Dean, Jazz Becomes Respectable," *Good Housekeeping*, June 1956, 120.

11. Radano, *New Musical Figurations*, 16 fn.

12. Henry Pleasants, "Modern Music: 'A Dead Art,'" *New York Times Sunday Magazine*, March 11, 1955, 57.

13. Whitney Balliett, "Pandemonium Pays Off," *Saturday Review*, September 25, 1954, 45.

14. Ibid., 45. See also Scott DeVeaux, "The Emergence of the Jazz Concert, 1935–1945," *American Music* 7 (spring 1989): 6–29, and *The Birth of Bebop: A Social and Musical History* (Berkeley: University of California Press, 1997), 279.

15. See Michel Ruppli, *The Clef/Verve Labels: A Discography (The Norman Granz Era, Volume 1)* (New York: Greenwood Press, 1986).

16. For an overview of jazz festivals, see the entry "Festivals" by Barry Kernfeld and Paul Laird in *The New Grove Dictionary of Jazz*, ed. Barry Kernfeld (New York: Macmillan, 1988). The data on the Newport festival are from "Summer Folk and Classical and Jazz Festivals," [unsigned], *Metronome* 77, no. 7 (July 1960): 12.

17. For discussion of changes in the economics of jazz after World War II, see Erenberg, *Swingin' the Dream*, 211–54; and DeVeaux, *The Birth of Bebop*, 273–317.

18. Alice Goldfarb Marquis, "Jazz Goes to College: Has Academic Status Served the Art," *Popular Music and Society*, summer 1998.; college Music Supplement to *Billboard*, March 28, 1964, section 2; Herm Schoenfeld, "Hottest B.O. on Campus," *Variety*, March 16, 1966, 55, 58.

19. Marquis, "Jazz Goes to College." Bruno Nettl, *Heartland Excursions: Ethnomusicological Reflections on Schools of Music* (Champaign: University of Illinois Press, 1995).

20. Peter Watrous, "A Conference (Hangout?) on ABC's of Jazz," *New York Times*, January 7, 1998, C1.

21. Gerald Early, *One Nation under a Groove: Motown and American Culture* (Hopewell, N.J.: Ecco Press, 1995), 95.

22. Unsigned entry, *Down Beat*, September 15, 1960, 11.

23. These statements were read at a tribute dinner commemorating Stephanie Barber and jazz at Music Inn. The dinner was held in Lenox on August 22, 1998.

24. The "fresh air and freedom" quote comes from the 1956 Music Inn program. For overviews of Music Inn's history, see Seth Rogovoy, "The Life and Times of Music Inn," *Berkshire Magazine*, summer 1995, 32–41; and Michael Fitzgerald, "The Lenox School of Jazz," http://www16.brinkster.com/fitzgera/lenox/lenhome.htm.

25. Marshall Stearns, "Roundtable on Jazz," *New York Times*, August 24, 1952; Nat Hentoff, "Counterpoint," *Down Beat*, June 1, 1955; transcript of Marshall Stearns

interview with Sheldon Harris, 1961 (IJS vertical file "Stearns"); Martin Williams, "The School of Jazz and the Acquisition of Things Past," *Metronome* 78, no. 2 (1960): 24.

26. Unsigned editorial, *Berkshire Eagle*, April 27, 1995, 16.

27. Letter from Pete Seeger to Stephanie Barber on the occasion of a reunion dinner commemorating Music Inn, August 22, 1998.

28. Rogovoy, "Life and Times of Music Inn," 34.

29. Hentoff, *The Jazz Life*, 171; Joe Goldberg, *Jazz Masters of the Fifties* (1965; New York: Da Capo, 1983), 113. For an overview of the MJQ in these years, see Goldberg, 113–31.

30. Bob Brookmeyer testimonial read at Music Inn commemorative dinner, August 22, 1998.

31. Miles Davis, quoted in Hentoff, *The Jazz Life*, 173.

32. Goldberg, *Jazz Masters of the Fifties*, 128.

33. The John Wilson quote comes from Goldberg, *Jazz Masters of the Fifties*, 120. Lewis's words come from a letter read at the August 22, 1998 dinner commemorating Stephanie Barber and jazz at Music Inn.

34. For a full listing of Lenox School of Jazz students and faculty, see Fitzgerald website links: http://www16.brinkster.com/fitzgera/lenox/lenhome.htm.

35. Jules Foster, "Newly-Formed Jazz School Has Diverse Student Body," *Berkshire Eagle*, August 20, 1957.

36. "The School of Jazz," *Down Beat*, October 3, 1957.

37. "A Case for the School of Jazz," Institute of Jazz Studies, vertical file "Lenox."

38. Undated letter from J. Peter Denny to Marshall Stearns, Institute of Jazz Studies vertical file "Lenox." The composition of the Lenox faculty was noted in many news clippings: for instance, "Top Jazz Musicians Will Teach at New Jazz School," *New York Amsterdam News*, February 9, 1957, 12; and "Leading Jazz Men on School Faculty," *New York Amsterdam News*, April 20, 1957, 12.

39. Quoted in Fitzgerald, "The Lenox School of Jazz."

40. Dizzy Gillespie [with Al Fraser], *To Be, or Not . . . to Bop* (New York: Da Capo, 1985 [1979]), 401, 404.

41. See, for instance, A. B. Spellman's discussion of Cecil Taylor's travails at the Five Spot in the East Village, in *Four Lives in the Bebop Business* (New York: Pantheon, 1966), 6–10.

42. Kenneth Rexroth, "What's Wrong with the Clubs," *Metronome* 78, no. 5 (May 1961): 21.

43. On Ornette Coleman's early career, see Spellman, *Four Lives in the Bebop Business*, 77–150; Ted Gioia, *West Coast Jazz: Modern Jazz in California, 1945–1960* (New York: Oxford University Press, 1992), 345–68; Mike Davis, *City of Quartz: Excavating the Future in Los Angeles* (London and New York: Verso, 1990), 62–65; and Martin Williams, "A Letter from Lenox, Massachusetts," *Jazz Review*, October 1959, reprinted in Williams, *Jazz Masters in Transition, 1957–1968* (New York: Da Capo, 1970), 33–36.

44. John McLellan, "The Jazz Scene," *Boston Globe*, June 11, 1959. McClellan identifies as winners of the F&M Schaefer Brewing Company Intercollegiate

Scholarship pianist Steve Kuhn (Harvard '59), trombonist and composer Herb Gardner (Harvard '60), flutist John Keyser (Princeton '61), drummer Paul Cohen (Pennsylvania '59), trumpeter Tony Greenwald (Yale '59), and flutist Ian Underwood (Yale '51).

45. Williams, "A Letter from Lenox, Massachusetts," 34.

46. Gunther Schuller, *Early Jazz* (New York: Oxford University Press, 1968) and *The Swing Era: The Development of Jazz, 1930–1945* (New York: Oxford University Press, 1989).

47. Gunther Schuller and Don Heckman, "Two Views on the School of Jazz," *The Jazz Review* 3, no. 9 (November 1960): 14.

48. Rogovoy, "Life and Times of Music Inn," 34.

49. Ibid.

50. Ira Gitler, "Randy Weston," *Down Beat,* February 27, 1964, 17.

51. Ibid., 17, 36; Rogovoy, "Life and Times of Music Inn," 36.

52. Fitzgerald, "The Lenox School of Jazz"; Balliett, *Collected Works,* 24; Eric Nisenson, "George Russell," *Music Sound Output,* July 1994.

53. Schuller and Heckman, "Two Views on the School of Jazz," 14.

54. Francis Davis, *Outcats: Jazz Composers, Instrumentalists, and Singers* (New York: Oxford University Press, 1990), 113; and Davis, *Bebop and Nothingness: Jazz and Pop at the End of the Century* (New York: Schirmer Books, 1996), 174–75.

55. Both quotations in this paragraph are from Goldberg, *Jazz Masters of the Fifties,* 127.

56. Rogovoy, "Life and Times of Music Inn."

57. George Wein interview with Christopher Lydon on radio program "The Connection," WBUR (Boston), July 14, 1997.

58. Lillian Ross, "You Dig It Sir?"*New Yorker*, July 1954; reprinted in *Jam Session: An Anthology of Jazz,* ed. Ralph Gleason (New York: Putnam, 1958), 252; 1954 Newport Jazz Festival program; George Frazier, "Blue Notes and Blue Stockings," *Esquire,* August 1955, 55–58; George Wein, "The Newport Jazz Festival: Notes from the Gent Who Started It All," *Playboy,* July 1956; Burt Goldblatt, *Newport Jazz Festival: The Illustrated History* (New York: Dial Press, 1977).

59. For an excellent discussion of Armstrong's film work, see Krin Gabbard, *Jammin' at the Margins: Jazz and the American Cinema* (Chicago: University of Chicago Press, 1996), 204–38.

60. News clippings on the 1954 festival and on festivals in subsequent years can be consulted at the Institute of Jazz Studies, Rutgers University-Newark, in the file labeled "Newport Jazz Festival." The reference to Wein's reception in Europe is from Frazier, "Blue Notes," 56. The *New Yorker* reference is to Lillian Ross's dispatch "You Dig It Sir?"

61. Frazier, "Blue Notes," 55, 56; George Wein interview with John Gennari, August 17, 2000.

62. Frazier, "Blue Notes," 55; Wein, "The Newport Jazz Festival," 22. In my interview with Wein, he confirmed the accuracy of Frazier's story about Jo Jones. "Jo Jones taught me a lot about rhythm," Wein said. "Jo said to me 'for crying out loud George, everything you play is like the Charleston. You need to stop comping the Charleston and learn how to swing." George Wein interview with John Gennari, August 17, 2000.

63. Frazier, "Blue Notes," 56; Ross, "You Dig It Sir?" 250.

64. 1954 Newport Jazz Festival Program; Ross, "You Dig It Sir?" 258.

65. "Jam in Newport," *Time*, July 25, 1955, 65; "Newport Jazz Festival," *Ebony*, October 1955, 10–12; Ross, "You Dig It Sir?" 259.

66. Minutes of the Newport Festival Executive Advisory Committee meeting, December 9, 1955. Institute of Jazz Studies vertical file "Newport Jazz Festival 1955."

67. Melvin Tapley, "Emotional and Musical Fireworks at Newport Jazz," New York *Amsterdam News*, July 13, 1957, 16; Langston Hughes letter to Arna Bontemps, dated July 9, 1958, in *Arna Bontemps—Langston Hughes Letters, 1925–1967*, ed. Charles H. Nichols (New York: Paragon House, 1990), 374; Langston Hughes, "Jazz," New York *Post*, June 28, 1963, 32.

68. *Down Beat*, June 30, 1966, 11; Leonard Feather, *The Jazz Years: Eyewitness to an Era* (New York: Da Capo, 1987), 198–99; "Big Jazz behind the Iron Curtain," *Look*, November 20, 1962, 61; Lawrence Elliot, "The World's Favorite American," *Reader's Digest*, July 1985, 95; John Gennari interview with Willis Conover, January 25, 1993.

69. Dizzy Gillespie [with Al Fraser], *To Be, or Not . . . to Bop* (New York: Da Capo, 1985 [1979]), 315, 402, 414.

70. George Wein interview with John Gennari, August 17, 2000.

71. John Hasse, *Beyond Category: The Life and Genius of Duke Ellington* (New York: Simon and Schuster, 1993), 318–22; "Mood Indigo and Beyond," *Time*, August 20, 1956, 54–62; George Avakian, liner notes to *Ellington at Newport* (Columbia CL 934, 1956), reprinted in *Setting the Tempo: Fifty Years of Great Jazz Liner Notes*, ed. Tom Piazza (New York: Anchor, 1996), 80–85.

72. Nat Hentoff's interview with Miles Davis in the November 2, 1955 issue of *Down Beat* was one plank in Davis's effort to regain the public spotlight. Gary Carner's headnotes to his reprint of this interview in *The Miles Davis Companion* offer an excellent summary of the significance of Davis's 1955 Newport appearance: Gary Carner, ed., *The Miles Davis Companion: Four Decades of Commentary* (New York: Schirmer, 1996), 58. "Jazz Dossier," *Vogue*, September 15, 1955.

73. The Stern quote is from George Hoefer, "Jazz on a Summer's Day," *Down Beat*, March 17, 1960, 19. Other quotations in the paragraph are from Jerry Tallmer, "Jazz on a Summer's Day," *Evergreen Review*, September/October 1960, 126–30.

74. George Avakian interview with John Gennari, September 20, 1992.

75. Donald Bogle, "Louis Armstrong: The Films," in *Louis Armstrong: A Cultural Legacy*, ed. Marc H. Miller (Seattle: University of Washington Press, 1994), 172–75. Leonard Feather, "Feather's Nest," *Down Beat*, April 17, 1958, 58. Ralph Ellison letter to Albert Murray, dated August 17, 1957, in *Trading Twelves: The Selected Letters of Ralph Ellison and Albert Murray*, ed. Albert Murray and John Callahan (New York: Modern Library, 2000), 175. For this allusion to the Blue Note record covers, I am indebted to the description proffered by Burton Peretti in *Jazz in American Culture* (Chicago: Ivan Dee, 1997), 117–18.

76. Harold Schoenberg, "Jazz Comes of Age in Newport," *New York Times*, July 18, 1955; Roger Maren, "A Few False Notes at Newport," *The Reporter*, September 8, 1955, 41–44. Mahalia Jackson is quoted in Sheldon Meyers, "Publishing Jazz Books: The Prospects Are Bright," *Publisher's Weekly*, 11 August 1958, 29.

77. Nat Hentoff and Whitney Balliett, letters to the editor, *The Reporter*, October 20, 1955, 7; Balliett, "Jazz at Newport: 1956," *Saturday Review*, July 28, 1956, 25; Richard Gehman, "The Newport 'News' of 1957," *Saturday Review*, July 28, 1957; Dan Morgenstern, "Jazz Festivals: Why Some Are and Some Aren't," *Metronome* 78, no. 7 (July 1961) 10; Nat Hentoff, *The Jazz Life*, 101–2.

78. Whitney Balliett, "Jazz at Newport: 1956," *Saturday Review*, July 28, 1956, 25; George Avakian, liner notes to *Ellington at Newport*. For a discussion and historical contextualization of the riot at the Fats Domino concert, see Brian Ward, *Just My Soul Responding: Rhythm and Blues, Black Consciousness, and Race Relations* (Berkeley: University of California Press, 1998), 113–14.

79. George Avakian interview with John Gennari, September 20, 1992.

80. Melvin Tapley, "Emotional and Musical Fireworks at Newport Jazz," 15–16. "Why whites will continue to insist on dragging our religious music in with jazz because it has a rhythm they are intrigued by, and why dedicated Negro artists consent to help them 'lump' the two together . . . is an interesting question," wrote Tapley. Ralph Ellison, "As the Spirit Moves Mahalia," in *Shadow and Act* (New York: Random House, 1964), 218–19; Ellison, *Trading Twelves*, 175.

81. George Wein, "Guest Editor: George Wein," *Metronome* 77, no. 7 (July 1960): 5.

82. I found a draft copy of this letter at the Institute of Jazz Studies in the vertical file labeled "Newport, 1958." The copy has handwritten marginalia I believe to be the work of Marshall Stearns, although there is no indication who authored the letter.

83. George Frazier, "Old Tricks for Young Critics," *Jazz: A Quarterly of American Music*, October 1958, 6.

84. Leonard Feather, "Feather's Nest," *Down Beat*, October 3, 1957, 29.

85. The 1960 riot was extensively covered in the jazz and general press. See Gene Lees, "The Trouble," *Down Beat*, August 18, 1960, 20–24; Thomasina Norford, "Newport Freezes Jazz Festival," New York *Amsterdam News*, July 23, 1960, 1, 34; Nat Hentoff, "Bringing Dignity to Jazz," in *The Jazz Life* (New York: Da Capo, 1961 [1975]), 98–116; "The Wild Newport Stomp," *Life*, July 18, 1960; Hsio Wen Shih, "Jazz in Print," *The Jazz Review*, September/October, 1960, 32, 34–35; Whitney Balliett, "Musical Events," *New Yorker*, July 16, 1960, 84–88; Robert Reisner, "The Newport Blues," *Village Voice*, July 7, 1960; Ken Sobol, "Beatnik, Stay Home," *Village Voice*, July 14, 1960, 7, 12. The Providence *Journal* quote is cited in Hentoff's account, in *The Jazz Life*, 107.

86. The "square collegian" quote is from an unsigned entry in *Down Beat*, September 15, 1960, 11. The Kempton quote is cited by Hentoff, "Bringing Dignity to Jazz," 104; Reisner, "The Newport Blues"; "only imported beer bottles" from Lees, "The Troubles," 22.

87. Reisner, "The Newport Blues"; Hentoff, "Bringing Dignity to Jazz."

88. Hentoff, *The Jazz Life*, 105.

89. Nat Hentoff interview with John Gennari, November 5, 1995. Charles Mingus, *Beneath the Underdog: His World as Composed by Mingus*, ed. Nel King (New York: Vintage, 1971), 325–54. The Providence *Evening Bulletin* report on Mingus's fee arrangement is cited by Burt Goldblatt, *Newport Jazz Festival: The Illustrated History*, 72.

90. Balliett, "Musical Events," 84–87; Hentoff, *The Jazz Life*, 109; Robert Reisner, "The Newport Blues," *Village Voice*, July 7, 1960. An album on the Candid label titled *Newport Rebels* was recorded in New York in November 1960 (Candid LP 9022; reissued on CD as Candid CCD 79022).

91. Hentoff, *The Jazz Life*, 111.

92. Reporting on the Kingston Trio concert, the *Berkshire Eagle* spoke of "a discontented mob . . . a bunch of rowdies shoving ushers and innocent bystanders around." Cited in Rogovoy, "Life and Times of Music Inn," 40.

93. Hentoff, *The Jazz Life*, 104–5, 111.

94. Lees, "The Trouble," 20–24.

95. Robert Cantwell, *When We Were Good: The Folk Revival* (Cambridge: Harvard University Press, 1996), 296–97.

96. George Wein interview with John Gennari, August 17, 2000.

97. For an overview of George Wein's accomplishments, see the special issue of *Billboard* (October 7, 2000) commemorating Wein's seventy-fifth birthday and the fiftieth anniversary of his career as a jazz producer.

98. Gene Santoro, "JazzFest Madness," *Nation*, August 24/September 1, 1997, 46.

99. George Wein interview with John Gennari, August 17, 2000.

100. Ibid.; Nat Hentoff interview with John Gennari, August 22, 2000.

101. Mingus quoted by Hentoff, *The Jazz Life*, 109.

Chapter 6

1. For an interesting discussion of Blue Note's visual aesthetics, see Burton Peretti, *Jazz in American Culture*, 117–18.

2. Sonny Rollins, *The Freedom Suite* (Riverside 12-258, 1958).

3. Orrin Keepnews, liner notes to Sonny Rollins, *Freedom Suite* (Riverside 12-258), reprinted in Tom Piazza, ed., *Setting the Tempo: Fifty Years of Great Liner Notes* (New York: Anchor Books/Doubleday, 1996), 215–19.

4. Frank Kofsky's 1960s jazz writings are collected in *Black Nationalism and the Revolution in Music* (New York: Pathfinder Press, 1970). His doctoral dissertation, "Black Nationalism and the Revolution in Music: Social Change and Stylistic Development in the Art of John Coltrane and Others, 1954–1967" (University of Pittsburgh, 1973) draws on the same material. Kofsky published a revised and expanded version of the project in 1997 under the title *John Coltrane and the Jazz Revolution of the 1960s* (New York: Pathfinder Press, 1997). He also wrote a new companion volume, *Black Music, White Business: Illuminating the History and Political Economy of Jazz* (New York: Pathfinder Press, 1997). Kofsky's book on the cold war is *Harry S. Truman and the War Scare of 1948: A Successful Campaign to Deceive the Nation* (New York: St. Martin's Press, 1993).

5. Kofsky, *Black Nationalism*, 14.

6. Ibid., 147.

7. John F. Szwed, *Jazz 101: A Complete Guide to Learning and Loving Jazz* (New York: Hyperion, 2000), 209–22.

8. John Tynan, "Take Five," *Down Beat*, November 23, 1961, 40. Dolphy and Coltrane responded to the "anti-jazz" charge several months later: see Don DeMichael,

"John Coltrane and Eric Dolphy Answer the Jazz Critics," *Down Beat*, April 12, 1962, 20–22. In contrast to the heated rhetoric of the critics, Dolphy and Coltrane showed little rancor in calling for the critics to consult more closely with the musicians over music they profess not to understand. Later, in a 1966 interview with Frank Kofsky (*Black Nationalism*, 242), Coltrane sounded somewhat more miffed by the "anti-jazz" controversy than he had let on at the time.

9. Philip Larkin, *All That Jazz: A Record Diary, 1961–1971* (New York: Farrar, Straus, and Giroux, 1985), 20–21.

10. This story was told to me by Jon Hendricks, in an interview on June 9, 2000.

11. Balliett, "The New Thing (1965)," in *Collected Works: A Journal of Jazz, 1954–2000* (New York: St. Martin's Press, 2000), 234. In his inaugural jazz column in the *New Yorker* in 1957, Balliett favorably reviewed the LP *Jazz Advance: The Cecil Taylor Quartet*. He praised Taylor for an "astonishing" musical imagination and called Taylor's drummer, Dennis Charles, and his bass player, Buell Neidlinger, "remarkable" (*Collected Works*, 15).

12. Dan Morgenstern, "The October Revolution," *Down Beat*, November 19, 1964, 15, 33. Doubting that the "new thing" could compete in the marketplace, Morgenstern called for it to be subsidized by private foundations and government grants. Frank Kofsky, in his attack on "Establishment" critics, singled out Morgenstern for not giving Cecil Taylor a gig at the Museum of Modern Art jazz series for which Morgenstern served as program consultant.

13. Williams, *The Jazz Tradition* (New York: Oxford University Press, 1983 [1970]), 229–33, 243–44.

14. Hentoff's review, which appeared in *Down Beat* (January 8, 1959), is cited by Farah Jasmine Griffin, *If You Can't Be Free, Be a Mystery: In Search of Billie Holiday* (New York: Free Press, 2001), 167.

15. Griffin, *If You Can't Be Free, Be a Mystery*, 171–72.

16. "Racial Prejudice in Jazz [Part 1]," *Down Beat*, March 15, 1962, 21.

17. Kevin Gaines, "Jazz and Black Diaspora Consciousness in the Era of Civil Rights and Anticolonial Movements," paper presented at American Studies Association conference, October 31, 1997.

18. "Racial Prejudice in Jazz," 22.

19. Gloria Oden, [untitled review of Nat Hentoff's *The New Equality*], *Down Beat*, October 8, 1964, 36. Oden also took exception to the publisher (Viking Press) claiming in a promotional blurb that Hentoff was an authority based on "research on the jazz scene [that] has given him a very special opportunity to observe Negro-white relationships . . . from close up." Oden wrote: "the southern white was saying much the same thing for years until the southern Negro undertook to show him how wrong he was." Leonard Feather jumped to Hentoff's defense, insisting on the distinction between "the white intellectual working in jazz, whose interracial relationships are based on social equality and mutual friendship," and "the southern cracker who says, 'Don't tell *me* about them niggers; I've worked with 'em; I understand 'em.'" Leonard Feather, "Feather's Nest," *Down Beat*, November 5, 1964, 34.

20. *Jazz* 1, no. 2 (November–December 1962): 3.

21. Kofsky first appeared in the mainstream jazz press in 1960 in Leonard Feather's *Down Beat* column, singled out as the most thoughtful reader respondent to a

twenty-question survey about the current jazz scene. Then a student at Berkeley and a habitual reader of "all the jazz magazines and Ralph Gleason's column," Kofksy voiced concern about jazz's commercialization—especially in the festival movement, excepting the musician-directed Monterey event—using even-tempered language that would soon elude him, and a logic very much similar to that employed by Gleason, Hentoff, and even Balliett in the late 1950s. He urged a friendly if skeptical tolerance toward critics: "I've found, inasmuch as every critic has some bias, that when reading reviews, it's best to keep an old Confucian proverb in mind: 'The mind is like a parachute; it only functions when it's open.'" In his otherwise comprehensive analysis of the jazz scene, Kofsky made no mention of race. Feather signed off amiably, "Mr. Kofsky, it was a pleasure to open my column to your open mind." Kofsky quoted in Leonard Feather, "Feather's Nest," *Down Beat*, May 26, 1960, 43–44.

Within the year, Kofsky was reviewing records for *Down Beat*. He quickly resigned the position, however, claiming that his pieces were being altered without his consent, and expressing sympathy with Gleason, who had left the magazine after a dispute with the editors and management. Gleason had written a column suggesting a favorable connection between the jazz avant garde and Fidel Castro's Cuban revolution. Gleason and Kofsky claimed that Gleason resigned after *Down Beat's* publisher, responding to advertisers' concerns, pressured Gleason to stop writing what they deemed pro-communist propaganda (Kofsky, *Black Nationalism*, 87–88). Gene Lees, who at the time was turning the *Down Beat* editorship over to Don DeMichael, tells a different story: "Don fired Ralph Gleason—and had I stayed at the magazine a few more weeks I would have done it myself—for being a prima donna about any editing done to his prose, which was usually slapdash, sometimes incoherent and sometimes even ungrammatical; for writing over length; and above all for missing deadlines. Castro had nothing to do with it." Gene Lees, "Down Beat Days," *Gene Lees Jazzletter*, February 15, 1982, 5.

22. Kofsky's article "Black Music: Cold War 'Secret Weapon'" is reprinted in *Black Nationalism*, 109–21.

23. Kofsky's article "Critiquing the Critics" is reprinted in *Black Nationalism*, 71–97.

24. Kofsky, *Black Nationalism*, 76.

25. Ibid., 5, 81–82.

26. Frank Kofsky, *Black Music, White Business*, chapter 1.

27. Each of these three examples is from Hentoff's "Second Chorus" column in *Down Beat* in 1966. The Cecil Taylor reference is from the May 5 issue, p. 14; the Lincoln Center reference is from June 30, p. 11; and the record company and NEA references are from October 20, p. 10.

28. Kofsky, *Black Music, White Business*, chapter 1.

29. Leonard Feather, "The Name of the Game," *Down Beat*, October 15, 1970, 11. Feather's accusation against Archie Shepp came in *Cavalier*, December 1966, cited by Kofsky, *Black Nationalism*, 82–83.

30. Dan Morgenstern, "It Don't Mean a Thing," *Down Beat*, December 10, 1970, 13, 37.

31. Martin Williams, "The Same Old Story," *Down Beat*, September 7, 1967, 6.

32. Martin Williams, "No Work in the U.S. for Ornette?" *Down Beat*, June 30, 1966, 12.

33. Martin Williams, "The Novelist and the Hornman," *Down Beat*, September 5, 1968, 14.

34. John Mehegan, "The Question of Coleman," *Down Beat*, December 24, 1959, 7.

35. Williams, "No Work in the U.S. for Ornette," 12.

36. A. B. Spellman, *Four Lives in the Bebop Business* (New York: Limelight Editions, 1985 [1966]), 142–43.

37. Arthur Taylor, *Notes and Tones: Musician to Musician Interviews* (New York: G. P. Putnam's Sons, 1977), 40.

38. All of the quoted phrases in this paragraph come from Kofsky, *Black Nationalism*: "jazz club-narcotics," 223; "Negro disaffiliation," 132; "nice, safe," 90; "doesn't want to be," 92; "another one of," 85.

39. Kofsky, *Black Nationalism*, 139.

40. Kofsky's "John Coltrane: An Interview," originally published in *Jazz*, September 1967, is in *Black Nationalism*, 221–43. The Coltrane testimony I see as most resistant to Kofsky's agenda is on 227 and 241.

41. Williams, *The Jazz Tradition*, 234.

42. Phil Watson, "Banal Identity Reasoning," *Weekly Worker*, December 16, 1999.

43. Houston A. Baker Jr., *Long Black Song: Essays in Black American Literature and Culture* (Charlottesville: University Press of Virginia, 1990 [1972]), xv.

44. Gerald Early, "The Case of LeRoi Jones/Amiri Baraka," in *Tuxedo Junction: Essays on American Culture* (Hopewell, N.J.: Ecco Press, 1989), 200.

45. Werner Sollors, *Amiri Baraka/LeRoi Jones: The Quest for a "Populist Modernism"* (New York: Columbia University Press, 1978), 2. Baraka tells the story of his discharge from the Air Force in Amiri Baraka, *The Autobiography of LeRoi Jones/Amiri Baraka* (New York: Freundlich Books, 1984), 120–23. He discusses his Newark upbringing, Howard University (after a short stint at Rutgers/Newark), and the Air Force in *The Autobiography*, 1–123.

46. Baraka, *The Autobiography*, 121.

47. Sollors, *Amiri Baraka/LeRoi Jones,* 14.

48. LeRoi Jones (Amiri Baraka), "The Beat Generation," *Partisan Review*, summer 1958, 472–73.

49. William J. Harris, review of *Selected Poetry of Amiri Baraka/LeRoi Jones* (1979), *The Greenfield Review* 8, nos. 3-4 (1980): 47. See also Harris's *The Poetry and Poetics of Amiri Baraka: The Jazz Aesthetic* (Columbia: University of Missouri Press, 1985).

50. "Cuba Libre" and other of Baraka's essays from 1960 to 1965 are collected in LeRoi Jones, *Home: Social Essays* (Hopewell, N.J.: Ecco Press, 1998 [1966]). Harold Cruse was another U.S. black intellectual on the 1960 trip to Cuba, and he made a point of closely observing Baraka. See Cruse, *The Crisis of the Negro Intellectual: A Historical Analysis of the Failure of Black Leadership* (New York: Quill, 1984 [1967]), 356–59.

51. Jones, *How I Became Hettie Jones*, 2.

52. Ibid., 22–23.

53. Baraka, *The Autobiography*, 140.

54. Ibid., 138–39.

55. This Ginsberg quote is from a 1988 interview with Josef Jarab (manuscript in author's possession).

56. Baraka, *The Autobiography*, 142.

57. Ibid., 129.

58. Baraka, *Home*, 6.

59. Baraka discusses his Greenwich Village period in *The Autobiography*, 124–201. For an overview of black artists in Greenwich Village during these years, see Jon Panish, *The Color of Jazz: Race and Representation in Postwar American Culture* (Jackson: University Press of Mississippi, 1997), 23–41. See also the essays by Norma Rogers, Lorenzo Thomas, Sarah Wright, Tom Dent, and Calvin Hernton in a retrospective on the Lower East Side in *African American Review* 27, no. 4 (1993): 569–98 Also useful on the cultural history of the Village during this period are Steven Watson, *The Birth of the Beat Generation: Visionaries, Rebels, and Hipsters, 1944–1960* (New York: Pantheon, 1995); Terry Miller, *Greenwich Village and How It Got That Way* (New York: Crown Publishers, 1990); Ronald Sukenick, *Down and In: Life in the Underground* (New York: Beach Tree Books/William Morrow, 1987); Dan Wakefield, *New York in the 50s* (Boston: Houghton Mifflin, 1992).

60. Jones, *How I Became Hettie Jones*, 172.

61. Baraka's liner notes for *Coltrane Live at Birdland* (1964) are reprinted in LeRoi Jones (Amiri Baraka), *Black Music* (New York: William Morrow, 1968), 63–68.

62. Stanley Crouch, *Always in Pursuit: Fresh American Perspectives, 1995–1997* (New York: Pantheon, 1998), 5–6.

63. Baraka, *The Music*, 259.

64. Amiri Baraka (LeRoi Jones), "Jazz and the White Critic," in *Black Music*, 11–20.

65. LeRoi Jones (Amiri Baraka), *Blues People: Negro Music in White America* (New York: William Morrow, 1963).

66. Baraka's discussion of Ellison's *Invisible Man* is in the *Jazz Review*, June 1959, 33. The citations from *Blues People* are on 124, 181, 200, and 220. For overviews of the 1950s mass culture critique, see Andrew Ross, *No Respect: Intellectuals and Popular Culture* (New York: Routledge, 1989), 42–64; and Thomas Frank, *The Conquest of Cool: Business Culture, Counterculture, and the Rise of Hip Consumerism* (Chicago: University of Chicago Press, 1997), 1–52.

67. Baraka, *Home*, 106.

68. Baraka, *Blues People*, 33, 134.

69. Ibid., 28–29.

70. Lorenzo Thomas, "Ascension: Music and the Black Arts Movement," in Krin Gabbard, ed., *Jazz Among the Discourses* (Durham, N.C.: Duke University Press, 1995), 262.

71. Joe Goldberg, "Music, Metaphor, and Men," *Saturday Review*, January 11, 1964, 69.

72. Baraka, *Blues People*, 137.

73. Ibid., 94.

74. Ibid., 207, 216.

75. Ibid., 149.

76. Ibid., 202–4.

77. Ibid., 151–54.

78. Ibid., 165.

79. Ibid., 210.

80. Ibid., 211.

81. Ibid., 229.

82. Ibid., 193.

83. Ibid., 188.

84. Ibid., 211.

85. Ibid., 176, 218.

86. Ibid., 173.

87. Ibid., 217–18; *Black Music*, 107.

88. Nat Hentoff, "The Square Route to Blues Is White," New York *Herald-Tribune Bookweek*, October 20, 1963.

89. Ralph Ellison, *Shadow and Act* (New York: Random House, 1964), 249.

90. Ibid., 253.

91. Ibid., 253.

92. Ibid., 256.

93. Baraka, *The Autobiography*, 58, 60.

94. Ben S. Page, "Relevant Opinions," *Jazz*, May–June 1964, 28.

95. Baraka, *The Autobiography*, 182–83.

96. Ibid., 194–95.

97. Gerald Early, "The Case of LeRoi Jones/Amiri Baraka," in *Tuxedo Junction*, 199. For Baraka's writing about Cecil Taylor, see "Present Perfect (Cecil Taylor)," and "Cecil Taylor (*The World of Cecil Taylor*)," in *Black Music*, 104–12. Baraka announced that Taylor was creating an orchestral language "as complete . . . as Ellington's"; that he was "an amazingly fresh musical personality" who nonetheless drew on traditional methods, such as inserting the rhythmic pulse of the music directly into the melody, as Thelonious Monk and Charlie Parker had done.

98. Bill Dixon's letter to *Down Beat* is in the January 2, 1964 issue.

99. Quoted in Sollors, *Amiri Baraka/LeRoi Jones*, 173.

100. See Harold Cruse, *The Crisis of the Negro Intellectual: A Historical Analysis of the Failure of Black Leadership* (New York: Quill, 1984 [1967]), 485–87, for a discussion of the Village Vanguard forums.

101. Baraka discusses this period of transition in *The Autobiography*, 189–229; and *Home*, 210–15, 238–50. Hettie Jones addresses her marital dissolution in *How I Became Hettie Jones*, 202–39.

102. Sollors, *Amiri Baraka/LeRoi Jones*, 2–4.

103. Baraka, *Black Music*, 134.

104. Ibid., 137.

105. Ibid., 174.

106. I am indebted here to Eric Porter's *What Is This Thing Called Jazz? African American Musicians as Artists, Critics, and Activists* (Berkeley: University of California Press, 2002). The Baraka quote comes from Porter's discussion of the 1965 jazz and Black Nationalism panel on 191. Comments from the panel were serialized in *Jazz* magazine over the course of fourteen issues between April 1966 and July 1967.

107. Phillip Brian Harper, "Nationalism and Social Division in Black Arts Poetry of the 1960s," *Critical Inquiry* 19 (winter 1993): 234–53. Eric Porter discusses Harper's essay in *What Is This Thing*, 198.

108. Werner Sollors discusses the exchange between Baraka and Kofsky in *Amiri Baraka/LeRoi Jones*, 191–92.

109. Quoted in Baraka, "New Tenor Archie Shepp Talking," in *Black Music*, 155.

110. "Chords and Discords," *Down Beat*, February 25, 1965, 8, 10.

111. Thomas Conrad, "Book Review: LeRoi Jones's *Black Music*," *Down Beat*, October 30, 1969, 19, 28.

112. Baraka, *The Autobiography*, 215.

113. A. B. Spellman, "Not Just Whistling Dixie," in LeRoi Jones and Larry Neal, eds., *Black Fire* (New York: William Morrow, 1968), 167. Brian Ward uses this Spellman passage in his discussion of these issues in *Just My Soul Responding: Rhythm and Blues, Black Consciousness, and Race Relations* (Berkeley: University of California Press, 1998), 411.

114. Baraka, *Black Music*, 124.

115. Ibid., 210.

116. Amiri Baraka, "The Changing Same (R&B and New Black Music)," in *Black Music*, 180–211.

117. Cruse, *The Crisis of the Black Intellectual*, 540.

118. Baraka, *The Autobiography*, 212.

119. Christopher Funkhouser, "LeRoi Jones, Larry Neal, and *The Cricket*: Jazz and Poets' Black Fire," *African American Review* 37, no. 2-3 (2003): 237–34, quotes from 238, 239.

120. Ibid., 241.

121. Thomas, "Ascension," 270–71.

122. This comes from Houston Baker's biographical note and statement of poetics in Sascha Feinstein and Yusef Komunyakaa, eds., *The Second Set: The Jazz Poetry Anthology, Volume 2* (Bloomington: Indiana University Press, 1996), 199–200.

123. Amiri Baraka, liner notes for *New Music—New Poetry* (India Navigation, 1048, 1981); Baraka (LeRoi Jones), *New York Art Quintet* (Esp, 1004, 1965). For treatments of Baraka's jazz/poetry performances, see Harris, *The Poetry and Poetics of Amiri Baraka*, and Barry Wallenstein, "Jazz and Poetry: A Twentieth-Century Wedding," *Black American Literature Forum* 25, no. 3 (fall 1991): 612–15.

124. Martin Williams interview with John Gennari, December 12, 1992.

125. Ron Welburn, "The Black Aesthetic Imperative," in Addison Gayle Jr., ed., *The Black Aesthetic* (Garden City, N.Y.: Doubleday, 1971), 132–49, quotes on 135, 136, 139, 148, 149.

126. Ron Welburn, "American Jazz Criticism, 1914–1940." (Ph.D. dissertation, New York University, 1983).

127. Ron Welburn interview with Charley Gerard, in Gerard, *Jazz in Black and White: Race, Culture, and Identity in the Jazz Community* (New York: Praeger, 1998), 140–51, quotes on 143, 144, 147, 149.

128. Janet Sommer, "Dan Morgenstern Interview," *www.allaboutjazz.com/journalists*, 5–6.

129. Dan Morgenstern, "A Message to Our Readers," *Down Beat*, June 29, 1967, 13.

130. Leonard Feather, "The Works of Mann," *Down Beat*, April 30, 1970, 12.

131. Leonard Feather, "The Name of the Game," *Down Beat*, October 15, 1970, 11.

132. Martin Williams, "The Bystander," *Down Beat*, October 8, 1964, 41.

133. Martin Williams, "White Blues," *Down Beat*, December 1, 1966, 14.

134. Martin Williams, "The Bystander," *Down Beat*, October 8, 1964, 41.

135. Martin Williams, "The Bystander," *Down Beat*, June 27, 1968, 15.

136. Martin Williams, "The Bystander," *Down Beat*, April 18, 1968, 15.

137. Ralph Gleason, "Like a Rolling Stone," *Jazz & Pop*, September 1967, 14.

138. Robert Draper, *Rolling Stone Magazine: The Uncensored History* (Garden City, N.Y.: Doubleday, 1990), 25–31, 46–49, 60–61, 74–76, 237–40; quote on 47.

139. "Ralph Gleason in Perspective," *Rolling Stone*, July 17, 1975, 42.

140. Ibid., 39–49.

141. Gleason, *Celebrating the Duke*, 143.

142. "Ralph Gleason in Perspective," 46.

143. Ralph Gleason, "A Brave New Whirl in the Park," *San Francisco Chronicle*, June 13, 1967, 39; "Ralph Gleason in Perspective," 46–47.

144. Ralph Gleason, "Perspectives: A Power to Change the World," *Rolling Stone*, June 22, 1968, 10.

145. Kenneth Keniston, "Young Radicals," *Life*, May 27, 1966, 75.

146. Martin Williams, "The Bystander," *Down Beat*, April 18, 1968, 15.

147. Draper, *Rolling Stone Magazine: The Uncensored History*, 235.

148. "Ralph Gleason in Perspective," 47.

Chapter 7

1. Julio Cortázar, "The Pursuer," in *Blow-Up and Other Stories*, trans. Paul Blackburn (New York: Pantheon, 1967), 182–247; Doris Sommer, "Grammar Trouble for Cortazar," in *Proceed with Caution, When Engaged with Minority Writing in the Americas* (Cambridge: Harvard University Press, 1999), 211–33.

2. Cortázar, "The Pursuer," 238.

3. Russell, quoted in a story by Robert Lawrence in the *San Diego Union* sometime after the 1973 publication of *Bird Lives!*. The date and page number are obscured on the copy of the article I read in Box 5, Ross Russell Collection at the Harry Ransom Humanities Research Center, University of Texas at Austin. I wish to thank the Harry Ransom Center for the use of this collection, which is hereafter cited as RRC/HRHRC.

4. Martin Williams letter to Ross Russell, March 3, 1973, Box 1B-35, RRC/HRHRC. Despite his admiration for Russell's grasp of Parker's character, Williams, not uncharacteristically, also had a litany of complaints about Russell's "carelessness" in matters of discographical detail.

5. After serving in the merchant marine in World War II and working briefly at Lockheed Aircraft, Russell opened a record store in Hollywood. Stocking the early jazz and swing music he had grown up on, Russell's Tempo Music Store was the West Coast analogue to Milt Gabler's Commodore shop in New York. Unlike Gabler and many other first-generation jazz entrepreneurs, Russell responded adroitly to bebop's convulsive emergence in the 1940s. Witnessing the face-off between Howard McGhee's Beboppers and Kid Ory's New Orleans band at L.A.'s Jade Palace, Russell saw artistic and commercial capital on both sides. Diversifying beyond its traditionalist clientele, Tempo became the place where young musicians like Joe Albany, Dodo Marmarosa, Stan Getz, Zoot Sims, and Dean Benedetti came to listen to new bebop releases like "Groovin' High," "Salt Peanuts," and "Shaw 'Nuff," spun by Russell on a turntable built into the shop's sleekly modernist front counter. In emulation of Gabler's Commodore label, Russell started Dial Records in 1945 as an adjunct to his retail operation. But as bebop became more popular and Russell began to squeeze marginally higher profits out of record production—Russell's financial returns, company records show, were never very substantial—the Dial label took precedence over the Tempo retail operation. Russell relocated Dial to New York in 1947, shifting its focus to contemporary classical music, recording Schoenberg, Webern, Berg, and Bartok, among others, and some calypso music he collected on a Caribbean trip in 1953. Moderate sales and high stress led Russell to close down Dial in 1954. Ross Russell, "Symposium Keynote Address," in *The Bebop Revolution in Words and Music*, ed. Dave Oliphant (Austin: University of Texas Press, 1994), 19–20; Richard Lawn, "From Bird to Schoenberg," in *Perspectives on Music: Essays on the Collections at the Humanities Research Center*, ed. Dave Oliphant and Thomas Zigal (Austin: University of Texas Press, 1985), 137–47; Edward Komara, "The Dial Recordings of Charlie Parker," in *The Bebop Revolution*, 79–103.

6. Komara, "Dial Recordings," 80.

7. Ross Russell, *Bird Lives!: The High Life and Hard Times of Charlie (Yardbird) Parker* (New York: Charterhouse, 1973), 214, 216.

8. For overall accounts of the "Lover Man" session and its aftermath, see Gary Giddins, *Celebrating Bird: The Triumph of Charlie Parker* (New York: Beech Tree, 1987), 94; Russell, *Bird Lives!* 228–41; and Ted Gioia, *West Coast Jazz: Modern Jazz in California, 1945–1960* (New York: Oxford University Press, 1992), 24–27. Miles Davis's remarks are in Davis (with Quincy Troupe), *Miles: The Autobiography* (New York: Simon and Schuster, 1989), 93. Howard McGhee's account came in an interview with Scott DeVeaux: see DeVeaux, "Conversation with Howard McGhee: Jazz in the Forties," *Black Perspective in Music*, spring 1987, 75.

9. For assessments of "Lover Man," see Giddins, *Celebrating Bird,* 94; and Gioia, *West Coast Jazz,* 24. For Russell's account of the Camarillo affair, see his testimony in *Bird: The Legend of Charlie Parker*, ed. Robert Reisner (New York: Da Capo, 1977 [1962]), 200–201. Grennard's claim is made in Reisner, *Bird,* 98. Parker's nightclub threat is reported by Leonard Feather, "Book Shows Life and Hard Times of 'Yardbird' Parker," *Huntsville (Ala.) Times* [syndicated from *Los Angeles Times* news service], March 11, 1973, 28.

10. Gioia, *West Coast Jazz*, 22.

11. Davis, *Miles: The Autobiography*, 89.

12. Ross Russell letter to David Amram, October 18, 1969, Box 1, folder 10, RRC/HRHRC.

13. Ralph Ellison, *Shadow and Act* (New York: Random House, 1964), 229.

14. Davis, *Miles: The Autobiography*, 65.

15. Ross Russell letter to David Amram, October 18, 1969, Box 1, folder 10, RRC/HRHRC.

16. Russell's essays were anthologized by Martin Williams in his edited collection *The Art of Jazz* (New York: Oxford University Press, 1959).

17. Ross Russell, *Jazz Style in Kansas City and the Southwest* (Berkeley and Los Angeles: University of California Press, 1971).

18. Ross Russell, *The Sound* (New York: MacFadden Books, 1962 [1961]), 34.

19. Whitney Balliett, "The Demon, The Tenderfoot, and the Monolith," *New Yorker,* July 8, 1961, 68; Martin Williams letter to Ross Russell, February 20, 1961, Box 1B-35, RRC/HRHRC.

20. Box 9 ("unpublished fiction"), RRC/HRHRC.

21. Martin Williams letter to Ross Russell, January 12, 1967, Box 1B-35, RRC/HRHRC.

22. Research notes and miscellany related to Raymond Chandler biography, Boxes 10, 11, and 12, RRC/HRHRC; Ross Russell letter to Albert Goldman, November 15, 1974, Box 1A-8, RRC/HRHRC.

23. Ross Russell letters to Albert Goldman, January 22, 1970 and August 29, 1977, Box 1A-8, RRC/HRHRC.

24. Ross Russell letter to Martin Williams, March 8, 1973, Box 1B-35, RRC/HRHRC. Russell wrote in the acknowledgments of *Bird Lives!*: "In 1970 Albert called me from Los Angeles, where he had gone to do research on [his] Lenny Bruce biography, to ask how my own work was progressing. It wasn't. He rented a car, drove to Escondido, and spent two days there going over materials and manuscript. Without his help and encouragement this book might never have been completed." (377).

25. Albert Goldman letter to Ross Russell, February 20, 1978, Box 1A-8, RRC/HRHRC.

26. Ross Russell letter to Albert Goldman, September 22, 1977, Box 1A-8, RRC/HRHRC.

27. Ibid.

28. Ross Russell letter to Albert Goldman, November 15, 1974, Box 1A-8, RRC/HRHRC. Russell met Kathlyn Sulk in Trinidad in 1951, and was married to her two years later.

29. Ross Russell letter to Albert Goldman, December 23, 1977, Box 1A-8, RRC/HRHRC.

30. Ross Russell letter to Albert Goldman, November 15, 1974, Box 1A-8, RRC/HRHRC.

31. Russell, *Bird Lives!*, 375.

32. Ross Russell letter to Myra Kuehl, March 31, 1978, Box 1A-15, RRC/HRHRC.

33. Ross Russell letter to Albert Goldman, March 31, 1978, Box 1A-8, RRC/HRHRC.

34. Lawn, 146; Ross Russell letters to Albert Goldman, August 10 and 20, 1977, Box 1A-8, RRC/HRHRC; Ross Russell letter to Chan Richardson, January 3, 1979, Box 4B-12, RRC/HRHRC.

35. Ross Russell letter to Albert Goldman, August 10, 1977, Box 1A-8, RRC/HRHRC.

36. For discussion of Parker's treatment by the mainstream media see Giddins, *Celebrating Bird,* 9–20; and Jon Panish, *The Color of Jazz: Race and Representation in Postwar American Culture* (Jackson: University Press of Mississippi, 1997), 44–45.

37. John A. Williams, *Flashbacks: A Twenty-Year Diary of Article Writing* (Garden City, N.Y.: Anchor Press/Doubleday, 1973), 228.

38. Ralph Ellison, "On Bird, Bird-Watching, and Jazz," in *Shadow and Act,* 228. Ellison's essay was a review, originally published in *Saturday Review* in 1962, of the Robert Reisner–edited collection *Bird: The Legend of Charlie Parker,* where the Art Blakey quote appeared.

39. Ibid., 228.

40. Nat Hentoff, *Jazz Is* (New York: Random House, 1976), 194.

41. Nat Hentoff, "Flight of Fancy," *American Film,* September 1988, 25–31.

42. Stanley Crouch, "Bird Land," *New Republic,* February 27, 1989, 25–31.

43. Ross Russell, *The Sound* (New York: MacFadden, 1962 [1961]). The page citations that follow are from the MacFadden 1962 edition.

44. Ibid., 22.

45. Ibid., 101.

46. Ibid., 55.

47. Ibid., 21.

48. Ibid., 30.

49. Martin Williams letter to Ross Russell, February 16, 1961, Box 1B-35, RRC/HRHRC.

50. Ross Russell letter to Martin Williams, March 24, 1961, Box 1B-35, RRC/HRHRC.

51. Albert Goldman, "The Art of the Bebopper," *New Leader,* October 2, 1961, 32.

52. Leonard Feather, "Book Review [*The Sound*]," *Down Beat,* June 8, 1961, 44.

53. Feather, "Book Shows Life and Hard Times of 'Yardbird' Parker," 28.

54. Russell, *The Sound,* 77.

55. Ibid., 120.

56. Ibid., 79.

57. Ibid., 50.

58. Ibid., 49.

59. Philip Durham, "The 'Black Mask' School,'" in *Tough Guy Writers of the Thirties,* ed. David Madden (Carbondale: Southern Illinois University Press, 1968), 78.

60. Russell, *The Sound,* 74.

61. Ibid., 128.

62. Ibid., 10–11.

63. Nat Hentoff letter to Ross Russell, February 19, 1961, Box 1B-17, RRC/HRHRC.

64. Robert Reisner, "The Sound," *Village Voice*, June 8, 1961, 11.

65. Collin Clark, "The Sound," *Library Journal*, July 1961, 2494.

66. "Books" [unsigned], *Saturday Review*, July 22, 1961, 59.

67. "Jazz and Junkies" [unsigned], *Newsweek*, June 5, 1961, 47.

68. "Summer Reading," [unsigned], Huntington (W. Va.) *Herald Advertiser*, July 2, 1961, 23.

69. Dan Morgenstern, "Books [*The Sound*]," *Metronome*, September 1961, 36–37.

70. Balliett, "The Demon, The Tenderfoot, and the Monolith," 68–69.

71. Whitney Balliett, *The Sound of Surprise: 46 Pieces on Jazz* (New York: E. P. Dutton, 1959), 13.

72. Reisner, "The Sound," 11.

73. Reisner, *Bird: The Legend of Charlie Parker*: 26; see also Gary Giddins, "The Death of a Hipster: Bob Reisner, 1921–74," *Village Voice*, February 28, 1974, 42–43, 47.

74. Reisner, *Bird: The Legend of Charlie Parker*, 19.

75. Russell, *The Sound*, 36.

76. Balliett, "The Demon, The Tenderfoot, and the Monolith," 68.

77. Jon Panish, in an insightful reading of *The Sound*, suggests that "Russell's construction of African American experience in the novel is hollow and primitivistic because it refers not to anything specific to African Americans in American history—for example, racism or their musical tradition—but to the universal experience of the misunderstood and suffering artist and to the existing stereotypes about African American musicians." Panish, *The Color of Jazz*, 63.

78. Russell, *The Sound*, 101.

79. Ibid., 181–82.

80. Ibid., 186.

81. Ibid., 184.

82. Ibid., 126-7.

83. Ibid., 131.

84. Ibid., 126.

85. Ross Russell letter to Albert Goldman, October 16, 1961, Box 1A-8, RRC/HRHRC; Safford Chamberlain letter to Ross Russell, June 19, 1961, Box 1-10, RRC/HRHRC.

86. Albert Goldman, "The Art of the Be-Bopper," *The New Leader*, October 2, 1961, 32.

87. Albert Goldman, *Freakshow: The Rocksoulbluesjazzsickhumorsexpoppsych Gig and Other Scenes from the Counter-Culture* (New York: Athenaeum, 1971), 278.

88. Ibid., 272.

89. Ibid., 274.

90. Ibid., 279.

91. Ronald Radano, "The Writing of Slave Spirituals, *Critical Inquiry* 22, no. 3 (spring 1996): 506–44.

92. Goldman, *Freakshow*, 300.

93. Ibid., 304.

94. Ibid., 303.

95. Ibid., 275.

96. Ibid., 304.

97. Ibid., 301.

98. Ibid., 302.

99. Krin Gabbard, "Signifyin(g) the Phallus: Representations of the Jazz Trumpet," in *Jammin' at the Margins: Jazz and the American Cinema* (Chicago: University of Chicago Press, 1996), 138–59, especially 140–45.

100. Amiri Baraka, "When Miles Split!" *Village Voice*, October 15, 1991, 87.

101. Quincy Troupe, "Up Close and Personal: Miles Davis and Me," *Conjunctions* 16 (1991): 77, 79.

102. Greg Tate, "Silence, Exile, and Cunning: Miles Davis in Memoriam," *Village Voice*, October 15, 1991, 87, 90. It is worth noting that only Tate among these writers takes a crack against Davis for his vicious misogyny.

103. Panish, *The Color of Jazz*, 44.

104. *Bird Lives!* treats Gillespie as an important but clearly second-rank contributor to bebop. In a letter to Chan Richardson Woods in 1979, Russell wrote: "I did a 20 minute segment for BBC on Bird and Diz, said the 1940s was Bird, that Diz was a brilliant trumpet player, performer, wonderful front man, but that he furnished very few of the ideas, composed practically nothing, and has since become a festival personality, which I suppose will probably piss him. He told the leading jazz critic in Finland [that] *Bird Lives!* was 'bullshit.'" Ross Russell letter to Chan Richardson Woods, January 3, 1979; Box 4b-12 , RRC/HRHRC.

105. Theodor Adorno, "On Jazz" [1936], trans. Jamie Owen Daniel, *Discourse* 12 (1989–90): 45–69; and "Perennial Fashion—Jazz," in *Prisms*, trans. Samuel and Sherry Weber (Cambridge: Harvard University Press, 1981). Andreas Huyssen, *After the Great Divide: Modernism, Mass Culture, Postmodernism* (Bloomington: Indiana University Press, 1986).

106. Gabbard, *Jammin' at the Margins*, 141; Steven Cohen, "'Feminizing' the Song-and-Dance Man: Fred Astaire and the Spectacle of Masculinity in the Hollywood Musical," in *Screening the Male: Exploring Masculinities in Hollywood Cinema*, ed. Steven Cohen and Ina Rae Hark (New York: Routledge, 1993), 46–69.

107. See the chapter "Caging Bird: Charlie Parker Meets the Postwar Construction of the Jazz Musician," in Panish, *The Color of Jazz*, 42–78.

108. Jack Kerouac, *The Subterraneans* (New York: Grove Press, 1971 [1958]) and *Mexico City Blues (242 Choruses)* (New York: Grove Weidenfeld, 1990 [1959]).

109. James Baldwin, "Sonny's Blues" (1957), in *Hot and Cool: Jazz Short Stories*, ed. Marcela Breton (New York: Plume, 1990).

110. Amiri Baraka, *Dutchman and The Slave* (New York: William Morrow, 1964), 35.

111. Norman Mailer, "The White Negro: Superficial Reflections on the Hipster," in *Advertisements for Myself* (New York: Putnam, 1959), 341. Arguments for Mailer's influence on the 1960s counterculture include Allen J. Matusow, *The Unraveling of America: A History of Liberalism in the 1960s* (New York: Harper and Row, 1984),

280–81; and Morris Dickstein, *Gates of Eden: American Culture in the 1960s* (New York: Basic Books, 1977), chapter 1.

112. "In the main," Whitney Balliett suggested, "jazz musicians are home-loving, television-watching, newspaper-reading innocents who dislike night clubs, late hours, buses, and all other discomforts their jobs force on them." Quoted by Goldman, *Freakshow*, 278. See also Nat Hentoff's "A Brief Note on the Romance of 'The White Negro,'" in *The Jazz Life*, 138–43; Hettie Jones, *How I Became Hettie Jones* (New York: Penguin, 1990), 33; and Nelson George, *The Death of Rhythm and Blues* (New York: Penguin, 1988), 61–63.

113. Panish, *The Color of Jazz*, 56.

114. Eric Lott, "White Like Me: Racial Cross-Dressing and the Construction of American Whiteness," in *Cultures of United States Imperialism,* ed. Amy Kaplan and Donald E. Pease (Durham, N.C.: Duke University Press, 1993), 483.

115. Eric Lott, *Love and Theft: Blackface Minstrelsy and the American Working Class* (New York: Oxford University Press, 1993).

116. For a sampling of the negative reviews, see Greil Marcus, *Village Voice Literary Supplement*, December 1991; Luc Sante, *New York Review of Books*, December 17, 1981, 22; John Lahr, *New York Times Book Review*, September 25, 1988, 3; Michiko Kakutani, *New York Times*, September 12, 1988. For more sympathetic reviews, see Mark Breslin, *Toronto Globe and Mail*, October 8, 1988; Paul Gray, *Time*, September 12, 1988, 77.

117. Tom Wolfe, *The Electric Kool-Aid Acid Test* (New York: Bantam, 1968), 158. My references here to Wolfe and Hunter Thompson are inspired by Eric Cummins's discussion of these journalists in his book *The Rise and Fall of California's Radical Prison Movement* (Stanford, Cal.: Stanford University Press, 1994), especially in his chapter "Eldridge Cleaver and the Celebration of Crime," 93–127.

118. Cummins, *The Rise and Fall of California's Radical Prison Movement*, 106.

119. Ross Russell, typed notes on telephone conversation with Albert Goldman, January 15, 1962, Box 1A-8, RRC/HRHRC.

120. Albert Goldman letter to Ross Russell, April 27, 1972, Box 1A-8, RRC/HRHRC.

121. John Clellon Holmes, "The Broken Places," in *Passionate Opinions: The Cultural Essays* (Fayetteville: University of Arkansas Press, 1988), 168. Quoted by Siva Vaidhyanathan in *"Bird Lives!* Constructing a Hero" (unpublished seminar paper, University of Texas, April 25, 1994; in author's possession).

122. Ross Russell, notes on telephone call to Albert Goldman, December 19, 1969; Russell letter to Goldman, February 16, 1970; Goldman letter to Russell, November 5, 1970; Russell letter to Goldman, December 5, 1970, Box 1A-8, RRC/HRHRC.

123. Goldman wrote to Russell on April 27, 1972: "What happened to the story that Reisner told you about Bird killing a man? Why can't this be presented as a well-founded report, a rumor, something that may not be true but is part of the underground legend. After all, Bird was part man, part myth. The myth counts for as much or more than the man." Box 1A-8, RRC/HRHRC.

124. Albert Goldman letter to Ross Russell, April 24, 1972, Box 1A-8, RRC/HRHRC.

125. Albert Goldman letter to Ross Russell, May 31, 1975, Box 1A-8, RRC/HRHRC.

126. Vaidhyanathan, *"Bird Lives!*: Constructing a Hero," 10.

127. Russell, *Bird Lives!* 376.

128. Ross Russell letter to David Amram, October 18, 1969, Box 1-10, RRC/HRHRC.

129. Russell, *Bird Lives!* 287.

130. Stanley Crouch, personal communication with Krin Gabbard, August 21, 1994. Cited in Gabbard, *Jammin' at the Margins*, 301.

131. Russell, *Bird Lives!* 271.

132. Ibid., 245.

133. Ibid., 5.

134. Ibid., 7.

135. Ibid., 12.

136. Daniel Patrick Moynihan was the author of the hugely controversial paper *The Negro Family: The Case for National Action* [U.S. Department of Labor Office of Policy Planning and Research, 1965]. Moynihan warned of "a new crisis in race relations" growing out of a "tangle of pathology" in the urban black family, especially an alleged inclination toward crime, delinquency, and welfare dependency in female-headed households. Moynihan's report, couched as an expert sociological and historical analysis, met with a firestorm of criticism from academics, notably Lee Rainwater and William L. Yancey, *The Moynihan Report and the Politics of Controversy* (1967). Two magisterial historical works, Herbert G. Gutman's *The Black Family in Slavery and Freedom, 1790–1925* (New York: Oxford University Press, 1976), and Jacqueline Jones, *Labor of Love, Labor of Sorrow: Black Women, Work, and the Family from Slavery to the Present* (New York: Basic Books, 1985), explicitly challenged Moynihan's basic assumptions. So too did African American writer Albert Murray, who with characteristic acerbity pointed out the "intellectual hypocrisy" of Moynihan's "white norm/black deviation folklore": "The Moynihan Report, which insists that Negro men are victims of a matriarchal family structure, makes no mention at all of the incontestable fact that aggressiveness of white American women is such that they are regarded as veritable amazons not only in the Orient but also by many Europeans and not a few people at home." Murray, *The Omni-Americans: Black Experience and American Culture* (New York: Vintage, 1983 [1970]), 34.

137. Russell, *Bird Lives!* 37.

138. Ibid., 132.

139. On "momism," see Elaine Tyler May's *Homeward Bound: American Families in the Cold War Era* (New York: Basic Books, 1988), 74. May writes, "It was in 1942 that Philip Wylie coined the term 'Momism' in his best-selling book, *Generation of Vipers*. 'Momism,' according to Wylie and many of his followers, was the result of frustrated women who smothered their children with overprotection and overaffection, making their sons in particular weak and passive." These "frustrated women" were assumed to be middle-class white women, the stereotyped counterpart of the Organization Man.

140. Russell, *Bird Lives!* 153.

141. I am drawing from Crouch's criticism of Clint Eastwood for giving only glancing attention to Parker's mother in *Bird*: "Though Parker was well taken care of as a child . . . and was quite attached to his mother, whom he called every weekend, she is only referred to once in *Bird*." Crouch appears to agree with Russell that Parker's

alcoholic, absent father and doting mother decisively shaped his psychology. "Convinced that she could keep young Charlie away from the things her husband loved by giving the boy everything he wanted, she reared him as a well-dressed prince who could do no wrong," Crouch writes, adding: "The treatment is far from unusual in the lives of Negro innovators. It gives them the feeling that they can do things differently from everyone else." Crouch, "Bird Land," 26, 28.

142. Russell, *Bird Lives!* 32.

143. Ibid., 34.

144. Ross Russell letter to Rudi Blesh, December 24, 1968, Box 1-B, RRC/HRHRC.

145. Russell, *Bird Lives!* 258.

146. Ibid., 256.

147. Ibid., 324.

148. Ibid., 258.

149. Ibid., 246.

150. Ibid., 257.

151. Ross Russell letter to Albert Goldman, August 19, 1968, Box 1A-8, RRC/HRHRC.

152. Ross Russell letter to Mickey Goldsen (Criterion Music), Box 1-10, RRC/HRHRC.

153. Albert Goldman letter to Ross Russell, May 20, 1978, Box 1A-8, RRC/HRHRC.

154. Albert Goldman letter to Ross Russell, May 22, 1978, Box 1A-8, RRC/HRHRC.

155. Kuehl's archive of Billie Holiday research eventually was purchased by Toby Byron, acting on the recommendation of Martin Williams. Robert O'Meally made excellent use of the archive in the writing of his book *Lady Day: The Many Faces of Billie Holiday* (New York: Arcade/Little, Brown and Company, 1991).

156. Ross Russell letter to Albert Goldman, June 24, 1978, Box 1A-8, RRC/HRHRC].

157. It is significant that Russell's private correspondence reveals no similar sentiments toward his black wife.

158. Albert Goldman letter to Ross Russell, March 27, 1978, Box 1A-8, RRC/HRHRC.

159. Russell, *Bird Lives!* 376.

160. Albert Goldman letter to Ross Russell, March 26, 1978, Box 1A-8, RRC/HRHRC.

161. Albert Goldman letter to Ross Russell, May 20, 1978, Box 1A-8, RRC/HRHRC.

162. Russell, *Bird Lives!* 257.

163. Richard Locke, "Chasing the Bird—At Last," *New York Times*, May 1, 1973; Stanley Dance, "The Fire, the Skillet, and the Cooking," *Jazz Journal*, April 1973, 10; Arthur Cooper, *Newsweek*, April 9, 1973. Two reviewers who were more skeptical of Russell's intentions offered penetrating criticisms of his positioning in the narrative. Despite praising *Bird Lives!* as "far and away the best jazz biography I've ever read," Harper Barnes, writing in the *Washington Post Book World*, characterized Russell's discussion of his relationship with Parker as bearing a "petulant air of wronged innocence." Suggesting that "perhaps it *is* harder to get inside a man's skin if you are a different color," Barnes chided Russell for assuming that musicians looked at him

differently than they did other representatives of the white-dominated jazz establishment. Melinda Abern's review in *Changes* sounded the same theme, saying that Russell was being obtuse if he expected Parker's response to him to differ from his response to other record producers. Fairly or not, Abern wrote, "Russell became one of Parker's Establishment symbols." Harper Barnes, "Bird of Paradox," *Washington Post Book World*, March 18, 1973; Melinda Abern, *Changes*, July 1973.

164. Hollie West, "The Bird: His Music and His Lifestyle," *Washington Post*, April 1, 1973, 1, 6.

165. Ishmael Reed, "Bird Lives!" *New York Times Book Review*, March 25, 1973, 3–4.

166. Lorenzo Thomas, "The Bop Aesthetic and Black Intellectual Tradition," in *The Bebop Revolution in Words and Music*, ed. Dave Oliphant (Austin: University of Texas Press, 1994), 117. This volume came out of a symposium held at the Harry Ransom Humanities Research Center at the University of Texas at Austin, where the Ross Russell Collection is located.

167. Ibid., 116.

168. Lorenzo Thomas, "Historiography," in *The Second Set: The Jazz Poetry Anthology, Volume 2*, ed. Sascha Feinstein and Yusef Komunyakaa (Bloomington: Indiana University Press, 1996), 170–71.

169. J. Lorand Matory, "The Other African-Americans," lecture delivered to the Talcott Parsons Conference on the Construction of Sociology, Harvard University, March 13, 1993.

170. Chan Richardson Woods letter to Ross Russell, November 14, 1972, Box 4B-12, RRC/HRHRC.

171. Ross Russell letter to Chan Richardson Woods, September 22, 1972, Box 4B-12, RRC/HRHRC.

172. Crouch, "Bird Land," 25.

173. Ibid., 26.

174. Chan (Richardson Woods) Parker, *My Life in E-Flat* (Columbia: University of South Carolina Press, 1993), 13.

175. Ibid., 20, 31, 34.

Chapter 8

1. Stanley Crouch, "Blues to Be Constitutional: A Long Look at the Wild Wherefores of Our Democratic Lives as Symbolized in the Making of Rhythm and Tune," in *The Jazz Cadence of American Culture*, ed. Robert O'Meally (New York: Columbia University Press, 1998), 155.

2. Crouch's poem, "Up on the Spoon," is reprinted in *The Second Set: The Jazz Poetry Anthology, Volume 2*, ed. Sascha Feinstein and Yusef Komunyakaa (Bloomington: Indiana University Press, 1996), 34–35. The comment on Eastwood's *Bird* is in Stanley Crouch, "Bird Land," *New Republic*, February 27, 1989, 26. Crouch's corpus of writing is represented in *Notes of a Hanging Judge: Essays and Reviews, 1979–1988* (New York: Oxford University Press, 1990); *The All-American Skin Game; or, The Decay of Race; The Long and Short of It, 1990–1994* (New York: Pantheon, 1995); *Always in Pursuit: Fresh American Perspectives, 1995–1997* (New York: Pantheon, 1998); and *Don't the Moon Look Lonesome: A Novel in Blues and Swing* (New York: Pantheon, 2000).

3. Gary Giddins, *Celebrating Bird: The Triumph of Charlie Parker* (New York: Beech Tree Books, 1987), 20.

4. Ibid., acknowledgments (unnumbered).

5. Ibid., 11, 15, 18, 66-7, 120.

6. Ben Ratliff, in *The Future of Jazz*, ed. Yuval Taylor (Chicago: A Capella Books, 2002), 26.

7. Stanley Crouch, "Jazz Criticism and Its Effect on the Art Form," in *New Perspectives on Jazz*, ed. David Baker (Washington, D.C.: Smithsonian Institution Press, 1990), 85. This volume collects papers from a National Jazz Service Organization conference held in Racine, Wisconsin in September 1986. Crouch's paper was a response to a paper by Amiri Baraka.

8. Wynton Marsalis, *The Majesty of the Blues* (CBS 45091).

9. Alexander Stewart discusses this issue well in a chapter titled "*Blood on the Fields*: Wynton Marsalis and the Transformation of the Lincoln Center Jazz Orchestra," in Stewart, *Jazz Worlds: Contemporary New York City Big Bands* (Berkeley: University of California Press, forthcoming).

10. For a leading example, see Frank Conroy, "Stop Nitpicking a Genius," *The New York Times Magazine*, June 25, 1995, 28–31.

11. Gunther Schuller, *Early Jazz: Its Roots and Musical Development* (New York: Oxford University Press, 1968), ix. Guthrie P. Ramsey Jr. offers a helpful contextual discussion of Schuller and others' text-based approach in his article "Who Hears Here? Black Music, Critical Bias, and the Musicological Skin Trade," *Musical Quarterly* 85, no. 1 (2001): 1–52.

12. The most complete discussion of Giddins's career is in an extensive interview he gave to the online site Jerry Jazz Musician (www.jerryjazzmusician.com).

13. Gary Giddins, "Defining the Jazzbox," *Village Voice*, August 22, 1974, 51.

14. Giddins's oeuvre includes *Riding on a Blue Note: A Jazz Chronicle* (New York: Oxford University Press, 1981); *Rhythm-a-ning: Jazz Tradition and Innovation in the 1980s* (New York: Oxford University Press, 1985); *Celebrating Bird: The Triumph of Charlie Parker*; *Satchmo* (New York: Da Capo, 1998 [Doubleday, 1988]); *Faces in the Crowd: Players and Writers* (New York: Oxford University Press, 1992); *Visions of Jazz: The First Century* (New York: Oxford University Press, 1998); and *Bing Crosby, A Pocketful of Dreams: The Early Years, 1903–1940* (Boston: Little, Brown, and Company, 2001).

15. Giddins, *Visions of Jazz*, 8.

16. Ibid., 623, 8.

17. Gary Giddins interview with Jerry Jazz Musician (www.jerryjazzmusician.com).

18. Crouch, *The All-American Skin Game*, x.

19. Albert Murray, "Preface," in *Trading Twelves: The Selected Letters of Ralph Ellison and Albert Murray*, ed. Albert Murray and John F. Callahan (New York: Modern Library, 2000), xxii.

20. Murray provides biographical details in his Preface and headnotes in *Trading Twelves*, and in his memoir *South to a Very Old Place* (New York: Vintage, 1971). See also Stanley Crouch, "Chitlins at the Waldorf: The Work of Albert Murray," *Village Voice*, March 3, 1980, in Crouch, *Notes of a Hanging Judge*, 42–47, and "Some Words about

Albert Murray: Universal Counterpoint from the Bass Clef," in *Always in Pursuit: Fresh American Perspectives*, 132–78.

21. Albert Murray, *Trading Twelves*, xxiii.

22. Albert Murray, *The Omni-Americans: Black Experience and American Culture* (New York: Vintage, 1983 [1970]): "folklore/fakelore", 7; "elastic individuality," 65; "Podhoretz/Basie," 224; Henry Louis Gates Jr., "King of Cats," in *Thirteen Ways of Looking at a Black Man* (New York: Random House, 1997), 21–46.

23. John A. Kouwenhoven's major works were *Made in America: The Arts in Modern Civilization* (1948) and *Beer Can by the Highway* (1961). In a 1984 letter that Murray deeply cherishes, Kouwenhoven told Murray that he was one of the few people "who comment on my work [who] seem to have any idea that it's the *interaction* of the vernacular with the learned tradition that in my view matters." Murray discusses Constance Rourke in *The Omni-Americans*, 15. Constance Rourke's pioneering works in American studies were *American Humor: A Study of the National Character* (1931) and *The Roots of American Culture* (1942). On Rourke's career, see Joan Shelley Rubin, *Constance Rourke and American Culture* (Chapel Hill: University of North Carolina Press, 1980).

24. Albert Murray, *Stomping the Blues* (New York: Da Capo [McGraw-Hill, 1976]), 3.

25. Ibid., 118–25, 250.

26. Ibid., 6. Murray worked through these ideas concerning the relationship between blues and literature in a set of lectures he delivered at the University of Missouri, published as *The Hero and the Blues* (Columbia: University of Missouri Press, 1973).

27. Crouch, "Chitlins at the Waldorf," 53; Murray, *Stomping the Blues*, 132; *The Omni-Americans*, 58.

28. Amiri Baraka, *The Autobiography of LeRoi Jones/Amiri Baraka* (New York: Freundlich Books, 1984), 58, 60; Amiri Baraka, "The Changing Same (R&B and New Black Music)," in *Black Music* (New York: William Morrow & Co., 1968), 180–211.

29. Murray, *Stomping the Blues,* 164–65; Murray and Callahan, eds., *Trading Twelves*, 202; Murray, *Stomping the Blues*, 186, 51. Murray's line about Coltrane comes from my interview with Murray on December 20, 1994.

30. Stanley Crouch, "Body and Soul," in *Notes of a Hanging Judge*, 244–65; quotations on 247, 249, 254–55, 255.

31. Stanley Crouch, "On the Corner: The Sellout of Miles Davis," in *The All-American Skin Game*, 166–85, quotations on 166, 175, 176.

32. Crouch's piece on Cecil Taylor appeared in the *Village Voice*, March 30, 1982, 59. Taylor recorded his poem on *Chinampas* (Leo LR-103).

33. Stanley Crouch, liner notes for World Saxophone Quartet, *Revue* (Black Saint, BSR-0056), 1980.

34. Greg Tate, "Blow on This," *Village Voice*, July 25, 1989, 81.

35. Greg Tate, in *The Future of Jazz*, 167.

36. Ibid., 61.

37. This language comes from Burnt Sugar's website, www.burntsugarindex.com.

38. Greg Tate, "The Electric Miles (Parts 1 and 2)," in *Flyboy in the Buttermilk: Essays on Contemporary America* (New York: Simon & Schuster, 1992), 68–85.

39. Ibid., 74–75.

40. Ibid., 69.

41. Ibid., 80.

42. Ibid., 72–73.

43. Francis Davis's essays are collected in *In the Moment: Jazz in the 1980s* (New York: Da Capo, 1986); *Outcats: Jazz Composers, Instrumentalists, and Singers* (New York: Oxford University Press, 1990); and *Bebop and Nothingness: Jazz and Pop at the End of the Century* (New York: Schirmer, 1996).

44. Francis Davis, "White-Anglo Saxon Pythagorean (Roswell Rudd)," in *Bebop and Nothingness*, 121–34, quotations on 123, 132.

45. Howard Mandel's work is collected in *Future Jazz* (New York: Oxford University Press, 1999). Gene Santoro's bibliography includes *Dancing in Your Head: Jazz, Blues, Rock, and Beyond* (New York: Oxford University Press, 1994), *Stir It Up: Musical Mixes from Roots to Jazz* (New York: Oxford University Press, 1997), and *Highway 61 Revisited: The Tangled Roots of American Jazz, Blues, Folk, Rock, and Country Music* (New York: Oxford University Press, 2004).

46. Will Friedwald, *Jazz Singing: America's Great Voices from Bessie Smith to Bebop and Beyond* (New York: Charles Scribner's Sons, 1990) and *Sinatra! The Song Is You: A Singer's Art* (New York: Charles Scribner's Sons, 1995). See also "Original Recipe vs. Extra Crispy: Jazz Vocals," in *The Future of Jazz*, 129–38.

47. Davis, *Bebop and Nothingness*, 141.

48. See Richard Sudhalter, *Lost Chords: White Musicians and Their Contribution to Jazz, 1917–1945* (New York: Oxford University Press, 1999), and "A Racial Divide that Needn't Be," *The New York Times*, January 3, 1999, Arts and Leisure section, 1, 31; Terry Teachout, "The Color of Jazz," in *A Terry Teachout Reader* (New Haven, Conn.: Yale University Press), 244–54; Gene Lees, *Cats of Any Color: Jazz, Black and White* (New York: Da Capo, 2001 [1994]), 187–246; Eric Nisenson, *Blue: The Murder of Jazz* (New York: St. Martin's Press, 1997), 11–46, 213–33; Stuart Nicholson, in *The Future of Jazz*, 36–37, 206, 216–17. A debate that took place between Wynton Marsalis and James Lincoln Collier is introduced and transcribed in André Craddock-Willis, "Jazz People: Wynton Marsalis vs. James Lincoln Collier," *Transition*, spring 1995, 140–78. Also helpful for background on the Lincoln Center debates are Tom Piazza, "Lincoln Center and Its Critics Swing Away," *The New York Times*, January 16, 1994, section 2, 26; and Jervis Anderson, "Medium Cool," *The New Yorker*, December 12, 1994, 72–82.

49. Martin Williams, "Nostalgia for Sale—Part III," *Down Beat*, November 26, 1970.

50. *Trading Twelves*, 195.

51. Scott DeVeaux, "What Did We Do to Be So Black and Blue?" *The Musical Quarterly*, Fall 1996, 392–430, especially 395–96.

52. Murray, *Stomping the Blues*, 196–99. The photograph is the legendary "Great Day in Harlem" shot by Art Kane that was published in *Esquire* in January 1959. The white musicians in the picture are Chubby Jackson, Miff Mole, Gene Krupa, Max Kaminsky, George Wettling, Bud Freeman, Pee Wee Russell, Marian McPartland, and Gerry Mulligan.

53. Martin Williams quotes these lines from Murray's review, published in the *New Leader*, in his *Down Beat* column on April 4, 1968, 13.

54. Murray quoted by Sanford Pinsker in "The Bluesteel, Rawhide, Patent Leather Implications of Fairy Tales," in *The Georgia Review* (1997), reprinted in Albert Murray, *From the Briarpatch File: On Context, Procedure, and American Identity* (New York: Pantheon, 2001).

55. This latest Crouch controversy began when Crouch published an essay, titled "Putting the White Man in Charge," in the April 2003 issue of *Jazz Times*, where he had been a regular contributor in recent years. Following the ensuing dustup, *Jazz Times* dropped Crouch from its list of contributors, editor Christopher Porter telling the *Village Voice* that Crouch's contributions had grown tired "alternating between vitriolic rants and celebrations of his buddies." Quoted in Adam Shatz, "Fight Club," *The Nation*, May 22, 2003. The website Jerry Jazz Musician hosted a roundtable discussion of the essay and its responses ("Blues for Clement Greenberg") on May 4, 2003, with Crouch, Martha Bayles, and Loren Schoenberg (*www.jerryjazzmusician.com/linernotes/clement_greenberg.html*). See also Francis Davis's review of new recordings by Dave Douglas and Wynton Marsalis in "Mr. Uptown and Mr. Downtown," *Village Voice*, March 3–9, 2004.

56. Eric Nisenson, *Blue: The Murder of Jazz*, 16, 132, 133.

57. Stanley Crouch, "Putting the White Man in Charge," 28.

58. Adam Shatz, "Fight Club."

59. Stanley Crouch, in "Blues for Clement Greenberg," *www.jerryjazzmusician.com/linernotes/clement_greenberg.html*.

60. Ron Welburn, "The Black Aesthetic Imperative," in *The Black Aesthetic*, ed. Addison Gayle Jr. (Garden City, N.Y.: Doubleday, 1971), 139.

61. Stanley Crouch, in "Blues for Clement Greenberg," *www.jerryjazzmusician.com/linernotes/clement_greenberg.html*.

62. See Graham Lock, *Blutopia: Visions of the Future and Revisions of the Past in the Work of Sun Ra, Duke Ellington, and Anthony Braxton* (Durham, N.C.: Duke University Press, 1999); and Ronald M. Radano, *New Musical Figurations: Anthony Braxton's Cultural Critique* (Chicago: University of Chicago Press, 1993).

63. Mark Jacobson, "Matt Shipp's Out," *New York Magazine*, May 3, 1999.

64. Ben Ratliff, in *The Future of Jazz*, 197.

65. John Szwed, in *The Future of Jazz*, 173.

66. In *The Future of Jazz*: Williams, 149–54; Nicholson, 126, 161–63; Macnie, 158; Friedwald, 33–34, 63; Tate, 160.

Conclusion

1. Gene Santoro, *Dancing in Your Head: Jazz, Blues, Rock, and Beyond* (New York: Oxford University Press, 1994), *Stir It Up: Musical Mixes from Roots to Jazz* (New York: Oxford University Press, 1997), and *Highway 61 Revisited: The Tangled Roots of American Jazz, Blues, Folk, Rock, and Country Music* (New York: Oxford University Press, 2004); Greg Tate, *Flyboy in the Buttermilk: Essays on Contemporary America* (New York: Simon and Schuster, 1992); *The Future of Jazz*, ed. Yuval Taylor (Chicago: A Capella Books, 2002).

2. Gary Giddins, *Bing Crosby, A Pocketful of Dreams: The Early Years, 1903–1940* (Boston: Little, Brown, and Company, 2001); David Hajdu, *Lush Life: A Biography of*

Billy Strayhorn (New York: Farrar Straus Giroux, 1996); Will Friedwald, *Sinatra! The Song Is You: A Singer's Art* (New York: Charles Scribner's Sons, 1995).

3. Francis Davis, *Outcats: Jazz Composers, Instrumentalists, and Singers* (New York: Oxford University Press, 1990), ix.

4. Gary Giddins, *Satchmo* (New York: Da Capo, 1998 [Doubleday, 1988]), 33.

5. Gary Giddins, "Jazz Styles of the Obscure and Neglected," *The Village Voice Jazz Special*, June 21, 1988, 3; "Jazz Obsessions," *Village Voice*, August 28, 1990, 57.

6. Whitney Balliett's work from that period can be found in *Collected Works: A Journal of Jazz, 1954–2000* (New York: St. Martin's Press, 2000). Martin Williams's bibliography includes edited volumes *The Art of Jazz: Essays on the Nature and Development of Jazz* (New York: Oxford University Press, 1959) and *Jazz Panorama* (New York: Collier, 1964); and *Jazz Masters in Transition, 1957–69* (New York: Macmillan, 1970), *The Jazz Tradition* (New York: Oxford University Press, 1993 [1970]), *Jazz Heritage* (New York: Oxford University Press, 1985), *Jazz in Its Time* (New York: Oxford University Press, 1989), and *Hidden in Plain Sight: An Examination of the American Arts* (New York: Oxford University Press, 1992). Nat Hentoff's jazz work includes *Jazz: New Perspectives on the History of Jazz* (New York: Da Capo, 1974 [Rinehart, 1959]), which he edited with Albert McCarthy; *The Jazz Life* (New York: Da Capo, 1985 [The Dial Press, 1961]); *Jazz Is* (New York: Random House, 1976); and *Listen to the Stories: Nat Hentoff on Jazz and Country Music* (New York: HarperCollins, 1995). Gene Lees's jazz books include *Meet Me at Jim & Andy's: Jazz Musicians and Their World* (New York: Oxford University Press, 1988), *Waiting for Dizzy* (New York: Oxford University Press, 1991), and *Cats of Any Color: Jazz, Black and White* (New York: Da Capo, 2001 [1994]). Ralph Gleason's jazz bibliography includes the edited volume *Jam Session: An Anthology of Jazz* (New York: Putnam, 1958). Ira Gitler's jazz work includes *Jazz Masters of the Forties* (New York: Macmillan, 1966) and *Swing to Bop: An Oral History of the Transition in Jazz in the 1940s* (New York: Oxford University Press, 1985). The jazz writing of Amiri Baraka (LeRoi Jones) is found in *Blues People: Negro Music in White America* (New York: William Morrow, 1963), *Black Music* (New York: William Morrow, 1967), and *The Music: Reflections on Jazz and Blues* (New York: William Morrow, 1987). Before starting Riverside Records, Orrin Keepnews was an editor of *The Record Changer* and wrote many pieces for the magazine. Some of those pieces from the late 1940s and 1950s, along with later writings, are collected in *The View from Within: Jazz Writings, 1948–1987* (New York: Oxford University Press, 1988). Dan Morgenstern's writings have been collected in *Living with Jazz* (New York: Pantheon, 2004).

7. Whitney Balliett, *The Sound of Surprise* (New York: E. P. Dutton, 1959), 14.

8. Gary Giddins, "How Come Jazz Isn't Dead," in *This Is Pop: In Search of the Elusive at Experience Music Project*, ed. Eric Weisbard (Cambridge: Harvard University Press, 2004), 47.

9. Davis, *Outcats*, 47, 148; Gary Giddins, *Visions of Jazz: The First Century* (New York: Oxford University Press, 1998), 477.

10. Howard Mandel, *Future Jazz* (New York: Oxford University Press, 1999), x–xii.

11. Francis Davis, *Bebop and Nothingness: Jazz and Pop at the End of the Century* (New York: Schirmer, 1996), 120, 171–90.

12. Giddins, *Visions of Jazz*, 9.

13. See, for example, Stanley Crouch, *Notes of a Hanging Judge: Essays and Reviews, 1979–1989* (New York: Oxford University Press, 1990), ix–xv.; "Blues to Be Constitutional: A Long Look at the Wild Wherefores of Our Democratic Lives as Symbolized in the Making of Rhythm and Tune," in *The Jazz Cadence of American Culture,* ed. Robert O' Meally (New York: Columbia University Press, 1998), 154–65.

14. Albert Murray quoted by Robert S. Boynton, in "The Professor of Connection," *The New Yorker,* November 11, 1995, 101.

15. For a sampling of critiques of the Lincoln Center jazz program, see Terry Teachout, "The Color of Jazz," in *A Terry Teachout Reader* (New Haven, Conn.: Yale University Press), 244–54; Lees, *Cats of Any Color,* 187–246; Eric Nisenson, *Blue: The Murder of Jazz* (New York: St. Martin's Press, 1997), 11–46, 213–33; Stuart Nicholson, in *The Future of Jazz,* 36–37, 206, 216–17.

16. Ben Ratliff, in *The Future of Jazz,* 25–26.

17. Peter Watrous, in *The Future of Jazz,* 185.

18. Ibid., 204.

19. Stuart Nicholson, in *The Future of Jazz,* 206.

20. Nisenson, *Blue: The Murder of Jazz,* 10.

21. Stanley Crouch, "Body and Soul," in *Notes of a Hanging Judge,* 246.

22. John F. Szwed, "Really the (Typed-Out) Blues: Jazz Fiction in Search of Dr. Faustus," *Village Voice,* July 2, 1979, 72.

23. Francis Davis, *Bebop and Nothingness,* xviii.

24. Balliett, "Dizzy," *New Yorker,* September 17, 1990, 48–58.

25. Balliett's *New Yorker* "portraits" are collected in *American Musicians: Fifty-Six Portraits in Jazz* (New York: Oxford University Press, 1986); *American Singers: Twenty-Six Portraits in Song* (New York: Oxford University Press, 1988); *Barney, Bradley, and Max: Sixteen Portraits in Jazz* (New York: Oxford University Press, 1989); *American Singers II: Seventy-Two Portraits in Jazz* (New York: Oxford University Press, 1996).

26. Lees's profile of Hank Jones is in *Waiting for Dizzy,* 53–66. The Billy Taylor profile is in *Meet Me at Jim & Andy's,* 176–93. Lees talks about Gerry Mulligan in the essay "The Last Days of Junior's," in *Meet Me at Jim& Andy's,* 213–42. The material quoted on Paul Desmond is from his Desmond profile in *Meet Me at Jim & Andy's,* 247.

27. Lees, *Meet Me at Jim & Andy's,* 142–43, 152–57.

28. Lees, *Waiting for Dizzy,* vi; *Meet Me at Jim & Andy's,* xvii.

29. Lees, *Cats of Any Color,* 218.

30. Jim Macnie, in *The Future of Jazz,* 35.

31. Nelson George, *The Death of Rhythm and Blues* (New York: Plume/Penguin, 1988), 108.

32. Greg Tate, in *The Future of Jazz,* 38–39.

Duke (magazine), 389n20
Duke Ellington (Ulanov), 82
Dulles, John Foster, 209
Dunbar, Paul Laurence, 202
Dyer, Geoff, 6–7
Dylan, Bob, 225, 245–46, 295, 297

Early, Gerald, 45, 47, 215, 264, 281
Early Jazz (Schuller), 221, 343
Eastwood, Clint, 307, 324–25, 337, 340,
    436n141
Ebony (magazine), 229, 230, 234, 385
Eckert, John, 219
Eckstine, Billy, 201
Edison, Harry "Sweets," 42
Edmond, Irwin, 83
education. *See* jazz education
Edwards, Teddy, 302
Ehrenreich, Barbara, 178
Eldridge, Roy, 22, 37, 56, 95, 107, 211,
    340
Eliot, T. S., 156, 186, 265, 350
Ellington, Duke: African American
    symphonic jazz of, 46, 49, 52–53; in
    American cultural landscape, 370;
    American Jazz Orchestra playing works
    by, 346; American students not
    knowing, 374; on Armed Forces radio,
    114; Balliett on, 194; Baraka on
    education of, 275; at Berkshire Music
    Barn concerts, 217; as beyond category,
    367; *Black, Brown and Beige,* 50, 52,
    53–55, 144, 238, 397n89; black
    identities in orchestra of, 10; Blesh on,
    136; Braxton influenced by, 367; in
    Burns's *Jazz,* 340, 341; as college
    student favorite, 212; at Cotton Club,
    29; Crouch on, 354; Dance and, 87;
    Frank Marshall Davis on, 107; death of,
    342; and death of jazz, 376; de Toledano
    on, 400n42; Dodge on, 127; *Down Beat*
    attack on Hammond by, 43, 51, 68,
    102; Ellison on, 156, 160; Feather's
    defense of, 53–54; Finkelstein on, 139,
    143–44; in France, 21; on Frazier, 102;
    Frazier on, 101; Gabler and, 92; Prince
    George collects records of, 21; Giddins
    on, 346; Gleason and, 198; Hammond
    and, 25, 43–55, 127; *Harlem,* 53;
    Hentoff and, 166, 168; Hobsbawm and,

62; Hodeir on, 188; "It Don't Mean a
    Thing If It Ain't Got That Swing," 49; on
    Jazz magazine International Advisory
    Council, 258; in jazz mainstream, 208;
    Jazzmen on, 127, 131; *Jump for Joy,* 54,
    397n96; at Left-oriented functions, 34,
    54; Locke and, 50; in Mandel's musical
    coming of age, 378; middle-class
    background of, 49, 50; Murray on, 349,
    350, 352, 353; *Music Is My Mistress,*
    397n96; *My People,* 53; at Newport Jazz
    Festival, 229, 230, 232–34; *New World
    a-Coming,* 53; as not integrating his
    band, 55; on racial authenticity, 51–52;
    racially integrated audience of, 97; in
    reader's polls, 68, 95, 403n79;
    Reminiscing in Tempo, 51; and Romantic
    tragic view of jazz, 7; on Stearns, 102;
    "Stormy Weather," 77; *Symphony in
    Black* score by, 50, 52, 396n87; on
    Tate on, 356, 357; Ulanov and, 82, 83,
    84, 141; virility attributed to music of,
    46; on white musicians, 100; Martin
    Williams on, 189, 191; as writer about
    jazz, 6
Ellington at Newport (album), 234, 238
Ellis, Don, 219, 223
Ellison, Ralph, 155–62; on African American
    "concord of sensibilities," 169;
    ambivalence about jazz's future,
    117–18; on Armstrong at Newport Jazz
    Festival, 236; Baraka on *Invisible Man,*
    271–72; on Baraka's *Blues People,* 162,
    277–79; Baraka's critical perspective
    and, 271, 275; on bebop, 159, 161,
    376; on the blues, 157–58, 162; and
    Cambridge ritualist school, 156; Crouch
    influenced by, 339; on Ellington, 156,
    160; firsthand testimony of, 156; "The
    Golden Age, Time Past," 117–19,
    158–59, 370; "Harlem Is Nowhere,"
    159; inspirational dimension of jazz
    writing of, 161–62; on jazz mainstream,
    207, 208; on jazz tradition, 118; on
    Lafargue Psychiatric Clinic, 159–60; in
    mainstream public life, 215; on
    Minton's, 117–18, 158–59; and Murray,
    347–48, 352; and Newport Jazz
    Festival, 230, 237, 238–39; on "noisy
    lostness" of jazz, 118, 121, 370; on